SLAYING THE DRAGON

The History of Addiction Treatment and Recovery in America

William L. White

A Chestnut Health Systems Publication

Chestnut Health Systems/Lighthouse Institute
Bloomington, Illinois 61701
http://www.chestnut.org

© 1998 by William L. White

Third Printing

Printed in the United States of America

Publishers/organizations that graciously provided permission to reproduce copyrighted material are cited in the text or in endnote citations of the included material. Particular thanks go to the World Service Office of Alcoholics Anonymous, Women for Sobriety, Alcoholics Victorious, and the Bishop of Books.

This publication may be ordered by sending $19.95 plus $4 shipping and handling to Chestnut Health Systems, 720 West Chestnut St., Bloomington, Illinois 61701. (Illinois residents add $1.40 sales tax.) Phone orders can be placed by calling toll free 888-547-8271.

Cover design by Jody Boles. Photographic credits for pictures on the cover can be found within the picture section of the book.

Library of Congress Cataloging-in-Publication Data

White, William L., 1947-
    Slaying the dragon : the history of addiction treatment and recovery
in America / William L. White.
        p. cm.
    Includes bibliographical references and index.
    ISBN 0-938475-07-X
    1. Alcoholism–Treatment–United States–History. 2. Drug abuse–Treatment –United States–History. 3. Rehabilitation centers–United States–History   I. Title.
HV5279.W48   1998
362.29'18'0973–dc21   98-11879
                                                   CIP

Dedication

Creating this work turned into a marathon far longer than I could have ever imagined when I began writing in the Spring of 1994. What sustained me through the journey were two quite remarkable people whose technical assistance and words of regular encouragement helped keep me moving forward when no end was in sight. This book is dedicated to my wife, Rita Chaney, whom I cherish, and to Ernest Kurtz, whose professional guidance and personal support on this project require words of appreciation that are beyond my ability to express. It is also dedicated to those who have written, and to those who will continue to write, this history with their lives.

Acknowledgments

In 1976 Dr. Ed Senay placed Dr. David Musto's book *The American Disease* in my hands with the admonition that I could not impact the future of the field of addiction treatment without understanding its past. Dr. Senay's sage advice and Dr. Musto's remarkable book marked the beginning of my search for deeper knowledge of a field that I had then worked in for nine years but in truth knew very little about. In the succeeding years, my researches into the history of addiction and its treatment led me to the works of Jim Baumohl, John Burnham, David Courtwright, Denise Herd, Mark Keller, John Kramer, Ernest Kurtz, Mark Lender, Harry Levine, Alfred Lindesmith, James Martin, Milton Maxwell, H. Wayne Morgan, Bill Pittman, Ron Roizen, Robin Room, W. J. Rorabaugh, Sarah Tracy, and Constance Weisner. I owe thanks to all of these individuals for laying the foundation upon which this book was constructed.

Many people read and critiqued portions of this book as it was being written. While most are acknowledged in particular chapters, I would like to offer special acknowledgment of my colleagues at Chestnut Health Systems, particularly Randall Webber, whose encouragement and recommendations were invaluable. The long task of locating the many rare books and obscure articles that were needed to construct this story was aided by a succession of research assistants—Darrell Jones, Jennifer Rose, and Amelia Goembel—and by the incredible skills and graciousness of many librarians and archivists. Particular thanks go to Laura Brosamer at St. Mary's Hospital Health Science Library, Pat Ruestman at Prevention First, Inc., Cheryl Schenerring of the Keeley Archives–Illinois State Historical Library, Al Epstein of the Frances E. Willard Memorial Library, Bill Pittman and Barbara Weiner of Hazelden, and Jane Kenamore, the Archivist for the American Medical Association and her Assistant, Robert Tenuta (The AMA's Historical Health Fraud and Alternative Medicine Collection was a goldmine of information). I also wish to thank Charlie Bishop, Jr. for his warm hospitality and access to his incomparable private library of alcoholism literature. (This collection has recently been transferred to Brown University and constitutes the primary holdings of the Chester H. Kirk Collection on Alcoholism and Alcoholics Anonymous.)

Several chapters of this book are based almost exclusively upon interviews. The individuals who gave so graciously of their time to participate in these interviews are acknowledged within the individual chapters.

Photographs and illustrations included in the book have been drawn from many individually cited sources but the following people and institutions deserve special acknowledgment: William Helfand, the late James H. Oughton Jr., Wally P., Penny B. Page, Bill Pittman, Vicki Sipe, the American Medical Association, Brown University, the Chicago Historical Society, the Department of Health and Human Services (Program Support Center), the General Service Office of Alcoholics Anonymous, the Illinois State Historical Society, the Illinois Addiction Studies Archives, the national office of Women for Sobriety, the Pittman Archives-Hazelden, and the Rutgers Center of Alcohol Studies Library.

Research for this book was subsidized by Chestnut Health Systems whose Board and leaders saw support for this project as a way they could honor the history of the field of addiction treatment and nurture its future. I would like to particularly acknowledge Rev. Russell Hagen, the Chief Executive Officer of Chestnut Health Systems, and Dr. Mark Godley, Director of the Lighthouse Institute, for their unflinching belief that this was a story that needed to be told.

Pamela Woll brought her remarkable editorial skills to this project, Amelia Goembel and Melissa McDermeit served as proof readers, and Joyce Thomas and Michele Hillary brought great care to the preparation of the final manuscript.

Slaying the Dragon
The History of Addiction Treatment and Recovery in America

Table of Contents

Section One
The Rise of Addiction and Personal Recovery Movements
in the Nineteenth Century

Section Two
The Birth of Addiction Treatment in America

Section Three
Evolving Approaches to Alcoholism Treatment: 1860-1940

Section Four
Treating Addictions to Narcotics and Other Drugs

Section Five
A.A. and the Modern Alcoholism Movement

Section Six
Mid-Century Addiction Treatment

Section Seven
Addiction Treatment in the Late Twentieth Century

Introduction

History cannot proceed by silences. The chronicler of ill-recorded times has none the less to tell the tale. If facts are lacking, rumors must serve. Failing affidavits, we must build with gossip.

Winston Churchill

History is the ultimate elder. We would do well to absorb the lessons confirmed anew in the tales of each generation. The story you are about to enter is a kaleidoscope of such instruction. It is the story of a problem and the professional field that was birthed to respond to it. It is the story of the dance between the problem and the profession—a dance choreographed within the rhythms of larger political, economic, religious and cultural forces. What follows is the captivating story of the people, institutions, events and ideas that constitute the history of addiction treatment and addiction recovery in America.

Intended Audience

This book is not written for scholars or academic historians though I hope it may stir their own inquiries into aspects of this subject. It is not written for addicts or their loved ones, although such readers will likely find their own stories mirrored in these pages. It is instead written for people who confront addiction every day in the performance of their professional roles. It is written for the counselors, physicians, nurses, outreach workers, and case managers working on the front lines of addiction treatment. It is written for judges, lawyers, police officers, probation officers, clergy, child welfare and child protection workers, public health workers, teachers, school counselors, youth workers, preventionists and all the other people whose jobs deal with the human and social consequences of addiction to alcohol and other drugs.

Each story was selected through a filter that asked: What does this event or this person's life tell us about the nature of addiction and recovery, the nature of ourselves, and the nature of our culture? This book provides a context through which professional helpers can better understand and respond to the myriad faces of addiction and recovery in America. To those who get up each morning and seek meaning in trying to touch the lives of alcoholics and addicts, here are the stories of those who came before you. Here is a

heritage that can be tapped for knowledge, courage, strength, humility, and, perhaps in the end, wisdom.

Scope of the Book

This book explores the history of addiction treatment and recovery in America. Coverage of persons, institutions, and innovations outside America are limited to those that exerted a profound effect on developments within the United States.

The definition of treatment used to determine the boundaries of this study was left purposely vague. Included in these pages are an enormous range of strategies that have been used to reform, rehabilitate, and redeem the addict. We will purposely move back and forth across this vague boundary until we approach the end of our journey, at which time we will more precisely define addiction treatment and determine it's birthplace in America.

It is important to note also what isn't here that might have been. The book does not include an in depth review of the history of alcohol and other drug prevention activities or the prevention field. While this history begs to be told, space limitations did not allow such a treatment within this current work.

Methods

Ernest Kurtz admonished me to adhere to three principles in my construction of this story: 1) provide evidence to support all your claims and conclusions, 2) draw your conclusions based on ALL of the available evidence, and 3) place each story within its broader historical context. The advice was invaluable and I have tried to follow it faithfully within the limits of space and my own abilities. In gathering this historical evidence, I have relied on the published and unpublished texts of the recorders of history that came before me. Where extensive research had already been done in key areas, I attempted to achieve an accurate and engaging synthesis of these secondary sources. In areas where there was little modern analysis, I relied on primary sources from various libraries and archives. There was also much of this story that had not been recorded on paper. Those who have worked in the field of addiction treatment have long favored action over self-reflection. The marked absence of memoirs by people working in the field often forced me to rely on oral traditions through which much of the history of the field has been passed to new generations of workers. This latter history was obtained through interviews with many pioneers within the field.

In analyzing the oral history of the field, Kurtz challenged me to ponder the following question: "Is memory a storehouse, or a reconstruction site?" The question was central to my approach to those chapters of the book that relied almost exclusively on interviews in which key participants in the history of the field were asked to "tell the story" of a person, an organization, an idea, an event or a period. As Kurtz suggests, there is always concern about the distortion that occurs in this recalling and retelling. Every effort was made to reconcile differences between objective history and recalled (reconstructed) history, between history and mythology, between fact and rumor. My primary goal was to weave the details of this written and oral history into an accurate, interesting and meaningful story. As Churchill noted, we must begin somewhere to tell the tale.

A Caution and an Invitation

I promise the reader many surprises in these pages—surprises that will trigger reflection, amazement, smiles, and, on occasion, sadness and anger. Your emotional as well as intellectual response to the material outlined in this book is inevitable. History can crush the zeal of a new idea or technique by cataloging the sheer volume of earlier failures that others advocated with zeal to match our own. There is potential disillusionment for the reader who confronts for the first time some of the more primitive forces that have shaped our national alcohol and drug policies and our own treatment field. On the other hand, history can empower us with its accounts of perfectly timed ideas and the potential enormity of a single individual's life. My goal for the reader is to share with me this walk through the fires of our history and close the last page with eyes open—committed to continuing our professional struggle in the absence of illusions about where we have been and the challenges that still lie ahead.

Structure of the Book

This book has been organized chronologically and thematically. The chapters and major stories unfold in historical sequence while the entire historical synopsis of some key topics can be found in one place within the book. This dual track will hopefully help the reader grasp historical trends and the synergy between various historical events while still allowing those in special settings or roles to find the history of their own area cogently summarized.

There are four pivotal events in this history that are referenced before they are formally introduced. These will be briefly noted here for the reader new to the field who may have only limited knowledge of their occurrence, timing or import. The first of these is the emergence of inebriate homes and asylums—the nation's first addiction treatment centers—during the second half of the nineteenth century. The second is the drug prohibition movements that resulted in passage of the Harrison Tax Act in 1914 and passage of the Eighteenth Amendment to the Constitution in 1919. This prohibition era marks a critical milestone in the criminalization of the status of addiction in America. The third event is the founding of Alcoholics Anonymous (A.A.) in 1935. A.A. will be used as a benchmark to measure mutual support societies that came before and after it. The fourth milestone event is the opening of two federal narcotics "farms" in 1935 (Lexington, Kentucky) and 1938 (Fort Worth, Texas). The opening of these facilities marked the beginning of the federal government's direct involvement in addiction treatment.

A Note on Accuracy and Sources

Like others who have tried to capture a tale that unfolded in fits and spurts across a continent, I have tried to be cautious in my designation of something as being the "first." Where such designation was used, I welcome the readers evidence of something or someone that came earlier. Every effort was made to verify the events, dates and other information included in the text. To any who believe errors have been made in fact or conclusions, I would invite you to communicate with me in care of Chestnut Health Systems, 720 West Chestnut, Bloomington, IL 61701. I would also extend the same invitation to readers who feel there are significant omissions in this history. I consider this work a first draft offered to the field for review and comment. I will be thrilled if many new discoveries pour in as a result of this critique.

My first goal in constructing this book was to tell the story and to have it read as a story rather than as a reference-cluttered dissertation. My secondary goal, however, was to provide future scholars access to the source material used to construct this story. To achieve these twin goals, I have used endnotes throughout the text to document all relevant sources and to provide background details that I judged not to be an essential part of the narrative.

On the Use of Names

Many people affiliated with Twelve Step recovery programs have made significant contributions within the history of addiction treatment in the U.S. Where affiliation with a Twelve Step program required acknowledgment, I have used the traditional first name and last initial for both living and deceased members except where their full identity has already been noted within both popular and professional literature. First and last names of people who were patients in treatment are used only where such people have themselves publicly acknowledged such treatment.

On the Title

The image of the dragon pervades the early history of addition and its treatment in America. "Chasing the Dragon" is a phrase that long ago made its way into the argot of the American drug culture. The phrase, first used by Chinese addicts in Hong Kong, came in America to denote the smoking of heroin. The story told of its origin is that the burning heroin creates a black smoke that twists and curls into dragon-like shapes and that the smoke itself appears as the dragon's breath. The user's face, as the story goes, chases this vaporous image, breathing in the dragon's intoxicating breath. This almost mythical image captured the promised pleasure (and masked pain) imbedded within the human specie's unrelenting attraction to intoxicants. In an equally mythical manner, references by addicts of their struggle to get free of a fiery, many-headed dragon also date from America's first inebriate asylum. The image of persons chasing and fighting dragons seemed to simultaneously capture societal efforts to suppress intoxicants and the addicts' efforts to slay the dragons of their own self-destruction. This is a book filled with the stories of people chasing dragons, being devoured by dragons, and taming or slaying dragons.

No book like this one is complete. There are still untold stories from our past to be uncovered and told. There are future chapters yet unwritten that will be created through the lives of those still working in the field and those yet to come. This book is dedicated to that future. It is hoped that the lessons contained in these pages can nurture our journey forward.

Prologue

The Problem of Language: A Professional Tower of Babel[1]

The very naming of something creates new realities, new situations, and often new problems.
—Thomas D. Watts[2]

We begin this story with a brief discussion of the language of *alcoholism*. Or should we say the language of *addiction*? Or *substance abuse*? Or *chemical dependency*? It is with that very question that we begin our historical journey.

The evolution of addiction rhetoric in America emerged out of what Harry Levine has called the "discovery of addiction"—a period in which those who consumed alcohol ceased being an homogenous group of "drinkers" and became separated into normal and abnormal drinkers.[3]

Drinking and Drunkenness: Early Distinctions

Alcohol use and occasional drunkenness were pervasive in colonial America, but it wasn't until per capita alcohol consumption began to rise dramatically between the Revolutionary War and 1830 that Americans began to look at excessive drinking in a new way and with a new language. The harbinger of this new view was Benjamin Rush's 1784 treatise *An Inquiry Into The Effects of Ardent Spirits* in which Rush referred to the "habitual use of ardent spirits" as an "odious disease."[4] In the 1840s the Washingtonians, America's first society of recovered alcoholics, spoke not of alcoholism but of drunkenness and referred to themselves as *confirmed drinkers, drunkards, hard cases, inveterate cases, sots, tipplers*, and *inebriates*.[5]

"Alcoholism" Coined

Drawn from the Arabic word *al-kuhl*–a name referring to an antimony-based eye cosmetic, *alcohol* later came to mean the essence or spirit of something.[6] It wasn't until the eighteenth century that the word *alcohol* came to designate the intoxicating ingredient in liquor. The Swedish physician Magnus Huss introduced the term *alcoholism* in 1849 to describe a state of chronic alcohol intoxication that was characterized by severe physical pathology and disruption of social functioning.[7] It took nearly a century for Huss's new term, and the accompanying term *alcoholic*, to achieve widespread usage in America.

The Inebriate Asylum Era

In the years following Huss's introduction of the term *alcoholism*, other terms emerged for consideration in professional and lay circles to describe the pathological craving for alcohol and the consequences of its excessive use. These terms included *intemperance, barrel fever, habitual drunkenness (drunk, drunkard), dipsomania (dipsomaniac), inebriety or ebriosity (inebriate)*, and the *liquor habit (victim of drink)*.[8] The two terms most frequently used at the end of the 19th century were *dipsomania* and *inebriety*.

The term *dipsomania*, taken from the Greek meaning "thirst frenzy," came to be associated with a pattern of binge drinking characterized by periods of abstinence interrupted by "drink storms." This pattern of explosive drinking was also sometimes called *Oinomania*—drawn from the word *oinis*, meaning wine.[9] *Dipso* (alcoholic) and *dip shop* (alcoholic sanatarium) were common slang terms among the affluent during the early twentieth century.[10]

Inebriety, derived from the Latin root *inebriare* —meaning, to intoxicate—was a generic term for what today would be called *addiction* or *chemical dependency*.[11] The type of inebriety was specified, as in *alcohol inebriety* or *cocaine inebriety*.

Psychiatric and Lay Therapy Influences

Huss's term, *alcoholism*, gradually began to take hold, first in professional circles and then in popular usage. Professional embrace of the term seems to have been marked by a 1908 essay by Karl Abraham, a prominent psychoanalyst.[12] Richard Peabody, a lay therapist, and Charles Towns, proprietor of a well-

known "drying out" hospital, were among the first prominent treatment specialists to use the terms *alcoholism* and *alcoholic* in articles written for the general public.[13]

Consensus on the public and professional language to be used in defining problems with alcohol was slow in coming. Addiction experts in the 1930s expressed preference for terms such as *problem drinking* and *problem drinker* on the grounds that the terms *alcoholism* and *alcoholic* were too stigmatizing and because of their belief that alcohol was a problem for many people who were not physically addicted to alcohol.[14] It was the founding of Alcoholics Anonymous in the mid-1930s, perhaps more than any other event, that solidified use of the term *alcoholism* and brought it into widespread popular use. In fact, the terms *alcoholism* and *alcoholic* were used frequently enough in the popular and professional press in the late 1930s that Dr. Edward Strecker and Francis Chambers complained that the terms were losing their meaning as a result of overuse. They recommended the terms be replaced with *abnormal drinking* and *abnormal drinker*.[15]

The Modern Alcoholism Movement

The rise of the "the modern alcoholism movement" in the 1940s under the leadership of the National Committee for Education on Alcoholism, firmly imbedded the terms *alcoholism* and *alcoholic* into scientific and popular use but did not stop the language debate. Many early leaders of this movement, including E.M. Jellinek, had misgivings about the term *alcoholism* and preferred such phrases as *alcohol addiction* or *compulsive drinking*.[16] Movement leaders expressed concern that the utility of the term *alcoholism* was being destroyed by its popularization.[17] In 1957, the World Health Organization, agreeing that the term *alcoholism* had lost its clinical specificity, proposed use of the term *alcohol dependence* and also explored application of the terms *alcohol addiction* and *alcohol habituation*. In 1960, Jellinek underscored this linguistic problem by noting the existence of more than 200 definitions of *alcoholism*.[18]

Continued Debate

At the end of a five-year research project in the 1960s, members of the Cooperative Commission on the Study of Alcoholism were still arguing over whether *person with a drinking problem* was preferable language to the term *alcoholic*. In 1967, they settled on use of the term *problem drinker*.[19] During this same period, the American Psychiatric Association (APA) recommended the term *alcoholic problems*. It was the APA's position that the terms *alcoholic* and *alcoholism* created the misconception that all persons with problems related to alcohol consumption suffered from a singular affliction. Other groups in the 1970s attacked the term *alcoholism* as stereotyping and stigmatizing and proposed that it be replaced with *Jellinek's Disease*.[20]

When a national institute was established in the early 1970s with the phrase *alcohol abuse* in its title, the semantic battle intensified. Mark Keller charged that *alcohol abuse* was "opprobrious, vindictive, pejorative" and an "inherently nasty" phrase.[21] Other terms that were used within the field's discourse during the 1970s included *problematic alcohol use, alcohol misuse, deviant drinking*, and *excessive drinking*.

Impact of Modern Diagnostic Classifications

The language debate was further played out in the development of the two modern systems of Diagnostic classification—the Diagnostic and Statistical Manual of Mental Disorders of the American Psychiatric Association (APA) and the International Classification of Diseases of the World Health Organization. *Alcoholism* first appeared in these evolving classifications as a subset of personality disorders and neuroses. This stance was later abandoned in favor of two new independent classifications: *alcohol abuse* and *alcohol dependence*. The APA in its latest diagnostic classification manual included generic categories of *substance intoxication, substance dependence*, and *substance-induced disorders*, as well as more drug specific diagnoses such as *alcohol dependence*.[22]

Creating Language to Embrace Drugs other than Alcohol

The development of consensus on a professional language that could embrace the problematic use of drugs other than alcohol has proved to be equally difficult. This language included such 19th century terms as *opium drunkenness, morphinism, morphinomania, chloralism and narcotism*. The "ism" suffix generally referred to perpetual states of drug use; the

"mania" suffix referred to a rabid craving that could incite periodic binges.[23]

There have also been attempts for more than a century to create a generic term that would encompass multiple drug choices: *inebriety, intoxicomania, drug addiction, drug habituation, drug abuse, alcohol-and-other-drug-abuse, drug dependence, substance abuse, and chemical dependency*. All of these terms and phrases have come under episodic attack. Concern with concurrent and sequential use of multiple drugs dates at least to nineteenth and early twentieth century inebriety literature in which we find such phrases as "mixed cases," "multiple inebriety," "combined inebriety," and "alternating inebriety."[24]

The term *addiction*, derived from the Latin root *addicere* meaning to adore or to surrender oneself to a master, has come into increasing popularity during the last decade. It first came into common usage in the professional literature of the mid-1890s—the same period the terms *dope* and *dope fiend* were coming into common slang.[25] *Dope* came into common usage first to refer to any syrupy preparation and later to designate products containing opium and cocaine. The changing view of drug use was reflected in the combining *dope* with the word *fiend*—a German derivative referring to a diabolically wicked and hated person.[26]

The term *addict*, or on occasion, *addictee*, emerged around 1910 to replace the earlier term, "habitué" used to designate a person suffering from addiction.[27] With the popularization of the term *alcoholism*, the words *addiction* and *addict* came to imply drugs other than alcohol, particularly the illicit drugs. But this distinction was not always clear. Some spoke and wrote of *addicts,* encompassing alcoholics within the meaning of this term, while others spoke of *alcoholics and addicts*. The umbrella terms *narcotic* and *narcotic addiction* further added to the language confusion when these terms came, through most of this century, to embrace cocaine, marihuana and other drugs whose pharmacological properties bore no resemblance to opiates. The American Medical Association's publication *Useful Drugs* even categorized alcohol as a "narcotic" during the first half of this century.[28]

From "Substances" to "Processes"

The 1980s saw an extension of addiction concepts to behaviors unrelated to drug use. *Co-alcoholism* and *para-alcoholism* were expanded to *codependence* and then to a broad category of so-called "process addictions" that included destructive relationships with food, work, people, sex, gambling, shopping and religion.[29] These new conceptual categories eventually came under a flood of criticism following their movement into the popular culture. Defining the boundaries of the term *addiction* became increasingly difficult as people began referring to themselves as being *addicted* to everything from television to bowling. *Addiction* came to be used in the popular culture to refer to any behavior that was excessive or repetitive. People similarly referred to themselves or others as chocaholics, workaholics, and various other "aholics."

Naming People, Helping Institutions and Naming Helping Interventions

Through all of the eras just reviewed, there has been disagreement about how to refer to people who are undergoing treatment for addiction. The terms *inmates, patients, clients, members, residents, guests*, and *students* have been the most common choices during the past century. There has also been confusion within the field and the larger culture about what to call persons who are no longer actively addicted. Debate over this designation has for the past 150 years included such adjectives as *redeemed, repentant, reformed, dry, former, ex-, arrested, cured, recovered*, and *recovering*.[30] The rather quaint term "sobriate" — perhaps a takeoff on inebriate, was also used in some quarters to describe the recovered alcoholic.[31] Individuals with prior histories of addiction have been variably characterized as *on the wagon, sober, drug-free, clean, straight, or abstinent*. There has similarly been no enduring consensus of what to call institutions that care for persons with alcohol and other drug problems. These institutions have been called *homes, asylums, reformatories, colonies, institutes, sanatoriums, sanatariums, hospitals, wards, lodges, farms, retreats, agencies, centers and programs*. There hasn't even been agreement on what to call what occurs inside these institutions: *reform, cure, rehabilitation, treatment, counseling, therapy*, or *reeducation*.[32]

The Language of Addiction Treatment

For nearly two centuries, Americans have struggled and failed to achieve sustained medical and social consensus on 1) how to refer to people whose alcohol and other drug consumption creates problems for themselves or society, 2) how to refer to people who are receiving some kind of intervention to correct these problems, 3) how to refer to this helping process, and 4) how to refer to people who once had, but no longer have, such problems. I have argued elsewhere that the reason for this failure of consensus lies in the multiple personal, social, economic, professional and political utilities such language must simultaneously serve.[33] Such failure of consensus is likely to continue well into the future. But we–author and reader–are stuck with a more immediate question: What language shall we use to tell this story?

The language of addiction is a coded language. Each word emerges as a means of signaling nuances of one's personal, professional and political values and affiliations. The rhetoric chosen to define and discuss alcohol and other drug addiction itself defines addicts in certain ways and rationalizes particular types of interventions into their lives. In this sense, the language of each era is an important part of this history. With that understanding, I have tried to tell each chapter of this story in the language that was popular within that era and to liberally quote from the leading thinkers of each era to convey not only the ideas but the words that dominated each of these periods. As we move into the modern era, my language of preference will include the phrases "alcohol, tobacco and other drugs," "alcohol and other drug problems," and "alcoholism and other addictions." When I speak of addict and addiction, these terms will encompass those harmfully impacted by the whole spectrum of legal and illegal intoxicants. Most importantly, the term *addict* will encompass alcoholics and the term *addiction* will encompass alcoholism. Individuals in treatment and in early recovery will be referred to as "recovering" and those with sustained periods of sobriety will be referred to as "recovered." (The use of both of these terms will take on significance as we move forward.) Now that we have settled on a vocabulary, let the story begin.

Section One
✠
Chapter One
The Seeds of Addiction Medicine
& Personal Recovery Movements

Addiction treatment in the United States emerged in the mid-19th-century out of the synergy among changing patterns of alcohol and drug consumption, social reform movements, personal recovery movements, and the rising professionalization of medicine. This chapter will detail that synergy.

Early American Drinking

Early American drinking patterns reflected a synthesis of cultural responses to psychoactive drugs.

Native Americans had little experience with alcohol before their contact with Europeans, and they had no experience with distilled alcohol. What most tribes did have was a highly sophisticated understanding of psychopharmacology and a long history of using psychoactive drugs in religious and medical rituals. The earliest Native American experiences with alcohol during European contact were not—as popular myth would have it—a history of drunken devastation. Many American Indians refrained from drinking on the grounds that alcohol was "degrading for free men," while others integrated alcohol into the rituals of use that had effectively controlled other psychoactive drugs.[1] However, alcohol was increasingly used against Native Peoples as a tool of economic, political, and sexual exploitation. This exploitation, along with the physical and cultural assault on Native American tribes, set the stage for rising Native American alcohol problems.[2]

The Africans who were brought to America as slaves came primarily from West African cultures that had blended alcohol into economic, social, and religious customs since antiquity. During their early years in America, Africans were so moderate in their use of alcohol that they were thought to be immune to its influence.[3] As the institution of slavery continued to develop, slave masters came to promote excessive alcohol use on isolated occasions as rituals of degradation, while Slave Codes prohibited slaves from owning stills or selling alcohol and prohibited others from selling alcohol to slaves.[4] There is little evidence of sustained heavy drinking by slaves. The major alcohol problem for early African Americans was the risk that they faced when Whites drank it.

The Spanish, English, Dutch, and French all brought alcohol to America and immediately set about ensuring its continued supply. What is striking about early colonial history is the utter pervasiveness of alcohol. It was consumed throughout the day by men, women, and children and integrated into nearly every ritual of social and political discourse. Alcohol was the "Good Creature of God"—a blessing used to bring cheer, relieve sorrow, and nurse the sick. Early Americans drank alcohol at home and at work, and alcohol was ever-present in colonial social life. While innumerable laws were passed to control public drunkenness, drinking itself was not perceived as a problem.[5]

As America moved toward its birth as a Republic, several factors made drunkenness more visible as a growing personal and social problem. The person who called America's attention to a growing alcohol problem was a most remarkable citizen.

Benjamin Rush and The Birth of the American Disease Concept of Alcoholism

No one writing on the subject of alcohol was more influential in early American history than Benjamin Rush (1746-1813). Rush was a prominent citizen in colonial America—a member of the Continental Congress, a signer of the Declaration of Independence, and Physician-General of the Continental Army. He was educated at Princeton, then in London and Paris, before accepting a position at the Philadelphia College of Physicians.

Rush had a profound influence on early American medicine. As one of the first and most prominent medical teachers in the colonies, he generated many ideas that dominated medical thinking for almost a century. He taught more physicians in his time than any other teacher, and his written tracts were published together as the first American medical textbook. Rush was a prolific writer and social activist. If a health or social issue arose during this period, Benjamin Rush was likely to be in the middle of the debate. He has often been called the "father of American psychiatry" and was unquestionably the first American authority on alcohol and alcoholism. His interest in alcohol and alcohol-related problems sprang from personal as well as professional experience. Rush's father was an alcoholic whose drinking led to his parents' divorce, and his mother's second husband was a distiller who abused her.[6]

Rush's first professional recognition of the problem of alcohol involved the level of drunkenness among soldiers of the Continental Army—an issue of concern to George Washington as well. In 1777, Rush issued a strong condemnation of the use of distilled spirits; his condemnation was published and distributed to all soldiers.[7] This was followed in 1782 with a newspaper article entitled "Against Spirituous Liquors," in which Rush recommended that farmers cease the practice of providing daily rations of liquor to their laborers. It was Rush's contention that the rationed liquor hurt the workers' health and productivity. Two years later, in 1784, Rush published a pamphlet entitled *An Enquiry into the Effects of Spirituous Liquors Upon the Human Body, and Their Influence Upon the Happiness of Society*. This 36-page tract was reprinted by the thousands and stands as the most influential piece of early American writing on alcohol and alcoholism.

Rush's words in *Enquiry* marked the beginning of a reassessment of alcohol, just when alcohol consumption was dramatically increasing in America. Rush's influence can be attributed to his mix of science, morality, and understanding of colonial psychology. At a time when the nation was reveling in its new-found freedom, Rush challenged in his tract that "a nation corrupted by alcohol can never be free."

Rush's Conception of Drunkenness

The article that would make Rush famous in the alcoholism field ranges from the scientific to the whimsical, the latter clearly evident in Rush's report of a rum drinker who belched too close to a flame and exploded. It was Rush's description of alcoholism itself that has continued to strike responsive cords for more than 200 years. While a fully developed disease concept of alcoholism would not emerge until the 1870s, Rush's writings stand as the first articulation of a disease concept of alcoholism by an American.

Rush first suggested that chronic drunkenness was a progressive medical condition. His "moral thermometer" was an early entry in a long series of depictions of this progression, from Currier's 1846 engraving *The Drunkard's Progress* to the modern "Jellinek chart." He then identified the characteristic behaviors of the alcoholic—radical personality

changes while drinking, for example—and noted the medical consequences of chronic drunkenness. He called the process through which the drunkard became progressively addicted to and finally destroyed by alcohol a "disease of the will." Rush further recognized that the tendency toward drunkenness was transmitted intergenerationally within families.

There is much in Rush's article that would seem strange today. Rush believed that distilled spirits exacerbated many medical conditions and recommended that beer, cider, and wine be substituted in their place. Rush's belief that distilled spirits were the cause of most drunkenness was so strong that he miscalculated the potential for similar effects from wine and beer. On the other hand, Rush may have recognized—even more than commentators today—the enormous significance of the advent of distilled spirits in the history of alcoholism. Rush perceived distilled spirits, more than alcohol, to be the culprits in addiction. He recommended that opium replace alcohol in medicine, on the grounds that opium caused less deterioration and posed less risk of addiction.

Rush's essay, which suggested that alcoholism should be viewed as a self-contained disease, broke from the traditional view that excessive drinking was either a reflection of moral depravity or a cause or symptom of mental illness.[8] Rush penned this essay with the full knowledge that he was swimming against strong cultural waters.

> *I am aware that the efforts of science and humanity, in applying their resources to the cure of a disease induced by a vice, will meet with a cold reception from many people.*[9]

Claims by Rush that drunkenness was a disease requiring abstinence were initially regarded as "ludicrous and impracticable" by a New Republic awash in alcohol. However, Rush's influence, both through his writings and through the generations of graduates he taught at the Philadelphia School of Medicine, laid the groundwork for the medical treatment of drunkenness and marked the birth of the American temperance movement.

Rush's writings on alcohol emerged in the same era in which an English physician, Thomas Trotter, published "Essay, Medical, Philosophical and Chemical, on Drunkenness." Working independently, Rush and Trotter both described alcoholism and characterized it as a disease. They are often cited as the originators of the "disease concept" of alcoholism. Although there may have been earlier advocates of a disease concept of alcoholism, it was Rush's prestige and full articulation of these beliefs in colonial society that marked a turning point in early America's relationship with alcohol.[10]

Rush's writings had a profound influence in both inciting and shaping the early temperance movement. In fact, one finds in the earliest days of this movement a unique blending of Rush's "disease" concept of drunkenness with the growing religious depiction of alcohol as a tool of the devil. "Disease" references helped buttress the move toward total abstinence from alcohol, as in the following 1811 pronouncement from an early temperance group in Fairfield, Connecticut:

> *The remedy we would suggest, particularly to those whose appetite for drink is strong and increasing, is a total abstinence from the use of all intoxicating liquors. This may be deemed a harsh remedy, but the nature of the disease absolutely requires it.*[11]

Rush's Views on the Etiology of Drunkenness

Rush believed that drunkenness could spring from many conditions. He believed that those whose occupations demanded constant and intense use of their mental faculties were particularly vulnerable to distilled spirits as a source of relief from mental exhaustion. He recommended tea as a more effective and less injurious remedy. For those who sought to drown their sorrows in distilled spirits, Rush recommended wine, beer, and opium as alternatives.

Rush referred to the disease of drunkenness as "suicide perpetrated gradually"—an idea that Dr. Karl Menninger would revive and elaborate on 152 years later.[12] In this pronouncement, Rush postulated that some people's drunkenness sprang from a hidden desire for self-injury, and he conceptualized the bottle as a potential instrument of self-harm.

Rush also noted the growing role of alcohol in medicine and anticipated self-medication theories of addiction in his observation that women were sometimes drawn into drunkenness in their use of ardent spirits to seek relief from what was then called "breeding sickness" (menstrual distress).

Rush's Views on the Treatment of Drunkenness

Rush's approach to treating medical disorders in general—and alcoholism in particular—must be viewed in light of the medical philosophy under which he operated. Like other physicians of his day, Rush believed that health and disease were determined by the relative balance or imbalance of the body's four humors (fluids): blood, phlegm, black bile, and yellow bile. Curing sickness involved re-establishing the balance between these humors, a state achieved by sweating, bleeding (via lancing or leeches), purging (via laxatives and emetics), blistering the skin, or ingesting various drugs.[13] Rush's treatment of acute intoxication included such methods as inducing perspiration and vomiting, inducing fright, and bleeding the patient. Rush advocated prodigious amounts of bleeding. He believed that all disease arose from a "morbid excitement caused by capillary tension" that could be relieved by bleeding.

Many of his primary medical interventions were clearly harmful. He poisoned his patients with mercury-laden calomel, dehydrated patients through excessive purging, inflicted pain through blistering, and threatened lives through bleeding.[14] Rush's use and advocacy of such remedies unquestionably threatened the lives of patients treated by these "heroic" methods. Rush's refusal to embrace less aggressive and more benign medical treatments led to a decrease in his medical practice and to potential economic disaster, averted only by Rush's appointment as Treasurer of the U.S. Mint.[15]

Rush was on much more solid ground when he made recommendations for the long-term reversal of chronic drunkenness. Rush was the first American physician to posit that continued abstinence from alcohol was the only hope for the confirmed drunkard. In his own words:

> *It has been said, that the disuse of spirits should be gradual; but my observations authorize me to say, that persons who have been addicted to them, should abstain from them suddenly and entirely. 'Taste not, handle not, touch not,' should be inscribed upon every vessel that contains spirits in the house of a man, who wishes to be cured of habits of intemperance.*[16]

Rush thought that this state of permanent sobriety could be achieved through numerous influences, "religious, metaphysical, and medical." In his description of treatment, Rush presented what today might be called a multiple-pathway model of alcoholism recovery. Rush laid out no less than 12 remedies that he had known to produce sobriety in the confirmed drunkard. These included: Christian conversion, acute guilt or shame, the linking of drink with some painful impression, vegetarianism, cold baths, acute disease, blistering the ankles, witnessing the death of a drunkard, and swearing an oath of abstinence.

One of the many interesting elements of Rush's 1784 tract was his description of the use of Pavlovian psychology—before Pavlov—in rendering a cure for drunkenness. Rush described how he cured a case of drunkenness by inducing vomiting through the use of tartar emetic mixed in with the alcohol. He reported that, for two years following this treatment, the fellow could not stand the sight or smell of alcohol. One hundred and fifty-six years later, Dr. Walter Voegtlin would pioneer a method of aversion therapy in the treatment of alcoholism using a technique very similar to the one described by Rush.

Rush recognized the difficulties involved in treating the confirmed drunkard. Having observed the failure of the jail and the hospital to effect the rehabilitation of the alcoholic, Rush in 1810 recommended the establishment of special institutions where alcoholics could be helped until they were cured. Rush called for the creation of a "Sober House," where alcoholics could be confined and rehabilitated upon evidence of drunkenness, neglect of business, and ill-treatment of family members. In Rush's view, rehabilitation at Sober House would consist primarily of religious and moral instruction. A committee appointed by the judge of the local court would decide when the alcoholic had been sufficiently rehabilitated to warrant discharge.[17]

Rush's proposal of a special institution takes on added meaning when one considers that hospitals were few and far between in colonial America. Like everyone else, confirmed drunkards had limited access to medical services in general—and their access to hospital services was particularly limited—but the alcoholic quite likely had additional obstacles. Given the scarcity of hospital beds, access was restricted to those who were "morally worthy." Drunkards, along with unwed mothers and those suffering from venereal disease, were routinely denied admission to America's earliest hospitals on the grounds that they were unworthy of community care. Like other patients of the day, alcoholics found themselves facing medical care rendered through sedating drugs, bleeding instruments, blistering salves, electricity machines, and an array of restraining devices. Juxtaposed on this back-ground, Rush's proposal for a "Sober House" looks indeed visionary.

A New Republic on a Binge

Benjamin Rush's concern about America's appetite for alcohol was a legitimate one. What Rush could not have anticipated was that he was seeing the

beginning of a 40-year period that would mark the highest alcohol consumption in American history. The New Republic was indeed about to launch itself into an extended alcoholic binge. Between 1790 and 1830, America fundamentally altered its pattern of alcohol consumption. In 1792, there were 2,579 distilleries in the U.S. and annual per-capita alcohol consumption was 2½ gallons. In 1810, there were 14,191 U.S. distilleries and annual per-capita alcohol consumption had risen to more than 4½ gallons. By 1830, annual consumption had risen to 7.1 gallons of pure alcohol per person.[18] Problems of public drunkenness and disorder, and the impact of drunkenness on family life, intensified in the midst of this collective spree.

The growth in America's alcohol-related problems stemmed, in part, from changes in availability and taste for particular types of alcoholic beverages. Most important was the shift in consumption from beer and wine to distilled spirits. The drink of choice was whiskey, and Americans were consuming it in unprecedented quantities. It was potent, cheap, and highly portable.[19]

A new type of drinker and a new drinking institution emerged in the 19th century. New immigrants, industrialization, and the movement into the Western frontier had all served to create a class of American men who organized their work life and leisure time around drinking. These men were virtually alone, unencumbered by duty to family or enduring community ties. America's changing drinking rituals were also reflected in the evolution from the tavern to the saloon. The tavern had been the center of village life, but the saloon—associated with violence, crime, vice, and political corruption—now emerged as a threat to community life.

The Rise and Evolution of the American Temperance Movement

The growing visibility of public drunkenness and other alcohol-related problems in the late 18th century forced a re-evaluation of alcohol and its role in American society. The "Good Creature of God" was about to be rechristened "Demon Rum." A growing number of prominent people joined Rush's call for change in American drinking practices. Prominent men like George Washington, Thomas Jefferson, Benjamin Franklin, and John Adams began to speak to the alcohol question. Religious leaders such as Anthony Benezet and Dr. Billy Clark condemned drunkenness and called for a new spirit of moderation. Benezet's 1774 publication of *The Mighty Destroyer*

Displayed, might well be considered America's first text on alcoholism. Billy Clark, for his part, founded the Union Temperance Society in Moreau, New York in 1808. The Moreau Society set the model for early temperance groups: a pledge to refrain from drinking distilled spirits, weekly temperance meetings, and a campaign of public education marked by meetings, speeches, and publications.[20] Momentum from these early temperance advocates was picked up by a broader spectrum of religious leaders—the Methodists, the Presbyterians, the Congregationalists. Isolated acts of social criticism regarding public drunkenness merged into a full-fledged social movement that sustained a century-long battle against alcohol.

The temperance movement's initial goal—the replacement of excessive drinking with moderate, socially approved levels of drinking—was reflected in its name. But a shift from this view of temperance-as-moderation to temperance-as-abstinence unfolded between 1800 and 1825. The position taken by the General Conference of the Methodist Episcopal Church in 1826 reflected this changing view.

> *We are the more disposed to press the necessity of entire abstinence, because there seems to be no safe line of distinction between the moderate and the immoderate use of intoxicating drinks; the transition from the moderate to the immoderate use of them is almost as certain as it is insensible; indeed, it is with a question of moral interest whether a man can indulge in their use at all and be considered temperate.*[21]

Deep strains of conviction emerged within the temperance movement regarding both of these goals (moderation and complete abstinence) and the strategies that might be used to achieve them (voluntary pledges of abstinence versus legal prohibition of alcohol). Between 1825 and 1850, the tide turned toward abstinence as a goal and legal alcohol prohibition as the means.

Moderate drinking was redefined from a goal that would prevent drunkenness to a newly defined cause of drunkenness. When alcohol was framed as an evil and inherently addictive substance, all use of alcohol was redefined as a stage in the inevitable decline toward intemperance. At a personal level, the only strategy to avoid the risk of becoming a drunkard was to follow Rush's dictum, "touch not, taste not, handle not." Temperance advocates became convinced that, at a societal level, only an alcohol-free land could produce families and communities free from the plague of drunkenness.

Alcoholics and the Evolution of Temperance Philosophy

The temperance movement's philosophical shift from moderation to total abstinence is an important influence on our continuing story, as is the primary reason behind this shift. With no concept of addiction, early temperance leaders had for decades encouraged habitual drunkards to moderate rather than completely stop their drinking. It was a common practice to encourage the drunkard to substitute wine and beer for distilled spirits—a practice that was believed to promote temperance in its original connotation, that of moderation. The Rev. W.H. Daniels explained why this practice had to be changed.

> *The relapse of multitudes of reformed men into drunkenness through the use of milder drinks, such as wine, ale and cider, led to the conviction that this, also, must be abandoned.*[22]

Efforts to convert whisky-drinking drunkards into temperate beer-drinkers failed, as did other efforts to convince drunkards simply to consume less alcohol. Elisha Taylor's 1830's account from Schenectady, New York, is typical. Taylor documented the case of 26 confirmed drunkards who within the local temperance society had taken the pledge not to drink distilled spirits. Nineteen kept the pledge, but of the seven who relapsed, all fell from grace through their continued use of fermented drinks. Like a growing number of temperance leaders, Taylor became convinced that reformation was possible only with complete abstinence from all alcoholic products.[23] Because of such failures, the target of the temperance movement shifted from the drunkard to the drinker. In what would be a call for the creation of the American Society for the Promotion of Temperance, Dr. Justin Edwards set forth this new position:

> *Our main object is not to reform inebriates, but to induce all temperate people to continue temperate, by practicing total abstinence....The drunkards, if not reformed, will die, and the land be free.*[24]

The temperance movement shifted its goal from the suppression of intemperance to the promotion of temperance. The plan was a simple one: prevent the creation of new drunkards and let the old drunkards die off.

The failure of alcoholics to moderate their drinking patterns—and the failure of early temperance societies to effect such a change—ensured that later reform societies organized by and for alcoholics would be almost exclusively based on abstinence. These failures also ensured that treatment institutions born in the mid-19th century would from their inception be based on the belief that the alcoholic's only option for long-term recovery was complete abstinence.

The temperance movement's advocacy of abstinence rather than moderation reflected both a growing understanding of what would later be christened *addiction*—this recognition of craving and compulsion not controllable by personal will. It also reflected a growing understanding of alcohol. The original pledge to abstain from distilled spirits was based on the belief that only spirits contained alcohol and that beer and wine did not. According to Carol Steinsapir, beer and wine were believed to contain only the "constituent ingredients of alcohol, not alcohol itself."[25] As scientists and habitual drunkards confirmed the presence of alcohol in beer and wine, it was inevitable that all alcohol products be embraced within a new, comprehensive temperance pledge.

Early Involvement of Alcoholics in the Temperance Movement

Alcoholics were drawn to the temperance movement from its earliest days; they continued to be drawn to this movement even when the movement began to view alcoholics with considerable contempt. Throughout the early decades of the 19th century, most temperance societies kept a recording of the number of their members who were reformed drunkards. Cherrington's research revealed that, in 1829, some 1,200 former drunkards participated among the 100,000 local members of such societies. Four years later, the number of former drunkards had risen to 10,000, out of a total membership of 1,250,000.[26] If Cherrington's figures are to be believed, alcoholics were joining temperance societies in increasing numbers even before new temperance groups were organized by and for drunkards. By the mid-1830s, drunkards were being drawn into the temperance movement, where their highly emotional accounts of their travails with alcohol stirred large audiences. At that time one could construct a social world and a daily lifestyle within the burgeoning temperance movement. Many desperate alcoholics sought shelter in the temperance meetings, temperance coffee houses, temperance reading rooms, and temperance hotels.[27]

From Individual Struggle to Shared Recovery

Many 19th-century alcoholics waged—as many do today—individual battles for recovery without professional assistance or the mutual support of other alcoholics. They made private promises and signed public pledges. They wrote confessionals and filled lecture pulpits in attempts to purge themselves of the appetite for alcohol and to strengthen their own commitment to abstinence. They sought the advice of others. They sometimes sought substitutes in other drugs. And they often sought the medium of religious conversion. But most important in terms of our story, they did all of this in virtual isolation from other alcoholics.

Our first evidence of individuals turning their own negative experiences with alcohol into a social movement of mutual support occurs within Native American tribes. There are several pre-Washingtonian examples of such movements. As early as 1772, Samson Occom, a Mohegan who had recovered from alcoholism through conversion to Christianity, penned a widely distributed attack on alcohol's effects on Indians.[28] In 1800, following an alcohol-induced near-death vision experience, Handsome Lake organized a successful total abstinence movement among the Iroquois. In 1805, a Shawnee Chief named The Prophet launched a total abstinence campaign that, for several years, reduced alcohol problems among western tribes. Stories of personal recovery come also from Kah-ge-ga-gah-bowh, a temperance leader of the Ojibways (Chippewas); and from William Apess, a temperance leader among the Mashpee Indians. Apess' 1829 *A Son of the Forest* was the first published autobiography of a Native American, one of the earliest American accounts of the effects of alcoholism on children (Apess was raised by alcoholic grandparents), and an eloquent early American account of personal recovery from alcoholism.[29]

Outside Native America, temperance societies composed exclusively of reformed drunkards began to appear as early as 1831 (in Norwich, New York). Typical of these early groups was the Reformers Benevolent Temperance Society of Schenectady, New York, which demanded abstinence from wine and beer as well as spirits. In the 1830s, some reformed drunkards followed the example of J.P. Coffin, who became active in temperance work and used his personal story on the lecture circuit to underscore the need for total abstinence.[30] Coffin's role as a paid temperance agent places him among the first recovered alcoholics working professionally to reclaim others.

Family members of alcoholics also played prominent roles in the emerging temperance organizations and probably found sources of healing and mutual support in such societies. Ruth Alexander and Ruth Bordin's separate studies of women involved in temperance societies in the 1840s revealed that many were wives and daughters of inebriates. It is quite likely that the temperance movement served as a therapeutic mutual-support group for these daughters, sisters, wives, and mothers of alcoholics.[31]

In the coming chapters, we will see a continued shift in this trend from individual recovery to shared recovery. Before we make this transition, we will explore the life of one 19th-century alcoholic whose story shows what it was like to try to recover without participation in formal treatment or shared involvement with other alcoholics in the recovery process.

The Tortured Saga of Luther Benson

The life of Luther Benson epitomizes the experience of the isolated alcoholic struggling to find a medium of self-cure while his drinking propels him inexorably toward insanity and death. Early alcoholism recovery in the United States began in one of two ways: as an assertion of personal will—a battle forged against a demon variably located inside the alcoholic or inside the bottle—or as an act of submission to God through individual religious experience. The struggle of men like Luther Benson to recover sometimes entailed both of these styles of attempted recovery. And quite often they failed.

Luther Benson penned the tale of his life, appropriately titled *Fifteen Years in Hell*, while locked in the Indiana Asylum for the Insane. He was born in 1847 the last of nine children, eight of whom lived sober, industrious lives. Benson vividly recalled his first drink at age six and the magic effect the warm liquor had on his body, mind, and emotions. The appetite for more was instantaneous and insatiable. His high tolerance for alcohol led to early episodes of lost memory—what today we know as alcoholic blackouts. Benson ordinarily experienced the most noble of ambitions but took on another character when the drink was upon him—a phenomenon that would later be described as the alcoholic's Dr. Jekyll/Mr Hyde personality. In school, he excelled during periods of abstinence but was eventually expelled for drunkenness. He later was licensed to practice law, but all that he attained professionally and financially

while sober was lost while he was drunk.

As his alcoholism roared out of control, Benson tried many means of cure, from self-will to religion. He even accepted the suggestion of a friend that he become a temperance lecturer. Use of the lecture pulpit as an attempted method of self-cure was not uncommon, and this was a role in which Benson seemed gifted. He traveled the country and through his impassioned eloquence persuaded many alcoholics to step forward and sign the pledge—all the while failing to master his own sustained battle with alcohol. Again and again, he threw himself into the work, hoping that its excitement would "take the place of alcohol."

> *I learned too late that this was the very worst thing I could have done. I was all the time expending the very strength I so much needed for the restoration of my shattered system.*[32]

Benson could live neither with alcohol nor without it. Drinking in moderation was impossible for him; he was either perfectly sober or perfectly drunk—nothing in between. In a poignant description of what would later be called "loss of control," Benson declared:

> *Moderation? A drink of liquor is to my appetite what a red-hot poker is to a keg of dry powder....When I take one drink, if it is but a taste, I must have more, even if I knew hell would burst out of the earth and engulf me the next instant.*[33]

When he was not drinking, Benson was like a ticking bomb. His autobiography is a tale of unending obsession and unrelenting craving:

> *During the period that I abstained....my agony was unbearable. I dreamed that I was drinking and.....drunk. Day by day my appetite grew fiercer and more unbearable...I would have torn the veins from my arms open, if I could have drawn whiskey from them....I was burning up for liquor. In just this condition I went to Indianapolis to address the Woman's Temperance Convention.*[34]

Often drinking before, after, and between temperance lectures, Benson could not help but be stung by his own hypocrisy—working to save other alcoholics while slipping off to another city for an extended spree. In his more sober and reflective moments, he could not help but reflect: "Depraved and wretched is he who has practiced vice so long that he curses it while he yet clings to it."[35] For three years Benson interspersed temperance lectures with highly intemperate drinking binges—binges that destroyed his reputation and drove away his most loyal friends. Benson's tale proceeds through a suicide attempt, another religious conversion, and a relapse that led to his legal commitment to the insane asylum. His written account—penned in a locked ward—ends with his continued search for a power in the universe that can give him hope, and with a request that

readers pray for his future.

The cumulative pain and vulnerability generated by a New Republic's drunken binge was reaching critical mass in the 1830s. What the Luther Bensons of the early 19th century desperately needed was a fellowship of kindred spirits whose shared suffering and collective strength would enable them to achieve together what they had so hopelessly failed to achieve alone. Just such a national movement was about to arise on the American landscape. And that movement would include the seeds out of which would rise the field of addiction treatment in America.

✠

Chapter Two
The Washingtonian Revival [36]

"They (Washingtonians) teach hope to all—despair to none."
—Abraham Lincoln, 1842.

The temperance movement was in dire need. In the years 1830 to 1840, its shift from moderation to total abstinence, its emerging advocacy of legal prohibition of alcohol, and the conflict surrounding its stand on abolition of slavery had hurt the movement's membership. The movement was fragmenting and in decline. In New York, for example, membership in temperance groups had declined from 229,000 in 1836 to 131,000 in 1839.[37] What was needed was something that could revitalize the American temperance movement. That revitalization was about to come from the most unlikely of sources.

It had also become clear even to hard-line temperance leaders like Justin Edwards that new drunkards were replacing the old and that the long-term success of the temperance movement had to include some means of reforming the drunkard. What was needed was a successful method of achieving that goal. The temperance movement, and America as a whole, were about to experience such a method, the likes of which they could never have imagined.

Founding and Growth of the Washingtonians

William Mitchell, John Hoss, David Anderson, George Steers, James McCurley, and Archibald Campbell were members of a drinking club of some 20 men who met nightly at the Chase Tavern on Lincoln

Street in Baltimore, Maryland. On April 2, 1840, an argument arose when the proprietor of the tavern declared that all temperance lecturers were hypocrites. Four of the above-named club members were sent out to investigate a temperance lecture that was being delivered that very night by the Reverend Matthew Hale Smith.[38] Upon their return, a lively debate began regarding the sentiments expressed at the lecture. In the midst of this discussion, George Steers proposed that they form their own temperance club. After sleeping on this idea, the earlier-named six individuals resolved to proceed with just such a plan. Each member joining this newly christened Washingtonian Total Abstinence Society[39] did so under the following pledge drafted by William Mitchell:

We, whose names are annexed, desirous of forming a society for mutual benefit, and to guard against a pernicious practice which is injurious to our health, standing and families, do pledge ourselves as gentlemen that we will not drink any spirituous or malt liquor, wine, or cider.

Leaders and members of the Washingtonian Society were drawn from the artisan and working classes—in marked contrast to earlier temperance groups, whose leadership and membership tended more toward the social elite.[40] The new society charged a 25-cent initiation fee and dues of 12 ½ cents per month. The society met nightly, just as its members had as a drinking club, but later shifted to weekly meetings.[41]

The Washingtonian meetings were high drama. Instead of the debates, formal speeches, and abstract principles that had been on the standard temperance meeting agenda, the main bill of fare at a Washingtonian meeting was *experience sharing*—confessions of alcoholic debauchery followed by glorious accounts of personal reformation. Following these opening presentations by established members, newly arrived alcoholics with bloated faces and trembling hands were offered the opportunity to join. As each newcomer came forward, he was asked to tell a little of his own story, then sign the abstinence pledge amid the cheers of onlookers. This ritual of public confession and public signing of the pledge carried great emotional power for those participating. It evoked, at least temporarily, what would be described one hundred years later as ego deflation or surrender.

With the zeal of the newly converted, the Washingtonians immediately sought to involve other alcoholics in their society. The operating pledge was, "*Let every man be present, and every man bring a man.*" Washingtonians were turned into what Tyrell called "secular missionaries."[42] New recruits were sought out among the membership's drinking friends, and Washingtonians entered the bars and tried through "moral suasion" to enlist new recruits to their cause. The effort was highly organized, with members divided into "ward committees" responsible for enlisting the involvement of drunkards from their assigned areas. It was through this sequence of drinker-recruiting-drinker that the movement grew rapidly. From their beginnings as a working-class movement, the Washingtonians recruited a growing number of the affluent and famous. The Washingtonians claimed among the reformed two men who became mayors, one who became governor of his state, and several members of Congress.[43]

The first Washingtonian meetings were closed to outsiders. These gatherings constitute the first widespread "closed meetings" of alcoholics banded together for mutual support and recovery. Because of interest in the meetings expressed by the general public, members of other temperance groups, and the clergy, the Washingtonians decided in November, 1840, to hold public meetings in addition to their membership meetings.

The public meetings had a significant influence on the evolution of the Society. While the charter of the Washingtonian Society defined it as an order for reformed drunks, the popularity of the public meetings led to a broadening of this vision. The only requirement for membership became the pledge of personal abstinence. Within two years of its founding, one of its leaders would note:

> *There is a prevalent impression, that none but reformed drunkards are admitted as members of the Washington Society. This is a mistake. Any man may become a member by signing the pledge, and continue so by adhering to it.*[44]

The speed with which the membership changed was quite remarkable. For example, by June of 1841, the Washingtonian Society in Worcester had 500 members, only 50 of whom had been "hard cases."[45] The public meetings brought large numbers of non-alcoholics under the Washingtonian influence. The emotional impact of the meetings seemed to be as riveting to abstainers and moderate drinkers as it was to drunkards. A report on a Washingtonian meeting in Boston suggests something of this power:

> *We believe more tears were never shed by an audience in one evening than flowed last night....Old gray haired men sobbed like children, and the noble and honorable bowed their heads and wept.*[46]

As the Washingtonian circle widened, well known people who were not alcoholic were also sometimes invited to speak. On February 22, 1842, Abraham Lincoln spoke before the Springfield, Illinois Washingtonian Society. Lincoln's comments that night offer an interesting perspective on the man (a life-long abstainer and former tavern keeper) and the times. He made suggestions on the physical cause of alcoholism: "In my judgment such of us who have never fallen victims (of alcoholism) have been spared more by the absence of appetite than from any mental or moral superiority over those who have." Lincoln went on to sing the praises of the Washingtonian movement and to criticize earlier temperance movements that had defined the alcoholic as incorrigible.[47]

News of the Washingtonian meetings spread by word of mouth and through the press. The Baltimore *Sun* proclaimed that the drunkard had "taken his cause in his own hands—analyzed his disease and wrought his own cure."[48] Alcoholics whom everyone had given up on were suddenly reforming themselves within the Washingtonian framework, with results so startling that the group was sometimes referred to as the "Resurrection Society."[49]

As word of the Washingtonian Movement spread, requests for Washingtonian speakers came to Baltimore from all over the country. Pairs of reformed men were sent out in all directions, some becoming quite well known. The team of J.F. Pollard and W.E. Wright toured the East, while the team of Jesse Vickers and Jesse Small toured the West.[50] These extended speaking tours had but one purpose: to spread the Washingtonian message of hope to the alcoholic. This missionary branch of the original Washingtonian Society spurred the creation of Washingtonian groups throughout the United States.

Never in history had an alcohol abstinence movement taken off so explosively. At its first anniversary celebration, the Washingtonian Society parade included 5,000 marchers, and among the marchers were 1,000 reformed drunkards.[51] A Washingtonian meeting in Boston drew some 12,000 people. Washingtonian societies spread to more than 160 towns and villages in New England, then spread West and South. At the height of the movement, more than 600,000 pledges were signed, thousands marched in Washingtonian temperance parades, and a weekly newspaper was launched.

Special meetings were organized for women and children. The first Martha Washington Society was organized May 12, 1841 in New York. The goals of the Martha Washington Societies were to provide moral and material support to reforming inebriates, and to provide special support to female inebriates and to the wives and children of inebriates. The groups provided food, clothing, and shelter to reforming inebriates, and some even served as employment clearinghouses for inebriates trying to get back on their feet financially. Although other temperance societies were quite conscious of the social class and reputation of those they recruited, the Martha Washington Societies extended support to some of "the most disreputable members of their communities."[52]

The Martha Washington Societies also encouraged women to set high standards regarding their associations and the banishment of alcohol from their homes—a stance well illustrated by one of their parade banners that read, "Total abstinence or no husband!" The Martha Washington Societies were the first organizations in the temperance movement in which women assumed leadership roles. They were also the first organized effort to focus on the needs of inebriate women, who were recruited, restored to health, and embraced as full members of the Martha Washington Societies. The Washingtonian Movement also spawned juvenile auxiliary groups. While the races did not mix in the Washingtonian societies—or

in hardly any other social organizations in the 1840s—separate Washingtonian societies were organized by freed Blacks.[53]

The Washingtonian movement generated its own genre of confessional literature, which grew to considerable popularity throughout the century. The roots of today's confessional books on addiction and recovery can be traced to the mid-19th century. Fortunately, modern titles are nowhere near as long as the titles of these books. One of the shorter titles of the time was James Gale's 1842 *Long Voyage in a Leaky Ship; or Forty Years Cruise on the Sea of Intemperance, Being an Account of Some of the Principal Incidents in the Life of an Inebriate.*[54]

The Washingtonian Movement rose like an emotional rocket over the American scene, sweeping up alcoholics and non-alcoholics alike in its wake. The Movement reached its peak in 1843, with its two best orators, John Gough and John Hawkins, on extended tours, organizing new Washingtonian Societies.

The Washingtonian Program

The Washingtonians did not have a fully articulated ideology of the nature of alcoholism and its recovery, but their core activities are clearly identifiable. The Washingtonian program of recovery consisted of 1) public confession, 2) public commitment, 3) visits from older members, 4) economic assistance, 5) continued participation in experience sharing, 6) acts of service toward other alcoholics, and 7) sober entertainment.

Washingtonians with more stable sobriety visited new converts to provide encouragement and bolster new members' resolve. Until new recruits could get on their feet, the Washingtonians also provided food, clothing, shelter, financial support to pay court fines, and employment. In turn, they provided pressure for the new recruit to clean himself up so that the difference between the old and new persona would be glaringly apparent to all who saw him. The Washingtonians tried to encourage the use of sober alternatives to the saloon, including reading rooms, temperance fairs, marches, concerts, balls, and picnics.[55] Involvement in the Washingtonian Society did provide social support to help people stop drinking and construct an abstinence-based identity and an abstinence-based social world. There is no doubt that many alcoholics attained sobriety in the Washingtonian Movement and sustained their sobriety long after the movement itself had dissipated.

Two people who played significant roles in

spreading the Washingtonian Movement were John Hawkins and John Gough.[56] Before exploring the fate of the Washingtonian Movement, we will pause to explore the personal stories of its two most famous proponents.

John Hawkins and John Gough

John Henry Hawkins lost two wives and a career as a hatter in his plummet into alcoholism. He would probably have fallen further, if it were not for the day his daughter Hannah approached him in his morning hangover and begged him not to send her for whiskey again. Her plea touched his heart. Hawkins would tell this story thousands of times, noting this event as the turning point that sparked his first visit to the Washingtonians and his subsequent recovery from alcoholism.[57]

Hawkins was recruited into the original Washingtonian group in June of 1840, two months after the group was founded. His organizational skills and charismatic speeches contributed to the spread of the movement. He became so convinced of the role of religion in long-term recovery that he became an ordained Methodist minister. Hawkins made a profession of lecturing on the temperance circuit and held a paid position with the Massachusetts Temperance Society. In the 18 years between his reformation and his death, Hawkins worked tirelessly in organizing total abstinence support groups for alcoholics. He is said to have traveled more than 200,000 miles and delivered more than 5,000 speeches during those years.[58]

John Gough came to America from England as a child and grew up to work as a bookbinder. He married and fathered a child, but his wife and child both died during his years of heavy drinking. John Gough was popular during his drinking years. His imitations, stories, and songs brightened many a tavern and street corner. Through the years of his drinking, he descended from a light-hearted man of the town to a drunken buffoon. In October of 1842, a Quaker named Joel Stratton invited Gough to a temperance meeting. Something touched Gough deeply in that meeting, and he signed a temperance pledge with a trembling hand. His career as a temperance lecturer began almost immediately. His emotional and highly dramatic presentations were in high demand. He was paid $2 for his first lecture, $10 per lecture in an 1844 tour of New York, and as much as $170 per lecture in the years following the Civil War. Thirty years after signing the pledge, John Gough had amassed a small fortune from his skills on the lecture stage.

Gough experienced at least two relapses. His first relapse occurred after he had been sober for five months. He believed his appetite had been fully conquered and thought little of taking the tincture of opium his physician prescribed for symptoms that today might be recognized as warning signs of relapse: physical exhaustion, extreme restlessness, irritability, and apprehensiveness. After a drinking binge of several days, Gough stopped drinking and confessed his fall in an open group meeting. He continued his lecturing with a new understanding of the insidious nature of addiction.[59] A later relapse occurred in New York in 1845. Gough was missing for several days and found unconscious in a "house of ill-repute." Gough responded by claiming that he had been drugged by a spiked glass of raspberry soda water and abducted by the enemies of temperance.[60] Gough bounced back onto the lecture circuit, and there were no further confirmed reports of his drinking.

Gough's relationships with his fellow Washingtonians grew progressively strained. Gough favored legal prohibition of alcohol and believed religion was an essential element of alcoholic reformation. As these themes entered his speeches, conflict with the Washingtonians inevitably increased. His popularity was resented, and some of his early Washingtonian colleagues accused him of exploiting the temperance cause for his own financial gain. Gough worked with all branches of the temperance movement and became less and less closely identified with the Washingtonians.

Gough's abilities as an orator were legendary. With every emotion revealed in his face, Gough could move people to tears one moment and have them holding their sides in laughter the next. Gough's exhortations were physical as well as emotional—he charged over the stage, sometimes tearing his clothes and striking tables with his hands. Early descriptions of Gough's animation reflect the vibrancy of his stage technique.

> *His hair was bushy and he tossed it about as a lion does his mane. The lithe form was always in motion, and needed a large platform for full effect. The restless, eager hands, supple as India-rubber, were perpetually busy flinging the hair forward, in one character, back in another, or standing it straight up in a third; crushing the drink-fiend, pointing to the angel in human nature, or doubling up the long coat tails in the most*

grotesque climaxes of gesticulation.[61]

Gough's presentations were as exhilarating for the audience as they were draining for him. Considering his skills as an orator, many were surprised to learn that John Gough always experienced almost paralyzing stage fright until he stood up and began talking. At the conclusion of his nightly presentations, Gough would be dripping with perspiration and on the verge of collapse, but it would still be hours before he could fall asleep. On February 15, 1886, John Gough collapsed and died while giving a speech. He was 69 years old. In his lifetime he had traveled more than 450,000 miles and delivered more than 8,600 temperance addresses. Gough's speeches were filled with some of the most vivid descriptions of the pathophysiology of alcoholism in American literature. Here, for example, is John Gough in one of his speeches, describing the onset of delirium tremens.

I turned to my work broken-hearted, crushed in spirit, paralyzed in energy, feeling how low I had sunk in the esteem of prudent and sober-minded men. Suddenly the small bar I held in my hand began to move; I felt it move: I gripped it: still it moved and twisted; I gripped it still harder; yet the thing would move till I could feel it tearing the palm of my hand; then I dropped it, and there it lay a curling, slimy snake....I knew it was a cold, dead bar of iron, and there it was, with its green eyes, its forking, darting tongue, curling in all its slimy loathsomeness! And the horror filled me....[62]

Gough also had taken the time to itemize and tabulate the social costs of alcohol to the country, a figure he placed at $2,000,000,000.

Men like Hawkins and Gough, who carried the Washingtonian message across the country, were not blessed with great education, but they became spellbinding orators by sharing openly and with great emotional intensity the story of their lives before and after they quit drinking. It was that intense and detailed sharing of experience that inspired many alcoholics to reach for the pledge card and step forward to tell their own stories.

Both Hawkins and Gough emphasized the role of religion in sustaining sobriety. Gough told the story of a man who, having heard him the night before, returned the next day and said that he had that morning been praying on his knees that he could sustain his commitment to not drink. Gough's reply to the man—"Keep there, my friend, and you will keep sober"—reflected not only Gough's view of the need for God's help with sobriety but also the posture of humility that Gough had learned was crucial to sustained sobriety.

Key leaders of the Washingtonian Movement such as John Hawkins and John Gough continued their travels long after the movement's demise, spreading the story of alcoholic reformation and helping draw large numbers of alcoholics into other temperance organizations. Hawkins and Gough were among the first recovered alcoholics working in paid roles to carry a message of hope to other alcoholics. Early roots of the roles of the alcoholism counselor and the prevention specialist can be traced to these temperance missionaries.

The Washingtonian Demise

The Washingtonian Movement rose like a brilliant fireworks display on the American horizon, then it was all over. By 1845, the Washingtonian movement's energy was spent. What it had initiated could not be sustained. Almost none of the Washingtonian Societies were active beyond 1847, with the exception of those in Boston, which continued until the 1860s.[63] The Washingtonian movement was like a cry of "Fire!" in a crowded theater. It had aroused great emotion to get everyone outside the theater, but then no one was sure what to do.

The demise of the Washingtonian movement remains shrouded in mystery. Analysis of this failure has spanned more than 150 years and is likely to continue. Because it was the first mutual-aid movement that focused on alcoholism, understanding its failure provides a framework for comparison with later, more successful mutual-aid movements. Factors cited in the demise of the Washingtonian movement can be summarized briefly in the following categories.

Moral Versus Legal Suasion: Contemporaries of the Washingtonians, particularly those representing temperance groups, cited the failure of the Washingtonians as evidence of the inherently flawed strategy of moral suasion. In their view, the Washingtonian failure was added proof that legal prohibition was America's only answer to its liquor problem.[64]

Conflict with Religious and Temperance Groups: Contemporary church leaders of the period suggested that the Washingtonians failed because they ignored the crucial role of religion in the reformation of the alcoholic.[65] While dissension on this point existed within the movement, most Washingtonians believed that social camaraderie was sufficient to sustain sobriety and that a religious component would only discourage drinkers from joining. Clergy were clearly threatened by the Washingtonians' popularity and miffed at their exclusion as speakers for Washingtonian meetings. Some critics even went so far as to charge the Washingtonians with the heresy of humanism—elevating their own will above God's by failing to include religion in their meetings.[66]

Damaged Credibility: There were charges of sensationalism and fabrication as Washingtonian speakers competed to outdo one another in describing the depths to which alcoholism had taken them. The meetings themselves were thought by many to have retained too much of the rawness and vulgarity of the saloon. The movement's reputation was also damaged when individuals who had publicly championed the movement returned to drinking. Relapse of those publicly linked with the movement was particularly damaging in light of excessive advertising promoting Washingtonian membership as a "never failing remedy in all stages of the disease."[67]

Weak Organizational Structure: Dissension arose among the founding leaders of the Washingtonian Society on such issues as the role of religion in long-term recovery and the group's stand on the legal prohibition of alcohol. They had no effective vehicle for making decisions and resolving conflict as the movement evolved. There was no central organizational authority through which the philosophy and program of the Washingtonians could be defined or disseminated. The extreme decentralization of the movement and its lack of a codified program led to the movement's rapid dissipation. In their study of the Washingtonians, Leon Blumberg and Bill Pittman properly concluded that "organizational ineptitude" was a primary source of the movement's downfall.[68]

Lack of a Sustainable Recovery Program: As early as 1844, James Baker noted that the flaw in the Washingtonian approach was that it relied on creating "a degree of excitement in which the human mind, from its very nature and constitution, cannot for any length of time remain."[69] In his modern study of the Washingtonians, Jonathan Zimmerman concluded—as had Jellinek and Baker before him—that the demise of the Washingtonians was ultimately a result of "their inability to develop a binding therapeutic ideology."[70]

These analyses raise a most interesting point in our narrative: What it takes to sustain sobriety is quite different from what it takes to initiate sobriety. They mistook the public confession and the decision to sign the temperance pledge as a program of ongoing

recovery. Because the movement lacked a therapeutic program capable of sustaining sobriety, it quickly dissipated.[71]

Distraction and Diffusion: Political controversies within the Washingtonian movement, particularly debates over the question of alcohol prohibition, splintered many groups, diverting the focus from the reformation of the individual alcoholic.[72] It would be a lesson for the future: service to individuals can be undermined through political involvement and political controversy.

The Washingtonians' focus on the alcoholic also dissipated as their membership became more diverse. As a result of the movement's unexpected public popularity, alcoholics became a small proportion of the total number of people drawn to its meetings. For example, by 1844 only 10% of the 20,000 members of Boston's local Washingtonian Society were reformed inebriates.[73] Milton Maxwell and Leonard Blumberg independently concluded that the Washingtonians were absorbed—"co-opted" and "colonized"—into the larger temperance movement.[74] The Washingtonians were the first recovery-focused mutual-aid group to die of diffusion.

Lack of Sustainable Leadership: In their analysis of the decline of the Washingtonians, Blumberg and Pittman noted that internal conflict and factionalism prevented the emergence of clearly identifiable charismatic leadership.[75] Key leaders of the Washingtonian movement pursued individual careers as professional temperance lecturers—shifting their energy from group survival to individual self-interest and raising divisive allegations that they were exploiting the cause.

Changing Economic Conditions: The harsh economic conditions of 1840-1842 contributed to the rise of a working-class mutual-aid society. The return of economic prosperity in 1843 may well have decreased the desperation of many alcoholics and drained both existing and potential members from the Washingtonian movement.[76]

All of the above-cited factors contributed to the demise of the movement as an identifiable institution, but particular emphasis should be placed on the themes of distraction and diffusion. The dissolution of the Washingtonian Movement occurred through a dilution and corruption of its mission and message. It died in part from organizational arrogance—a fatal character flaw induced by the American phenomenon of super-success.[77] The explosive expansion and fame of the Washingtonians obscured the fact that the movement's original purposes were being lost—that those who were the centerpiece of the birth of the movement had been abandoned. When the novelty and emotional titillation phase passed, little of the movement was left. But as we shall shortly see, all was not lost.

The Washingtonian Legacy

The Washingtonian Society contributed many firsts. It was the first widely available mutual-aid society organized by and for alcoholics in American history. The experiences of the Washingtonian Movement—at its best and at its worst—laid a foundation of experience that guided alcoholism mutual-aid movements that followed. The Washingtonian legacies included 1) the importance of maintaining a focus on the welfare and reformation of the individual alcoholic, 2) the potential power of a personal and public commitment to total abstinence from alcohol, 3) the benefit of regular sober fellowship for the newly recovering alcoholic, 4) the power of experience sharing —the vivid recounting of the ways in which one's life was affected by drinking and the benefits that one had received from sobriety, 5) the use of recovered alcoholics as charismatic speakers and in service work to other alcoholics, and 6) the use of a religious/spiritual foundation for sustained recovery (not part of the official program but incorporated by key Washingtonian leaders).[78]

The Washingtonian decline added several elements to this legacy: 1) Personal reformation movements may be exploited by outsiders and insiders for both ideological and personal gain. 2) Concerns with politics, leadership, publicity, and money can undermine and destroy personal reformation societies. 3) Addiction recovery movements are vulnerable to disruption when they focus on anything other than the personal reformation of their members. This personal recovery focus is best reflected in exclusivity of membership (addicts only) and in a refusal to become

involved in political or professional debate. 4) Personal reformation movements can be harmed by the indiscretions (relapses) of their members and leaders when such people are publicly identified with the movement. 5) Personal recovery may be initiated by a charismatic leader speaking to thousands, but personal recovery is best sustained through personal interaction in small groups.

A careful reading of the following chapters might lead to the interpretation that this movement was, not a failure, but the opening move in an evolving organization of alcoholics into a personal reformation movement. Most "self-help" history tells of the Washingtonian demise and the rise of A.A. a century later. A more careful review will lead to the conclusion that nearly continuous threads linked the Washingtonians with the founders of Alcoholics Anonymous. Considerable evidence points to the possibility that the Washingtonian movement did not end, but went underground by rapidly evolving into a more viable organizational structure—the fraternal temperance society.

As experience accumulated in the Washingtonian Societies, it became clear that many alcoholics needed more than public confession and public commitment to sustain sobriety. Sober Washingtonians began to become more involved with their new recruits. They helped alcoholics clean themselves up and get back on their feet physically, emotionally, and financially. They stayed involved and performed many of the services that a century later would be performed by people called sponsors and counselors. And they sought out new structures that would prove a more viable framework for long-term recovery. The most significant of these structures were the fraternal temperance societies and the reform clubs.

✠

Chapter Three
Fraternal Temperance Societies and Reform Clubs

In the 1840s, many types of fraternal orders in the United States served as mutual-aid societies. Most provided social activities and emotional and financial support to members during difficult times. Members paid regular dues, and out of those dues, benefits were paid for illness and funeral expenses. In the wake of the Washingtonian Revival, it became apparent that a support structure of this kind was needed for drunk-

ards trying to reform. There were two problems: The existing fraternal societies did not require abstinence, and many late-stage alcoholics were excluded from those societies because of their reputations. What was needed was a fraternal organization of reformed alcoholics and other sober-minded individuals.

Out of the dissipation of the Washingtonian Movement, fraternal organizations emerged within the temperance movement between 1842 and 1850. Groups like the Independent Order of Rechabites, the Sons of Temperance, the Order of Good Templars, the National Temple of Honor, the Order of the Good Samaritans, and the Order of Friends of Temperance were born to fill the existing need. The links between the Washingtonians and the fraternal temperance societies were quite human ones. Careers in sobriety could actually be marked by the evolution of one's participation in these evolving sobriety-based support structures. Typical of such evolution was the story of Nathaniel Curtis, a hotel keeper who went from years of drunkenness to sustained sobriety through membership, then leadership roles, first in the Washingtonian movement and later in the Sons of Temperance and the Independent Order of Good Templars.[79]

These new "secret temperance societies" provided both mutual support for sobriety and financial support for the newly reformed. Some, such as the Rechabites and the Samaritans, avoided political involvement and maintained their focus on personal reformation of the drunkard, while others eventually were drawn into the drive for prohibition.[80]

The fraternal temperance orders used group cohesion, mutual surveillance, and elaborate cultural trappings—secret handshakes, secret passwords, symbols, elaborate uniforms, and ceremonies—to bolster their resolve to keep the pledge. The secrecy of the societies—a break from the Washingtonians' emphasis on public confession—allowed many to enter without fear of public stigma regarding their affliction and prevented any public relapses from damaging group credibility.[81] The tradition of anonymity in today's Twelve-Step programs has its historical precedent in these societies. The fraternal temperance orders were also secular orders. Where the mainstream temperance leaders held out religious conversion as the sole means of personal reformation, the fraternal temperance orders focused more on the role of mutual support and surveillance as a means of achieving and maintaining sobriety.

The Sons of Temperance: The Sons of Temperance, founded in 1842 by a group of 16 men, grew to more than 250,000 members in the next decade, with chapters in every state. According to the Rev. R. Adler Temple's 1886 account, the Sons were born directly out of the decline of the Washingtonians. Noting the relapse of 450,000 of the 600,000 men reformed in the great Washingtonian awakening, Temple declared:

A society was, therefore, needed which should offer a refuge to reformed men and shield them from temptation; a brotherhood which should attract them by the cordiality of its sympathies, interest them by the variety of its functions, and strengthen them by its moral support—in a word, which should, by its living spirit of love and fraternity, unlock the wards of their heart and reach the elements of humanness which lay buried there and rehabilitate and re-enthrone them.[82]

The official goals of the Sons of Temperance were to shield members from the evils of intemperance, to provide mutual assistance in case of sickness, and to elevate their character as men. At its most practical level, the Sons helped the inebriate who emerged from his alcoholic haze in a state of abject poverty. The Sons provided relief that helped the newly sober get on their feet and introduced the idea of providing sickness benefits and death benefits through a fraternal temperance society. For example, members of the New York chapter of the Sons of Temperance paid weekly dues to support a sickness benefit of $4 per week and a death benefit that paid $30 for the funeral expenses of a deceased member. The Sons also provided a rich variety of social diversions to help members avoid the siren call of the saloon. These diversions included plays, picnics, bands, small vocal groups, and organized sports. The most controversial of these diversions was dancing, which was officially banned in 1878.[83]

Membership in the Sons rose and fell in the decades following the Washingtonian collapse, but in 1882 the organization still claimed a membership of 73,000 men.[84] The Sons ran what would today be called "closed" meetings and were criticized by such mainstream temperance leaders as John Marsh because they would not allow non-members to attend their meetings.[85] From the organization's inception, two factions arose within the Sons: reformed men who believed that moral suasion and mutual support were the answers to the problem of intemperance and "old temperance men" who were advocates of legal prohibition of alcohol.[86] This split was played out throughout the Sons' history. Some Divisions of the Sons of Temperance joined the political agitation for legal prohibition and lobbied for the Sons' support of this position, support that they won in the late 1840s. Other Divisions of the Sons channeled their political activism into advocacy of the development of state-funded inebriate asylums.[87]

Good Templars and Good Samaritans: The largest fraternal temperance society, the Independent Order of Good Templars, was founded in 1851 with a platform committing its members to total abstinence from all intoxicating liquors and support for the legal prohibition of the manufacture, importation, and sale of alcohol. By 1876, the Templars had initiated more than 2.9 million members. A former Templar leader estimated that more than 400,000 recovered drunkards were among that membership—and that more than half of them had kept their pledges.[88]

Some of the fraternal organizations had smaller numbers but were composed exclusively of reformed alcoholics. One example of such an organization was the Independent Order of Good Samaritans and Daughters of Samaria. This New York-based organization had only 14,000 members, but nearly all were reformed. The Good Samaritans had the distinction of being one of the first racially integrated groups, and one of the first groups that banned political discussions such as debates—particularly those regarding prohibition—from their meetings.

Organization and Practices: The fact that the fraternal temperance societies are often mentioned as part of the mainstream temperance movement actually disguises their true function. The secret temperance societies were the first places where newly recovering alcoholics in America could gather for mutual support and know that their anonymity was ensured. They were among the first sustained "closed meetings" of alcoholics in the United States. Alcoholics who would have been very uncomfortable in the more public atmosphere of the Washingtonians could seek membership in one of the fraternal societies, with the knowledge that their anonymity and their confidential statements would have much greater protection. The major danger to this anonymity was the fact that so many reformed men were drawn to the secret temperance societies that the public came to view them as societies that **only** reformed men could join.[89]

In marked contrast to the highly disorganized Washingtonians, the new fraternal orders provided organizational hierarchy and stability. Their focus also shifted from the individual pledge to a process of mutual vigilance and mutual surveillance. They focused not so much on getting sober as on remaining sober. Within these orders, group conformity demanded complete abstinence. Breaches of this rule could and did lead to expulsion.[90]

One Washingtonian tradition that was extended to the new fraternal temperance societies was the emphasis on service to the alcoholic. Groups like the Good Templars believed that the only way the re-

formed alcoholic could strengthen his own resolve was to pass encouragement and strength on to other alcoholics.[91] While members of many fraternal temperance organizations sought out other alcoholics to whom they could carry a message of hope for personal recovery, some of these societies also carried a countervailing force. In their study of the fraternal temperance societies, Blumberg and Pittman note that classist pretensions began to undermine people's efforts to reach out to the late-stage alcoholic. They report that many of the societies began to explicitly include a membership requirement of "high moral character and good reputation" as a device to screen out lower-class alcoholics.[92] The Independent Order of Rechabites refused membership to anyone with an infirmity that would render him "burdensome" to the group, and the Sons of Temperance rejected anyone who had no visible means of support.[93] It seems that some alcoholics, once sober and economically stable, were prone to turn their backs on those still in need.

Some fraternal temperance societies opened their membership to women. Some, such as the Templars and the Good Samaritans, admitted women to full membership, while others encouraged women to develop parallel independent societies. When the Martha Washington Societies dissipated in the overall demise of the Washingtonian Movement, some of their members migrated to these gender-integrated temperance benevolent societies or started such societies of their own, like the Daughters of Rechab, the Daughters of Temperance, and the Sisters of Samaria. However, the focus on work with and inclusion of inebriate women was lost in the transition to these newer societies. It would be more than a century before alcoholic women would participate in any significant numbers in a mutual-aid movement for alcoholics.[94]

The issue of inclusion of women and Blacks was a highly controversial one within the temperance societies of the 1870s and 1880s, particularly as these societies began to spread into the South. In his well researched book, *Temperance and Racism*, David Fahey describes the schism that divided the Independent Order of Good Templars over the issue of whether or not to include Blacks. While a small number of African-American men and women participated in integrated temperance groups, most African Americans actively involved in the temperance movement preferred to create their own organizations. Separate Black temperance societies like the Black Templars and the True Reformers reinforced abstinence but did not serve as reform institutions for

Black problem drinkers.[95] However, the literature holds little evidence of chronic drunkenness among Blacks during the immediate post-Civil War period.

While some fraternal temperance societies continued to focus on the reformation of the individual alcoholic, many were eventually drawn into the debates generated by the drive toward national alcohol prohibition. As political debate rose, membership in many of the temperance societies declined. In 1882, membership in the Sons of Temperance had fallen to 49,732, and the Independent Order of Good Templars was down to 310,115 members. The fraternal temperance societies' requirement of dues and their somewhat exclusive membership criteria limited the range of alcoholics who could make use of these support structures. Some of the societies also fell prey to dictatorial leadership.

As fraternal temperance societies developed restrictive membership criteria, became caught up in heated political debates about the question of alcohol prohibition, or fell victim to authoritarian leadership, those trends created a vacuum. Once again a mutual-support framework was needed whose sole focus was the reformation of the alcoholic. Reform clubs emerged in many areas to fill this need.

The Reform Clubs

The reform club movement was born in Maine, where men like J.K. Osgood, Dr. Henry Reynolds, and Francis Murphy originated an idea that swept across the country with less fanfare than the Washingtonian Movement had, but with greater durability. Here are the stories of key figures in the reform club movement.

Osgood's Reformed Drinkers Club: J. K. Osgood returned to his home in Gardiner, Maine in August of 1871, following one more in an unending string of drunken sprees. Looking through the window of his home, he saw his wife awaiting his arrival with a look of pained desperation on her face. Deeply touched by this scene, Osgood vowed never to drink another drop of whiskey. He shook off the first miserable days that followed, sought out a lawyer friend whose drinking was as bad as his own, and enlisted his friend's participation in a vow to stop drinking. In January, 1872, the two men posted the following notice:

REFORMERS' MEETING.—There will be a meeting of reformed drinkers at City Hall, Gardiner, on Friday Evening, January 19th, at 7 o'clock. A cordial invitation is extended to all occasional drinkers, constant drinkers,

hard drinkers, and young men who are tempted to drink. Come and hear what rum has done to us.[96]

Osgood and his friend spoke to a large crowd and, at the end, offered an opportunity for others to join them in their pledge. Eight of Gardiner's most notorious drinkers accepted the invitation and organized the Royal Purple Reform Club. The Reform Club movement began with ten alcoholics pledging mutual support for their continued sobriety. Within months, Osgood's reform clubs had spread through much of New Hampshire, Vermont, and Massachusetts and had enlisted the involvement of more than 20,000 heavy drinkers.[97]

Reynolds' Red Ribbon Reform Clubs: Dr. Henry A. Reynolds graduated with honors from medical school at Harvard University in 1864 and, after serving in the Civil War, established a medical practice in Bangor, Maine. Everything he achieved in that practice deteriorated through the progression of his alcoholism. As he would later say of himself, "I am one of the unfortunate men who inherited an appetite for strong drink. I love liquor the way a baby loves milk." In a posture of complete surrender, Dr. Reynolds fell on his knees in 1873 and asked God to deliver him from the ravages of alcoholism. He rose from his knees vowing to sign a pledge at a large meeting of the Women's Temperance Crusade that was being held in Bangor. After he had completed this task, Reynolds immediately sought a source through which he could support his own commitment to sobriety and help others as well. For months, he sought out alcoholics in a haphazard manner, but he finally resolved that he and they needed something more organized. He ran an advertisement in the paper asking reformed drinkers to meet with him on September 10, 1874. Eleven people responded and participated in the organization of the Bangor Reform Club.

Reynolds was asked to visit other communities and share the work of the reform club. Through this process clubs were started all over Maine, with a membership that reached 46,000. Based on the success of the Maine reform clubs, Dr. Reynolds began traveling to other states and organizing similar clubs. Combining the emotional power of his personal recovery and the prestige of his medical degree, Reynolds was a natural on the lecture circuit. The first "Red Ribbon" reform club in Massachusetts was organized in Salem on September 19, 1875. Within a year, more than 70 Red Ribbon Clubs operated in cities across Massachusetts, including larger cities like Gloucester, New Bedford, Lowell, Haverhill, and

Charlestown, all with more than 1,000 members each.[98]

Membership in Reynold's reform clubs was open to any person 18 years of age or older who had been "addicted to strong drink." The reform clubs were religious in nature, and like alcoholic support groups that preceded and followed, focused on a recitation of the trials and tribulations of drinking and the changes that had come with sobriety. Regular meetings were held one night during the week, and a public meeting was held jointly with the Woman's Christian Temperance Union on Sunday afternoons or evenings.[99]

Dr. Reynolds traveled from community to community and state to state (particularly in Massachusetts, Michigan, and Illinois) organizing reform clubs and sharing his own story and the success stories of other reform club members. Reynolds had a unique gift of calling forth the best from men who had been pitied and condemned, first by identifying with them and then by describing their best qualities.

> *I am a graduate of Harvard College, and received a thorough medical education; but I have been drunk four times a day in my office, and if there is any worse hell than I have suffered I don't want to be there. No nobler class of men walk the earth than some who are drinking men. They are naturally generous, wholesome, genial, jolly; but by intemperance their minds become diseased. They become scorned and degraded outcasts in the ditch, kept there by thoughtless people, less generous and honorable by nature than themselves. But for rum, these might be on the throne instead of in the gutter.*[100]

Each member carried a signed pledge card that bore the reform club slogan ("Dare to do Right!") and said:

> *Having seen and felt the evils of intemperance, we, the undersigned, for our own good, and for the good of the world in which we live, do hereby promise and engage, with the help of Almighty God, to abstain from buying, selling, or using Alcoholic or Malt Beverages, Wine and Cider included.*[101]

The term "Red Ribbon Reform Club" derived from the members' practice of wearing a red ribbon on their clothing as a badge of membership. The red ribbon not only helped members identify each other but also provided a visible reminder of their commitment to sobriety. More than one man had his mind changed about reverting to drink in the moment he stopped to remove the red ribbon before entering a saloon. In this way, the red ribbon served much the same purpose as the tokens—ceremonial chips, coins, marbles, keys—used in today's mutual-aid groups and addiction treatment centers.

The reform clubs, like their counterparts today, reached individuals in significant positions of prestige and power. Harold Hughes, the esteemed Iowa Senator who championed the cause of alcoholism in the 1970s and 1980s, is often thought of as the first congressman who openly proclaimed his recovery from alcoholism. But Edwin Willets of Monroe, Michigan walked into the House of Representatives with a red ribbon on his lapel almost 100 years before Hughes' arrival in Washington.[102]

Sometimes very young drinkers felt the call to join a reform club. Since membership was limited to people 18 years of age and older, young drinkers in places like Lawrence, Massachusetts organized their own reform clubs.[103] These reform clubs specifically organized for youthful drinkers are quite likely the earliest predecessors of today's young people's A.A. meetings.

Dr. Reynolds' tactics as a reform club organizer differed considerably from those of his Washingtonian predecessors. He focused on organizing small groups of alcoholics who wanted recovery rather than on filling auditoriums and newspaper headlines. His style was not that of the charismatic speaker. He wanted the focus of attention to be on the work of the local participants, not on a traveling celebrity.

As Dr. Reynolds traveled the country organizing reform clubs, funds to support his work came from donations collected at the public meetings. There is no record of the amount of this income.

Francis Murphy's Blue Ribbon Reform Clubs: Irish-born Francis Murphy migrated to the United States as a teenager. He later lost nearly everything he had achieved as an adult as a result of his alcoholism. Following bankruptcy he opened a bar, but he accidentally killed a customer when, in the midst of a drunken brawl, the two tumbled down a stairway. Murphy was acquitted of murder, but his drinking continued to escalate. While he was confined in jail for drunkenness in July 1871, he received a visit from Captain Cyrus Sturdivant, who cried for him as "a mother sometimes weeps for her child."[104] Praying on his knees in a jail cell with Captain Sturdivant, Murphy was converted to Christianity and the cause of temperance. He promised his wife, who died of typhoid fever shortly after his release from jail, that he would never take another drink. History records that he kept this pledge.

Murphy gave his first temperance speech in Portland, Maine in 1871 and established the Portland Reform Club. The goal of the Reform Club as set forth by the founding members was to "protect ourselves and others from the evils of intemperance."[105] The club was open to all people—women as well as men. The rules governing the club included the threat of fines or expulsion as penalties for drinking, although the club did have procedures for reinstating expelled members.

Murphy's success as a speaker and reform club organizer carried him throughout New England and the Midwest. Impressive numbers of drunkards were brought into the reform clubs: 50,000 in Philadelphia, 40,000 in Pittsburgh, and on and on.[106] Murphy was known both for his organizational skills and for his power and eloquence on the stage. One of his biographers described his commanding presence: "There was something about him, a look, an air that attracted all to him, and made each one feel as though he had just issued from a holy place."[107]

Murphy refined the practice of turning the newly reformed into orators. People with all degrees of education—and with no education—were coaxed to the lectern by his warm invitation to share their stories. The moment someone made a commitment to reform, he or she was put into service helping others. People who had not spoken in front of ten people, with Murphy's encouragement, spoke before a thousand. Slouched men began to straighten, and unclean men groomed themselves in the knowledge they that they could be called on to speak at any moment. Murphy understood that, above all, reformation involved a reawakening of self-respect. Many people scoffed at the idea that yesterday's town drunks were being organized into clubs and presenting temperance lectures, until they began to see many of these men restored to responsible citizenship.

Reform clubs did not promote any particular religion, but they did strongly encourage church and prayer. Murphy always linked religion with personal reformation of the alcoholic. He used to tell his followers:

Too many temperance reforms have led men away from the Churches, but this reform is to bring them into the church. Fill up the Churches, boys. The Church is your mother.[108]

Murphy had a special compassion for children who had been raised amidst the horrors of alcoholism, so he organized formal children's meetings. Here children heard temperance stories, shared their stories about the wounds that alcohol had inflicted on their homes, and were given an opportunity to sign a promise of abstinence not unlike the one signed by their parents.

The reform clubs launched by Murphy were to a great extent born and nurtured out of his own personality and passion. In spite of Murphy's protestations, his work became known as the "Murphy movement," and members often referred to themselves as "Murphyites" and wore the blue ribbon that signaled their membership in one of Murphy's reform clubs.

The travels of Francis Murphy were supported by various religious and temperance organizations, which paid him a stipend of approximately $125 per week.

Reform Clubs' Operation and Spread: Like their predecessors, the reform clubs had to find a way to manage issues that might divert and disrupt their singular purpose. Francis Murphy refused to get involved in ideological or political debates and organized his movement under Lincoln's motto: "With malice towards none, and charity towards all." However, politics did arise as a potentially disruptive and divisive force within the Red Ribbon Reform Clubs. At a meeting in Boston, debate arose over legal prohibition and resulted in many members' leaving the meeting in disgust. Those who remained passed a resolution proclaiming:

We emphatically condemn the introduction, discussion, or agitation of politics in our meetings.[109]

Dr. Reynolds consistently cautioned about mixing politics with the personal reform movement.

Let everything else alone. You reformed men have enough business on your hands to take care of yourselves, without being made cat's-paws for politicians to pull their chestnuts out of the fire.[110]

Reform clubs had a life of their own. They spread far beyond the reach of Osgood, Reynolds, and Murphy—their most famous organizers. There were other noted organizers of reform clubs, including John Drew, Eccles Robinson, Professor Bontecon, Will Knott, Father O'Halloran, and Colonel Rowell. Like John Fisch, who organized reform clubs all over Nebraska, most provided informal leadership within a particular geographical region. Others were organized by employees of railroads and police and fire stations. Most reform clubs were started without fanfare by people whose names were never recorded for history. What the beginnings of all these clubs had in common was one alcoholic reaching out to another alcoholic in support of sobriety. The need to find another who understood and the need to carry the message of recovery to others were at the heart of the reform club movement. The historical fate of the reform club members seems to have been tied to its leaders. Local groups were usually inspired and sustained through the energy of a single leader, and the demise of these groups often paralleled the relocation or death of these leaders.

The Business Men's Moderation Society

For people experiencing problems related to alcohol in the last half of the 19th century, there were alternatives to the abstinence-based fraternal temperance societies and reform clubs. These alternatives took the form of moderation societies. One such society, the Business Men's Moderation Society, was organized on March 11, 1879 "for the encouragement of moderation" in drinking. The major tenets of the society were a pledge not to drink during business hours, adherence to a "blue pledge" that banned "treating," and general encouragement of responsible drinking.

There is suspicion that alcoholics seeking an alternative to abstinence were influential in the founding of this society. In 1884, Daniel Dorchester reported that these societies "organized on the imperfect basis of moderation, all died of drunkenness, and more radical methods were found necessary."[111]   Later temperance texts made light of the moderation societies by noting examples such as the society in which members pledged not to drink more than 14 glasses of wine per day.[112] In general, the moderation societies sought to define when, where, and under what circumstances one should drink, as well as how much one should drink. Most of these societies were short-lived, and it would be a century later before mutual-support groups would reappear with moderate drinking specifically defined as their ultimate goal.

In these first three chapters, we have seen how personal recovery movements emerged into tenuous existence as a response to the rise of alcohol-related problems in 19th-century America. We have also seen how some of the more gifted among the reformed turned their tragedies into professional credentials and a launching pad for new movements organized by and for alcoholics. The continued thread of mutual-aid societies for alcoholics will be picked up later in the alumni associations of inebriate asylums, recovery groups organized within the religious missions, the Jacoby Club of the Emmanuel Clinic, the Oxford Groups, and the birth of Alcoholics Anonymous in 1935. Many alcoholics' struggle to get sober in these earliest mutual-aid groups led to the call for new institutions made up of varying mixtures of religion, medicine, and business. These new institutions were the inebriate homes and inebriate asylums.

Chapter Four
The Rise and Fall of Inebriate Homes and Asylums [1]

"God forbid that we should erect asylums for our children! But God forbid, if our own children become drunkards, that they should fail to find asylums for seclusion and recovery!"[2]

The idea of a place where people addicted to alcohol or other drugs could be cared for by those who specialized in the treatment of this disorder is quite old. Egyptian records dating back some 5,000 years indicate the presence of people who provided care in their own homes for people who were "mad from wine or beer." Recommendations for public and private asylums for inebriates also appear in early Greek and Roman writings.[3] In America, the idea of creating special institutions and special professional roles for the care of inebriates began in the late 18th century and blossomed in the mid-19th century. Dr. Benjamin Rush was the first American physician to propose that the chronically intemperate were diseased and should be medically treated. Similar recommendations came in the years 1830-1860 from Drs. Eli Todd, Samuel Woodward, and Joseph Turner.[4][1]

Dr. Samuel Woodward, America's leading authority on mental disease in the early 19th century, published an 1833 essay in which he set forth his conviction that half the country's drunkards could be cured by treatment in well-conducted institutions.[5] In 1840, R. Grinrod proposed the development of asylums for the intemperate as an alternative to the almshouse and the jail.

Let the experiment be fairly tried; let an institution be founded; let the means of cure be provided; let the principles on which it is to be founded be extensively promulgated,

and I doubt not, all intelligent people will be satisfied of its feasibility....At the head of this institution place a physician of zeal, medical skill and enlarged benevolence; let the principle of total abstinence be rigorously adopted and enforced....let appropriate medication be afforded; let the mind be soothed....let the certainty of success be clearly delineated to the mind of the sufferer....Let good nutrition be regularly administered; let perfect quiet be enjoined while the prostration of strength and energy continue—this course, rigorously adopted and pursued, will restore nine out of ten in all cases.[6]

All of those calling for reform declared it a public duty to care for the inebriate on both moral and practical grounds, and many went further in positing that such institutions should be supported through income generated from the sale of alcoholic beverages.

Pre-Asylum Days: Knowledge of Addiction

Other than the early discovery that rum made in lead stills resulted in lead poisoning, there was very little recognition of alcohol-related physical maladies until the late 18th-century writings of Dr. Benjamin Rush.[7] During the 19th century, the effects of heavy drinking on the liver, the stomach, the blood, and the nerve and muscle tissue of the extremities were discovered and in turn christened *alcoholic cirrhosis*, *alcoholic gastritis*, and *alcoholic polyneuropathy*.[8]

The 19th century also witnessed a growing recognition of alcoholic psychoses. Samuel Burton Pearson and John Armstrong described an alcohol-induced "brain fever" that was later named *delirium tremens* by Thomas Sutton. American accounts of "D.T.s" between 1819 and 1831 by physicians Walter Channing and John Ware offered quite complete depictions of the symptoms of delirium tremens: hand tremors, restlessness, loss of appetite, violent vomiting, excessive perspiration, impairment of memory, confusion, and terrifying hallucinatory and illusory experiences.[9]

In 1881, Carl Wernicke described a psychosis accompanied by polyneuritis that was the result of

---

[1]Sources used to construct this chapter that deserve special acknowledgment include Jim Baumohl's and Sarah Tracy's seminal work on the early inebriate asylums. Their respective dissertations and many subsequent papers provided the foundation of scholarship for this chapter. Their ground-breaking research; their critiques of early drafts of the chapters in this section; and their sustained encouragement of my work on this book are gratefully acknowledged.

chronic alcoholism and its accompanying vitamin B_1 deficiency. Six years later, Sergei Korsakoff described an organic condition emerging during late stages of alcoholism that was characterized by polyneuropathy, confusion, impairment of recent memory, confabulation, visual and auditory hallucinations, and superficial and stereotyped speech. These conditions came to bear names reflecting their discovers: *Wernicke's syndrome* and *Korsakoff's psychosis*.

Nineteenth-century physicians also recognized that alcohol, even in small quantities, could ignite explosive violence in some individuals. This condition, which was often accompanied by disorientation and paranoid delusions and sometimes followed by amnesia, was know variously as "drunken furor," "mania a potu," or "pathological intoxication."[10]

In addition to the growing recognition of the physical pathology of alcohol in the 19th century, there was also a growing understanding of the primary condition of alcoholism. One man, a Swedish physician named Magnus Huss, played a significant role in introducing the term *alcoholism* and synthesizing and cataloguing what was being learned about alcoholism around the world. His text, *Chronic Alcoholism,* was at that time the most definitive exploration of alcoholism that had ever been written.[11]

While the above breakthroughs in knowledge were significant, the primitive state of the knowledge about alcohol and alcoholism is well illustrated by the amount of discussion within 19th-century professional and lay circles of a most unusual phenomenon: the spontaneous combustion of alcoholics.

Within the temperance era in which the inebriate asylums arose, there were many retold tales of alcoholic debauchery and demise. None quite compares, however, with the legend of drunkards becoming so saturated with alcohol that they ignited by spontaneous combustion. "Well authenticated" cases of inebriates burning to death from "internal fires" filled the pages of the *American Temperance Magazine* in the 1850s.[12]

This legend had numerous sources. There were so many reports of spontaneous combustion of humans in France and Germany that the notion became a generally accepted fact in 19th-century European medicine and literature.[13]

The person most responsible for the spread of this idea in the United States was Robert MacNish. He included a whole chapter on "Spontaneous Combustion of Drunkards" in his 1835 treatise, *Anatomy of Drunkenness*. In his review of published cases of spontaneous combustion in humans, MacNish noted that nearly all were inebriates. Typical of these reports was the case of Mary Clues, a fifty-year-old woman long

addicted to drink, who went to sleep in close proximity to a burning candle and fireplace. When neighbors responded to the sight of smoke coming from Ms. Clues' window, they reportedly found the deceased woman's skin and muscle severely burned while her clothes, the bedding, and surrounding furniture were not charred. It was concluded that she had burned, from the inside out.[14] Such tales of flaming drunks made great fare on the temperance lecture circuit, and the sustained prevalence of these reports in 19th-century medicine provide a measure of the level of technical knowledge of alcohol and alcoholism as we enter the era of the inebriate asylum.[15]

Pre-Asylum Days: Care of the Addicted

Before the development of institutions specializing in the treatment of addiction, alcoholics and addicts landed in all manner of institutions—the almshouse, the charitable lodging home, the jail, the workhouse, and the newly created lunatic asylum.[16] None of these institutions desired the inebriate's presence, and none were equipped to treat addiction. Under such circumstances, many—particularly those addicted to narcotics—kept their addictions hidden until the circumstances of their death revealed what for each had been the central secret of his or her life.[17]

There was no adequate response to the medical needs of inebriates in the mid-19th century, but this inadequacy was part of a more pervasive range of unmet health-care needs. In the first half of the 19th century, these conditions spawned a number of reform movements that sought to improve the nation's health and respond to growing social problems through the creation of new American institutions: the prison, the reform school, the orphanage home, the insane asylum, the tuberculosis sanatorium, and the leper colony. During the same period, and out of this same reform sentiment, came a drive to create special institutions for the treatment of alcoholism and other drug addictions.

The movement to create specialized care for inebriates incubated within a series of failed attempts to bring the problem of intemperance under control. First was the failure of the temperance movement to induce inebriates to moderate their patterns of excessive drinking. This failure lead to a radicalization of the temperance movement, the legal drive toward prohibition, and proposals for the development of abstinence-based institutions that could specialize in the treatment of inebriety. Second was the failure of other social institutions—medicine, religion, public charity, the courts, and the jails—to reform the alcoholic. The relationship between these institutions and inebriates was often one of mutual contempt and avoidance. In the vacuum of this failure rose the need for a specialized institution that could transcend this barrier of contempt to reach alcoholics on a medical and moral basis.

The Earliest Institutions

During the second half of the 19th century, there was a rapid growth in the number of institutions specializing in the treatment of inebriety. When a professional association of inebriate home and inebriate asylum managers—the American Association for the Cure of Inebriates—was launched in 1870, only six institutions were in operation. By 1878, 32 institutions were represented in the association, and by 1902 there were more than 100 facilities in the U.S. that specialized in the treatment of alcoholism and other addictions.[18] The early pioneers included the New York State Inebriate Asylum, the Pennsylvania Sanitarium for Inebriates, the Washingtonian Homes in Boston and Chicago, the Kings County Inebriates' Home, and Walnut Lodge. Some of these facilities quickly distinguished themselves by the sheer numbers of people they were treating. The Washingtonian Home in Boston, for example, had treated more than 10,000 alcoholics by 1899.[19]

Types of Institutions

Institutions that cared for those addicted to alcohol and other drugs during this period went by many names: lodging houses, inebriate homes, inebriate asylums, sanataria, reformatories, retreats, institutes, and —later—inebriate farms and inebriate colonies. Most fell into two categories: inebriate homes and inebriate asylums.

Inebriate "homes" were those institutions that provided a minimal level of treatment activity in addition to room and board. Some evolved out of the temperance movement's "dry hotels" or out of "lodging houses" like Washingtonian Hall in Boston and Dashaway Hall in San Francisco, which gave the down-on-his-luck inebriate a place to stay while the temperance meetings did the work of moral reformation. The Washingtonian Homes in Boston and Chicago were among the best known of these facilities.

Inebriate asylums tended to be large medically directed facilities. The first of these facilities, the New York State Inebriate Asylum, was opened in 1864. While many of the asylums were organized

privately, a trend at the turn of the century was the emergence of state-operated facilities for the treatment of inebriety. The states of New York, Iowa, Wisconsin, Connecticut, and Minnesota were among the pioneers in the creation of such specialized facilities. By 1909, there were nine such facilities in the country.[20] Notable among these state initiatives was the Massachusetts State Hospital for Dipsomaniacs and Inebriates in Foxborough, and later Norfolk. It opened in 1893 as the first completely government (state)-funded and- operated inebriate institution in the country. Massachusetts continued to provide specialized institutional settings for the treatment of inebriety until such services were terminated in 1920, on the eve of national alcohol prohibition.[21]

While movements for state centralization of charities, prisons, and psychiatric asylums were well underway by the end of the 19th century, plans to fund and centralize the management of inebriate asylums through state control never gained nationwide momentum. Many states discussed inebriate asylum proposals without acting upon them, while others like Texas and Washington, D.C. chartered but never funded the construction or operation of an inebriate asylum. Even where such asylums were opened, state support was inconsistent.[22]

Another phenomenon that emerged at the end of the 19th century was the development of private sanitaria that cultivated an affluent clientele who were seeking, if not addiction treatment, at least periodic drying out. Facilities, variably christened "Sanitarium," "Lodge," "Institute," or "Retreat," offered discreet detoxification and recuperation for the affluent. While the primary focus of all of these facilities was on the treatment of alcoholism, the first treatment facilities in the country cared for people addicted to a wide variety of intoxicants. One of the first facilities devoted exclusively to treating addiction to drugs other than alcohol was Dr. Jansen B. Mattison's Brooklyn Home for Habitués, which opened in 1891.[23]

Inebriety treatment consisted of physicians who ministered to the addict's medical problems and attempted ambulatory detoxification, a variety of residentially based treatment services in the inebriate asylums and homes, and occasional experiments in what today would be called "day treatment" or "intensive outpatient treatment." Many of the addiction cure "Institutes" used a treatment protocol whereby patients came for medicines three or four times a day while they were living at home or being boarded in a hotel. One quite notable experiment in outpatient treatment was conducted in Massachusetts between 1909 and 1917. During this period, the Massachusetts Hospital for Dipsomaniacs and Inebriates operated 29 outpatient offices across Massachusetts that provided counseling to alcoholics. Each year, physicians and social workers operating out of these clinics visited and maintained regular correspondence with more than 3,000 patients.[24]

The first efforts to initiate addiction treatment services in America produced what was clearly a patchwork of specialty institutions. Proposals to implement a more consistent and better-organized approach to the treatment of inebriates were often advocated. Dr. T.D. Crothers, for example, advocated the creation of three types of facilities: 1) specialized hospitals that would treat acute cases of inebriety on a voluntary and involuntary basis through residential stays of up to one year, 2) institutions that would treat chronic cases of inebriety through residential stays of one to three years, and 3) workhouses or farm colonies where incurable inebriates could be forced into "military habits of life and work, and kept in the best conditions of forced healthy living." Crothers envisioned that acute care would be provided in urban population centers and that treatment for chronic and incurable cases would be located in rural areas.[25] Proposals like Crothers' were the among the first suggestions to move beyond isolated institutions to create a system of services that in our modern vernacular could provide a "continuum of care."

Sponsorship and Financing

The earliest addiction treatment programs in America were supported through self-payment by patients and their families, legislative grants, special alcohol taxes, charitable contributions, and selling patient-generated products and labor.

From their earliest days, inebriate homes and asylums sought to garner state funding to support their efforts, but only a few states provided such support. Even where this seemingly stable funding flow was available, there was a danger that earmarked funds would be diverted to other areas during times of economic hardship. In the end, 19th-century efforts did not succeed in winning public funding for the treatment of inebriates. Legislators facing funding requests for such treatment efforts weighed them against what was, at the time, portrayed as a more permanent solution: the prohibition of alcohol.

Most of the inebriate homes and asylums attempted to be self-supporting by charging fees for room and board and for special treatment procedures.

Many, however, did make provision for the indigent, usually by designating one or two beds for "charity cases."[26]

Addiction treatment institutions found several other sources of subsidy. Some were supported through liquor-related taxes. The Kings County Inebriates' Home in New York, for example, received 12% of the county's annual liquor license revenues. Early advocates of specialized institutions for the care of inebriates sought to bolster support for the allocation of liquor revenues to such institutions by proposing the principle that "every business should be obliged to provide for the accidents which grow out of it."[27] This principle led to such legislation as Ohio's Adai Laws holding saloonkeepers responsible for the behavior of their patrons and to recommendations that liquor taxes should be used to subsidize the treatment of inebriety.[28] However, only in a few localities did they win direct support of alcoholism treatment institutions through alcohol-related tax revenue or fines for drunkenness; and even where such support did exist, funds could be cut back quickly during times of local economic hardship. Some early inebriate homes, like the New York Christian Home for Intemperate Men and the Good Templars Asylum in Quincy, Illinois, were financially supported by religious or temperance organizations. Other homes, such as the San Francisco Home for the Care of the Inebriate, were fortunate enough to receive substantial endowments from private philanthropists.[29]

Many inebriate asylums—particularly those catering to the middle and working classes—were organized according to the "industrial plan." The industrial plan involved using the patient workforce to conduct much of the work of the institution, to raise the crops and livestock used to feed the asylum community, and to operate patient industries that generated products or services that could be sold to support the institution.[30] Each home had to use whatever means were available to sustain itself. When the Appleton Home in South Boston was denied state aid, the home was supported by fees earned from the lecture tour of its administrator, D. Banks MacKenzie.[31]

Despite private donations, sporadic state and religious support, and the designation of a small number of "charity beds," very few inebriate paupers were treated within the inebriate asylums.[32] Treatment was most accessible to people of affluence, who could afford the $40-$600-per-month fees charged by the inebriate institutions.[33] America's first addiction treatment leaders were concerned about the ways in which these financial considerations could affect admission decisions. In 1871, one inebriate asylum director advocated state funding of treatment facilities so that admission decisions would not be biased by an institution's need for a particular patient's financial support.[34]

Relationships With Other Community Institutions

As inebriate asylums came into existence, they sought to formalize relationships with other community institutions. While the public at large was skeptical and ambivalent about this new institution, many formal community agencies supported the work of the inebriate homes and asylums. This support stemmed from the belief that these new facilities could relieve the burden that alcoholics and addicts placed on both general and psychiatric hospitals, as well as on almshouses, jails, and charitable organizations. Communities were also concerned about alcohol-impaired workers and the growing presence of drunkards in the local courts. Jim Baumohl has described how the early fire and police departments of San Francisco referred their alcohol-impaired employees for treatment at the San Francisco Home for the Care of the Inebriate.[35] The country's new addiction treatment agencies tried to establish their niche within the communities they served.

Finding such a niche for these institutions was, however, not without its conflict. The inebriate asylums experienced a variety of relationship problems: 1) tension with temperance organizations, springing from differing views of the etiology of, and remedy for, drunkenness; 2) tension with political authorities over requests for state subsidy of treatment, and 3) conflict with other community institutions over philosophy, methods, and mutual responsibility for care of the inebriate.

Perhaps the sharpest point of conflict was between inebriate institution leaders and the superintendents of psychiatric institutions. State psychiatric asylums had established a pattern of excluding alcoholics and addicts. When new inebriety institutions were opened, disagreements inevitably occurred over which institutions bore responsibility for people who presented dimensions of both insanity and inebriety. The psychiatric institutions not only acknowledged that they were ill-equipped to care for the inebriate, but went so far as to declare that mixing inebriates within their institutions would prove "prejudicial to the welfare of those inmates for whom the institutions were designed."[36]

A hidden source of this conflict was the fact that the inebriate constituted a direct confrontation of America's earliest psychiatric practices. It is hard to imagine how inebriate patients would have fit within institutions known for their free and liberal use of whiskey, opium, and other narcotics as medicines, and for the use of chemical restraints, also a common practice in 19th-century insane asylums.[37] First-person accounts of life in 19th-century insane asylums are also replete with references to the drinking and drug problems of staff working at these facilities. This problem was so great that the following was among the reform recommendations offered in 1883:

> *That excessive use of opium or intoxicating liquors by Superintendents and subordinates in insane hospitals is such a crime as calls for legislative prohibition....*[38]

The new inebriety institutions operated in a community fishbowl on what might be called a probationary status.

Early Professionalization: The American Association for the Cure of Inebriates

The rise of movements to create specialized institutions for the care of the indigent, the orphaned, the mentally ill, and the inebriate was followed by a secondary movement to bring those working in such institutions into professional affiliation. This was particularly the case in the decade of the 1870s, which saw the birth of such organizations as the National Association for the Protection of the Insane, the National Conference of Social Work, the American Public Health Association, the Charity Organization Society, and the National Prison Association. It was within this fever to organize human service professionals that those directing America's earliest institutions for the treatment of inebriety first came together.

Early History and Philosophy: On November 29, 1870, 14 physicians, trustees, and lay people affiliated with six inebriate asylums met together at the New York City YMCA to found the American Association for the Cure of Inebriates. The Association was the dream of Dr. Joseph Parrish, director of the Pennsylvania Sanitarium for Inebriates. Dr. Parrish enlisted the aid of Dr. Willard Parker of the New York State Inebriate Asylum in launching the first professional organization within the addiction treatment field.[39] Other Institutions represented at this first meeting were the Kings County Inebriates' Homes, the Washingtonian Home of Boston, the Washingtonian

Home of Chicago, and the Greenwood Institute. Also in attendance were C.L. Ives from the Yale Medical School and Dr. Alonzo Calkins, author of *Opium and the Opium Appetite*.[40]

The first four tenets articulated in the American Association for the Study and Cure of Inebriety (AASCI) statement of principles and purposes declared that: *1. Intemperance is a disease. 2. It is curable in the same sense that other diseases are. 3. Its primary cause is a constitutional susceptibility to the alcoholic impression. 4. This constitutional tendency may be inherited or acquired*.[41] The statement of principles went on to criticize the penal approach to inebriety and to call for the creation of special medical institutions in which the inebriate could be treated scientifically.[42]

The notion that alcohol inebriety (alcoholism) was a disease worthy of medical treatment was not a concept discovered by the leaders of the inebriate asylum movement. What the inebriate asylum leaders did that had not been achieved by any of their predecessors was to develop a *well-articulated* disease concept of addiction and to operationalize this concept within a system of institutional care for the alcoholic. This is not to say that there was unanimity of belief in a disease concept among the directors of inebriate asylums and homes. The proposition that inebriety was a disease continued to be argued within the Association and in broader professional circles. Some institutions, such as Philadelphia's Franklin Reformatory Home for Inebriates, withdrew from the Association after repeatedly challenging the Association's principles through such remarks as the following:

> *We do not, either in our name or management, recognize drunkenness as the effect of a diseased impulse; but regard it as a habit, sin and crime, we do not speak of cases being cured, as in a hospital, but "reformed."*[43]

There was also wider public and professional criticism of the Association's founding principles, and particularly of its advocacy of specialized medical treatment for the inebriate. Some of these critics viewed inebriety as a hereditary weakness and advocated that alcoholics should be left to die so that alcoholism would eventually disappear. Others, particularly the clergy, saw this new disease theory as a medicalization of sin and as an invitation for medically excused moral transgressions.[44]

Activities: The Association for the Study and Cure of Inebriety was involved in three primary activities: 1) professional information exchange, 2) political advocacy of legislation establishing and supporting the work of inebriate asylums, and 3) the publication of a professional journal and a small number of treatises on addiction treatment.[45]

Political activities of the Association included lobbying for state financial support of asylums, advocating the passage of commitment laws that would provide for the involuntary treatment of the inebriate, and encouraging states to regulate the addiction treatment industry. Members of the association were acutely aware of the growth of quack addiction cures and sought state regulation of institutions, practitioners, and medicines involved in the treatment of inebriety.[46]

The most significant activity of the Association was its publication of meeting proceedings, and the publication of *The Quarterly Journal of Inebriety* from 1876 to 1914. The first 5,000-copy edition of the *Journal* was issued in December, 1876, under the guidance of Dr. T.D. Crothers, who served as editor of the Journal during its entire 38-year history.

The Journal struggled to establish professional credibility by weeding out wildly controversial papers and supposedly scientific papers that were little more than thinly masked advertisements for a particular physician or treatment facility. Under Crothers' guidance, the *Journal* did begin to achieve some degree of professional credibility. By 1891, more than 2,000 physicians subscribed to the Journal.[47]

A perusal of articles in the *Journal of Inebriety* reveals some material of remarkable sophistication, even by today's standards, and other material that is surprising and outlandish. The Journal included advertisements for drugs—including Glyco-Heroin and Veronal (a barbiturate) —and referenced many unusual cures. For example, an article in the January-February, 1914 issue suggested that bee stings could reverse alcohol intoxication, could make one immune to the effects of alcohol, and could destroy the alcoholic's desire for alcohol.

The creation of the Association and *The Journal of Inebriety* signaled a growing market for a broader body of professional and lay literature on addiction. Beginning with Dr. Albert Day's *Methomania (1867)* and Dr. George Calkins' 1871 text, *Opium and the Opium Appetite*, a number of texts detailing approaches to addiction treatment began to appear, including Hubbard's *The Opium Habit and Alcoholism* (1881), Parrish's *Alcoholic Inebriety* (1883), Wright's *Inebriism* (1885), and Crothers' classic 1893 work *Diseases of Inebriety*.

What this professional literature presented was a

conflicting array of theories and approaches to addiction treatment that could befuddle practitioners and thoroughly confuse the addicted citizen in need of assistance. Addicts were confronted then, as now, with a large number of addiction experts and institutions, each claiming a special knowledge of the cause and cure of addiction. Many addicts, suffering repeated setbacks after hopes of cure, found themselves disillusioned with the treatments of the day—and with themselves. One addict in the 1880s described his experience with such cure purveyors with pointed eloquence:

> *I have borne the most unfair comments and insinuations from people utterly incapable of comprehending for one second the smallest part of my suffering, or even knowing that such could exist. Yet they claim to deliver opinions and comments as though better informed on the subject of opium eating than anybody else in the world. I have been stung by their talk as by hornets, and have been driven to solitude to avoid the fools.*[48]

Patients were not the only ones critical of the many new and widely advertised treatments. An editorial that appeared in the *Journal of Inebriety* in 1900 called for the development of what in today's language might be called accreditation standards for institutions treating alcohol and other drug addictions. The editorial complained of "irregular homes and sanitariums" managed by "unknown and so-called reformed men" and the proliferation of "secret drugs and so-called specifics" for the cure of addiction.[49]

The Decline of the Inebriate Asylums

The field of addiction treatment was booming in 1890, and the future looked exceedingly bright. Pronouncements on the future of institutions for the treatment of inebriety were profuse with optimism. There was similar optimism about the role of physicians in this treatment. In 1900, Dr. Charles Parker predicted in the pages of *The Medical Record* that the treatment of alcoholism and drug addictions would "soon be rated among the most important specialties in the medical profession."[50] But forces were unfolding that would decimate the field of addiction treatment just when it seemed that its future was ensured.

Inebriate asylums and homes were inherently unstable organizations that emerged more out of the passion of visionary individuals than out of a groundswell of public support. The shaky political and economic foundation upon which the homes and asylums were built led to a very tenuous existence for these institutions. Some institutions, like the Southern California State Asylum, were founded but never built or opened. Other institutions closed after short periods of operation or redefined their institutional mission. The mixed interests which came together to support these new institutions sometimes erupted into conflict that threatened their very existence. Even those inebriate asylums that thrived in the last half of the 19th century struggled as they moved into the new century.

A series of surveys underscored the dramatic decline of the inebriate asylum as a social institution between 1890 and 1920. In 1893, Crothers noted that, of the first 50 institutions that had been founded to treat inebriety, only 30 remained open, and that only in a few of these was "inebriety studied and treated on a scientific basis".[51] A 1917 survey of institutions in the United States conducted by Pollock and Furbush found only 23 private institutions providing treatment exclusively for alcoholism and other addictions.[52]

In 1922, members of the Scientific Temperance Federation sought to discover the effect of prohibition on admissions to alcoholism treatment institutions. They found pre-prohibition advertisements and listings for 275 institutions treating alcoholics and tried to contact each to determine its current status. They were able to secure information on 184 of the listed institutions, of which only 51 remained in business. Their survey revealed that most of the institutions had changed their focus or had gone out of business due to decreased demand for treatment. In 1922, only 27 institutions specializing solely in the treatment of inebriety could be found in the whole country. The survey documented the manner in which whole chains of addiction treatment centers had closed or been dramatically reduced in number. All five Gatlin Institutes were closed, 60 of the 62 Neal Institutes were closed, and the number of Keeley Institutes had dropped from more than 100 to 12. Most of the treatment facilities that remained open in 1922 also reported a decline in the total number of patients treated since the beginning of prohibition. For example, admission of men to the Chicago Washingtonian Home had plummeted from 1,114 in 1919 to 171 in 1921.[53]

By the mid-1920s, most of the inebriate homes, inebriate asylums, and private sanitaria specializing in addiction treatment were gone. Many had evolved into insane asylums, private health sanitaria, or correctional institutions. The institutional response to the inebriate was shifting from the private, specialized facility to the public psychiatric or correctional facility. The decline of the inebriate home and asylum as specialty institutions was mirrored by the progressive collapse of the addiction treatment field as a professional arena. In 1904, the American Medical Temperance Association and the Association for the Study and Cure of Inebriety merged under a new name, the American Medical Association for the Study of Alcohol and Other Narcotics.[54] This merged Association withered along with the field it represented. The *Journal of Inebriety* was sustained only by the individual efforts of the aging T.D. Crothers. The last issue was published in 1914. The Association's full demise occurred unnoticed in the 1920s.[55]

By 1925, America's network of inebriate homes and asylums had all but collapsed, with only a handful of the original 19th-century specialty institutions surviving into the modern era. The only widely available institutional placements remaining for alcoholics and addicts were the exclusive private hospitals that few could afford and state-operated psychiatric hospitals that were being described as places of "inhumanity and neglect."[56]

The fact that a national network of addiction treatment programs was born, was professionalized, then disappeared—all within the span of a few decades—should give the reader pause for serious reflection. What factors led to this demise, and might the current treatment system be subject to such a decline? We will answer the first of these questions here and hold the second for a later discussion.

A Post-Mortem of the Inebriate Asylum Movement

No single factor led to the demise of the inebriate homes and asylums. Rather, forces both from outside and from within the field contributed to the rapid deterioration and collapse of inebriate homes and asylums.

Economic Forces: The private treatment facilities that constituted the inebriety movement existed as independent businesses or charitable enterprises. There existed no central mechanism—no federal, state or private authority—that took over the role of planning, funding, and evaluating these facilities. The failure of inebriate asylums and homes to achieve broad public support and the lack of centralized bureaucratic support at the state level—support that prisons, orphanages, and insane asylums had achieved to a substantial degree—contributed to the vulnerability of the inebriate asylum and home as a social institution. Many died amidst promises of public funding that failed to materialize or funding that was cut during a period of local or state fiscal crisis.

Nineteenth- and early 20th-century addiction treatment institutions were threatened both when the economy was at its best and when it was at its worst. The boom economy absorbed large numbers of marginal alcoholics and addicts into the workforce, decreasing the demand for treatment services. The troubled economy decreased people's ability to pay for treatment and intensified competition for public dollars needed to support addiction treatment. Three economic depressions (the mid-1890s; 1913-1916; and the late 1920s and early 1930s) had this dual effect upon many inebriate homes and asylums.[57] But economic forces were not nearly as devastating as was the growing perception of addiction in criminal rather than medical terms.

Social and Political Forces: The inebriate asylum movement rose alongside other social institutions in an atmosphere of optimism that David Rothman has described as a *"grand and almost utopian vision."* This vision was based on the widespread belief that people could be changed profoundly if they were isolated for a period of time from harmful influences and placed in an environment in which their values and beliefs could be "rigorously reprogrammed."[58] The rise of the inebriate asylum and related reform institutions was accompanied by promises that great cures would be effected through these bold experiments in social engineering.

By the early 20th century, this optimism about personal reformation had faded and left in its wake a more pessimistic and fatalistic view of the problems that the reform movements had promised to eliminate. Americans came to view addiction less in terms of disease and more in terms of defects of character and morality. There was also a growing portrayal of social problems as dangerously contagious. In this view, the carriers of such social infections had to be quarantined for the good of the larger community. This triggered a shift toward solving social problems through legal restraint, punishment, and sequestration.[59] Offers of material and spiritual support to inebriates gave way to legal coercion and containment. Proposals to cure alcoholics and addicts were increasingly replaced by proposals to prohibit alcohol, tobacco, and the non-medical use of opiates and cocaine.[60] As we shall see in coming chapters, this criminalization of addiction exerted a profound influence on our continuing story.

Poorly Developed Clinical Technology: The inebriate asylum field failed to develop a coherent philosophy and technology (clinical protocol) of addiction treatment that was capable of achieving and sustaining scientific credibility or public confidence. The field simply was never able to establish the soundness of its theories or the effectiveness of its interventions. Lacking a central therapeutic ideology and a core addiction treatment technology, the field's existence was socially, professionally, and politically tenuous.

Howard Hall, in his study of the demise of the American Association for the Study and Cure of Inebriety, has underscored the way in which the Association and its institutional members came under severe criticism for the lack of scientific validation of their theories and treatment methods. In response to this criticism, rather than acknowledge itself as a young field that had not yet had time or resources to complete such scientific studies, the Association instead argued against the usefulness of such scientific methods. Association leaders consistently argued that clinical observation and case-study methods were more valuable than experimental or laboratory procedures in understanding inebriety and its treatment. As a result of this stance, when its very existence was threatened, the field had no scientific data that it could use to justify its methods or its very existence.[61]

Patient Selectivity: Patient selectivity worked two ways to undermine the viability of the inebriate homes and asylums. First, public facilities were often burdened by their lack of control of who entered their facilities. The forced admission of court-ordered incorrigibles into these institutions proved particularly disruptive.[62] Second, many of the private facilities were quite proficient in a practice known today as "creaming": the recruitment and admission into treatment of clients who have the greatest financial resources and the best prognosis for recovery—and the simultaneous exclusion of those who fail to meet such criteria. While this latter practice led to the efficient and profitable management of the treatment institution, it also led to the public perception that such facilities were for the rich—an image that generated little support for them among the general citizenry. Inebriate homes and asylums failed to seek out and care for the inebriates who were burdening community hospitals, courts, and jails. Because they failed to serve these institutional clients and to treat the alcoholics and addicts who were contributing the most to public disorder, many inebriate homes and asylums were perceived as having no viable value to the communities and states they approached for financial support. All too often the public perceived the inebriate home as a luxurious retreat where people who had behaved very badly were not just treated well, but coddled.

Modality/Environment Bias: The asylum movement was based on the premise that inebriates required physical isolation from their natural environments and a sustained period of physical and psychological/moral rehabilitation. The leaders of this movement competed, not only with each other, but with a host of cures and treatments that the inebriate could undergo while living at home. The fact that the clinical technology was residentially based, with its enforced period of isolation, all but ensured that inebriate homes and asylums would primarily serve individuals in the latest stages of addiction, whose physical and emotional pain was sufficient to overcome their natural resistance to sequestration from work and family. This modality bias restricted the percentage of addicts who could ever be reached by the movement. The institutional model also committed the movement to an extremely high per-capita treatment cost, which it failed to reconcile with its perceived poor recovery rates.

Conflict Within the Field and With Allied Fields: Inebriate asylums and homes were also made vulnerable by dissension among various branches of the field, dissension within particular institutions, and conflicts with allied professions.

Conflicts among leaders, staff, board representatives, and the broader community actually led to the closing of some early inebriate facilities. Such was the fate of America's first inebriate asylum, the New York State Inebriate Asylum, whose story will be told in Chapter Six. The whole field seemed to lack a model for conflict resolution. Acrimonious debates were played out in public rather than professional forums, in a manner that tarnished the image of the entire field. The lack of professional standards particularly of a foundation of science through which the field could test its many theories—and the lack of a professional etiquette that could guide the field's discourse undermined the very viability of the field. Lacking such a foundation, the field struggled to compete with home cures that claimed to be faster, safer, cheaper and more effective.

The professional legitimacy of inebriety treatment as a medical specialty was undermined by allied professions that saw these new treatment facilities as a threat to their own preeminence. For example, when the AASCI was founded, the editor of the *American Journal of Insanity*, the official organ of the insane asylum managers, criticized the very idea of an inebriate asylum.

Congregating such people (drunkards) together, and subjecting them to the moral treatment of idleness, indulgence in the use of tobacco, and card playing, with a moral lecture, once or twice a week, on the evils of intemperance will never cure disease.[63]

Ethical Abuses: Lacking any articulated ethical code of professional practice, the field of inebriety treatment found itself plagued by highly publicized ethical abuses. As competition among treatment institutions tightened in the 1890s, charges and counter-charges of charlatanry and fraud filled the pages of the *Journal of Inebriety* and the popular press. Unfortunately, these charges all too often proved accurate.[64] In reviewing this period, Terry and Pellens noted the following about the private hospitals and addiction-cure sanitaria: "Many of these were fraudulent in character and made no effort to cure their cases, discharging them when their funds were exhausted still suffering from that which they sought relief."[65] In response to such exposés, a public that little understood the various branches of this new treatment field tended to paint the field with one brush.

Practices that led to the perception that addiction specialists were charlatans included aggressive and fraudulent marketing techniques (including exorbitant claims for cure rates); excessive lengths of stay; unlimited admissions for wealthy clients; the use of medicines that were themselves loaded with alcohol, opiates, and cocaine; and a wide variety of reported patient abuses.

The range of allegations of ethical abuse within inebriate homes and asylums is illustrated by turn-of-the-century events in Massachusetts. In 1906, the governor of Massachusetts launched an investigation into the operation of the state's Hospital for Dipsomaniacs and Inebriates, in response to what had been a long series of charges that included medical incompetence, patient neglect and abuse (including charges of the overuse of restraints and solitary confinement in the "prison ward"), unsanitary conditions, corruption in the award of lucrative contracts to trustees (board members) of the hospital, and charges that the superintendent was living an extravagant lifestyle that included gourmet food at state expense. What was unique about this investigation is that it was prompted by patients, who had organized themselves to bring formal charges against the institution. Accounts of these abuses were highly publicized and resulted in some criminal indictments.[66]

The charges against the staff of Foxboro were not unique. When T.D. Crothers wrote a defense of Foxboro following earlier allegations, he opened his editorial in the *Quarterly of Inebriety* by noting:

Cruelty to patients, poor food, neglect of proper care, and free whiskey, and patients running away all the time, bad, immoral influences from attendants, and unfit patients, are the common charges that have been urged against every asylum in the country.[67]

Crothers went on to deny that such charges were justified at Foxboro or at any other inebriate asylum. In spite of overwhelming evidence of ethical abuses within the field, Crothers claimed that such complaints were always levied by the most "disreputable of witnesses" and that the charges of such abuses within inebriate asylums were uniformly "unsupported and malicious."[68] Crothers' stance typified a pervasive inability of inebriety specialists to listen to patients' comments regarding their treatment. The field was hurt by the ethical abuses committed by treatment providers, by the denial of the reality of such abuses, and by its own failure to create and enforce standards of professional practice.

The Problem of Leadership Succession: Challenged by outside forces, many inebriate homes, asylums, and private sanitaria actually closed when their founders retired or died. It appears that the field had a group of leaders who had birthed a treatment movement, guided that movement into maturity as the leaders themselves matured, then aged and died together. The lack of mentorship—a system for recruiting and developing new leaders—contributed to the demise of the treatment of inebriety as a professional specialty during the early decades of the 20th century.[69]

Legacy

During their collective existence, the achievements of the inebriate homes and asylums were not insignificant. First and foremost was the support that such institutions provided to a large number of citizens who were addicted to alcohol and other drugs during this era. These institutions marked the first broad-scale professional movement to medicalize excessive drinking and drug use in America. The movement's leaders posited biological explanations of inebriety and pioneered physical methods of treatment. To speak of the disease of inebriety with references to its hereditary and biological roots helped move inebriety culturally and professionally from the realm of morality to the realm of medicine and shifted the definition of the root of addiction from that of moral defect to physiological and psychological vulnerability. For the physicians who entered this new specialty, the "disease" concept transformed drunkards into legitimate patients and provided a core concept upon which a new field of addiction medicine could be built. These pioneers produced a significant body of literature that included typologies and models of differential diagnosis (foreshadowing Jellinek's work by almost a century). Modern concepts of tolerance, withdrawal, craving, and loss of control can all be found described repeatedly in the *Journal of Inebriety*. The concept of "inebriety" itself, fore-shadowing later concepts of "chemical dependency" and "substance abuse," provided an integrated framework for treating people addicted to a wide variety of psychoactive drugs within the same professional specialty and institutional milieu. The fall of the inebriate homes and asylums marked the collapse of the concept of inebriety and the shift to drug-specific social policies and treatment philo-sophies. It would take most of the next century to recreate a conceptual umbrella for all chemical addictions.

Summary

Inebriate homes and asylums found themselves without a sustainable identity. The field lived on the fringe of medicine, the fringe of religion, the fringe of charity, and the fringe of law enforcement. It was a field that lived on the fringe of everything but that could not find and sustain its own center. More powerful movements that demonized drugs and those who used them engulfed America's first serious flirtation with the disease concept of addiction and extinguished the country's first network of addiction treatment programs. The country eventually fell sway to the argument that, if alcohol and other drugs were effectively prohibited, there would be no need for addiction treatment programs.

Only a handful of the earliest inebriate homes survived. In the end, the function of the inebriate home and asylum was taken over by more enduring institutions: state psychiatric asylums, city hospitals, private hospitals and sanitaria, inebriate farms and colonies, and prisons. This transition was also marked by changing views of addiction itself. The notion of addiction as a primary and treatable disease gave way to two views. The first posited that addiction was a symptom of underlying emotional disturbance, and thus within the purview of the newly burgeoning medical specialty of psychiatry. An alter-native view was that alcoholism represented willful misconduct and should be punished within the criminal justice system. The seeds for the growing contempt with which psychiatrists would come to regard addicts, and the seeds for what would become for the alcoholic a "revolving door" through the criminal justice system, were sown in this transition.

The 19th-century inebriate homes and asylums, as a whole, simply could not survive as a viable social institution. The inebriate asylum movement came to an end, and many of its lessons and legacies have been lost. A century later, an addiction treatment field —also facing internal and external conditions that threaten its existence—is rediscovering, and perhaps re-experiencing, this history.

Chapter Five
Inebriate Homes and Asylums:
Treatment Philosophies, Methods, and Outcomes

It is possible that the cure of inebriates may become a specialty of medical practice, to which those, gifted with the requisite talent, will devote their lives.[70]

This chapter will provide for the reader an insider's view of the treatment experience in 19th- and early 20th-century inebriate homes and asylums. We will look at how these programs were staffed, the demographic and clinical profile of the clients who were treated there, the philosophies and methods of treatment, and the treatment outcomes reported by these institutions. The chapter concludes with a special look at how addicted women were perceived and treated in these institutions.

The Staff

The superintendents of the 19th-century inebriate asylums and homes were usually physicians, clergy, or reformed alcoholics, depending on whether the institution saw itself as treating a physical disease or saw itself involved in a process of moral reformation. Other staff roles within the inebriate homes and asylums included those of nurses, orderlies, attendants, and building-and-grounds maintenance personnel.

The perceived qualification to perform these roles was influenced by the Washingtonians', fraternal temperance societies,' and reform clubs' discovery of the value of alcoholic-to-alcoholic identification and mutual support. There were three levels at which recovered inebriates were brought into the 19th-century professional arena of addiction treatment. The first was as managers and physicians—roles that recovered inebriates were filling in inebriate homes and asylums by the 1880s. Among the more visible of such leaders were D. Banks McKenzie, Superintendent of the Appleton Home; and Charles Bunting, founder of the New York Christian Home for Intemperate Men.

Recovered inebriates also frequently worked within inebriate homes and asylums as personal attendants —a role that was a cross between what today might be called a psychiatric aid and a counselor. This practice evolved out of observations of the benefit of mutual support provided among patients in treatment. The rationale for placing one inebriate patient in a helping relationship with another was expressed in 1875 by Dr. Henry Bowditch, an inebriate asylum advocate in Massachusetts. Bowditch believed that those inebriate patients better blessed with intelligence and education had a moral duty, commensurate with this advantage, to help educate those patients less amply blessed.[71] It was only a matter of time and expanded patient census before these indigenous patient-helper roles evolved into paid jobs. Current or former inebriate home and asylum patients also worked in a variety of unskilled or technical-support areas. This grew out of the practice of having indigent inebriates work off part of their keep by assuming various jobs within the asylum.[72] According to Sarah Tracy's study of the Massachusetts Hospital for Dipsomaniacs and Inebriates, there was a very thin line between care and employment within the early inebriate asylums.[73]

Many patients had....skills in baking, electrical work, accounting, or farming that

were useful to the institution. These men often were encouraged to stay on at a modest salary, and even if they left and drank again, they were almost always welcomed back for care and employment.[74]

Having recovered inebriates fill paid roles at all three of these levels was thought to enhance the prospects for sustained recovery for the more hopeful cases, and to provide appropriate role models for incoming patients. The skills acquired through such work also could be used outside the inebriate asylum. Sarah Tracy reports that a significant number of former inebriate asylum patients went on to pursue careers as nurses, orderlies, and attendants within hospitals. Inebriate asylum superintendents, aware of the staff shortages in hospitals and private sanitaria, often helped place their more successful patients in such positions.[75]

The movement of recovered people into leadership and direct-care positions within inebriate homes and asylums was not without its controversies. From the very birth of the addiction treatment field, a strain existed between people whose credibility sprang from personal experience of addiction and recovery and those whose credibility was derived from medical or religious training. The debate over the advisability of allowing recovered people to fill care-giving roles for alcoholics and addicts was a heated one. Dr. T.D. Crothers set forth his views on this issue in an 1897 editorial in the *Journal of Inebriety* entitled "Reformed Men as Asylum Managers":

> *It is confidently asserted that a personal experience as an inebriate gives a special knowledge and fitness for the study and treatment of this malady. While a large number of inebriates who have been restored engage in the work of curing others suffering from the same trouble, no one ever succeeds for any length of time or attains any eminence....Physicians and others who, after being cured, enter upon the work of curing others in asylums and homes, are found to be incompetent by reason of organic defects of the higher mentality....In the history of the asylums in this country, no reformed man has ever continued long in the work, or succeeded as a manager or physician in the medical and personal cure of inebriates.*[76]

This observation was likely part of Crothers' sustained

attack on the "gold-cure empires," whom Crothers associated with the practice of hiring former patients.

Crothers expressed concern that the emotional strain placed on recovering people who accepted paid positions in inebriate institutions would cause the newly recovering person to "break down and return to spirits or drugs after a time"[77] Crothers' objection to the employment of reformed people in inebriate asylums may have stemmed, in part, from his vision of inebriety treatment as a fully professionalized branch of mainstream medicine.

There was as much controversy about the behavior of employees who weren't "reformed" as there was about the status of treatment graduates working in the asylums. There were reports of proprietors of inebriate homes who periodically humiliated themselves by issuing various orders to patients while they were themselves in a state of profound intoxication.[78] Scandals created by the drunken comportment of some employees led to the general expectation that even workers without a history of alcoholism who worked in inebriate institutions were expected to be total abstainers.

There is very little available information on the role of attendants in the inebriate asylums, but it might be possible to infer something about their working conditions from independent studies by Gerald Grob and David Rothman that include information on attendants in psychiatric asylums during this same era. Grob's and Rothman's research notes that attendants had no training, worked 12-hour shifts, were required to sleep on facility grounds, and were given only three days off every four weeks. Under these conditions, it is not surprising that Superintendents found themselves finding replacements for each of these positions an average of three times per year.[79] Given this context, it might be that the selection of recovered people to fill attendant roles in inebriate homes and asylums was a bold experiment to create a more stable and higher-quality workforce.

The Patients: Demographic Profile

Enough reports from early inebriate homes and asylums are available to construct a general profile of the demographic and clinical characteristics of the typical client in treatment in the 19th century.

We know that asylum patients were drawn from a broad geographical area. Because local addiction treatment services were rare, alcoholics and addicts traveled great distances in search of a cure. In 1872 the Washingtonian Home of Boston admitted more patients from other states (and countries) than from Massachusetts.[80] In the opening years of the inebriate asylum movement, the stigma of addiction was so great that many patients came to treatment under assumed names, keeping their true identities secret even from those responsible for their care.[81]

Most clients admitted for treatment within the inebriate asylums were between the ages of 30 and 50. Almost all were White, and they were drawn primarily from the middle and upper socioeconomic classes.[82] There are almost no references to treatment of African Americans or other people of color within the early reports of the inebriate asylums.[83] While racial segregation would have barred the entrance of African Americans into most of the residential treatment centers of this period, the rationale for their absence was most often couched in terms of their lower incidence of inebriety.[84]

The inebriate asylum-era literature is replete with interesting observations about the incidence or likelihood of alcoholism in particular occupational groups. For example, Dr. R.P. Harris reported in the 1870s that "shoemakers are especially difficult to reform as they incite each other to drink, and club together and send out for beer and whiskey."[85] Crothers indicated that the incidence of inebriety was high among those exposed to inclement weather and irregular hours, such as conductors and drivers. Among the skilled trades, painters, bartenders, liquor dealers, butchers, stone-cutters, and plasters were well represented among those entering treatment. In her investigations of the occupational status of patients admitted to the state inebriate hospital in Massachusetts, Sarah Tracy found teamsters, salesmen, shoemakers, painters, carpenters, bookkeepers, machinists, waiters and printers heavily represented.[86] The professions most frequently admitted to the inebriate institutions (in descending order of frequency) included physicians, lawyers, engineers, druggists, journalists, artists, students, reporters, clergymen, and actors.[87]

The Patients: A Clinical Profile

Many of the pioneers of inebriate asylums developed elaborate patient-classification systems. The Fort Hamilton Home, for example, was designed so that patients could be grouped into "separate communities, of kindred tastes, sympathies and culture."[88] Clinical classification systems were developed in order to help staff make decisions regarding who could and could not be treated, and to determine what in today's language would be called the "patient mix" most conducive to treatment.

There were classification systems based on the perceived cause of inebriety, the pattern of drinking (daily versus periodic), drug choice, and personality type.[89] In 1894, the Massachusetts Hospital for Dipsomaniacs and Inebriates placed patients in three categories, based on how each responded to treatment: intractable, somewhat trustworthy, and trustworthy.[90] The most elaborate classification systems were set forth by Dr. T.D. Crothers, who proposed classification based on a mixture of perceived etiology and drinking pattern. His system included: 1) "accidental inebriates" who, due to weakness of character, were temperate or intemperate according to the dictates of their social environments; 2) "emotional inebriates," who used spirits in an attempt to restore order to frequently unstable emotions; 3) "solitary inebriates," whose drinking was carefully hidden and masked behind positions of social and political importance; 4) "senile inebriates", whose drinking began late in life; and 5) "pauper inebriates," whose drinking resulted from general moral degeneracy.[91]

Nearly all of the classification systems had means of identifying what today would be called personality or character disorders. Asylum directors made particular effort to exclude people who were at that time called "criminal degenerates" or "reckless characters." Inebriate asylum reports of the 19th century often noted the ability of such people to "demoralize the whole house," and recommended that the place for such people was not the asylum or sanitarium but the penitentiary.[92] Typical of these views were those expressed by Dr. W.S. Osborn, superintendent of the Iowa State Hospital for Inebriates in Knoxville:

> *So long as the indiscriminate commitment of incurable, depraved and criminal types continues...just so long will the very purpose for which the institution was established be defeated. The increasing proportion of this class admitted to our hospital makes of it a reformatory and not a hospital....The hopeful cases must be removed and isolated to protect them from harmful influences resulting from association with other classes.*[93]

Early inebriate homes such as the Franklin Reformatory Home for Inebriates established policies that refused admission to men known to have "vicious or criminal natures" and admitted only "men of good character, in all but intemperance."[94]

Arguments abounded over who could and could not be treated. Class influences entered heavily into these definitions, with the more affluent often defined as curable and channeled to private sanitaria, while the working class and poor were shuttled off to publicly financed state inebriate asylums. It was in this social context that the drunken affluent were seen as victims of a disease, while the drunken working class and poor were seen as exhibiting willful misconduct deserving of punishment. Clinical classi-fication systems—then, as today—served to salve the consciences of staff who excluded indigent and treatment-resistant inebriates from admission while providing esteem-salvaging metaphors through which affluent and motivated inebriates could understand their condition.[95]

This use of patient-classification systems did generate some controversy. As early as 1871, Dr. D.G. Dodge of the New York State Inebriate Asylum proclaimed:

> *I can conceive of no classification of patients in an inebriate asylum which would not be attended with disastrous results. If patients are classified according to character, culture, pecuniary means, or social standing, those who are ranked or think they are ranked in inferior groups will naturally be wounded.*[96]

Treatment Philosophies

While the philosophies that guided the treatment of addiction in the 19th century differed from institution to institution, as they do today, these philosophies fell into two large schools of thought. One school was exemplified by the inebriate asylums, and the other by the Washingtonian-influenced inebriate homes. These differences will become apparent as we examine key elements of 19th-century treatment philosophy.

Inebriety: If one central idea was shared across the spectrum of early treatment programs, it was the concept of "inebriety." "Inebriety" encompassed a wide spectrum of disorders that resulted from acute or chronic consumption of psychoactive drugs. "Inebriety" was the term that captured the morbid craving, the compulsive drug-seeking, and the untoward physical, psychological and social consequences of drug use.

Inebriety was broken down into its numerous forms through elaborate classification systems that included "alcohol inebriety," "opium inebriety," "cocaine inebriety," "tobaccoism," "ether inebriety," "chloroform inebriety," and the "inebriety produced by "chloroform inebriety," and the "inebriety produced by coffee and tea."[97]   Since a central disorder—inebriety—linked all these destructive patterns of drug use, it followed that people who used these various substances could be treated together within the same facilities and through quite similar methods. Alcohol inebriety and cocaine inebriety were simply seen as different variations of the same disease—the disease of inebriety.

Etiology: Nineteenth-century inebriety specialists debated the root causes of inebriety at both social and clinical levels. At a social level, there was a heated cultural debate about whether inebriety was a vice, a crime, or a disease. The American Association for the Study and Cure of Inebriety issued a resolution in 1871 proclaiming that the effects of intoxicants were "the same in the virtuous, as in the vicious, and that antecedent and subsequent moral conditions are incidental to the main fact of disease."[98]   There was inevitable tension between temperance leaders' portrayal of the problem of drunkenness and this new scientific approach to the study of alcohol inebriety.[99]

Temperance advocates who placed the roots of drunkenness within the realm of morals forced inebriety specialists to differentiate in their classification and treatment approaches between the vice of alcohol and other drug use and the disease of inebriety. The most graphic example of such delineation is evident in the work of George Beard. Beard saw drunkenness as a moral vice of the lower classes, and inebriety as a disease of higher social and intellectual classes. When people in the first category were drunk, it was a sign of moral weakness, irresponsibility, and hedonistic lifestyles. When people in the second category were drunk, it was a "disease of refinement" resulting from the pressures and strains of modern civilization. Where the former needed punishment and moral education, the latter needed rest and physical and emotional renewal.[100]

What is most striking by today's standards is the incredible variety of causes thought to operate within the condition of inebriety. Most treatment experts believed there were multiple etiological roots to the disorder. The Washingtonian-style inebriate homes tended to view the etiology of inebriety in religious, moral, and characterological terms, while the inebriate asylums tended to emphasize genetic, biological, and psychological causes. The reader will note in the following discussion that some of the identified causative agents are not reflected in current models of addiction treatment, suggesting that errors of fact and perception were weeded out as the field advanced—or that important discoveries and understandings were

lost as the field evolved.

During the 19th century, there was considerable discussion about the role of heredity in inebriety. In his 1835 essay *Anatomy of Drunkenness,* MacNish depicted drunkenness as a condition passed by predisposition from parents to their children.[101] Most of the 19th-century addiction specialists concurred that heredity was a causative or contributing factor in inebriety. Other causes cited by these experts include: social approval of alcoholic indulgence; the growing use of opium- and alcohol laced medicines; poverty;[102] the search for pleasure;[103] lax parental training; physical disease; injury to the brain;[104] use of alcohol or other drugs to self-medicate physical pain; emotional trauma; sexual excess; weather extremes;[105] the use of opiates to medicate alcoholic hangover; insomnia; family and business troubles;[106] sunstroke; nerve exhaustion;[107] "dietary disturbances;" tapeworms; weakness of character;[108] and the stress produced by the telegraph, printing press, and railroads.[109]

As the inebriate asylum movement gained momentum, there was an increased belief in the role of physiology as the etiological basis of inebriety. The physiological factors that were believed to cause inebriety were of three varieties: heredity, trauma, and disease. Dr. Norman Kerr, whose writing exerted a profound influence on the American inebriate asylum movement, regularly cited family histories that illustrated an "unbroken chain of reckless inebriates" and spoke of people "branded with the hot iron of alcoholic heredity."[110]   This belief in the hereditary influence on alcoholics also extended to other drug choices, particularly the opiates.[111]

Another prominently discussed cause of inebriety —particularly narcotic inebriety—involved debilitating injuries or diseases that caused the sufferer to seek chemical relief from pain and discomfort. Inebriate asylum literature is replete with cases of narcotic addiction that began through physician treatment or self-medication of illness or injury. Physicians such as Asa Myerlet in the 1880s spoke passionately of the need to recognize hidden illnesses underlying addiction: *"....if this disease be not cured the habit is not cured."*[112]

While inebriety was described as being caused by varied patterns of use, commonalities were noted that seemed to exist across these different cases. Crothers and others noted the great "uniformity of symptomology" and the propensity of these symptoms to "follow a uniform line of progress." There was already a clear understanding of the pattern of self-acceleration that characterized most cases of inebriety. Noting its characteristic progression, Dr. Franklin

Clum referred to inebriety in 1888 as "a disease that feeds on itself."[113] Many of the 19th-century specialists in the treatment of inebriety struggled to explain the "morbid craving" and "ungovernable appetite" that seemed to fuel the addict's self-destruction. Clum suggested that this innate craving resulted from a disordered nervous system—that the longing for narcotics and stimulants was the nervous system's request for self-correction.[114]

<u>Voluntary Versus Coerced Treatment</u>: There were two broad schools of thought on the treatment of inebriety in the late 19th Century, one emphasizing an enduring period of restraint and medical care, and another that emphasized the "moral treatment" of prayer, pledge, and encouragement. Professional debates of the day often centered around the issue of coercion—the relative value of involuntary commitment for treatment.

The directors of large asylums generally preferred involuntary treatment. Asylum directors lobbied state legislatures to pass laws providing for the legal commitment of inebriates. Typical of these commitment laws was Pennsylvania's 1903 "inebriate law," through which inebriates could be legally committed for up to one year to an asylum, after a legal hearing in which two physicians certified the need for such action. While many asylum directors supported the legal commitment of patients, there was growing concern that the facilities themselves had no right to select who would be committed or when such commitment would end— powers reserved by the judges who ruled on the commitments.

One of the major factors influencing views on the role of coercion in treatment was the problem created by the high "escape rate" of inebriates committed to the care of these facilities.[115] Another, more pervasive problem was the skill with which legally committed inebriates continued to drink while institutionalized. Dr. Charles Dana commented on this problem in 1891:

When we get good laws and successfully commit the patient, he proceeds to get drunk at the very place which he is sent for cure. And the more specifically the sanitarium is devoted to inebriates, the easier it seems to be in some instances for the inmates to get what they want.[116]

The directors of the smaller treatment facilities that emphasized moral suasion objected to such coercion, believing that the inebriate could be successfully treated only with his or her own voluntary participation. Many of the Washingtonian-style homes and private addiction-cure "institutes" accepted only voluntary patients who remained for a course of treatment that lasted, in most such facilities, about four weeks.

<u>Treatment Versus Cure</u>: Many writers in the inebriate-asylum period made a distinction between "treatment"—the alleviation of acute intoxication, the medical management of withdrawal, and the care of acute medical problems—and "cure"—the elimination of the morbid craving for the drug. This distinction was introduced to correct the mistaken belief that a temporarily detoxified body represented a successful and sustainable elimination of addiction—a mistake that is still occasionally made today.

<u>Treatment Goal</u>: If there was one thing that 19th-century treatment institutions of all varieties agreed upon, it was that the goal of inebriety treatment was the patient's complete and continuing abstinence. Writers across the spectrum cautioned about the use of any intoxicants. This admonition extended to all drug choices. Kane, in 1882, noted this rule for opium addicts:

Under no circumstance should these people be given opiates in any form or for any complaint, save when life can be saved in no other way, for a relapse is almost certain to occur if this is done....A single dose may undo the work of years.[117]

Dr. Albert Day pronounced the dominant position of the 19th-century inebriate asylum leaders:

....they (inebriates) can never safely touch one drop of any liquor containing alcohol in any form or degree....The condition will always remain. Time will never obliterate it.[118]

What is most interesting by modern standards is the fact that this call for total abstinence often included tobacco. D.G. Dodge, Superintendent of the New York State Inebriate Asylum, typified this position in 1877 when he declared that "The treatment of inebriates can never be wholly successful til the use of tobacco in all forms is absolutely dispensed with."[119]

<u>Individualized Treatment</u>: One of the most striking aspects of the stand taken by the inebriate asylum leaders was their belief in a highly individualized approach to the treatment of inebriety. The 19th-century inebriety literature posited that alcoholism and

other addictions sprang from multiple causes, presented themselves in different patterns of use and choices of intoxicants, and required highly individualized treatment approaches.

Treatment Philosophy: There were two broad schools of philosophy governing the management of institutions that cared for the inebriate. Asylum leaders saw recovery as an act of somatic/neurological regeneration achieved through the application of scientific (physical) treatment methods. On the other hand, the Washingtonian-style homes viewed recovery from inebriety as a process of moral regeneration. The Washingtonian-style institutions emphasized "moral treatment"—voluntary stays in home-like country shelters in which the inebriate, while being treated with courtesy and respect, was subjected to a disciplined regimen of food; exercise; and uplifting music, conversation, and leisure. The Washingtonian-style homes focused on a reconstruction of character and viewed recovery as an act of self-will strengthened within a milieu of shared moral and spiritual renewal. In this view, recovery was an educational process that occurred in the context of trusting and supporting relationships. This debate over physical versus moral methods of treatment, large versus small facilities, and coercive restraint versus non-restraint was already underway within the newly emerging field of psychiatry and heavily influenced discussions within the field of inebriety treatment.

Length of Stay: While the managers of inebriate asylums and homes differed in their beliefs about ideal lengths of stay, time requirements sometimes varied by prognosis, with six months or less recommended for more hopeful cases and one to two years for less hopeful cases.[120] Dr. Norman Kerr believed that most patients were so advanced in their addiction that the shortest ideal period of treatment was one year. While conceding that a few might be able to succeed with shorter stays, he further noted that some patients would require terms of two, three, four, and five years.[121] Apparently some patients did stay this long. In his 1883 treatise *Alcoholic Inebriety*, Dr. Joseph Parrish noted the cases of a number of alcoholics who stayed at an asylum for years to protect themselves from relapse and to save their families from annoyance, danger, and shame. The inebriate asylum leaders were quite adamant in their assertion of the ineffectiveness of what in their time might have been considered "brief therapy." In his 1902 text on addiction treatment, Crothers declared:

It is clearly impossible to expect any results from two or four weeks' treatment by any

conceivable method or plan. The degenerations and injuries following and associated with the use of spirits cannot be repaired in that time. No treatment should be for less than from six months to a year.[122]

Treatment Methods

Nineteenth-century inebriety specialists spent considerable time trying to conceptualize and construct what would today be called a continuum of care. Crothers' vision of such a continuum began with local physicians' referral of addicts to a local detention hospital for detoxification and evaluation, moved to placement of the then-medically stabilized patient in longer-term treatment in the asylum or farm colony, and finally returned the patient back to the physician who would follow the client's case in the community.[123] Other inebriety specialists conceptualized this continuum in terms of the linkage among urban detention hospitals, small homes providing short periods of extended convalescence, and larger rural asylums providing long-term treatment and colonization.

One of the most important technologies within inebriate homes and asylums was a means of enhancing treatment retention. Persuading patients to remain through and beyond the period of acute detoxification was a challenge in both the Washingtonian-style homes and the large inebriate asylums. Some inebriate asylums, such as Massachusetts' state asylum in Foxborough, actually established a "prison ward" in an effort to contain patients who had a history of "eloping."[124] Others used financial manipulation. Dr. Albert Day, Superintendent of the New York Inebriate Asylum, described how this strategy worked.

The newcomer subscribes to the rules, pays his board three months in advance, and surrenders all the rest of his money. The paying in advance is a good thing....It is one more inducement to remain until other motives gain strength....[125]

The voluntary nature of the Washingtonian-style homes forced them to rely on support and encouragement, but they sometimes reverted to quite creative strategies to get the inebriate through detoxification. The Appleton Home in South Boston simply undressed the arriving patient, put him to bed, and hid his clothes in order to prevent flight.[126]

Treatment methods within the inebriate homes and asylums varied greatly from facility to facility. Like today's treatment programs, these institutions used a mixture of physical, psychological, and spiritual methods to treat addiction.

Isolation of the inebriate from the stresses and temptations of normal life was viewed as the first essential step in the inebriate's physical and moral regeneration. For both the incoming patient and the staff, the major concern was detoxification. Methods of detoxification ranged from "cold-turkey"[127] withdrawal to phased detoxification using a wide variety of pharmacological adjuncts that could include whiskey, beer, sherry, chloral hydrate, strychnine, atropine, coca, cannabis indica, atropin, hyoscyamus, belladonna, quinine, iron, and placebos. The elimination of "toxins" was often speeded by the use of soap-suds enemas and other purgatives. Following detoxification there was a focus on physical restoration of the patient. Methods of achieving this restoration included treatment of medical problems, rest, Turkish baths, massage, phototherapy (exposure to sunlight), electrotherapy (electrical stimulation), nourishing meals and vitamin supplements, high fluid intake, exercise, and lots of fresh air.

Religious/spiritual influence was brought to bear on inebriate patients through the use of chaplains, daily religious services, Bible readings, prayers, and—in some homes—explicit religious instruction.

Social support of each patient included mutual encouragement from people in similar circumstances. Asylum Superintendents like Dr. D.G. Dodge noted the therapeutic chemistry that developed among patients living in the inebriate asylum and recommended that "the most intimate association should be encouraged."[128] This camaraderie and support was often organized formally through patient associations. Such associations can be traced to the very first inebriate asylum in New York, where patients formed the Ollapod Club for purposes of mutual education, support, and entertainment. Membership in the Ollapod Club required, among other things, a pledge that the patient "not offend or bring disrepute upon our fellowship by presenting himself at any time or place under the influence of liquor."[129] A patient in 1869 described the kind of closeness and safety that marked the Club's milieu.

> *In this candid little lodge of ours the masks and dominos of character are dropped, and the man, morally naked, regards himself in the clear, true glass of his own confession.*[130]

These clubs constituted both a structure for personal support and an early mechanism of patient government within the institutions. Some of these patient associations evolved into aftercare clubs or community-based temperance organizations. Social supports for inebriate patients were also generated from other sources. The Franklin Reformatory Home for Inebriates maintained an auxiliary board of 26 "lady managers," who not only provided moral encouragement to men in the home, but also visited and provided religious and material support to the families of those residing in the home.[131]

Work and recreation, including manual labor and such diversions as billiards, croquet, games, music, theatrical events, debates, and private (non-alcoholic) parties, were also a routine part of early treatment activities. In many institutions, patients were expected to contribute the skills from their trades to the institutions, or to acquire new skills. Patients were expected to work as many as seven hours a day within the institutional routine of some asylums.[132] The goal was to create a milieu that was socially and intellectually stimulating. Here is a description of the atmosphere of an inebriate asylum in 1868.

> *No one, it is true, ever saw a college so handsomely arranged and provided; but the tone of the thing is college-like, especially when you get about the rooms of the inmates, and see them cramming for next Monday's debate, or writing a lecture for the Asylum course.*[133]

Music was used regularly for its perceived therapeutic value. Inebriety specialists like Dr. Franklin Clum were adamant about the need for the presence of pianos, organs, violins, and harps in every asylum.[134]

Patients were encouraged to engage in a process of self-reflection—what today might be called self-inventory—and some institutions, like the Pennsylvania Sanatarium, recommended journaling.[135]

A central treatment method of most institutions included what was called moral suasion—the exposure of patients to motivational talks, inspirational literature, wholesome conversation, artistic works, information on addiction, and religious services. The use of lectures to teach inebriates about the nature of their disease was the centerpiece of the efforts at moral suasion. A visitor to the New York State Inebriate Asylum in 1868 noted Dr. Albert Day's teaching style.

> *It is the intention of the superintendent, that every inmate of the Asylum shall become acquainted with the precise effects of alcohol upon the human system....He accordingly opened this meeting with a*

short lecture upon some branch of the subject, and then invited the patients to illustrate the point from their own experience.[136]

The visitor went on to point out the major points of Dr. Day's lecture on the day of her visit—a distinctly modern message. His three points were:

1. No hope for an inebriate until he thoroughly distrusts the strength of his own resolution; 2. No hope for an inebriate except in total abstinence as long as he lives, both in sickness and in health; 3. Little hope for an inebriate unless he avoids....the occasions of temptation, the places where liquor is sold, and the people who will urge it upon him.[137]

Counseling, as we know it today, was rarely provided, although there was occasional recognition that a form of mental treatment could be provided through talks between the patient and the asylum superintendent.[138] These seem to have been primarily motivational and advice-giving.

Also a part of treatment were efforts to involve patients in acts of service, ranging from help for newly arrived patients to more sustained service involvement in temperance and religious work.

Three commonly used physical methods of treatment within the inebriate asylums were aversion therapy, electrotherapies, and hydrotherapies, methods that will be outlined in greater detail in Chapter Eleven. Induced aversion involved developing an aversion to alcohol, either through classical conditioning or through post-hypnotic suggestion. In his 1892 review of alcoholism treatments of the day, Calhoun described the "Swedish Treatment," in which patients staying at the sanitarium were encouraged to drink all of the whiskey they wished. In fact, that is all they could drink—whiskey, whiskey-saturated coffee, whiskey-saturated tea, and whiskey-saturated milk. All meals and all snacks, regardless of fare, were saturated with whiskey. Patients wore whiskey-sprayed clothes and slept in whiskey-saturated sheets. The goal was to satiate and sicken the appetite for alcohol and leave one begging for pure water.[139] Others used classical methods of inducing revulsion to alcohol. In 1902, Crothers noted the therapeutic effect of using apomorphine, ipecac, and other emetics to induce nausea, "to break up the recollection of the past and to impress the memory of spirits with disgust," and to break the morphine addict's "needle ad-

diction."[140]

A variety of electrotherapies were also used within the inebriate asylums. One such technique in 1868 was described as follows:

....the galvanic battery is judiciously administered by placing both feet in contact with a copper plate constituting the negative electrode, while the operator grasps the positive in one hand, and having wetted the fingers of the other, follows the spine downward, exerting gentle pressure with them as he goes.[141]

By far the most common physical method of treatment in the inebriate asylums, other than the administration of drugs, was hydrotherapy. In 1868, F. Ludlow incorporated many hydrotherapeutic techniques into his depiction of the ideal inebriate asylum. He spoke of Turkish baths, Russian baths, galvanic baths, foot baths, steams of every variety, wet packs, body sponging, mild exercise followed by special massage techniques—all to induce the chemical toxins from the body and quiet the addict's frayed and pulsating nerves. In his 1881 text *Drugs that Enslave,* H.H. Kane recommended hydrotherapy baths to reduce excitement, to reduce pain, to improve the circulation, and to induce sleep.[142]

The daily institutional milieu was considered an essential part of the treatment experience within the inebriate home or asylum. Rules and regulations governing daily conduct were viewed as an essential means of maintaining order and helping the inebriate regain a proper capacity for self-discipline. Patients were expected to follow the rules and daily regimen with "military regularity." In 1865, the house rules for the Chicago Washingtonian Home demanded attendance at all meals and devotional meetings and included the following injunctions:

As cleanliness is a virtue, and as spitting upon the floor, or ejecting tobacco juice upon the stoves and grates is obnoxious, this filthy habit is forbidden.

As profanity is always shocking, even to those who are habituated to the vice, the avoidance of this habit is requested.[143]

While most inebriate asylums had provision for the expulsion of "refractory" cases (those who continued to drink while in treatment) and for the disobedient, this extreme measure was taken only rarely.[144]

For patients in the well-ordered inebriate asylum, daily life began with the "rising bell" calling them out of bed. Following the expected rituals of personal hygiene, patients joined the staff at a communal breakfast (although staff members usually ate at their own table). Breakfast was followed by prayers in the Chapel; a walk on the grounds; a visit to town; or such activities on the grounds as billiards, bowling, exercise in the gymnasium, or reading in the library. Patient association meetings were often held in the morning. Patients also had work assignments and interviews with the Superintendent interspersed throughout the mornings and afternoons. Following communal lunches (at 1 p.m.) and dinners (at 6 p.m.) and two anxiously anticipated mail calls (at 11 a.m. and 6 p.m.), patients looked forward to evenings filled with readings of poetry and literature, talks by the superintendent, community receptions, and plays put on by their fellow patients. Weekends were usually designated as times for family visits and religious services.

While there were significant differences in philosophies and treatment methods among inebriate homes and asylums, these differences tended to dissipate over time. The medically oriented asylums often incorporated spiritual and religious remedies within their treatment milieus. The Walnut Hill Asylum, for example, had a full-time chaplain living on the grounds, whose sole responsibility was cultivating religious sentiment among the patients. Patients attended religious services daily in this medically oriented treatment facility.[145] In a parallel manner, many of the inebriate homes operating on religious and moral principles increasingly integrated medical and psychological treatments.

The Family and the Inebriate Asylum

Nineteenth- and early 20th-century inebriety literature expressed enormous ambivalence toward the family of the alcoholic and addict. Wives of patients often took up temporary residence in the city nearest the inebriate asylums, so they could provide daily support to their husbands.[146] Although these wives were viewed as loyal angels by those undergoing treatment, the staff of the inebriate asylum often viewed them quite differently. They might have noted the importance of the family's role in such activities as committing the alcoholic, taking guardianship of the inebriate's financial affairs, visiting and supporting the inebriate in treatment, but it is obvious that many early treatment professionals and students of addiction saw the family as hostile interlopers. Dr. H.H. Kane

noted in 1881 that many failures were due to what today would be called family enabling.

Very often the relatives, not understanding the meaning of certain symptoms, distressed beyond measure by the pitiful pleadings of the sufferer, will interpose and at once put an end to treatment, thus unwittingly and with well meaning doing the patient injury of the gravest kind.[147]

Charles Palmer, in his 1896 treatise *Inebriety*, was perhaps one of the earliest to actually suggest that wives played some hidden role in the alcoholism of their husbands.

The universality of good wives to intemperate husbands suggests an inquiry into the connection they may bear and the influence they may exercise, however innocently, in the downfall of their husbands.[148]

Nine years later, George Cutten in his *Psychology of Alcoholism* text wrote words that could have come from a recent article on family enabling: "The kindest wife and most indulgent parents are very much in the way of numerous cures, and prove to be, instead of the best friends, the worst enemies the alcoholic has."[149] Wives of inebriates were afforded much more empathy and understanding within mainstream temperance groups than in the addiction treatment institutions of the 19th century.

Aftercare

As America's new humanitarian institutions arose in the mid-1800s, concern began to increase about the plight of people when they left these institutions. Between 1840 and 1870, special groups were founded that specifically focused on how institutionalized people might best be integrated back into productive roles in society. These groups ranged from the Quakers "Prisoners' Friend Associations", an organization for those leaving prisons in the 1840s, to special support and aftercare associations for those leaving insane asylums and inebriate asylums.[150]

In spite of the general awareness of the problems of community re-entry following institutionalization, by today's standards, aftercare in the inebriate homes and asylums was poorly developed. Aftercare generally involved placing the patient with sober friends and encouraging the patient's affiliation with a church or fraternal temperance society.[151] Some institutions evolved special rituals through which the patient could stay emotionally linked with the institution. Most patients at the New York State Inebriate Asylum participated in the practice of writing the superintendent each year on the anniversary date of their discharge, to provide an account of themselves for the past year.[152] In Massachusetts, this practice came to be known as the "cure by correspondence."[153]

Some of the inebriate asylums and homes organized ongoing systems of support for people treated at their facilities. Inebriate homes and asylums also tried to link their patients to sobriety-based support structures in the community. Many patients leaving inebriate asylums used temperance groups as their primary sobriety-based support structures following treatment. In his 1869 report on the Washingtonian Home of Chicago, Dr. J.A. Ballard, the Superintendent, noted that former residents involved in temperance organizations were "thus helping to raise others from the depths of sin and degradation from which they themselves have been raised."[154] In a similar manner, the staff at Foxborough State Hospital linked their inebriate patients to the Boston Jacoby Club—a voluntary fellowship of recovered alcoholics—and later organized their own "men's club" as part of their aftercare program.[155]

The Chicago Home was one of the first homes to use a monthly newspaper as a vehicle of communication for and among people who had left their facility. This paper, *The Washingtonian*, recounted stories of the successes and struggles of men and women following their treatment. Such newspapers were emulated by other homes and asylums, and their utility was expanded to include public relations and marketing by private addiction cure institutes.

Reported Treatment Outcomes

Inebriate homes and asylums rose in United States during the middle to late 19th century, under a banner proclaiming that inebriety was a curable disease. Estimates of cure rates presented in the directors' reports at the first meeting (1870) of the American Association for the Cure of Inebriates ranged between 33% and 63 percent.[156] The Association's report for the following year indicated that 33% of the patients treated in the Association's member facilities had achieved a permanent cure.[157] In 1874, Turner reported on the first follow-up study of addiction treatment in America, noting that 66½% of patients discharged were found to be "temperate

and total abstainers" five years after treatment.[158] In 1870 the Chicago Washingtonian Home reported its outcomes at discharge in the following categories: Discharged: 71; Cured: 39; Hopeful: 15; Doubtful: 8; and Hopeless: 9.[159]

In 1892, H.R. Chamberlain reported on the fate of 3,212 men who had been admitted to the New York Christian Home for Intemperate Men over a span of 13 years. Of those admitted, 2,716 claimed religious conversion; and of these, 2,026 were reported to have "remained steadfast as far as can be ascertained."[160]

In 1893, Thomas Crothers reported on the treatment outcome of 3,380 inebriates treated at Fort Hamilton. Of those discharged, 19½% could not be accounted for; 43% were doing well; 16½% were improved; 16½% had been readmitted; 2½% had died; and 2% had been transferred to other institutions.[161] Former patients of the Massachusetts Hospital for Dipsomaniacs and Inebriates were monitored during the year following their discharge. The percentage of those reported to be "doing well or abstinent" in the years 1894 to 1918 ranged from a low of 22% to a high of 55 percent.[162]

There was early concern about those factors that contributed to a poor prognosis for recovery. Albert Day's 1877 report on the Boston Washingtonian Home noted that the following conditions were associated with unfavorable treatment outcomes: inebriety resulting from hereditary predisposition or brain injury, the lack of an occupation, the absence of family connection, limited education, concurrent nervous disorders, and the use of narcotics or chloral as an aid in sleep.[163] Inebriety specialists were concerned about the future disposition of chronically relapsing patients. As early as 1877, proposals emerged calling for the establishment of state-run inebriety institutions, to which such chronic recidivists could be legally committed.[164]

Treatment outcomes were reported to vary by drug choice. Because cocaine users could be detoxified easily—without the difficult withdrawal associated with narcotic or alcohol addiction—but were so prone to relapse, the psychological hold that cocaine had on its victims was often viewed as more insidious than that addictions that were considered more physical in nature.[165]

The characterization of patients who relapsed after leaving treatment changed over time. The early attitude is indicated by the following March 9, 1858 journal entry at Boston's Washingtonian Home:

> ....*he is determined to prostitute them [his abilities] to his inevitable destruction, as he*

had no sooner left the institution than all his professions of reformation vanished, and with the blackest ingratitude, he violated his pledge, thereby forfeiting all claim to further sympathy.[166]

By the 1890s, most treatment facilities had a much deeper understanding of the chronicity of most addictive disorders and the continuing risk of relapse for clients. In 1898, Dr. T.D. Crothers reflected: "Even under the most skillful care, with the best appliances known to science, it [inebriety] is often incurable and only temporarily influenced by therapeutic measures."[167]

Then, as now, most reports of treatment outcome were not based on carefully controlled studies and were subject to many influences. Early figures of success may have been inflated under the pressure of these new institutions to succeed, just as in later years competition among institutions may have similarly worked to artificially inflate the degree of reported success. In her study of the state inebriate hospital in Massachusetts, Sarah Tracy suggests that follow-up studies to evaluate patient success during this era might have been conducted on purposely short-term bases to avoid the erosion of abstinence rates that was likely to occur over time.[168]

Interspersed among such professional positioning and marketing claims were rare episodes of rather remarkable insight and candor. In 1874, D. Banks MacKenzie of the Appleton Home in Boston, Massachusetts offered the following advice to those working with inebriates:

> *....do not be hasty in giving up a victim as incurable. Your patience will be sadly tried, those you had the most confidence in will betray you, lie to you, deceive you and fall. Do not give up, forgive seventy times seven, so long as the prodigal comes back, acknowledges willingness to try again, the spark is there. This is a work of great trials but great rejoicings....the good seed is planted, and will bring forth fruit sometime.*[169]

The Treatment of Alcoholism and Other Addictions in Women

This chapter has portrayed the philosophies, methodologies, and outcomes of addiction treatment within 19th- and early 20th-century inebriate homes and asylums. We would be remiss, however, if we failed to acknowledge that these views do not fully reflect the perceptions of inebriety in women or the experience of women in treatment during this era. We will close the chapter with an exploration of this more detailed story.

The Social Context: At the time the inebriate asylums were being founded, women were viewed as fragile but morally superior creatures, who needed the physical and economic protection of their husbands while they focused on the domestic duties of running the household and bearing and raising children. Both insanity and inebriety in women were viewed as arising from the biological and psychological vulnerabilities associated with menstruation, pregnancy, childbirth, lactation, gynecological diseases, and menopause. The moral idealization of women contributed to the early denial of alcohol and other drug problems, and at the same time gave women a venue for social action outside the home via the temperance movement. By the time the inebriate asylums were in decline at the end of the 19th century, a "New Woman" was emerging: young, educated, intellectual, socially active, and committed to bettering the community. Women who pursued traditionally defined roles and women who challenged such constrictions both found themselves increasingly vulnerable to problems in their relationship with alcohol and other drugs.[170]

Prevalence of Inebriety in Women: The number and potency of drugs increased through the 19th century. Women were over-represented among their consumers, but at the same time, such use was hidden. The efforts of the temperance movement, along with the growing conceptualization of opiate dependence as a vice, had attached a stigma to intoxication that many women wished to avoid. This created a veil of secrecy around women's use of alcohol, opiates, chloral hydrate, chloroform, and other psychoactive substances. Dr. Asa Myerlet described how the opiate addiction of women in the 1880s was hidden even from those closest to them—their husbands and families.

> *They notice that she is queer, that her memory is impaired, that she frequently loses articles of value—hiding them and forgetting where they are; that she sometimes invites friends to dine with her, but forgets to provide for them, and is evidently perplexed at their coming; that she does not make calls, and is seldom prepared to receive; that her household duties are neglected, her children uncared*

for, her friends almost forgotten. But they say she has never been the same since she was sick a few years ago....[171]

In their classic study of opiate addiction, Charles Terry and Mildred Pellens reviewed all available survey data and concluded that the overwhelming preponderance of opiate addicts in the 19th century were affluent, educated women.[172] However, such addiction was commonly hidden behind a mask of other publicly proclaimed physical and emotional ailments. Addicted women could seek help for neurasthenia, hysteria, or melancholy in psychiatric institutions, where their irritability and discomfort would often be "treated" with opiates.[173] This practice allowed women to deny their opiate addiction and still sustain themselves on opiates.[174]

Alcohol consumption, like the consumption of opiates, tended to be hidden within the home and masked behind women's use of "medicines." The need to sustain one's consumption during prolonged periods in public created a market for some clever devices. In the 1880s, thin India-rubber capsules resembling grapes, which were filled with wine or spirits, were marketed to women. Placed in an opera glass case, the capsules could be surreptitiously slipped into the mouth and crushed with the teeth. The liquid could be swallowed and the skin slyly discarded.[175] There were also popular accounts of women who became "slaves to cologne" by drinking alcohol-based perfumes and toilet waters.[176]

This presentation does not mean that all inebriety in women was hidden behind the genteel walls of homes and private medicine cabinets. An 1874 report from the Albany Penitentiary noted that more than 6,000 women had been confined there, "nearly all inebriates."[177] There was clearly a rise in the number of women who presented themselves intoxicated in public during the last quarter of the 19th century. For example, by 1900 the number of arrests of women for drunkenness in New York City had reached 8,000 per year.[178]

The inebriety of women also became visible and caused concerns when it threatened the welfare of their children. An 1899 article in *The Catholic World* noted:

The matron at one of the New York day nurseries, which cares for the children of that class (poor) of women, says that the mothers are frequently under the influence of drink to such an extent when they call for the babies at night that the nurses are afraid to trust the little ones with them.[179]

Perceptions of the Causes of Inebriety in Women: During the era of the inebriate asylums there was much speculation about the causes of inebriety in women. Here is a sampling of opinions regarding such causes expressed over a span of some 75 years.

One of the earliest references to inebriety in women by a recognized addiction expert was an 1835 report by Robert MacNish, in which he suggested that the practice of encouraging women to drink ale as an aid to nursing had given women a socially approved reason to consume large quantities of alcohol and led to growing numbers of women acquiring the appetite for alcohol.[180]

During the 1870s, George Beard made a number of pronouncements about the vulnerability of women to addiction. He began in 1871 by proclaiming that women were more vulnerable to inebriety than men because women had a more "nervous" organization.[181] By 1874, Beard had completely reversed his position on women's innate vulnerability to intoxicants.

Chronic alcoholism is a masculine disease. Freedom from it is one of the compensations of being born a woman....The organization of civilized woman, and notably of the American woman, is so sensitive and impressible that it cannot bear alcohol....Very few of our finely organized American women have any desire to drink, and those who do have such desire, are but rarely able to drink enough to induce symptoms of chronic alcoholism.[182]

In 1875, Dr. T.D. Crothers suggested that women were "more liable to inebriety than men, because they have feebler organizations, and suffer more from functional disorders, and organic degenerations."[183] Crothers also noted the popular view that problems of inebriety in women were caused by the shock produced by drinking wine after the heat of dancing.[184] In his 1881 treatise *The Opium Habit and Alcoholism*, Dr. Fred Hubbard noted that uterine and ovarian complications contributed to more cases of opium addiction in women than all other causes combined. Hubbard also noted the special complications of addiction in pregnant women. He warned that precipitous withdrawal could threaten the life of both mother and child and recommended low-dose maintenance followed by detoxification of both mother and child following delivery.[185] In 1883, Dr. Lucy Hall, Physician in Charge of the Reformatory Prison in Sherburne, Massachusetts, reported on 204 inebriate women, 109 of whom had two or more prior commitments to the prison for drunkenness-related offenses. One woman had been committed more than 100 times. The inebriate women Hall profiled began drinking intemperately before they were aged 21, drank not alone but usually with other young women, and began drinking alcohol-laced tonics and then progressed to beer and distilled spirits. Hall's report emphasized the relationship between female alcoholism and domestic battery. Of the married inebriates studied by Hall, more than one third had scars upon their heads resulting from violent assaults from drunken husbands.[186]

In 1894, Norman Kerr observed that "The great functional disturbance undergone by many women at the approach of each period, especially by individuals of highly nervous temperament, has been a prolific cause of the inebriety tendency."[187] He went on to note another source of vulnerability: "This unwanted physical commotion at the menopause leads to mental excitement which, in the minds unstable by heredity or some other predisposition, and at times even by its own force, explodes now into insanity, now into inebriety."[188]

Dr. Agnes Sparks of Brooklyn, New York—one of the earliest women working within addiction medicine—observed in 1898 that women suffered less genetic risk of inebriety than men, but greater somatic risks. Sparks believed there were two primary causes of inebriety in women: 1) a neurasthenic weakening of energy resulting from poor nutrition and the rigors of domestic and social responsibilities, and 2) painful disorders of their sex. In Spark's view, the former cried out for stimulants, as the latter demanded anesthesia.[189]

In 1901, Dr. Heywood Smith offered his opinion that the increasing independence of women was a likely factor in rising inebriety, particularly in women who could not bear the stress that such independence brought. He also noted that the growing practice of champagne drinking among the higher classes and the growing availability of alcohol in grocery stores probably contributed to rising inebriety among women.[190]

Partridge observed in 1912 that "....the motive which in women leads to drinking is likely to be pain, that her use of intoxicants is more likely to be solitary; that the narcotic effects of drugs are more pronounced in her, and are more often sought."[191]

What is perhaps most remarkable in this just-completed review is not the wide divergence in these views, but the assumption that unique factors influenced the differences between inebriety in men and in women, and the quite active search for the nature of those factors in women. This quest was swept away in the overall demise of the inebriate asylum movement and would not be raised again in the mainstream of addiction treatment until the 1970s.

Treatment of Inebriety in Women: Women in the 19th century, like women today, faced special obstacles in getting help for addiction-related problems. Addiction treatment programs in many areas of the country did not treat women, and even where the doors to such treatment were open, social stigma often kept women from seeking help. In 1877, Thomas Doner compared the fate of men and women who suffer from alcoholism:

> *Men can reform; society welcomes them back to the path of virtue....their promises to reform are hailed with great delight. But, alas! for poor women who have been tempted to sin by rum. For them there are no calls to come home; no sheltering arm; no acceptance of confessions and promises to amend.... How seldom we attempt to reach and rescue her! For her there is no refuge.*[192]

Stigma and shame also shaped the nature of treatment for women. Inebriate asylums that catered to women made special note of the separate quarters and entrances for women whereby the secrecy of their presence could be guaranteed.

The roots of addiction treatment services for women can be traced to the temperance movement. The short-lived Martha Washington Societies that sprang up in the early 1840s represent the first efforts that focused specifically on the needs of alcoholic women. Johnson's 1843 account of the Martha Washington Societies includes the success stories of many female inebriates who initiated their recovery within these organizations.[193] The Martha Washington Societies mark the emergence of an enduring theme in addiction treatment—the organization of addiction recovery support structures by and for women as a response to their exclusion from or maltreatment within mainstream service institutions.

Other temperance groups, such as the Ladies Dashaway Association in San Francisco, also sustained a focus on help for the female inebriate.[194] While large numbers of mothers, wives, sisters and daughters of alcoholics were drawn into these temperance societies, the overall number of alcohol- and other drug-addicted women who joined these groups remained relatively small. For example, Ruth

Bordin's study of the Women's Christian Temperance Union membership concluded that very few women entered temperance groups because of their own struggles with addiction.[195]

Institutional programs for inebriate women began in 1841 when temperance programs first opened "industrial homes" for women.[196] There is evidence that women sought admission for addiction treatment from the earliest days of the asylum movement in the U.S. For example, of the first 4,000 requests for admission to the New York State Inebriate Asylum, 400 were from women.[197]

Concern about the need for special approaches and special institutions for the treatment of female inebriates paralleled similar concerns about the needs of women in prisons and insane asylums. The early mixing of men and women in all of these institutions led to many abuses and scandals, and eventually to the segregation of women within inebriate, psychiatric, and penal institutions.[198]

Special women's units were organized within existing programs. One example was the Female Department of the Washingtonian Home in Chicago, which opened in 1869 and admitted 50 women in its first 18 months of operation. Other independent facilities built specifically to treat inebriate women included the New England Home for Intemperate Women, opened in Boston in 1879, and the St. Saviors Sanitarium in New York, which opened in the early 1890s under the leadership of Dr. Frederick Peterson. St. Savior's, which is still part of the Episcopalian House of Mercy, enticed the state legislature to pass a law that allowed inebriate women to be committed to the St. Savior's Sanitarium for up to two years.[199] There were also a growing number of inebriate treatment institutions that admitted both men and women, such as the Kings County Home in Brooklyn, Massachusetts and the Fort Hamilton Home in Long Island, New York. Of the 4,663 cases of addiction treated at the Fort Hamilton Home by 1893, 579 were

women. When Mark Lender conducted his review of alcoholism admissions of women to treatment institutions in the years 1884-1912, he found the male-to-female ratio of such admissions ranging from 3:1 to 9:1.[200]

Even in co-educational facilities, women were treated separately from men, and there was strong condemnation of any fraternization between the sexes during treatment. Interesting rationales were used to justify the exclusion or separation of women. Dr. Norman Kerr's justification for separating women was that their dresses afforded greater opportunity to smuggle liquor and other contraband to male inmates. He rationalized his recommendation for refusing to admit women to inebriety institutions on the grounds that such exclusion was needed to protect the male patients.[201]

By the end of the 19th century, literature on the special needs of women had grown, as the number of inebriate women treated within the asylums had increased. Observations from a sampling of this literature include the following:

- Women have a lower genetic vulnerability to alcoholism than men.
- The progression of alcoholism is different in women. (There was disagreement over whether it was slower or faster.)
- Excessive alcohol consumption in women leads to "a diseased, depraved progeny."
- Women require longer periods of treatment than do men.[202]

There was considerable disagreement on the question of treatment prognosis for women. For example, Agnes Sparks reported that women had a better prognosis than men, but T.D. Crothers believed that women were harder to cure because their alcoholism was concealed for so long before they sought treatment.[203]

Chapter Six
Four Institutional Histories

The 19th-century inebriate homes and asylums scattered across America varied greatly in the conditions that spawned their birth, their treatment philosophies and methods, and their eventual fate. This chapter will provide a brief account of four such institutions: the New York State Inebriate Asylum,

the Washingtonian Home in Boston, the Washingtonian Home for the Cure of Inebriates in Chicago, and the San Francisco Home for the Care of the Inebriate. A picture of the struggles, successes, and failures of the early inebriate homes and asylums is reflected in these profiles.

The New York State Inebriate Asylum[204]

Dr. Joseph Edward Turner developed an interest in alcoholism in medical school and spent years championing the creation of a national asylum for the treatment of inebriety. He queried physicians, clergy, and judges across the country and studied approaches to the treatment of inebriety in Europe. To raise money for his proposed inebriate asylum, Turner tried to sell private stock at $10 per share. Unfortunately, only 66 of 3,000 prospects were willing to invest in his proposed institution. This was indicative of the great resistance to this new idea of an asylum for inebriates. Turner approached more than 140 noted personages before he found 20 who would agree to serve on the board of this new venture.[205] Due in great part to Turner's own tenaciousness, support for the idea of an inebriate asylum slowly grew, in spite of strong opposition from various religious and temperance leaders.

In 1854, the New York State Legislature granted Turner a charter for the "United States Inebriate Asylum for the Reformation of the Destitute Inebriate." When funders were not forthcoming, the charter was amended with the more humble goal of creating the New York State Inebriate Asylum. Ground was broken for this new facility in 1858. While the New York Legislature initially refused to fund the construction of the facility or its services, in 1859 it succumbed to the argument that "if the State permits a revenue to arise from this traffic (in liquor), it should amply provide for the disease it creates."[206] The Legislature granted the Asylum one tenth of alcohol-related revenues collected in the state, and by 1862 Dr. Turner's dream was close to fruition. Some 250 acres of land were acquired, and the cornerstone was laid on an institution that was to include patient wards, a gymnasium, a chapel, a conservatory, riding stables, a library, and a billiards room.

By the time the home opened in 1864 under the direction of Dr. Turner and Dr. Valentine Mott, some 2,800 people had applied for admission.[207] During the same year, the New York legislature added further support by passing legislation prohibiting the sale of alcohol within one-half mile of the asylum, prohibiting people who were not staff or patients from trespassing on the asylum grounds without permission, and providing for the legal commitment of chronic inebriates to the asylum for up to one year.[208]

A year after the asylum opened, Dr. Mott died and was replaced by a Dr. Willard Parker. Clashes of temperament and treatment philosophies between Turner and Parker escalated into a destructive power struggle. At the center of this struggle was a controversy over the degree of freedom and autonomy afforded patients. Turner's position was that the inebriate must be subjected to absolute control and restraint until there were strong indications that the disease had been cured. Under this philosophy, rules governing patient behavior were large in number and even included prohibitions against possessing money or stamps. Patients and their family members bristled at this authoritarian environment. They particularly objected to the seemingly inflexible requirement that all patients had to stay at least one year at the institution. The internal conflicts over the treatment and management philosophy of the institution led to a confusing mixture of treatment policies and practices. There was also external hostility toward the asylum, which arose from Turner's refusal to allow Christian revivalists access to patients so that the revivalists could attempt their conversion cure.[209]

When the Asylum's main building burned down in 1867, Turner was forced out of his position, the target of legal charges of arson. (The charges were later dropped.) Conflict abounded. Turner's enemies claimed that $80,000 in insurance money paid to Turner after the fire had never been put back into the facility. There were continual rumors that Turner was an arsonist, a thief, and a bigamist and that he called himself "Dr." but had no medical degree. There were charges that he was morally unfit to direct the asylum.[210] The conflict, which split the board and spread into the daily newspapers and eventually into the courts, resulted in the temporary closing of the facility to patients.

Although the facility re-opened for a short time under the leadership of Dr. Albert Day, Dr. Parker closed and deeded the Asylum to the State of New York for a modest sum of $1. The State used it as a psychiatric hospital—the Binghampton State Hospital. Alcoholics continued to be treated at the State Hospital well into the 20th century, in stays of three months to a year.[211] But as an institution specializing in the care of inebriety, the New York Asylum had a short existence.

Dr. Turner went on to try to establish "The Woman's National Hospital for Inebriates and Opium Eaters" in Connecticut, but rumors related to his past conduct in New York eventually doomed this effort. Dr. Turner's 50-year struggle to create a hospital for the treatment of alcoholism produced no lasting institution. His contemporaries varied in their characterization of Dr. Turner. Some called him a charlatan and crook, while others viewed him as a martyr who pioneered the drive for specialty institutions for addiction treatment.[212] His work was carried on by men like Drs. Albert Day and T.D. Crothers, who both worked with Turner at Binghamton and went on to make significant contributions to the inebriate asylum movement. These men consistently acknowledged Turner's role as a pioneer within the field. Turner died in 1889, a year after writing a book on the "First Inebriate Asylum in the World."[213]

The New York State Inebriate Asylum rose and fell amidst intense conflicts of personality, conflicts over treatment philosophy, and charges of mismanagement and fraud. Other more enduring addiction treatment institutions would take its place, but the themes surrounding the demise of the New York State Inebriate Asylum provided bold illustration of the forces that could undermine the successful operation of an addiction treatment program. Variations on the experience of the New York State Inebriate Asylum would be played out again and again in the century following its closing.

The Boston Washingtonian Home

In 1841, the Washingtonian Society of Boston provided rooms under its meeting hall, to accommodate men who were struggling to achieve sobriety within the Washingtonian movement. Dr. Charles Jewitt, the famed temperance reformer, reported on a visit to Washingtonian Hall in Boston during the early 1840s. He described descending stairs at the rear of the large Washingtonian meeting hall and wrote of seeing "a dozen or more bunks, or coarse beds."[214] This humble room was the first lodging home for inebriates. In 1844 and 1845, the Boston Washingtonian Total Abstinence Society opened three houses to lodge new recruits who, in the language of a later generation, had "hit bottom." These lodging homes closed down for lack of funds after a short period of operation. No treatment as such was provided in these houses, as all lodgers were expected to be fully participating in the Washingtonian meetings. But the homes did constitute a special form of support for men in the Washingtonian Society who failed to keep their pledges due to recurring relapses. Similar houses of refuge were being attempted in New York during the same period.

The need for an institution that could provide more active support than the lodging house had long been discussed within the Washington Temperance Society of Boston. A Mrs. Charles Spear launched a legislative drive for the opening of an inebriate asylum in Boston. She and the Reverend Phineas Stone opened the Home for the Fallen on the corner of

Fulton and Richmond Streets in 1857. In 1858 the home moved to new facilities at 36 Charles Street and came under the direction of Dr. Albert Day. The home moved to a newly erected facility at 41 Waltham Street in the mid-1870s. It was incorporated by the State of Massachusetts as the "Washingtonian Home." This home was supported by annual appropriations from the state legislature between 1859 and 1871.

During the early years of the Washingtonian Home, treatment methods were more moral and religious than medical or correctional. In his 1860 account of the Washingtonian Home in Boston, Harrison emphasized the "entire absence of any compulsory restraint upon the movements of the inmates, they being allowed to go and come at pleasure walking the city....under the sacred parole of honor." The philosophy of the home was that "The unfortunate victim of inebriety requires kindness, sympathy and love—not force, violence and restraint." In the Home's approach to treatment of the inebriate, the emphasis was on "drawing out his inherent goodness of character."[215]

Days in the home consisted of morning and evening prayers, and testimonial meetings in which current and former inmates shared their experiences. The pledge each patient was asked to sign read as follows:

> *Believing that the use of intoxicating drinks is not only useless, but injurious to health and destructive to peace and happiness; therefore, being sober and in my right mind, I do, in the presence of God, solemnly swear, that I will not use any intoxicating drinks as a beverage, during my natural life.*[216]

The only documentation of treatment within the Washingtonian Home during these early years was a journal that provided few-sentence biographies of the patients, along with their dates of arrival, notation of their signing the pledge, and the dates on which they left.

The Boston Washingtonian Home emphasized that what it was doing did not constitute a cure in the usual sense of that term:

> *Until the evidence is conclusive that the desire for strong drink, which is the last symptom of their disease, has been removed, they (inebriate patients) are regarded and reported as convalescent, but on no account*

dismissed as cured.[217]

Dr. Albert Day and his associates discovered that this type of personal reformation took time. By 1871, the average length of stay had been extended from 21 days to a span of three to six months. Much of what would today be called "aftercare support" was handled by the prolific correspondence maintained between Dr. Day and his former patients.

In 1873, $100,000 was raised to build a new facility. Between 250 and 1,000 alcoholics per year were treated in the expanded facilities of the Boston Washingtonian Home.

The Boston Washingtonian Home continued to operate through the years that saw many other treatment institutions close. The number of admissions dropped at the beginning of prohibition and reached their crest at 1,314 in 1926. Adaptations in treatment approaches were also made during this period, such as an Outpatient Department that was officially opened in 1914. In 1938 the home was reorganized and became the Washingtonian Hospital.

After detoxification, treatment at the hospital in the 1940s consisted of "psychological classification," "psychological therapy," experimental shock therapy, drug therapy, and teaching about alcohol. (The reader will note the shift from moral reformation to medical treatment reflected in this list of treatment methods.) Each patient's treatment ended with a period of "working parole," in which the patient worked out of the facility every day but returned to the hospital at night. Patients were then encouraged to continue in long-term outpatient treatment. Inpatient and outpatient treatment was provided by an interdisciplinary staff of physicians, nurses, a social worker, and a consulting psychologist.[218]

The Boston facility was the first of its kind in the country and became a model for many similar facilities across the country. The Washingtonian Home in Boston evolved into the Boston Washingtonian Hospital, which evolved into a modern addiction treatment program: the Washingtonian Center for Addictions.[219]

The Chicago Washingtonian Home

The Washingtonian Home for the Cure of Inebriates in Chicago was established in 1863 under the leadership and patronage of Robert (Rolla) A. Law, a prominent Chicago publisher. Law, a temperance advocate and member of the Independent Order of Good Templars of Cook County, had befriended a highly valued alcoholic employee by taking the employee into Law's own home. The employee had stopped drinking and returned to his former level of productivity. Based on this success, Law approached his fellow Templars with a proposal to open a home to help inebriates.

Through the support of the Templars, the Washingtonian Home for the Cure of Inebriates was opened December 10, 1863 at 547 State Street. The Home occupied what had once been the Bull's Head Tavern until 1875, when a new facility was built on the corner of Madison Street and Ogden Avenue. Twenty-three men were treated during the first year, including two clergymen, two lawyers, an editor, and a surgeon. The Home was incorporated in 1867 by a special act of the Illinois legislature. It was the first institution in Illinois established specifically for the treatment of alcoholics. A residence for women was opened in June of 1869 and christened the Martha Washington Home. Prior to 1869, female inebriates were taken into the home of Charles Hull—a home that was later to become the first settlement house in America under the leadership of Jane Addams.[220]

During the 1880s, Superintendent Wilkins introduced a series of eight lectures that all residents of the Washingtonian Home were required to attend. The topics listed in the lecture schedule were as follows.

1.   *The cause why nations and individuals use narcotics, and especially alcohol and opium.*
2.   *Why do these narcotics affect some more than others?*
3.   *What is physical life, and the cause of physical heat?*
4.   *Give the effects that alcohol has upon physical tissue.*
5.   *The effects of alcohol upon the intellectual, moral and animal man.*
6.   *The reconstruction of the physical man.*
7.   *The reconstruction of the intellectual and moral, and the control of the animal man.*
8.   *The means to be used to render reformation thorough and permanent.*[221]

The Home also held prayer meetings hosted by the Grand Lodge of Good Templars and the Sons of Temperance, although these meetings were sometimes poorly attended.

The Home operated on a budget that would be incomprehensible by today's standards. In 1871, the Home took in $12,101 and expended $10,937.[222] One of the unique features of the Washingtonian Home was its early strategy to generate funds. Ten percent of a tax on saloons in Chicago and Cook County went directly to the Washingtonian Home until an 1875 court decision declared the use of public funds for this purpose unconstitutional. Facing a dramatic depletion of operating funds, administrators of the Home sold "Life Memberships" to the public for $25.00 to sustain its operations. Men and women who could afford to pay for their treatment in Chicago's Washingtonian Homes were charged between $5 and $15 per week. Free services were provided to the indigent.

The homes continued to expand in size until the turn of the century. A report in 1900 noted that 26,000 men and 1,300 women had been treated since the homes were opened. The daily census of alcoholic patients often ran between 300 and 400. The full course of treatment was two to four weeks for the men and two to four months for the women. No rationale was given for the much longer duration of treatment for women. The report noted that 20% of the men achieved complete reformation, with a higher success rate for the women attributable to the fact that they were "less inclined to the habit." Women did play a unique role while in residence, helping tend the vegetable gardens and the chickens that fed the patients and were sold to raise funds for the center. A 1914 report on men admitted for treatment revealed that most were between 30 and 50 years of age and that the most frequent occupations were painters, printers, salesmen, and railroad men.[223]

When alcohol prohibition slowed the demand for treatment services to a trickle and the patient census dropped below 20, the program was closed and the building sold in 1922. Proceeds from the sale were used to erect the Martha Washington Hospital, which contained a ward that continued the Washingtonian Home's mission of treating the alcoholic. More than 300,000 alcoholics were treated at the Washingtonian Home of Chicago between 1867 and 1922. Martha Washington Hospital continued its service to alcoholics until the hospital's closing in the summer of 1991.

The San Francisco Home for the Care of the Inebriate

While most early historical accounts of alcoholism treatment describe facilities in the East or Midwest, Jim Baumohl has constructed an excellent history of the San Francisco Home for the Care of the Inebriate. The home, like those in Boston and Chicago, grew out of a temperance organization—in this case, the Dashaway Association. The Dashaway Association was founded in 1859 by volunteer firemen in San Francisco with the sole purpose of

reclaiming the drunkard. With almost 5,000 members in 1862, the Dashaways built a facility that contained a large auditorium and reading and club rooms.

Lectures, support meetings, and social events were hosted within the facility, almost on a daily basis. Recovery was based on a renewable pledge of abstinence, "experience sharing" in the Washingtonian style, recruitment of those still addicted, exposure to inspirational speakers, and a reconstruction of lifestyle and social relationships within the Dashaway Association. Members who relapsed were subjected to trials called by the "Vigilance Committee," in which the fallen member either renewed the pledge to reform or faced expulsion. Membership in the Dashaways expanded beyond firemen, and the granting of charters to start new chapters spread the Dashaway influence northward into Canada and as far East as St. Louis.[224]

On June 1, 1859, the Dashaways opened the San Francisco Home for the Care of the Inebriate on the fourth floor of the facilities which they were then renting. This floor housed up to 56 men, who were referred by the local courts or recruited by men in the Dashaway Association. Baumohl describes the Home's four-week treatment regimen.

> *Treatment consisted of bed rest, nourishment, ministrations by consulting physicians drawn from among the Dashaways, self-improvement exhortations....and for those who joined the Dashaways....supportive services.*[225]

The Home was first staffed by a superintendent and his wife, who were later helped by a small number of aides. While this staffing pattern is meager indeed by today's standards, the Home's location above the Hall rented by the Dashaways ensured a rich supply of daily volunteers.[226]

The Home was funded by grants from the state and from a portion of police court fines for public drunkenness. In 1863, the Home moved to a separate facility and hired an attending physician for the fee of $25 per month. The only real alternative alcoholics had to treatment at the San Francisco Home was involuntary commitment to California's lunatic asylums. In contrast, the San Francisco Home used friendly persuasion both to engage residents and to keep them in the Home.

The Home came under increasing criticism over its methods. It was criticized for accepting only a small number of people and choosing only those with the highest commitment to personal reformation. It was criticized for the small percentage of its clients who continued in the Dashaway Association following discharge. The relapse of many of the people who stayed in the Home contributed to a growing belief that brief, voluntary treatment of the alcoholic was futile.[227] The Home progressively declined during the years of debate about whether alcoholics should be voluntarily treated for short periods in homes or involuntarily treated in large asylums for long periods of time. Financial support for the Home also deteriorated as a result of an economic depression.

The Home was also made vulnerable by the internal conflicts within, and eventual demise of, its parent organization, the Dashaway Association. Baumohl described this transformation:

> Whereas in the '60s the Dashaways were the fair-haired champions of lofty ideals and individual integrity, they became by the late '70s a "small band of schemers," speculators and capitalists for the most part, intent on dividing a substantial amount of loot.[228]

During the 1880s, the Dashaways were riddled with public charges ranging from cruelty to patients to improper use of funds. Conflicts between the home's executive director and the board were also prominent during this decade. The entire atmosphere of the home took on the tenor of a soap opera when reports surfaced of attempts at murder and suicide by key figures in the conflict. In the face of such turmoil, the Dashaways disappeared as an organization by 1890, and the San Francisco Home for the Care of the Inebriate progressively deteriorated into a "private prison" that was closed in December 1898. Between its opening in 1859 and its closing in 1898, the home provided a source of support to a large number of recovering alcoholics and operated as one of the more prominent homes for the treatment of inebriety on the West Coast.[229]

This chapter has reviewed four 19th-century institutions that specialized in addiction treatment. In the next chapter, we will visit a treatment institution that was not part of the Association for the Study and Cure of Inebriety, and, in fact, was regularly under attack by the Association. If any one of the treatment centers for inebriety took center stage in America's consciousness—both in its popularity and in its controversy—it was unquestionably the Keeley Institutes. The Keeley story marks one of the most fascinating chapters in the history of addiction treatment in America.

Chapter Seven
Franchising Addiction Treatment: The Keeley Institutes [230]

Addiction cures grew at prolific rates during the last quarter of the 19th century. The drive toward alcohol and other drug prohibition whetted America's appetite for sobriety and opened business opportunities for those who promised aid in achieving this goal. Along with the religiously influenced inebriate homes and more medically oriented inebriate asylums came a growing number of business-oriented addiction cures. These included private sanitaria that catered to alcoholics and addicts, as well as various home cures—medicinal "specifics" that claimed the power to quell the craving for strong drink and narcotics. Newspapers and magazines advertised such treatments as the Fittz Cure, Tiplicuro, and the Bellinger Cure —the last of these promising to cure opium addiction within 24 hours.[231]

Some of these business-oriented inebriety cures of the late 19th century achieved such popularity that they developed into what today would be called "chains" or "franchises." There were several such popular chains—the Leyfield Cure, the Hagey Cure, the Empire Institutes, the Oppenheimer Institutes, the Gatlin Institutes, and the Neal Institutes—but none was more famous, more geographically dispersed, more widely utilized, and more controversial than Leslie Keeley's Double Chloride of Gold Cure for the treatment of alcoholism, drug addiction, and the tobacco habit. Between 1880 and 1920, more than 500,000 alcoholics and addicts took the Keeley Cure. This treatment was lauded as a cure of miraculous potential—and at the same time attacked as a fraud. This is its story.[2]

---

[2]The work constructing the history of the Keeley Institute was enriched by discussions with James Oughton, Jr. and Mrs. Anne Withrow, and by three unpublished manuscripts by Ben Scott, Paul Weitz, and Mary Sigler. Paul was a bubbling fountain of information and resources on Keeley, and his help is gratefully acknowledged.

The Humble Beginnings of a National Phenomenon

Dr. Leslie E. Keeley studied medicine with a doctor in Beardstown, Illinois. He went on to complete his medical education at Rush Medical College in Chicago and serve as a surgeon in the Civil War. It was during his military service that Keeley first became interested in the causes of and potential cures for inebriety. According to oral folklore passed down within the founding families of the Keeley Institute, Keeley organized treatment for alcoholism in an East Coast Union hospital during the war. His cured patients, according to this legend, later sent their friends and relatives with similar problems in search of Keeley's aid.[232]

Following his discharge from the military in 1864, Keeley settled in the small rural village of Dwight, Illinois, some 70 miles south of Chicago. Keeley's interest in a cure for inebriety led to a collaboration with Frederick B. Hargreaves, a former minister and temperance lecturer.[233] After some experimentation in Dwight, Keeley and Hargreaves believed they had discovered a cure. The first people exposed to the Keeley cure were a few local alcoholics who were considered "bums" by most of the local folk in Dwight.[234] With some early success under their belt, Keeley and Hargreaves opened the first Keeley Institute in 1879. Proclaiming that "drunkenness is a disease and I can cure it," Keeley publicly announced his discovery of the "Double Chloride of Gold Remedies" for inebriety, tobacco-ism, and neurasthenia (nervous exhaustion) and invited people who suffered from these conditions to come and be cured at the Leslie E. Keeley Gold Cure Institute for the Treatment of Inebriates in Dwight, Illinois.

Within a year, the Leslie E. Keeley Company was incorporated, and John R. Oughton, a chemist; Curtis J. Judd, a businessman and Keeley brother-in-law; and Father James Halpin were added as founding partners. The interests of Hargreaves and Halpin were bought out by the other partners in 1886, and the company was reincorporated. Hargreaves, from whom we will hear a bit later, went on to become a Keeley critic and competitor.

The launching of the Keeley Institute was interrupted by two events. In June of 1881, The Illinois State Board of Health revoked Keeley's medical license for "unprofessional" advertising. Governor Joseph Fifer later restored the license on the grounds that the revocation decision had been impulsive and prejudicial.[235] The second event was Dr. Keeley's temporary withdrawal of his treatment, from December of 1885 to June of 1887. This action was taken in response to serious side effects that some patients were experiencing, reactions to ingredients in the Keeley medicines. The Institute re-opened when —according to Keeley—an Irish physician showed him a way to eliminate the buildup of gold that had produced these adverse effects.[236] The Keeley Institute underwent rapid growth from 1890 to 1893, and it was during this period that Keeley achieved national and international recognition. In 1890, when the Dwight facilities were bursting with requests for admission, Keeley decided to franchise the treatment by organizing Keeley branches around the United States. The first branches were opened in Des Moines, Iowa; Atlanta, Georgia; White Plains, New York; and Media, Pennsylvania.[237] By the end of 1891, 26 new Keeley Institutes had been opened, and 75 new Institutes opened in 1892. By mid-1893, there were a total of 118 Keeley Institutes spread across the U.S., as well as Keeley Institutes in England, Finland, Denmark, and Sweden.[238]

The Keeley branches were franchises, owned by private individuals or investment groups who contracted to use the Keeley name and the Keeley methods of treatment. Franchise owners paid the Keeley company a buy-in fee (some as much as $50,000), paid a percentage of each patient's fees to the Keeley Company, and purchased all medicines used in the treatment from the parent Institute in Dwight. All of the Keeley branches used the Double Chloride of Gold treatment, and the key staff from each branch were trained by Dr. Keeley in Dwight.

The explosive growth that took place between 1890 and 1893 evolved primarily from an event in 1891 that brought the Keeley Cure into the National limelight and put Dwight, Illinois on the map. The event was a challenge that Dr. Keeley issued to Joseph Medill, the publisher of the *Chicago Tribune:* "send me six of the worst drunkards you can find, and in three days I will sober them up and in four weeks I will send them back to Chicago sober men." Medill took up this challenge and sent a steady stream of Chicago's worst drunkards to Dwight. When Medill reported on the pages of the *Tribune* that "they went away sots and returned gentlemen," Keeley's fame spread throughout the nation and beyond. The Keeley treatment also gained public recognition when its cure was positively portrayed by former patients in two books published in 1892-1893: C.S. Clark's *The Perfect Keeley Cure* and Alfred Calhoun's *Is It "A Modern Miracle?"*

Leslie Keeley also responded to the growing recognition of the problem of alcoholism among the disabled veterans of the Civil and Mexican Wars, who filled 28 national and state veterans' homes around the country. When the United States surgeon general wrote to Dr. Leslie Keeley in 1892, Keeley offered to train the physicians of these homes and to offer them the medicines used at the Keeley Institute. Keeley's methods were introduced into several of these homes, and more than 1,500 veterans were treated at the Fort Leavenworth Home, with reportedly good results. This success led to the introduction of the "Keeley Cure" for alcoholic enlisted men at Fort Leavenworth and Fort Riley.[239]

These widely publicized events, plus the Keeley Company's extensive use of magazine and newspaper advertising, bold billboards, and touring speakers (including the famed temperance veteran Francis Murphy), injected Keeley into the consciousness of the American public. Dr. Leslie Keeley and his Keeley Institutes became so well known that a Keeley Day was held as part of the official program of the 1893 World's Fair in Chicago. Keeley's financial records also confirm his success during the early 1890s; 1892 was the Keeley companies' most profitable year, with gross earnings of $727,094 and a net profit of $508,966.[240] Between 1892 and 1900, the Keeley Company generated income of more than $2.7 million ($1.6 million profit), with half of this income generated in the peak years of 1892 through 1894.[241]

Keeley: On the Causes of Inebriety

Dr. Leslie Keeley championed the view that alcoholism and other addictions were diseases whose causes were biological in nature. His opinion about the nature of these biological causes, however, evolved during his career. In the 1880s, he regularly suggested that heredity played a major role in the etiology of alcoholism, but by 1892 he had softened this position.[242] Increasingly, Keeley came to believe that the roots of inebriety could be incited by childhood contact with intoxicants. In this view, exposing children to alcohol-laced medicines and giving children alcohol as a beverage created a craving for, and a vulnerability to, alcohol that was then activated by later drinking experiences.[243]

As early as 1882, Keeley proposed that the chronic ingestion of morphine created an "isomeric change in the structure of the nerve and its action," which then required the continued presence of the drug for the normal functioning of the nervous system.[244] By the mid-1890s, Keeley had begun to attribute the cause of alcoholism and opiate addiction to the poisons found in these substances that altered the character and workings of human cells.[245] Keeley proclaimed that his Double Chloride of Gold cured all these forms of inebriety by speeding up the restoration of poisoned cells to their pre-poisoned condition.

The Keeley Patients

Dr. Keeley's penchant for meticulous record-keeping makes it possible to sculpt a general profile of the Keeley patient, particularly of one treated at the parent Institute in Dwight. The Keeley Institute was a predominately male institution. Women were treated at Keeley, but were sequestered through much of their stay and never appeared in early Keeley photos. In Dwight, female inebriates stayed in separate quarters—"the Ladies Home"—some two blocks away from the Livingston Hotel, where most of the male Keeley patients stayed. Female patients used a separate entrance and parlor at the Institute, even though they often received their treatments in the privacy of their own lodgings. Such sequestration ensured that female patients would not have to fear possible public exposure of their condition.[246]

The Keeley Institute in Dwight logged the occupations of those entering treatment, broken down into 55 occupational categories, ranging from capitalists to cooks, from inn-keepers to insurance agents. In the year 1900, the log book noted 795 admissions, with admissions in 52 of the 55 occupational categories. Only the categories for actors, cooks, and sailors showed no admissions during that year. The largest occupational groups represented that year were farmers (111), salesmen (46), clerks (44), housewives (38), mechanics (38), physicians (34), and lawyers (31). Other professional groups included druggists (20), clergy (3), dentists (3), and engineers (3). Only 31 of the 795 admissions were listed as having no employment.[247] The number of physicians reported to have been treated at Keeley was impressive—some 17,000 by the 1940s.[248] Articles and promotional materials on Keeley often made note of the prominence of their patients' status as physicians, judges, senators, and business tycoons.[249]

Patients came to Dwight through attraction by Keeley's extensive advertising, through referral by physicians, and—not uncommonly—through recommendation by former Keeley patients.[250]

The Keeley Staff

The Keeley Institutes were staffed by physicians,

nurses, and personal attendants. There were also Keeley offices, in which individuals served as agents and public relations representatives for Keeley. These employees screened interested parties and arranged transportation to one of the Keeley Institutes. A significant portion of the Keeley physicians, attendants, and agents were themselves graduates of the Keeley program. The Keeley archives contain references to attendants who had in the Keeley language "reformed," and J.L. Kenney—the Keeley agent in Chicago during the 1930s—was a self-proclaimed Keeley graduate.

The most interesting dimension of the staffing of the Keeley Institutes involves the unprecedented number of physicians working who had themselves been treated for addiction. Alfred Calhoun's 1892 account of the Keeley cure noted that more than 100 of the physicians working at the Keeley Institutes around the country had undergone treatment for alcohol or opium addiction and been cured.[251] Other evidence of the use of recovered physicians at the Keeley Institutes comes from the Leslie E. Keeley Company Physician's Record. This Record, which contains a brief biographical sketch of each physician hired to work at a Keeley Institute between 1891 and 1950, also profiles each physician in a category marked "Addiction." This category notes whether or not the physician had been addicted, notes by code the nature of the addiction—such as "D" for drunkenness, "O" for opium, "C" for cocaine—and the time and place the physician was treated. Of 418 physicians listed in the Physician's Record, 131 had been addicted and treated, 226 had no reported history of addiction or treatment, and 61 had no notation after the heading "Addiction." All of those treated had been patients at one of the Keeley Institutes.

The high percentage of physicians who were former Keeley patients raises the question of whether Dr. Leslie Keeley routinely recruited physician-patients and entrepreneur-patients to spread the establishment of Keeley Institutes across the United States. The highest percentage of recovering physicians worked at the Keeley Institutes during the expansionist phase of the Keeley Institutes, 1891 through 1894. (Fifty-three were hired during 1892 and 1893.) Many of these physicians were hired and trained immediately following their own treatment, and most were hired within one year after they completed treatment.

The Keeley Institutes' practice of hiring recovering physicians was abandoned at the turn of the century. After 1900, only 12 recovering physicians were hired, and only one of these was hired after 1910.

There is no definitive answer to the question of why this practice stopped, but this author would suggest three reasons. First, there were problems related to the performance of some former-patient physicians. Buried within the 60-year record of the Keeley physicians can be found isolated notations such as, "Suicided—drinking heavily," "gave up because of much impaired memory," and "relapsed, was rejected for treatment here—dead." In her study of a Keeley Institute in New Brunswick, Canada, Cheryl Warsh described the scandal that hit the Institute there in 1895. At that time the house physician disappeared, and he was subsequently found "in a badly decomposed state" suffering from "despondency and the excessive use of cocaine."[252] Second, as noted earlier, Keeley's use of "reformed men as asylum managers" was subject to intense professional criticism from such leaders as Dr. T.D. Crothers.[253] Third, Keeley records show that after 1895 the supply of physicians applying for work was much greater than the number of available positions in the declining number of Keeley Institutes. It is quite likely that, under these circumstances, Dr. Keeley and subsequent Keeley administrators chose the path of least controversy in their selection of medical staff.[254]

The primary role of the physicians was to supervise detoxification, treat acute medical problems, administer the four shots a day to each patient, and conduct patient education in the form of lectures. Personal attendants accompanied newly arriving Keeley patients throughout the day, attending to their needs and monitoring their compliance with Institute rules. Attendants developed quite close relationships with their charges, taking meals with them and sleeping on cots in the patients' lodging rooms. The Keeley Institute "Instructions to Attendants" detailed the proper method of preparing malted milk for patients, demanded confidentiality regarding patient disclosures, prohibited roughness and crudeness, cautioned against over-familiarity, and prohibited the acceptance of gifts from patients. These kinds of instructions—which were common within the inebriate asylums, inebriate homes, and private addiction treatment institutes—constitute the earliest historical remnants of what we now call professional codes of ethics for addictions counselors.[255]

The Keeley Treatment

Treatment at the parent Institute in Dwight, Illinois was the model for treatment in all the Keeley franchises. Although patients arriving at Keeley Institutes may have experienced the coercive pressure of family, employers, or fear of impending insanity, few came under legal commitment or duress. The atmosphere was informal and friendly, with a marked absence of the bars and restraints that were typical in most inebriate asylums of the period. Patients stayed in Dwight for four weeks (longer for opium addicts), housed in the adjoining Livingston Hotel or boarded with families in this small rural community. Patients entering in a state of intoxication were assigned an attendant, often a recovered alcoholic, who stayed with the newcomer during this most difficult period. There was no confinement, and the requirement most often emphasized was the need to be in line four times a day for injections of the Keeley remedy. In between, patients were left to commune among themselves with a minimum of staff supervision.

This image of laissez faire supervision belies the fact that Keeley patients often entered a total milieu of treatment. The "Rules, Regulations and Instructions" given to each patient upon arrival at the Keeley Institute noted the times at which the remedy would be administered; required participation in all lectures; and prohibited cigarette smoking, sodas, gambling, the use of cars, and fraternization between male and female patients. The consumption of coffee and tea were permitted only in very limited quantities.[256]

The town of Dwight was itself an extension of the Keeley treatment milieu. In its earliest years, the Keeley Institute was the largest and most successful industry in Dwight and the heart of the local economy. Widows supported themselves by taking in Keeley patients as lodgers, and the patronage of Keeley patients fattened the coffers of the city's hotels, restaurants, and retail stores. In a town as small as Dwight, it was only a matter of a few days before everyone became acquainted with the latest arrival. There were also former Keeley patients who chose to remain in Dwight, living close to the birthplace of their sobriety. (Some aging former Keeley patients continue to live in Dwight today.) Mrs. Anne Withrow, who worked for the Keeley company for 47 years, noted the following relationship between the town and the Keeley patients.

> *The whole town got to know the patients. The town lodged the patients, fed the patients, and watched out for them. Even tavern owners would call the Institute to report a patient who had tried to purchase alcohol. There would be patients and townspeople at the train station every day to greet new Keeley arrivals.*[257]

James Oughton, Jr., who grew up in one of the founding families of the Keeley Institute and worked at the Institute throughout his life, says the following about this special relationship between the Keeley patients and the citizens of Dwight:

> *Treatment didn't stop when the someone left the Institute grounds. Keeley turned the whole town of Dwight into a kind of therapeutic community. Treating alcoholism and other addictions became the town mission. ....This came about because of the Keeley staff who lived in Dwight, former patients who chose to remain in Dwight's protective healing environment, and the townspeople of Dwight who developed a great sympathy for the distinguished visitors who came to their city for treatment.*[258]

During 1891, patient bills for four weeks' treatment at the Keeley facility in Dwight ran between $100 and $200. Housing was an additional $21 per week, and the assistance of a personal attendant cost $3 per day. The states of Colorado, Louisiana, Maryland, Minnesota, North Dakota, and the Oklahoma Territory passed "Keeley Laws," which subsidized treatment for indigent alcoholics at the Keeley Institutes.[259]

Newcomers were provided all the whiskey they needed or demanded until they lost the appetite for it—usually within three or four days. Those entering addicted to opium were set up on a schedule of decreasing doses of the drug. There was no prohibition against drinking, but smuggling in alcohol, cigarette smoking, and gambling were grounds for dismissal.[260]

The centerpiece of the Keeley cure was four daily injections of the Double Chloride of Gold remedy, whose content was adjusted slightly for each patient, plus a tonic medicine that the patient had to take every two hours during the waking hours. Patients lined up every day at 8 a.m., 12 noon, 5 p.m., and 7:30 p.m. in a building that patients had dubbed "the shot tower." There they received injections drawn in various quantities from three bottles containing, red, white, and blue liquids.

The founders, along with all those who became part of the Keeley franchises, signed a pledge never to reveal the formula of the Double Chloride of Gold treatment. Medical and popular journals and press accounts of laboratory tests of the formula varied widely in their reports of the alleged composition of the cure. They suggested such diverse ingredients as alcohol, strychnine, apomorphine, aloin from the aloe plant, willow bark, ginger, ammonia, belladonna, atropine, hyoscine, scopolamine, coca, opium, and morphine. While the daily injections may have served to alleviate the discomfort of withdrawal, the elaborate rituals may also have constituted a psychological sleight-of-hand, designed to keep the addict engaged while Keeley's other admonitions —daily rest, nutrition, mutual sharing, and alternative diversions worked to improve the patient's physical and psychological health.

While the Keeley cure is most often associated with alcoholism, Keeley extensively advertised the applicability of the Double Chloride of Gold cure for opium and tobacco addiction. In 1897, he claimed that the product was equally successful in curing "other toxic habits, such as cocaine, chloral, hasheesh, atropia, strychnia, and such others as are formed by humanity."[261]

Each patient leaving the Keeley Institute was given a pamphlet entitled "To the Keeley Graduate." This pamphlet began with the following proclamation:

You are now numbered among thousands of men and women who have broken the shackles of alcohol and drug addictions by the Keeley method of treatment. Your cure will be as permanent as your life, you will never have any craving for alcohol or other sedative drugs as long as you live, unless you create it by returning to their use, thus re-poisoning your nerve cells.

The pamphlet went on to emphasize the importance of sustaining the new Keeley habits: regular patterns of sleep, regular and balanced meals, regular consumption of water, abstinence from tobacco and caffeinated drinks, healthy recreation, and care in the selection of personal associates.[262] Graduating patients were also expected to participate in a well established Keeley ritual: regularly writing to the Keeley Institute, the Keeley Leagues, and one or two of their fellow patients.[263]

Treatment at the branch institutes was strictly controlled and monitored from Dwight. All physician-managers of the Keeley Institutes were brought to Dwight for training. All of the Institutes followed carefully detailed procedures regarding all aspects of their clinical operation. Letters from Dwight to the branches reveal how carefully these operations were monitored:

- An October 13, 1894 letter to the Keeley branch in Charleston, West Virginia admonished the staff for failing to conduct clinical examinations of all patients within three days of admission and to forward these reports to Dwight for review.[264]
- A February 13, 1895 letter to the Keeley Branch in Excelsior Springs, Missouri, chastised staff for their recent practice of shortening treatment from four weeks to three weeks.[265]

The tone of these letters was quite directive in stating standards and expectations for compliance by branch staff. Some letters went so far as to prohibit admission of particular patients, as was the case in two 1896 letters to Institutes in Benton Harbor, Michigan and Buffalo, New York. The Benton Harbor letter noted the multiple admissions of a particular patient and directed the Institute to refuse the patient all further treatment. The Buffalo letter suggested great care in the treatment of a particular patient, because "evidence from Philadelphia and other points is that he is of no account and is only using our remedies and Institutes for temporary benefit." The use of the Keeley remedy at the Branch Institutes came under particularly strict review. The majority of the letters that went out from Dwight to the branches noted discrepancies between the number of patients the branch treated during the month and the amount of remedy that they used. These letters expressed concern over the use of too few or too many bottles of the remedy.[266]

The Mail-Order Business

For some time, the Double Chloride of Gold Cure, in addition to being the center of treatment for those who came to the Keeley Institutes, was also sold by mail order. The uniquely shaped and ornately labeled bottle came in pairs, the tobacco cure costing $5, the neurasthenia cure $8, the alcoholism cure $9, and the opium cure $10. Keeley defended the mail-order business as a way to help people who could not afford or were too ashamed to seek institutional treatment. The advertised promise for the mail-order cure was bold and unequivocal:

In four days the habit will be checked, in a week the desire to drink will be gone, in nine days it will be impossible to take alcohol into the system, and the manacles which bound the man for ten, twenty, or thirty years will be shattered and broken forever.[267]

The mail-order business gave the illusion, if not the reality, of individualized treatment. Patients sent in detailed reports of their pattern of daily use and were sent in return numbered bottles, which they were expected to use in careful sequence. At any sign of relapse in the correspondence, patients were admonished to return all unused bottles of the remedy. Whether this admonition was based on clinical or business concerns is unclear. Dr. Leslie Keeley's methods and his remedies extended beyond the more than 100 Keeley Institutes, as the Keeley remedies were sent to many private sanitaria that were not publicly affiliated with the Keeley Institute. The mail-order business to individuals and institutions faded over the years. In a letter to a Professor Gowdy dated January 25, 1895, Leslie Keeley remarked that he was withdrawing the home cure because "fakirs" were using that cure to sober up their patients in direct competition with the Keeley Institutes.[268]

The Keeley Leagues

An account of the Keeley method of treatment would be incomplete without a description of what may have been the most influential element of the treatment experience: participation in the Keeley League. By early 1891, the milieu surrounding the Keeley cure in Dwight was reaching critical mass. The numbers of patients had grown rapidly, forcing longer periods of interaction between the patients who were waiting in lines four times a day for their shots. Out of this chemistry of shared vulnerability arose a unique mutual-aid group, birthed within the milieu of a treatment center.

On April 6, 1891 a group of Keeley patients—led by Samuel Moore, a Pittsburgh businessman, Grant Richardson, a journalist, and the novelist Opie Read—organized a club for Keeley patients. Meetings were held daily, with officers serving during the month of their stay. New patients were introduced, patients leaving were asked to make speeches and were bid fond farewell, and letters of encouragement from former patients were read. Religious meetings and social events were also hosted by the club. One of the League rituals in Dwight was to go to the train station each day—as many as 200 strong—to greet the new Keeley arrivals as they walked—and sometimes stumbled—off the train.

Keeley League meetings quickly spread from Dwight to other Institute communities. In many of the Institutes, the Keeley League activities were centered in clubhouses where patients shared their time when they were not engaged in treatment activities. In

1892, Calhoun described the Keeley League club-house—a former church—in White Plains, New York:

The club is the great point of rendezvous. Often entertainments are given at night, and a meeting is held every morning at nine. At these meetings, men who have finished the treatment have an opportunity to say goodbye to their friends, and then also are read letters from those who have been "graduated" some time. These letters are always encouraging, and their moral effect on the patients, still anxious about themselves, is invaluable.[269]

Calhoun went on to describe the genuine affection that developed among patients and the emotional intensity of the Keeley League meetings.

....the names of new members are read and each one is called on for a speech, and then the farewell speeches of men who expect to go home are listened to with much interest. When the farewell words are spoken and the last good-byes are being said I have seen men break down and cry like babies, while the entire audience would appear to be afflicted with sudden colds; and these are men, too, who only a few weeks ago were all strangers to each other.[270]

A contagious enthusiasm held sway within the Keeley treatment milieu, and this enthusiasm spread outward when patients graduated. Former members began getting together following treatment to extend the Keeley League's activities to the provision of continuing support for sobriety following their discharge from a Keeley Institute. Former patients wrote letters and articles for their local newspapers, describing their Keeley treatment and Keeley League experiences with effusive praise.

First known as the Bi-Chloride of Gold Club, the Keeley Leagues grew to a membership of more than 30,000 former patients in 370 chapters across the U.S. The majority of the Keeley Leagues were concentrated in the states of Tennessee, Illinois, Pennsylvania, Colorado, Missouri, New York, Iowa, Maine, and Michigan.[271] The multiple purposes of the Keeley League, set forth in its constitution, included 1) "curing the drunkard of the disease of intemperance" 2) "preventing the youth of the country, by education and example, from contracting it," 3) binding "together in one fraternal bond all who have taken the Keeley treatment," and 4) "extending public knowledge of the Keeley cure."[272]

Between 1891 and 1897, the Keeley Leagues held seven national conventions. Claiming no rivals, the leagues were promoted as the "only organization in the world composed exclusively of men who confess themselves to have been drunkards and cured." Their motto was an unequivocal invitation: "We were once as you are; come with us and be cured."[273] Their members wore a "K" imbedded in a horseshoe bearing the letters B.C.G.C. on their lapels, as an open sign of their freedom from addiction.[274] A newspaper, *The Banner of Gold*, linked the Leagues and their members. In addition to providing mutual support, League members identified and referred alcoholics to the Keeley Institutes, then welcomed them into League membership on their return. In 1897, League chapters referred 831 alcoholics to the Keeley Institutes and raised funds to pay for the treatment of 322 alcoholics.[275] The Keeley Leagues were also the primary source of political advocacy supporting passage of "Keeley Laws," which provided public funds to send indigent alcoholics for the Keeley cure.

Separate Women's Keeley Leagues were established for "a band of brave, true-hearted and noble women, some of whom have themselves been delivered from slavery of drunkenness, or opium." Joining the women who had themselves been treated at the Keeley Institutes were wives, daughters, sisters, and mothers of Keeley graduates.

The Leagues began to dissipate in the late 1890s, as part of the overall decline of the Keeley Institutes. This decline was also hastened by scandal that touched the League through its president, Andrew J. Smith. Smith, manager of the National Soldiers' Home in Leavenworth, Kansas, was the subject of a congressional investigation following highly publicized accusations that he appeared in the Home drunk, coerced patients into taking the Keeley cure, accepted a salary from the Keeley Institute at the same time he was drawing his federal salary, and mixed Keeley funds with The Post fund (the latter fund generated from the sale of beer to patients). Regarding the Post fund, the government report noted, "There seems also a glaring inconsistency that the sale of beer and the administration of the Keeley Cure should both be found running at the same Government institution, and both at a profit...."[276] Additional adverse publicity arose in 1894, when the national secretary of the Keeley League, John Kelly, charged that Dr. Leslie Keeley wanted the League to die out because Keeley could no longer control it. Kelly

further contended that Dr. Keeley had offered him a bribe to let the League lapse.[277] Kelly claimed that the focus of the National Keeley League had shifted from mutual support to "a great advertising medium."[278]

Interest in the Keeley League waned in tandem with the declining tides of the Keeley Company. In 1896 the Keeley League received only $119.30 in membership dues. The last Keeley League National Convention was held in 1897, in Minneapolis, Minnesota.[279]

Reported Treatment Outcomes

Dr. Leslie Keeley and the physician-entrepreneurs who were Keeley's primary competitors made incredible claims regarding the success of their addiction cures. (One Keeley competitor, Dr. B.E. Neal, who oversaw more than 60 Neal Institutes, actually provided a signed contract with each incoming patient, promising that the appetite for liquor would be completely destroyed for at least one year after discharge from the Neal Institute.)[280] In 1880, Keeley proclaimed that his methods effected "a cure in every instance, provided he [the alcoholic] takes the remedy implicitly according to instructions."[281] Keeley Institutes boasted a 95% cure rate, although Dr. Leslie Keeley suggested in various publications that the rate was actually higher.[282] Dr. Keeley made equally remarkable claims for success in the cure of morphine addiction, proclaiming that "It (The Double Chloride of Gold Opium Cure) is the only antidote known to the world for the opium habit....By the magic of the Gold Remedy the opium habit is cast out easily and permanently."[283] In a follow-up study of 1,000 patients treated at Dwight, reported in Keeley's 1897 treatise on opium, three died while in treatment and 44 left before treatment was completed. Of the 953 addicts who completed treatment, only 4.7% of the opium and morphine cases were reported to have relapsed after treatment—an unprecedented success rate of 95 percent.[284]

Other Gold Cures

The success of the Keeley Institutes in the 1890s spawned other addiction treatment "Institutes" and other gold cures for treatment of alcoholism, morphinism and tobaccoism. Among Keeley's primary competitors were the Garten Cure, Dr. Haines Golden Remedy, the Geneva Gold Cure, the Boston Bichloride of Gold Company, the Kelly Bi-Chloride of Gold Cure, the National Bi-Chloride of Gold Company, the Baker-Rose Gold Cure, and Monroe's Gold Cure.[285] One of

Keeley's early partners, Frederick Hargreaves, left and started his own inebriety cures known variously as "Dipsocura," the "Hargreaves Cure," and the "Dwight Cure." Many of the Keeley competitors, like the Key Cure that operated in the 1890s out of offices in Chatanooga, Tennessee and Lowell, Massachusetts, mirrored Keeley's use of hypodermic injections and liquid tonics.[286]

Early Controversies and Critics

The pulp image of Dr. Leslie Keeley—that of the country physician who had stumbled onto a revolutionary cure for the inebriety problem that had stumped the best medical scientists—contributed to the early popularity of the Keeley treatment.[287] Although early criticism of Keeley by his medical peers could be written off as "sour grapes," the sheer volume and specificity of this criticism began to take its toll. This criticism grew in intensity during 1891 and 1892 and reached a crescendo in mid-1893. Leslie Keeley's critics focused on five broad issues.

First, they quite rightly challenged Keeley's claim that he had originated the treatment of drunkenness as a disease and from a medical standpoint.[288] These critics noted that an association of inebriate asylums based on the premise that inebriety was a disease and curable with proper medical treatment had been founded nearly a decade before Keeley's announcement of his new cure.

Second, the critics argued that the Double Chloride of Gold was not a specific cure for inebriety and that no such "specific" had ever existed or was likely to exist in the future. Such criticisms attacked the theoretical foundation of the Keeley cure: that inebriety was caused by a singular biological process that could be reversed by a medicinal "specific."

Third, the critics objected to the secrecy surrounding the Keeley remedy. They argued that, if the Keeley cure really was a cure for alcoholism, then withholding the nature of the formula—so that the cure could not be subjected to scientific peer review, replication studies, and, if warranted, wide dissemination—was a gross breach of medical ethics.[289] Keeley's response to this argument:

> ....my cure is the result of a system, and cannot be accomplished by the simple administration of a sovereign remedy. It involves the intelligent use of powerful drugs, gradations to suit the physical condition of particular patients, changes in immediate agents employed at different stages of the

> cure and an exact knowledge of the pathological conditions of drunkenness and their results.[290]

Keeley argued that the release of the general formula would, therefore, lead to its misapplication and over-simplified use.[291]

A fourth professional and public criticism was that the Keeley Double Chloride of Gold contained no gold but contained powerful and potentially harmful drugs including, according to various analyses, strychnine, atropine, cocaine, codeine, and apomorphine. The critics contended that the Double Chloride of Gold produced serious side effects. Among the data cited was a report of 88 cases of insanity, allegedly the results of taking the Keeley remedy.[292] Medical critics argued that it was unethical to have Keeley Institute physicians administering powerful drugs with potential adverse reactions, when the physicians were unaware of the medicine's contents and thus stymied in their treatment of adverse symptoms. Dr. Leslie Keeley countered such arguments by denying the presence of these substances in the Keeley cure and denying that the Double Chloride of Gold remedy produced any toxic side effects.

One of the most strident critics of the Keeley cure was Dr. T. D. Crothers, a leader in the inebriate asylum movement. Crothers attacked the gold cures for inebriety as quackery.

> There is no gold cure for inebriety. There are no facts to show that gold has any value in this disease. All the assertions and statements concerning gold as a remedy are delusions, and will not bear the test of critical examination.[293]

The fifth and final theme of the Keeley critics was that the Keeley cure was a fraud intended only to make money. After a stinging 1893 indictment of the Keeley cure in *The Chicago Medical Record*, Dr. Chauncey Chapman concluded:

> I desire to state in a most emphatic manner that the Keeley cure is a shameless, barefaced, money-making scheme, as practiced, and the men engaged in it are totally devoid of ethical honor.[294]

There is little question that many of Keeley's critics may have been reacting out of financial as well as scientific interest. Keeley defenders, such as J. Gilmer Speed, were quick to point out that many critics of the Keeley cure operated asylums that were in direct competition with Keeley. Their criticism, he suggested, stemmed from the fact that Keeley's success was hurting them financially.[295] However, criticism of Keeley and the gold cure went far beyond those who could be accused of reacting out of self-interest.

Keeley spent considerable time on the lecture circuit responding to his critics. The Keeley Company also responded to attacks by filing lawsuits against its critics. This tactic made journals leery of articles attacking Keeley, so they softened the tone of their criticism. However, when the Keeley Company developed a pattern of dropping these suits for unstated reasons before going to court, Keeley's credibility was further called into question.[296]

Former Keeley patients were also quick to come to the defense of Dr. Keeley and the Keeley treatment. When four highly respected physicians attacked the gold cure as a fraud in a series of 1891 articles in *The North American Review*, J.F. Mines, a well known author and Keeley graduate, launched a notable defense. Mines used his own life story as proof of Keeley's methods, claiming that he had lost all desire to drink as a result of the Keeley cure. After depicting the depths of alcoholic depravity to which he had sunk, Mines proclaimed that he had "conquered the black lion of the desert" and now possessed a "sense of freedom and happiness no man can paint."[297] This highly visible gesture of support backfired when Mines later relapsed and died—events covered heavily by the American press.

Some journalistic bystanders in the debate over the Keeley cure thought they could settle the controversy by polling Keeley graduates to assess the effectiveness of the Keeley treatment. When the Rev. James Buckley, editor of the *Christian Advocate*, polled 534 Keeley graduates, he found that 51% had remained free of alcoholism; the remaining graduates were reported to have relapsed, died, or gone insane.[298]

Given the extensive media coverage of the Keeley debate, one is compelled to wonder what it must have been like for potential consumers of addiction treatment services in the 1890s. It must have been difficult and confusing for the person seeking a place to go for treatment to sort out the charges and counter-charges publicly thrown about by the addiction experts. While the Keeley cure was being depicted as a fraud, Keeley himself was writing eloquently about addiction cure frauds:

The market is literally crowded with nostrums of all kinds, which contain as active principles, coca, cocaine, chloral, morphine, atropia, the various so-called hypnotic remedies, etc., all of them concealed under seductive names and guaranteed to cure obstinate cases. Many of these preparations are employed by quasi-sanitariums as substitute remedies for the opium habit, the patient being finally dismissed as "cured," but taking more morphine or cocaine than when he entered for treatment ....Such unfairness tends to dishearten the patient and causes him to lose faith in all remedial agencies.[299]

Of all the charges and countercharges that filled the newspapers and lay and professional journals of the mid 1890s, the strangest story of the Keeley Institute surfaced after the most intense period of public controversy. In 1902, The Keeley Company filed a breach-of-contract suit to prevent the Memphis Institute (formerly a Keeley Branch) from continuing to advertize that they were using the Keeley remedies to treat alcoholism and drug addiction. The suit is irrelevant to our story except for the exceptional testimony of Frederick B. Hargreaves, noted earlier as a former partner of Keeley and subsequent competitor in the inebriety cure business. In his Memphis testimony, Hargreaves first established his involvement in the very beginnings of the Keeley cure by revealing a partnership agreement that predated the participation of Dr. Keeley's existing partners, Oughton and Judd. Hargreaves' remaining testimony, which was excerpted and published in the *Journal of the American Medical Association* in 1907, contained the following claims drawn from his early involvement with Dr. Keeley at Dwight:

- The only patient who ever received Keeley medicine that actually had gold in it almost died. A far superior ingredient was found, but the use of gold in the product name was kept to enhance sales.
- Although Hargreaves would not name the ingredient that was found to replace gold in the Keeley remedy, he did report that he and Keeley had discovered its potential use from a newspaper article in which it was mentioned.
- Hargreaves and Dr. Keeley spiked a few bottles of Double Chloride of Gold and had them tested, so they could show laboratory verification that the product did contain gold.
- The early patient testimonials that appeared in the Keeley Institute advertisements were written,

not by patients, but by Hargreaves and Dr. Keeley.

- Dr. Keeley's early books and articles were not written by Keeley, but were written by Hargreaves and a Dr. R.J. Curtis of Joliet, Illinois.
- The hypodermic injections given at the Keeley Institutes were a placebo designed to keep patients in residence for the three to four weeks of treatment; only the oral tonic actually contained ingredients that Dr. Keeley believed would suppress the craving for alcohol.[300]

Amidst the controversies surrounding the Keeley methods, there seems to be one unarguable fact, acknowledged even by Keeley's most vociferous critics, and that is "the undisputed fact that a large proportion of the Keeley patients do lose their appetite for liquor."[301] What baffled all of Keeley's critics was the apparently large contingent of sober Keeley graduates who loudly sang the praises of the Keeley treatment and its effect on their lives. We will shortly return to a discussion of this point.

Turn-of-the-Century Decline

As criticism of the Keeley cure mounted, Dr. Leslie Keeley attempted to sell the company to a New York syndicate. After this transaction fell through, Keeley spent most of his time defending his methods and medicines. The decline of the Keeley institutions began in the mid 1890s, first with a consolidation of branches and then with a closing of nearly all the branch offices. A loss in public confidence in the Keeley methods contributed to this decline. The loss in confidence came from a recognition of higher-than-proclaimed relapse rates among Keeley patients, a public backlash against Keeley's exaggerated claims of success, and the relentless medical criticism of the gold cure. The number of Keeley Branch Institutes declined from 118 in 1893 to less than 50 at the turn of the century.[302]

After 1893, as the Keeley Institute went into a progressive decline, Leslie Keeley spent more time traveling and writing. As his energy and health declined, Keeley spent more and more time away from Dwight. He died February 21, 1900 of a heart attack at his winter home in California. He died a millionaire. Shortly afterward, Curtis Judd retired, leaving the Keeley legacy in the hands of the Oughton family.

At the time of Dr. Leslie Keeley's death, more than 400,000 men and women had been treated at 126 Keeley Institutes scattered across the United States.

The Later Keeley Years: 1900-1966

Most accounts of the Keeley Institute read as if the Institute folded with the death of Dr. Leslie Keeley in 1900. Paul Weitz has provided one of the few accounts of the continuing story of the Keeley Institute. Following Keeley's death in 1900, John Oughton, the surviving founding partner, became president of a shrinking Keeley empire. The medical direction of the Keeley Institute was turned over to Oughton's son, James H. Oughton. A 1902 fire destroyed the Keeley Laboratory and Office Building, along with the adjacent Livingston Hotel, where the majority of Keeley patients resided during their treatment. A new hotel, laboratory, and general offices were built and opened in June of 1903. At that time the Keeley Institute still retained enough influence to have President Theodore Roosevelt present at the ceremony to open the doors of the new facilities. Along with new facilities in Dwight, which continued to treat a steady stream of alcoholics and addicts, 44 Branch Institutes were operating in the U.S. in 1907. As more states passed state alcohol prohibition laws, the demand for alcoholism treatment declined. This resulted in a further decrease in the number of Keeley Institute Branches. From 44 Branches in 1907, the number had fallen to 35 in 1916, and to just four in 1935.[303] One of the strangest stories of the Keeley Institute closings of this era came out of Kansas City, where the former Keeley Institute building was raided and found to have hidden in its basement a large bootleg liquor manufacturing operation.[304]

On the assumption that the demand for services would decline as a result of prohibition, the Keeley facilities in Dwight were sold in 1920 to the Veteran's Administration for use as a hospital for World War I veterans.[305] However, the home Institute in Dwight—perhaps as a result of the closing of the other Institutes—continued to receive demands for treatment throughout prohibition. To provide these services, the original Oughton family home was converted into a "lodge," a new administration building was erected, and an old carriage house (known as "the Clubhouse") was used as a recreation, treatment, and meeting room.[306] Eighteen patients at a time resided in the former Oughton Home, while other patients were housed in private residences in Dwight. Weitz's analysis of admission figures for the years 1920 to 1933 reveals steadily increasing admissions throughout these prohibition years. Admission to the Keeley Institute in Dwight rose from 186 patients in 1920 to a peak of 869 admissions in 1930.[307]

The treatment of alcoholics at Dwight continued after prohibition, under the direction of Dr. James Oughton, who had taken over the Presidency of the Keeley Company from his father in 1925. Dr. Oughton eliminated the use of the Double Chloride of Gold remedy at the Institute. While he believed that the original treatment was a beneficial specific in the treatment of alcoholism, he became concerned that the body's inability to metabolize the heavy metals in the medicine might have long-term medical effects on Keeley patients. The formula was changed for the third time in Keeley history, but the contents of this final formula were also never revealed. Dr. Oughton was shot and killed in a burglary in August, 1935, and administration of the Institute was taken over by his son, James Oughton, Jr., who had just graduated from Dartmouth. James Oughton, Jr. served in this role for the next 31 years.[308]

During the 1930s and 1940s, most of the male Keeley patients continued to stay in the lodge, which today is a restaurant in Dwight. Readers learning of an addiction treatment institution located in an all-white rural community might wonder if African Americans had access to such private facilities during a prolonged era of racial segregation in America. When questioned, former staff reported that African Americans were in fact treated at Keeley, and with a minimum of special accommodations. While African-American patients were housed in private residences rather than in the lodge, they participated fully in all the regular dining, social, and treatment activities of the Institute. In response to the further query about whether or not there were any difficulties arranging accommodations for African-American patients in a rural, white community in the middle decades of the 20th century, I was told, "Oh my, no. You see they [the African-American patients] were almost all doctors and lawyers." It seems the main criterion for ease of inclusion was one of social class, rather than race. While it is not possible to ascertain the number of African Americans treated at Keeley, the numbers could not have been high. The group pictures of patients throughout the Keeley years are filled with white men. Female patients during the 1930s and 1940s were housed at a cottage near the Institute. Most of their treatment activities occurred at the cottage, which continued the long tradition of minimizing their contact with male patients.[309]

Treatment of alcoholism and other addictions at the Keeley Institutes during the 1940s and 1950s was very similar to the early Keeley treatment. The Institute's head attendant, anywhere from six to ten patients, and a few townspeople met arriving patients each day at the train station. Fully detoxified patients seemed to relish viewing the horrible condition of the new arrivals—a condition that reflected their own status just a few days earlier. There was also always the possibility of the unexpected at the train station, such as the time a famous model arrived wearing her fur coat and nothing else. Each arriving patient was still assigned an attendant—a "jag boss"—who stayed with him or her day and night through the first few days. These attendants, mostly middle-aged men and many of them former Keeley patients, administered decreasing doses of whiskey mixed in malted milk to detoxify the new patients. Detox did not always go well, as reflected in the story of the famous football player who had to be strapped to his bed, but who a few hours later came down the stairs of the lodge with the bed still strapped to his back.

When detox was completed, continued responsibility for the patients remained with the two or three full-time Keeley physicians. Patients were given three physicals during their stay at Keeley, were given three to five individual consultations (counseling sessions), and received daily medications. Although the Double Chloride of Gold was no longer used, patients still received injections of a pink solution four times a day—then called "tonic medicines"—and consumed a bitter yellow fluid in water every two hours (in bottles numbered from one to three), which patients were told was "a laxative tonic which eliminated the poisons produced by alcohol."[310] Daily life for a patient at Keeley included attendance at a morning lecture presented by one of the physicians; receiving the four injections; leisure activities such as exercise, tennis, and volleyball, planned by an athletic instructor; and large quantities of good food. Patients also spent a good deal of their free time talking with one another and going for walks in downtown Dwight. Attendance at church services was recommended but not required. One change in this later era was the introduction of A.A.

During the 1940s, representatives of A.A. approached the Keeley Institute about integrating A.A. into the Keeley treatment, and A.A. meetings were sometimes held at Keeley. By 1946, Keeley patients were actively encouraged to affiliate with A.A. in their home communities. By 1950, only two Keeley Institutes remained (in Dwight and in Greensboro, North Carolina). The Institutes cooperated more fully with A.A. in the 1950s. The first regular A.A. meetings at Keeley began in 1956, and Keeley hosted A.A.'s Midwest Summer Round-up from 1958 to 1966. According to Weitz's interview with a former patient (and the Keeley literature of this era), the

Keeley treatment during the mid-20th century was quite similar to that given in the early days of Keeley, with a few modern twists: medical detoxification, shots four times a day, a fixed daily schedule (rising early and retiring early), a ban on smoking (tobacco treatment was included at no extra charge), nourishing food, vitamin supplements, physical exercise, lectures, a weekly visit with a psychiatrist, and participation in a weekly A.A. meeting. By 1960, the Keeley Institute had lowered its claim of success from the 95% repeatedly quoted by Dr. Keeley at the turn of the century to a claim that "50 percent of the patients adjust permanently to their new life without beverage alcohol."[311]

Admissions to the last two Keeley Institutes declined in the 1960s as an increasing number of states opened state-operated alcoholism treatment facilities, and as more communities developed local alcoholism treatment services. The Institute in Greensboro closed in 1965, and the original Keeley Institute at Dwight stopped accepting patients for treatment in 1966.

The Keeley Company continued to be active in the state and national alcoholism movement during these later years through the activities of James H. Oughton, Jr. Oughton stayed involved in the alcoholism field after the Keeley Institute closed and, until his death in 1996, regularly regaled visitors to Dwight with stories of the days when the rich and famous came to take the "Keeley Cure."

The Keeley Legacy

So what shall we make of one of the most publicly recognized and controversial alcoholism and addiction treatments in American history? Do we christen Dr. Leslie Keeley an entrepreneur, a pioneer, or a predatory charlatan—or something in between? Plotting the truth is difficult, because the majority of the surviving literature comes from four distinctly biased sources: 1) the Keeley literature itself, which some might suggest is as much promotional mythology as historical fact; 2) a body of confessional literature from a small number of Keeley patients, effusive with their praise and gratitude; 3) a body of highly critical literature from the medical establishment, written mostly by competitors objecting to Keeley's homeopathic philosophy, his financial success, and his public acclaim; and, finally, 4) the charges of an embittered former employee and competitor. Having sorted through all of this literature, the author would suggest the following conclusions.

First, the remedy: Dr. Leslie Keeley died without ever revealing the contents of the Double Chloride of

Gold and the tonics used at the Institutes, and he never confirmed any of the varied analyses of these products that were published.[312] (He did specifically deny that the Double Chloride of Gold contained strychnia, atropine, or apomorphine.)[313] While John Oughton acknowledged after Keeley's death that the injections contained antagonists, emetics, and tonics, the exact composition of the Double Chloride of Gold has never been revealed. Many of Keeley's medical contemporaries noted that the symptoms[314] that patients described while first taking the Double Chloride of Gold were consistent with the symptoms of atropine intoxication.[315]

Leslie Keeley claimed he had discovered a "specific"—a drug protocol that cured inebriety by permanently eliminating the morbid craving for intoxicants at the cellular level. The Keeley treatment did initiate many recoveries, but no such "specific" existed. If such a specific had existed, Keeley's refusal to disclose the formula would have been an unconscionable breach of medical ethics, justifying all of the criticism ever aimed at him. The likely ingredients of the Double Chloride of Gold remedy and tonics—alcohol, atropine, strychnia, apomorphine—did aid detoxification, and the shots did engender a revulsion for alcohol (at least among those whose shots came from the mysterious and greatly feared blue bottle).[316] The Keeley cure was one of many 19th-century alcoholism cures that—often without the patient's informed consent—relied upon the power of aversive conditioning to destroy the appetite for alcohol. Keeley introduced an approach that carried an aura of scientific truth and all the emotional support and intensity of a revival meeting—a combination to which many addicts continue to respond positively today.

It is unfortunate that the controversy surrounding the Keeley approach focused on the nature of the Double Chloride of Gold treatment, because Dr. Keeley's true legacy lay in other areas. He shares credit or blame (depending on the reader's philosophical orientation) for setting forth physiological explanations for the etiology of inebriety. These ideas helped build a foundation for what would emerge in the next century as a modern "disease concept of alcoholism." In a similar manner, Keeley's advocacy of what might be called a disease model of narcotic addiction anticipated ideas that would be set forth nearly a century later as the theoretical foundation of methadone maintenance.

The Keeley story has many unique aspects. Keeley was remarkably successful in enticing large numbers of alcoholics and addicts into treatment. By declaring that their condition was a product of disease rather than vice, by promising to alleviate the physical discomfort of sobering up, and by allowing them freedom from constraint, the Keeley Institutes brought unprecedented numbers of alcoholics and other addicts into treatment. Leslie Keeley's aggressive marketing campaigns also helped educate the public. These campaigns served to decrease the stigma of addiction and provided a counterbalance to the demonization of the addict that was occurring within the drug prohibition movements of the same era. At a time when addiction treatment was focused on long-term institutional care, the Keeley Institutes provided a large-scale day treatment/intensive outpatient model—a legacy of some importance in light of recent trends in the field. The Keeley Institute also was among the first treatment systems to manage quality control at multiple facilities through centralized training of key staff, monitoring of clinical procedures, and clinical documentation. And then there was the treatment milieu itself.

The Keeley Institutes were among the first American institutions that hired recovered alcoholics and addicts to work in the treatment industry, and the Keeley Institutes employed more recovered physicians than any program in history. This fact alone should ensure the Keeley Institute a most fascinating footnote in the history of addiction medicine. From its beginning in 1879 to its closure in 1966, Keeley treated hundreds of thousands of alcoholics and addicts with a staff that never included a counselor. During all those years, the activities we would today define as counseling were performed by Keeley's full-time physicians.

Keeley's creation of a supportive atmosphere in which addicts were treated with trust and respect and encouraged to support one another predated modern uses of the "dynamic milieu" by nearly a century. The Keeley Institutes combined the home-like atmosphere and effusive optimism of the Washingtonian homes with the physical methods of treatment of the inebriate asylums. The Keeley critics often referred to the general enthusiasm of the patients—which gave the place the feel of a camp meeting or revival—as a way of suggesting that it was this power of positive suggestion that accounted for the cures, rather than the mysterious medicines that were administered.[317]

Keeley's creation of a long-term sobriety-based support structure, through which his graduates across the United States could experience mutual support, would be one of the largest of such networks between the collapse of the Washingtonian movement in the mid-1840s and the rise of Alcoholics Anonymous in the 1930s. The Keeley Leagues and the patient clubs and aftercare associations of other treatment programs historically link the fraternal temperance organizations and reform clubs with the later involvement of alcoholics in the Oxford Group and the emergence of Alcoholics Anonymous.

Dr. Leslie Keeley's legacy is to be found, not in his medical elixir, but in the social milieu that surrounded his remedy. A special chemistry occurred in the relationships among those standing in line four times a day for their shots, and between those getting and giving the shots: As we now know, many of the physicians were themselves recovered. Jim Baumohl and Cheryl Walsh have independently suggested that part of the effectiveness of this milieu was its appeal to male camaraderie and manly dignity. Keeley men were coached to face their shots courageously, then to publicly proclaim in the boldest manner their recovery from alcoholism. In the Keeley milieu, men were challenged to restore their identity and personal pride as men—Keeley men—by heroically casting off the curse of drunkenness and engineering their own personal reformation.[318]

The spirit of mutual support born within the Keeley Institutes and formalized in the Keeley Leagues was the source of many permanent recoveries. Keeley put together elements that continue through this history: medically supported detoxification, the conceptualization of addiction as a disease, a milieu of mutual support among those being treated, the guided restoration of physical and emotional health, and, not insignificantly, a gimmick that engaged addicts' propensity for magical thinking and helped them through the early weeks and months of recovery. So much attention was focused on the mysterious medium of Keeley's cure—the Double Chloride of Gold formula—that most critics failed to appreciate the healing power of the treatment milieu within each Keeley Institute. In the end, it was the milieu, not the medicine, that was Dr. Leslie Keeley's greatest legacy.

Chapter Eight
Miracle Cures for Alcoholism and Other Addictions

I know of no class of people who have been so victimized by the quack as the inebriate.[319]

There were four main branches of specialized treatment for inebriety in the 19th and early 20th centuries: inebriate homes; inebriate asylums; proprietary hospitals, sanitaria, and institutes; and mail-order cures. There was considerable overlap between the last two categories, with many of the gold cure institutes and physician-directed sanitaria offering both residential care and mail-order cures. Although we will not ignore this overlap, our focus in this chapter will be primarily upon the mail-order services that offered medicinal cures for alcoholism and other addictions. Since this is a relatively unique branch of addiction treatment, the time period covered in this chapter will extend from the 1860s to the 1960s.

The Context

The rise of commercialized addiction remedies in the 19th century occurred in tandem with the rise of nostrums and remedies for every conceivable ailment. Medicine as we know it today had not yet established itself as a legitimate science in spite of new breakthroughs in anesthesiology, bacteriology, pharmacology, and surgery. Midwives, folk chemists, traveling medicine men, and local "apothecaries" (druggists) were as likely to prescribe treatment as were ill-trained physicians or people whose title of "doctor" was more likely to have been adopted than earned.[320] In this climate, debilitating conditions like alcoholism and opium addiction that had no specific medical cure offered fertile ground for fraud and exploitation.

The patent-medicine industry flourished in a century filled with newly discovered psychoactive drugs and few if any legal controls on such substances. Opium-, morphine- and cocaine-laced products were widely available and aggressively promoted. Opium derivatives were the primary ingredients in such products as Dovers Powder, Laudanum, Godfrey's Cordial and McMunn's Elixir. Even infants and children were heavily dosed with opium in concoctions like Mrs. Winslow's Soothing Syrup and Mother Bailey's Quieting Syrup. Patent medicines such as Wine of Coca, Coca Beef Tonic, and Dr. Birney's Catarrh Powder were popular cocaine-laced products. And of course there was alcohol. Products such as Dr. Kilmer's Swamp Root, Paine's Celery Compound, Hostetter's Stomach Bitters, and Faith Whitcomb's Nerve Bitters ranged from 20% to 45% alcohol by volume. Much of the addiction in the 19th century resulted from citizens' dosing themselves with such drug-laced products.[321]

Inebriates in the 19th century, like those in this century, regularly sought chemical relief for their chemically induced physical and mental anguish. In the 1880s, druggists reported a high demand on Monday mornings for chloral, acid phosphate, tincture of capsicum, and laudanum—all products known to be used by alcoholics to ward off the anguish that followed a weekend binge.[322] Alcoholics and addicts also made enduring attempts to find in a new drug a solution to their growing drug-related problems. And there to exploit that search were the unscrupulous purveyors of miracle cures for addiction.

For more than a century, alcoholics and addicts and their family members have responded to false promises of quick cures. The addict's combination of physical and emotional anguish and propensity for magical thinking—and the unending desperation of the addict's loved ones—constituted a vulnerability to sustained exploitation. What made these varied cures particularly alluring, in contrast to the inebriate homes and inebriate asylums, were their promises of: 1) treatment in secrecy even from one's closest friends and family members, 2) treatment at a radically reduced cost, 3) treatment that did not require institutionalization, and 4) treatment that did not interfere with one's routine business and personal affairs.

The Products [323]

The same patent-medicine industry that brought opium, morphine, cocaine, chloral hydrate, and innumerable alcohol-based preparations into American households and fed the daily habits of many addicts also offered cures for addiction to these same drugs. Advertisements promoting such cures appeared as early as 1850 and were common by the 1880s. What follows is a guided tour of a century of such offerings.

Hangover Remedies: While there have long been folk remedies to cure the immediate aftermath of over-indulgence in alcohol, the commercialization of these products did not gain solid footing until the 20th century and, interestingly, flourished primarily following the repeal of prohibition. What is amazing is the sheer number of such remedies available in the 1930s. Alka-Nox, HR5, Miracle Compound, Pix-Up, Res-U-Rex, Mrs. Moffat's Shoo Fly Powders, S.L.'s Powders for the Morning After, Sobrosal, Sober-Up Pills, Vi-Vo, and Wink were among the more prominent 1930s hangover remedies. While most of these products promised to relieve the pain of overindulgence the morning after, one such product, Good Samaritan, claimed that it could actually prevent hangovers if taken while drinking.[324]

Alcoholism Cures: There were many advertised home cures for alcoholism between 1860 and 1930. The Hay-Litchfield Antidote, patented in 1868, promised to eliminate the appetite for liquor by inciting "disgust and nausea" at the very sight of alcohol. The concoction contained various quantities of calamus root, gum-guiacum, beef gall, eel-skin, codfish, milk, cherry-tree bark, poke root, cow's urine, and *alcohol*.[325] Typical of the cures offered by reformed inebriates was Knights' Tonic for Inebriates, which was widely promoted during the 1870s. The product was placed on the market by Samuel C. Knights of Cambridge, Massachusetts and promised to "remove that craving for a stimulant that those who have been addicted to the use of ardent spirits so well know." The product was advertised as a "temperance bitter."[326] The White Star Secret Liquor Cure came in boxes of thirty capsules selling for 94 cents a box. The primary ingredient in these capsules was erthroxylon coca—cocaine. Cures like the Boston Drug Cure for Drunkenness could be ordered by mail for $1 a box—and it took four boxes to complete the cure. In 1901, one could even order a 50-cent cure for drunkenness from the Sears and Roebuck catalogue. Some of the more popular early 20th-century home treatments for alcoholism included Alcoban, Alcola, Alcodyne, Anti-Jag, Antol, Antialkaholin Drink Cure, Aurmino, Blackstone Treatment for Alcoholism, Cravex, Dr. Chambers' Celebrated Remedy for Intemperance, Dr. Haines Golden Specific for the Cure of Drunkenness, Frank's Cure for Inebriety, Golden Treatment for the Liquor Habit, Mickey Finn Powders, White Cross Anti-Liquor Treatment, and Wooley's Cure for Alcoholism.

Cures For the "Drug Habit": Like the alcoholism cures, cures for drug addiction came from individual physicians, from various institutes, from drug companies, and from lone individuals—many of whom proclaimed to have been saved by their own products. Mrs. Baldwin's Home Cure, for example, promised a "never-failing" remedy for anyone addicted to cocaine, morphine, opium, or laudanum, a remedy that Mrs. Baldwin had developed and successfully used to cure herself. Those in need could order the cure from her home address in Chicago. The St. Paul Association Cure offered free trial treatments of a "painless and permanent home cure" for anyone addicted to morphine, cocaine, opium, or laudanum. The Compound Oxygen Association, promoted by Dr. J.W. Coblentz of Fort Wayne, Indiana, offered a morphine addiction cure that sold for $11. "Antidote," also sold as "Collins Painless Opium Antidote," was a bottled cure offered by Dr. Sam Collins, who spent more than $300,000 to advertise its benefits.[327] Antidote and Restorative was the product of Dr. Henry Brown, who prepared each bottle individually after the patient sent in a detailed survey of his or her daily drug consumption.[328] Habatina, offered by the Delta Chemical Company of St. Louis, promised to provide "pleasant stimulation and perfect support" while curing morphine addiction—and all for a mere $2 per bottle. Other cures widely advertised between 1880 and 1930 include: the Acme Drug Co. Home Cure for the Morphine and Opium Habits, Carney Common Sense Treatment for the Morphine Habit, Four Famous Formulae Opium Cure, Hyo-Sco-Phine Tablets, Maplewood Drug Habit Cure, Starnes' Drug Habit Cure, St. Anne's Morphin Cure, Waterman Institute Morphin Cure, and Weatherby's Opium Antidote. Opiate cures often came numbered or were sent in sequence with ever-decreasing doses of narcotics—providing either sustained maintenance or gradual withdrawal without direct medical supervision.

Cures For the "Tobacco Habit": The progressive accumulation of information on the role of tobacco in a variety of diseases—coupled with America's periodic anti-tobacco campaigns—has long promoted an enduring line of home cures, booklets, and smoking-cessation clinics. Some of the earliest of these products (before 1930) included Anti-Cigarette League Treatment, BACO-CURE, Dr. Ravely's Guaranteed Remedy for the Tobacco Habit, Gustafson's Tobacco Remedy, James Home Remedy, Nicotol, Nix-O-Tine, Superba Tobacco Remedy, Tobacco Boom, and Tobacco Redeemer. New generations of smoking-cure products have arisen in every decade of the 20th century. The contents of these smoking cures have varied. Early 20th-century products like Celebrated Tobacco Specific and Tobacco Bullets contained cocaine, but most of the later products have contained astringent mouth-washes (including alum or silver salts to give tobacco a bad taste), local anesthetics, nicotine substitutes (primarily lobeline), and cures that progressively administer decreasing amounts of nicotine through lozenges, gum, or skin patches.[329]

Generic Cures: While most addiction cures were drug specific, some companies offered a single product that they claimed would cure any type of addiction. The Ensor Institute Vegetable Cure, for example, offered a single product that promised to cure all opium, alcohol, and tobacco habits. Another product, RE-VI-VO, promised a cure for alcohol, opium, and tobacco habits while simultaneously curing "Nervous, Stomach, Liver, or Sexual Troubles"—all for only $1.[330]

Promotional Schemes

The miracle-cure purveyors relied on a variety of promotional techniques to sell their products.[331] Such promotion began with the very naming of the product. There were names that conveyed medical, religious, or academic authority. There were lots of "Dr. This" and "Dr. That" cures (Dr. Meeker's Antidote). There were cures named after Saints (St. James Society Cure), Fathers (Father Mathew Remedy), and Professors (Prof. M.M. Waterman Cure). There were names that seemed to promise great value (the gold cure institutes), comfort (Richie Painless Cure), and confidence (Reliable Cure for the Opium and Morphine Habits). There were cures offered by places that sounded like charities rather than companies—lots of Associations and Institutes, and even a Drug Crave Crusade. And there were even cures that promised supernatural intervention, like Neal Institute's depiction of its 3-day addiction cure as "more like a miracle than a medicine."

Many common themes emerged within the addiction-cure advertisements. Announcements of a just-discovered breakthrough in science and medicine by this doctor or that professor—whose name was often attached to the product—were particularly common. There was the ever-present "secret formula" that emphasized what the product did NOT contain: alcohol, opiates, or cocaine. There were the required testimonials from physicians, clergy, and former patients singing the praises of the product. The addiction cures presented their remedies as infallible or—in the advertising copy for Dr. Collin's Genuine Painless Opium Antidote—"never a failure in a single case."[332] The cures' infallibility were underscored by claims of the numbers cured—claims that generally ranged between 10,000 and 400,000 people. There was also the open solicitation of "complicated" or

"refractory" cases, promising that this treatment was different from all the others they have tried. There were the regular attacks on addiction-cure charlatans who offered fake imitations of the true product now being offered. There were promises of secrecy (promises that packages would arrive in plain wrapping), speed (there was clear competition on which product could cure addiction in the smallest number of days), and freedom from discomfort (promises of "no vomiting" or "no injections").

Most addiction-cure companies offered something of a gimmick—elaborate personal assessment forms, a written money-back guarantee, elaborate procedures for use of the medication—all designed to arouse the addict's magical thinking. Denarco—a "popular home treatment for opium, morphine, laudanum, paregoric, chloral, cocaine, opium smoking and kindred habits"—provided an elaborate system of medications, with careful instructions for stepping down the dose over a period of 74 days. Not surprisingly given these instructions, the product was later found to contain morphine.[333] Pandora Laboratories, Inc. manufactured and sold a product called "Thirty-Two," which consisted of 32 elaborately encased bottles (costing $32) advertised as "a complete course of alcoholism treatment" that could be completed at home in 48 days.[334] Addiction cures often promised some bonus effect that would accompany their cure. The most common of these was enhanced sexual functioning. Dr. Patterson of Atlanta, Georgia promised that his morphine and opium habit cure would restore impaired sexual organs and "make you happy in the love for the opposite sex."[335] No-To-Bac was even more direct in its claims: "No-To-Bac cures impotency and is used with magical effect by men advanced in years."[336] This bonus effect was evident in many addiction-cure advertising slogans, such as Oxien's slogan: "Cures Drunkards and Makes Weak Women Walk."

These promises came not only through newspaper, magazine, window display, and billboard advertising, but also through direct-mail campaigns. The White Cross Anti-Liquor Society, after procuring names of potential alcoholics and addicts, launched an aggressive direct-mail campaign that began with a low-key letter offering a home trial of their cure for only $5. If it brought no response, it was followed by a second letter emphasizing the long-term devastation resulting from alcoholism. If there was still no response, this was followed by a letter offering a payment plan through which the prospective patient would be sent the cure for $3 and could pay the remaining $2 in installments. Lacking any response to this offer, the Society sent a final letter and enclosed a check for $2, which could be sent along with just $3 to purchase the cure.[337]

Appeals to Wives and Family Members: Many addiction-cure advertisements targeted wives and family members of alcoholics. The most insidious of these claimed that the alcoholic could be cured without his voluntary cooperation and, in fact, without his knowledge. Instructions that came with Formula A, for example, directed that 15 to 20 drops of Formula A be surreptitiously placed within the drinker's first drink of the day, and that if this did not induce vomiting, another 15-20 drops were to be added to the second or third drink. These were to be supplemented by sprinkling the contents of Formula A capsules in the drinker's food. Formula A, like many such cures, contained a nauseant—usually fluid extract of ipecac.[338] Among the alcoholism-cure products that advertised that they could be given secretly were the White Star Secret Liquor Cure, The Boston Drug Cure for Drunkenness, Vantox, and Tescum Powders. Such products often came in two forms: tablets for voluntary administration and powders for secret administration in food or drinks.[339]

Appeals to Druggists and Physicians: Efforts to get physicians and druggists to recommend particular addiction-cure products went far beyond the traditional sales pitches on the potential benefits of the products. The cure purveyors offered strong financial incentives for druggists and physicians to refer patients to them. The primary technique used to enlist such cooperation was what is today called "fee splitting." In 1910, Dr. K.F. Purdy, owner of the Purdy Sanitarium for Drug Addictions and Alcoholism, was promising in a mass mailing to physicians:

If you will send me a list of people addicted to opium in any form, I will mail them my literature and try and interest them in my treatment. For each case taken I will promptly mail you a money order for $5.00. For cases coming to our sanitarium, your commission will be $20.00.[340]

The Neal Institute in Chicago sent promotional letters to physicians in 1911, promising to pay $12.50 for each addicted patient whose name the doctor referred to the Institute. The letter further promised the physician that the Institute would keep the physician's status as informant "sacredly confidential."[341] Patients so identified would then be targeted for direct-mail campaigns like the one described above.

Exposés and Legislative Reform

Concern about fraudulent medicines promoted the Medical Society of the City of New York to create a Committee on Quack Remedies as early as 1827. The first wave of agitation for reform began in the 1880s. Dr. J. B. Mattison wrote an 1886 expose on "opium antidotes" in the *Journal of the American Medical Association,* in which he found opium in 19 of 20 advertised opium cures subjected to laboratory testing.[342] In 1888, the Massachusetts State Board of Health reported the following analyses, which they undertook to determine the presence and quantity of alcohol in various advertised cures for inebriety.

Product	Percentage Alcohol
Scotch Oats Essence	35.0%
Golden's Liquid Beef Tonic	26.5%
The "Best" Tonic	7.5%
Carter's Physical Extract	22.0%
Hostetters Stomach Bitters	44.3%
Hoofland's German Tonic	29.3%
Hop Tonic	7.0%
Howe's Arabian Tonic	13.2%
Jackson's Golden Seal Tonic	19.6%
Liebig Co's Cocoa Beef Tonic	23.2%
Mensman's Peptonized Beef Tonic	16.5%
Parker's Tonic	41.6%
Schenck's Seaweed Tonic	19.5%

This 1888 study found some 49 products advertised for "usefulness in the reformation of intemperate habits" that contained alcohol. Parker's Tonic promised that "inebriates struggling to reform will find its tonic and sustaining influence on the nervous system a great help to their efforts." Browns Iron Bitters advertised itself as "perfectly harmless—not a substitute for alcohol." But perhaps most blatant was Hoofland's German Bitters, which advertised itself as "entirely vegetable and free from alcoholic stimulant."[343] In his account of these Massachusetts findings, Frederick Peterson noted that people occasionally achieved success with these fraudulent cures—a success that he attributed not to powers within the product, but to "the support by faith and suggestion given the weak will of the patient."[344]

In 1889, the American Association for the Study and Cure of Inebriety appointed a Committee on Nostrums, Proprietary Medicines, and New Drugs to investigate 50 advertised cures for alcoholism and 20 advertised cures for the opium habit. The Committee found that all of the alcoholism cures contained alcohol (from 6% to 47%), and 19 of the 20 opium habit cures contained opium. These products not only contained the drugs they were alleged to cure, but they also cost more than the original drugs to which their consumers were addicted. In 1893, the Association officially condemned all secret formulas used in treating addiction and called for state regulation of the treatment industry.[345]

Taking on the purveyors of fraudulent addiction cures was not easy, because it meant taking on the larger patent medicine industry. As the primary source of advertising revenues in newspapers and magazines, the patent medicine industry wielded enormous political power. This power was exerted quite blatantly in advertising contracts that included a "red clause," nullifying the contract if the state in which the newspaper was published passed any legislation designed to control patent medicines. For years, these contracts provided a built-in media machine to oppose patent medicine reform.[346] Only in an era of great social reform could challenges be launched against a patent medicine industry that by 1906 was grossing $75 million per year. Such a task required the combined efforts of the American Association for the Study and Cure of Inebriety, the American Pharmaceutical Association's Committee on Acquirement of the Drug Habit, the American Medical Association, and some muckraking journalists.[347]

The first blow struck against the patent medicine industry targeted products containing alcohol. In 1905 the Internal Revenue Service issued a regulation requiring that manufacturers of medicines containing alcohol had to apply for a liquor license—a requirement that was more an irritant and an embarrassment than a threat to profits. But more changes followed public exposure of industry practices in *Collier's Magazine* and *Ladies' Home Journal*.[348]

Collier's ran a series of exposés on the patent medicine industry written by Samuel Hopkins Adams, a free-lance reporter. Beginning October 7, 1905, the series of articles combined meticulous documentation with fiery rhetoric to expose abuses within the patent medicine industry.

In an article entitled "The Scavengers," Adams exposed the fraudulent patent-medicine cures for the liquor and drug habits. To research this article, Adams ordered many advertised cures for morphine addiction and had them sent to laboratories for testing. The result of his tests of the morphine cures is illustrated in the following table, which appeared in the article.

The Cure	What It Contained
Richie Painless Cure	Morphine
St. Paul Association Cure	Morphine
Tri-Elixiria (Charles B. James)	Morphine
The Purdy Cure	Morphine
Maplewood Institute	Morphine
St. James Society Cure	Morphine
O.P. Coats Co. Cure	Morphine
Harris Institute Cure	Morphine
Morphina-Cure	Morphine
Opacura	Morphine
Prof. M.M. Waterman	Morphine
Drug Crave Crusade	Morphine
Denarco	Morphine
Dr. J.C. Hoffman Cure	Morphine
Dr. B.M. Woolley Cure	Morphine
Dr. J. Edward Allport System	Morphine

Source: "The Scavengers," *Colliers Weekly*, September 22, 1906.

He found that most of the cures contained large quantities of the drugs they were alleged to cure—or substituted other substances. Many of the alcohol cures, for example, contained opium, morphine, or cocaine. When Adams wrote to the St. Paul Association of Chicago requesting a cure for his 12-grain-per-day morphine habit, he was sent a cure that taken at its prescribed dosage would have given him eleven and one third grains of morphine per day, without even an acknowledgment that the cure contained morphine.[349] Less-individualized cures could result in an addict's increasing rather than decreasing his daily dosage of narcotics.[350]

Other cures just contained a high dose of booze—most ranging from 40 to 80 proof.[351] The purveyors of the addiction cures were quite brazen in their promotional efforts, often denying that their products contained alcohol, opium coca, or other intoxicants that tests would later prove to be present. One addiction-cure promoter, Dr. Samuel Collins of LaPorte, Indiana, even used quotes from early addiction-cure exposés in his articles. Many of the proffered addiction cures contained combinations of drugs. Scotch Oats Essence, for example, contained morphine and cannabis.

The extent of the addiction-cure trade was dramatically illustrated when Charles Towns exhibited 76 American opium-cure products at the Shanghai Opium Conference. Exposés like Adams' series, a growing cadre of agricultural chemists who were regularly publishing their tests of the contents of proprietary drugs, and linked charges of filthy conditions in the food industry stirred calls for action against the patent medicine and food industries. Dr. Harvey Wiley, the chief chemist for the Department of Agriculture, introduced what would became the Pure Food and Drug Act of 1906. President Theodore Roosevelt signed the bill into law on June 30, 1906.[352]

The Pure Food and Drug Act did not ban the inclusion of alcohol, morphine, opium, cocaine, heroin, chloroform, cannabis indica, or chloral hydrate in patent medicines, but it did require that the presence and dosage of such substances be indicated on the label of products sold in interstate commerce. This act at least temporarily eliminated the worst of the miracle-cure frauds that exploited addicts. Some continued to sell their now-truthfully labeled products, numbering the bottles in a manner similar to the way we now number sunscreen products, to indicate the gradually lowering concentration of opiates. While many addicts attempted this reduction method of self-treatment to lower their tolerance, few were able to achieve complete abstinence.[353]

Continued Presence of Fraudulent "Cures"

In spite of the reforms implemented under the 1906 Pure Food and Drug Act, miracle cures for the addictions continued to come and go in the years that followed. In 1921—the second full year of alcohol prohibition—the American Medical Association's *Nostrums and Quackery* exposed a number of fraudulent alcoholism and addiction cures. With blaring advertising copy proclaiming "Drunkards Cured Secretly" and "Drunkards Cured in 24 Hours," these products preyed on alcoholics and their families, draining their financial resources while providing nothing but placebos or substitute drugs. Some of the products exposed by the AMA included:

- Antialkolin Drink Cure (Containing nothing but milk sugar)
- Carney Common Sense Opiate Cure (Containing morphine)
- Coho Drink Cure (Containing cinnamon flavored alcohol)
- Harrison's Opium Cure (20 per cent alcohol; 5% opium)
- Normyl Treatment (An alcoholism cure that was 75.5% alcohol)
- St. Anne's Morphine Cure (Containing morphine and caffeine)

- Starnes Drug-Habit Cure (Containing morphine)
- Tucker's Drug-Habit Cure (Containing alcohol and morphine)

The continued presence of fraudulent addiction cures prompted the National Better Business Bureau, Inc. (NBBB) to issue a press release in 1929 on such cures. The NBBB warned consumers against fraudulent products and declared that there were no medicines known to science that alone constituted an effective treatment that could remove the craving for alcohol or other drugs.[354]

Accounts of miracle cures continued into the 1930s and 1940s. Masters described two interesting alcohol-laced products promoted as cures for alcoholism during this period. The first, "Teetolia Treatment," was 30% alcohol; and the other, the alcohol-laced "Prescription Brand Whiskey," was promoted as a non-intoxicating substitute for alcohol.[355] The latter product was distributed by a Chicago-based company using the trade name, "Rx Medicinal Spirits." A group by the same name operated out of Peoria, Illinois and offered a similar non-intoxicating whiskey called "RMS Private Formula." Those distributing these products claimed that the harmful intoxicating properties had been removed from the whiskey. Their advertising copy claimed:

> *Used as a prophylactic, it will prevent the possibility of ever becoming an inebriate. Used as a remedial whiskey in chronic alcoholism, it tends to make a moderate and sane drinker.*[356]

A 1939 warning in the *Journal of the American Medical Association* regarding these products noted that this treatment approach to alcoholism would not lead to sobriety in spite of its potential popularity among alcoholics.[357][358] Dwight Anderson inventoried alcoholism cures that were advertised in magazines and newspapers during the late 1940s. Products like "Dr. Haines' Golden Specific," "Health Anti-Liquor," "Alcoban," and "Alconox" promised to cure drunkards in 24 hours. Many of these products, like those that came a generation before, could be given without the drinker's knowledge. They supposedly induced a distaste for alcohol in the inveterate drinker. Most such products appeared in a blaze of advertising, soaked money from their desperate victims, then disappeared before charges of mail fraud could be lodged—only to reappear later under new company names and addresses. The majority of cures, like the more than 30 bottles sent as part of the "McTaggert Method," contained alcohol; or, like the product "Cravex," contained nothing that would stop or satisfy one's craving for alcohol or anything else. Anderson's 1950 investigation revealed that companies were selling bottles of booze "from which the poisons had been removed." This alcohol, the buyer was led to believe, could be ingested without harm.[359]

There were also self-help books and pamphlets for sale that promised home cures for the drink habit. These ranged from those giving simplistic advice to one that offered a step-by-step method of self-administered aversion therapy using emetine hydro-chloride.

At times decisive action has been taken against companies that offered medically unsupervised home cures for addiction. The makers of Habatina—an early 20th-century remedy for the morphine habit—were found guilty of selling poisonous drugs through the mails and using the mails to defraud the public. It turns out that Habatina contained 16 grains of morphine, eight grains of heroin, and a quantity of alcohol within each ounce of this alleged addiction cure.[360] The Federal Trade Commission has also taken action against addiction-cure purveyors. Typical of this action was its 1941 order that the Gates Medicine Co. of Charleston, West Virginia cease its false advertising of the White Ribbon Remedy for the Liquor Habit.[361] As recently as the 1960s, the FTC banned the continued advertising of "Soberin" as a new medical discovery that could cure alcoholism.[362]

Fraud as a Theme in the Early History of Treatment

The charge of quackery and fraud in the early history of addiction treatment extends beyond those purveyors of miracle cures in a bottle. Between the years 1880 and 1920, open arguments among treatment practitioners over which methods were most effective often extended to charges of fraud and unethical practice. A few such charges are illustrative.

In 1881, H.H. Kane, reacting to the "deceitful lies" that filled the advertising for various addiction "cures," wrote: "*It is about time that the people found out that honest, honorable, and trustworthy physicians, who have only the good of the patient at heart, do not advertise.*"[363] Paradoxically, Kane himself developed a home treatment for opium or chloral habits and alcoholic inebriety, for which he both advertised and charged ($60). He also sold such ancillary products as his Oleo-Dermatine ($10) for the

healing of hypodermic abscesses and his Electric Innervator ($10), which served as an "artificial nerve force for debilitated patients."[364]

T.D. Crothers regularly attacked financial profiteering by those who peddled fraudulent addiction cures. In 1902, Crothers claimed that most quack treatments for addiction relied on hidden drug ingredients and the principle of drug substitution. He concluded: "This is not curative in any sense. It is simply drug restraint, and masking of symptoms which break out with greater force when the restraint is removed."[365] In 1914, G.H. Benton, Superintendent of the Sterling Worth Sanitorium in Miami, Florida, launched an attack on institutions that held themselves up as curing the inebriate, but whose care was marked by incompetence and fraud. Benton called for the state to license and inspect all facilities that provided care to the inebriate.[366] In 1915, Charles Towns—who himself was later criticized for promotion of his "Towns Cure"—attacked these institutions for what he considered financial exploitation.

The sum annually spent in the United States upon useless sanitorium treatment must certainly amount to millions....Wealthy people are specially likely to become victims of this form of rapacity....The ingenuity with which a sanitorium manager devises "extras" is worthy of the name genius. And the physically incurable patient is often retained in the sanatorium till his money or the money of his friends is exhausted in a needless sacrifice to greed.[367]

The fact is that allegations of fraud constitute an enduring theme within the history of addiction treatment. The lack of a defined treatment science, the proliferation of many schools of competing thought and practice, and the desperate vulnerability of the addict and the addict's family all create a climate ripe for exploitation. It seems that each era of addiction treatment begins with claims of enormous scientific breakthroughs. These claims are then converted into marketable commodities or services that initially generate high praise. Then when the clamor dies down, there is a discovery that the product or service did not live up to its original expectations. From these crashed hopes occasionally arise charges of quackery and fraud.

What is surprising is how rarely these charges break public. We know very little about what it was actually like to experience such remedies. People who hid their addiction in secrecy pursued these cures with equal secrecy. The open solicitation of "refractory cases" by the remedy merchants suggests that this path was paved with failure, but these cases represented a silent, hidden population of addicts within American history.[368] After all, how could one protest one's exploitation without revealing one's status as an addict? Shame silenced the voices of the suffering, preventing public accounts of their unrelenting efforts at self-cure and their exploitation at the hands of profiteers. In some cases, shame even silenced reports of enduring recoveries—recoveries whose success was aided, not by the ingredients of the curative agent but, by a well-timed placebo effect.

Since fraud is such a cyclical theme in this history, one is forced to stop and reflect how the pages of history will judge those treatments offered during our contemporary period. This chapter, in particular, suggests the need for healthy skepticism and close scrutiny of the next drug or gimmick that comes along lauded as a cure for alcoholism or other addictions. It is quite possible that some current products and services being sold as aids in the treatment of alcohol, tobacco, and other drug addictions will in the future be added to this chapter's list of fraudulent remedies. The question of how each of us and our institutions will be judged by this history is one worthy of serious self-reflection.

Chapter Nine
Religious Conversion as a Remedy for Alcoholism [369]

In earlier chapters, we made passing note of how religious influences led many alcoholics to the temperance pledge, and we noted the nature of religious influences within the 19th-century alcoholic mutual-aid societies and inebriate homes and asylums. In this chapter we will take a more direct look at the role of religion in addiction recovery during America's 19th and early 20th centuries. We will see how the personal transformation inherent in religious conversion initiated the process of recovery for many addicts, and we will see how religious institutions served as sobriety-based support structures that helped sustain the long-term process of addiction recovery. We will identify the religious institutions that actively reached out to alcoholics and summarize the way in which early alcoholism treatment specialists viewed the role of religion in alcoholism recovery.

Religion and Recovery: Historical Roots

Many of those who were first concerned with the rise of inebriety in America also noted the potential role of religion as a remedy to the problem of chronic drunkenness. Dr. Benjamin Rush, in a letter to Jeremy Belknap, reflected this sentiment when he observed:

> I am disposed to believe that the business [temperance] must be effected finally by religion alone. Human reason has been employed in vain....Let these considerations lead us to address the heads of the governing bodies of all churches in America.[370]

Nineteenth-century temperance leaders in America consistently advocated the religious experience as an antidote to alcoholism. The reform institutions that evolved through the 19th century—the almshouse, the insane asylum, the orphanage, the prisons and reformatories, and the inebriate asylum—often similarly recognized the potential role of religion in personal reformation. Katherine Chavigny has suggested that the entire underlying theme of the therapeutic temperance movement was evangelical religion. This attempt to exert religious influence upon the inebriate existed, not just within the addiction-specific mutual aid societies, but also in the mainstream religious movements of the 19th century.[371]

The image of former drunkards standing at religious revivals of the 1850s and 1860s proclaiming that God had taken away their appetite for alcohol was a common one. These religious movements were also part of a broader network of lodges, conventions, tent meetings, missions, and informal helping services within which the newly reformed drunkard could become enmeshed.[372] The practice of "experience sharing" that had been so galvanizing within the earlier Washingtonian meetings was itself influenced by the religious practice of publicly declaring one's faith. The three-part story style–the past, the turn-around experience, and life since then–was modeled on a similar story style that Christians had evolved to qualify themselves as converted. The Washingtonians grabbed so much attention, not by introducing a new story style, but by virtue of the fact that their stories of sin were so much more far ranging and vivid. The

Washingtonian awakening of the early 1840s refined the ritual of bold public confession of the alcoholic's transgressions, and alcoholics continued this tradition in the religious revival tents long after the collapse of the Washingtonians.

One of the most significant factors in the rise of religious approaches to alcoholism recovery was a change in the urban landscape, more specifically, the rise of America's Skid Rows.

Skid Row, the Bowery and the Birth of the Rescue Mission

The term "Skid Row" dates to 1852 in Seattle, Washington. A sawmill built in Pioneer Square near Puget Sound used skids (tracks of peeled logs) to get the timber to the mill. This area, which later became home to vagrants and destitute alcoholics, was known as Skid Road, and later as "Skid Row." Another equivalent term, "the Bowery," originally referred to a 16-block street on the lower East Side of Manhattan in New York City. The terms "Skid Row" and "Bowery" were picked up by the national press to describe the blighted city areas frequented by alcoholics. These terms were used to denote that portion of any city characterized by vagrants, alcoholics, cheap hotels and lodging houses, bars, brothels, temporary employment agencies, pawn-shops, second-hand stores, soup kitchens, and missions. The Skid Row and Bowery neighborhoods—and those who lived there— seemed to be in a state of accelerating decline.[373] The number of these areas in America grew dramatically between 1870 and the turn of the century.

The Skid Row alcoholic, and the broader phenomenon of increased public intoxication, consumed a growing quantity of civic attention and civic resources during the last half of the 19th century. Concern with the chronic alcoholic was at the centerpiece of growing worries about public disorder. The pressure that public inebriates placed on local police departments in turn exerted pressure to create new remedies to the problem of chronic alcoholism. The climate was ripe for the emergence of a new institution: the urban rescue mission. At the forefront of launching this new institution was a most unlikely candidate: Jerry McAuley.

Jerry McAuley's Water Street Mission [374]

A counterfeiter's son, a runaway, a thief, a drunkard, a brawler, and a convict. Those were the credentials that Jerry McAuley brought to his religious conversion in Sing Sing Prison, where he had been sentenced for 15 years for highway robbery. Although McAuley was an unlikely candidate for religious sentiment, his conversion burst forth in a series of wrenching emotional experiences. The first came in response to the story of another drunkard, a former professional fighter named "Awful" Gardner, who shared his own story of degradation and religious rebirth. Gardner's story softened the hardened veneer within which McAuley had encapsulated himself. A short time later, McAuley described what happened when a religious volunteer visiting the prison prayed for him:

All at once it seemed as if something supernatural was in my room. I was afraid to open my eyes. I was in agony and the tears rolled off my face in great drops. How I longed for God's mercy! Just then, in the very height of my distress, it seemed as if a hand was laid upon my head and these words came to me: "My son, thy sins, which are many, are forgiven."[375]

Following almost a year-long slip into his old life upon his discharge from prison, McAuley experienced a third spiritual breakthrough that an observer described:

There was a shock which came into the room, something similar to a flash of lightning which every one present saw and felt. Jerry fell down on his side prone on the floor with tears streaming from his eyes.[376]

McAuley renewed his faith and his sobriety behind a bold new idea: provide a haven for people like himself, where they could find basic sustenance, words of encouragement, and an opportunity for personal and religious reformation. Born Roman Catholic, McAuley launched the evangelical Protestant rescue mission movement. He and those around him had little inclination to capture the accounts of their experiences on paper, but we do have McAuley's 1876 autobiographical pamphlet, *Transformed: The History of a River Thief*, and Arthur Bonner's 1967 biography of McAuley. This is a brief synopsis of the story these documents tell of the Water Street Mission.

McAuley's vision of a sanctuary for outcasts was well-timed. By 1870, religious groups in New York City were writing about the growing "tramp problem"—a reference to the growing number of homeless men and "fallen women" whose public intoxication was causing growing alarm within the city. While existing institutions offered shelter and food for the "deserving" (defined as respectable people who had fallen on hard times through circumstances beyond their control), none sought out or accepted those viewed as undeserving. The failure of traditional religious and charity institutions to reach these individuals created a vacuum that could be filled only by a new type of institution—one that McAuley himself was about to create.[377]

In October 1872, McAuley founded the first and most famous of the rescue missions that served alcoholics: the Water Street Mission in New York City's notorious Fourth Ward. The resources used to start the mission were raised through McAuley's own testimony and pleas for donations to support the new institution. The staff at the mission included Jerry, his wife Maria, and a janitor. Maria was herself a former drunkard and prostitute, who by all accounts played a major role in the success of the Water Street Mission. The need filled by the Mission was evident in the 5,144 men provided lodging and the 26,262 meals served during the mission's first year of operation.

The first thing McAuley offered those who came through the doors of the Mission was respect. He treated people like ladies and gentlemen—people who were used to being treated like whores and derelicts. The Water Street Mission met people's concrete need for food and shelter within a relationship free of condescension and contempt. The advertisement for the Water Street Mission that appeared in each Saturday's newspaper said it all: "Everybody welcome, especially drunkards."[378]

The religious meetings at the mission were attended by anywhere from 100 to 400 people. The framework for these meetings was an interesting one. First, there were no long sermons. The meetings opened with singing, a Bible reading, and a brief comment from Jerry. His remarks usually contained a spiritual message couched in a material promise. Rather than proffer the traditional hell-and-brimstone sermon, McAuley simply pointed out the "rewards of righteousness."[379] But the heart of the meeting was not McAuley, but the "testimonies" of the participants.

One after another they spoke of their fall and their rebirth, or of their need for hope and change. The only structure to this "experience sharing" (to remind the reader of the Washingtonian parallel) was McAuley's time limit of one minute per speaker. He even used a bell to rein in the long-winded. When a desperate man came requesting that McAuley pray for him, McAuley often placed his hands on the penitent and encouraged him to pray out loud for himself. This wasn't a place where people "got" religion; it was a place where people had to go after it.

Behind it all stood the example of what Jerry McAuley had done with his own life. But McAuley's life story was generally passed along by others, rather than by his own words. McAuley had a unique story style. While his life could have provided a wealth of details of drunkenness and crime, he kept his vow to disclose his past only in the most general manner. In his talks, the emphasis was not on the details of what he had been, but on the details of what he had become and how the transformation had occurred.[380] McAuley may have recognized the lack of benefit to others—and to himself—of what would more than half a century later become known as a "drunk-alogue."

While some religious institutions had made superficial overtures to drunkards, prostitutes, thieves, and the homeless, McAuley's Water Street Mission was the first institution that opened its doors day and night to truly welcome those branded as social outcasts. The Water Street Mission grew in the size and scope of its service mission, and it influenced many other, parallel ventures. McAuley himself later opened the Cremorne Mission—an institution that sought to reach the women working in New York City's brothels, dance halls, and gambling houses. There is some evidence that McAuley's demonstration that the alcoholic could be reformed by religious conversion also contributed to the founding of the New York Christian Home for Intemperate Men in 1877.[381]

McAuley carried his message of Christian salvation as a cure for alcoholism until he died in 1884 of the tuberculosis he had contracted in Sing Sing Prison. His funeral, one of the largest in New York City history, was attended by people of all walks of life who had been touched or inspired by his work. He is quite rightly acknowledged as the driving force behind the emergence of urban missions in the U.S. McAuley's torch was passed to Samuel Hadley.

In April, 1882, Samuel Hadley had been on a continuous binge when, in a moment of wrenching self-disgust, he swore he would die before he took another drink. Hadley asked to be locked in jail, where he traded the bottle for an extended bout of D.T.s . From the jail, he went to the Water Street Mission, where he experienced a kind of spiritual collapse. In a manner similar to what the co-founder of A.A. would describe 52 years later, Hadley reported that the room was flooded with light and he was overwhelmed with a spiritual presence. Hadley woke the next day wondering if the experience had been a dream. He convinced himself that the experience was genuine and went on to a lifetime of service within New York City's rescue missions. Samuel Hadley died in 1906, but his son, S.H. Hadley, carried on his father's missionary work. In a most interesting touch of historical continuity, the younger Hadley later ran the Calvary Mission, where a just-sober Bill Wilson sought support in the days before his meeting with Dr. Robert Smith marked the beginning of Alcoholics Anonymous.[382]

The work of McAuley, Hadley, and the other pioneers of the urban rescue missions were inspired by such Protestant revivalists as Dwight L. Moody and Ira D. Sankey. These revivalists advocated Christian conversion as a vehicle of reformation and rebirth for the alcoholic. They often called upon reformed men to give testimony at their meetings and emphasized that God could take away a man's appetite for spirits. Evangelists such as Moody saw pledge-signing as a rather superficial and misdirected act and placed emphasis instead on the conversion experience. In Moody's view, abstinence was not an act of individual will to be pledged, but a consequence of one's religious rebirth. The revival meetings held by Moody and Sankey in the 1870s touched many alcoholics and sent them to the rescue missions in search of continuing support.[383]

Urban missions were an outgrowth of Evangelical Protestantism and its missionary societies. These societies, witnessing the growing numbers of urban immigrants, established city missions in the hopes of winning religious converts among these new Americans. In the decades following the Civil War, immigrants from all corners of the world were drawn to America's cities, and by the 1920s more than 3,000 missions had been formed to serve them.[384] Although McAuley's Water Street Mission marked the beginning of the urban rescue mission movement, the organization that became most extensively involved in this work was the Salvation Army.

The Salvation Army

The Salvation Army grew out of the pastoral work of a Methodist minister, William Booth. It was founded in 1865 as the Christian Revival Association and rechristened the Salvation Army (SA) in 1878. The SA came to the United States in 1880, represented by a group of seven women and Commissioner George Railton. Later Booth's own daughter, Commander Evangeline Booth, worked with the SA in

America. In recounting the SA's mission of serving alcoholics, we will extend this story beyond our current period of focus, to show how the SA evolved into its current philosophy of operation.

Booth declared in 1890 that alcoholism was "a disease often inherited, always developed by indulgence, but as clearly a disease as opthalmia or stone." His plan for bringing salvation to the alcoholic involved attracting him with food and shelter; then providing stability through temporary employment; and finally transferring him to rural colonies, where he would learn the values of sobriety and responsibility. The vision was that Christian salvation and moral education in a wholesome environment would save the body and soul of the alcoholic.[385]

Salvation Army workers began street outreach with alcoholics as early as 1891. Their first convert was Jimmy Kemp, known as "Ash-Barrel Jimmy" for having become frozen to a barrel while in a drunken stupor. Although the SA offered no specialized treatment services, alcoholics made up a large portion of the clientele when the SA's first "Cheap Food and Shelter Depot" opened in 1891 in New York City. These early depots—called "Lighthouses"—turned away men who were overtly intoxicated, but the sheer number of intoxicated men seeking services over the years led to the development of special detoxification programs with the SA's Social Services Department. In facilities like the San Francisco Lifeboat, the SA created special quarters where intoxicated men could sober up in safety. By 1900 there were more than 700 corps of the Salvation Army scattered across America's cities. From these humble roots, the Salvation Army served alcoholics for more than a century, going on to become what McKinley called in 1986 "the largest and most successful rehabilitation program for transient alcoholic men in the United States."[386]

The Salvation Army tried many innovative approaches in its efforts to reach alcoholics. In 1911 Major W.W. Mitchell organized the "Boozers Brigade" in Jersey City, a makeshift ambulance that picked up drunken men and brought them back to the Industrial Home to sober up on the Major's special detox cocktail—a delicious concoction of raw eggs, Worcestershire sauce, and Epsom salts. Another such approach was "Boozers Day" in Manhattan. On such days, more than 1,000 alcoholics were picked up in Skid Row and transported by buses to a great hall, where they were exposed to a recovery-oriented gospel meeting. In 1914, a band of these converts organized themselves into the United Order of Ex-Boozers, a self-described "fraternal group devoted to the reclamation of other drunkards." Accounts of successful Christian conversion of alcoholics during the early 20th century is recounted in Harold Begbie's *Twice-Born Men.*

During the middle decades of the 20th century, the Salvation Army came to see itself as having a special mission in the reclamation of alcoholics and began to reach out for specialized knowledge that could help it with this mission. In 1939 the Salvation Army opened its first facility specifically designed as an alcoholism treatment center—the Detroit Harbor Lights Corps— under the leadership of Lt. Colonel James Murphy. That same year, the first Alcoholics Anonymous group within an SA center was started in Philadelphia.[387] In the 1940s, the SA committed itself to a broadened approach to treating alcoholism that integrated medical assistance, professional counseling, Alcoholics Anonymous, and Christian salvation. This new vision led to the initiation of formal casework and counseling services for alcoholics in many SA centers. The SA work during this period was heavily influenced by SA officers' participation in the first Summer Schools of Alcohol Studies at Yale. By the 1950s, several of the SA centers had begun to professionalize their alcoholism treatment services by hiring social workers to implement more structured therapy programs.

This move toward professionalization was not an easy one. There remained some conflict within the SA about the nature of alcoholism and its appropriate treatment. Some SA members rebelled against the disease concept of alcoholism in the belief that it reduced the alcoholic's "moral responsibility." A formal SA position paper on alcoholism struck this balance of the spiritual and the scientific:

> *The Salvation Army believes that every individual who is addicted to alcohol may find deliverance from its bondage through - submission of the total personality to the Lordship of Jesus Christ.*
>
> *The Salvation Army also recognizes the value of medical, social and psychiatric treatment for alcoholics and makes extensive use of these services at its centers.*[388]

The Salvation Army developed a practice of hiring some of its own "success stories." In one such story, Tom Crocker sobered up at the Detroit Harbor Lights Corp and, after four years of SA work with alcoholics in Detroit, went on to carry his ministry to Chicago's Skid Row—the Army's Harbor Lights Corps on West Michigan Avenue. Crocker developed a unique involvement with the Chicago courts. Those alcoholics judged to have the best chance at recovery were turned over each day to Crocker's custody. He took more than 3,000 such people in during one six month period.

In 1961, the SA operated 124 men's social centers, with a total daily bed capacity of 10,388—unquestionably the largest alcoholism rehabilitation service in the United States. During the 1970s, the SA expanded its services to alcoholic women and operated a number of social-setting detoxification programs that diverted alcoholics from the drunk tanks of city jails to alcoholism counseling within the SA centers. In spite of such contributions—and perhaps because of its religious orientation—the Salvation Army's work has been little known either by the public or within professional alcoholism-treatment circles. Today, the Salvation Army uses a $200-million budget to treat more than 50,000 alcoholics per year in 150 facilities spread across the United States. What these facilities consistently offer to the alcoholic includes food, shelter, work, counseling, and evangelical Christianity.[389] From its beginning, the SA emphasized elements of experience that would be later incorporated into more formal and professionalized approaches to alcoholism treatment: public confession, spiritual conversion, transformation of personal identity, the construction of sobriety-based social networks, and service to others.

America's Keswick Colony of Mercy

William Raws emigrated from England to the United States in 1889 in an effort to outrun his alcoholism. Following the sudden deaths of his mother and wife—the latter from alcoholism—William Raws underwent a profound religious experience that checked his own alcoholism and incited a desire to carry the message of religious salvation to other alcoholics. He carried this message in the rescue missions of Philadelphia, then founded the Whosoever Gospel Mission and Rescue Home. In 1897, along with his assistant John R. McIntyre, he founded the Keswick Colony of Mercy in Whiting, New Jersey.

The Keswick Colony was inspired by a book entitled *Colonies of Mercy*, which described how a German pastor had established small communities called "Colonies of Mercy," where people who shared similar physical and social handicaps lived and worked together. The Keswick Colony of Mercy provided a program of "spiritual therapy" for recovery from alcoholism. When William Raws died in 1910, his ministry was carried on by his son, Addison Raws—a ministry that he in turn passed to his own son, the Rev. William Raws.

When the number of alcoholic men seeking help from Keswick dramatically declined during prohibition, Keswick expanded its mission to serve as a Christian conference facility. Since 1924, it has continued its twin missions as a spiritual retreat for alcoholics and a conference center for religious renewal. Alcoholics who have the desire for help and are willing to commit themselves completely to the 90-day program of religious education continue to enter America's Keswick Colony. Up to 39 men at a time reside at the colony, undergoing bible study, prayer, and personal counseling. Each man leaving is linked with a religious mentor, and together they form a "pastoral covenant" for continued religious education and support. Men leaving the Colony are also expected to seek continued support through religious recovery groups such as Alcoholics Victorious, Mountain Movers, or High Ground. More than 17,000 alcoholic men have sought shelter and comfort at the Keswick Colony since its founding in 1897.[390]

Like many of the programs described in this chapter, alcoholism recovery at the Keswick Colony was believed to be predicated upon the experience of religious conversion. The Colony is an extension of the 19th-century urban mission movement. There are many other free-standing spiritual retreats in the U.S., mostly in the South, that today specifically serve alcoholics.[391] Many of these facilities are linked within the Christian Alcoholic Rehabilitation Association (C.A.R.A.), which was founded in 1967.

The charismatic branch of Christianity holds out the story of Saul's conversion on the road to Damascus as a metaphor of the personal transformation that was possible for the alcoholic. To be reborn holds out the possibility of a new body and spirit freed from the morbid craving for alcohol and other drugs. The Christian view of addiction has also included the theme that addiction constitutes a worship of the flesh that separates one from other human beings, and from God. In this view, recovery comes both through a respect for the flesh as the "temple of God" and through a transcendence of the flesh.

Early Professional Views on Religion and Recovery

The developmental years of the urban rescue missions and the Salvation Army, which spanned the last half of the 19th century, stimulated increased thinking about the psychology of religion and the role of religion in alcoholism recovery. Many of the late-19th-century addiction experts increasingly came to recognize the potential role of religion in recovery. In 1892, Dr. H.M. Bannister of the Illinois Eastern Hospital for the Insane observed that, "In my opinion, the only chance of reform in many cases of apparently hopeless inebriety is through some powerful stimulus of the higher nature, such as religious conversion."[392] Four years later, J.H. Leuba included in his treatise on the psychology of religion seven case studies of alcoholics who had permanently stopped drinking as a consequence of religious conversion.[393]

George Cutten's 1907 treatise *The Psychology of Alcoholism* included a whole chapter on religious conversion as a cure for alcoholism. Cutten, a Yale psychologist, studied the conversion experiences of alcoholics at the Water Street Mission and at the New York Christian Home for Intemperate Men. He believed that the cure of alcoholism by religious conversion could be attributed to three factors: 1) conversion stimulated a deep desire for reform, 2) the social world of the alcoholic was transformed as a result of conversion, and 3) the spiritual ecstasy accompanying conversion provided a substitute for chemical intoxication. Cutten's description of alcoholic conversion uses such words as "deliverance," "self-surrender," and "rebirth"— words that would fill addiction-recovery literature throughout the century.[394]

Two other texts of note during this period —Starbuck's *The Psychology of Religion* and Monroe's *Twice-Born Men in America*—also noted the role of religious conversion in recovery from alcoholism. Starbuck's writings on the stages of conversion (conflict, crisis, surrender, conversion, regeneration) bear striking resemblance to many tales of alcoholic reformation and recovery.[395] Monroe's text included detailed accounts of the conversion experience of alcoholics within urban missions in America.[396]

While all of these studies shed light on the potential role of religious experience in recovery from alcoholism, none could approximate the significance of William James' *The Varieties of Religious Experience.*

Conversion and Recovery: The Ideas of William James

In 1901 and 1902, William James, a Harvard psychologist and non-practicing M.D., delivered a series of lectures on the psychology of religion at the University of Aberdeen in Edinburgh, Scotland. Published in 1902 under the title *The Varieties of Religious Experience,* these lectures explored—among many issues—the potential role of religious conversion as a cure for alcoholism. Highlights from James' lectures can help us understand how his book would, more than three decades, later play such an important role in the birth of Alcoholics Anonymous.

There was much in James writings that could have touched the alcoholic. He began by suggesting a common thread ran through the quest for religious experience and the quest for intoxication.

> *The sway of alcohol over mankind is unquestionably due to its power to stimulate the mystical faculties of human nature, usually crushed to earth by the cold facts and dry criticisms of the sober hour. Sobriety diminishes, discriminates, and says no; drunkenness expands, unites and says yes.*[397]

James spoke a great deal about melancholy and the lost capacity for pleasure. He spoke of the need to square one's account—to start anew with a clean page— through confession and absolution. He spoke of the healthy-minded who needed to be born only once, and of those with sick souls who needed a second birth to achieve happiness. He spoke of two styles of religious transformation, one gradual and the other sudden and dramatic. It was his writing on the latter—this powerful conversion experience—to which alcoholics would be drawn for decades to help them determine whether they were experiencing a spiritual awakening or a mental breakdown.

James spoke of the "hot place in a person's consciousness....the habitual center of one's personal energy" and noted that it was this center that was the target of the religious conversion.[398] James described in great detail the nuances of the conversion experience and the supra-normal elements often found within such experiences: voices, visions, photisms (lights), awareness of some superior power, overpowering insights, a melting of emotions, a sense of cleansing, raptures (an ecstasy of joy), close connectedness to others, a new and brilliantly clear sense of purpose, and a new spiritual enthusiasm and zest for life.

James was impressed that whole lives could be shaped by conversion experiences that lasted only moments. He believed that the center of the alcoholic's energy—alcohol—could be displaced and a new center could be substituted that could remove the craving for alcohol.

James cautioned the professional helper that intrusive intervention could abort the conversion process. He noted:

> *When the new center of personal energy has been subconsciously incubated so long as to be just ready to open into flower, "hands off" is the only word for us, it must burst forth unaided!*[399]

James believed that conversion experiences should be evaluated based on their fruits. Where the consequences were good, the experience should be celebrated and venerated; where the consequences were bad, it should be ignored, "no matter what supernatural being may have infused it."[400] He cited many examples of alcoholics who were cured via the vehicle of religious conversion, and he offered his oft-quoted dictum that "The only cure for dipsomania is religiomania."

Thirty two years after the publication of *The Varieties of Religious Experience,* a copy of this text was handed to an alcoholic who had just experienced an overwhelming breakthrough that had left him simultaneously hopeful and questioning his sanity. What he found in the pages of James' book helped him label and use this experience to continue his destiny as a co-founder of Alcoholics Anonymous. The alcoholic who received the book was Bill Wilson, whose story we will explore in Chapter Fifteen.

Later Professional Perspectives

Contributions on the role of religion in addiction recovery did not stop with James. In 1912, Partridge studied the work a number of missions in New York and concluded:

> *Facts gathered at the McAuley Mission and at other missions in New York leave no doubt in the mind of the writer that conversion, under the conditions in which the missions are able to accomplish it, is a powerful means of controlling drunkenness.*[401]

Dr. Robert Fleming noted in 1937 that alcoholism treatment involved two stages: 1) medical detoxification and stabilization and 2) substitution. Flemming believed that religious conversion provided an ideal substitute for alcohol—one that transformed the patient's feelings of self-value and provided companionship and emotional exaltation.[402] Dwight Anderson concurred with Flemming by noting that "the conversion (of the alcoholic) must be *to* something as well as *from* something." In this view, addiction turned the beloved drug into an object of worship—a God. The spiritual transformation that is the basis of so many recoveries must help the addict grieve the loss of this God through the discovery of something of greater value.[403]

Critics of Religious Approaches to Alcoholism Recovery

Early critics of the use of religion as a method of curing alcoholism generally fall into two categories.

1. *Religious experience as a vehicle of alcoholism recovery is open to only a small percentage of alcoholics.*

Some of the critics who noted the limited value of religion in alcoholism recovery were themselves religious people. The Reverend J. Willet, in his 1877 text *The Drunkard's Diseased Appetite,* suggested that there was a difference between those drinkers for whom religious conversion would and would not check the drink habit. In his view, many people who drank heavily but were not truly addicted could and often did thrown off drinking and reported that the appetite for alcohol was lost at the moment of conversion. Willett proclaimed that such men were not true inebriates and that religious teachers "possessing more zeal than knowledge" were using these accounts to set forth the "strange and dangerous delusion" that inebriety could be treated simply by religious conversion. During the same period Reverend Willet was writing, the Reverend Charles Warren also challenged the number of inebriates believed to be capable of reformation through religious conversion.

> *It is hard to believe that any man in such a state of voluntarily-induced imbecility, too drunk to hold intelligent converse with men, can be competent enough to transact business with God."*[404]

2. *Religious conversion can actually be harmful to the alcoholic.*

Not everyone viewed the birth of religious fervor as a positive influence on the alcoholic. A Connecticut report recommending the creation of state-sponsored treatment programs for alcoholics cautioned that treatment for some might have effects more harmful than beneficial. Those preparing the report made particular note that the alcoholic might be vulnerable to the substitution of other patterns of behavior for drinking, patterns which might be "equally unrealistic and immature." The authors of the report included religious fanaticism in this category.[405]

In reading religious writings of the late 19th century, one also senses an ambivalence about this power of conversion to cure alcoholism. While some viewed such conversions as affirmation of the power of religious belief, others seemed worried about the potential of transforming religion into a medium of cure—the transformation of a spiritual experience into a secular or domestic tool. Because they considered conversion itself the goal, rather than recovery from alcoholism, these critics seemed concerned that spirituality might be turned into a product or process of the marketplace, to be purchased and used to achieve other ends. That concern would resurface in the 1980s and 1990s.

This chapter has described the potential role of religious conversion in initiating recovery from alcoholism and other addictions. While this potential has been known for some time, it is an option that seems to have been open to only a small percentage of the total pool of actively using alcoholics and addicts. As our history continues, we will see how other groups have met the challenge of trying to expand the number of alcoholics and addicts who would avail themselves of this style of addiction recovery. We will also see in our continuing story the expanding role of the church in training clergy about alcoholism, initiating specialized alcoholism-treatment programs within communities of faith, and developing sobriety-based support structures for recovering alcoholics and addicts within and outside the church.

Chapter Ten
Alcoholism Treatment Settings: 1900-1940

Several 19th-century social institutions that had borne the brunt of care and control of the alcoholic —the almshouse, the inebriate home, and the inebriate asylum—faded in the early decades of the new century. As almshouses evolved into institutional settings for the care of the aged and inebriate asylums closed or evolved into psychiatric hospitals, a vacuum was created that for a time left many communities without any significant resources for the care or management of the alcoholic. Newly emerging and existing community institutions bore an increased burden of responsibility for the care of alcoholics. These institutions included 1) the inebriate farm (colony), 2) the local general hospital, 3) the local psychopathic hospital, 4) the state insane asylum, and 5) the private hospital or sanitarium. In this chapter we will describe how these institutions responded to the alcoholic in the first four decades of the 20th century.

The century opened with growing concerns about a highly visible group of indigent alcoholics. A turn-of-the-century social welfare journal, *The Survey*, noted the explosive growth of public intoxication and posed a question that became a consistent refrain within the culture: "What shall be done with this large and ever-increasing body of men who are a menace to the public at large and an enormous expense if arrested and kept confined?" Although proposals set forth in answer to this question pointed out the need for the psychological rehabilitation of the alcoholic, nearly all efforts of intervention deteriorated into programs of social control. Municipal courts came to be increasingly clogged with "old rounders"—chronic alcoholics who were repeatedly arrested for public drunkenness and related offenses. A 1916 study of 100 people arrested for public drunkenness revealed that these people had a total of 1,775 prior arrests. The growing visibility of the public inebriate sparked calls for specialized hospitals and farm colonies for inebriates.[1]

The Inebriate Farm/Colony [2]

The very idea of an inebriate colony grew out of the perceived failure of the inebriate asylum to address problems created by a growing mass of drunken and often homeless men and women. The asylums'

successful treatment of a small number of well motivated, affluent alcoholics and their frustrated efforts to reform those court-committed to their care had done very little to relieve the growing burden that drunken men and women placed on public hospitals and public jails.

Proposals for Alternative Institutions: A central figure who set forth new proposals for the treatment of the public inebriate was Dr. T.D. Crothers. The ways in which Crothers' ideas evolved demonstrate the growing pressure for an institution that could divert chronic alcoholics from both health care institutions and the criminal justice system.

In 1891, Crothers advocated the creation of industrial hospitals for alcoholics, located close to all large cities. He suggested that these facilities be supported by taxes levied on the manufacture and sale of alcohol.[3] Two years later, he advocated the creation of reformatories, hospitals, or work-houses for "pauper inebriates," institutions that would recognize the inebriate "as a diseased person, not a criminal."[4] By 1902, Crothers was advocating a more elaborate system of care for inebriates that consisted of involuntary hospital detoxification followed by placement in a rural "farm colony" for sustained rehabilitation.[5]

This push for an alternative system of care for the chronic inebriate began to be picked up by civic and legislative bodies. A 1910 report entitled *Drunkenness in Massachusetts* called for the creation of a farm colony for incurable inebriates, where they might be "kept at productive labor apart from criminals and under medical care."[6] Dr. Frederick Peterson called for the creation of a "Temperance Island," funded by alcohol taxes, where inebriates could be sequestered and made to live productive lives.[7]

Proposals for "farm colonies" and "industrial hospitals" for alcoholics were, in part, a vehicle of quarantine through which it was believed the contagious quality of addiction could be checked. Early 20th-century farm colony proposals drew support from a growing eugenics movement that believed sustained quarantine, if not conducive to rehabilitation, might provide a means of birth control that would prevent alcoholics from creating new generations of social misfits.

Another source of support for the sequestration of

alcoholics came from the leaders of charitable institutions, who believed that alcoholics were unworthy of public charity and that they misused charitable resources to support their drinking. It was thought that the social quarantine of alcoholics would ensure that scarce charitable resources would go to the truly deserving—those whose problems were not a result of moral lassitude.[8]

Of all of these proposals, the one that came closest to fruition was the inebriate farm. During the early 20th century, states such as Massachusetts, Iowa, and Minnesota created state farms for the punishment and rehabilitation of criminal offenders. The representation of alcoholics in these farms grew so high that there were inevitable calls for specialized farms for inebriates. Inebriate farms were operated in Connecticut, Massachusetts, New York, Iowa, Minnesota, Pennsylvania, and California.[9]

The Operation of an Inebriate Farm: The New York City Hospital and Industrial Colony was initiated in 1912 by the New York Board of Inebriety—a board established in 1910 for the express purpose of providing for New York City "a hospital and industrial colony for the care, treatment and occupation of inebriates."[10] The inebriate farm occupied 697 acres in Warwick, New York and accommodated 100-200 men, who were committed to the facility for periods ranging from one to three years. The eventual capacity of the inebriate colony at Warwick was projected at 1,000 inebriates.[11] The farm colony was an effort to reduce the problems and costs of public drunkenness, and an effort to provide a milieu that might contribute to the alcoholic's rehabilitation. The farms gave the alcoholic a mix of medical care, moral encouragement, and hard work as an alternative to a jail cell.[12]

From Inebriate Farm to County Farm: The inebriate colony never fully emerged as a viable institution. What did endure for many decades was the use of other institutions to control—"treat" is probably not an appropriate word—the chronic alcoholic in the municipal or county jail, the county farm or workhouse, and—for some—the state psychiatric hospital.[13] These institutions provided brief reprieves for the physical restoration of many alcoholics. The back wards of aging state psychiatric and correctional facilities are as close as the U.S. ever came to the widespread implementation of inebriate colonies.

Criminal justice approaches to alcohol inebriety themselves regenerated calls for specialized treatment institutions. When Austin McCormick reviewed social response to alcoholics during the first four decades of the 20th century, he noted that "a veritable army" of alcoholics was passing through police stations, courts,

and jails every year—and that alcoholics were more often harmed than helped by this treatment. Noting that the practice of sentencing alcoholics repeatedly to probation or to jail for short sentences was creating a "revolving door," McCormick claimed that alcoholics would be helped only by the application of scientific treatment.[14]

While the police, courts, and jails were increasingly called upon to socially control the public inebriate, another institution took up the brunt of the physical care of alcoholism, in spite of its reluctance to assume this role. That institution was the city hospital.

Alcoholism and City Hospitals

Long before being admitted to inebriate farms or state psychiatric asylums, most alcoholics had gone through dozens, if not hundreds, of admissions to these local hospitals. Care of the alcoholic in the community hospital consisted primarily of medical detoxification, treatment of acute alcohol-related trauma and diseases, and—in some cases—treatment of alcohol-induced psychiatric disorders. A brief look at how two hospitals—Boston City Hospital and New York City's Bellevue Hospital—responded to demands placed upon them by alcoholics will illustrate the growing importance of this institution in the lives of alcoholics. Like many hospitals, Boston City Hospital officially excluded alcoholics but found itself forced to admit them. The alcoholic was a difficult and expensive medical-management problem for the large city hospital. Such management usually consisted of isolating alcoholics into "foul wards"— as Boston City Hospital did in the 1870s—or of acts like the 1908 directive that declared: "No people having acute venereal disease or alcoholism, shall be admitted except as a paying patient." These kinds of practices reflected the view of alcoholism as a self-induced condition that was more a reflection of moral weakness than medical illness. This attitude had changed very little three decades later, when Drs. Merrill Moore and Mildred Gray reflected that—in spite of the lack of welcome—more than 70,000 alcoholics had been admitted to Boston City Hospital since it opened.[15]

At Bellevue Hospital in New York City, the story was not much different. Alcoholics and the mentally ill were treated in the same wards until 1879, when a separate "Insane Pavilion" was erected and an "inebriate ward" was organized.[16]

The care of alcoholics placed an incredible demand on Bellevue Hospital, a demand that called for their placement in one of two basement suites known as "the cells." The diagnosis of alcoholism accounted for

3,428 admissions to Bellevue in 1889; five percent of those patients died from the sheer exhaustion of sustained delirium.[17] The number of annual admissions rose from 4,190 in 1895, to as high as 11,300 during the opening years of the 20th century. These admissions dropped to 2,000 per year during the early prohibition years (1920-1921), but climbed to more than 8,000 by 1930. By 1936, alcoholics constituted 40% of Bellevue Hospital's 25,000 annual admissions.[18]

By the late 1930s, staff at most hospitals expressed great pessimism regarding recovery from alcoholism.[19] One of the hospitals that responded to a 1944 national survey of treatment resources reported that its staff viewed alcoholics as "a disgusting, disagreeable annoyance." Only a handful of doctors expressed interest in treating alcoholism. But amidst this bleak landscape, a few treatment specialists were beginning to develop a vision of the future of the medical treatment of alcoholism. One of the most remarkable of such visions was set forth by Dr. Robert Fleming in the pages of the prestigious *New England Journal of Medicine* in 1937:

> *If there could be created an Institute for the Study of Alcoholism where the biochemist, the internist, the psychologist, the anthropologist, the psychiatrist, and, possibly, the theologian working cooperatively could each bring to a common focus, on the manifold problems of alcoholism, his own special knowledge, then it should be possible to remove from this field some of the ignorance, prejudice and charlatancy that characterizes it today.*[20]

With those words, Fleming anticipated the multidisciplinary approach to the treatment of alcoholism that would emerge in the 1940s and 1950s.

Alcoholics in Local Psychopathic Hospitals and State Psychiatric Hospitals

In an era of progressive reform that roughly spanned the years 1880 to 1920, alcohol and the disordered behavior of the alcoholic were defined both as threats to public health and as forces that could undermine the new middle class's search for stable community life.[21] As the number of public inebriates increased at the turn of the century, concern focused as much on treating the alcoholic's disordered and disruptive behavior as on treating the alcoholism itself. As a result, many alcoholics were routed through the general hospital or police authorities to two other

institutions: the local psychopathic hospital and the state psychiatric hospital.

While 19th-century psychiatry was dominated by large insane asylums, the first move toward community psychiatry was the creation of an intermediate step between the home and the state psychiatric hospital. That step, the local psychopathic hospital, emerged between 1890 and 1920. The psychopathic hospital served as a local "receiving" facility, where those suffering from acute mental illness could be assessed, stabilized, and— if possible—treated and discharged to return home. When discharge was not a good option, the patient was sent on to the state psychiatric asylum. Where it was available, the local psychopathic hospital assumed responsibility for the assessment of the alcoholic and management of alcohol-induced psychiatric disorders. Communities that lacked these local resources relied on the state psychiatric hospitals to provide this service.

Nearly all early 20th-century addiction specialists believed that sequestering alcoholics within a medically supervised milieu was essential to the effective treatment of the alcoholic. However, one of the major problems faced in such treatment was the fact that most alcoholics would not voluntarily remain in such institutions long enough to be treated. Some states found a way to solve this problem.

Legal Commitment to Insane Asylums: As the inebriate asylums declined and were replaced by psychiatric asylums, efforts were made to increase the access of alcoholics and addicts to the latter. States like Illinois, New Jersey, Pennsylvania, and Delaware broadened their admission criteria to include state psychiatric facilities, so that alcoholics and addicts could be admitted and treated.[22] The statutes provided for the legal commitment of alcoholics for periods ranging from one year to the term defined in states like Iowa and Montana: "until the patient is cured."

Institutional Surveys: In 1917, the National Committee for Mental Hygiene conducted a national census of 571 institutions that cared for the insane, "feebleminded," epileptics, and inebriates in the United States. Twenty-three institutions provided specialty care for inebriates, while some 120 institutions provided care for a mix of the above-mentioned groups of patients. At the time of the survey, 4,891 inebriates were receiving institutional care. The survey revealed that four states (Connecticut, Iowa, Massachusetts, and Minnesota) and one municipality (New York City) had publicly sponsored specialty institutions for the treatment of inebriety. The states with the largest numbers of inebriate patients in private treatment in the survey were New Jersey, Illinois, New York,

Pennsylvania, Massachusetts, and Connecticut.[23]

E.H. Corwin and Elizabeth Cunningham's 1940 post-prohibition survey of alcoholic admissions to state psychiatric facilities revealed no state-sponsored institutions specifically for the treatment of alcoholism. Their survey revealed 5,840 admissions to state psychiatric facilities for "alcoholism without psychosis" and another 4,621 admissions for "alcoholic psychoses." The states with the largest number of alcoholic admissions included California, Illinois, Virginia, North Carolina, Wisconsin, Iowa, Texas, and Kentucky. Corwin and Cunningham identified 72 private psychiatric institutions that had treated a total of 4,754 alcoholic patients during 1940, but 12 of these institutions accounted for 3,497 of the patient admissions. The survey found only 22 private institutions that specialized in addiction treatment. With a total bed capacity of 389, these institutions admitted 6,689 patients for treatment during the year 1940.[24]

Treatment in State Psychiatric Hospitals: The majority of alcoholics admitted to state psychiatric facilities were admitted for acute alcoholic withdrawal or for alcohol-induced psychoses. Many states prohibited the admission of alcoholics into state psychiatric facilities if they were not psychotic, and a few states—such as New Mexico—prohibited their admission even if they were psychotic. Most non-psychotic alcoholics in the U.S. did not have access to such facilities. When they did have access, what was treated was not alcoholism, but the psychiatric consequences of alcoholism. Stays for non-psychotic alcoholics were quite short. Even states such as California, which had inebriate commitment laws, could not keep addicts and alcoholics hospitalized. The superintendents of these facilities, irritated by the institutional shenanigans of detoxified alcoholics, merely pronounced them cured and precipitously discharged them—to the delight of most patients and the chagrin of many communities.[25]

There were two groups of alcoholics and addicts who found their way into state hospitals—and both groups, once detoxified, were among the highest-functioning patients in the hospitals. Alcoholics in the first group, branded as incurable psychopaths, were an unending source of mischief to other patients and to staff. State hospital administrators had struggled for a century to keep this group out of their institutions. A second group of alcoholics and addicts made a much more peaceful adjustment to institutional life. These individuals developed long-lasting relationships characterized by a cycle of 1) periods of stable institutional adjustment, in which they operated as a

highly valued unpaid labor force, 2) interruptions in this stability produced by periodic binges following either discharge or elopement, and 3) re-admission.[26]

Treatment for alcoholism in state psychiatric hospitals was based on the view that alcoholism was a symptom of underlying emotional disturbance—a view that subjected alcoholics to whatever psychiatric treatments were in vogue. These treatments ranged from the ineffective but benign "rest cures" to more physically intrusive treatments that will be described in detail in the next chapter.

Overall, alcoholics fared poorly in state psychiatric hospitals. These institutions had experienced explosive growth between 1890 and 1940—a growth that had left them over-crowded, understaffed, and increasingly serving a custodial function. The staff of most state psychiatric facilities had no training in alcoholism treatment, and few specialized alcoholism treatment units existed. It is not surprising that treatment outcomes for alcoholics at these facilities were described by their own staff as "uniformly poor" and that there were calls for special institutions to treat alcoholism.[27] Alcoholics were warehoused in these environments until they could be released and free once again to resume their drinking careers—or until they became highly institutionalized and lived out their lives in the back wards of these institutions.[28] Horatio Pollock's 1932 review of national alcoholism admissions to state psychiatric facilities noted that 25% of first admissions died in the hospital and that another 20 to 25% faced future readmission.[29]

Drying Out the Rich and Famous: A Continuing Story

While indigent alcoholics filled beds in community hospitals, local jails, county farms, and the back wards of public psychiatric hospitals, affluent alcoholics sought discreet assistance in an all-but-invisible American social institution: the private sanitarium. The small private sanitarium or private hospital replaced the large institutional inebriate asylum, and did so with little public recognition of this transition.

Some private sanitaria specialized in the treatment of addictions, while others included addictions within a broader umbrella of care for various physical and "nervous" disorders. There were a large number of private sanitaria and hospitals that specifically advertised their ability to treat alcoholism and other addictions between the years 1900 and 1940.

In the early decades of the 20th century, private

sanitaria catering to alcoholics found themselves facing a shrinking clientele, due to the growing number of states implementing alcohol prohibition. The response was an increased aggressiveness in their advertising campaigns. Facilities such as Dr. Sheldon's Sanitarium in Springboro, Pennsylvania advertised their cures for the liquor and drug habits with the bold proclamation: "We have no failures."[30] Although these private facilities struggled in the early years of prohibition, they began to flourish during the later years of prohibition and the post-repeal period.

One should not assume that sanitarium treatment was of uniformly high quality simply based on the fact that they served an affluent clientele. In their review of the private sanitaria, Corwin and Cunningham emphasized the importance of seeing such facilities as offering a service not otherwise available:

Whatever their virtues and failings, it must be remembered that, one and all, they offer a refuge to patients who are frequently refused help by other more sanctimonious hospitals.[31]

Two stories illustrate the workings of these private facilities. The first is an account of one alcoholic—Willie Seabrook—who underwent treatment at a private psychiatric hospital that occasionally and reluctantly admitted alcoholics; the second is the story of one very special private institution, the Charles B. Towns Hospital for the Treatment of Drug and Alcoholic Addictions.

The Saga of Willie Seabrook

The attitudes toward alcoholics and the techniques used to treat alcoholism in private psychiatric hospitals during the early decades of the 20th century are well illustrated in the story of William Seabrook. A reporter turned adventurer, Seabrook used his travels to generate such popular books as *The Magic Island* and *The White Monk of Timbuctoo*. Like many successful American writers of his day, Seabrook was drawn to the literary world of Paris, where he lived for many years, associating with the likes of Aldous Huxley, Gertrude Stein, and Thomas Mann. And Willie drank—eventually two bottles of Courvoisier Brandy a day. His drinking eventually crossed over the line that Seabrook himself had defined as alcoholism. With the help of friends, he made arrangements to return to America, where he voluntarily committed himself on December 5, 1933—the day Prohibition was repealed—to the Bloomingdale Asylum for the Insane.

Willie Seabrook's treatment, his views about his alcoholism, and his psychiatrist's view of alcoholism are well documented in a book that Seabrook later wrote about his experiences. He was first detoxified with the aid of sedatives and bromides, and by a hydrotherapy technique commonly referred to as "wet packs."

My nerves jangled like cracked fire alarms....pretty soon the prize-fighter and another husky came in, carrying what looked like the hotel wet-wash. They fixed the bed so it wouldn't soak through to the mattress, then laid me straight and naked on the bed with my arms pressed along my sides like a soldier lying at attention and began swathing me, rolling me on one side and then the other, in tight wet sheets....I was flat on my back. Except that my head stuck out and lay comfortably on a pillow, I was the mummy of Rameses....This was the famous 'pack.'....After a while my mind began to work, and I discovered that I liked it.[32]

Once detoxified, Seabrook entered the ward life of the asylum—days filled with various crafts (occupational therapy), exercise, books, movies carefully selected so as not to inflame the emotions, nutritious meals, and periodic visits with various psychiatrists. The attitude of psychiatrists toward alcoholism in the 1930s is exemplified by Dr. Quigley, who complains to Seabrook, "Every time we've taken a drunk in this place, we've regretted it."

Willie's keepers, like most psychiatrists of this era, viewed alcoholism as a symptom of underlying emotional disorder—a view that implicitly held out the potential for regaining control over one's drinking if such underlying problems were resolved. After spending six months in the Asylum, Willie was discharged with the agreement that he would abstain from all forms of alcohol for at least another six months before he tested himself by exposure to drinking. Willie kept this agreement but began drinking in the months following his year of self-imposed sobriety.

During the months of sobriety and the months of resumed drinking, Willie completed a book on his experience in treatment, in which he expressed great confidence that the emotional difficulties that caused his alcoholism were now successfully resolved. His best evidence of this cure was that he was writing again and had not returned to his pattern of binge drinking. In the closing paragraph, he notes his capacity to drink now and then without difficulty and proclaims: "I seem to be cured of drunkenness."

The book, *Asylum*, was published and widely read—offering many alcoholics and their family members renewed hope for a "cure." Unfortunately, Willie Seabrook's ability to drink without problems was not sustainable. His drinking reverted to its former pattern. In the years that followed the success of *Asylum*, he visited many other asylums for treatment but never achieved sustained sobriety. William Seabrook committed suicide with an overdose of sleeping pills in 1945. He was 59.[33]

The Charles B. Towns Hospital for the Treatment of Drug and Alcoholic Addictions

The saga of the Charles B. Towns Hospital is the story of a most fascinating institution created by a most fascinating man.

Charles B. Towns was a tall, well built man who "radiated an animal vitality." He was so personally persuasive and dominating that some observers even questioned whether the results of his treatment for addiction might be more attributed to the power of his personality than to the medical protocol used at his hospital.[34] As one physician noted, "The Towns treatment would be all right if you could mix in about a grain of Towns with every capsule of the specific."[35]

The Hospital's Founding: With a background in farming, railroading, life insurance, and the stock market, Charles B. Towns—according to his own self-constructed mythology—became interested in addiction through a mysterious stranger he met in a bar shortly after he had left Georgia in 1901 to seek his fortunes in New York City. The unnamed stranger told Towns that he had the formula for a cure for the drug habits that had been discovered by a country doctor, and that he and Towns could make a lot of money selling the cure.[36] Intrigued with the possibilities, Towns began reading about addiction and experimenting with the stranger's formula. A racetrack worker whom Towns persuaded to take the cure—and who was then held against his will until the cure was complete—became Towns' first success.

This serendipitous beginning led in 1901—the year of Leslie E. Keeley's death—to the opening of the Charles B. Towns Hospital for Drug and Alcoholic Addictions. The hospital operated out of humble quarters on 82nd and 81st streets before settling into its permanent quarters at 293 Central Park West in New York City. Other hospitals that used the Towns

Treatment were established later, including one that opened near Boston in 1910.[37] His first patients came by word of mouth—the word spreading among the addicted, telling of a new cure for their affliction.

When Towns first opened his hospital, addiction treatment came in the form of several-month asylum stays, in the form of several-week stays in a small inebriate home, or through various outpatient clinics or home cures. Towns attacked nearly all of these options as ineffective and fraudulent. He created a unique niche for himself and his institution by providing short-term medical detoxification and treatment in a hospital-oriented setting that welcomed and comforted the alcoholic and addict. Towns' initial specialty was the treatment of opiate addiction, but when patients who were also addicted to alcohol reported losing their craving for strong drink following their treatment, Towns began to formally solicit alcoholics to enter his hospital.[38]

Early Recognition: The "Towns Treatment" received little professional recognition until 1904, when Towns introduced Dr. Alexander Lambert to his procedures. Lambert was the perfect instrument to help spread this new treatment. He worked at Bellevue Hospital, served as a Professor of Clinical Medicine at Cornell University, and was politically active in the American Medical Association. Lambert's patronage brought Towns and his treatment some degree of professional credibility and led to its frequent designation as the "Towns-Lambert Treatment."

Lambert was also a friend of Theodore Roosevelt, and this connection brought Towns in contact with Secretary of War Taft for discussions regarding the opium problem in the Far East. While his hospital continued to operate, Towns, stirred by Taft's portrayal of the Chinese opium problem, went to China in 1908 and spent 13 months trying to organize hospitals to use his treatment. His efforts were frustrated by the Chinese government and led to a confrontation that saw Towns sitting on the steps of his Charles B. Towns Anti-Opium Institute, one revolver in hand and one on his hip, defying a governmental order to take down the sign advertising his Institute. Eventually, a compromise was reached that allowed Towns to remain in China for several months while he established hospitals in Peking and other cities. He claimed to have treated more than 4,000 Chinese opium addicts before returning to America and the management of his own hospital.[39]

Unlike Keeley and other purveyors of treatment "specifics" for addiction, Towns revealed the nature of his addiction cure, under the encouragement of Dr.

Lambert. He first shared the formula at the International Opium Conference in Shanghai in 1909, and followed this with publication of the full clinical protocol in articles published through Dr. Lambert and other physicians in mainstream medical journals between 1909 and 1911.[40]

The Hospital and Its Promotion: The Charles B. Towns Hospital operated across from New York City's Central Park and boasted of its exclusive view of "Millionaire's Row" on Fifth Avenue. The building itself was a five-story apartment building with a solarium on the roof. No sign declared that this building nestled in among residential apartment buildings was a hospital whose primary purpose was the treatment of alcohol and drug addictions. Entering the building gave one the feeling of entering, not a hospital, but a private and quite exclusive hotel.

While many other addiction treatment establishments operated in competition with mainstream physicians, Towns desperately sought mainstream medical credibility for his facility. He published his treatment protocol in the *Journal of the American Medical Association* and marketed almost exclusively to physicians. His marketing materials reinforced the idea that the Towns facility was a "hospital" in every sense of the word and invited physicians to participate openly in the treatment of their patients at the Towns Hospital.[41]

Towns walked a fine line in promoting his hospital to physicians. On one hand, he wanted potential patients and their physicians to know that this was an exclusive hospital. The promotional literature explicitly promised individual rooms or suites, absolute privacy, individualized meal service, private telephones, and—if the patient so desired—the services of a personal nursing attendant, valet, or florist.[42] All of this could be theirs, along with relaxation in a heated solarium that boasted of easy chairs and couches, singing birds, a library and a billiards table, and a panoramic view of Central Park. While such comforts beckoned many an affluent patient, Towns was also aware that too much comfort could be a source of criticism. Promotional literature from the same decade declared:

> *My hospital is no homelike place with broad verandas, sunlit lawns and spreading shade trees, where patients are made comfortable by coddling, urged to feel at home and tacitly implored to come again....my institution is a hospital....it is not in the most remote sense a sanitarium.*[43]

Perhaps sensitive to the growing image of his Hospital as a drying-out place for the wealthy, Towns later opened an Annex (immediately behind his Central Park facility) at 119 West 81st Street, where he provided treatment to patients of moderate means.

Through Towns' knack for garnering public and professional recognition, the Towns Hospital became an exclusive drying-out place for the political, social, and economic elite. Through most of the hospital's years of operation, each patient was assessed a specific fee at admission that covered all costs of treatment. In 1914, fees at Towns Hospital ran from $200 to $350 for drug treatment ($75 in the Annex) and $75-150 for alcoholism treatment ($50 in the Annex).[44]

Charles Towns claimed that some 7,000 patients had been treated at his Hospital in its first 27 years of operation.[45] The diversity of the types of addictions presented by the patients entering Towns Hospital is indicated by the patient-admission data for the year 1915. In that year, the hospital treated 693 men and 189 women, 573 of whom were addicted to alcohol, with the remaining patients addicted to other drugs, most of the narcotic family.[46]

Towns' Views on Addiction: Charles Towns attacked nearly every prevailing approach to the treatment of alcoholism and other addictions. He attacked the constant recycling of alcoholics and addicts through the courts and jails and characterized repetitive episodes of "drying out" as "foolishly futile."[47] He characterized home treatment as an assured failure and sanitarium treatment as a form of exploitation, but was adamant in his claim that addicts could be successfully treated in hospitals.

Towns viewed the etiology of alcoholism and drug addiction as a problem of cell pathology. And yet, interestingly, Towns considered the notion that alcoholism was a disease an "absolutely absurd" proposition. In Towns' view, alcoholism was the product, not of some underlying disease pathology, but of the body's systematic poisoning by alcohol and other drugs. In Towns' view, this poisoning of the alcoholic's tissue "set up a craving that in its cumulative effect, sweeps him along like a piece of driftwood on the surface of a stream." Towns called for treatment methods that could "unpoison him (the alcoholic) physiologically and thus set him free psychologically."[48] While physiological factors dominated Towns' views of the etiology of addiction and its treatment, he did acknowledge that addiction was "highly individualistic" and that recovery required that the "defects in the personality be laid bare."[49]

Towns believed that his treatment could unpoison the addict, free the addict from his or her morbid cravings, and restore physical and emotional stability, leaving the addict then to his own choices and consequences.[50]

Towns was quite visionary in many of his ideas about addiction treatment. Consider his anticipation of the modern employee assistance movement in the following recommendation from 1916:

I would like to see the state authorities unite with the municipal authorities in this matter: they could begin with the employer by trying first to save the man who has a job but will lose it unless he stops drink; educate the employer to his responsibility in trying to save such a man.[51]

More than 50 years later, federal and state alcoholism authorities funded occupational alcoholism specialists to do precisely what Towns had advocated.

The Towns Treatment: Dr. Alexander Lambert described the Towns Hospital treatment in several medical articles published between 1909 and 1912.

The treatment which was given me by Mr. Charles B. Towns....is the one which seems in my experience to more quickly and thoroughly unpoison the mind and system from alcohol than any other treatment....Briefly stated, it consists of belladonna, hyoscyamus and xanthoxylum. This mixture is given every hour, day and night, for about fifty hours. There is also given about every twelve hours a vigorous catharsis of C C pills and blue mass. At the end of the treatment....castor oil is given to clean out the intestinal tract, and the reconstruction treatment of tonics is begun.[52]

Alcoholics were treated with the same formula as were morphine addicts, but the treatment took less time, and greater care had to be taken in monitoring the alcoholic's response to the treatment, because they were more susceptible to experiencing delirium under the influence of belladonna.[53] Alcoholic patients admitted to Towns were quickly phased off alcohol (with the alcohol replaced by sedatives), while the regime of Towns medications was begun.

Towns referred to the remedy-aided detoxification as "treatment," and to the inpatient physical rehabilitation that followed it as "rational

after-treatment" or "recuperative treatment." This after-treatment involved combinations of specialized diets, exercise, massage, hydrotherapy, and "electrical baths."[54] One's overall stay at Towns Hospital could be as short as four to five days for alcoholism or as long as eight to fourteen days for various drug habits. Upon discharge, each patient was referred back to his or her original physician for follow-up.

There was one particularly striking difference between the milieu of the Towns Hospital and that of the other treatment institutions we have described. While other institutions sought to promote camaraderie between patients in addiction recovery, the Towns Hospital almost barred such contact. The Towns promotional literature emphasized that patients did not come into contact with one another. This practice seems to have been aimed at ensuring patient privacy.[55]

Reported Success Rate: The success rate of the Towns treatment was variably reported by Charles Towns to be between 75% and 95 percent.[56] As in many treatment institutions of this era, success was often defined as the percentage of clients who did not return for additional treatment.

Dr. Alexander Lambert claimed that this treatment not only provided successful detoxification, but also resulted in a "cessation of desire" for intoxicants. But Lambert's calculation of success was quite different from that offered by Charles Towns. In a follow-up report of patients treated at Bellevue Hospital using the Towns method, Lambert reported that 18 (21%) of 85 patients had remained abstinent 18 months following treatment. Lambert noted that this was a "far better result than one could expect from the usual method of treatment."[57]

Towns Hospital—The Later Years: Charles Towns died on February 20, 1947. Towns Hospital continued into the modern era as an exclusive addiction hospital under the direction of Charles' son, Colonel Ed Towns. The hospital in these later years continued to serve as an exclusive drying-out hospital for wealthy alcoholics, who would sometimes call ahead to schedule a bed before they began a drinking spree, or after they had set the termination date for their current binge.[58]

John White, in his autobiographical account *Ward N-1*, described the way in which most mid-century alcoholics viewed the Towns Hospital.

I could check in for a week in Towns Hospital, where bored but expert doctors and nurses knew how to tide you over the horrors of a hangover—if you had the price....You walked out of Towns a bit shaky—but clear-minded, the alcohol wrung out of your tissues, ready to face the world—until your next binge.[59]

The Legacy of Charles B. Towns: Charles Towns deserves note in this text for many contributions to the addictions field.

There is Charles B. Towns the thinker. Towns' writings on addiction described and brought to popular understanding the most essential elements of physical addiction: 1) increased tissue tolerance, 2) an identifiable withdrawal syndrome following cessation of drug use, and 3) craving and compulsive drug-seeking behavior. Towns was also an astute observer of the nature of various drugs. He was adamant in his belief that cocaine would turn out to be one of the most dangerous and addictive of drugs and was one of the first to recognize the addictive potential of the new "hypnotic" barbiturate and non-barbiturate sedatives.[60]

There is Charles B. Towns the critic and activist. He was one of the most vocal advocates of federal drug-control legislation and was the author of New York's Boylan Law, upon which the federal Harrison Narcotic Act was based. He advocated alcohol prohibition, control and monitoring of the production and distribution of all psychoactive drugs, control of access to hypodermic syringes, and universal access to treatment for all addicts. He believed that large cities should establish "alcoholic clearinghouses," where alcoholics could be properly classified and treated, and that each state should set aside one institution for the specialized treatment of alcohol and other drug addictions.[61]

There is Charles B. Towns, proprietor, promoter, huckster. His medical protocol is not part of his lasting legacy, but his institution safely detoxified thousands of alcoholics—although the number of permanent cures is open to question. The Charles B. Towns Hospital does, however, play a most unique role in our continuing story of addiction treatment in America. An alcoholic was admitted to Towns Hospital in 1934 whose enduring recovery changed America's very conception of alcoholism, profoundly touched the lives of millions of alcoholics and their family members, and redefined the very nature of alcoholism treatment in the 20th century. We will pick up the thread of this aspect of the Towns legacy in Chapter Fifteen.

We have seen in this chapter how the void left by the collapse of the 19th-century inebriate homes and asylums was filled—in part—during the early 20th century, by new social experiments (inebriate farms and colonies) and by the assumption of expanded responsibility for the care of alcoholics by local psychopathic hospitals, state psychiatric hospitals, and private hospitals and sanitaria. We will pause in our review of the evolution of the system of alcoholism treatment to explore in greater depth the physical and psychological methods used to treat alcoholism and other addictions.

Chapter Eleven
Physical Methods of Treatment and Containment

This chapter will detail the physical methods used to treat alcoholism between 1840 and 1950. The methods described were used in a wide variety of settings: the private physician's office, the general hospital, inebriate homes and asylums, the psychopathic hospital, the state psychiatric asylum, and the private hospital and sanitarium.

Physical Treatments for Alcoholism Between 1840 and 1950: An Overview

In the 19th and early 20th centuries, physical methods of treating alcoholism unfolded within the broader evolution of American medicine. During this period, the medical field was struggling to establish itself as a science, in the face of conflicting schools of theory, treatment, a plethora of health fads, and sects. Having escaped the era of blistering and bloodletting, and the pervasive use of harsh cathartics and emetics, American medicine was seeking to distinguish itself from the quacks, imposters and folk healers. This chapter will detail the dominant beliefs and methods that marked the physical treatment of alcoholism between 1840 and 1950—both the science and the fads—and their current scientific status. Physical methods used in the treatment of narcotic addiction, particularly the drug therapies, will be discussed in a later chapter. From the mid-19th to the mid-20th centuries, physical approaches to the treatment of alcoholism came and went and sometimes returned again as if newly discovered. This period saw the introduction of drug therapies, mechanical manipulation, surgical alteration, natural therapies (water, air, sunlight), and chemical- and electro-convulsive therapies. Many of these methods were used in combination, particularly where the popularity of an older method continued as a new method was being introduced. As far as possible, we shall try to tell this story in the sequence in which it unfolded. But first, we shall explore one of the most physically invasive solutions to the problem of alcoholism ever proposed: mandatory sterilization.

Eugenics: Sterilization and Benign Neglect

In 1883, Francis Galton, cousin of Charles Darwin, coined the term "eugenics" to describe a new field that sought to improve the human race through the scientific manipulation of heredity. The initial strategy advocated to create this gifted race was the careful selection of marital partners across successive generations. Later, a "negative eugenics" branch of this movement sought to decrease or eliminate breeding by those judged to be the most unfit of the human stock. Negative eugenics grew out of the 19th-century notion of degenerationism: the belief that most social problems, such as alcoholism, crime, feeblemindedness, insanity, laziness and poverty, were passed on biologically in more severe forms in each new generation. Seriously flawed degeneracy studies, from Richard Dugdale's 1877 study of the Jukes family to Henry Goddard's 1912 study of the Kallikak family, added an aura of scientific validity to the notion that social problems and their resulting social costs were a product of bad breeding. The idea of cumulative degeneracy produced by alcoholism provided a foundation for bold strategies for using social engineering to reduce alcoholism and its social costs.[62]

Views on Alcoholic Degeneracy: The idea of hereditary degeneracy permeated the writings of many turn-of-the-century addiction experts. These experts, whose opinions filled the *Journal of Inebriety* as well as the popular press, pushed the notion that parents addicted to alcohol and other drugs begat children with vulnerability to inebriety, feeblemindedness, prostitution and criminality, psychic manias, and an unending list of physical infirmities. As early as 1888, Clum identified inebriety as the primary cause of insanity, idiocy, pauperism, criminality, and disease. The notion that parental inebriety led to the

hereditary transmission of physical and mental diseases to their progeny regularly appeared in hygiene texts of the day.[63] T.D. Crothers' 1902 depiction of the moral degeneracy of the offspring of alcoholics is typical of this literature.

Often the higher moral faculties of the person are undeveloped, and the children of alcoholized people are born criminals without consciousness of right and wrong, and with a feeble sense of duty and obligation[64]

Turn-of-the-century medical and temperance reports claimed that unchecked parental alcoholism would lead to "racial suicide." Reports of miscarriages, still births, imbecility, and a wide spectrum of other physical defects in the alcoholic's progeny led to calls for radical intervention.

There was a general belief at the turn of the century that alcohol contributed to natural selection by helping to kill off weaker members of the human species. Eugenists such as Popenoe and Johnson argued that, through the principle of natural selection, alcoholism actually weeded out weak racial stock.

By killing off the worst drunkards in each generation, nature provides that the following generation shall contain fewer people who lack the power to resist the attraction to the effect of alcohol, or who have a tendency to use it to such an extent as to injure their minds and bodies.[65]

This position provided a rationale for benign neglect of the alcoholic, in the optimistic view that time and natural selection would eliminate the problem. Proposals in this category included denying degenerate individuals and their families public relief, as a means of speeding their demise.[66] A growing number of people, however, were suggesting that this natural process be speeded up through marriage bans; sexual segregation; exclusion of degenerate immigrants; and mandatory, state-funded sterilization of degenerates.[67] Dr. Agnes Sparks spoke directly to this last recommendation in an 1898 *Journal of Inebriety* article:

Granting the [alcoholic] woman has been given treatment, proper, persistent, and prolonged, without avail, she should be desexualized....It might be curative; it surely would be preventive, and better, by far, unsex the woman, than have her beget a brood tainted with this curse of the world.[68]

Archibald Reid's 1901 text, *Alcoholism,* further typified this view.

It is in our power by copying Nature, by eliminating not drink but the excessive drinker, by substituting artificial for natural selection, to obviate much of the misery incident with the latter, and thus speedily to evolve a sober race.[69]

It was argued that the costs of these various proposals would be supported by the reduced need for state institutions and state services. The arguments for purification of the race and a reduced burden on public resources struck a responsive cord. The most radical of all eugenics proposals was that of involuntary sterilization. Surgical breakthroughs, such as the development of the vasectomy, gave the eugenics movement new technologies that its leaders believed could weed out the bad genetic seed within the American culture.

The "Surgical Solution": Broader social forces also generated momentum for mandatory sterilization of particular groups of people. The eugenics movement of the early 20th century tapped some of the most primitive issues within the changing American culture: growing fears about the explosive rate of foreign immigration, repugnance toward what was perceived as increasing miscegenation between Blacks and Whites, and a rising fear that a shrinking able population would be responsible for growing hoards of the mentally defective, the insane, the criminal, the infirm, and the chronically drunk.

This was the primitive soil in which the eugenics movement flowered. Involuntary sterilization laws sprouted next to restrictionist immigration laws, legal bans on interracial marriages, and laws providing for the prolonged social segregation (institutionalization) of people who were likely to pass on defective genes. Involuntary sterilization laws came in two waves: 1907-1913 and 1923-1929. Fifteen states passed sterilization laws before 1922, and two thirds of all states went on to pass some type of involuntary sterilization law. As a result, more than 60,000 Americans were subjected to involuntary sterilization during the first 60 years of the 20th century.[70]

In the opening decades of the 20th century, sterilization of the chronically addicted was proposed as a strategy of treatment and prevention. According to its advocates, involuntary sterilization would achieve two goals simultaneously. It would reduce the "irritating physical causes" of alcoholism, and it would eliminate the genetic transmission of alcoholism and other defects to subsequent generations.[71]

Such proposals increased at the turn of the century. In 1899, Dr. S. Vines advocated the "the castration of all drunken men and the spaying of all drunken women."[72] In his 1903 presentation to the Iowa State Medical Society, Dr. George Boody outlined his medical view on the role of alcoholism in genetic degeneracy and declared that the propagation of physical and moral degenerates by their alcoholic parents was a "crime against the race and 20th-century civilization." He advocated the passage of laws that would "compel the administration of such treatment as would prevent them (alcoholics) from reproducing their kind, and yet leave them able to live useful lives."[73]

Sterilization of Alcoholics: Involuntary sterilization laws caught the alcoholic and addict in their net because the language of these laws frequently gave administrators and officers of asylums discretionary power to sterilize those people who in their judgement (as provided in the 1913 Iowa law) "would produce children with tendency to disease, deformity, crime, insanity, feeble-mindedness, idiocy, imbecility, or alcoholism."[74]

Some eugenics-inspired laws specifically targeted alcoholics and addicts. Indiana passed a law in 1905 which prohibited marriages of any people who were mentally deficient or habitual drunkards. Iowa passed a law in 1911 that made inmates of public institutions who were involved in crimes or drug addiction eligible for sterilization.[75] Male alcoholics were not primary targets for sterilization, due to the fact that most were single, were middle aged or older, suffered from multiple medical problems, and were often impotent.

While sterilization of alcoholics was "voluntary" in many states, by mid-century there existed a coercive influence that could be brought to bear on such individuals. In the 1960s, this author interviewed a number of alcoholic women who had been committed to state psychiatric facilities in the 1940s and 1950s. Many of these women reported that they were not discharged until they submitted to "voluntary" sterilization. In reviewing the medical records of these women, it became apparent that they were subjected to pressure for sterilization the moment that excessive drinking appeared in their history.

The institutional pressure for sterilization of

alcoholic women was, according to the patients I interviewed, based on three concerns: 1) the fear of defective progeny (and a stereotyped presumption of promiscuity), 2) the belief that these women's psychiatric impairment would render them unfit parents, and 3) the view that the demands of parenthood would likely exacerbate psychiatric illness and result in repeated hospitalizations. Philip Reilly's studies confirm that this pervasive practice of "de-institutionalization contingent upon sterilization" was common in state psychiatric hospitals.[76] The actual number of alcoholic men and women subjected to mandated or coerced sterilization procedures in the United States is unknown.[77]

Ideas about alcoholism drawn from the American eugenics movement reached their most extreme application in Nazi Germany. The problem of alcoholism as viewed by the Nazis was that it wreaked enormous social costs before it finally killed the alcoholic or, in their words, "alcoholism harms too many but kills too few." The Nazis identified more than 200,000 people considered to be hopeless because of constitutional vulnerability to alcoholism. They passed laws in the mid-1930s that denied alcoholics the right to marry and provided legal authority for judges to include mandatory sterilization in their sentencing of alcoholics. Between 20,000 and 30,000 German alcoholics were subjected to forced sterilization during the Nazi reign—an incredible number, but far short of the total number targeted by the Nazis for such treatment.[78]

Natural Therapeutics

Many inebriate homes in the 19th century evolved methods of treatment that were based on the assumption that a process of natural recovery would unfold within many alcoholics if only they could be sequestered in an environment that promoted physical and moral health. This approach evolved out of a broader philosophy of treating health problems known as Natural Therapeutics. Dr. Henry Lindlahr, the author of a 1919 text entitled *Natural Therapeutics,* described this approach to alcoholism treatment.

The active treatment of alcoholism must include everything that is good in natural methods. Of primary importance is a strict vegetarian diet, alternating between raw food, dry food, milk diet and fasting regimen. Tonic cold water treatments, massage, Swedish movements, neurotherapy, curative gymnastics, air and sun baths and every-

thing else conducive to a thorough regeneration of the system must be applied systematically.[79]

Natural therapeutics, which also relied upon educating and strengthening the "moral nature," grew out of the "moral suasion" branch of the asylum movement. What this meant in terms of physical methods of treatment was that alcoholics were isolated from their normal environments, detoxified, then exposed to a wide spectrum of "natural" treatments intended to spark a process of physical and moral regeneration. These methods included the following:

Specialized Diets: Between 1840 and 1940, many alcoholism treatment facilities prescribed special diets that they believed would speed the physical recovery of the alcoholic. These diet regimens tended to lean toward vegetables and grains. Some facilities were completely vegetarian and told their patients that alcoholic cravings would continue to be excited by their exposure to red meat. The emphasis on diet did serve to mollify the malnutrition that most alcoholics experienced. Diet treatments for alcoholism included the widely proclaimed salt, orange, apple, lemons, date, grape, banana, watermelon, raisin, and onion cures.[80] Most such "cures" used a particular dietary product that its advocates claimed cleared the system of toxins and reduced cravings by serving as a substitute for alcohol.[81]

Exercise: Exercise was a common part of the regimen of early inebriate homes and asylums. Daily life in these homes often involved walks on the grounds. Some medical directors even prescribed special types of exercises that they thought particularly conducive to recovery. In his 1913 text *The Narcotic Drug Disease and the Allied Ailments,* Dr. George Pettey recommended physical training as an essential part of the addiction treatment regime. His text included 22 exercises that his patients had found helpful in speeding their recovery from addiction.[82] Specialized exercises were often combined with steam baths and body massage as means of extracting the poisons out of alcoholics and addicts who were detoxifying. Private sanataria and hospitals catering to alcoholics boasted of their extensive array of exercise equipment.

Leisure: There were three fairly distinct stages in the use of leisure activity as a part of alcoholism treatment. In the inebriate asylums, constructive leisure was thought to have a positive physical and moral effect, so most asylums came equipped with libraries and billiard rooms. Literature, music, and lectures were all carefully selected to simultaneously educate and uplift, while being careful not to overstimulate the physical appetites. During the following era of the private sanataria, leisure focused more on activities that could provide pleasing entertainment for their affluent clientele. In the era of alcoholism units in state psychiatric hospitals, structured leisure became almost non-existent, as daily life in many such units deteriorated to an agonizing boredom—a condition that by the middle of this century sparked discussion of the need for recreational therapy on such units.

Work: The idea that work had therapeutic value, and the practice of assigning responsibilities as a part of one's daily life in treatment, ebbed and flowed between 1840 and 1940. Work responsibilities (chores) were a normal part of early asylum life. In the Washingtonian Homes, male residents assisted with the daily upkeep of facilities while female residents tended to the vegetable gardens and helped with food preparation. It is open to question whether such work was assigned for its therapeutic benefit or was absolutely essential to run these institutions with only a few paid staff members.

Although work as a therapeutic endeavor seems to have disappeared from the regimen of the private sanataria, it returned within the inebriate colonies and alcoholism units of state psychiatric hospitals. Alcoholics sentenced to inebriate farms or industrial colonies worked every day. In fact, they did little else, because few therapeutic activities existed in these facilities. The theory behind this design was a belief that productive work in the open air, such as in tending crops and livestock, gave the body and mind time to return spontaneously to a healthy pre-drinking state. Many alcoholics in state psychiatric facilities became quasi-staff, performing many needed facility-maintenance details and support functions for other patients. While this activity may indeed have had therapeutic effects, there is little question that alcoholics were exploited as an unpaid labor force.

Natural Elements: Inebriate homes, asylums, and most private sanataria that treated addictions were run on the premise that healing could be speeded by exposing alcoholics and addicts to the natural elements. "Elements" could be defined here as sun, air, and water, or cures involving elements from the earth, such as the bark, iron, steel, and gold cures. Private sanataria that served primarily to detoxify and physically renew alcoholics often used a combination of very benign treatment interventions. For example, in the mid-1930s, methods of treating alcoholism at the Bloomingdale Hospital in White Plains, New York included rest, special diets, increased fluid intake, warm baths, and wet packs.[83]

Many treatments for inebriety emphasized the importance of exposure to the sun, and one finds "sun baths" occasionally listed as a treatment method in the advertisements of private sanataria catering to inebriates. Others emphasized exposure to air—which ranged from extended periods out of doors and sleeping with open windows to exotic mechanical devices called "air boxes." But exposure to sun, air and metallic cures paled in comparison with the role that water played in the treatment of alcoholism and other addictions from the mid-19th to the mid-20th centuries.

The Water Cures

Water as a therapeutic agent long preceded its application to the treatment of alcoholism and other addictions. The use of water in Native American medicinal and religious rituals dates to antiquity.[84] Known first as "hydropathy" and then more popularly as "hydrotherapy," the application of water as a commercialized healing agent was brought to the United States from Europe by Dr. Simon Baruch and popularized by such health reformers as Dr. J.H. Kellogg. More than 200 water cure institutions were founded between 1840 and 1900.[85]

The buildings of the water cure institution were often divided into a lodging hall, the bath areas, and—not infrequently—a gymnasium and dance hall. Often combined with special diets, exercise, massage, electro-therapeutic treatments, natural medicines, and exposure to sun and fresh air, the water cure treatments promised hope for disorders ranging from piles to tuberculosis. The water cure itself consisted of baths, douches, sprays, steams, vaporizers, hot and wet packs, and inhalers. Water was taken into and drawn out of the body through every possible orifice.

Water and Inebriety: Water and its relationship to inebriety has a long history in America. In his 1774 essay, *The Mighty Destroyer Displayed,* Benezet recommended using water to progressively dilute alcoholic drinks, as a way of weaning alcoholics from the habit. Dr. Benjamin Rush, during the same period, recommended cold showers in the treatment of alcoholism and cold water as an alternative to alcohol. During the years in which hydrotherapy was becoming an American craze, water came to symbolize abstinence in a flourishing temperance movement. Temperance groups were part of the "cold-water army" who enlisted men to take the "cold-water pledge," and those going into treatment for inebriety were sometimes said to be taking the "water cure."

Temperance workers felt so strongly about the power of water that they lobbied cities to provide safe drinking water as an alternative to alcohol.[86]

When one spoke of taking the "water cure" for addiction, those words had numerous potential meanings. First, the phrase could refer to the shift from alcohol as a drug to water as a beverage—a practice frequently referred to as "going on the water wagon." There were also various mineral waters advertised as specifics in the treatment of alcoholism —consumed orally as restoratives and suppressants of alcoholic cravings. There were also the hydro-therapies: baths, sprays, steams, douches, and hot and wet packs used to relieve the inebriate's pain, induce perspiration, and generally sedate or stimulate (depending on the choice of hot or cold sprays/packs.)[87]

Hydrotherapy Institutions: Alcoholics received hydrotherapies in four institutional settings: the water cure establishment, the inebriate asylum, the lunatic asylum (which became the large state psychiatric hospital), and the private sanitarium. Water cure institutions caught the attention of many alcoholics during the mid-19th century, for two reasons. First, the fact that the water cure institutions treated so many health problems meant that they could be used for physical remediation of addiction to alcohol and other drugs without any public acknowledgment of the nature of one's problem. Many alcoholics sought out water cure institutions while masking their true condition behind such vague labels as "neuralgia" or "nervous exhaustion." Second, water cure institutions specifically cultivated the alcoholic's business through various advertising media. Water cure institutions served as "drying out" facilities before and during the early years of the inebriate asylums. Inebriate asylums and private inebriety homes incorporated water therapies into their treatment regimens to compete with the water cure establishments.

Water cure institutes seemed a logical choice for alcoholics because hydrotherapy practitioners demanded abstinence from the most popular stimulants of the day (alcohol, tobacco, coffee, and tea) and provided a reasonable regimen of detoxification for all but the most severe cases of alcohol addiction.[88] The attention of many alcoholics was caught by writings such as the 1859 pamphlet entitled "The Turkish Bath: An Antidote for the Cravings of the Drunkard," which promised that the craving for strong drink would disappear under the baths' influence.[89] Places like the Jackson Health Resort in Dansville, New York claimed that their pure spring water could reverse the "systemic poisoning and accumulated waste matters"

produced by the over-indulgence in alcohol. Articles and advertisements in *The Water Cure Journal* noted that large quantities of water had a cleansing and sedating effect on the constitution of the inebriate. Water cures were held out to be the "open sesame" of temperance—a medium of both treatment and prevention.[90]

Alcoholics found themselves drinking and being injected with mineral water while they were bathed, showered, steam-bathed, and wet-packed. But the expense of the water cure institution had physicians complaining that only one in 20 of their patients could afford such treatment. The water cure sanitarium served primarily as a place where the affluent addict could periodically (and ironically) dry out and bolster his or her resolution to refrain from future bouts.[91]

The use of hydrotherapy in the treatment of alcoholism can be traced from the mid-19th century water cure establishments to the inebriate asylums, then on to the early-20th-century private sanataria and insane asylums. If there is a single institution that bridged these eras, it would most assuredly be Dr. John H. Kellogg's Battle Creek Sanitarium in Battle Creek, Michigan. Dr. Kellogg incorporated many of the methods of the water cure institutions, participated actively in the American Association for the Study and Cure of Inebriety, and continued to treat inebriates long after other, more specialized inebriate asylums had closed their doors. Kellogg's hydrotherapy techniques included: steam baths; hot, cold and neutral baths; needle spray showers; hot and cold water sponging; douches; towel rubs; wet packs; and frequent water-drinking—all combined with electric light baths, hot enemas, electrical stimulation, massage, manual exercise, specialized diets that eliminated the meats and spicy sauces (which were thought to stimulate cravings for intoxicants), and fresh air. These methods were used, not only for the rapid detoxification preferred by Kellogg, but also during the following months of convalescence at the sanitarium.[92]

The therapeutic value of water—both its internal and external use—in the treatment of addiction continued for more than a century. As late as the 1940s, addiction specialists were still advocating water (plain or mixed with lemon or orange juice) as the only effective substitute for drugs, and into the 1950s, alcoholics and other addicts were routinely being "wet packed" in state psychiatric hospitals.[93]

Drug Therapies: 1860-1930

As noted in our earlier discussion of treatment in

the inebriate asylums, many early drug therapies were used in the treatment of alcoholism. In his 1868 text *On Chronic Alcohol Intoxication,* Marcet noted Huss' recommendation of the use of fusel oil and opium in the treatment of acute alcoholic withdrawal. Dr. W. Marcet preferred oxide of zinc as an agent of detoxification and continued fortification.[94] In his 1890 text *The Homeopathic Treatment of Alcoholism,* Dr. Gallavardin recommended 14 remedies, claiming that—administered in high potencies—these remedies would "destroy the inclination to get drunk." His remedies included nux vomica (strychnine), sulphur, opium (especially recommended for Brandy drinkers), mercury, and arsenic.[95] Drugs used to detoxify and treat alcoholics between 1860 and 1930 also included such agents as whiskey and beer; cannabis indica, chloral hydrate, paraldehyde, veronal and other sedatives; coca; hyoscyamus, belladonna, and atropine; nauseants such as apomorphine; and a wide assortment of other pharmacological concoctions. Treatments ranged from the mainstream to the exotic. We will briefly review a few of both kinds.

The search for effective drug treatments for alcoholism focused for a brief period on one fascinating possibility: the development of an alcoholism vaccine.

The Search for an Alcoholism Vaccine: Between 1899 and 1903, there were reports that temporarily stirred hope of the discovery of an alcoholism vaccine. The initial idea put forth by Sepalier and Dromard was that certain antibodies were produced in response to alcohol exposure, in a manner similar to the way the body responds to infection. They thought that these antibodies might prove useful in the treatment of alcoholism. To test this hypothesis, they gave horses high doses of alcohol until physical dependence was established. Those horses' blood was then injected into other horses, who were reported to respond with a revulsion for alcohol. An anti-alcohol antibody named "equisine," extracted from horse blood, was developed by Evelyn in San Francisco. The antibody was applied to the scarified skin of alcoholics over a period of nine weeks. Human trials using this method proved inconclusive.[96]

Morphine as an Alcoholism Treatment: One of the most unusual of the drug therapies for alcoholism, by today's standards, was the substitution of opiates for alcohol. By far the most outspoken advocate of this approach was Dr. J.R. Black, who, in an 1889 article in the *Cincinnati Lancet-Clinic,* advocated addicting incurable alcoholics to morphine. Black began his article with the pessimistic conclusion that he had never seen a case of permanent reformation of

an alcoholic in his 40 years of medical practice. He noted that many claims of such reformation were really a form of hidden drug substitution—the replacement of alcohol with opium. While noting that alcoholics themselves often made this surreptitious switch, Black went on to recommend that physicians aid their alcoholic patients in such substitution. Black advocated the systematic replacement of alcohol with morphine on the following grounds: 1) morphine is cheaper and less socially and economically devastating to the alcoholic and his family, 2) morphine replaces the alcoholic's uncleanliness, cruelty, profanity, and boisterous public comportment with a quieted, soothing demeanor, 3) morphine is far less damaging to the organs and the patient's longevity than is alcohol, and 4) there is less hereditary degeneration associated with morphine than with alcohol. Black boldly raised the duty of the physician to pursue what today would be called "harm-reduction" strategies when attempts at cure have failed. Black urged the "substitution of morphine instead of alcohol for all to whom such a craving is an incurable propensity."[97]

Sedatives, Tonics, and Specifics: Two other products used during the late 19th and 20th centuries in the treatment of alcoholic withdrawal were paraldehyde and chloral hydrate—substances that themselves became drugs of abuse. Chloral hydrate was used in the sanitarium treatment of alcoholism as early as 1879, and paraldehyde was used in the treatment of alcohol withdrawal in the early 1880s. Most physicians preferred to treat alcoholism using a combination of drugs that produced a tonic or stimulant effect with drugs that were purported to destroy one's appetite for alcohol. Dr. C. McBride recommended a series of treatments aimed at removing the craving for alcohol and instilling a distaste for alcohol. McBride's regimen called for injections of a mixture of nitrate of strychnine, sulfate of atropine, and tincture of capsicum. The effectiveness of this therapy was tested by giving each patient a four-ounce bottle of whiskey, along with the communication that the patient could drink the whiskey if he or she so wished.[98] Drs. Albright and Smith recommend the following as tonics in the treatment of addiction: passiflora, hydrastis, gentian, and cinchoma.[99] In his 1918 article on the treatment of addicted soldiers at Camp Lee, Major J.M. Scott noted the frequent use of hyoscin, scopolamin, and atropin in private sanitarium cures for addiction.[100]

Early Resistance to Drug-Based Therapies: Not all addiction specialists used drugs in their treatment regimens. Dr. J.H. Kellogg, for example, was unequivocal in his opposition to such intervention.

> *I have no hesitancy in saying that any system of treatment of the opium or alcohol habit, or any other form of drug addiction which depends for its success upon the administration of a substitute drug is, and must be, a failure....I find no advantage whatever in the use of potash, chloral, hyoscyamus, and the numerous other drugs which have been so largely used in these cases.*[101]

Those who objected to drug interventions were a small but vocal minority among 19th- and early 20th-century addiction experts.

Convulsive Therapies

Convulsive therapies resulted from the 1934 observation by Dr. J.L. Meduna that agitation and depression in a patient subsided following a seizure. During 1935 and 1936, seizures were induced through the use of a drug such as metrazol or cardiazol, in an effort to achieve this effect. This practice was discontinued when patients complained of the extreme terror they experienced just before onset of the seizure. Metrazol injections were replaced after the 1938 discovery by two Italian doctors, Cerletti and Bini, that an alternating electrical current passed through the brain could produce the same seizure without the terror associated with the metrazol.[102] This marked the beginning of electroconvulsive therapy, commonly called "ECT" or "shock therapy." The use of these therapies increased through the 1930s, and they were widely used in the 1940s and 1950s. The convulsive therapies were used primarily in the treatment of depression, but were also applied to the treatment of alcoholic psychoses. They were sometimes used experimentally in an effort to alter the pathological craving for alcohol or to alter the personality that was viewed as the root of a patient's alcoholism.[103]

Several reports exist on the use of convulsive therapy in the treatment of addictive disorders. A number of alcoholics whom I interviewed in the 1960s and early 1970s reported having received ECT while in state psychiatric institutions. Their stories reveal a rationale for such use that included the treatment of depression, a condition that was thought to undergird their alcoholism. There were also reports of capricious use of ECT in response to the antics of alcoholics who embarrassed, frustrated, or challenged the institutional staff. Unfortunately, there seem to have been non-fictional counterparts to Ken Kesey's character Randle Patrick McMurphy in *One Flew Over the Cuckoo's Nest.*

Psychosurgery and Addiction: The Lobotomy Era[104]

One of the earliest recommendations for surgery (other than sterilization) as a treatment for addiction came in a 1902 article in the *Journal of Inebriety* written by Dr. H.A. Rodebaugh of the Park View Sanitorium in Columbus, Ohio. Rodebaugh described a number of inebriety cases he had treated at Park View, in which the patients had developed alcohol or other drug problems in an attempt to self-treat painful medical conditions. Rodebaugh demonstrated that, when such conditions as hemorrhoids and rectal fissures were corrected surgically, the patient's excessive use of anesthetizing drugs stopped.[105] While Rodebaugh's suggestion of surgery as an addiction treatment tool might sound bizarre by today's standards, he was actually operating out of a mainstream tradition in the inebriate asylum era, in which the self-medication of acute and chronic medical problems was viewed as a major etiological factor in the onset of inebriety. Rodebaugh's surgical procedures were a logical extension of the inebriate specialists' propensity to treat the underlying exciting cause of inebriety. The surgical procedures that resurfaced at mid-century proved to be much more controversial.

In 1935, the Portuguese neurologist Egas Moniz introduced a surgical technique, the prefrontal leucotomy, into the field of psychiatry. In this procedure, an instrument was introduced into the prefrontal lobes, to destroy the nerve fibers that link the frontal lobe with the thalmus. After refinement with 20 patients, the procedure was renamed prefrontal lobotomy and described broadly as psychosurgery. The first psychosurgery procedures in the United States were conducted by Drs. Walter Freeman and James Watts in 1936. Their 15th lobotomy patient was an alcoholic who had been subjected to this procedure on the grounds that the surgical alteration of personality would alter the patient's pathological craving for alcohol. Following this procedure, the patient dressed and, pulling a hat down over his bandaged head, slipped out of the hospital in search of a drink. Freeman and Watts spent Christmas Eve, 1936, searching the bars for this patient, whom they eventually found and returned to the hospital in a state of extreme intoxication.[106]

Another case is noted in the autobiography of Dr. William Sargeant, who records the following observations of his interview with a chronic alcoholic who had been lobotomized in the early 1940s:

> *The alcoholic commended the operation highly: he said he could now drink half his ordinary amount of whiskey and get twice as tight! Obviously, it had done his alcoholism no good and perhaps a great deal of harm: he was much less tense but of course did badly later on as he continued drinking heavily. I remember his broad smile...saying, "My! it had been a first-class operation."*[107]

Alcoholics also became candidates for psychosurgery under different circumstances. The view that the etiology of chronic alcoholism was an aberration of character—the alcoholic personality, or an attempted escape from psychic pain—opened up the theoretical potential that psychosurgery could eliminate the fueling passion for excessive drinking. There are also anecdotal reports of psychosurgery being used as the ultimate tool of retaliation in the power struggles between psychiatric staff and alcoholic patients, who as a group were notorious for their challenges to authority in institutional settings.

The only systematic study of the effects of lobotomy upon drinking behavior is that of Talbot, Bellis and Greenblatt. These Harvard researchers studied the post-surgical effects of 473 bilateral prefrontal lobotomies performed at the Boston Psychopathic Hospital. Of the total sample, 179 post-surgical patients were discharged into the community and had access to alcoholic beverages. Of those, 20 patients had prior diagnoses of alcoholism. Of the 20, ten showed increased severity of alcoholism after surgery, five showed improvement following surgery, and five revealed no change in their pre- and post-surgical drinking patterns. What is interesting is that some patients who had not had alcohol problems before surgery developed alcohol problems following the surgery. Other observations of the effects of lobotomy upon alcoholism included reports that patients' alcohol tolerance decreased after surgery and that many lobotomized patients exhibited a bland, unconcerned attitude toward their alcoholism following surgery.[108]

Between 1944 and 1960, 100,000 psychosurgery procedures were performed in the U.S. The number of alcoholics and addicts who underwent this procedure is unknown, but the literature on psychosurgery noted the viability of this technique in treating "compulsive hedonias:" alcoholism, drug addiction, excessive eating and sexual deviations.[109] Following the heyday of psychosurgery in the U.S., reports of the potential use of brain surgery as a treatment for alcoholism have continued.[110]

Psychosurgery as a treatment for alcoholism stopped primarily due to consistent reports that such procedures had only a "negligible" effect on the alcoholic's drinking behavior. The use of psychosurgery in the treatment of addiction provides a cautionary tale that shows how great harm can be done in the name of good. The elaborateness and eloquence of the clinical rationales used to perform such procedures could not long mask the fact that this was clinical power gone mad.

Miscellaneous Treatments

Other physical treatments for alcoholism employed between the mid-19th and mid-20th centuries included the application of electrical current believed to stimulate the growth of damaged nerve tissue and the exposure of alcoholics to hot-air boxes and light boxes that mimicked the climatic conditions of the equator, where alcoholism was rare. There were massage treatments and vibrating machines. There were treatments involving oxygen inhalation and injections of calcium salts. There were treatments involving injections of glucose and insulin, and sugar taken by mouth. There were treatments involving spinal puncture. There were institutions that used combination treatments involving the sequenced use of sedatives, purgatives, tonics, apomorphine, hydrotherapy, and "electric" treatments "as needed." There were institutions that reported treating alcoholics with "typhoid fever therapy "and "colonic irrigation therapy."[111]

Indeed, many unusual physical treatments were proposed for alcoholism, but perhaps none was as unusual as that proposed by a physician in a 1900 medical journal. Based on his observation that alcoholics lost interest in drinking while suffering from an active case of gonorrhea, the physician suggested inoculating alcoholics with gonorrhea as an economical alternative to institutional treatment.[112]

✠

Chapter Twelve
Psychological Approaches to Alcoholism and Addiction

While physical approaches to treating the alcoholic and the addict evolved as described in the last chapter, a number of psychological approaches also began to be woven into the treatment technology. In differing degrees, all of these approaches left legacies that can be found in contemporary treatment. In this chapter we will look at three therapeutic models: psychoanalytic approaches to addiction and recovery, the lay therapy movement, and aversion therapy.

The Psychoanalytic Approach

During most of the 20th century, psychoanalytic thinking exerted a profound influence on the perception and treatment of alcoholics and addicts by physicians, psychiatrists, and other helping professionals. Psychoanalytic theory was introduced into the United States in the first two decades of the century and gained particular cultural prominence by mid-century. The infusion of psychoanalytic ideas into the American culture at large, stimulated in great part by Freud's lectures at Clark University in 1909, enhanced the view that a wide variety of behaviors could be the results of hidden forces over which the individual had no conscious control.

The first psychoanalytic interpretation of habitual drunkenness was a 1908 essay by Karl Abraham. Abraham attributed chronic drunkenness in men to an unresolved oral dependency that resulted in alcohol's replacement of women as a sexual object. According to Abraham, drinking was the sexual activity of the alcoholic.[113] He proclaimed that "every drinking bout is tinged with homosexuality" and that men grasp at alcohol as a substitute for their "vanishing procreative power."[114] This view of alcoholism as a manifestation of latent homosexuality continued well into the second half of the 20th century. In an interesting note, this view was frequently applied to male alcoholics, but only rarely applied to female alcoholics.

What most distinguished the psychoanalytic view of addiction was the belief that alcoholic drinking and addictive drug use were not primary disease entities, but symptoms of neurotic conflict or underlying psychosis, or manifestations of a disordered personality. The evolving psychoanalytic literature linked substance abuse to a wide variety of maladies:

"arrested psycho-sexual development," "impulse neuroses," "character disorders," "perversions," "oral-narcissistic fixations resulting from forced weaning," "primary maternal identification," "compulsion neuroses," "masochism," "slow suicide," "infantile narcissism," "mother fixation," "fear of castration," and "latent homosexuality."[115] Most psychoanalysts viewed addiction, not as a self-contained disorder, but as a failed strategy of self-help—an alternative to emotional maturation. Addiction to a drug was viewed, not in terms of psychopharmacology, but as a repetitive, maladaptive behavior in the same symptomatic category as kleptomania, gambling, Don Juanism, pyromania, or bulimia.[116] To elaborate, we will review the key ideas of some of the early proponents of psychoanalytic theories of addiction.

Psychoanalytic Theories of Alcoholism and Other Addictions

Freudian and Early Neo-Freudian Theories: Freud and many of his followers viewed addiction as a sign of distorted psychosexual development. Freud referred to masturbation as the one "primary addiction" and believed that all the other addictions were a substitute for this activity. He also described alcoholism as a fixation at the oral stage of psychosexual development and as a symptom of repressed homosexuality. He did note its practical effect of "keeping misery at a distance."[117] Psychoanalytic writings contend that the retarded psychosexual development that was the basis of alcoholism was itself caused by maternal neglect or overindulgence. Such aberrant parenting, as the theory went, created an "alcoholic personality" characterized by strong dependency needs, grandiosity, low frustration tolerance, and impulsiveness. Neo-Freudians, such as Alfred Adler, viewed the etiology of alcoholism not in terms of disordered sexuality but in terms of the alcoholic's overwhelming feelings of inferiority and social discomfort.[118]

William Stekel: The views of Dr. William Stekel, a close associate of Freud, are typical of early thinking about the disorder that Stekel called "narcotomania."

The drink craving....is always a serious

mental conflict....Morbid sexual life plays the chief role. Drunkards suffer from serious paraphilias (sadism, necrophilia, paedophilia, zoophilia, etc.). Nearly all of them are latent homosexuals; they are incestuously fixed; in milder instances they are victims of an unhappy love affair. They are unable to obtain their sexual objective or have lost it.[119]

Stekel also noted the ease with which other symptoms could coexist with or replace the drink habit. He noted how the alcoholic's "impulsive temperament" also revealed itself in kleptomania, pyromania, gambling, or excessive spending. Stekel, like most of his early psychoanalytic counterparts, concluded that the "only rational method for the treatment of dipsomania and narcotomania is psychoanalysis."[120]

Ernst Simmel: Simmel suggested that drug use was an effort to resolve castration anxiety. He believed that drug use was an aggressive act that sought to symbolically poison the source of such anxiety: the mother.[121]

Sandor Rado: Sandor Rado, a psychoanalyst who devoted considerable time to the study of addiction, coined the term "pharmacothymia" to represent his view of the craving for drugs and the "craving for magic" that were at the heart of addictive disorders. Rado focused on the ability of drugs to induce euphoria and alleviate emotional discomfort. He saw addiction as meeting progressive needs: 1) a "pharmacothymic regime" that combated depression and provided a shield against internal stimulation; 2) an autoerotic ritual that substituted the more widely available pharmacological orgasm for the more complicated interpersonal orgasm; and 3) a self-destructive reflection of masochism and the death instinct. According to Rado, it was only when the addict had reached a point of "pharmacothymic crisis"—when internal pain surpassed the pharmacological defense—that successful treatment and recovery were possible. He went on to note that, even in such crises, many addicts wish, not a drug-free state, but to "rehabilitate the depreciated value of the poison."[122]

Karl Menninger: Karl Menninger, like most psychoanalysts, focused on alcoholism as a deadly but superficial symptom. Menninger stated unequivocally that alcoholism was not a disease but "a suicidal flight from disease, a disastrous attempt at self-cure of an unseen inner conflict."[123] His speculations on this alcoholism-generating inner conflict include references to childhood injury, unspeakable terrors

and fears, repressed hostility, and oral fixations (alcohol as "mother's milk"). Menninger viewed alcoholism as a vehicle of self-cure, as a strategy of infantile revenge, and as a medium of self-destruction ("chronic suicide"). Menninger believed that the only appropriate treatment for alcoholism was "a complete and thoroughgoing reconstruction of the entire personality," and that the only treatment that could achieve such a goal was psychoanalysis.[124]

The influence of psychoanalytic thinking about alcoholism—and a whole spectrum of other problems—spread rapidly through American culture in the first half of the 20th century. Under this influence, alcoholism came to be seen as a symptom of underlying psychological pathology. It was in this context that investigations such as a 1943 study of drunkenness in wartime Connecticut concluded that this condition was "a late-appearing symptom of a complex maladjustment."[125] This view that alcoholics were abnormal before they started drinking, and that the only way to treat alcoholism was to treat the underlying psychological disturbance which spawned alcoholism, carried forward into the modern era and overlapped the re-emergence of the counter-view that alcoholism was a primary disease. Modern psychoanalysts have come to view alcoholism and drug addiction as springing from multiple etiological roots, all interacting in a "vicious circle of mutual reinforcement and malignancy."[126]

Psychoanalytic Treatment Methods

Robert Knight described the psychoanalytic approach to treating alcoholics at the Menninger Sanitarium in Topeka, Kansas in the late 1930s. Knight believed that alcoholics could be treated only in a controlled and restricted environment. As to the Menninger Sanitarium's understanding of alcoholism in this period, Knight was adamant: "alcoholism is only a symptom, not a clinical entity."[127] Given Knight's view of addiction as a symptom of severe characterological disturbance, the goal of treatment was nothing less than the reconstruction of the alcoholic's personality. But Robert Knight and Karl Menninger emphasized that the traditionally detached role of the psychoanalyst had to be changed in treating alcoholics. They believed that the alcoholic's great need for affection had to be met within the treatment relationship, rather than merely analyzed and interpreted. The treatment relationship was itself viewed as a substitute for drinking.

Knight described three subgroups of alcoholics seen at the sanitarium in the 1930s. First of all, there were "essential alcoholics," whose oral fixations and dependency conflicts were solved through excessive drinking. Knight referred to this group as psychopaths and noted their poor prognosis for recovery. Second, there were "reactive alcoholics," whose onset of excessive drinking could be traced to a precipitating event. These alcoholics had greater histories of success prior to the onset of their alcoholism and had a better treatment prognosis. Finally, there were the "symptomatic alcoholics," whose drinking was "only incidental, not the major symptom." Treatment was described as a process of working through unconscious conflicts and then reeducating the patient, first in an inpatient setting for several months, and then with continued outpatient psychoanalysis.

Treatment of addiction via the psychoanalytic model varied by practitioner but generally involved the use of psychotherapy to bring unconscious motivations to the conscious level. The general model has been described by Richard Blum and Eva Blum to include the following approaches. For the neurotic symptomatic drinker, the analyst seeks to develop the patient's insight into the underlying problems that trigger drinking episodes. Destructive drinking is eliminated by resolving neurotic conflict and enhancing the patient's capacity for emotional expression. With the character-disordered addict, the analyst imposes external controls that the patient can internalize over time. The overall goal for this patient is to enhance emotional maturity through the development of self-control and the acquisition of socially appropriate values.[128]

The focused goal of therapy was also different in the psychoanalytic approach to alcoholism treatment. Rather than demand abstinence from drinking as an explicit goal, analysts have traditionally asked patients to "postpone" drinking and drug use during the treatment process. Knight even suggested that enforcing sudden and complete abstinence on the alcoholic might be harmful without adjustment of the underlying personality disorder. Earlier psychoanalytic thinkers had suggested that forcing the alcoholic into abstinence might magnify a "crippling neurosis which may drive him to suicide."[129] Eva Blum's 1966 description of the psychoanalytic view of alcoholism was quite explicit on this issue of treatment goal. She clearly stated that total abstinence had never been a goal in psychoanalytically oriented therapy of alcoholism and that therapeutic success was defined as the ability to "drink moderately, when and where he chooses and with whom." She went even further by criticizing the goal of total abstinence on the grounds that it would "move the patient toward the substitution of one defense for another" and stimulate resistance in the therapeutic relationship.[130]

The psychoanalytic literature of this period describes the hope of recovery from alcoholism as quite bleak. Dr. Karl Menninger noted that the prognosis for recovery was better for schizophrenia than it was for alcoholism and that, if given a choice, he would prefer that one of his own family members be schizophrenic than alcoholic.[131]

Criticisms of Psychoanalytic Approaches to Addiction

It is perhaps appropriate here to note why psychoanalysis proved such a poor choice for the treatment of most addictive disorders. One of the best critiques of psychoanalytic and psychodynamic approaches to alcoholism treatment was provided by the psychiatrist Harry Tiebout. In his view, psychiatry had failed by approaching the alcoholic with the patently false assumption that alcoholism was symptomatic and peripheral to the primary underlying psychopathology, and that to focus on this superficial symptom reflected a naive and inappropriate approach to treatment. In a fascinating article entitled "Direct Treatment of a Symptom," Tiebout recounted how he had "searched energetically" for the unconscious forces and underlying problems of which alcoholism was merely a symptom. He eventually concluded that alcoholism was a symptom that had itself become a life-threatening, primary disease. Tiebout argued to his fellow psychiatrists that "the alcoholic must be brought to accept that he is a victim of a disease and that the only way for him to remain healthy is to refrain from taking the first drink."[132]

While many criticisms of psychoanalytic thinking about alcoholism point to errors in the theoretical construction of alcoholism, others suggest that the problem might be more attitudinal. Tiebout noted that psychiatrists tended to view the alcoholic, not just as a poor psychotherapy candidate, but also as an "out and out nuisance." He described most psychiatrists attempting to treat alcoholics as "fish out of water" who have little ability to understand, let alone help, the alcoholic.[133] There has rarely been a treatment method more poorly matched to a problem than that of the use of psychoanalysis in the treatment of addictions. Psychoanalysts found that they had little that could intervene meaningfully to abort the addiction cycle. For their part, alcoholics were often resentful and defiant in response to being coerced into treatment.

Alcoholics also brought many other traits that made them unsuitable for psychoanalysis. They had little regard for time schedules. They often escaped the discomforts of therapy through relapse. They constantly acted out and tested boundaries. They presented an unending list of emotional and environmental crises. They were at times excessively dependent. They presented with a multiplicity of problems. They often stopped participating in treatment. All of these characteristics placed alcoholics and addicts on the bottom of the list of desired candidates for psychoanalysis. Many alcoholics and addicts also came from ethnic and class cultures that were poorly understood by most psychoanalysts. And if those characteristics were not enough, alcoholics and addicts spent their available money, not on therapy, but on their drugs of choice.[134]

Psychoanalysis was quite simply not accessible to the majority of alcoholics and addicts, and it was not particularly successful for those for whom it was available and affordable. While psychoanalysis exerted great influence on American psychiatry, it had little influence on the day-to-day treatment that alcoholics and addicts received in state psychiatric hospitals. There was neither the time nor the money to provide psychoanalysis to alcoholics treated in state psychiatric hospitals. Subtleties of treatment philosophies and techniques in these settings often lost out to the more mundane and practical concerns of managing large, overcrowded institutions.

In the end, psychoanalysis was long on its description of the etiological roots of alcoholism but woefully short on its prescriptions for treating alcoholism. Benjamin Karpman's 1948 text on three alcoholic women, whom he had treated through psychoanalytically oriented psychotherapy at St. Elizabeth's Hospital, is typical in its lengthy speculations on etiological dynamics and its sparse description of treatment technology. The treatment outcomes of the three cases presented in this text, which was published as a guide for other therapists, were as follows: 1) Mrs. C. reported at follow-up that she was making a nice living and that, although she drank socially, she no longer drank the way she used to; 2) Mrs. R. continued to drink and died a year and a half after treatment of alcoholism-related medical diseases; and 3) Mrs. E. reported that she was "more stable" but did admit to periodic admissions for alcoholic detoxification following her one and one half years of institutional treatment at St. Elizabeth's.[135]

As America moved into the second half of the 20th century, it was becoming painfully clear that traditional psychoanalytic and psychodynamic approaches to individual therapy were not effective methods of treating alcoholism and other addictions. In 1978, Sheldon Zimberg reviewed the state of alcoholism treatment in this century. He concluded that "Physicians, psychiatrists and other mental health professionals have been ineffective in the treatment of alcoholics and have lost interest in attempting to treat them."[136] The primary influence of the psychoanalytic movement on the treatment of alcoholism was to place the question of why the alcoholic drank at the very center of the treatment process. For most alcoholics, this approach provided pseudo-scientific speculation (or justification) as to why they drank, but no sustainable program of sobriety. This failure influenced the emergence of a new professional field that treated these disorders outside the parameters of the traditional mental health disciplines and institutions.

Freud's Influence upon the Modern Alcoholism Movement and Lay Therapy

Freud's most significant contributions to addiction treatment came in three areas. The first seminal contribution of psychoanalytic thought was the widely disseminated view that disturbances in behavior reflected unconscious motivations and that people with disturbed behavior were in a psychological sense suffering from an illness or disease. It was this broader framework of cultural belief which created a window of opportunity to re-introduce the idea that excessive drinking was a manifestation of a disease. It was in laying this foundation that Freud and the popularization of his ideas laid an intellectual and cultural foundation for the rise of a mid-century alcoholism movement predicated on the view of alcoholism as a disease.[137]

The second key contribution of psychoanalytic thinking to the treatment of alcoholism involved the people qualified to conduct psychotherapy. When Freud's approach to psychoanalysis was introduced into the United States in the early 20th century, debate arose over who was qualified to conduct this new technique. American psychiatrists advocated that only physicians should be able to conduct psychoanalysis, but Freud argued that only people performing psychoanalysis have proper training in the technique. Freud's position opened the door to what came to be called "lay analysts"—people training to perform psychoanalysis who were not trained in medicine or psychiatry.[138] This position influenced and added credibility to the rise of lay therapists in the alcoholism treatment field.[139] The third contribution was a model of outpatient psychotherapy that focused on character reconstruction. Essential elements of these seminal ideas would be adapted for the treatment of alcoholism, not in the psychiatrist's office, but in a most unusual setting: the Emmanuel Church in Boston.

The Emmanuel Clinic and the Lay Therapy Movement[140]

In 1906, the Rev. Drs. Elwood Worcester and Samuel McComb, along with the physician Dr. Isador Coriat, opened a clinic in the Emmanuel Church in Boston, that for 23 years, integrated religion, medicine, and psychology in the treatment of various disorders. McComb offered the following description of the clinic in 1909:

> *The fundamental idea of our effort is that of the co-operation of physician, psychologically trained clergyman and expert social worker, in the alleviation and cure of certain disorders of the nervous system that are generally regarded as involving some weakness or defect of character....*[141]

The Clinic's service to alcoholics evolved out of an initial program of education and mutual support for people suffering from tuberculosis. When significant numbers of alcoholics were found within this latter class, the clinic developed a specialized approach to the treatment of alcohol problems.[142]

The clinic required that alcoholics seeking service: 1) have a personal desire to stop drinking, 2) possess a willingness to accept total abstinence as a treatment goal, and 3) show up sober for the first interview and commit to not drinking for one week. The abstinence requirement was added after Worcester's attempts to teach alcoholics to "drink like gentlemen" resulted in a 100% failure rate.[143]

The clinic integrated many elements of modern addiction counseling: medical screening and treatment, psychological counseling, spiritual inspiration, a mutual-support structure, and the involvement of the recovered alcoholic in acts of service to others. The clinic employed a specially trained staff, placed great emphasis on the importance of correct diagnosis, and maintained individual case records. The Jacoby Club, started by Ernest Jacoby in 1910, provided formal support meetings and social events for alcoholics in treatment. Its motto was "A club for men to help themselves by helping others."[144]

The structure of help provided through the Emmanuel Clinic consisted of three elements: 1) group therapy, 2) individual counseling, and 3) sup-

port and mentoring. Groupwork consisted of a series of educational classes, each followed by discussion and a social hour. Individual counseling was provided every day during each client's early weeks of recovery. Each client was also assigned a "friendly visitor" (some paid, some volunteer) who provided social work services similar to those of today's outreach workers or case managers.

W.A. Purrington described the Clinic's methods as consisting of "conversation, counsel, suggestion, to some extent of hypnosis, encouragement, prayer, restoration of hope, and finding work and support for those needing it." The method was referred to as "psychotherapy," which at the time was defined as "the attempt to help the sick through, mental, moral, and spiritual methods."[145] In the founders' view, the essential elements of alcoholism recovery were the diminishment of guilt through confession to a sympathetic listener; the acquisition of religious faith; the development of positive emotions; and the implanting of positive attitudes through hypnosis, prayer, and daily self-talk.

Although many alcoholics used the Emmanuel Movement to establish stable recovery from alcoholism, the Movement dissipated following the death of Worcester in 1940.

There is much in the Emmanuel Clinic that influenced the future of alcoholism treatment. Its integration of psychology and religion foreshadows the current use of spirituality in addiction treatment. It was the first outpatient alcoholism clinic whose primary methods were those of psychological counseling. Its focus on self-inventory and confession foreshadowed the Oxford Groups and Alcoholics Anonymous. The use of "friendly visitors" and "lay therapists" foreshadowed A.A.'s Twelfth Step and system of sponsorship, the emergence of the professional role of the alcoholism counselor, and the more recent role of the case manager. Elements of the methods developed at the Emmanuel Clinic were incorporated into the mid-century development of outpatient alcoholism counseling clinics.[146]

One of the more historically significant contributions of the Emmanuel Clinic was the use of recovered alcoholics as what came to be called "lay therapists."

References to the "lay therapy movement" spawned at this Clinic generally indicated both the people who were providing the therapy—recovered alcoholics without formal training as psychiatrists, psychologists or social workers—and the kind of therapy that was being provided—therapy that followed the general guidelines set forth by early lay-therapist pioneers at the Clinic, particularly Richard Peabody.[147] Courtenay Baylor, Richard Peabody, Francis Chambers, and Samuel Crocker were among the outstanding lay therapists of the Emmanuel Movement. They devoted their lives to counseling alcoholics. The story of the lay therapy movement can be told through their individual stories.

Courtenay Baylor

Courtenay Baylor began working with Dr. Worcester in the treatment of alcoholics in the Emmanuel Clinic in 1913. He is, to the best of this author's research, the first recovered alcoholic to work as a *professionally paid alcoholism counselor*. Baylor believed that the craving for alcohol was fed by mental tension and emphasized the "necessity of working primarily, not upon the surface difficulty, but upon the condition behind it and upon the cause of the underlying condition."[148] His antidote was to teach alcoholics how to lower this tension and how to prevent it from building up. He taught techniques of relaxation that today would go by such names as thought stopping, progressive relaxation, self-hypnosis, autogenic training, and guided visualization.

Baylor's therapeutic style involved teaching, encouragement, and a high degree of mutual self-disclosure. Because of Baylor's emphasis on self-disclosure, his treatment contract required a *mutual* commitment to confidentiality. Baylor tried to cultivate in the client the development of a new focus in life. To Baylor, sobriety required a purpose, a philosophy, and a plan. He spoke, not of recovery, but of "reconstruction." He believed that the life-transforming reconstruction of the alcoholic took considerable time, and he asked each alcoholic seeking his help for a commitment of at least one year. Baylor's approach to this work is summarized in his 1919 book *Remaking a Man*—one of the first texts written specifically on the technique of alcoholism counseling.[149]

Richard Peabody

Richard R. Peabody was one of Courtenay Baylor's clients who recovered from alcoholism and went on to study abnormal psychology. He participated as a client at the Emmanuel Clinic in 1921 and 1922, worked as a volunteer in 1924, and went on to establish a private alcoholism counseling practice in New York, where it is said he "effected some remarkable cures."[150]

Peabody's goal was to incorporate the growing knowledge of the field of psychology into the treatment of alcoholism. He elaborated on the earlier work of Baylor and presented his ideas about alcoholism and his approach to alcoholism counseling through a series of articles and in his 1931 book, *The Common Sense of Drinking*. This book served for years as a kind of professional "Bible" for alcoholics and their therapists. In spite of his reported intoxication at the time of his death, Peabody's teachings significantly influenced the evolution of alcoholism treatment in the years that preceded and followed the origin of Alcoholics Anonymous. Therapists were continuing to cite and emulate Peabody's alcoholism treatment techniques in the 1950s.[151]

Peabody believed there were three basic causes of alcoholism: 1) inheritance of a nervous system that was not resistant to alcohol, 2) the effects of the early family environment, and 3) the influence of later experiences in marriage, college, or work. Peabody emphasized the parental role as a causative agent of alcoholism (his followers were more specific in blaming mothers). In this view, maternal domination —often in combination with the presence of a shy, despondent father—led to feelings of inferiority, nervousness, and inadequate personality development that provided the foundation for the development of alcoholism. Alcoholism was thus viewed as a "disease of immaturity."[152] While Peabody's understandings of the causes of alcoholism are interesting and clearly show a psychoanalytic influence, he and other practitioners in the Emmanuel tradition became much better known for their methods of treatment than for their theories.

Peabody's approach to counseling alcoholics involved 1) analyzing the causative agents, 2) teaching the client to use relaxation and suggestion in the counseling session, 3) extending the use of autorelaxation and autosuggestion outside the counseling session, 4) conducting persuasive discussions, 5) encouraging the development of new interests and activities, 6) assigning inspirational reading, 7) helping the client operate on a regular schedule and participate in daily exercise, and 8) teaching the client thought-control techniques.[153]

According to Peabody, these steps had to be carefully sequenced. In the analysis of causative factors, Peabody helped his client identify the historical fears, conflicts, doubts, and patterns of thinking that were at the core of the client's alcoholism. Peabody also saw this analysis as a process of emotional surrender and emotional commitment to sobriety. Peabody placed great emphasis on surrender—the unconditional acceptance of the goal of total and enduring abstinence—as the first step in alcoholism recovery. He thought this surrender experience resulted from the alcoholic's telling and analyzing his life story. Peabody emphasized the importance of moving beyond being "on the water wagon," where one was physically dry and mentally drunk, to a resolute commitment to remove alcohol permanently from one's life.

The second step involved the lowering of physical tension and mental anxiety through relaxation techniques and suggestion. Peabody taught Dr. Edmund Jacobson's technique of progressive relaxation and used hypnotic suggestion to bolster esteem and sobriety. His hypnotic suggestions included such messages as "You are learning to relax," "You are maturing," and "The craving for alcohol is leaving you." He taught the client how to use these same messages as a kind of meditative mantra before sleep each night.

Peabody was not the only practitioner of the time to use hypnotic suggestion. Hypnosis was widely used in the 1890s and early 1900s in the treatment of alcoholism, and reports of its use in a variety of addiction disorders continue up to the present. At the turn of the century, alcoholic patients were repeatedly put under hypnosis and given post-hypnotic suggestions designed to prevent relapse. Some of the reports of successful treatment of alcoholism using hypnotism and suggestion were quite remarkable. In 1903, J. Bramwell reported 28 cases of full recovery and 36 cases of marked improvement (only rare episodes of relapse) out of a total of 76 alcoholic patients treated with hypnosis.[154] In 1908, Dr. John Quackenbos claimed that he had treated more than 800 alcoholics over nine years, with 80% to 90% experiencing a permanent cure.[155]

Along with its psychological assessment and relaxation techniques, Peabody's therapeutic model had a strong teaching and motivational component. He saw recovery as mastery over one's thinking process. It was Peabody's view that rehabilitation required between 50 and 100 hours of individual and group instruction. He focused on teaching clients how to eliminate negative thoughts and replace them with positive thoughts. He was quite directive in helping the client reconstruct the rituals of daily living. Peabody insisted that his clients develop and live by a daily schedule that focused on hygiene, productivity, self-expression, and thought control. He recommended daily exercise, daily reading, and the development of alternative hobbies and life pursuits.[156] Peabody conveyed hope to his clients by teaching

them that the forces of excessiveness that had driven them to the brink of self-destruction could be channeled to create great personal success and happiness.[157]

Peabody trained many recovering alcoholics to become lay therapists. Samuel Crocker, James Bellamy, Francis T. Chambers, William Wister, and Wilson McKay were among the better known. The experience of this first group of recovering alcoholic therapists underscored the risk of relapse for those working professionally in the field. Several of these therapists (Wister, Crocker, and McKay), as well as Peabody himself, experienced relapses after they began their work as counselors.[158] This experience underscored two lessons that history has borne out: 1) working as an alcoholism counselor does not ensure sobriety, and 2) working professionally with other alcoholics and addicts can pose threats to an otherwise stable program of recovery.

Edward Strecker and Francis Chambers

One of the more interesting approaches to psychotherapy with alcoholics was developed out of the collaboration of a psychiatrist, Dr. Edward Strecker, with Francis Chambers, a Peabody-trained lay therapist.

Dr. Edward Strecker, Chair of Psychiatry at the University of Pennsylvania, became open to alternative approaches to the treatment of alcoholism as a result of observing the constant recycling of alcoholics through hospitals, asylums, and sanataria. Before he met Chambers, Dr. Strecker had concluded that treating alcoholics was a "thankless and somewhat humiliating task."[159]

Francis Chambers had been treated for alcoholism at 11 different institutions before he entered counseling with Richard Peabody. After he became sober, Chambers decided to pursue a career as a lay therapist. Where Peabody became one of the first non-physician private-practice therapists to treat alcoholism, Chambers always worked in a larger medical-psychiatric team.

Strecker and Chambers began their collaboration in 1935, when Chambers accepted a position as a lay therapist at the Institute of the Pennsylvania Hospital, a private psychiatric facility. They worked to develop a formal system of treating alcoholism on an outpatient basis in the broader milieu of a psychiatric clinic. They later described this approach in their book, *One Man's Meat*.

Strecker's and Chambers' approach to alcoholism counseling was heavily influenced by Chambers' therapy and training under Richard Peabody. Chambers distinguished normal drinkers (even heavy drinkers) from abnormal drinkers in that the former sought the pleasurable effects of alcohol, where the latter sought alcohol's "psych-medicinal" properties. The former was a search for pleasure; the latter was a search for escape from pain and discomfort. Chambers believed that the alcoholic sought, not normal alcohol intoxication, but anesthetic oblivion.[160]

Strecker and Chambers were struck by the alcoholic's paradoxical dilemma. In their words, "The abnormal drinker is the man who cannot face reality without alcohol, and yet whose adequate adjustment to reality is impossible as long as he uses alcohol."[161] The primary etiological mechanism in alcoholism was, in their opinion, emotional regression—an emotional escape chosen by people who experienced an "incomplete formation of a personality" during their critical developmental years. Strecker and Chambers believed that this regression was caused by a heightened faculty for self-criticism and a sense of social discomfort that manifested itself in introversion. In this view, what the alcoholic sought was not a chemical pathway to extroversion but an even deeper and more profound introversion.

The antidote to this pharmacological regression was a therapeutic process that enhanced emotional maturity. Strecker and Chambers criticized prolonged inpatient treatment as overprotective—as an isolation that buffered the alcoholic from the very experiences that would most likely enhance maturity. Their system of treatment required that alcoholics commit themselves to complete and enduring abstinence and participation in 60 to 100 hours of treatment. Counseling sessions were held two to three times per week for the first months, followed by a gradual reduction in visits over a total course of one year.[162]

Chambers used self-disclosure of his own condition from the first interview. He briefly told the story of his alcoholism and recovery, then asked each client to tell his or her story in his or her own way. The first stage of therapy involved clarifying precisely what the goal was. Chambers used the same direct approach Peabody had used on him:

> *If you have any idea that you can still drink in moderation, there is absolutely no use in your consulting me. If you really believe that you can drink in a controlled manner despite what you have been through, the best thing for you to do is to go out and try. Then if you fail, come back to me and I will be glad to go into the matter further.*[163]

Therapy with Chambers was a process of instruction; he referred to this therapy as "re-education." This instruction focused on conducting a "psychological inventory," discussing daily problems and drinking themes in dreams, selecting and assigning outside study, teaching systematic relaxation, and helping the client prepare a daily routine—methods that clearly reflect Peabody's influence. Chambers taught his patients that their abnormal relationship with alcohol was the result of their having inherited a nervous system that was "non-resistant to alcohol," and that they should be no more ashamed of their inability to drink than diabetics should be ashamed of their inability to eat sugar.[164]

Strecker and Chambers articulated three objectives of alcoholism therapy: 1) analyzing the exciting cause, 2) inculcating a non-alcoholic philosophy of living, and 3) instilling a different "conditioned reflex" to alcohol. They considered therapy successful if the following three elements had been achieved: 1) the client believes that his or her drinking is abnormal, 2) the client has made a resolution to quit drinking once and for all, and 3) the client is practicing new habits of living every day.[165]

Strecker and Chambers had a number of ideas that the current practitioner might find interesting. They believed that the foundation of recovery from alcoholism was the hope of the therapist. In their view, the lack of true hopefulness on the part of the therapist would always be discovered by the hypersensitive alcoholic and, in a kind of self-fulfilling prophesy, lead to failure. They noted the tendency of many alcoholics early in treatment to experience what they called a "flight into recovery." Such a flight was a transient suppression of drinking and a gross oversimplification of what recovery would entail. The flight into recovery was a style of escaping the treatment experience with inevitable future relapse. Chambers, like Peabody, also spent considerable time—the last 15 minutes of every session with his patients—teaching them autosuggestion and relaxation. Strecker and Chambers spent considerable time with their patients on a reconstruction of daily lifestyle. They emphasized the need for new hobbies and relationships to fill the periods of boredom, restlessness, and dissatisfaction that occurred when one gave up drinking.[166]

Strecker and Chambers gave copies of Peabody's *The Common Sense of Drinking* to their alcoholic patients, asking each to mark the passages that fit their individual experience. They called this assignment a form of self-analysis. Chambers also used "notes" that had been passed on to him from Peabody. These notes (pamphlets of sorts) included written-out ideas that Chambers used in individual sessions with patients, much like those Peabody had used in Chambers' own therapy. Chambers went over each note with his patients, asking them to rewrite each one in their own language and in light of their own experience. The sequenced notes focused on such things as: 1) an inventory of what prompted the patient to seek treatment, 2) the need for nonalcoholic oral gratification (e.g., candy, tea, coffee), 3) the identification of high-risk drinking situations and preparation of defensive responses, 4) the exploration of "not-drinking" as a way of life, 5) errors in thinking—rationalizations—that could cause relapse, 6) countering the regressive "spoiled-child" syndrome with self-honesty, 7) responding to ill-formed advice from friends, 8) focusing on self-motivation for recovery (as opposed to becoming sober for others), 9) early sources of danger in recovery (e.g, fatigue, geographical changes, overconfidence, sex), 10) filling the emotional vacuum created by the loss of drinking, and 11) finding new sources of pleasure.[167]

Figures other than Courtenay Baylor and Richard Peabody also populated the lay-therapist movement. One prominent west-coast figure was Sam Leake. A notorious alcoholic who had also consumed prodigious quantities of sedative pills, Leake simply woke one morning with the realization that he had no desire for whiskey. As he would later report, "I didn't leave drunkenness; drunkenness left me."[168] Without involvement in, or support from any organization, Sam Leake began seeking out and counseling alcoholics. His work touched individual lives but created no broader movement of lay therapy in San Francisco.[169]

It is worth noting how these therapists viewed the alcoholic's family members. Most saw the family of the alcoholic as a nuisance or a threat. The views of Strecker and Chambers are typical. They noted that the pride of wives of alcoholics was wounded by successful therapy and that wives often resorted to sabotage to reassert their power and control of the relationship. They complained of having to deal with the wife's "childish resentments." In their view, the goal of working with the family was not engaging the family's involvement, but obtaining the family's agreement for noninterference in the alcoholic's treatment.[170]

In these men's stories, we have seen several common themes. First, there was a shift from doing something to the alcoholic to entering into a relationship with the alcoholic. In particular, there was an emphasis on alcohol-to-alcoholic identification

that led to the emergence of recovered alcoholics working as lay therapists. We also saw throughout these stories a view of alcoholism, not as a primary disease, but as a symptom of failed emotional development—a clear influence of psychoanalytic thinking. Although this view would later come into disfavor, the roots of modern alcoholism counseling are clearly evident in the structure and techniques used by Baylor, Peabody, and Chambers. In 1944, Dwight Anderson reviewed the history and status of lay therapy in the treatment of alcoholism and drew the following prophetic conclusion: "They can be made increasingly of use in the future if we learn how to select them, how to train them, and recognizing the scope of their function, learn how to use them in cooperation with the social worker, the psychologist, the physician and the psychiatrist." [171]

What many of the lay therapists of the 1930s had in common was the integration of psychoanalytic and psychodynamic understanding of behavior into solutions to the particular problem of alcoholism. This emphasis was also evident in the literature on alcoholism of the 1930s and 1940s. For example, Charles Clapp, Jr. wrote two books on alcoholism —*The Big Bender* in 1938 and *Drunks are Square Pegs* in 1942. The first described his own recovery from alcoholism, and the second set forth his philosophy of alcoholism recovery. Clapp believed that alcoholics drank to escape "the pain of being jammed into a round hole when they should be in a square one," and that alcoholics were not cured until they discovered why they drank and corrected that root cause.[172] One interesting aspect of Clapp's writings was his position that alcoholics after a sustained period of emotional adjustment—finding their square holes—could drink in moderation without experiencing their past difficulties.

It is my belief an alcoholic is not completely cured until he or she has made the entire alcoholic cycle, arrived in the square hole and can drink in moderation.[173]

Clapp's own personal experiments with moderate drinking continued until 1945, when he acknowledged their failure. Based on his own failed efforts at controlled drinking, he concluded that no alcoholic could ever again drink in a normal fashion regardless of his or her degree of emotional adjustment.[174]

Durfee's "Practicing Farm"

Another leading practitioner of alcoholism

treatment who was greatly influenced by the earlier work of Worcester, Baylor, and Peabody was Charles Durfee, Ph.D. Durfee conducted alcoholism treatment at a "practicing farm" in Wakefield, Rhode Island, in collaboration with his wife, who was a clinical psychologist. Durfee's male "students of living"—usually six to eight at a time—lived unattended in a "Guest House" on his farm. The structure of Durfee's treatment consisted of three months to a year of psychotherapy integrated into social and work activities on the farm. Students were phased back into their normal environments, with periodic refresher visits to the farm. While they were at the farm, Durfee's students were free from all constraint and could go into town or continue to pursue some of their occupational responsibilities. The milieu of the farm was shaped by Durfee's belief in "self-government under guidance"—the practice in which every interaction and activity was used as a process of self-awareness. Similarities between Durfee's farm, earlier Washingtonian-style homes, and later therapeutic communities are striking.[175]

Durfee believed that the failure of most alcoholism treatment could be attributed to three causes. The first was a failure to differentiate adequately between those who could and could not be helped by treatment. Durfee screened out the psychotic, the feebleminded, those with deep unconscious conflict who were more appropriate for psychoanalysis, and the psychopath. He looked for candidates who came freely and who brought a high degree of commitment to seek insight into their problem. The second cause of failure was the inevitable resistance ignited when the problem drinker was placed under institutional control. Noting how problem drinkers bristled at such efforts at control, Durfee emphasized the principle of self-development and self-direction in a peer-governed milieu. He saw the third cause of treatment failure as the placement of too much emphasis on the symptom of drinking and insufficient emphasis on the total mental health of the problem drinker. Durfee believed that the target of treatment should be, not the drinking behavior, but the personality factors that rendered the person vulnerable to drinking. When these personality factors are addressed, he believed, "the drinking will take care of itself."[176]

Durfee taught his patients that they suffered from a constitutional or acquired intolerance to alcohol, that they could never return to normal drinking, and that their futures hinged on an emotional growth that would render alcohol unnecessary, along with a total reconstruction of their lifestyle. In what today would be called a strategy of "relapse prevention," Durfee helped his clients define "zero hour"—those times and circumstances more likely to elicit craving and drinking—and helped them develop alternative activities to respond to these critical times.

Durfee perceived treatment as a process of maturation—an enhanced integration of the personality. The therapist's personality and relationship with the client was often the most important stimulant to this process of maturation. This maturation consisted of developing alternatives to the satisfactions previously experienced through alcoholic intoxication.[177] Rather than coddle his alcoholic patients, Durfee tried to harden his patients against the temptations they would later face. Durfee thought, for example, that the alcoholic needed to learn in treatment how to decline alcohol during social occasions where drinking was prevalent. To this end, Durfee invited his patients to small social gatherings at which alcohol was served—a sort of rehearsal for declining the invitation to drink.

Aversion Therapy: Early Efforts

All of the methods described in this chapter reflected a growing interest in psychological techniques of influencing human behavior. One such technique that received some prominence in the first half of the 20th century was aversive conditioning. Attempts to disrupt alcoholic drinking by associating alcohol with some noxious stimulus—later called aversion therapy or a conditioned reflex treatment—began early in American history. Benjamin Rush's experiments with aversion therapy for alcoholism date from the 1780s. In the early 1800s, a Dr. Kain used tartar emetic as an aversive agent to link the taste and smell of alcohol with nausea.[178] In their separate reviews of the substances used to induce a distaste for alcohol, Drs. J.D. Rolleston and Joseph Thimann named a number of substances, including rotted sea grapes, mole blood, and sparrow's dung. Some attempts involved elaborate procedures such as forcing the patient to drink wine in which a live eel had been suffocated or having the alcoholic consume powderized pork that had secretly resided in the bed of a Jew for nine days.[179] Relatives of alcoholics have at various times been coached to place worms or insects into the alcoholic's bottle or to saturate with alcohol everything the alcoholic ate. Some specialists advocated that drunkards be forced to drink their own urine. The purpose of all such strategies was to induce a revulsion toward alcohol.

One of the earliest experiments with the use of a

scientifically based aversive conditioning technique with human beings was conducted by the Russian researcher N.V. Kantorovich. Kantorovich treated 20 alcoholics in the late 1920s by pairing the sight, smell, and taste of alcoholic products with electrical shock.[180] The first aversive agent used in the modern treatment of addiction was apomorphine, which, after being introduced by Dr. John Dent of England, became widely used in Europe as an agent for treating alcoholism.

The best-developed and -publicized use of aversion therapy in the treatment of alcoholism in the United States was pioneered at the Shadel Sanatorium in Seattle. The conditioned-reflex, or aversion treatment provided in Shadel was developed and refined during its early years by Dr. Walter Voegtlin, a gastroenterologist; and Dr. Frederick Lemere, a psychiatrist. The Shadel Sanatorium opened in 1935, and descriptions of its treatment techniques first appeared in the professional literature in 1940. This story, like the birth of A.A. in the same year, begins with an alcoholic in desperate need.

In 1935, Charles Shadel was a Seattle business-man suffering from alcoholism, when his search for help led him to a young physician named Walter Voegtlin. Dr. Voegtlin had just formulated a treatment for alcoholism based on Ivan Pavlov's discovery of conditioned reflexes. Voegtlin believed that nausea could serve as a conditioning agent that could simultaneously eliminate the desire for alcohol and induce a revulsion towards alcohol. Shadel volunteered for the treatment and was so impressed with the results that he and his wife opened their home to treat other alcoholics. Shadel later used his own funds to buy a house, so they could start a sanatorium where others could be treated with the technique. The success of the Seattle institution spurred Charles Shadel to build a second institution in Portland, Oregon.

Treatment Procedures

The technique pioneered by Dr. Voegtlin includ-ed the following steps. Alcoholics were screened for admission, to ensure that all those entering understood the necessity of permanent abstinence from alcohol for the rest of their lives. It was further explained that the first phase of treatment would take between five and ten days, and that this would have to be followed by periodic return visits over the next year. Those admitted were detoxified, medically stabilized, then brought to a special treatment room that was arranged as a bar.

In the hours prior to the treatment, patients were given neither food nor other medication. Great care was taken to eliminate all stimuli except the sight, smell, and taste of alcohol—and the drug-induced nausea. A sound-proofed room, along with special lighting and mirrors, focused the alcoholic's attention on the alcohol and its effects. The patient was seated in front of bottles of alcohol, glasses, and ice, while staff discussed with the patient his or her normal drinks of choice. The patient's attention was focused on the sight of the alcohol bottles and the drink, on the sounds of ice in the glass, and on the smell of alcohol. The patient was then given an injection of Emetine and asked to drink. The patient drank and vomited, and continued to drink and vomit until the drinking was stopped (just before the nausea wore off). Great care was taken to ensure that absorption of alcohol was prevented, so that the patient did not feel any intoxication from the alcohol consumed.

The patient was then put to bed for two to three hours. The procedure was carefully administered by trained technicians. It was so powerful that some patients reported that they could not even look at an advertisement for alcohol without experiencing nausea.[181]

This procedure was repeated every other day until four or five treatments of increasing intensity had been completed. Follow-up treatments that repeated the procedure occurred at 1 month, 2 months, 6 months, and one year after discharge. During the days on which aversion therapy was not used, patients were given sodium pentothal (the "truth serum" of spy-story fame) and were interviewed under its influence about their emotional problems. Shadel's treatment, like most of the programs that used aversion therapy, also provided other elements of treatment: a sympa-thetic staff, encouragement of sharing and mutual support within the treatment milieu, counseling and support for the family, patient education, nutritional advice, individual and group counseling, and encouragement of self-help group participation. Voegtlin and Lemere believed that alcoholics could never return to moderate drinking, and believed they had found a technique that could keep many alcoholics from taking that first drink. Ten rules for recovery were presented to patients as part of their educational experience in treatment at Shadel.

1. Never take that first drink.
2. Do not experiment with drinking.
3. Remember that alcoholism is an illness.
4. Do not look upon alcoholism as a personal weak-ness.

5. Do not think of alcohol as a challenge.
6. Prove that you do not need alcohol.
7. Develop other outlets.
8. Do not work too hard.
9. Develop an adequate philosophy of life.
10. Be proud of having stopped drinking.[182]

The Shadel Sanatorium gave each departing client what came to be thought of as a diploma: a thermometer that they were asked to hang where they would see it every day. The thermometer read: *There is just one thing that I can't do* —a daily reminder not to take the first drink.[183]

The average patient stay at the Sanatorium in its early years was ten days, with costs ranging from $450 to $750.

The Sanatorium also provided support following discharge. Shadel used a system comparable to A.A.'s Twelfth Step, whereby former patients, called "field-men," stayed actively involved in working with newly discharged patients. Six field men worked full time, visiting and encouraging former patients, returning vulnerable patients to the sanatorium for a "recap," and interviewing new prospects for treatment.

The staff at Shadel was composed mostly of former patients who had been sober several years before their employment and, in some cases, relatives of former patients who brought both maturity and sensitivity to the needs of alcoholics.[184]

Reported Treatment Outcomes

In the 1940s, follow-up studies of patients treated with aversion therapy reported recovery rates of 45% to 60%. The largest of these was a 1948 study by P. O'Halloren and F. Lemere of 2,323 alcoholics who had been treated at Shadel between 1935 and 1945. Of the 2,323 people interviewed from six months to ten years following their treatment, 48.8% were abstinent at the time of the follow-up.[185] This high success rate was likely influenced by the fact that all of the patients were voluntary and committed to the goal of permanently eliminating alcohol from their lives. The Shadel patients most likely to remain abstinent following treatment were over 35 years of age, married, employed, of middle or upper income, and small-town residents.[186]

Reports in the 1940s of patients dying while undergoing aversion treatment for alcoholism led to more careful medical screening to identify those who were not appropriate for this treatment. By 1957, reviewers of the aversion therapy treatment of alcoholism were noting an additional list of psycho-

logical characteristics of patients for whom this therapy was unsuitable. The list included the indigent, the poorly motivated, the psychopath, those of borderline intelligence, those who drank to escape, those with a criminal record, drug addicts, women, and professional men.[187]

Subsequent Developments

Aversion therapy for alcoholism was used in a large number of alcoholism treatment institutions in the 1940s and 1950s, including State of Wisconsin General Hospital, the Hospital of the University of Virginia, and Meyer Memorial Hospital in Buffalo. Corwin and Cunningham, in their 1940 survey of alcoholism treatment programs, found that aversion therapy was the most popular technique used in the 20 surveyed institutions that specialized in addiction treatment.[188] The procedure was even used in such traditional treatment institutions as the Washingtonian Hospital in Boston, which combined these treatments with a special "Abstinence Club" (often called "Conditioning Club" by the patients) that provided a sober social milieu for newly discharged patients.[189]

As aversion therapy spread beyond Shadel, there were numerous variations on the technique. These included:

- the use of alternative aversion agents, e.g., apomorphine, disulfiram (Antabuse), metronidazole (Flagyl);
- the use of hypnosis to induce aversion to drinking alcohol and to encourage the substitution of non-alcoholic drinks; and
- the use of a device that allows the alcoholic to self-administer a mild electrical shock whenever he or she experiences thoughts about drinking or cravings for alcohol.

In the 1960s, an even more extreme conditioning process was proposed that involved linking the sight, smell, and taste of alcohol with the terrifying experience of respiratory paralysis. The drug used to induce this terror was succinylcholine chloride (Scoline or Anectine). That drug, which is closely related to the substance South American Indians use to poison the tips of their arrows, creates a temporary (60-second) but complete paralysis, including an inability to breathe and speak. In short, the patients believe and feel as if they are dying. The procedure involved placing alcohol on the lips of patients as they were injected with the apnea-inducing drug. The Canadians who pioneered this technique—Dugal

Cambell, S.G. Laverty and R.E. Sanderson—believed that the intensity of this trauma would heighten the terror associated with drinking and improve treatment outcomes.

Cambell's and Laverty's reports provide no discussion of the potential ethical issues involved in inducing this terror for the patient's own good with this "therapeutically useful noxious stimulus." This technique was used in isolated cases to treat alcoholics in the United States. Reports of such experiments include 25 alcoholics treated at the Iowa Psychopathic Hospital and 12 alcoholics treated at the Galesburg State Research Hospital in Galesburg, Illinois.[190] A follow-up report of 23 alcoholics treated with this technique at Mendocino State Hospital in California noted that, in spite of the fact that 22 required oxygen to reverse severe bradycardia, all but two had resumed drinking within four months.[191]

Dr. John Hsu, the Director of Research at Pontiac State Hospital In Pontiac, Michigan, added another chapter to the story of the use of conditioning as a treatment for alcoholism. In 1965, Hsu reported on the use of electric current to induce an aversion to alcohol in patients being treated for alcoholism. In this technique, patients were presented a tray filled with one-ounce cups of milk, wine, water, beer, whiskey and fruit juice, and were told to drink them in any order they chose. Patients were shocked with an electrical current only after drinking the alcoholic beverages. The treatments were given five days in a row, with a recommendation that patients return for reinforcement treatments at four weeks and six months following the initial series of treatments. Hsu reported that the degree of unpleasantness experienced by electrical shock far exceeded other methods that relied on nausea, vomiting, headaches, or a shock-like state in their conditioning treatments. Thirteen of the 40 patients completed both the initial series and the first reinforcement treatment. Seven of these were known to have resumed drinking once they left the hospital.[192]

Patrick Frawley, the self-made millionaire associated with Schick razors and Papermate pens, was successfully treated for alcoholism in 1963 in Shadel's aversion therapy program. He founded Schick Laboratories to find a cure for alcoholism, but when this effort failed, he went back to champion the method that had helped him get sober. He purchased the Shadel Sanatorium in 1964, then opened additional aversion treatment units in Texas and California. Modern refinements in the methods used at Schick's Shadel Hospital were overseen by Dr. James Smith.[193] In more recent years, Schick's Shadel expanded the use of this technique to include smoking cessation and the treatment of eating disorders.

Another thread of the Shadel history that extends into the modern era of addiction treatment involved Shadel's Portland facility. The Portland program began operations in 1942 under the management of Baldy Miles (who had been treated at Shadel in 1938) and Dr. John Montague. This facility later separated from Shadel and operated under the name "Raleigh Hills." Montague served as Raleigh Hills Medical Director for the next 34 years.

Raleigh Hills changed hands several times over the years, in 1946 and 1948, and then through mergers, first with Neuro-Psychiatric and Health Services, Inc, then in 1972 with Advanced Health Systems, Inc. By 1982, Raleigh Hills had franchised its method of treatment through its operation of 21 hospitals in ten states.[194]

Aversion therapy was the longest enduring behavioral technique used in alcoholism treatment in the first six decades of the 20th century, but other behavioral technologies would be added in the closing decades of the century, as would other psychological approaches to the treatment of addictions.

Our discussions of treatment approaches through most of the earlier chapters have focused primarily on the treatment of alcoholism. In the next two chapters, we will explore some of the specialized treatment approaches for addiction to drugs other than alcohol that evolved between 1880 and 1950.

Section Four

✠

Chapter Thirteen
The Treatment of Addiction to Narcotics and Other Drugs: 1880-1925

The next two chapters will provide a detailed outline of the methods used in the United States to treat addiction to narcotics and other drugs between 1880 and 1950. We will begin our story with two fascinating episodes in this history. In the first episode, the father of psychoanalysis will advocate and then retract the recommendation that cocaine be used in the treatment of morphine addiction. In the second, the father of American surgery will be found to have "cured" himself of cocaine addiction by secretly sustaining decades of morphine use.

The Use of Cocaine as an Addiction Cure—and Freud's Retraction

As early as 1878, Dr. W.H. Bently of Valley Oak, Kentucky, advocated the use of cocaine in the treatment of morphine addiction. In an 1889 article in the *Detroit Therapeutic Gazette*, Dr. Bently reported that he had prescribed some 25 pounds of cocaine over a span of two years in his treatment of patients suffering from morphine addiction and from alcoholism. Although Bently's article claimed successful cures through such substitution, the article also contained warning signs of problems to come. First was Bently's seemingly benign account of what occurred when he prescribed one pound of cocaine to a woman addicted to morphine.

> I received a note from her when she had used this. She was much encouraged and had ordered two pounds more....I saw her recently when she assured me that she had no desire for morphine.[1]

A second case reported in this same article was that of an alcoholic physician whom Bently had treated with cocaine. As a testimony to the effectiveness of the treatment, Bently cited a letter from the patient which contained the following passage.

> I am perfectly cured of the whisky habit, thanks to you and erthoxylon coca, but I can scarcely keep from forming a coca habit, becoming a "coquero."[2]

Such reports of the use of coca preparations in the treatment of various forms of inebriety were common in the 1880s, although there were fewer such reports in the United States than in Europe. Reports of cocaine's effectiveness as a remedy for opium addiction came from both the patent medicine and from mainstream physicians.[3] While Dr. J.T. Whitaker and a number of other American physicians claimed in the mid-1880s that cocaine was the "best remedy for the morphia habit that we have," the person most often linked with the use of cocaine in the treatment of alcohol and opiate addiction was a young Viennese physician.[4]

In 1884, Sigmund Freud was intrigued by a medical report on the use of cocaine to suppress fatigue in soldiers in the Bavarian Army. He ordered a supply of cocaine and began to experiment with its effects—on himself and on many of those close to him. Freud became infatuated with the drug's potential and issued a paper entitled "Ueber Coca" (On Coca), which was published in the *St. Louis Medical and Surgical Journal*. In this article, Freud recommended the use of cocaine as a stimulant; an aphrodisiac; an anesthetic; and a treatment for nervous disorders, digestive problems, syphilis, and asthma. He also extolled the potential role of cocaine in the treatment of morphine addiction.[5]

Based on the pronouncements of Freud and others, the Parke-Davis Company was confident about cocaine's future role in the treatment of alcoholism and morphine addiction. Their promotional literature cited Freud's claim that "inebriate asylums can now be entirely dispensed with because of cocaine's curative powers."[6]

Freud's initial observations on the potential role of cocaine occurred after he gave Dr. Ernst von Fleischl cocaine in 1884 as a recommended cure for the latter's addiction to morphine. While the early response was positive—the cocaine was effectively substituted for morphine—Dr. Fleischl escalated his dosages of cocaine and within a year was injecting a gram a day. Fleischl experienced the classic paranoia and hallucinations of cocaine psychosis, the most vivid being the experience of white snakes creeping over his skin: what we know today as formication syndrome. Unfortunately, Dr. Fleischl was not the only case to appear in the medical literature documenting the shift in addictions from morphine to cocaine. Freud came under attack from many quarters, particularly in a series of articles by Dr. Friedrich Erlenmeyer. Erlenmeyer called cocaine "the third scourge of the human race" (behind alcohol and morphine) and implied that Freud was responsible for its spread. Erlenmeyer, in noting the risk of developing cocainism in the morphine addict, likened the treatment of morphine addiction with cocaine to casting out Satan with Beelzebub.[7] In 1887, Freud published "Remarks on Craving for and Fear of Cocaine," in which he responded to his critics by noting the risk of cocaine addiction in morphine addicts.

The patients began to get hold of the drug themselves and become addicted to it as they had been to morphine....Cocaine used in this way is far more dangerous to health than morphine. Instead of a slow marasmus, we have rapid physical and moral deterioration, hallucinatory states of agitation similar to delirium tremens, a chronic persecution mania.

In this, his last publication on cocaine, Freud insisted that the use of cocaine for people not previously addicted to morphine was not habit forming. Finding his first venture into the arena of psychopharmacology a bit discomforting, Freud went on to new areas of investigation, for which he became world famous.

Cocaine, Morphine, and the Father of American Surgery [8]

William Stewart Halstead attended Yale in the mid-1870's, distinguishing himself more on the athletic field than in the classroom and giving little evidence of his future as a medical pioneer. Halstead went on to graduate with honors from the College of Physicians and Surgeons in New York, and to study surgery in Europe before returning to the U.S. in 1880. Halstead became the first Professor of Surgery and then Surgeon-in-Chief at Johns Hopkins Hospital. He revolutionized surgery by introducing methods of sterilizing surgical instruments and clothing, pioneering a number of new surgical techniques and procedures, and developing a new system of training surgeons. For such accomplishments, he earned the unchallenged title of the "Father of American Sur-

gery." After a long and distinguished career, William Stewart Halstead died in 1922 at the age of 70.

What is missing from that story remained hidden until 1969, when a sealed diary of Sir William Osler, one of the co-founders of John Hopkins, was opened to commemorate the Hospital's 80th anniversary. The diary revealed the following missing pieces of the Halstead biography.

Reports of Dr. Sigmund Freud's paper on cocaine and Dr. Karl Koller's use of cocaine for anesthesia sparked William Halstead's own experiments with cocaine in 1884. Halstead, along with a small group of colleagues and medical students, used themselves as test subjects to explore the anesthetic properties of cocaine. Their methods, which involved injecting cocaine into nerves, confirmed cocaine's potential as an anesthetic, but also introduced them to the drug's euphorigenic effects.

Halstead and several of his colleagues became addicted to the drug and, according to one biographer, Sherwin Nuland, in all cases but Halstead's their medical careers were destroyed. Halstead made several early attempts at curing his addiction: self-exile on a boat and two hospitalizations at the Butler Hospital in Providence, Rhode Island.[9] In one of his attempts to shake his cocaine addiction, Halstead became addicted to morphine. The amazing secret that Osler revealed was not that America's foremost surgeon was addicted to cocaine early in his career, but that he was addicted to morphine for almost his entire medical career. Osler noted:

He had never been able to reduce the amount (of morphine) to less than three grains daily; on this he could do his work comfortably and maintain his excellent physical vigor.[10]

Opiate Addiction: A Hidden Disease

The rise in opiate addiction in the 19th century was shrouded in myth and caricature. While the dominant profile of opiate addiction was that of the woman addicted to the use of opiate-laced medicines, the image of the drug addict was one centered around the Chinese opium dens. The former was considered to be suffering from a disease, while the latter was viewed as perpetrating a heathen vice. While Chinese opium users were subjected to considerable persecution, affluent White opium and morphine users were embraced in a growing medical conceptualization of their disorder.

The disease concept of inebriety, which rose to

cultural consciousness behind the efforts of the inebriate asylum pioneers, extended not only to alcoholism but also to opiate addiction. This view of opiate addiction as a disease was first introduced through professional medical literature. Addiction experts like T.D. Crothers set forth the proposition that drug addiction was primarily a physical disease.[11] As evidence of the growing incidence of opium and morphine addiction became apparent, the popular press embraced a more disease-oriented conceptualization of mainstream opiate use and called for the medical treatment of addiction.[12]

Medical support for this idea declined during the campaign to pass the Harrison Act and the years following its enactment. The American Medical Association's 1920 Report of the Committee on the Narcotic Drug Situation included the following sentiment:

> The shallow pretense that drug addiction is "a disease" which the specialist must be allowed to "treat," which pretended treatment consists of supplying its victims with the drug has caused their physical and moral debauchery....[13]

As we shall see, 19th- and early 20th-century treatments for drug addiction rose and fell among these vacillating cultural perceptions of addiction.

Drug Treatments and Drug Cures Before the Harrison Act

While drug addiction was not criminalized in the 19th century, its progressively stigmatized status led addicts to hide their addictions and only as a last resort risk public exposure by seeking treatment. Two stories of addicted preachers illustrate the status and fate of many 19th-century opiate addicts. The first is the story of an affluent preacher who became addicted to opium and entered an insane asylum for treatment in 1840. He described being in the throes of withdrawal amidst the "muttering and gibbering, the howling and the horrid execrations of the mad creatures" who surrounded him. He confessed to leaving the institution "more shattered physically than when I entered."[14] In a later account, Crothers shares the account of a preacher whose medical examination following his sudden death in a hotel revealed the long-standing needle scars that were the telltale signs of morphine addiction.[15]

Opiate addiction in the 19th century was hidden, not in illicit, subterranean subcultures, but in the secrecy of one's own home. Slowly, addicts were coaxed from this secrecy, to be treated by an expanding legion of addictionologists and specialty institutions. What these specialists focused on was the problem of narcotic withdrawal. This problem was so critical that most practitioners defined treatment as withdrawal.

Three approaches to addict withdrawal were used during this period. There was the sudden termination of drug ingestion, which came to be known as "cold turkey" because of the common occurrence of piloerection (goose flesh) during narcotic withdrawal. Few addicts could tolerate this procedure in an era of easy drug availability in which most had reached phenomenal levels of tissue tolerance. Sudden withdrawal in the face of such high tolerance could be life threatening, depending on the age and health of the addict. Specialists such as Dr. J.B. Mattison characterized this method as so cruel and inhumane as to be "utterly unworthy of a healing art."[16]

The second approach was withdrawal utilizing a step-down of drug dosage over a short period of time (generally a week). Such rapid withdrawal left the addict drug free but physically and psychologically prostrate. Relapse under such circumstances was quite high. A third method involved prolonged withdrawal—a gradual weaning of the addict over an extended period of time ranging from weeks to months. This method could also involve considerable agony, as the following 1868 account attests:

> The fifty-sixth day of suffering without sleep found me at a Water Cure. Warm baths, sometimes with battery, then packs, then sitz baths, for ten more long, suffering days and nights—but sleep never came to me and pain never left me.[17]

All of these methods usually combined the cessation of narcotic use with the simultaneous application of various tonics and stimulants to help bolster the addict's weakened system. Pharmacological agents to aid both rapid and prolonged narcotic detoxification were used within the inebriate asylums, were available through local physicians, and were available by mail order. Those with legitimate intent, if not effective execution, included:

- narcotic substitutes, such as codeine, to aid withdrawal;[18]
- non-narcotic substitutes such as cannabis indica, nux vomica (strychnine), belladonna, atropine, cocaine, quinine, whiskey, and even coffee—all

thought to serve as tonics to sustain strength during withdrawal;[19]
- purgatives to speed the elimination of "drug toxins";
- sedatives to enhance comfort during withdrawal, e.g., chloral hydrate, the bromides, and newer hypnotics such as sulphonal, trional, and veronal;
- drugs intended to create an aversion to opiates, e.g., tartar emetic;
- drugs that at higher doses induced confusion and forgetfulness, e.g., hyoscine or atropine, and
- plant specifics believed to destroy narcotic craving, e.g., Avena sativa or Viola sagittata.[20]

Several dominant addict-withdrawal protocols were available between 1900 and 1930. There was the Lambert-Towns treatment, described in Chapter Ten, which consisted of rapid withdrawal of the drug accompanied by the administration of combinations of belladonna, xanthoxlyun, hyoscyamus, strychnine, and digitalis. There was the Petty method, which combined purging, forced fluids, and vapor baths with the administration of atropine, scopolamine, sparteine sulphate, and sodium thiosulfate. There was the Sceleth method used in the Chicago House of Corrections, which combined rapid withdrawal with the administration of scopolamine, pilocarpine, ethylmorphin, strychnine, and various cathartics.[21] There was the Nellens and Massee method used at the United States Penitentiary at Atlanta, which involved complete and rapid withdrawal combined with the use of mercurous chloride, magnesium sulphate, chloral for sedation, and orange or lemon juice to reduce nausea.[22] And there was the "Narcosan" treatment of Lambert and Tilney, which was reported to be made up of a mixture of lipoids, proteins, and vitamins.[23]

It can be seen that the protocol for withdrawing addicts varied widely and included many exotic and potentially dangerous ingredients. Such treatments continued for decades, with no formal testing of their safety or efficacy. As late as 1927, an expert medical panel appointed by Mayor James Waler of New York to assess treatments available for addicts in the New York Department of Corrections advised Waler that the then-popular hyoscine and "Narcosan" cures were both useless and potentially harmful. The only method of effectively detoxifying narcotic addicts they had found was the controlled reduction in narcotic intake.[24]

Shortly after passage of the Harrison Act, a D.F. MacMartin published his confessional *Thirty Years in Hell,* in which he described, from the bed of a psychopathic hospital, his three-decade addiction to mor-phine, cocaine, chloral, and hashish. His addiction to these drugs began as a search for relief from the physical pain of alcoholism. MacMartin attributed his vulnerability to addiction to his having been born a hedonist. His autobiography makes only brief references to his eight treatments (detoxifications) but includes much about his feelings toward those providing the treatment.

> *These croakers had the gall of a bullock, the heart of a hyena, the brains of a peacock....They indulge in fables to hide the baldness of a fact. They are a rabble of quacks....The fifty-six hour cure, known as the Lambert cure, is a defunct wheeze, the Keeley cure, a species of elephantine charlatanerie, psychotherapy is snarled nonsense, and it is the parable of a moral truth that they produce but negative results.*[25]

Most narcotic addicts did not have the financial resources to gain access to the treatments that MacMartin so bitterly criticized. Nearly all of the cures were provided by private practitioners or private agencies that only the affluent could afford. It was this lack of access that created a vacuum for the fraudulent patent-medicine cures that were described in Chapter Eight. But even these limited resources were about to be challenged by a new federal law.

Drug Treatment, The Harrison Act, Drug Enforcement, and The Supreme Court[26]

Following a prolonged campaign for federal drug control legislation, the Harrison Anti-Narcotic Act was passed in 1914. This act, as written, used the vehicles of registration and taxation to restrict the use of opiates and cocaine to legitimate medical purposes. America went from uncontrolled access—under federal law—to access regulated by physicians. Subsequent interpretations and enforcement of this law altered both its intent and its effect and exerted a profound influence on addiction treatment that extends to the present.

Whatever hardships addicts may have experienced prior to passage of the Harrison Act were nothing compared to those they experienced afterwards. When the law first went into effect in 1915, addicts scrambled to apply for "registration permits" from the Department of Treasury, until the realization sank in that no such permits would be issued to them. But they still believed that they would be able to sustain access to narcotics through the auspices of medical treatment. After all, the Harrison Act stated specifically that the prohibition of the distribution of opium derivatives and cocaine did not apply:

> *to the dispensing or distribution of any of the aforesaid drugs to a patient by a physician, dentist, or veterinary surgeon registered under this act during the course of his professional practice.*

But this was not to be the case. Treasury Department Decision 2200, issued May 11, 1915, required that physicians' prescriptions to addicts for opiates had to specify progressively decreasing doses. The orders became increasingly restrictive until the prescription of any opiate or cocaine to an addict was interpreted by the Treasury Department as a violation of the Harrison Act. What could have been the motivation behind such an administrative interpretation?

Lacking any substantive knowledge of the relapse phenomenon in opiate addiction, the Treasury Department took a stand against what was called "ambulatory treatment." Ambulatory treatment consisted of the addicted patient's arriving each day at his or her physician's office or clinic to receive a prescription for morphine that was, in theory, progressively reduced until the patient was weaned from the drug.

The Treasury Department opposed ambulatory treatment because, for many patients, it turned into sustained maintenance, and also because the remaining inebriate hospitals and asylums of the day were still boasting 95% success rates. After all, leaders of the Treasury Department argued, why should someone be maintained on morphine when all he or she had to do was to take the cure? It was through such misrepresentation of success rates that the inebriate asylums and private treatment sanitariams contributed inadvertently to the criminalization of narcotic addiction in the U.S.

The restrictive intent of the Treasury Department regulations and their aggressive enforcement led to legal challenges and Supreme Court decisions that dramatically changed the status of the addict in America. In 1916, in the *U.S. v. Jin Fuey Moy,* the Supreme Court ruling in this case affirmed that an addict's possession of smuggled drugs was a violation of the Harrison Act. With this decision, the only way an addicted person could possess a drug was to obtain the drug through a physician. In 1919, in *U.S. v. Doremus,* the Court ruled that the Act was constitutional in spite of the fact that it had been implemented

for purposes other than revenue. In a critical decision announced the same day, the Supreme Court ruled in *Webb v. United States* that a physician prescribing morphine to an addict "not in the course of professional treatment in the attempted cure of the habit," but at a dosage "sufficient to keep him comfortable," was not within the meaning of the physicians' exemption of the Harrison Act, and was therefore illegal. Douglas Kinder, in his analysis of these decisions, concluded that the court was strongly influenced by the alleged association between illicit drug use and "undesirables" (anarchists, radicals, and foreigners) and the fear that illegal drug use might increase as a result of the advent of alcohol prohibition.[27]

The Webb decision threw the entire system of treating addicts into flux. Most doctors simply refused to treat addicts following the Webb decision. This condition was not relieved when a 1919 bill to appropriate money for drug treatment facilities was defeated in the senate as a result of lobbying by the AMA, which saw such funding as government intrusion into the practice of medicine.[28] In the 1922 decision *U.S. v. Behrman*, the Supreme Court went even further by declaring that it was a violation of the Harrison Act for a physician to prescribe drugs to an addict regardless of the purpose or the "good faith" of the doctor. This decision shut off all legal access to drugs for those addicted and redefined the addict's status from that of patient to that of criminal. The Treasury Department immediately threatened with prosecution those few doctors still treating addicts.[29]

One of the doctors prosecuted after the Behrman decision was Dr. Charles Linder of Seattle. Dr. Linder treated one addict in withdrawal with a single prescription for four tablets. The addict turned out to be a Department of Treasury informant, and Dr. Linder was indicted. After spending more than $30,000 and losing his license to practice for two years, Dr. Linder was eventually exonerated by the Supreme Court. In the 1925 decision *Linder v. U.S.*, the Court, reversing its earlier position in the Behrman case, overturned the conviction of the highly respected physician. The court declared that addicts were "diseased and proper subjects for treatment" and that it was not illegal for a physician acting in good faith and according to fair medical standards to prescribe moderate amounts of narcotics for purposes of alleviating withdrawal symptoms.[30] Federal court interpretations of the Linder decision further noted that the Department of Treasury enforcement of the Behrman decision would likely be unconstitutional, on the grounds that such enforcement constituted, not an issue of tax revenue, but a regulation of the practice of medicine.

The Linder decision did not alter public policy, quite simply because the Department of the Treasury continued to intimidate physicians with threats of criminal prosecution.[31]

The enforcement of the Harrison Tax Act altered the relationship between physicians and their addicted patients for more than a half century. Doctors who treated addicts risked losing their medical practice through arbitrary interpretations of "good faith" and "proper treatment." If one were to inquire why the modern physician is so ambivalent about the addicted patient, one would only have to look at the history of 20th-century medicine. More than 25,000 physicians were indicted under the Harrison Act between 1914 and 1938. Some 3,000 actually went to jail, while another 20,000 paid substantial fines.[32] The practical effect of such enforcement was that physicians stopped treating their addicted patients.

What is perhaps most ironic about this period of drug enforcement is the use of addicted informants—themselves often cooperating under threat of indictment—to entrap physicians who were willing to prescribe to addicts to alleviate withdrawal or to provide regular drug maintenance for their condition. The Department of Treasury regularly doled out narcotics to their informants to ensure their cooperation—then indicted the physicians who would have done the same thing.

This period of drug criminalization, which would prove so influential on the continuation of our story of addiction and recovery in America, was driven primarily by fear. The specter of racial violence, addicted soldiers, children falling prey to drug peddlers, drug-emboldened criminal gangs, people switching to drugs after alcohol prohibition, and foreign enemies using drugs as a weapon against America were all among the images floating in the cultural stew of the Harrison Act and its enforcement.

The Morphine Maintenance Clinics

The aggressive enforcement of the Harrison Act generated the need for a response to addicts who no longer had access to narcotics. Proposals of what should be done varied, and arose among the addicts' own demands for immediate treatment. The crisis was usually brought to the fore as a result of the arrest of physicians or druggists who supplied narcotics to large numbers of addicts. In 1918, when authorities arrested four physicians and five druggists in Memphis, Tennessee for violation of the Harrison Act, the community had to decide overnight how to respond to its addicted patients—including many medically

fragile patients—who suddenly faced precipitous withdrawal. Memphis responded by designating one doctor to manage the more than 350 addicts (mostly middle-aged married women) who arrived daily to procure their prescriptions for morphine. In the larger cities, the problem was even more acute. When the 1919 indictment of several physicians in New York City prompted the opening of a drug clinic, more than 3,300 addicts enrolled within the first week.[33]

Many of the proposed responses to the situation argued for the mandatory detention and treatment of addicts for as long as would be required to alter the threat that the addict posed to society.[34] In 1920-1921, Sara Graham-Mulhall and the American Medical Association called for the establishment of a colony system of care for narcotics addicts.[35] The problem was that, in the aftermath of the Harrison Act, there was confusion and conflict over who bore responsibility for the treatment of addicts unveiled by the Harrison Act.

Officials of the U.S. Public Health Service resisted assuming responsibility for addicts, claiming that they had neither the authority nor the resources to provide addiction treatment on such a scale. In 1919, Senator France of Maryland introduced a bill allocating $3 million for a federal narcotics program that would have assisted states in the development of narcotic treatment and prevention programs. The bill never came to a vote.[36] The burden of addiction treatment fell upon the states and local communities.

When the Supreme Court's 1919 Webb decision closed addicts' legal access to narcotics from local physicians, there was a scramble to formulate a response to the needs of addicted citizens. In Illinois, for example, the Governor ordered that restrictions barring the admission of addicts to state psychiatric hospitals be removed. To protect the reputation of people who were secretly addicted, the superintendents of Illinois' state hospitals were allowed to admit addicts under assumed names.[37] As individual physicians ceased to treat addicts due to the threat of indictment, most of the larger communities organized public-health clinics to treat addicts. Some clinics, such as the one in New Haven, Connecticut, were even operated by the local police department.[38] Some offered step-down cures, through which the addict was slowly withdrawn from narcotics. Others offered maintenance.

According to Dr. David Musto, the clinic era begins with the opening of the Jacksonville, Florida Clinic in 1912 and extends through the closure of the last clinic in Knoxville, Tennessee in 1925.[39] There were more than 40 such narcotic treatment clinics (various accounts place the number from 44 to 60). The clinics were concentrated in the Northeast (particularly in New York) and in the South (particularly in Kentucky, Tennessee, and Louisiana).[40] The clinics were closed when their medical staff was threatened with indictment by federal authorities. The closing of the clinics led to a flourishing illicit drug market. In some areas, the prices of narcotics in the illicit market increased by as much as 50 % immediately following the closure of the local clinic.[41]

Communities tried to respond to the needs of addicts in the midst of sometimes conflicting interpretations of what was and was not legal. Physicians were being indicted for prescribing narcotics to addicts, at the same time federal courts were throwing out many such indictments on the grounds that the arrests constituted an unconstitutional federal infringement of medical practice.[42]

The turmoil, at that time, regarding what the federal response to addiction should be at this time was revealed in the response of the Bureau of Narcotics within the Treasury Department. The Bureau announced a regulation in October 1921 that allowed physicians to use narcotics to detoxify addicts, to sustain addicts too old and infirm to face detoxification, and to treat acute and chronic pain within their general practice. However, this policy was later tightened to render illegal the prescription of any narcotic to an addict if its purpose was not the cure of addiction.[43]

The clinics came under severe criticism by law-enforcement groups. The clinics produced few "cures," and it was discovered that addicts were moving from clinic to clinic to prolong their maintenance. Led by a recently created Narcotic Division within the Prohibition Unit of the Department of Treasury, critics attacked the clinics with the following arguments.

1.   Supplying addicts with their customary doses of narcotics is not "good-faith" medical practice and should be prohibited.
2.   The only effective way to eliminate drug addiction is to eliminate the addict's access to the drug supply.
3.   Addicts should not be maintained on drugs when acceptable cures are available.[44]

The Treasury Department began to threaten clinic physicians with arrest. Nearly all the clinics closed in the face of such threats during 1921 and 1922, while a few hung on into the mid-20s. Physicians, acting individually and collectively through their medical societies, also played a role in condemning the operation of the clinics and recommending an end to this "ambulatory" treatment of addicts.[45]

Dr. Marie Nyswander later noted that the closing of the clinics in the early 1920s transferred medical responsibility for America's addicts from physicians to criminal syndicates. Sarah Graham-Mulhall noted the following status of the addict three years after the last clinic closed:

Addicts are not only turned away from hospitals, but they are shunned by civic and philanthropic organizations. Every one is afraid of them; no one cares what becomes of them. They are hardened and embittered by their ostracism; they are driven to places where their drug habit is commercialized.[46]

As the clinics were closing amidst this climate of rigorous legal attack on narcotic addiction, Congress passed the Jones-Miller Act of 1922. This act increased fines for narcotics violations to $5,000 and extended imprisonment to as much as ten years. In less than a decade, the status of the addict had shifted from that of legitimate patient to that of willful criminal.

The experience and quality of the clinics varied considerably, from the New York clinic, universally regarded as the worst managed, to clinics in New Orleans, Los Angeles, and Shreveport that were very highly regarded. The goals of the clinics were to relieve addict suffering, reduce illegal drug trafficking, contain the spread of addiction, and reduce drug-related criminal behavior.[47] Where the clinics were well-managed, available data suggests they were able to achieve these goals. Where the clinics were poorly managed, they quite likely contributed to the problem they were allegedly treating. The history of three of these clinics is illustrative.

The Jacksonville Clinic: Dr. Charles Terry served as City Health Officer in Jacksonville, Florida between 1910 and 1917. Terry studied the growing drug problem in Jacksonville and concluded that an important remedy to this problem lay in the registration and maintenance of addicts. In 1912, two years before the Harrison Tax Act was passed and seven years before most of the maintenance clinics opened, Terry championed the passage of a municipal ordinance that required prescriptions for all narcotics and cocaine, permitted no prescription refills for these drugs, required the recording of all narcotic and dangerous drug transactions, and required that copies of all prescriptions for more than three grains of opiates or two grains of cocaine be forwarded to the Health Department—a practice that amounted to an addict registry. In cases where there was sufficient evidence of habitual use, the ordinance also permitted physicians to provide prescriptions that would allow addicted individuals to be medically maintained on the drug. The Health Department identified 887 cases of habitual use of narcotics and/or cocaine. The majority of those identified were White women. These individuals were given drug prescriptions, in order to provide medical supervision of their addiction and to discourage the illicit drug market in Jacksonville. Terry supported the intent of the Harrison Tax Act and believed that strict enforcement might bring the addiction problem under control. His views changed when he discovered the exorbitant relapse rate of people who were detoxified following termination of the maintenance program, and when he viewed the growth of an illicit drug market that sold adulterated drugs at exorbitant prices in the Jacksonville area.[48]

Charles Terry later moved to New York, chaired the American Public Health Association's Committee on Habit Forming Drugs, and co-authored a Bureau of Social Hygiene study entitled *The Opium Problem.* Terry's personal fate was a sad one. He developed an alcohol problem, *The Opium Problem* was a commercial disaster, and, when he died in 1945, most of his views about addiction had been publicly criticized and discredited. Years later, Terry would be recognized as a pioneer, and *The Opium Problem* would be recognized as one of the most comprehensive and important works on addiction published in the 20th century.[49]

The New York City Clinic: On April 8, 1918—only two months after the New York Narcotic Drug Control Commission was created and one month after the Supreme Court declared the Harrison Act constitutional—federal agents arrested six physicians and four druggists in New York City who were maintaining some 2,000 addicts on narcotics. After the arrests, questions arose immediately concerning the possible ways of caring for these addicts. In response, the Commission set up a noble goal: establish a system of statewide clinics that could provide narcotic maintenance for addicts until institutions could be established to provide treatment and sustained aftercare.

The first of these clinics was opened by New York City officials on April 10, 1919. Sarah Graham-Mulhall, the Deputy Commissioner of the State of New York Department of Narcotic Drug Control, reported that the "clinic was organized for the humane purpose of saving the addict from the profiteering

doctor and the profiteering druggist and to prepare him for hospitalization." Several problems stood in the way of achieving these objectives. First, addicts resisted hospital detoxification due to its exorbitant cost and the suffering involved in rapid detoxification. The hospitals were equally reluctant to admit addicts for such care. When addicts reached the minimum dosage allowed through a clinic and faced pressure for detoxification, many went to another clinic and registered under an assumed name rather than face hospitalization. When they had exhausted the resources of the clinics and faced increased pressure for hospitalization and detoxification, many addicts escaped into a growing illicit drug culture.[50]

The profile of the addicts served by the clinic and those referred for hospital treatment revealed that dramatic changes were occurring in the characteristics of addicts in some American cities. Compared to earlier reports that most addicts in America were affluent middle-aged women, most (over 75%) of the addicts seen at the New York City Clinic were young males. A third of the addicts treated at the clinic were under 20 years of age, a fact that had been unthinkable only a few years earlier. Those treated at the clinic were overwhelmingly White (86%). Most had been addicted for two to five years and attributed their addiction to "bad associates and evil environments" rather than to medical treatment of illness or injury. The earlier morphine addicts (more likely to be seen as medical patients) gave way in the clinic population to young "heroinists." Those addicts treated at the New York City clinic were viewed primarily as underworld types, social misfits, and mental defectives banded together in subterranean cliques found on the fringes of "dance halls, pool rooms, roller skating halls, and movies."[51]

In its nine months of operation, the New York City Clinic illustrated the worst administrative and clinical practices of all the drug maintenance clinics of this era. Numerous state and municipal agencies waged endless turf battles over authority and responsibility. A long list of hospitals refused to open their doors to provide the institutional and aftercare phases of the treatment scheme. Only Riverside Hospital emerged as a primary addiction treatment facility, but 90% of the 2,600 addicts treated there quickly relapsed back to regular drug use.[52]

Efforts by both New York City and the State of New York to provide community clinics, institutional treatment, and follow-up treatment collapsed. To add insult to injury, Governor Miller introduced an austerity budget that called for the elimination of the Narcotic Drug Control Commission.[53]

Dr. Marie Nyswander's modern study of the failure of the New York City Clinic revealed that:

- There was no organized way to respond to the 7,464 addict/patients who sought help from the clinic: Confusion reigned, with as many as 500 addicts per day showing up at the clinic. With no controls, some clients stood in line repeatedly to receive several take-home doses of narcotics.
- Only 2,800 of the addicts agreed to undergo detoxification in a hospital, and most of these quickly relapsed.
- No physicals were given at the clinic, nor was there any other method of verifying addiction before drugs were disseminated.
- Drugs were given only to patients who agreed to withdraw, and there was no provision for treatment of relapsed clients.
- Excessive daily doses of narcotics were distributed (15 grains to patients for whom 1/4 grain would have prevented withdrawal). This led to an intensification of physical addiction and diversion of drugs into the illicit market.
- No provisions were made for treatment of the physical and psychological problems that often accompanied addiction.[54]

The clinic closed January 15, 1920. In 1921, Sara Graham-Mulhall, New York's Deputy Commissioner of the Department of Narcotic Drug Control, characterized the clinic as an "enormously expensive and colossal failure,"[55] but softened this view in 1926, when she looked back on the closing.

After a trial of less than a year, it became necessary to discontinue this clinic not because the idea was unsound, but because the administration and the financial support were inadequate to cope with the tremendous volume of a complex business that required scientific classification and sympathetic, individualized treatment.[56]

Graham-Mulhall reported with great sadness and disillusionment that, of the thousands treated, she could cite only three cases who stayed off drugs as a result of being treated at the clinic.[57] Dr. S. Dana Hubbard, who was also involved in the clinic experiment, concluded that cures were so rare with ambulatory treatment that the method should be legally prohibited.[58]

The situation for addicts in New York City was particularly problematic at the time the clinic closed. Riverside Hospital took no relapse cases, Bellevue Hospital closed its drug addiction unit, and Metropolitan Hospital refused to admit addicts—leaving only the workhouse or the penitentiary as destinations to which addicts could be sent.[59]

The Treasury Department used the mismanagement of the New York clinic to argue that the ambulatory treatment of addiction was a failure and should be stopped everywhere.

The Shreveport Clinic: If New York's was the worst of the nation's maintenance clinics, the clinic at Shreveport was unquestionably one of the best. Shreveport, Louisiana was affected by the Supreme Court's 1919 Doremus and Webb decisions, as were many American cities. When the hidden policy of drug maintenance abruptly stopped under the law-enforcement demand that physicians stop prescribing narcotics to their addicted patients, Shreveport's addicted citizens—a mixture of the very ill, the productive, and the very prominent—began clamoring for help. The State Board of Health responded by assigning one physician to prescribe to addicts, but this physician resigned within a month, due to the sheer volume of work. In response, the State Board asked a Shreveport physician, Dr. Willis P. Butler, to propose a response to the local addiction problem. Butler was experienced in treating addicts in jail through his role as county physician. He visited the New Orleans clinic and returned to Shreveport, impressed with the idea of a clinic but convinced that the methods of treatment used in New Orleans could be improved upon in this clinic.

The Shreveport clinic opened May 3, 1919, under Dr. Butler's administrative and medical supervision. Treatment of patients was initiated, and local response—including the editorial support of the *Shreveport Journal*—was positive. However, under pressure from the Prohibition Unit of the Department of the Treasury, the Louisiana State Board of Health in 1921 voted to close its three addiction treatment clinics in New Orleans, Alexandria, and Shreveport. Dr. Butler closed the clinic, but with support from local physicians he re-opened it the same day under city (rather than state) authority. The City Council of Shreveport gave Butler the authority to treat addicts and provided funds to support his work. Seven-hundred forty addicts were treated at the clinic during its first year, with about 120 addicted patients regularly enrolled. Most patients were White, male, and middle aged. The average length of addiction was 13 years prior to their entering the clinic, and most patients had experienced multiple failures in their prior efforts to get drug-free. In 1922, Dr. Butler published a report on the clinic and its methods in *American Medicine,* in which he set forth his maintenance philosophy.

The amount of morphine dispensed to each patient is the smallest amount that we believe that the patient can get along on and keep in drug balance. The dispensary is not intended as a treatment department for a cure, but only as a means of caring for the incurables, and those not at present curable or treatable, but who must have the medicine.[60]

Patients whose addiction was caused by or exacerbated by other medical conditions first were treated for those conditions, then were withdrawn from the drugs to which they were addicted. For these patients, maintenance continued until the underlying or complicating medical factors were fully treated. A second population of "healthy addicts" (addicts with no concurrent medical conditions) who had become addicted primarily through association with other addicts were immediately detoxified. A third group included addicts who had chronic medical conditions or long addiction histories and who were unlikely to sustain abstinence following detoxification. These "incurables" were placed on a stable dose of narcotics and maintained indefinitely, without expectation that they participate in active treatment or become drug free. Patients paid six cents a grain for morphine at the clinic; the price of the same drug obtained from street peddlers was one dollar a grain. The average dose for maintenance patients was eight grains per day.

Between 1921 and 1923, numerous investigations were launched and many threats made by the Treasury Department in efforts to close the Shreveport clinic.[61] The extended life of this clinic was due to strong support from a community that viewed the clinic as providing a valuable service—a service that not only cared for suffering addicts but also eliminated conditions under which drug trafficking and drug-related crime could flourish. In spite of this support, the clinic was finally ordered to close. Most patients were transferred to a hospital program for rapid detoxification, while some were referred to private physicians. Dr. Butler took 23 "incurables" into his own medical practice. The clinic closed February 10, 1923, and the hospital treatment unit continued to provide some detoxification services until its closure in March, 1925.

A modern re-evaluation of the Shreveport records draws the following conclusions:

The Shreveport staff found no particular innate psychological maladies in their addict-patients. Nor did they find any deleterious effects from maintaining addicts on large doses of morphine for long periods. These addicts were able to live, work, and lead quite normal and productive lives while being maintained....the differences between the productive, citizen-addicts of Shreveport in the 1920s and the maligned, criminal addicts of today appear to be a function of our morals, laws and treatments rather than of addicts themselves.[62]

Many analysts mark the closing of the clinics as the final wedge driven between physicians and their addict patients. Many physicians refused to allow this relationship to be severed and continued to explore medical avenues for the treatment of confirmed addicts.

It was not enough to close the clinics. The very idea of the clinics had to be destroyed. From the closing of the last clinic until the opening debates about methadone in the early 1960s, federal law-enforcement authorities railed against the clinic approach to treating addiction. When the states of California and Washington seriously considered reviving a maintenance clinic approach to managing narcotic addiction, the Bureau of Narcotics marshaled incredible forces to suppress this option. A brief experiment with a narcotics dispensary in Los Angeles ended with the coerced closing of the clinic, and with the eventual indictment of three physicians who continued to prescribe to addicts after the clinic was closed.[63]

Harry Anslinger, Commissioner of the Bureau of Narcotics, openly castigated the clinics, calling them "supply depots" or "barrooms" for addicts. Anslinger claimed that clinics turned doctors into dope dealers, led to a proliferation of crime and drug trafficking, and produced no lasting cures. In an interesting rewrite of history, Anslinger claimed that the clinics had been closed, not due to Federal law enforcement pressure, but due to the actions of local officials.[64] To destroy the very idea of the clinic-based approach to addiction treatment required the destruction of the linked belief that addiction was a disease. For this, Anslinger called upon Dr. Dana Hubbard of the New York City Department of Public Health. Hubbard —sounding more like a law-enforcement official than a public health official—declared:

> ....*drug addiction is not a mysterious disease....drug addiction is simply a degrading, debasing habit, and it is not necessary to consider this indulgence in any other light than an antisocial one.*[65]

By enlisting public-health authorities to declare addiction a voluntary, self-indulgent, malevolent behavior, Anslinger laid the groundwork for what he hoped would be the complete criminalization of addiction. In his view, there was only one way to treat addiction: Don't let it start. And it was his sincere belief that strict enforcement and severe penalties could dry up addiction in America.

The criminalization of addiction did not come as the result of sustained public debate and legislation that clearly expressed this intent. It was a result of the administrative fiat of one federal agency. What was even more remarkable was that this agency—the Department of the Treasury—formulated its position based on its view of what the medical treatment of addiction should and should not consist of, and did so without direct consultation with the mainstream medical community.

✠

Chapter Fourteen
The Treatment of Addiction to Narcotics and Other Drugs: 1925-1950

We ended our last chapter with the administrative criminalization of addiction in the United States, the enforced closing of the narcotics clinics, and the wide-scale exclusion of physicians from the treatment of narcotics addicts. We begin this chapter with the voices of those who protested this abrupt shift in social policy, move into a period in which few addiction treatment resources existed, and then detail the opening and operations of two federal "narcotics farms."

Voices of Protest

For the most part, physicians were silent about the new narcotic laws and their enforcement. It was universally understood that physicians had played a significant role in the development of this problem through their excessive administration of narcotics to their patients. This historical complicity and the awareness that some doctors were still profiteering from the narcotics business contributed to this silence. In fact, their complicity in the criminalization of addiction (in spite of its obvious government invasiveness into the practice of medicine) may have been an essential step in further enhancing the professional credibility of physicians. The other category of professionals closest to the problem of opiate addiction, the druggists, may have been in precisely the same position.

Not all physicians chose this position of silence. Some took great personal risks in protesting efforts to

move the care of addicts from the arena of medicine to that of the police, courts, and prisons. In his 1920 book, *The Narcotic Drug Problem*, E.S. Bishop claimed that this new federal policy left the addict vulnerable to exploitation by two equally reprehensible forces: the criminal underworld and the purveyors of fraudulent drug cures. In his call for the establishment of treatment clinics and a program of basic research as an alternative to criminal and commercial exploitation, Bishop stated:

> *The worst evils of the narcotic drug situation are not rooted in the inherent depravity and moral weakness of those addicted. They find their origin in the opportunity for commercial exploitation of the suffering resulting from denial of narcotic drugs to one addicted....Such exploitation would become unprofitable if the disease were recognized and its physical demands comprehended and provided for in more legitimate and less objectionable ways.*[66]

One year later, Dr. Charles Terry proclaimed that a grievous error was being made in replacing scientific study and medical treatment with a drastic experiment in the legal control of narcotics. Terry proclaimed:

> *Any activity which tries to handle individuals as "addicts" instead of as "patients"*

will fail as it always has and will serve to increase the very evils which it pretends to help.[67]

Dr. Terry went on to declare the source of this grievous error.

The one fundamental reason for the failure ...is the complete misconception on the part of these administrators as to the true nature of the conditions they are seeking to control and alleviate.[68]

In Terry's view, the addiction problem could be effectively managed only if the concept of addiction as a transient "vicious habit" chosen by criminal degenerates was replaced by one that viewed and treated addiction "upon a true disease basis."[69]

In 1925, the Los Angeles County Medical Association protested the conditions under which "any physician who attempts to devote his time to the treatment of narcotic addiction disease....no matter how conservative he may be, or conscientious, or careful, or no matter how humanitarian his purpose, will invariably come into conflict with the laws."[70]

One of the voices of protest against America's response to drug addiction was Dr. Henry Smith Williams, whose brother Dr. E.H. Williams had been indicted for maintaining addicts after the California maintenance clinic was closed. In two books, *Drugs Against Men* (1935) and *Drug Addicts are Human Beings* (1938), Henry Smith Williams stated in no uncertain terms that America's drug problem was created by flaws in American drug-control policies. Smith charged that the administrative misinterpretation of the intent of the Harrison Act had: 1) turned law-abiding, addicted American citizens into outcasts and criminals, 2) created a billion-dollar-a-year illicit-drug industry, 3) led to the persecution and prosecution of some 25,000 physicians whose only crime was fulfilling their pledge to relieve the suffering of their patients, and 4) filled federal prisons with addicts who did not deserve to be there and could not be adequately cared for there. Williams challenged the portrayal of addicts as vicious criminals and claimed that there was nothing inherently more immoral in the use of morphine than in the use of cigarettes or alcohol.[71]

Williams referred to the persecution of addicts, who he suggested suffered from a "deprivation disease" similar to diabetes, as comparable to the burning of witches. He characterized the national shift in drug policy as an "American Inquisition."

Williams recommended that incurable addicts, like their diabetic counterparts, be given medicine under doctors' supervision that would allow their systems to stay "in balance" and function normally—in the same manner in which the "nicotine addict gets his tobacco."[72]

Most of the voices of protest came from moral crusaders—individuals and organizations that had taken up the plight of addicts as a social cause. Included in this group were organizations like the American White Cross Association, the World Narcotic Research Foundation, and Everett Hoffman's Anti-Narcotic Bureau. In 1937, the White Cross Society of Seattle prepared a bill that would have empowered the state medical association to maintain confirmed addicts on narcotics as a way to bring these individuals under medical care and out of the clutches of drug peddlers. The position of the White Cross was that addiction was a medical disease and that addicts should be treated like people suffering from cancer, typhoid, or tuberculosis.[73] The voices of these lone critics, while poignant in their pleas, were quickly absorbed and deflected in this shift toward criminalization of addiction.

Some physicians protested these new policies, not with their voices, but with their prescription pads.

1920-1950: Medical Detoxification and Hidden Drug Maintenance

With the closing of the last maintenance clinic, treatment of addiction consisted primarily of the management of addict withdrawal. Medical arguments proliferated on the relative merits of sudden versus gradual withdrawal. There were also arguments over the best chemical agents to aid this withdrawal process. The choices included chloral hydrate, bromides, alcohol, paraldehyde, belladonna, scopolamine, caffeine, cannabis, and castor oil. During this period, little if anything was done to treat the addiction itself, and medical supervision of withdrawal occurred in spite of the overwhelming likelihood of subsequent relapse.

However, the closing of the clinics did not result in the precipitous withdrawal of all American addicts. Instead, it elicited the heightened degree of deviousness that the desperate addicts needed in order to acquire drugs until an illicit economy emerged to fill this need. Physicians continued to be the main sources through which addicts sustained their need for narcotics. Some addicts, as they do today, received simultaneous prescriptions from many physicians, each physician unaware of the others' involvement. Some addicts moved from doctor to doctor, staying with each physician until the stepped-down dosage reached a point of intolerable discomfort and forced them to seek a new physician and start the process all over. Others mastered the art of presenting symptoms of back injury or other medical problems that could generate brief respite via injections of or prescriptions for narcotics. (These skills included self-inflicted wounds that would place blood in the urine, confirming the addicts' fabricated stories of kidney stones.) Still others resorted to stealing and forging prescriptions or relied on legally exempted elixirs containing small amounts of heroin, codeine, or other opium-based preparations.[74]

Who made up this new class of criminals? While they differed by state and city, Dr. Thomas Blair noted that the Pennsylvania violators were men over 50, including a significant number of aging people with chronic illnesses, some of whom had been addicted as long as 40 years. Their diseases included neuralgia, chronic diarrhea, asthma, chronic bronchitis, tertiary syphilis, tuberculosis, diabetes, and cancer.[75] Some addicts whose addictions were linked to incurable diseases found legal loopholes that allowed them to be maintained on narcotics. Once these conditions were certified by their physicians, the physicians legally maintained these individuals on narcotics. Such exclusions in the application of the law existed by means of administrative interpretation and are mentioned in the autobiographical accounts of narcotics agents. It was not that prescribing narcotics was not technically illegal. It was that local narcotics agents sometimes made exceptions where they perceived that addiction resulted from a search, not for pleasure, but for relief from pain.[76]

On the surface, it seemed that the closing of the clinics had eliminated all but the above-noted exceptions to physicians' maintenance of addicts. A fact that remained hidden for more than 40 years was that numerous addicts were secretly maintained on drugs without legal intervention, particularly in certain areas of the South. When John O'Donnell conducted his landmark 1969 study, *Narcotic Addicts in Kentucky*, he discovered a hidden world of drug maintenance. Of the 266 addicts studied by O'Donnell, nearly three fourths had received prescribed narcotics during part of their careers as addicts, and a quarter had received prescribed narcotics during their entire addiction careers. Many of these people resided in small villages and rural areas that often escaped the close scrutiny of law enforcement authorities. In other instances, law enforcement authorities overlooked cases in which aged and infirm addicts were being maintained on narcotics. Some of this latter group came to the attention of authorities when their physicians died and they could not find new legal sources for drug maintenance. O'Donnell's study confirms the continued role of physicians in providing narcotics to addicts even after such practices were legally prohibited.[77] But not all doctors prescribing to long-term addicts achieved invisibility. Some, like Dr. Thomas Ratigan, Jr., were thrust into the public spotlight.

Dr. Thomas Ratigan, Jr.: Villain or Hero?

In the years following the Supreme Court decisions that, in effect, criminalized addiction in the United States, few urban doctors made themselves available to treat addicts. One exception was a Seattle physician, Dr. Thomas Ratigan, Jr., who in the 1930s began caring for a large number of Seattle's addicts. Charging $1 per visit for those who could afford it and providing free services to others, Dr. Ratigan gave addicts on-site injections of morphine out of his Public Health Institute, never allowing drugs to leave the premises or giving addicts prescriptions to obtain their own supplies. Upon his arrest in 1934, Dr. Ratigan admitted that he had treated 7,000 addicts per year out of the Institute, and that he had done so because there were no formal programs of treatment available to addicts in the state. Dr. Ratigan was convicted, sent to McNeil Island Penitentiary, and stripped of his medical license. Dr. Ratigan served his full prison sentence of seven years and was denied his request for reinstatement of his medical license. He died in 1961.

To some, Dr. Ratigan was a profiteering charlatan who made money from the suffering of addicts. To others, Dr. Ratigan was a courageous and pioneering professional ahead of his time. Dr. Ratigan never wavered from his belief in what he was doing. He said: "I have the solution to the narcotics problem and I am carrying it out. I am proud of my conviction. If administering morphine to confirmed addicts is a crime, I am a criminal." In a final interview before going to prison, Dr. Ratigan reflected: "My solution to the narcotics problem, by administering to addicts, is the only real solution and will be adopted in the future." Thirty-five years later, more than 70,000 addicts received daily doses of methadone in newly opened government-funded treatment programs. An added irony to this story is found in a later disclosure by Harry Anslinger, head of the Bureau of Narcotics, that he personally helped keep an addicted member of Congress (identified by at

least one source to be Joseph McCarthy) and a prominent matron of Washington society out of the hands of
police by regularly supplying narcotic drugs to each of
them.[78]

Phantastica and Narcotics Research

In spite of the closing of the narcotics clinics,
some valuable research studies on narcotic addiction
were still conducted in the 1920s and 1930s. In 1924,
the German chemist and poison specialist Louis
Lewin published *Phantastica*, unquestionably one of
the most significant contributions in history to the
study of psychoactive drugs. The accuracy of Lewin's
studies has held up over a remarkable long period. He
classified psychoactive drugs into five categories: 1)
euphoriants (sedating), 2) phantastica (hallucinogen-
inducing), 3) inebriantia (intoxicating), 4) hypnotica
(sleep-inducing), and 5) excitantia (stimulating).
Some of Lewin's observations and pronouncements
read as if they came from this morning's headlines
rather than from a text written more than 70 years ago.
Lewin's text included a full account of what he
referred to both as "cocainism" and "cocainomania."
Lewin compared cocaine's addictive potential to that
of morphine and provided a fully detailed depiction of
cocaine psychosis, including an account of a woman
who suffered severe self-injury attempting to remove
the "cocaine bugs" from beneath her skin with a
hypodermic needle.[79]

During the year after Lewin's *Phantastica* was
published, The New York Committee on Drug Addiction sponsored research on the biology of narcotic
addiction, in a study headed by Dr. Charles Doane of
Philadelphia. Doane's group provided a detailed
description of the narcotic abstinence syndrome and
went on to note that narcotic addicts suffered no major
physical deterioration other than that attributable to
malnutrition. These were among the first American
studies to apply modern laboratory science to the
study of addiction.

Binghma Dai's 1937 study of opiate addiction in
Chicago provides a glimpse of what treatment of
addiction was like in the Midwest during the mid-
1930s. There were private treatments offered by
particular physicians. Dai notes one ten-day "cure"
promoted all over the world by a Chicago physician,
Dr. C.E. Sceleth, who described his methods in a
promotional pamphlet entitled: *A Rational Treatment
of the Morphine Habit*.[80] The addicts in Dai's study
reported many attempts at cures in private sanataria,
state psychiatric institutions, and municipal hospitals.
The Chicago Psychopathic Hospital routinely detoxi-

fied people in what was reported as "the customary
ten days." The interviews in Dai's study reveal
addicts speaking with great frustration about their
multiple attempts at institutional cures—all of which
were followed by relapse.

The sparseness of addiction treatment in America changed in the mid-1930s, with what in the
context of our history might seem an unlikely event:
the opening of two federally sponsored addiction
treatment hospitals.

The Federal Narcotic Farms [81]

The U.S. Public Health Service's involvement in
the problem of addiction began in the early 1920s.
Dr. Lawrence Kolb conducted field studies to esti-
mate the number of addicts in the United States. He
concluded that there were between 110,000 and
150,000 addicts. Viewing addiction as a psychiatric
problem, Kolb called for the creation of specialized
psychiatric hospitals for the treatment of addiction.
While there was no immediate response to this
scientific proposal, the need for a more effective
response to narcotic addiction was becoming evident
in many ways. By the late 1920s, most states had
provided a legislative mechanism for the involuntary
commitment of addicts for treatment, mostly within
state psychiatric institutions that provided no specialized addiction treatment services. Only California
had a specialized addiction treatment facility: the
State Narcotics Hospital at Spadra, which operated
from 1928 to 1941.

The resources of state psychiatric facilities and
state prisons were being strained due to the growing
numbers of addicts, and federal prisons were being
overcrowded with addicts sentenced for violations of
the Harrison Act. The numbers of addicts committed
to federal penitentiaries increased from 63 in 1915 to
1,889 in 1929.[82] By 1928, more than two-thirds of
the inmates at Leavenworth, Atlanta, and McNeil's
Island were addicts, and staff of these facilities were
describing the incoming addicts as "quite troublesome to handle."[83] Following a riot at Leavenworth
that was attributed to overcrowding, and investigations of drug-smuggling operations at the federal
prisons, the need for change was clearly evident.
Pleas from federal prison officials, an exposé on
prison conditions by the Hearst newspapers, and a
reform study (Wickersham Committee Report)
recommending classification and segregation of
federal prison inmates into specialty facilities all
helped add momentum toward action.

In 1929, Congress passed the Porter Act, which

allocated funds for the U.S. Public Health Service to construct and operate two "narcotic farms," which would house and rehabilitate addict/offenders who had been convicted of violating federal drug laws.[84] In testimony during hearings for the Porter Act, the Surgeon General of the Public Health Service stated that the Service did not support this enterprise, but Congress bowed to the influence of James Bennet, superintendent of the federal prison system, who was a strong advocate of segregation and specialized care for addicts.

A year after "addiction" appeared for the first time in the American Psychiatric Association's Standard Classified Nomenclature of Disease, the Lexington Narcotics Farm opened in Lexington, Kentucky in May, 1935. The second facility opened in Fort Worth, Texas in November, 1938. The Lexington facility treated addicts who lived east of the Mississippi. The Fort Worth facility treated those who lived West of the Mississippi. The Lexington facility was renamed the U.S. Public Health Service Narcotics Hospital in 1936, but references to the federal narcotics "farms" continued for several decades.

Like most innovations, the Lexington and Fort Worth facilities represented a synthesis of a number of social and political agendas. While one can speak of the practical relief of prison overcrowding and an increased openness to the notion of addict treatment, these facilities also symbolized the breach between alcohol polices and policies related to other drugs. In the late 1930s, processes unfolded to redeem and mainstream the alcoholic, while the narcotic addict would be subjected to continued social isolation. Lexington and Fort Worth were as much instruments of quarantine as they were instruments of active treatment.[85] As late as 1956, Dr. James Lawry, the Medical Officer of Lexington, would define his facility's purposes as follows:

Hospitalization is a public health measure that prevents the spread of addiction by isolating a principal agent of dissemination—the narcotic addict.[86]

Admission: The Lexington and Fort Worth facilities were open to people addicted to drugs covered under federal law—most, to narcotics. Addicts admitted to the Lexington and Fort Worth facilities were admitted via two avenues: legal commitment through a federal court or voluntarily application for treatment. Voluntary patients were required to submit a completed application, which was re-

viewed by staff who then informed the applicant of the decision to grant or refuse admission. The term "voluntary," as applied to people entering the Lexington facility, requires some qualification. Many of those admitted as voluntary, while they were not committed under federal law, came in under various forms of duress, such as threatened prosecution by local authorities or pressure from family members.[87] All patients were first placed on an admission unit. Each entering patient was photographed; cleaned up; and issued pajamas, robes, and the "scrip" that was used for money on the hospital grounds.

Facilities: The Narcotic Hospital was located five miles outside of Lexington, Kentucky. When the newly arrived addicts entered the huge steel gates of "K.Y." (as it was often called by addicts) and viewed the barred windows and security procedures, they had no doubt they were entering a prison. The emphasis on security at Lexington lessened as staff gained experience in working with addicts, and the Fort Worth facility was designed with a less prison-like atmosphere. Inmates coming from other prisons often referred to Lexington as "the country club." The security at Lexington and Fort Worth was designed more to keep drugs and contraband from coming in than to keep prisoners from escaping.

The grounds of the Lexington Narcotics Farm facilities housed administration, library, and laboratory facilities. There were cells for 1,200 prisoners, which were expanded in 1941 with the addition of a separate building for women. There was a dairy farm, small furniture and garment factories, and an auditorium for recreation—all scattered across 1,000 acres of Kentucky bluegrass.[88] The Fort Worth facility sat on 1,400 acres and, like Lexington, contained a farm and dairy. It was designed to hold 1,000 prisoners. Except for a five-year period (1947-1952) in which women were treated at Fort Worth, addicted women from all areas of the United States were treated at Lexington.

The Staff: The staff of both facilities included physicians, psychiatrists, nurses, social workers, recreational therapists, chaplains, and aids. The administrative physicians assigned to coordinate the individual patients' care were psychiatric residents supervised by staff psychiatrists. The professional staff of Lexington was headed by Dr. Lawrence Kolb, who conducted the earlier-noted research on addiction at the U.S. Public Health Service Hygienic Laboratory in Washington, D.C.

The Patient Profile: Lawrence Kolb described the addicts entering Lexington and Fort Worth as making up five clinical subpopulations, each distinguished by different causes and presenting characteristics. Here is Kolb's own description of these five classes of addicts.

> *Class I was comprised of mentally healthy people who had become addicted accidentally or necessarily through the use of narcotic drugs for the treatment of an illness. Class II consisted of hedonistic individuals who both before and after their addiction had spent their lives seeking pleasure, new excitements and sensations....Class III were psychoneurotics who exhibited mild hysterical symptoms, various phobias and compulsions, and other neurotic pathology. Class IV was made up of habitual criminals with severe psychopathology which was expressed in extreme antisocial behavior. Class V comprised addictive personalities, who had an ungovernable need for intoxicants.*[89]

The demographic profile of the typical addict admitted to Lexington was described in a 1936 study as that of a 38-year-old white male prisoner plagued with chronic health problems, who became addicted to morphine at age 27 and later entered the prison system with a two-year sentence for illegal sale of narcotics.[90]

Treatment Methods: Three phases of treatment were provided at Lexington: withdrawal, convalescence, and rehabilitation. Gradual detoxification occurred over two weeks. The addict's discomfort was aided by hot baths during the day and chloral hydrate as an aid to sleep at night. After 1948, methadone was utilized to detoxify those addicted to morphine and heroin. Withdrawal from narcotics was usually achieved in four to seven days. A period of convalescence allowed the addict to regain strength and allowed staff to conduct individual interviews and formulate a plan of rehabilitation.

Following withdrawal, patients were moved to wards and integrated into various vocational and recreational activities. These movements also reflected different degrees of security and supervision, from maximum to minimum. During the initial period of orientation on a ward, each patient identified the types of activities that he or she was interested in pursuing while at Lexington. The list contained such items as individual therapy, group therapy, Alcoholics Anonymous meetings, school, church, and vocational training. A psychiatric evaluation was also completed during this orientation period. Information gathered

from each patient was integrated into a plan of treatment that usually included periodic interviews with the Lexington staff (only about one fourth actually had individual psychotherapy) and ward meetings, at which the patients were expected to discuss their personal problems and their plans to avoid relapse when they returned home.

A great portion of the daily activity at Lexington and Forth Worth consisted of assigned work in the various industries on the grounds: crop production, animal husbandry, landscaping, construction, and tailoring. Addicts at Lexington spent four times as much time in labor as they did in therapy-related activities. Patients were paid for their labor in cigarettes. All of these activities were subsumed under the rubric of "milieu therapy."[91]

Progress of patients at Lexington was defined in terms of signs of increased maturity: self-comfort and self-reliance, ability to get along with others, ability to handle stressful daily situations, and ability to control impulses. Patients who exhibited these characteristics were thought to be able to return home without succumbing to the temptation of drugs.[92]

There were two populations of addicts at Lexington. Inmates from other prisons were transferred to Lexington because of their addiction status. These inmates stayed a year or longer at Lexington. More than two thirds of the addict/offenders at Lexington were sentenced to more than one year, with many sentenced to between two and ten years.[93] The "voluntary" clients, who were assessed a daily fee for their treatment, could sign themselves out of Lexington with or without the agreement of the staff. One of the major problems at Lexington was the lack of control over length of stay for both of these groups. The involuntary patients with long prison sentences were hard to motivate—they stayed too long—and the voluntary population of addicts rarely stayed for the recommended time.

Boredom was a problem for both groups, in spite of the daily work schedule and staff efforts to provide various entertainments, such as billiards and movies. Most "down-time" at Lexington was spent sharing street tales and scheming imaginative ways to get to the facility's drug supplies or get to the patients of the opposite sex.[94]

Voluntary patients posed a special problem for the Lexington staff. When the courts ruled that voluntary patients could not be held against their will, the Lexington staff lobbied the Kentucky legislature to pass a "Blue Grass" law making "habitual narcotic use" a crime. When that law was passed, addicts wishing to enter Lexington were forced to plead guilty to the new law and were sentenced to one year of treatment in Lexington. Problems with involuntary patients were never fully resolved and, in fact, became worse as prison sentences for addicts lengthened throughout the 1950s and 1960s. The challenge posed to the staff at Lexington was well articulated by Dr. Robert Rasor:

> *The Hospital was in the position of being required to furnish treatment of a kind it considered to be inadequate to patients selected by others, for periods of time over which it had no effective control.*[95]

Another obstacle to the effectiveness of Lexington was the lack of any systematized contact with families and the lack of a way to follow addicts into their home communities.

Family involvement in treatment at Lexington and Ft. Worth was plagued by problems of distance. The addicts treated at these facilities came from all over the United States. The lack of community-based treatment resources meant that family members were rarely involved in the treatment process. There is a striking absence of family perspective in the addiction literature produced during this era. References to family in the literature are drawn primarily from addicts' own reports of their family circumstances.

The farms isolated addicts, in the belief that such isolation checked the contagious spread of addiction into communities. This rural isolation, it was thought, also took the addict away from the urban pressures and temptations that many believed led to addiction. But upon their release, addicts returned to those pressures and temptations—and did so with no reasonably accessible support for their continued recovery.

Treatment Outcome Studies: Results of follow-up studies of addicts leaving Lexington were disappointing. Almost all of the studies documented that 90-96% of addicts treated at Lexington returned to active addiction, most within six months of discharge. Dr. James Maddux, a former Chief Medical Officer at the Fort Worth facility, offered the following evaluation of the Lexington and Fort Worth programs:

> *At least nine of ten patients resumed use of a morphine like drug within five years after discharge. Few enduring cures of the drug-using habit were achieved. In widespread professional and public opinion, the hospitals came to be considered failures; measured by a criterion of enduring cure of most patients, they failed.*[96]

As poor treatment outcomes became evident and the percentage of re-admissions increased, the Public Health Service increased its recommended length of stay for addicts.

Internal staff explanation of this high failure rate tended to place blame on the addict population's lack of motivation for recovery and on the failure of medical science to discover a way to instill such motivation.[97] The most positive face was placed on these studies by Dr. Victor Vogel. In critiquing poor treatment outcomes for narcotics addicts, Vogel declared:

> *I do not share the authors' apology for reporting only a moderate degree of success, considering that drug addiction is a chronic disease with a tendency to relapse. If treatment results are compared with those in other chronic or recurrent diseases, such as tuberculosis, arthritis, hypertension, diabetes, or cancer, results in this field are good.*[98]

In spite of Vogel's optimistic assessment, studies of addicts treated at Lexington and Forth Worth underscored the limited role of hospital treatment in the total rehabilitation of an addict. By underscoring the high incidence of relapse and the circumstances associated with relapse, the studies laid the foundation for a community-based treatment system that incorporated programs of legal supervision and sustained aftercare services. They also challenged the prevailing view that addict relapse was a conscious choice made by moral weaklings. The overwhelming incidence of addict relapse suggested that they needed more intense and more enduring treatment efforts—and perhaps a fundamentally different type of treatment.

The Lexington and Fort Worth facilities provided the primary sources of treatment for narcotic addiction between 1935 and the early 1950s. The importance of these facilities diminished as more state- and community-based programs were initiated. The documentation of high relapse rates following treatment at Lexington and Fort Worth set the stage for the emergence of two new treatments for narcotic addiction, which will be described in Chapters Twenty-Four and Twenty-Five: the ex-addict-directed therapeutic community and methadone maintenance. As new community-based models of addiction treatment arose, the institutions in Lexington and Fort Worth became viewed as obsolete.

The Addiction Research Center

Although the treatment conducted at Lexington and Fort Worth may have been of questionable value, few would argue with the assertion that much of the foundation upon which modern treatment advances were built came from research conducted at Lexington and Fort Worth.

The Addiction Research Center was created at the Prison Annex at Leavenworth Penitentiary in 1933, while the Lexington and Fort Worth facilities were being built. The Center was later transferred to Lexington, Kentucky when the Public Health Service Narcotic Hospital opened there. The Addiction Research Center constructed psychiatric and psychological profiles of addicts, described and developed reliable ways of measuring drug withdrawal, pioneered the use of methadone as a withdrawal agent, and documented the need for aftercare services for addicts leaving institutional treatment. Staff of the Center discovered animal models to test the addiction liability of new drugs. By studying morphine and heroin addicts who had shifted to barbiturate use in the early 1940s when they could not obtain opiates, the Research Center (through the studies of Harris Isbell) was able to document that barbiturates were addicting drugs.[99] They pioneered research on the development of non-addictive pain killers. They discovered several narcotic antagonists, such as nalorphine, and investigated their use in addiction treatment. Administrative responsibility for the Addiction Research Center was transferred from the Public Health Service to the National Institute of Mental Health in 1948. In the 1950s, the ARC conducted studies on adolescent narcotic addiction—a phenomenon that was sparking great public concern at the time.

For decades, the Addiction Research Center was at the center of addiction research in the United States. People who made significant contributions to our understanding of addiction by working for or with the ARC included Lawrence Kolb, Clifton K. Himmelsbach, Harris Isbell, William Martin, and Nathan B. Eddy. Many people who would go on to make significant contributions to the field of addictions treatment, such as Marie Nyswander, Jerry Jaffe, George Vaillant, Patrick Hughes, and Joel Fort, worked early in their careers as clinicians or researchers at Lexington. The work of the ARC continued under the auspices of the National Institute on Drug Abuse after the Lexington treatment facilities were closed. Today, nearly 100 scientists work within the ARC's six research branches located in Baltimore, Maryland.

The World Outside Lexington and Fort Worth

The fact that, by 1938, the nation had two facilities that specialized in the treatment of narcotic addiction should not blur the reality that most mid-century addicts in America did not have access to addiction treatment services and were exposed to every conceivable type of experimental treatment. Typical of such experiments was an announced "serum cure" for addiction, reported to have been discovered at the Colorado State Penitentiary. The cure involved raising blisters on the skin of the addict with heat plasters, withdrawing serum from the blisters, and re-injecting the serum into the muscles of the addict. This procedure was repeated four to five times over a span of a week to ten days, and was said to have effected some remarkable cures.[100] Such was the world of addiction treatment in America outside the walls of the Lexington and Fort Worth facilities in the 1940s and early 1950s.

During the same year in which the Lexington facility opened, two alcoholics were about to meet each other and form the beginning of a fellowship that would profoundly shape the history of the treatment of both alcoholism and narcotic addiction.

Chapter Fifteen
The Birth of Alcoholics Anonymous: A Brief History [1,2,3]

Many people believe that mutual support groups for alcoholics began in 1935 with the founding of Alcoholics Anonymous (AA). This is clearly not the case. From the Washingtonian Movement through the fraternal temperance societies, the reform clubs, the Ollapod Club, the Keeley Leagues, the United Order of Ex-Boozers, the Jacoby Club of the Emmanuel Clinic, and on to the Oxford Group, alcoholics struggling to get sober and stay sober found places to band together for mutual support. But A.A. has a distinctive place in this history. No mutual-aid movement other than A.A. involved such large numbers of alcoholics, spread to so many corners of the earth, sustained itself so long, and so profoundly shaped the evolution of alcoholism treatment. It is a testament to this influence that every subsequent sobriety-based support structure is evaluated using A.A. as the standard of comparison.[1]

There were many things about the mid-1930s in America that made this time and place ripe for the rise of a society of self-professed alcoholics banded together for mutual support in their struggle to recover. For nearly a century, a succession of religious, temperance, and prohibition movements had framed the character of the alcoholic in a language of moral degeneracy. But forces were building that would reverse the pendulum of public thinking about alcohol and alcoholics. Conditions were emerging that would lessen the stigma of alcoholism by redefining the alcoholic in a language that was at once more medical and more likely to evoke compassion.

The prohibition of alcohol through the 1920s and the sustained depression of the 1930s both placed their strain on America's alcoholics. Prohibition and the hardships of the depression provided a unique context for the rise of A.A. During the early 1930s, the woes of America's alcoholics were increasing, just as traditional sources of help for the alcoholic had all but vanished. By 1930, most of the early-20th-century "drying-out" institutions had closed their doors, and those that remained were closed to all but the most affluent or well-connected alcoholics. Overcrowding in city hospitals and state psychiatric hospitals in the early 1930s made it increasingly difficult for alcoholics to get admitted. For many, what remained were impulsively purchased home cures that uniformly turned out to be frauds. A.A. was born amidst the inability of more formal helping institutions to respond successfully to the problem of alcoholism. Alcoholics entered the mid-1930s in need of help, but highly skeptical. Their families—whose suffering had also intensified amidst the drying-up of public and private charities—were at their wits' end, but equally skeptical that anything could help. A vacuum of need existed that begged to be filled with a source of hope.

One must also remember that prohibition had just been repealed—an event that many alcoholics must have foreseen as an omen of their own quickened destiny. President Roosevelt had just given a State of the Union Address that launched New Deal programs for the sick and aged, while calling upon Americans to band together and pull themselves up by their bootstraps. For those whose boots had long been filled with flasks, there were surely rising aspirations (grandiose though they may have been) for a new beginning. The climate was ripe for a new movement—a movement of self-regeneration launched by and for alcoholics. It had to be a movement that did not require scarce federal, state, or municipal funds —or equally scarce personal financial resources. It had to be a movement that could achieve credibility with alcoholics. It had to be a movement that altered America's very conception of the alcoholic. It had to be a movement that could last. The movement that came met all of these criteria.

The historical thread that leads to the birth of the largest fellowship of recovered alcoholics in history begins in Zurich, Switzerland; winds through Oxford Group meetings in New York City and Akron, Ohio; and settles on a meeting between two desperate men struggling to find a way out of the alcoholic labyrinth.

---

[1] Ernest Kurtz provided helpful critiques of several drafts of this and the following three chapters. His assistance is gratefully acknowledged, as is that of Mel B. and Wally P., who also provided helpful suggestions on these chapters.

Carl Jung and Rowland H.'s Failed Psychotherapy[2]

Rowland H.'s prominence could not hide the ravages of his alcoholism. His money and political influence had done nothing to slow the progression of his alcoholism. In desperation, this investment banker went to Zurich in 1931 and placed himself under the care of the noted psychoanalyst Carl Jung. After being treated by Jung, he returned to the United States, believing himself cured. After quickly relapsing, Rowland returned to Jung, only to be told that there was nothing left that medical or psychiatric treatment could do for him. Jung went on to say that Rowland's only hope was some kind of "spiritual awakening" or religious experience. With great candor, Jung also told him that such experiences were quite rare.

Jung understood that alcoholism created a spiritual void. He understood the way in which, for a blessed few, a spiritual experience seemed to fill this void and stem the alcoholic's voracious appetite for the very thing that promised self-destruction. Perhaps most important, Jung understood that such a spiritual experience was not in the realm of psychotherapy. Accepting the limits of his new science, Jung gave Rowland his pessimistic prescription. Rowland's search for a spiritual experience led him to the Oxford Group in England, then to the center of the Oxford Group in America—Sam Shoemaker and the Calvary Episcopal Church in New York City.[4]

The Oxford Group

The Oxford Group was a popular spiritual

_____

[2] This account of Rowland H. represents the summary of A.A.'s earliest seeds as it has been recounted in A.A's basic texts. These accounts note Rowland's treatment under Jung's care for a year, a subsequent relapse, and a return to Europe to hear Jung's above-noted advice. A just-completed review (continuing Wally P.'s initial investigations) into the Rowland H. Papers at the Rhode Island Historical Society reveals no evidence that Rowland was treated by Jung and suggests that, if such treatment did occur between 1930-1934, it was for a much shorter period (a few weeks). These same records do contain evidence that Rowland H. was treated twice for alcoholism at Doctor's Hospital in Yorkville, New York (February-March 1932; July, 1932) and that he was under the care of lay therapist Courtenay Baylor (see Chapter 12) between December, 1933 and October, 1934. (Personal Correspondence to the author, January 15, 1998, Rick Stattler, Manuscripts Curator, Rhode Island Historical Society.)

movement of the 1920s and 1930s started by Frank Buchman, a Lutheran minister from Pennsylvania. The movement began in the early 1900s, peaked in the late 1930s, and declined in the 1940s. Also called "Buchmanism," the Oxford Group was an outgrowth of the First Century Christian Fellowship started by Buchman some years earlier. The Episcopal clergyman Dr. Sam Shoemaker was most directly responsible for conveying and refining from the Oxford Group the concepts that would have the greatest utility for alcoholics. The central idea of the Oxford Group was that the problems of the world could be healed through a movement of personal spiritual change. This change came about through a set of core ideas and practices for daily living. Key concepts within the Oxford Group were reflected in their "four absolutes": absolute honesty, absolute purity, absolute unselfishness, and absolute love. There were also the "five C's" (confidence, confession, conviction, conversion, and continuance) and the "five procedures" (Give in to God, listen to God's direction, check guidance, restitution, and sharing through witness).[5]

The Oxford Group was not explicitly a program of alcoholism recovery, but many desperate alcoholics like Rowland were drawn to the Group. The Oxford Group did not require total abstinence from alcohol, as many religious sects did. What they did ask for were visible signs of change in the lives of their members. It was within this context that many Oxford group members stopped using alcohol and tobacco.[6] The future co-founders of A.A.—one in New York and one in Ohio—were each exposed to the Oxford Group before their history-making meeting.

The Oxford Groups, Ebby T., and Bill Wilson's "Hot Flash"

Rowland H.'s involvement in the Oxford Group temporarily quelled his appetite for alcohol and restored a semblance of sanity. The Group's emphasis on spiritual surrender (admitting that one had lost the battle to booze), relying on God as a source of strength, self-inventory, confession of one's wrongs, and helping others struck responsive chords in Rowland.

When Rowland heard that an old friend of his, Ebby T., was threatened with commitment because of drinking, Rowland and two other Oxford Group members visited Ebby in jail. There was something about Rowland's personal story that touched Ebby. He was released from jail through Rowland's intervention, stopped drinking, and began regular participation in the Oxford Group. Boiling over with the energy and confidence of the newly converted, Ebby sought out an old school friend who he knew was killing himself with alcohol. In November, 1934, Ebby visited Bill Wilson. A message about the potential for spiritual rebirth was once again about to be passed from one alcoholic to another.[7][8]

In 1934, Bill Wilson's alcoholism was raging out of control. He stole money from his wife, binged for days, brawled, suffered extensive blackouts, experienced delirium tremens, and required sedatives to sleep. And afterwards there were always the shame, the self-indictments, and the tearful apologies and promises.[9] Bill's drinking continued until December 11, 1934, at the age of 39, when he took what he would never have thought to be the last drink of his life. Ebby and other Oxford group members visited Bill Wilson and tried to sober him up enough to get him to an Oxford Group meeting, but Bill's medical condition interrupted the process. On December 11, 1934, he was admitted to the Charles B. Towns Hospital—a well known drying-out facility in Manhattan.[10] It was his fourth such trip in recent years, and the doctors had begun to talk to his wife, Lois, about the possible need to "put Bill away"—a polite euphemism for psychiatric commitment. Bill's alcoholism and his quest for a solution to it had reached a turning point.

A few days into his stay at Towns Hospital, Bill Wilson had an experience of enormous intensity that he would later refer to as his "Hot Flash." Wilson, who had been fighting the idea of a Higher Power since his early discussions with Ebby, later described what happened as his depression deepened in the hospital.

The last vestige of my proud obstinacy was crushed. All at once I found myself crying out, "If there is a God, let Him Show Himself! I am ready to do anything, anything!" Suddenly the room lit up with a great white light. I was caught up into an ecstasy which there are no words to describe....And then it burst upon me that I was a free man.....All about me there was a wonderful feeling of Presence, and I thought to myself, "So this is the God of the Preachers!"[11]

Thinking that this experience might be a hallucination and further indication that he was losing his mind, Bill sought the advice of his physician. That physician happened to be Dr. William Silkworth, who had come to work at the Towns Hospital in 1930 at a salary of $40 a week, after losing all his financial resources in the stock market.[12] Bill pointedly asked Silkworth, "Have I gone crazy?"[13] It would have been easy for Silkworth to attribute Bill's experience to the drugs he was being given: his belladonna-laced medications were known to produce hallucinations and delirium in some patients. As in the case of Dr. Jung before him, what Silkworth did not do (provide sedating medication) and did not say are as important to this history as what he did do and say. After listening to Bill Wilson's account, Silkworth told Bill that what he had described might be a conversion experience and that such powerful experiences sometimes released people from alcoholism. The man who would become known as "the little doctor who loved drunks" convinced Bill Wilson that what he had experienced was not a hallucination, but a spiritual breakthrough.[14] Writing of this event later, Bill observed, "If he had said 'hallucination' I might now be dead. To him I shall be eternally grateful."[15]

The change that had taken place in Bill was immediately evident to others. His wife Lois wrote:

The minute I saw him at the hospital, I knew something had happened. His eyes were filled with light. His whole being expressed joy and hope. From that moment on I shared his confidence in the future. I never doubted that at last he was free.[16]

Ebby brought Bill Wilson a copy of William James' book, *The Varieties of Religious Experience*, in the hope it might help Bill understand what had happened to him. Ebby was right. It was in the pages of this book that Bill came to understand how out of calamity and pain could come surrender—"deflation at depth"—and an opening of oneself to the experience of a hope-infusing Higher Power. James' description of the elements of conversion validated for Bill what he later called "the sublime paradox of strength coming out of weakness."[17] He undoubtedly also noticed James' observation that the only cure for "dipsomania" (alcoholism) was "religiomania."

Another aspect of Bill's seven-day stay at Towns hospital was his exposure to Silkworth's unrelenting message that Bill had developed an allergy to alcohol and could never again drink in a normal manner. While no such allergy had (or has) been scientifically validated, Silkworth's message provided Bill with a powerful and guilt-assuaging medical metaphor to understand what had happened to him. He left Towns Hospital with a new belief that he had a biological illness that would not allow him to drink.

Following his discharge, Bill and Lois Wilson

began attending Oxford Group meetings led by Dr. Sam Shoemaker, while Bill began to seek out the alcoholics who had started to gather in Stewart's Cafeteria after the regular Oxford Group meetings.[18] Bill also started trying to carry his message of hope to alcoholics being treated at the Towns Hospital and those he found at the Calvary Mission. Bill began to envision a movement of alcoholics carrying the message that the words of Silkworth and James had brought him. In a fashion that would be repeated thousands of times in other times and places, Bill got sober and decided he was going to sober up the world—all by himself. For six months, his efforts to sober up others had kept no one but himself sober. Then came the trip to Akron.

Bill W. Meets Dr. Bob

In 1935, Bill Wilson went to Akron, Ohio, on what turned out to be a failed business trip. On Saturday, May 11 of that year, Bill found himself alone in the lobby of the Mayflower Hotel, with the beckoning sounds of celebration coming from the bar. With a rising sense of panic, he sought the public phone and frantically tried to reach an Oxford group member to quell his impulse to drink. Believing that a conversation with another similarly afflicted individual might help, Bill began a series of phone calls that led from Rev. Walter Tunks to Mrs. Henrietta Seiberling. Bill told her he was a "rum hound from New York" who needed to help another drunk in order to stay sober. As fate would have it, Mrs. Seiberling knew just such a person, Dr. Robert Smith. "Dr. Bob" (as he would become known with affection in A.A.) had been trying unsuccessfully to stay sober in the local Oxford Group. At a meeting arranged at her home on May 12, 1935, Henrietta Seiberling introduced the two men. Dr. Bob was tentative, saying he could stay only 15 minutes, but the men talked and drank coffee for the next five hours. It was there that a stockbroker educated a surgeon about the medical nature of alcoholism. Dr. Bob would later say of Bill Wilson, "He was the first living human with whom I had ever talked who knew what he was talking about in regard to alcoholism from actual experience."[19]

Their relationship held a special chemistry from the beginning. As in the case of many other perfectly timed events that seem to mark the history of A.A., Bill was given more work in Akron and an opportunity to continue his meetings with Dr. Bob during the summer of 1935. A few weeks after their initial encounter, Dr. Smith attended a medical convention in Atlantic City. He returned drunk, and Bill and Anne

(Dr. Bob's wife) tapered him off in time to perform a scheduled surgical operation. Dr. Bob consumed a final beer to steady his nerves before the operation and never took another drink in his life. The day was June 10, 1935—the day noted as the founding date of Alcoholics Anonymous.[20] The next day, Dr. Bob suggested to Bill that together they begin reaching out to other alcoholics in need. Their search took them to Akron City Hospital and to A.A. Number Three. The process of multiplication had begun.[21]

A.A. Identity and Early A.A. Growth

That summer, Bill Wilson moved into Dr. Bob's and Anne's home on Ardmore Avenue in Akron. Slowly a group began to form, a group of alcoholics who were maintaining sobriety by working together and reaching out to other alcoholics. Week by week the number of alcoholics trying to get sober with Bill and Dr. Bob increased, but there were many failures. When Bill Wilson returned to New York late in the summer of 1935, there were only four sober members in Akron. Bill began his own recruitment in New York, contacting alcoholics in the Oxford Group, at Calvary Mission, and at the Towns Hospital. A.A. was growing from two points on the map—Akron and New York City—and then, in 1937, from a third: Cleveland, Ohio. Developments in Cleveland would prove particularly significant.

These first years have been called A.A.'s "flying blind" period. There were no Twelve Steps. There were no Twelve Traditions. Everything was being defined on a day-to-day and person-to-person basis. Bill, Dr. Bob, and other early members experimented until they discovered what worked. They would later say that they broke their own rules so often that there weren't any rules left, except "Don't Drink!" Something very exciting was happening through this experimentation—something that Bill Wilson's spiritual advisor, Father Ed Dowling, would later call "regeneration."

There was still no conscious A.A. identity. The fledgling groups met within the larger framework of the Oxford Group, but there was increasing strain between the alcoholic and non-alcoholic members of the Oxford Group. The Oxford Group leaders discouraged Bill's exclusive preoccupation with working with drunks, suggesting that this fixation was an indication that he and Lois were "not maximum"—an Oxford Group phrase intimating someone who was, in the language that A.A. would later develop, "not getting the program." The Calvary Mission even issued an order that prohibited alcoholics who lived at the Mission from attending Bill's Clinton-Street meeting.[22] Still, Bill and his rag-tag group of struggling alcoholics persevered to maintain their group identity.

Clear differences existed between the alcoholic and non-alcoholic groups. The Oxford Group insisted on periods of extended silence, which gave alcoholics the jitters. The Oxford Group valued personal publicity and public prominence as a kind of advertising, while the alcoholics were developing the practice of anonymity.[23] The Oxford Group members could be coercive in their zealous imposition of spiritual beliefs, while the alcoholics welcomed believer and non-believer alike and allowed their members to define the concept of Higher Power in their own manner and in their own time. There were also concerns that the Oxford Group association would lead to a perception of the group as a religious sect and that the Oxford Group's Protestant associations would discourage Catholic alcoholics from seeking help from the group. Another concern was that the negative publicity about the Oxford Group, such as alleged pro-Nazi comments made by Buchman, could damage the willingness of alcoholics to seek out this new movement. While all of these factors contributed to the inevitable split between the Oxford Group and the unnamed group of alcoholics, the most fundamental cause still rested with the different visions of their primary missions that the two groups held. Bill Wilson would later say of this difference, "The Oxford Group wanted to save the world, and I only wanted to save drunks."[24]

Bill was under considerable pressure to let go of his focus on alcoholics, particularly his hosting of the all-drunks meetings. And this pressure was coming from the very people who were helping Bill maintain his sobriety. The manner in which this tension was resolved turned out to be a crucial turning point in the history of addiction recovery in America. If Bill had abandoned his fixation on drunks and redefined his vision to that of carrying the Oxford Group message, what we know today as A.A. might never have existed.

The formal separation from the Oxford Group occurred in New York in 1937 and in Akron in 1939. The now-separate group of alcoholics continued to use many of the precepts and practices of the Oxford Group but quickly began adding and deleting beliefs and practices, toward the support of one singular goal: sustained recovery from alcoholism.[25]

During and after its separation from the Oxford Group, this emerging group of former drunks did not know how to refer to itself. Some members referred

to the group as "the alcoholic squad," while others thought it should be called "The James Club," because of favored Bible readings drawn from the book of James.[26] While membership rose to 40 in 1937 and survived the relapse of some key members, including Ebby, the group still had not really defined or named itself. There was some use of the name "The One Hundred Men Corporation" in 1938,[27] but it wasn't until 1939—when discussion focused on the name of the book describing this new movement—that "Alcoholics Anonymous" emerged and stuck. The name came from one of the members, a former writer for the *New Yorker* magazine who recast in more poetic terms the New York group's reference to itself as "a bunch of nameless drunks."[28] The first group meeting to officially call itself "Alcoholics Anonymous" met May 18, 1939, in Cleveland, Ohio.

Grandiose Visions

With the group's success confirmed by a growing number of sober members, two conditions spurred the search for financial support for A.A.: the legitimate financial needs of the founders and the grandiose vision and drive of Bill Wilson. The financial needs emerged from the fact that both Bill Wilson and Dr. Bob were spending the majority of their time on A.A. business and were barely supporting themselves financially. Some source of support had to be found if the organizing efforts were to continue. Bill envisioned the establishment of a chain of profit-making hospitals that would care for alcoholics. He envisioned traveling missionaries who would spread the A.A. message and a book that would share the A.A. experience. Group members' less-than-warm responses to such proposed schemes did little to dampen Bill's vision of raising millions of dollars in philanthropic support to carry a message of hope to alcoholics.

Just as these visions were emerging, a sudden opportunity presented itself. In 1936, Charles Towns, the well known proprietor of the Towns Hospital, offered to hire Bill as a lay therapist and move the entire A.A. operation into Towns Hospital. Charles Towns' business of drying out the wealthy had diminished during the prohibition years, and Towns saw Bill and his new group as a way to re-energize his business. He offered Bill a job and a "healthy slice" of the hospital's profits.[29] As will be remembered from Chapter Twelve, a precedent for the lay therapist role had already been set by Richard Peabody and his protégés. Bill's initial response to Towns' offer was one of tremendous excitement. In his view, this offer would not only solve his own financial difficulties, but also give A.A. a stable organizational foundation from which to grow. When the option was presented to the A.A. group, a member speaking for the group responded to Bill:

> *Don't you realize that you can never be professional? As generous as Charlie has been to us, don't you see that we can't tie this thing up with his hospital or any other? You tell us that Charlie's proposal is ethical. Sure, it's ethical. But what we've got won't run on ethics only; it has to be better....This is a matter of life and death, Bill, and nothing but the very best will do.*[30]

The group conscience of A.A. had spoken. Bill declined Charles Towns' offer. A.A. had escaped its first temptations—money and the promise of professional legitimacy. But Bill's dream of an expansionist A.A. movement continued to fuel a search for financial support.

The search for philanthropic support for A.A. led to a request for funds from John D. Rockefeller, Jr. Rockefeller was an obvious choice for such solicitation, given his earlier support of projects that focused on the alcohol problem. Fearing that money would spoil this spontaneous movement, however, Rockefeller refused to provide the $50,000 that his own staff were recommending. Instead, he placed $5,000 in the treasury of Riverside Church, out of which $3,000 went to pay off Dr. Bob's mortgage, while the remainder was doled out at $30 per week to Dr. Bob and Bill Wilson.[31] This modest fund supported the co-founders' living expenses during this early period of A.A. organization.

They escaped the temptations of money and property, not out of their own volition but through the wise counsel of a wealthy man who knew that money could destroy as well as create. A.A. literature would later acknowledge that Rockefeller's refusal saved A.A. from itself.[32]

The experiences with Towns and Rockefeller confirmed the potential of money and property to divert A.A. from its mission. As a result of this recognition, A.A. pledged itself to corporate poverty and to the goal of being completely self-supporting. The organization did, however, get something more valuable than money from Rockefeller and his staff: advice on how this new movement might structure itself. As a result of this consultation, A.A. created the Alcoholic Foundation in 1938—a five-member trust made up of two alcoholic members and three non-alcoholic members. The Alcoholic Foundation

provided some structure to oversee this growing movement. A.A. also created an A.A. Central Office and—most important for its future growth—made a decision to proceed with the development of a book that would outline the A.A. program.[33]

The "Big Book"

Plans for the book proceeded as the number of sober members increased. The book that would come to be the centerpiece of A.A. was written primarily by Bill Wilson, beginning in May of 1938. It was during this same period that Bill began to give up his notions of returning to a business career and focus instead on working full time to shape the future of A.A. The book consisted of two sections: an outline of the A.A. program and a collection of recovery stories. A just-sobered newspaper reporter helped get the individual stories (16 from Akron and 12 from New York) pulled together in publishable form. But the first half required formal definition of a program that had not yet been codified. This is the story of the creation of the Twelve Steps of A.A.

When the fledgling group of recovering alcoholics that would come to be known as Alcoholics Anonymous began to see itself as separate from the Oxford Groups, the group articulated six principles of recovery:

1. *We admitted we were powerless over alcohol.*
2. *We got honest with ourselves.*
3. *We got honest with another person, in confidence.*
4. *We made amends for harms done others.*
5. *We worked with other alcoholics without demand for prestige or money.*
6. *We prayed to God to help us to do these things as best we could.*[34]

When Bill Wilson was writing the book *Alcoholics Anonymous*, these six principles were expanded to the current Twelve Steps (See p.155). Bill attributed the Twelve Steps to three sources: 1) the Oxford Group, 2) Dr. William Silkworth, and 3) William James.[35]

Refinements occurred as the Steps written by Bill were reviewed and debated—word by word—by A.A. membership. In Step Two, the word "God" was replaced with the phrase "Power greater than ourselves." The phrase "as we understood Him" was added to references to God in Steps Three and Eleven. The phrase "on our knees" was eliminated from Step Seven. And finally, an introductory sentence was added to the Steps, reading: "Here are the steps we took which are suggested as a program of recovery." These changes were defined as helping to widen the "gateway" of entry into A.A.[36] The title of the book evolved through many considered choices: "One Hundred Men," "The Way Out," "The Wilson Movement," and the final choice, *Alcoholics Anonymous*.[37] The book was often referred to as "The Big Book"—a reference to a bulkiness produced by the heavy-weight paper used in the first edition. The choice of this heavy stock was conscious: It was thought the trembling hands picking the book up for the first time could more easily turn the thicker pages.[38]

A private corporation, the Works Publishing, Inc., was established to sell stock to publish the book. The money raised from selling $25 shares and a loan from Charles Towns supported the writing of the book and lent some support toward the book's printing. The first edition (4,730 copies) of *Alcoholics Anonymous* was published in 1939. A loan of $1,000 from the grateful sister of an A.A. member helped transport the stored books from the printer. Another $1,000 loan from Bert T. helped save Works Publishing when sales were slow. Copies of this first edition, which today sell for thousands of dollars, were sold for what in 1939 was considered a high price: $3.50. While the price of the Big Book may seem a pittance by today's standards, some of the earliest letters received in response to national publicity about A.A. were inquiries about where the book could be "rented."[39]

Sales of the Big Book were slow at first. A direct-mail announcement of the book sent to 20,000 physicians produced only two book orders. Reviews in the *Journal of the American Medical Association* and the *Journal of Nervous and Mental Disease* —which judged the book as having "no scientific merit or interest" and called the book a "curious combination of organizing propaganda and religious exhortation" and a "rambling sort of camp-meeting confession of experiences"—were also sources of great disappointment.[40] In spite of a few positive reviews, sales of the book did not take off until A.A. later received national publicity and experienced explosive growth.

The Alcoholic Foundation later paid off the original stockholders in Works Publishing, the company that had been formed to publish the Big Book. In doing so, A.A. took over ownership of its primary text and, by granting a royalty on the book to Bill and Dr. Bob, provided lifetime incomes for its founders. The Big Book of Alcoholics Anonymous itself marks a milestone in history. The book *Alcoholics Anonymous* broke the mold on earlier books by writing, not only about alcoholism, but *to* alcoholics.

Early Rituals

As A.A. completed its developmental separation from the Oxford Group and moved toward publication of the Big Book, other significant but less observable milestones occurred. Rules evolved (rules that were later relaxed) governing when a potential member, known variably as a "prospect," "baby," "pigeon" "fish," or "suspect," could first attend a meeting. Several Cleveland groups, for example, would not allow any prospective member to attend a meeting until he had either been detoxified in a hospital or talked to by ten members. A Denver Group would not allow prospects to attend meetings until they had taken the Steps.[41] Meeting rituals varied across groups and localities. It became standard meeting fare to have chairpersons (serving on a rotating basis) open meetings by "qualifying" themselves—providing a brief "lead" in which they talked about how they had come to A.A. and what had happened since they came to "the program"—then open the meeting up for discussion from those attending. The length of meetings, meeting closings, dress for meetings, and "meeting-after-the-meeting" rituals (usually at a restaurant or coffee shop) all evolved into unspoken traditions. Many things about the early meetings are interesting by today's standards. Wally P.'s research describes the nature of the early Akron groups. Everyone dressed up for meetings. No one smoked during meetings. There were no refreshments or basket passed for donations. No one read from the Big Book. Also interesting is the fact that the ritual of introducing oneself by first name and declaring "I'm an alcoholic" was not present during this era.[42] Other dimensions of A.A. also unfolded during this era, dimensions that were not part of A.A.'s formal program but constituted part of what might be called the "A.A. milieu." These included parties, softball and bowling leagues, and a plethora of social activities that one could avoid, choose selectively, or immerse oneself within.[43]

As A.A. grew, there was a recognition that people were entering A.A. at different points in the progression of alcoholism. Alcoholics entering A.A. were designated as either "high-bottom" or "low-bottom" drunks, depending on how far their alcoholism had progressed.[44] During the late 1930s, A.A. also evolved an approach to mentoring new members that came to be called "sponsorship." This practice began within the Cleveland A.A. groups. Sponsorship originated in part out of the procedures involved in admitting prospective members to hospitals for detoxification. In its earliest form, the "sponsor" was the A.A. member who guaranteed to the hospital that the pigeon's bill would be paid.[45] During the 1940s, sponsorship rituals became more formalized and more varied. The early focus of sponsorship was on introducing a new member to A.A.—a relatively short-term relationship. Later practices included the distinction between temporary and permanent sponsors and the use of multiple sponsors.

It was necessary for this developing fellowship to define how it would respond to members who returned to drinking—people who were known in the early days as "retroverts" and later as "slippers." Group responses to a member's slip varied but often included two elements. First, A.A. members reached out to a fellow member who had resumed drinking, with encouragement to get back into recovery. Second, A.A. welcomed back members who had slipped, and did so with little recrimination. A.A. found a way to encapsulate a slip, use a slip to reaffirm the fallen member's commitment to sobriety, and provide evidence to the whole membership that this business of sobriety was not easy.[46] Some early members, such as Marty M., spoke of their slips publicly in ways that helped other members avoid pitfalls that could lead to a resumption of drinking. Another milestone was the process through which new A.A. groups could be formed within an area. This usually occurred through one of two processes. The first was growth. Expansion often occurred when groups got too large. When this happened, members were encouraged to split off into smaller units—some reflecting meeting-style preferences, and others simply reflecting geographical areas. Many cities used a neighborhood plan to help ensure the geographical accessibility of meetings. The second way new A.A. groups started was conflict. Early A.A. history is replete with references to "warring factions" who sought the mediation of Bill Wilson and others. Such conflicts often resulted in "splitting"—the creation of new local A.A. groups. It was in this period that A.A. discovered that "all you need to start a new A.A. group is a resentment and a coffeepot." A.A. learned through its early years that it could survive this growth-by-division process. Alcoholics discovered that they could survive conflict and separation while still remaining sober and under the umbrella of A.A.

The Period of Explosive Growth

A.A.'s growth continued at a steady pace, reaching 100 members in 1939—the year in which

Alcoholics Anonymous was published. A.A. also spread geographically from its two bases in New York and Ohio to other cities in the Midwest and the East Coast. The first wave of growth was spread by the travels of early members and from the inquiries that came from publicity about the group. Such publicity was increasing. First, there was an interview on a prominent radio program. Then came the 1939 *Liberty* article, "Alcoholics and God," which generated more than 800 pleas for help.[47] A series of articles on A.A. appearing in the Cleveland *Plain Dealer* generated 500 calls for help and a jump in local A.A. membership from 15 to 100.[48] In 1940, Rollie H., star catcher for the Cleveland Indians, publicly announced that his past indiscretions were due to alcoholism and that he had been sober for a year through his involvement in A.A. Such disclosures triggered inquiries from a wide area and intensified internal discussions within A.A. about the issue of anonymity at the level of the press. Six articles on A.A. that appeared in the *Evening Star* brought news of A.A. to Washington D.C. in May, 1940. But all this was just a prelude to what was to unfold after the publication of a *Saturday Evening Post* article.

On March 1, 1941, an article on A.A. by Jack Alexander appeared in the *Saturday Evening Post*. The effect of the Alexander article was stunning. A.A. membership opened in 1941 at 2,000 and closed the year at 8,000.[49] From A.A.'s beginnings in Akron, New York City, and Cleveland, the fellowship spread outward to Chicago, Detroit, Philadelphia, Baltimore, Los Angeles, Houston, San Francisco, and innumerable points in between.

This growth brought conflict and painful learning experiences. Conflict arose within A.A. over the Big Book as rumors spread that the book was a racket designed to make Bill Wilson and Dr. Bob rich. One specific rumor in 1942 had it that Bill and Dr. Bob had split $64,000 in royalties from the book. The rumor continued even when the financial books were opened and showed that such royalties didn't exist. Suspicion, jealousy, and resentment became more visible within the group dynamic of A.A. There was conflict over every conceivable issue: the use of money, the operation of clubhouses, misuse of A.A.'s name, leadership, and personal romances. It was as if sobriety had brought a release of long-suppressed passions for money, recognition, power, and sex. It was open to question whether A.A., like other groups before it, would self-destruct from within. Bill Wilson, sensing the fragility of A.A.'s collective existence, began to think through "codes" to guide the operation of the fellowship. These codes evolved into the principles of self-government within A.A. that came to be known as the Twelve Traditions.[50] How A.A. handled this first period of rapid expansion was crucial to its ability to handle future periods of growth more explosive than any could have envisioned.

Growth of A.A. groups was so rapid that there were inevitable concerns about dilution and distortion of the A.A. program. In his biography of Bill Wilson, Robert Thomsen revealed a story of the fledgling A.A. group in Richmond, Virginia that held meetings to "get away from their wives and talk things over, but saw no reason not to drink beer at their meetings."[51] Forest Richeson, in his history of A.A. in Minnesota, tells the story of an A.A. group in Red Wing, Minnesota during the same period that succumbed to the summer heat and used the A.A. "kitty" to fund a "beer bust."[52] Such periods of instability were part of A.A.'s growing pains. Rumors of the most malicious variety were rampant. There were threats of secession, particularly from some Cleveland groups. In 1940, a San Francisco group threatened to leave A.A. and start an alternative society called "Dipsomaniacs Incognito" if it didn't receive more frequent communication from A.A.'s central authority, the Alcoholic Foundation.[53] There were also tensions regarding the proper relationship between A.A. and the informal clubhouses that were springing up around the organization. An early report on an A.A. Clubhouse in San Francisco made note of the strain from "over-crowding at meetings" and the problem of "drunks, panhandlers, wolves, and Red Riding Hoods upsetting the meetings."[54] All of these situations reflected A.A.'s growing pains.

A.A.'s growth was also reflected in its work with institutions. Members were influential in initiating many hospital-based alcoholism treatment programs—a subject that we will soon explore in some depth. Although A.A. members were already working with hospitals, the first A.A. groups to hold meetings in state psychiatric hospitals were organized in 1939 and 1941 in New York and Illinois. The first A.A. prison group was started at San Quentin in 1942, with the encouragement of the warden, Clinton Duffy, a progressive prison administrator. These early relationships formed the basis of the integration of A.A. and other Twelve-Step programs into modern addiction treatment programs.

The *A.A. Grapevine* began its distribution in June of 1944, originally to communicate with members in the armed services. There had been other local newsletters, but this New York City-spawned newsletter quickly went national. Conceived originally as a "meeting in print," it became the central vehicle

linking A.A. members and A.A. groups across the country—and later, around the world. The *Grapevine* was also the primary means of connection between A.A.'s founders and the A.A. membership. The driving forces behind the initiation and early production of the *Grapevine* were six volunteers, all women. The book *Alcoholics Anonymous* and the *A.A. Grapevine* provided a means of consistently defining and interpreting the A.A. program during the explosive growth of A.A. that took place in the 1940s. The *Grapevine* became an actual instrument of evolution when A.A.'s Twelve Traditions, the A.A. Preamble, and later changes in A.A. practices and structure were introduced in its pages.[55]

A Maturing A.A.

The decade of the 1950s opened on a sad note, produced by Dr. Bob's death at the age of seventy-one. The loss of one of A.A.'s co-founders was softened by the incredible growth and public acknowledgment A.A. was experiencing. The early 1950s saw A.A. membership surpass 90,000 and saw awards and recognition coming to A.A. from such groups as the American Psychiatric Association and the American Public Health Association. There were also positive portrayals of A.A. in *Reader's Digest* and *Time Magazine* and increased interest in A.A. by a film industry that had discovered the dramatic appeal of the subject of alcoholism. As *The Lost Weekend* heightened public understanding of alcoholism, films such as *Days of Wine and Roses* and *Come Back, Little Sheba* portrayed A.A.'s potential role in alcoholism recovery. All of this followed a decade in which alcoholism had played a prominent role in popular works of fiction, including Charles Jackson's *The Lost Weekend* (1944), Eliot Taintor's *September Remembers* (1945), Louis Paul's *Breakdown* (1946), Langston Moffett's *Devil by the Tail* (1947), Harold Maine's *If a Man be Mad* (1947), and—perhaps the best fictional account of alcoholism ever written—Malcolm Lowry's *Under the Volcano* (1947).

A.A.'s growing public visibility raised heated discussions about how supposedly anonymous A.A. members should relate to the press. Breaches of anonymity with the press by Rollie H., Marty M., and Bill Wilson himself forced a re-examination of the organization's stand on publicity.[56] This burst of media attention, with all of its potential for personal recognition and fame, was A.A.'s third temptation—a temptation that gave birth to the practice of anonymity at the public level.

While A.A.'s leaders began to push the anonymity standard, local groups often disregarded this request. After Bill Wilson arranged a visit to Oregon in 1943, the Portland A.A. group sent a letter to A.A.'s New York office informing them that they were going to publicize the event in the newspapers, and that they were not going to keep their names out of it. They asked to be informed if there was any reason to keep Bill's full name out of the papers.[57] The growing policy of anonymity at the level of press was sometimes breached inadvertently and brought as much laughter as serious debate. Such was the case in Springfield, Missouri, where a 10-cent-limit poker game at the A.A. Clubhouse was raided by the local vice squad. Newspaper accounts of the raid listed the names and addresses of the previously anonymous A.A. members who were arrested and later convicted of illegal gambling.[58]

In the 1940s, the media-sparked growth in A.A. was so explosive that a constant stream of correspondence flowed between A.A. Headquarters and new groups. Much of this correspondence sought advice related to group practices and problems. The idea of articulating a statement of A.A. traditions grew out of this correspondence. Although the book *Alcoholics Anonymous* had defined the personal program of recovery advocated by A.A., a new document was needed to help guide the organization's group life. The need to create such a document, first suggested to Bill Wilson by Earl T. of Chicago, became apparent as Bill witnessed the struggles of early A.A. groups and came to learn how earlier support structures for recovering alcoholics had failed.

A.A.'s Twelve Traditions were first formulated and disseminated in 1946 and formally adopted at the first International Convention of A.A. in 1950. There was considerable resistance to this innovation which many members viewed as Bill's peculiar obsession. "Who needs all those damned traditions?" was an oft-posed question by A.A. members in the late 1940s.[59] A more elaborate presentation of the Traditions appeared with the 1953 release of *Twelve Steps and Twelve Traditions*. The Traditions established principles designed to guide and protect the group life of A.A. The traditions provided a framework that could bring under control the circumstances that had destroyed other alcoholic mutual-aid efforts. The will to follow these articulated principles to the letter was quickly tested when an A.A. member died and left $10,000 to the organization. A.A. announced its refusal to accept the $10,000 bequest and its unequivocal intent to refuse any such gift in the future. At the end of the 1940s, Bill Wilson reflected back on the forces that A.A. had sought to manage through the traditions.

Naturally, the explosive potential of our rather neurotic fellowship is enormous. As elsewhere, it gathers closely around those external provocators: power, money and sex. Throughout A.A. these subterranean volcanoes erupt at least a thousand times daily; explosions we now view with some humor, considerable magnanimity, and little fear at all.[60]

A.A. also struggled with the issue of structure within the organization. As the groups continued to grow, there emerged a need for some method of communication between groups, even at the local level. This led to the development of "Intergroup Associations," or what were also sometimes called "Central Offices" or "Central Committees." These local structures handled calls coming to A.A., maintained an updated listing of all A.A. meetings, assisted in getting A.A.-sponsored people hospitalized for detoxification, hosted periodic Intergroup Association open meetings, planned annual banquets, and distributed both local and A.A.-approved literature. Formal intergroup structures often grew out of local A.A. clubhouses. These new structures experienced their own growing pains, particularly related to the financial needs of A.A.'s new formal (Central Committee) and informal (clubhouse) structures. For example, the Seattle Central Committee solved its financial needs by installing slot machines in the local clubhouse.[61] In spite of local struggles for solvency, by 1945, local groups were contributing to the financial support of A.A.'s central office in New York.

A.A. was often criticized, even by its friends, for failing to develop a more traditional organizational structure, with a central authority and rules governing membership. Outsiders complained of A.A.'s "anarchy," and even Dr. Harry Tiebout—one of A.A.'s strongest professional advocates—saw this lack of traditional structure as an immature abdication of responsibility.[62] If one asked about the lack of structure and rules within A.A., or about the lack of a clearly identifiable authority, one was simply told that when basic principles of the A.A. program were broken, members returned to drinking and groups disintegrated. Alcoholism, not leadership authority, was the enforcer of A.A. principles.

Drunkenness and disintegration are not penalties inflicted by people in authority; they are results of personal disobedience to spiritual principles. We must obey certain principles, or we die.[63]

A.A. committed itself to corporate poverty, group authority rather than personal authority and leadership, and the lowest level of organization necessary to carry A.A.'s message of recovery.[64]

A.A.'s structure did evolve as it moved out of the 1940s. The Alcoholic Foundation that had been created in 1938 was changed from a trust to a corporation in 1942, and all assets were transferred to the new corporation.[65] The Foundation was dissolved in 1954 and replaced by the General Service Board of Alcoholics Anonymous. What had been the Alcoholic Foundation's office in New York City became the General Service Office of A.A. At the 1955 International Convention of A.A., responsibility for world service was transferred to the A.A. membership through the vehicle of the General Service Conference. The four-year experiment with General Service Conferences, which had begun in 1951, had resulted in the decision that A.A. membership would itself take responsibility for the future of the fellowship. Although authority within A.A. during its early years had been heavily invested in the founders and the trustees of the Alcoholic Foundation, the 1955 Convention marked the transition of authority to A.A. members themselves. A.A. membership began directing the General Service Office through state and provincial delegates who met annually in a General Service Conference. At the 1955 Convention, Bill Wilson formally turned A.A. over to the General Service Conference and its trustees in the form of A.A.'s three legacies: Recovery, Unity, and Service. When A.A. celebrated its 20-year anniversary, its membership had reached 133,000.[66] Two years later its membership had grown to 200,000 alcoholics in 70 countries. A.A. had truly "come of age."

During the 1950s, A.A.'s growth sparked increased service and publishing activities and the creation of an A.A. publishing company, A.A. World Services, Inc. The book *Twelve Steps and Twelve Traditions* was published in 1953; a second edition of *Alcoholics Anonymous* was released in 1955; and a book detailing A.A.'s history, *Alcoholics Anonymous Comes of Age,* was released in 1957. The second edition of the "Big Book" reflected changes in A.A. membership. The stories in the book showed a membership that was younger and included more women, as well as members who were entering A.A. earlier in the progression of alcoholism. A.A. Headquarters in New York also increased its service activities during the 1950s. In addition to all of its publishing and literature-distribution activities, this office became the central point of support and consultation for Loners (men and women who had no access to A.A. groups), for fledgling A.A. groups, and for hospitals and prisons seeking information on how to begin cooperative relationships with A.A.

In 1956, a committee was set up to take over the public relations and correspondence previously conducted by Bill Wilson. In 1965, he asked A.A. membership to assume a renewed pledge of personal responsibility for the still-suffering alcoholic: The pledge read: "I am responsible. When anyone, anywhere, reaches out for help, I want the hand of A.A. always to be there. And for that: I am responsible." He spoke to the A.A. membership for the last time at the Thirty-fifth Anniversary Convention in 1970. Bill Wilson died January 24, 1971. His full name and picture appeared for the first time, accompanying the announcement of his death in the world press. The structures he had helped put in place ensured that Alcoholics Anonymous would continue in his absence.

Those Who Shaped the A.A./Treatment Relationship

One could construct a large cast of individuals who played significant roles in the history of A.A. Henrietta Seiberling, Sam Shoemaker, Jack Alexander, Father Edward Dowling, Dr. Harry Emerson Fosdick, Charles B. Towns, John D. Rockefeller, Jr., and Dr. A. Wiese Hammer are among those who would be included on this list. But five people in particular played, not only significant roles in the development of A.A. and its program, but also significant roles in defining the relationship between A.A. and alcoholism treatment programs in the United States: Bill Wilson, Dr. Bob Smith, Dr. William Silkworth, Sister Ignatia, and Dr. Harry Tiebout. Before moving on to a description of the A.A. program, A.A.'s influence upon treatment, and A.A.'s relationship with treatment institutions, we will briefly profile these individuals.

Bill Wilson

William Griffith Wilson was born November 26, 1895, in a small room located behind the bar in the Wilson House—an inn his parents managed in East Dorset, Vermont. His father had taken the temperance pledge (though he failed to follow it), and Bill was exposed to temperance education in school. He was raised by his maternal grandparents after his mother and father divorced. Bill's closest early childhood friend, Mark Whalon, introduced Bill to the world of ideas and the warm comfort of the New England

Tavern. Bill would later find that he liked both very much.

There were many developmental milestones in Bill Wilson's pre-drinking years that would give any psychiatrist a fertile field for exploration. There was his abandonment by his father at age nine, his parents' subsequent divorce, and his separation from his mother. During his boarding-school years he experienced athletic, academic, and social success, but he was heart-stricken by the sudden death of Bertha Bamford—his first love. Then there was the mysterious onset of mild seizures that forced Bill's temporary exit from Norwich University and his entry-expulsion-re-entry in military college. Two final milestones were his engagement to Lois Burnham and their mutual sadness over their inability to have children. Periods of sustained depression had already visited Bill, and they continued to plague him during his drinking years and the first 16 years of his recovery.

The summer after the U.S. entered the First World War, Bill Wilson entered military service. Until this period, he had eschewed drinking because of passed-on stories of what alcohol had done to other Wilson family members. Shortly after his commission as an officer, Bill experienced in a single evening his first drink of alcohol and his first episode of intoxication. He later described how he experienced this first drink as "magic," "the elixir of life," and "the missing link." Problems with alcohol, however, were the farthest thing from his mind when he married Lois Burnham in 1918.

Bill's drinking increased following his return from the service, a fact he attributed to his "fits of depression." He completed law school (but never picked up his diploma) while working as a stock investigator on Wall Street. In the 1920s, Bill experienced periods of great financial success, but his drinking continued to spin out of control amidst the most sincere pledges of reform. At Christmas in 1923, he wrote to Lois: "I make you this present: No liquor will pass my lips for one year." His adherence to the pledge did not last two months.[67] In January, 1927 Bill penned to Lois the short-lived resolution, "There will be no booze in 1927."[68] The next year he wrote, "To my beloved wife that has endured so much, let this stand as evidence of my pledge to you that I have finished with drink forever."[69]

The 1920s were filled with increasing alcohol-related problems for Bill: binges that progressed to daily oblivion, fights, physical sickness, failed efforts at sobriety, a strained marriage, and financial disaster in the market crash of 1929. He bounced back financially in a move to Canada, but he returned to New York when he was fired because of alcohol-inspired altercations at a country club. The instability of Bill's and Lois's life is indicated by the more than 50 addresses the couple had shared by the early 1930s.[70]

By early 1933, Bill had begun to think of himself as an alcoholic. Many failed attempts at sobriety and numerous hospitalizations set the stage for Ebby's visit and the chain of events that resulted in the founding of Alcoholics Anonymous.[71]

Bill's early years in A.A. reflected his incredible drive and his effort to rein in his own grandiosity and desire for fame and glory—an effort in which he was greatly aided by his spiritual advisor, Father Ed Dowling. His refusal of an employment offer as a lay therapist in spite of his acute poverty at the time marked a milestone in both Bill Wilson's and A.A.'s history. This seems remarkable when one considers that, from 1939 to 1941, Bill and Lois were so poor that they virtually lived out of suitcases with friends and A.A. members. And yet something of Bill's generosity is evident in his appeal for financial support from the Guggenheim Foundation during this period—not for himself, but for Dr. Bob and Anne. [72]

While continuing his recovery and work within A.A., Bill suffered from serious bouts of depression from 1944 to 1955. In 1944, he began undergoing psychotherapy twice a week with Dr. Harry Tiebout, and in 1947 was in therapy with Dr. Frances Weekes. Bill's battle with depression gave him a deep appreciation for the psychological problems that can sometimes accompany and be masked by alcoholism. Bill's bouts of depression were very hard to bear, particularly when some fellow A.A. members attributed Bill's depression to his not working the steps.[73]

Bill was quite interested in religion and even took Catholic instruction for a period, but he never joined or regularly attended any particular church. Bill, like the program he helped create, could be described as deeply spiritual, but not religious. To outsiders who think that Bill Wilson was deified within A.A., it may come as some surprise that Bill was often the subject of severe criticism within the fellowship. He was most often criticized for his obsessions—the traditions and A.A. self-government—and for not attending regular meetings.[74]

In accord with A.A.'s tradition of anonymity, Bill turned down many offers during his lifetime: an honorary Doctor of Law degree from Yale University, a listing in *Who's Who in America*, and an opportunity to appear on the cover of *Time* magazine. In spite of the personal recognition that had come to him and to A.A., he continued during the last 15 years of his life to explore new approaches that might help people who struggled with, or failed to understand and accept, the A.A. program. While the overall A.A. program moved toward stability and maturity, Bill seemed still obsessed with those who somehow weren't able to make A.A. work for them. Warning of the dangers of pride and complacency, he challenged A.A. membership at the fellowship's 30th anniversary meeting with the question: "What happened to the six hundred thousand who approached A.A. and left?"[75]

It was a search for an answer to that question that led to Bill's later interest in Vitamin B-3, and to his most controversial interest—LSD. (Both of these subjects were explored outside of his official position within A.A.) Bill became interested in these areas through his encounter with two psychiatrists, Dr. Humphry Osmond and Dr. Abram Hoffer, who were pioneering the use of Vitamin B-3 and LSD in the treatment of alcoholism.[76]

Bill took Vitamin B-3 (niacin) in hopes it would help his depression[77] and first took LSD in 1956 under the supervision of Dr. Sidney Cohen. The LSD experiments began at a time when LSD was being widely proclaimed as an experimental adjunct in the treatment of alcoholism and before LSD had surfaced as a drug of abuse. Bill reported that his first experiment with LSD produced a spiritual experience comparable to the "hot flash" that had marked the beginning of his recovery. He even persuaded others to try LSD, including his wife Lois, his secretary Nell Wing, and his spiritual mentor Father Dowling. Bill saw in LSD the potential for a kind of drug-induced ego deflation that could open the door to recovery—something more accessible than his own "hot flash," which he had come to recognize as rare even among A.A. members. Bill continued LSD experiments (the actual number of times he used the drug is unknown) with a small group of fellow explorers, but later discontinued them, primarily out of concern for how this activity could harm A.A.[78] Nell Wing notes in her memoir that Bill came to realize that such experiments conflicted with his "father image in A.A."[79] There is, however, some evidence that Bill's experiments with LSD continued into the early 1960s. As late as 1967, the *A.A. Grapevine* reported on studies that showed positive results from using LSD in the treatment of alcoholism.[80]

When Bill turned the fellowship over to the General Service Board, he noted that A.A. was now safe even from him. This point is a crucial one. What is most striking to this author about the life of Bill Wilson is his admirable struggle to set aside personal ambition for the broader good of A.A. His refusal of employment at the Towns Hospital, correction of his

early breaches of anonymity, his admonishment that A.A. leaders had to be "on tap, not on top," and the ability to resist his need for control and allow A.A. to mature beyond its founders are all testaments to his success in this struggle. What is even more remarkable is how conscious his efforts were: Bill talked often about how his efforts to dampen his insatiable pursuit of money, fame, and power with alcohol had almost killed him, but he also talked about his awareness that the dreaded "neurotic germ of the power contagion" had survived inside him.[81] Nell Wing said of Bill:

He devoted a large part of his energy and time to trying to divest himself of power and authority, instead of trying to hang onto them.[82]

Through guidance from people like Father Dowling and his struggle to master the very program he helped found, Bill Wilson achieved enough detachment to allow A.A. to grow into its own. There will probably be future revelations about Bill's character and actions that some will interpret as attacks on A.A. But such revelations will in the end only reinforce Bill's humanness and—most important—the extent to which Bill acted, in the end, to protect A.A. from himself.

Bill Wilson died January 24, 1971 of emphysema. He quit smoking during the year he died, but not before his emphysema was well advanced. There are many critical milestones and contributions in Bill Wilson's life in A.A. that influenced the fellowship's relationship with alcoholism treatment programs; most important, he was the first A.A. member to get sober within a hospital that specialized in caring for alcoholics. His refusal of the offer to go on the payroll and move A.A. into the Charles Towns Hospital prevented the professionalization and commercialization of A.A. His conceptualization and articulation of the Twelve Steps defined a program of recovery that would be integrated into treatment programs throughout the country and beyond. His formulation of the Twelve Traditions defined the principles that would be used to define the relationship between A.A. and treatment programs.

Dr. Bob Smith

Robert Holbrook Smith was born August 8, 1879 in St. Johnsbury, Vermont. At the age of nine, he stumbled onto a jug of home brew and later he vividly recalled his instantaneous fascination with its smell, taste, and effect. He graduated from St. Johnsbury Academy, where he met Anne Robinson Ripley, with whom he would carry on a 17-year courtship before their 1915 marriage. After he left St. Johnsbury, Bob entered Dartmouth College, where he majored in drinking. He had a prodigious capacity for alcohol and drank at first with a complete absence of the aftereffects suffered by his peers.

After he left Dartmouth, Bob spent the next three years pursuing various jobs in Boston, Chicago, and Montreal, while the intensity of his drinking continued to escalate. In 1905, he enrolled in pre-med at the University of Michigan, where he went on sustained binges interspersed with bouts of academic productivity. When he was asked to leave in 1907, he transferred to Rush University in Chicago. On the verge of failing at Rush, Bob managed two quarters without drinking, which allowed him to graduate. This was followed by a two-year internship at Akron City Hospital, in which he was almost too busy to drink.

After he set up his medical practice in Akron, Ohio, in 1912, Dr. Bob's problems with alcohol began anew. Within a few years, he was periodically checking himself into the local sanitarium to dry out. In 1914, his father brought him to Vermont to sober up, and he remained sober enough over the next months to marry Anne Ripley and return to his medical practice in Akron.

Dr. Bob stayed sober until the brink of prohibition. Then he started drinking again and continued drinking after prohibition by forging prescriptions for alcohol. As his alcoholism progressed, Dr. Bob also began medicating himself with powerful sedatives. Dr. Bob's health, financial, and family problems intensified in tandem with his drinking. He signed himself into a local sanatarium more than a dozen times, but all with the same eventual result. When beer became legal in 1933, Dr. Bob was drinking a case and a half a day and often spiking the beer with spirits. His medical practice almost gone, Dr. Bob and Anne were on a quest for a solution that took them to the local Oxford Group, where they met Henrietta Seiberling. For nearly two and one half years Dr. Bob attended Oxford group meetings *and* continued to get drunk, until Ms. Seiberling called and said there was someone from New York she wanted him to meet—a man named Bill Wilson.

Beginning on June 10, 1935 when Dr. Bob had his last drink, A.A. became the centerpiece of his life. Dr. Bob never had the "hot flash" of spiritual conversion like that described by his co-founder, but he demonstrated that the spiritual connection necessary to sustain sobriety can be acquired through conscious effort over a lifetime, as well as by a blinding flash.

As a physician, Dr. Bob played a special role in the link between A.A. and alcoholism treatment. Although his medical specialty was surgery, Dr. Bob worked with Sister Ignatia of St. Thomas Hospital to treat thousands of alcoholics, who were then channeled into A.A. He provided all of these services without charge.[83] Many early members of A.A. traveled to St. Thomas Hospital and stayed for a time in Akron to learn about A.A. first-hand where it had begun.

Dr. Bob and Bill Wilson brought interesting differences in personal character to their roles as co-founders of A.A. Bill had incredible vision and a grasp of the "Big Picture," while Dr. Bob seemed always to be grounded in the here and now. Where Bill brought a capacity for synthesizing ideas, Dr. Bob brought common sense and an instinct for that which was most important. Where Bill brought energy, ambition, and a willingness to risk, Dr. Bob brought stability and caution. Bill preferred the public arena, but Dr. Bob preferred the private chat. Bill always had a sense of what to say; Dr. Bob always seemed to know when to listen. Where Bill seemed to be always on the edge of controversy, Dr. Bob was the consummate peacemaker. Asked to compare how Bill and Dr. Bob complemented one another, a long-time A.A. member told the author: "Without Bill, A.A. would never have left Akron; without Dr. Bob, A.A. would have been franchised like McDonalds." Each of these men could have failed alone. Together, they succeeded—each bringing unique strengths and each tempering what could have been the other's fatal flaws. The success of A.A. can, in part, be attributed to the unique synergy and enduring friendship between these two men.

Dr. Bob died of cancer on November 16, 1950. Although his fifteen-year involvement with A.A. seems short from today's vantage point, his influence endures to the present. He is probably best known for his sustained humility. Regarding his co-founder status he always said he had done nothing—merely been used. When lauded, he demurred by claiming he was simply "another alcoholic trying to get along."[84] Dr. Bob is also known for his continuing admonition: "Let's not louse this thing up; let's keep it simple." His most significant contribution to the field of alcoholism treatment, in addition to his role in co-founding A.A., was the treatment regimen he helped establish at St. Thomas Hospital.

Dr. William D. Silkworth

Dr. William Silkworth ("Silky") graduated from Princeton and completed his medical training at New York University. After an internship at Bellevue Hospital, he pursued specialty training in neuropsychiatry. Early in his medical career, Silkworth developed an interest in, and knack for, working with drunks. That knack led him in 1930, at the age of 59, to accept the job of physician-in-charge (and later Medical Superintendent) at Charles B. Towns Hospital.[85] Silkworth played a significant role in articulating the conception of alcoholism within A.A. He described alcoholism as an *allergy of the body* and an *obsession of the mind*. He stated clearly and unequivocally that those who had developed this allergy could never drink any alcohol without disastrous consequences.

Silkworth's suggestion of a constitutional vulnerability which prompted alcoholics to drink—out of necessity rather than choice—became the cornerstone of the modern disease concept of alcoholism. It was Silkworth's belief that this vulnerability was a biologically determined hypersensitivity to alcohol, and that this characteristic was never lost, no matter how long the alcoholic refrained from drinking. To Silkworth, the primary evidence of an allergic response to alcohol was an insatiable craving for it that was excited by even the smallest exposure to the substance. He believed that there was only one way for those allergic individuals to avoid an "attack" of alcoholism: complete and enduring abstinence.[86]

William Silkworth helped Bill Wilson understand and articulate the nature of alcoholism and helped shape Bill's approach to working with other alcoholics. Silkworth confronted Bill about his early approach to reaching out to other alcoholics, telling Bill to stop preaching and talking about his "Hot Flash" and start confronting the alcoholic's ego by teaching him about alcoholism. He reminded Bill of what Bill had learned from William James and Carl Jung: alcoholics must be deflated before they are open to spiritual experiences.

Dr. Silkworth's contributions to A.A. and the treatment field included enlisting financial support for and writing the introduction to the first edition of *Alcoholics Anonymous*, involving A.A. members as visitors to patients at the Charles Towns Hospital, writing the first medical papers that introduced A.A., and—perhaps most important for his role in the birth of A.A.—offering words rather than drugs when Bill Wilson thought he was going insane.[87] What another doctor might have viewed as psychopathology or a medication side-effect, Dr. Silkworth saw as a potential spiritual breakthrough.

Between his work at the Towns Hospital and his work at the Knickerbocker Hospital in New York, it is estimated that Dr. Silkworth cared directly for more than 50,000 alcoholics. In spite of these numbers, alcoholics who were cared for by Dr. Silkworth reported that he never seemed to be in a hurry, nor did he respond to his patients with stock answers or formulas. "He came to each new case with a wonderfully open mind."[88] Dr. William Silkworth died in 1959, after more than 50 years of medical practice with alcoholics.

Sister Ignatia[89]

She was born Bridget Della Mary Gavin, became Sister Mary Ignatia of the Sisters of Charity of St. Augustine, and was known as "the Angel of Alcoholics Anonymous."[3] She emigrated from Ireland to America with her family when she was six, and she pursued formal studies in music until her decision to enter the Sisters of Charity of St. Augustine at the age of 25. Overworked and emotionally distraught, Sister Ignatia arrived at St. Thomas Hospital in Akron, Ohio, in recovery from a nervous breakdown. She was herself a "wounded healer." She had earlier been hospitalized for bleeding ulcers, partial paralysis, and complete exhaustion. Her own recovery provided a deep understanding of the process of physical, emotional, and spiritual regeneration.

Sister Ignatia pioneered the modern hospital-based treatment of alcoholism. Between 1934 and 1939, she collaborated with a Dr. Thomas Scuderi in treating alcoholics at St. Thomas. Then Dr. Bob confessed his own alcoholism to Sister Ignatia and asked for her help in treating others with the disorder. She was particularly struck by the spiritual approach to the treatment of alcoholism that Dr. Bob was proposing. She and Dr. Bob conspired to "bootleg" increasing numbers of alcoholics into the hospital under various diagnoses. To prevent discovery, their alcoholic patients were placed in a room that previously had been used only to prepare flowers and to temporarily hold patients who had died and were awaiting removal to the morgue. From the first patient admitted on August 16, 1939 until Dr. Bob died in 1950, they treated 4,800 alcoholics at St. Thomas. Together, they pioneered a five-day model

------

[3] This brief sketch of Sister Ignatia is drawn primarily from Mary Darrah's well-researched and delightful book *Sister Ignatia: Angel of Alcoholics Anonymous*.

alcoholism treatment that became a model for A.A./hospital collaboration. In 1952, Sister Ignatia left St. Thomas to administer the alcoholic treatment unit at St. Vincent's Charity Hospital in Cleveland.

While professionals were awakening to the problem of alcoholism, Sister Ignatia was already seeing a broader problem. Referring to the increased use of prescribed psychoactive drugs, she said in a 1954 speech that we had entered an "age of sedation."

Her sustained work with alcoholics and their families was acknowledged by many. One can only speculate about the private feelings Sister Ignatia must have experienced when in 1960, at the age of 71, she stood to address an audience of 17,000 A.A. members gathered to celebrate A.A.'s 25th birthday. Toward the end of her life, she, like Dr. Bob, was concerned that professionalism within a growing alcoholism treatment field would somehow destroy the philosophy and simplicity of what A.A. had brought to the world. Sister Ignatia died April 1, 1966.

Dr. Harry M. Tiebout

The psychiatrist Harry Tiebout played two primary roles in A.A.'s development in the 1940s. First, he exerted a profound influence on key individuals within A.A.'s early beginnings. As chief psychiatrist at the Blythewood Sanitarium (from 1935 to 1950), Dr. Tiebout read with great interest a pre-publication copy of the book *Alcoholics Anonymous*. Impressed by its potential import, he passed the copy along to two of his alcoholic patients—one of whom became the first woman to achieve continuing sobriety within the fellowship (Marty M.) and who would later emerge as one of the alcoholism movement's most dynamic leaders. He also served a more personal role in A.A. history by treating Bill Wilson for his continuing episodes of depression during the 1940s.[90] As friend and confidant, Harry Tiebout provided a sounding board on issues facing A.A. and Bill Wilson's evolving role in the fellowship.

Tiebout was A.A.'s first friend and advocate from the field of psychiatry. He paved the way for Bill Wilson to give presentations on A.A. at a New York state medical society meeting, and later at a meeting of the American Psychiatric Association. For a lay person—to say nothing of a self-proclaimed alcoholic—to address such groups was unprecedented in the 1940s and 1950s, and a testament to Tiebout's influence. Even more unprecedented was the publication of Bill's talk in the *American Journal of Psychiatry*. It was Harry Tiebout who opened the professional doors through which A.A.'s legitimacy was acknowl-edged by medical and psychiatric authorities.[91]

The second and equally far-reaching role Dr. Tiebout played was in enhancing A.A.'s legitimacy by providing a psychiatric interpretation of the fellowship's success. When Tiebout came face to face with the transformative power of A.A., he decided to "discover what made A.A. tick."[92] Through a series of what have become classic articles in the alcoholism treatment field, Harry Tiebout established himself as one of the premier innovators and interpreters of Alcoholics Anonymous and alcoholism treatment.[93] Tiebout believed that psychiatry's historical failure in treating alcoholism was based on "faulty theoretical assumptions" about the nature of the disorder. He called alcoholism a symptom that had assumed "disease proportions" and articulated how the program of A.A. worked to bring this disease into remission.[94] Tiebout described alcoholics as characterized by "egocentricity, rebellion against restrictions, a search for pleasure, a demand for special consideration, a peculiar twisted logic, and finally a marked irresponsibility and immaturity."[95] He further posited that this posture of immaturity was the major stumbling block to recovery. Where Tiebout differed from his psychiatric colleagues was in viewing these characteristics, not as enduring traits of personality that had caused alcoholism, but as shared adaptations to the progression of alcoholism. In Tiebout's view, treatment of alcoholics involved softening the infantile, egocentric shell of the alcoholic so that they could become amenable to influences outside themselves. As he noted, "The fundamental problem of any therapy of alcoholism, whatever its guise, is to help the individual mature."[96] Tiebout believed that A.A. provided four elements in the transformation of alcoholics that traditional psychotherapy had failed to provide: "hitting bottom, surrender, ego reduction, and maintenance of humility."[97] He viewed the transformation of the alcoholic within A.A. as a "rapid psychological reorientation"—a conversion process—and believed that it was the spiritual force within A.A. that had the power to break through the alcoholic's "narcissistic egocentric core."[98]

The "Tiebout papers" have provided guidance to generations of clinicians in their counseling and psychotherapy with alcoholic clients. His depiction of such stages of transformation as narcissistic grandiosity, hitting bottom, surrender, the "pink cloud" (honeymoon) in early sobriety, the dangerous resurrection of ego, the need for continuing surrender as a "disciplinary experience," and the movement into mature sobriety predates the research-based developmental models of alcoholism recovery that will be summarized in later chapters. Tiebout was one of a small group of mid-century psychiatrists who recognized the potential power of spiritual transformation in the alcoholic. When Marty M. approached Tiebout following a powerful spiritual experience, she asked him, "Do you think I'm really crazy?" Reminiscent of Dr. Silkworth's response to a similar question posed by Bill Wilson, Dr. Tiebout responded, "No, you've only found what we've all been looking for."[99]

In the 1950's, Tiebout lamented that people working in the alcoholism treatment field did not stay long enough to truly contribute to the field. He called upon clinicians to stay involved in the treatment of alcoholism and to speak and write about their clinical experiences so that "a body of accepted practice can be acquired." Tiebout was, in short, calling for the rise and full professionalization of an alcoholism treatment field.[100]

Dr. Tiebout went on to serve as the president of National Council on Alcoholism and as a Trustee of Alcoholics Anonymous. He died in the spring of 1966.

✠

Chapter Sixteen
The Program of Alcoholics Anonymous [101]

In this chapter, we begin with a reminder of the short life of the mutual-aid movements for alcoholics that preceded A.A. A.A.'s predecessors rose and fell primarily because of two fatal flaws: 1) their failure to develop a fully codified program of alcoholism recovery and 2) their failure to develop viable organizational structures and procedures. To understand how A.A. proved to be more resilient than its predecessors, we will explore A.A.'s recovery ideology and the unique structure and principles that evolved to govern A.A.'s life as an organization.

Defining the A.A. Program

Promoters, interpreters, and critics of A.A. have created many misconceptions about what A.A. is and is not. These misinterpretations themselves constitute an enduring theme in A.A. history and have spawned a minor industry of armchair analysts of the A.A. experience. Misinterpretations can sometimes be traced to overzealous A.A. members, particularly recent initiates, who themselves have not yet grasped the very principles and practices that they so aggressively promote to any who will listen. Misinterpretations of A.A. also come from outsiders. People who would never think of judging a country by one city or a city by one citizen encounter one A.A. member or visit one A.A. meeting and speak as if they know the whole of A.A. People who have never read A.A. literature, never attended an A.A. meeting, or never even known an A.A. member speak with great authority when the subject of A.A. arises in social and professional arenas. Such rush to judgments are typical of cultural phenomena like A.A. in which

knowledge is not a prerequisite for personal or professional opinion. Descriptions of A.A. from within and without reinforce the notion that this "simple" program is characterized by complexities so deep that more than 3,000 professional articles and books have been written on it. Reading the widely varying depictions of A.A. in this literature, one must inevitably conclude that A.A. is a chameleon whose character changes dramatically when viewed through the lens of any professional discipline—or that A.A. constitutes a Rorschach of sorts whose depiction reveals as much about the observer as about A.A.

Because of the many misconceptions about A.A., those within A.A. and those who have closely studied the fellowship spend considerable time talking about what A.A. is not. A plethora of *A.A. Grapevine* articles and A.A. brochures have tried to reinforce that A.A. is <u>not</u> a religious or temperance movement, a social service organization, an educational agency, a cure or cure-all, or an employment agency. This literature states that A.A. does <u>not</u> solicit or accept outside funds, run hospitals, prescribe treatment for alcoholics, or pay for the hospitalization of alcoholics.[102] Alcoholism conferences and the professional literature on alcoholism are also replete with references to misconceptions about A.A. In his presentations on A.A. to professionals, Ernest Kurtz frequently clarifies that A.A. literature does <u>not</u> assert that: "1) There is only one form of alcoholism, 2) moderate drinking is impossible for everyone with alcohol problems, 3) alcoholics should be labeled, confronted aggressively or coerced into treatment, 4) alcoholics are riddled with denial, or 5) Alcoholism is a purely physical or hereditary disorder." Miller and

Kurtz have even countered the common designation of A.A. as a "self-help" group—a term that implies a "pull-yourself-up-by-the-bootstraps" approach to recovery. They point out that the source of strength that propels the A.A. member's movement into recovery is not within the self, but in resources outside the self. As such, A.A. is the antithesis of self-help—an acknowledgment that all efforts at self-help have failed.[103]

What is clear is that the several decades worth of literature noting misconceptions about A.A. begs for caution in our approach to this chapter. So how do we define the program of A.A. and describe this fellowship as an organization? We will attempt such definition and description relying on two things. First, we will rely on A.A.'s own definition and description of its program as represented in its basic texts and the *A.A. Grapevine*. Second, we will try to describe A.A. in terms of its common practices, recognizing that such descriptions will not always fully encompass the growing diversity of A.A. experience. The latter will be based on independent studies of A.A. and the author's professional observations of A.A. over the past three decades. A focus on A.A.'s literature can help avoid misinterpretations of A.A. based on regional or local nuances, while a description of common A.A. practices can help illuminate dimensions of A.A., such as meetings and sponsorship rituals, that are not fully detailed in the organization's basic texts.

A.A. Steps and A.A. Practices

The essential program of alcoholism recovery within A.A. is the Twelve Steps. Everything else described in this chapter is a way of actualizing or protecting these Steps. A.A. meetings, sponsorship, literature, and all of the other dimensions of A.A. structure and experience described in this chapter evolved as ways of helping people work and live the Twelve Steps. The activities in A.A. are not ends in themselves, but vehicles through which the recovery process embedded within the Twelve Steps unfolds.

A.A. Experience and A.A. Logic

A.A. has long made a distinction between *not drinking* and *sobriety*. The former implies removing, usually briefly, a highly destructive behavior from an otherwise unchanged life. The latter implies a spiritual transformation of personal identity within which alcohol no longer has a place. A.A.'s remedy of abstinence as a step to sobriety involves four elements: 1) surrender, 2) identification, 3) hope, and 4)

daily prescriptions for living. All of these elements are integrated within a unique set of beliefs about the nature of alcoholism and alcoholism recovery.

A.A. Logic

What underlies the experiences of surrender, identification and hope within A.A. is an unrelenting logic that details the nature of alcoholism and the very real potential for recovery. Every A.A. interaction and every piece of A.A. literature conveys explicitly or implicitly five points: 1) You have a sickness—your loss of control while drinking and your inability to abstain from drinking in spite of its consequences are evidence of that sickness. 2) This illness is incurable and fatal. As long as you drink, the progression of the illness will accelerate toward madness and death. 3) Though incurable (you can never drink normally), the illness can be arrested with complete abstinence from alcohol and other intoxicants. 4) To initiate and sustain abstinence you must reconstruct your personal identity and daily lifestyle. 5) By keeping this sickness in remission through a daily program of spiritual recovery, you will be blessed with far more than just not drinking. The seeds of the alcoholic's surrender and hope are buried within this unrelenting sequence of propositions. It is these propositions that help each arriving alcoholic come to grips with what A.A.'s co-founder defined as the "age-old alcoholic dilemma": "our obsession guarantees that we shall go on drinking, but our increasing physical sensitivity guarantees that we shall go insane or die if we do."[104]

Surrender

Many A.A. observers—Dr. Harry Tiebout and Dr. Milton Maxwell among the most prominent —have noted the unique combination of pain and hope that marks the alcoholic's entrance into recovery. The turning point, according to Maxwell, is the alcoholic's simultaneous disillusionment over failed efforts to control his or her drinking and the hope inspired by identification with sober alcoholics.[105] With the First Step of A.A. ("We admitted we were powerless over alcohol—that our lives had become unmanageable."), A.A.'s logic is experienced within the innermost core of the alcoholic self. This "deflation at depth" experience of surrender can come through a climactic conversion experience—a kind of psychological or spiritual seizure similar to Bill W.'s "hot flash"—or it can come in the more typical one-inch-and-one-day-at-a-time process referred to in A.A.

as "spiritual awakening." In what will be the beginning of many paradoxes within the A.A. program, the alcoholic begins to succeed by admitting his or her absolute failure.

In an early First-Step ritual in Akron, the new prospect would get on his knees in prayer, confessing his powerlessness over alcohol and pledging that he would turn his life over to God. This ritual, completed in the presence of other A.A. members, was quite powerful, as reflected in descriptions of new members often coming downstairs "pale and shaken" following the experience.[106] The emotional effect of this process of surrender must be viewed in light of the characteristics of those who made up A.A.'s first generation. Robin Room has pointed out that A.A.'s first generation was composed of men whose motto, "I am the master of my fate, I am the captain of my soul," had been sorely tested by depression economics.[107] These were men bred in a tradition of rugged individualism, who had aspired to and often achieved personal success. But they were also men who had lost most of their personal power through the progression of their alcoholism, and who had tried to hide this decline in a bluster of grandiosity and a growing obsession with power and control. One can only imagine the intensity that an act of complete surrender would hold for such men. While such an act must have been exceedingly difficult, the spiritual nature of the A.A. program posited this act as the eye of the needle through which these men had to pass into recovery.

Identification and Hope

What surrender opened up in the A.A. program was the capacity to experience resources and relationships beyond the self. It opened the capacity for listening and, out of listening, the capacity for identification. What one listened to was not theory or proffered advice but personal stories. If there was a psychology to this new A.A. program, it was a psychology of experience transmitted in the form of story from one alcoholic to another. Recognizing oneself in others' stories began the movement out of fear and isolation. The language of self-disclosure and the language of A.A.'s steps was a language couched in "we." It reflected an implicit understanding of the alcoholic's desperate estrangement and equally desperate need for "we."

Hope came to the newcomers in A.A. through seeing alcoholics like themselves living sober, reasonably happy lives. It was in witnessing such transformed lives that the alcoholic approached A.A.'s Second Step. Step Two acknowledges the fear of insanity experienced by every alcoholic. Step Three of A.A. further extends the experience of surrender and introduces a paradox: by letting go of control, one becomes free of the need to control. Kurtz notes the way in which the alcoholic in A.A. reframes the prohibition "I cannot drink" into the liberating declaration, "I *can* not-drink."[108] This mixture of logic, paradox, and mystery is at the heart of A.A.-supported recovery from alcoholism.

Prescriptions for Daily Living

What is sometimes lost in recounting the spiritual dimensions of the A.A. program is the fact that they are supported by cognitive and behavioral prescriptions that are powerful in the sheer repetition with which they are offered to the newcomer. The first prescriptions are clear: don't drink, go to meetings, get a sponsor, read the "Big Book," and "work the steps." The program of recovery as practiced is reduced to what one does in each 24-hour period. It is a liberating mantra that says, in essence: "You can do anything today but drink: DO ANYTHING, BUT DON'T TAKE THE FIRST DRINK!" Other common forms of prescriptive advice given to the newcomer include hints about how to avoid relapse and achieve some degree of emotional stability. A.A. folklore also provides a plethora of rituals, meditations (the serenity prayer), thought-stopping and thought-substitution techniques (the slogans), and behavioral alternatives to taking a drink. Where earlier mutual-aid societies like the Washingtonians pushed the alcoholic to make a decision to stop drinking, A.A. constructed a daily program of recovery that empowered the alcoholic with the freedom to not start drinking.

Identity Reconstruction Within A.A.

In A.A., identity reconstruction happens in many ways. There is the implicit definition of oneself as alcoholic in the First Step and the usual ritual of introduction at meetings: "My name is ____. I'm an alcoholic."[109] This ritual undermines the alcoholic's propensity to redefine his or her problem as something other than alcoholism as soon as the acute pain subsides. It also embraces another paradox: a declaration of one's alcoholism—something that one could never make while actively drinking—is made with a clear mind and unslurred speech.

But the reconstruction of the alcoholic's identity in A.A. requires more than acknowledging the nature of the disorder. The alcoholic enters recovery with a spoiled identity—an identity stained by every past act of injury and every failed promise to self and others. It is the stain of what one did and failed to do, but it is also the more indelible stain of what one is. What emerged out of the collective experience of A.A.'s early members was a recognition that the alcoholic's guilt and shame, left unattended, would lead to continued self-destruction, most frequently through a return to drinking. A.A.'s prescription for these conditions, derived from the Oxford Groups, was a program of self-inventory, confession, and restitution.

Cleansing the alcoholic's stained identity begins with A.A.'s Fourth Step. This Step requires a rigorous review of one's past actions and an inventory of one's assets and deficits of character. It is through this step that rationalizations and other projections of blame give way to a clear acknowledgment of personal liability and responsibility. It is one more step in the refutation of arrogance and grandiosity—one more step in the acknowledgment of one's "Not-Godness."

Step Five adds a new dimension to this experience through three separate admissions of one's culpability for past wrongs. Doing a Fifth Step is a way to shed alcoholism's emotional legacy and to exorcize secrets that hauntingly whisper, "You are not worthy of recovery." In A.A. language, the Fifth Step is a way to bury the "ghosts of yesterday."[110] In these steps the alcoholic struggles with the values of courage and honesty.

If Steps Four and Five scrub a stained self, Steps Six and Seven are about the more enduring process of character reconstruction. The goal of this reconstruction of character is, in the words of the Big Book, "spiritual progress rather than spiritual perfection."[111] Many clinical observers have noted the personality changes that unfold through participation in A.A. Maxwell noted that eventually, through A.A.'s influence, the alcoholic's tendencies toward intolerance, jealousy, resentment, self-pity, selfishness, conceit, and fear of failure give way to humility, confidence, appreciation, enjoyment, honesty, humor, relaxation, and peace of mind.[112]

Reconstruction of Personal Relationships

While the alcoholic is working on his or her own personal reconstruction, there is another issue lurking in the shadows. This issue concerns the scores of past and enduring relationships that bear the taint of the alcoholic's transgressions. These ghosts must be metaphorically buried, and continuing relationships must be brought into the present tense—but without the contamination of yesterday's emotional agendas. The mechanism for this purging, which follows on the

tale of confession, is restitution. A.A.'s Steps Eight and Nine provide the framework for such restitution. Taking these Steps diminishes the power of the past to undermine current efforts at recovery.

Reconstruction of Daily Lifestyle Within A.A.

The reconstruction of the alcoholic's personal identity in A.A. is further reflected in a reconstruction of his or her daily activities. Many actions are implied within the steps of A.A.: admitting, believing, deciding, confessing, requesting, listing, making restitution, self-examining, praying, meditating, and serving. These are blended into four core activities that dominate life in A.A. and other sobriety-based support structures: 1) centering rituals, 2) mirroring rituals, 3) acts of personal responsibility, and 4) acts of service.[113]

Centering rituals are habitual behaviors that keep the alcoholic recovery-focused during his or her day-to-day activities. Such behaviors are prescribed in A.A.'s Step Eleven. Centering rituals, usually performed alone, provide a means of self-focusing and a means of bringing into heightened congruity one's aspirational values and one's daily conduct. These rituals include carrying various recovery symbols ("chips," pins, silver dollars), reading inspirational literature, praying, and meditating. They also include "time-out" periods during the day, through which one can assess one's personal conduct. These daily rituals of self-evaluation provide a mechanism for Step Ten, "Continued to take personal inventory and when we were wrong promptly admitted it." [114]

Mirroring rituals serve much the same function as centering rituals, but they involve interaction with others who share the alcoholic's recovery-based values. These rituals can be formal, such as attending A.A. meetings and regular face-to-face contact and phone contact (referred to early on as "nickel therapy") between sponsor and sponsee, or informal activities such as the plethora of social interactions that surround A.A.: roundups, retreats, celebrations, dinners, dances, athletic events, and a wide variety of other leisure contacts among A.A. members.[115]

Mirroring rituals involve three prominent features within A.A. that are not evident from a reading of A.A.'s Steps or Traditions. One cannot understand A.A. without understanding the role of the "story," the role of slogans, and the role of laughter.

The story is the centerpiece of A.A. experience. A.A. developed a narrative style of self-presentation referred to as "qualifying" or "telling one's story." The story provides a framework through which the alcoholic can use the recovery ideology of A.A. to reconstruct his or her personal identity as a recovering person. It provides a means of transforming a stained personal history into a meaningful and even sacred story. A.A. recovery involves the construction, ritual retelling, and constant refinement of a three-part personal story.

The first part of the story provides answers to two questions: 1) "Who was I before I became alcoholic?" and 2) "Who and what did I become through the progression of my alcoholism?" The middle part of the story describes what happened to break this pattern. It depicts the turning point—for many, the "hitting-bottom" experience—and the early encounters with A.A. The third part of the story, describing how one's life has changed as a result of A.A., answers two more questions: 1) "Who and what am I now?" and 2) "Where am I going, and what do I need to do to get there?"[116]

Another question that is also often addressed within the A.A. member's personal story is, "Why me?" Many people entering A.A. struggle to come to some understanding of how they became alcoholic. The answers to "Why me?" include genetic explanations ("I came from a long line of drunks and took to booze early and hard."), biological explanations ("I developed this allergy to alcohol—every time I drank, I broke out in a drunk."), characterological explanations ("Everything I've done in my life I did to the extreme—including my drinking."), and psychological or situational explanations ("I was so crushed after my son died, I tried to drown myself in a river of gin."). Personal answers to the "Why Me?" question usually appear in A.A. member stories only as oblique references, and the "Why me?" question raised by a newcomer is often greeted by the pronouncement of the question's irrelevancy or unanswerability.

The stories themselves seem to have spiritual power. They are filled with themes of sin and redemption, death and resurrection, and despair followed by hope and gratitude. The recitation seems to serve as a life-saving incantation that quells cravings and compulsions. And story telling, in its need for an audience, links the alcoholic to others.

Stories within A.A. and the broader discourse in A.A. are filled with slogans—crystallized proverbs of A.A. experience. Slogans enhance personality and life-style reconstruction and serve as a source of social glue within A.A. Their peppered presence in one's language serves as a recognizable symbol of A.A. membership—the verbal equivalent of the secret handshake.

Slogans constitute a form of self-talk that can be used for self-inventory and self-correction. There are slogans designed to rein in the alcoholic's propensity for excess, impulsivity, and intolerance: "Easy does it," "Think, think, think," "Live and let live," and "Keep an open mind." There are slogans designed to enhance the alcoholic's emotional connection with others: "But for the grace of God," "Identify, Don't compare," "Stick with the winners," and "Pass it on." There are slogans that help the alcoholic stay focused: "First things first," "One day at a time," and "Keep It simple." There are slogans that help handle adversity: "Let go and let God" and "This too shall pass." There are slogans of warning: "One drink, one drunk" and "There's no situation so bad that a drink couldn't make it worse." There are slogans that seem to be antidotes for such common alcoholic defenses as projection and rationalization: "Take your own inventory" and "Your best thinking got you here." In general, the slogans serve as what Mel B. has called a "shorthand for the Twelve Steps" that serves to "tranquilize unstable emotions and suggest better thinking."[117]

An interesting thing about A.A. slogans is that members often initially see them as rather ridiculous and superficial cliches, but then grow to view them as highly meaningful. It is clear that the slogans are onion-like in the way in which their meanings seem to unfold in layers over time. One can also find within the slogans the deep appreciation of paradox that is so prevalent within the culture of A.A. These truth-filled, seemingly incongruous nuggets are regularly reflected in such twists as "To win, you must surrender," "to keep it, you have to give it away." Paradox is even used to describe alcoholism—"the disease that says you don't have a disease."[118]

If the story and the slogan are the main courses of A.A. experience, *laughter* must surely be the dessert—one taken before, during, and after the main courses. When non-alcoholic professionals first attend open A.A. meetings, many things capture their attention. But inevitably, one of their most striking responses is their shock at the pervasive presence of laughter. Expecting recovery from such a deadly disorder as alcoholism to be a quite somber affair, professionals are surprised—if not offended—by the unrestrained laughter that pervades the meetings. The laughter within A.A. is not the superficial tittering of the cocktail party or the gallows laughter of the actively addicted. This is the boisterous, knowing belly-laugh of healing.[119]

Acts of Personal Responsibility, along with centering rituals and mirroring rituals, constitute the third core daily activity of recovery within A.A.

These rituals may involve establishing new habits of hygiene, eating, sleeping, dressing, exercising, or leisure. Peer modeling and sponsor admonitions help the new member develop better habits of personal accountability and self-care. In interpersonal relationships, acts of personal responsibility include the development of positive qualities that often deteriorated as a result of alcoholism, including predictability, reliability, truthfulness, and courtesy.

Acts of Service make up the fourth core ritual of daily living within A.A. Service serves many functions in A.A. The first goal of a Twelfth-Step call is not the service rendered to the new prospect, but the opportunity for the Twelfth-Step caller to reaffirm his or her commitment to sobriety and a spiritual way of life. In witnessing the suffering of the still-drinking alcoholic, the Twelfth-Step caller confronts what might have been—and still might be—his or her own fate. The Twelfth Step is also a boost to the alcoholic's newly budding esteem. Implicit within the Twelfth Step is the recognition that the Twelfth Stepper has something of value to offer. However, this Step also contains the element of the "giving that asks no rewards."[120] Acts of service within the framework of A.A.'s Twelfth Step constitute a form of generic restitution for past wrongs—an attempted balancing of the karmic scales. Acts of service also function as antidotes to narcissism and bridges to connection with others.

Reframing: The Curse that Became a Blessing

Kurtz has posited that the acceptance and transcendence of limitation is the beginning of A.A. spirituality—something he calls the "spirituality of imperfection." This theme of limitation rests as a pervasive philosophical foundation within the A.A. experience. It is the axis upon which turns the alcoholic's personal and interpersonal transformation. First there is the profession of limitation—the open acknowledgment of being alcoholic (flawed)—a refutation of one's claim to Godhood. Professing this limitation is not necessarily acceptance. Acceptance of limitation—"I am an alcoholic"—requires getting through the anger and the grief related to this status. This limitation-as-curse phase gives way to a quiet acceptance that one is not whole and that this lack of wholeness is the essence of being human. It is in this state that the alcoholic can move beyond his or her own narcissistic self-consciousness to realize than no one else is whole either, but that others, not recognizing this condition, continue their drives for perfection and control. It is here that the alcoholic experiences

a shift in psychological perspective in which what was once seen as a curse is now seen as a gift or a blessing. Within this new perspective, alcoholism—in its inducement of suffering and self-confrontation—is seen as a window of passage from the material world to the spiritual world. The phrases "having had a spiritual awakening as the result of these steps" and "practice these principles in all our affairs" in A.A.'s Twelfth Step suggest an interesting phenomenon: Most people come to A.A. in a desperate effort to escape pain; most stay because that very pain opened a pathway to a deeply satisfying spiritual way of life.[121]

The Recovery Program of A.A. and Its Predecessors: Shared Characteristics

The early A.A. Program had many elements in common with earlier mutual-aid societies of alcoholics, including the following:[122]

- recognition of the physical, mental, and spiritual dimensions of alcoholism;
- acceptance of total abstinence as a method and goal of recovery;
- the use of charismatic speakers to bolster one's resolve for recovery;
- a focus on self-reflection, self-inventory, confession, and restitution;
- service to other alcoholics as a means of strengthening one's own sobriety; and
- an emphasis on establishing an enduring sobriety-based social network (sober fellowship).

A.A. also extended—and, perhaps more than any of its predecessors, recognized the importance of—alcoholic-to-alcoholic experience sharing. The idea of "wounded healers"—this belief that two people who share the same pain can experience healing through the mutual sharing of their stories—achieved its highest level of historical development in Alcoholics Anonymous.

Innovations in A.A.'s Program of Recovery

In the 1930s and 1940s, A.A. implemented a number of refinements and innovations that broke precedent with its predecessors. Some of the more interesting points of comparison between the A.A.'s program of recovery and that of its predecessors include the following:

Anonymity: A.A. was the first mutual-aid group for alcoholics that practiced anonymity both as a device to counter the stigma associated with alcoholism and as a spiritual exercise. This practice widened the gateway of entry into A.A. and reduced the power of key people to harm the fellowship in the eyes of the public.

Lack of Barriers: A.A. eliminated economic and social barriers to participation. A.A. meetings were free, and there were no admission requirements barring people of "poor character or reputation." The "free" policy also helped separate A.A. from various for-profit alcoholism cures that were perceived by most alcoholics as "rackets."

Exclusivity: A.A. maintained an exclusive and sustained focus on the recovery of alcoholics and the importance of alcoholic-to-alcoholic communication. It was the first mutual-aid society that did not significantly compromise its "closed meeting" structure.[123]

Equality: For a fellowship of alcoholics hypersensitive to condescension and judgment and ambivalent about authority, A.A. created a democratic structure that emphasized the equal status of all members. A.A.'s democratic egalitarianism led to a program of suggestions rather than rules—a historical shift from "thou shalt not" to "It has been our experience that...."

Intimacy: A.A. enhanced member comfort and safety by establishing the small group as its basic unit and by creating the expectation that most members would attach themselves to a "home group." A.A. institutionalized the intimacy that was missing within the large Washingtonian meetings but had worked well within the reform clubs and Oxford Group meetings.

Detoxification: A.A. provided linkages to medical detoxification that were further supported by contact with recovering alcoholics. No previous mutual-aid society had adequately addressed the alcoholic's need for detoxification.

Program Codification: A.A. introduced a codified program of recovery. Its basic message was captured in writing, making it less susceptible to dilution and distortion. The book *Alcoholics Anonymous* provided "experience sharing" on paper—a portable meeting and a portable sponsor.

Mutuality Versus Self-Will: Many of A.A.'s predecessors placed emphasis on recovery as an act of will, exemplified by public signing of the pledge. A.A. focused instead on resources and relationships beyond the self. In Kurtz's view: "A.A.'s revolutionary contribution was not medical diagnosis of the 'disease' of alcoholism but its insistence that the most important reality in the life of any alcoholic, sobriety, could not be attained alone."[124]

Spirituality: Where most of A.A.'s predecessors either eschewed religion or advocated a particular religion as a recovery framework, A.A. took a middle path—defining its program as "spiritual rather than religious." What was perhaps most important was its creation of a spiritual program in which spirituality was open to personal interpretation. A.A.'s disaffiliation from the Oxford Groups and its non-religious, non-sectarian approach widened the pathway of entry for those alcoholics who came to A.A. with negative feelings about conventional religion.

Duration of Involvement: A.A.'s predecessors focused on the sobriety decision. Theirs tended to be a psychology of conversion that focused on taking the pledge. A.A., in contrast, provided an ideology and a long-term support structure for living sober. What A.A. appreciated that almost none of its predecessors did is that many of the elements needed to sustain sobriety are different from those needed to initiate sobriety.

Sponsorship: While previous mutual-aid societies had provided fellowship, none had formulated a plan of individual mentorship like the one that evolved in A.A. Sponsorship was one of hundreds of experiments within the developing fellowship of A.A. which were retained simply because they worked. This key relationship within the A.A. experience provided the newcomer with a guide, teacher, confidante, coach, and consultant, all wrapped into one person. Sponsorship styles—which varied from authoritarian and dictatorial to *laissez faire,* and all points in between—allowed an instinctive match between sponsor style and sponsee needs.

Culture Versus Club: Earlier mutual-aid groups had operated essentially as clubs; A.A., on the other hand, defined itself as a shared way of life and as a community.

Time Orientation: A.A. shifted the focus on recovery from the lifetime pledge to a focus on not drinking for 24 hours. A.A. recognized the danger of the alcoholic's preoccupation with either the past or the future, and so focused the alcoholic's attention on the present—not drinking and "practicing these principles" "one day at a time." At the same time, the A.A. culture did evolve ways to celebrate enduring recovery through the use of sobriety dates as a means of "qualifying" oneself and the honoring of sobriety birthdays.[125]

Public Versus Private Confession: A.A. replaced public confession and the promise of reform with a more private ritual of confession. "Closed meetings," to be attended only by members, gave alcoholics an opportunity to discuss "personal problems concerning alcohol" that "one does not feel free to discuss in the presence of non-alcoholics."[126] Public disclosures in A.A. meetings were also of a more general nature; more detailed and personal disclosures were relegated to one-to-one communications, sponsor-sponsee meetings, or Fifth-Step communications. This framework simultaneously heightened emotional safety and emotional intimacy.

Feedback (Cross talk): A.A. constructed each experience-sharing meeting as a series of self-disclosures (monologues). Members support each other, not by offering direct advice, but by sharing their own experiences. This general avoidance of "cross talk" separated A.A. from its immediate predecessor, the Oxford Groups, and from most subsequent group-oriented treatment approaches that relied heavily on advice-proffering or confrontation as therapeutic techniques.[127] In the words of A.A. researcher Klaus Makela, "The lack of cross talk and negative feedback creates space for candid self-revelations that in other contexts would signify a total loss of face."[128]

Response to Relapse: Prior to the advent of A.A., most mutual-aid societies engaged in a practice of mutual surveillance and fined and expelled relapsing members. In contrast, the relapse of an A.A. member brought an acknowledgment that staying sober was difficult and encouragement to recommit oneself to working a daily program of recovery. A.A., more than any of its predecessors, recognized that recovery for many alcoholics would unfold in a process of fits and spurts, plagued at times by episodes of continued "research" (relapse).

Imperfection Versus Perfection: A.A.'s response to relapsing members illustrated a broader distinction between itself and its predecessors, in its clear recognition and acceptance of human imperfection and of the damage done to alcoholics who evaluated themselves by arbitrary standards of perfection. The standard of "progress, not perfection" marked a significant break from A.A.'s predecessors.[129]

A.A.'s Organizational Structure and Practices

It is not enough that a mutual-aid society have a program of recovery that meets the long-term needs of its membership. Like other organizations, such societies can endure only if they find ways of transcending the foibles of their organizational leaders, managing leadership succession, and managing the processes of organizational growth and decay. More than any mutual-aid society before or since, A.A. found unique ways of resolving these challenges.

A.A.'s Mission

A.A.'s predecessors were sometimes sidetracked through a shift in focus from personal reformation to broader social and legislative reforms. A.A. developed a clear and narrowly defined mission set forth in Tradition Five. History suggests that, for alcoholic mutual-aid societies, survival involves escaping the danger of defining a mission that is either too narrow or too diffuse. When the circle of focus is drawn too wide, mutual-aid movements often shift from personal reformation to social reformation. When the circle is drawn too small, these societies are vulnerable to becoming closed therapeutic cults accessible to only a small number. Of all the sobriety-based support structures in history, A.A. is the institution that most clearly defined and sustained an exclusive focus on the individual alcoholic. A.A. further set its goal as, not just helping people abstain from drinking, but providing a program through which the alcoholic could achieve "quality sobriety," serenity, and a meaningful life. In fact, the limited achievement of "just not drinking" was dismissed in A.A. with such terms as "dry bender" or, more recently, "dry drunk."

A.A.'s Philosophy of Addiction

In the 50 years before the birth of A.A., texts on alcoholism consisted primarily of long theoretical speculations about the possible causes of alcoholism, with sparse references to how the condition should be treated. At the time of A.A.'s birth, professional and lay psychoanalysts were speculating endlessly on the "why" behind every conceivable malady. Within this context, it is noteworthy that A.A. spent so little time on the question of why one became an alcoholic. Its primary concern was with the solution, rather than the source.

A.A. literature provides only passing glimmers as to the etiology of alcoholism. A.A. literature suggests biological, psychological, and spiritual dimensions to one's vulnerability to alcoholism. The alcoholic is described as "a very sick person," and alcoholism is referred to as a fatal "illness."[130] But in A.A. literature, emphasis on the roots of alcoholism focuses on characterological rather than biological influences. The two basic texts of A.A. suggest that "liquor was but a symptom," the "bottles were only a symbol," and alcoholism was at base the result of "self-will run riot" or "instinct run wild."[131] A.A. literature is replete with references to the alcoholic's "emotional deformities," "Dr. Jekyll and Mr. Hyde" personality, and "childish, emotionally sensitive, and grandiose" nature.[132] Dr. Bob himself referred to the "selfishness which played such an important part in bringing on my alcoholism."[133]

The references to the etiology of alcoholism in A.A. literature stem from a search for metaphorical truths that could incite and strengthen recovery, rather than a search for scientific truth. A.A. members' use of the terms "allergy," "illness," "sickness," and "disease" provided labels that were metaphorically true in the experience of its members (and esteem-salvaging), regardless of the labels' scientific status. In a similar vein, A.A.'s simultaneous focus on characterological vulnerability provided a rationale for a program of recovery that focused on the alcoholic's defects of character. A.A.'s biological and character-ological explanations drew, not on empirical science, but on an experiential truth confirmed in the lives of A.A. members.

A.A. also served as a refutation of psychoana-lytic and psychological approaches to the treatment of alcoholism. These approaches posited that the way to treat alcoholism was to alter the underlying emotional architecture, after which the outer manifestation of pathology (compulsive drinking) would cease. In contrast, A.A. said "change the behavior ('Don't take the first drink') and the internal emotional architecture will change."[134] In making this shift, A.A. recognized that the problem of alcoholism was not how to stop drinking: alcoholics stopped drinking all the time. The problem was how to live life in such a way that drinking would no longer be necessary. The problem was how to not start drinking. A.A. provided an answer to these problems: "Don't take the first drink AND work a program of spiritual recovery."

A.A.'s Prescription for Short- and Long-Term Recovery

We noted earlier that A.A.'s codification of its program of recovery in the book *Alcoholics Anonymous* provided an invaluable personal aid to its members. But publication of the Big Book also met broader organizational needs. A.A. had published a definitive outline of its program of recovery within four years of its founding. In the same length of time (1840-1844), the Washingtonian Movement had exploded to a membership of some 600,000, then disappeared from the scene—lacking an essential definition of what alcoholics were supposed to do after they signed the pledge. Blumberg & Pittman suggest that part of A.A.'s success was its slow rate of early growth. This slow growth allowed A.A. to self-correct and survive early mistakes and to clearly spell out its philosophy and approach in a singular piece of

literature before it experienced rapid growth.[135]

Carrying the Message of A.A. Recovery

The Washingtonians had no way to carry their message other than the emotional intensity generated by their charismatic speakers. The fact that the fame of these speakers, particularly Hawkins and Gough, outlived the Washingtonian Movement is indeed revealing. In a frenzy of zealous promotion, the Washingtonians achieved the fleeting, almost uniquely American, and often lethal experience of super-success. They were caught up in their own success, and their fall was as rapid as their rise. A.A. chose another path–one set forth in Tradition Eleven, which called for a public relations policy "based on attraction rather than promotion." To ensure this policy, the tradition went on to demand "personal anonymity at the level of press, radio and film." No one who spoke for this new society could be identified by name. A.A.'s philosophy of attraction rather than promotion separated the fellowship from the style of aggressive recruitment and grandiose claims that marked earlier and contemporary alcoholism cures that were widely perceived by alcoholics as frauds.

Internal A.A. Relationships

From the emotional frenzy of the Washingtonians to the more formal titles and rituals of the fraternal temperance societies, each sobriety-based support structure in American history has been marked by a particular organizational climate. A.A.'s atmosphere, as well as its program of recovery, drew heavily from the Oxford Group. The core of the Oxford Group experience was one of personal intimacy nurtured within an informal, non-professional atmosphere. The informal give-and-take atmosphere of the A.A. meet-ing had its roots in the Oxford Group "houseparty," and A.A.'s stance of remaining forever non-profes-sional in its service orientation also drew on a similar Oxford Group tradition. Clark's descriptions of lasting and satisfying friendships within the Oxford Group and his depiction of the group as a "closely-knit and soul-satisfying fellowship" are equally true of A.A.[136] A.A. found a way to turn the pseudo-camraderie of the bar into a similarly informal, but more genuine, intimacy.

Defining A.A. Membership

Given that identification is the hallmark of the initial recovery experience within A.A., the fellowship—out of necessity—developed a practice of exclusivity. In contrast, nearly all of A.A.'s predecessors had succumbed to pressure to widen the boundary of participation. The consequence of this distraction and dilution was the alcoholics' diminished ability to identify with others in the movement—a fact indicated by decreasing percentages of alcoholics within the total membership. In contrast, A.A. has strictly maintained its exclusivity as set forth in Tradition Three.

A.A. took quite a novel approach to the issue of membership, but it first had to weather its early experiments with exclusionary criteria. Some groups, such as those in Rochester, New York and Little Rock, Arkansas, developed rigid rules for A.A. membership. Some groups even practiced "blackballing"—the extrusion of members who slipped more than once. After reviewing the collective lists of local definitions of who couldn't be an A.A. member, the conclusion was clear: "If all those rules had been in effect everywhere, nobody could have possibly joined A.A...."[137] By articulating its membership criteria within the single statement of Tradition Three, A.A. maintained its exclusive focus on the alcoholic, but eliminated the specter of all other forms of exclusion. In short, A.A. said that "Any alcoholic is a member of our Society when *he says so.*"[138] "We may refuse none who wish to recover."[139] A.A. set but one criterion for membership, and steadfastly refused to suspend that criteria. In essence, what A.A. has said to the more than 400 different non-alcoholic groups that sought its program was, "You may take what we have and adapt it to fit your own needs, but you may not join us. A.A. is for alcoholics."

A.A.'s philosophy of exclusivity was most often challenged regarding the inclusion of people in the fellowship who were addicted to drugs other than (rather than in addition to) alcohol. *Grapevine* correspondence in 1944 noted the existence of people who used A.A. to free themselves from narcotic addiction as well as alcoholism. Doc N. suggested that the *Grapevine* start a "hophead's corner," and Doc M. proposed starting an A.A. group at the federal narcotics hospital in Lexington, Kentucky.[140] As A.A. experience increased, it became clear that alcoholics were vulnerable to troubles with drugs other than alcohol. Members had begun referring to such use as "chewing your booze."[141] Many A.A. members, like the co-founders, had abused drugs in addition to alcohol, and others found themselves in trouble with drugs other than alcohol after their involvement with A.A. A.A.'s ultimate answer was to reinforce its position of exclusivity as stated in Tradition Three. In essence, A.A. said that the "only requirement for A.A. membership is a desire to stop drinking," but that a desire to stop drinking IS a requirement for A.A. membership.[142] [143]

The Expected Duration of A.A. Participation

A critical dimension in the stability of any mutual-aid organization is the expected length of member participation. In the field of addiction recovery, one might ask whether lifelong affiliation with a mutual-aid society is essential for sustained sobriety. At an individual level, the answer is likely to be yes for some, and no for most.[144] While the expectation of long-term member participation may not be essential to everyone's individual sobriety, it may be essential to the survival of a mutual-aid society of recovering alcoholics and addicts.

A.A.'s predecessors did not communicate a clear expectation of how long their members were expected to sustain their affiliation and active participation. There was perhaps an implicit understanding within A.A. (based on the failure of earlier movements and the high attrition of its own new members) that a mutual-aid group whose membership consisted only of people in early recovery was inherently unstable and unlikely to endure. A.A.—in practice, if not in theory—communicated to its members an expectation of lifelong involvement. Continued involvement in meetings is designed to achieve four things: 1) to provide continued support for recovery and reduce the risk of relapse, 2) to provide sober fellowship, 3) to provide ongoing support for stress reduction and spiritual growth, and 4) to ensure the continued availability of the A.A. group to the still-suffering alcoholic.

It is unclear whether a formal decision was ever made that A.A. affiliation should be for life. References within A.A. literature link individual sobriety to group affiliation,[145] but this pronouncement is unclear as to whether group affiliation is required as much for sustaining long-term sobriety as it is for initiating sobriety. *Grapevine* articles have also periodically reinforced the necessity of meeting attendance for high-quality sobriety and raised the specter of what would happen to still-suffering alcoholics if all stable members of A.A. stopped attending meetings.[146] Perhaps the ultimate Twelfth-Step act is remaining in A.A. to return to newcomers what one once received. If "personal recovery depends on A.A. unity," as the First Tradition suggests, perhaps the ultimate contribution to that unity is one's continued presence and participation.[147] [148] [149]

While speculations on this question continue, a new A.A. member asking, "How long do I have to go to meetings?" is likely to hear the following enigmatic quip from an A.A. elder: "Until the question is no longer important to you."

Power and Decision-Making in A.A.

Like its parental model, the Oxford Group, A.A. took a minimalist approach to organizational structure—only one membership requirement, no formal membership roll, no required financial contributions, no centralized authority, and minimal distinctions between leaders and members.[150] Having defined its therapeutic program, A.A. chose through its Fourth Tradition to leave the implementation of this program up to each local group. It further dealt with the issue of leadership succession by using a constantly rotating leadership that minimized the power and potential destructiveness of a single person. Power was placed within the group, rather than within the leader (Tradition Two). A.A.'s decision-making process was further defined as one of consensus or "group conscience" rather than majority rule—a stance that further decreased the risk of divisive leadership and splintering. A.A.'s overall structure might be referred to as a spiritually driven anarchy. It is a testament to its spiritual strength that an organization claiming a worldwide membership of some 2 million people can declare that "A.A. as such ought never be organized...." (From Tradition Nine) Several observers have noted the degree to which A.A.'s decentralized structure and rotating leadership have enhanced its survivability. Room makes the acute observation that A.A.'s lack of exclusive local territory turned interpersonal conflict that might otherwise have threatened A.A. into "an instrument of organizational growth."[151]

The Voice of A.A.

A.A.'s predecessors got in trouble either when their spokespersons became bigger than the movements they represented or when those singing the praises of the program were witnessed to have clearly plunged head-first off the "water wagon" on which they had apparently been so precariously balanced. In contrast, A.A. said that no one "with a name" could link him- or herself with A.A. at the public media level. In this way, A.A. protected itself from the fame or fall of its members.

A.A. Relationships with Allied Fields and Related Causes

A.A.'s predecessors were in open competition and conflict with outside organizations or were dominated by outside organizations and issues. The Washingtonians and fraternal temperance societies were all caught up in prohibition politics, and even the Oxford Group found itself embroiled in political controversy in 1936, when its founder was alleged to have made pro-Nazi statements.

To ensure its potential for survival and its singular focus on its mission, A.A. pledged itself to a position of absolute autonomy and disengagement from outside organizations and issues. This question was so important that four of A.A.'s Twelve Traditions address it. Tradition Six prohibited involvement in giving support to outside ventures. Tradition Seven prevented local groups from accepting support from outside bodies. Tradition Eight ensured that A.A. would not move into direct competition with professionals who cared for alcoholics. A.A. further reinforced this position of autonomy and disengagement by unequivocally declaring in Tradition Ten that A.A. had "no opinion on outside issues."

Managing Member Growth

Following the rapid growth in Cleveland sparked by the *Plain Dealer* articles on A.A., and the national growth sparked by the *Saturday Evening Post* article, A.A. discovered—to its surprise—that it could survive the rapid absorption of large numbers of new members. The crucial tools for managing such growth have been both the codification of the A.A. program within the book *Alcoholics Anonymous* and the codification of A.A.'s organizational principles within the book *Twelve Steps and Twelve Traditions*. A.A. learned—first in Cleveland and, later, across the world—that the A.A. message of recovery could be carried by the most imperfect of instruments. When barely sober men and women guided others into enduring recovery, it became apparent that the power of A.A.'s message could transcend the imperfections of its messengers.

Leader Development

A.A.'s predecessors tended to be leader focused and gave little attention to issues of leadership development or leadership succession. A failure to address this question was particularly fatal to the reform club movement. Each branch of this movement had its own national leader, and local clubs were often fed by the singular passion of a local leader. When these individuals died or left the area, the movement quickly dissipated for lack of sustainable leadership. By de-emphasizing the role of leaders and simultaneously developing many leaders through the practice of constant leadership rotation, A.A. found a way to enhance local groups' potential for survival. A.A.'s ability to achieve this at a national level is best illustrated by the continuity and stability of the fellowship following Bill Wilson's death in 1971.

Managing the Issues of Money, Property, and Personal Ambition

A.A. managed the distracting power of money and property through its pledge of corporate poverty—the secular equivalent of removing the tempting fruit from the Garden of Eden. A.A. protected itself from the influence of outside money by declaring itself completely self-supporting. The problems created by the ownership and management of property were eliminated by declaring that A.A. would own no property. The temptation of personal prestige and fame was handled by pledging the entire membership to anonymity at the public level. The potential temptation to move to the paid speakers' circuit that drew Hawkins and Gough out of the Washingtonian movement was eliminated by A.A.'s tradition of anonymity. The person who would exploit A.A.'s name on the speaker's circuit would by this very act disqualify him- or herself as a legitimate representative of A.A. The practice of anonymity, while serving as the "spiritual foundation" of A.A., also reduced opportunities for individual profiteering. Anonymity ensured that the focus of the fellowship would "place principles before personalities." The potential disruptiveness of the emergence of an elite group of "star

speakers" within A.A. was further minimized (compared, for example, to the potential that existed in the Washingtonians) by the fact that the basic unit of gathering within A.A. was not the large speaker's platform, but the small discussion group.

Social Context and Organizational Endurance

All of what we have discussed—A.A.'s unique program of recovery (the Twelve Steps) and its equally unique approach to ensuring organizational resilience (the Twelve Traditions)—contributed to A.A.'s success. But there may have been other contextual factors that also contributed to this success. Harry Levine has suggested a broader political and social context that contributed to A.A.'s acceptance. In the years following the repeal of prohibition, the country was searching for a new paradigm that could help it understand alcohol and alcohol-related problems. A.A.'s shift in focus from the evil of alcohol to the individual vulnerability of the alcoholic was a concept that could be politically embraced by the culture as a whole, and even by the liquor sellers who had been under cultural attack for the past 100 years.[152]

A recovery movement's core ideology must function at multiple levels. It must provide an organizing framework for personal transformation for addicts and their families. It must provide a framework for internal organization. It must provide a framework for organizing the interventions of professional helpers. And it must help the community and the culture define the nature of alcohol-related problems and formulate social policy prescriptions that hold out hope of resolving such problems. A.A.'s core ideology, in contrast to those of its predecessors, was able to perform all of these functions.

The Twelve Steps of Alcoholics Anonymous

1. We admitted we were powerless over alcohol —that our lives had become unmanageable.
2. Came to believe that a Power greater than ourselves could restore us to sanity.
3. Made a decision to turn our will and our lives over to the care of God *as we understood Him.*
4. Made a searching and fearless moral inventory of ourselves.
5. Admitted to God, to ourselves, and to another human being the exact nature of our wrongs.
6. Were entirely ready to have God remove all these defects of character.
7. Humbly asked Him to remove our shortcomings.
8. Made a list of all persons we had harmed, and became willing to make amends to them all.
9. Made direct amends to such people wherever possible, except when to do so would injure them or others.
10. Continued to take personal inventory and when we were wrong promptly admitted it.
11. Sought through prayer and meditation to improve our conscious contact with God *as we understood Him*, praying only for knowledge of His will for us and the power to carry that out.
12. Having had a spiritual awakening as the result of these steps, we tried to carry this message to alcoholics, and to practice these principles in all our affairs.

The Twelve Traditions of Alcoholics Anonymous

1. Our common welfare should come first; personal recovery depends upon A.A. unity.
2. For our group purpose, there is but one ultimate authority—a loving God as He may express Himself in our group conscience. Our leaders are but trusted servants; they do not govern
3. The only requirement for A.A. membership is a desire to stop drinking.
4. Each group should be autonomous except in matters affecting other groups or A.A. as a whole.
5. Each group has but one primary purpose—to carry its message to the alcoholic who still suffers.
6. An A.A. group ought never endorse, finance, or lend the A.A. name to any related facility or outside enterprise, lest problems of money, property, and prestige divert us from our primary purpose.
7. Every A.A. group ought to be fully self-supporting, declining outside contributions.
8. Alcoholics Anonymous should remain forever nonprofessional, but our service centers may employ special workers.
9. A.A., as such, ought never be organized; but we may create service boards or committees directly responsible to those they serve.
10. Alcoholics Anonymous has no opinion on outside issues; hence the A.A. name ought never be drawn into public controversy.
11. Our public relations policy is based on attraction rather than promotion; we need always maintain personal anonymity at the level of press, radio, and films.
12. Anonymity is the spiritual foundation of all our traditions, ever reminding us to place principles before personalities.

✠

Chapter Seventeen
A.A. Critics and the A.A. Legacy

One challenge that all sobriety-based mutual-aid societies face is the need to outlive their internal and external critics, and A.A. has had its share of both over the years. These critics have offered an unending list of recommendations for improving A.A. or have condemned A.A. *in toto*. Analyzing all of the criticisms of A.A. is beyond the scope of our story, but the story of A.A. should include both the fact that it has been criticized and the general nature of the criticism.

Criticism of A.A. generally revolves around one or more of the following ten propositions.[153]

1) *A.A. treats only the symptoms of alcoholism without getting at underlying causes.* This was one of the earliest criticisms of A.A., espoused primarily by psychiatrists who viewed alcoholism, not as a disorder, but as a symptom of underlying psychopathology. Dr. Harry Tiebout responded repeatedly to this charge by suggesting that A.A. simultaneously removed a life-threatening symptom and nurtured a level of spiritual development that altered the "inner source of discord" that was the source of the disorder.[154]

2) *A.A.'s relative effectiveness has not been scientifically validated.* This is a relatively benign criticism that decries the lack of scientific study of A.A.'s effectiveness compared to that of other interventions. There have actually been large numbers of evaluation studies that have looked at A.A. as a recovery variable. William Miller and Chad Emrick conducted separate reviews of the empirical research on A.A.'s effectiveness. Miller concluded that "the alleged effectiveness of A.A. remains unproven," and Emrick concluded that "while A.A. membership is associated with relatively high rates of abstinence, we are as yet unable to predict with any certainty who will affiliate with A.A. and who will be helped by participation in the organization."[155] A.A.'s singleness of purpose and anonymity traditions severely complicate if not preclude the kinds of research many scientists would like to do on A.A.

3) *A.A. is generally unsuccessful or is successful with only particular types of alcoholics.* This criticism goes beyond the call for more research by concluding that the research is already in and has proven that A.A. has limited effectiveness. Typical of these criticisms are the charges of Herbert Fingarette and Stanton Peele that most people with alcohol problems are never exposed to A.A., that most of those who are exposed quickly drop out, and that A.A. has not been found to be effective with "the general population of alcoholics."[156] Some critics even suggest that success stories within A.A. are not attributable to A.A.'s program of recovery. Charles Bufe, for example, attributed recovery through the use of A.A.'s Twelve Steps to "placebo effect." For its part, A.A. has never claimed to be the answer for all alcoholics. But it has periodically made statements regarding its effectiveness. A.A.'s basic text notes:

> *Of alcoholics who came to A.A. and really tried, 50% got sober at once and remained that way: 25% sobered up after some relapses, and among the remainder, those who stayed on with A.A. showed improvement.*[157]

4) *A.A.'s religious language and concepts keep many alcoholics from seeking affiliation.* This criticism comes particularly from some of the more recently developed sobriety-based support structures that use a non-spiritual framework of recovery. The perceived religious dimension of A.A. is often a source of objection for atheists or agnostics who are legally mandated either to A.A. or to an alcoholism treatment program that incorporates A.A.'s philosophy of recovery. A.A. has sought to address this issue by creating literature for the agnostic and by encouraging members to develop highly personal definitions of God—as in reliance on G.O.D.—group of drunks.

5) *A.A.'s reliance on "Higher Power" undermines the development of internal strengths and competencies essential to addiction recovery.*[158] This criticism can be most frequently heard within "rational" frameworks of recovery or within women-specific recovery frameworks. Psychiatric interpretations of A.A. have also raised concerns about A.A.'s emphasis on members' maintenance of their alcoholic identities. Some critics propose that the "once an alcoholic, always an alcoholic" ideology that is conveyed to members "obstructs their independence and their further personal growth."[159] A.A. members counter that total reliance on self is itself a sign of immaturity and that recovery hinges not on self-reliance but on the relationship with people and powers beyond oneself.

6) *People who become dependent upon A.A. are*

just substituting one dependence for another. This criticism can periodically be heard in casual conversation or on radio or television talk shows. The criticism is an interesting one in that it is based on an inherent assumption that all forms of dependency are bad. This criticism is also found in professional circles. In a modern critique of A.A., Alan Ogborne criticized what he viewed as an "infantalism" cultivated in A.A. members and the manner in which A.A. members tended to let A.A. become "their whole lives."[160] Extreme versions of this criticism have included outright characterizations of A.A. as a cult or references to "A.A. brainwashing," "A.A. Clones" —or "Step Zombies," or to A.A.'s "cult-like tendencies."[161] The "cult criticism" is balanced by findings that those alcoholics who do best in A.A. "become more actively involved in the organization, adopt its beliefs more completely, and follow its behavioral guidelines more carefully."[162] In a parallel finding, Henry Montgomery, William Miller, and Scott Tonigan found that, while mere attendance of A.A. meetings was not predictive of abstinence, increased intensity of A.A. involvement—as measured by frequency of meeting attendance and actively working A.A.'s Twelve Steps—was predictive of abstinence.[163]

7) *A.A.'s advocacy of a disease concept of alcoholism undermines personal responsibility.* This criticism of A.A. is first based on a misattribution of the disease concept to A.A. Such criticism has periodically come from religious leaders who perceive the "disease" concept as a refutation of the concept of "sin," from political leaders who view the disease concept as a strategy of escape from legal responsibility for personal behavior, and, more recently, from a variety of behavioral-health professionals. A.A. members who have been struck by the enormous emphasis on personal responsibility within A.A. find such criticism incomprehensible.

8) *A.A.'s placement of the cause of alcoholism within the individual ignores environmental factors that contribute to problems with alcohol and is "inherently supportive of the socioeconomic status quo."*[164] This criticism of A.A. is an invitation to political action. It implies that A.A. colludes with or is used by broader social institutions to focus on individual responsibility for alcohol problems rather than broader promotional forces (e.g., alcohol advertising and the targeting of vulnerable populations) or contextual factors that can influence alcohol problems (e.g., alcohol advertising, poverty, racism, sexism). A related invitation pulled many of A.A.'s earliest predecessors into the drive for alcohol prohibition.[165]

9) *A.A.'s political influence has retarded the*

scientific advancement and clinical integrity of the alcoholism treatment field. This criticism usually takes one of two forms. The first is the suggestion that A.A.'s influence has resulted in the application of the label "alcoholic" to persons with a broad spectrum of problems that may require different interventions.[166] The second is that A.A. has inhibited innovation within the treatment field by denouncing or working to suppress scientific discoveries that contradict its beliefs.[167] [168]

10) *The creative spirit that marked A.A.'s beginnings has been replaced by growing rigidity.* This criticism was leveled by Arthur Cain in 1963 and Jerome Ellison in 1964. Ellison charged that A.A.'s national headquarters had been "captured by an ultraconservative clique that was doing the society great harm." He claimed that the spiritual foundation of A.A. was being eroded by people inside the movement who wanted to establish A.A. "on a business basis" and by fanatics who were turning A.A. into a "hostile, fundamentalist religion." Ellison suggested that the A.A. program was stagnating due to the fear of changing or re-interpreting the program's canonized literature.[169] While grateful newcomers and a few crusty old-timers deservedly earn their depiction as "rigid," it is my experience that the presentation of A.A. as the "one and only way" to recovery from alcoholism is more likely to come from alcoholism treatment professionals than from A.A. members. Early A.A. had a respect for diverse styles of recovery from alcoholism. For example, when Bill Wilson was asked to respond to a September, 1944 *Grapevine* article by Philip Wylie describing his own solo recovery from alcoholism without benefit of any organized support group, Bill said simply, "the roads to recovery are many."[170]

When A.A. was attacked by Arthur Cain in a series of articles in the 1960s, Bill Wilson's response was to write an article in the *A.A. Grapevine* entitled, "Our Critics Can Be Our Benefactors." In the article, Bill challenged A.A.'s membership to reflect on how any criticism of A.A. could be used to strengthen the organization, and asserted that the public response to such criticism should be one of silence, lest A.A. be caught up in public controversy that could divert A.A. from its service mission. Bill further noted that A.A. ought never become a "closed corporation" and that critics who provided justified criticism should be thanked.[171]

One of the sustained criticisms of A.A. within the alcoholism treatment community regards the appropriateness of A.A. for women and people of color—a criticism that goes back to Ellison's 1964 article in

The Nation. We will now summarize what is known about the history of women and people of color within A.A.

Stretching A.A.'s Gateway of Entry: Women and People of Color in A.A.

One does not have to travel far within the addictions field to hear the criticism leveled at Alcoholics Anonymous that it is a program for White, affluent men. Such critics contend that A.A.'s utility is limited because the core experience out of which the A.A. program evolved was narrowly defined by the gender, race, and social class of its early members. Our brief historical analysis of this criticism will focus on three questions: 1) Were the experiences of women and people of color instrumental in shaping the Twelve Steps and Twelve Traditions of A.A.? 2) Has A.A. adapted its program to address the special needs of women and people of color? 3) What is the degree of participation of women and people of color in A.A.?

Were the experiences of women and people of color instrumental in shaping the Twelve Steps and Twelve Traditions of A.A.?

In its early years, Alcoholics Anonymous was much more than a meeting. It was a sobriety-based community of mutual support. The wives of early A.A. members—particularly Anne Smith and Lois Wilson—participated in and made immense contributions to this developing community. Anne's support and counsel to many of the early alcoholics is legendary. The seeds of many key ideas that emerged within A.A. began in the pages of her journal and in her conversations with early members. Both co-founders noted the role that wives played in the founding of A.A., Dr. Bob even suggesting that there would have been no A.A. without these women.[172] Following close on the heels of the wives of early A.A. members were the first alcoholic women seeking assistance from A.A. Accounts of early women in A.A. appear as brief references in A.A. literature: an unnamed Indian waitress; Sylvia K., the "glamorous divorcee;" Jane, the wife of a wealthy industrialist; Lelia M., the heiress; Ruth T. of Toledo; Ethel M. and Kaye M., who came into the program with their husbands; and Nona W. There was also Florence R., whose story appeared in the first edition of the Big Book, and who objected to one of the book's proposed titles, "One Hundred Men."[173] She later returned to drinking and died of alcoholism. Lil, the very first woman to seek help from A.A., got loaded with Victor, another early

prospect, pioneering what would come to be christened "thirteenth stepping" (sexual or romantic involvement with someone whose sobriety is relatively new and therefore potentially unstable). Lil, like many of the women who contacted A.A. in the early years, did not get sober during this period.

Women like Nona, Bobbie, and Ila appeared one at a time during 1939 and 1940, and then women seemed to appear at the New York meetings in greater numbers in the early 1940s. Marty M., who entered A.A. in New York in 1939 and went on to become the first woman to achieve enduring sobriety within A.A., noted that many of these women failed to get sober, not because they were so much sicker, but simply because they were women.[174] Marty M. played an important role in bringing women into A.A., although she raised considerable controversy in the process regarding A.A.'s policy of anonymity. When she talked openly about her affiliation with A.A. in speeches and radio addresses, she spurred many women on to seek help in A.A. One speaking event alone brought twelve women into local A.A. groups.[175]

Many early A.A. members did not believe women could be alcoholics, and most were uncomfortable with female alcoholics. Some were not quite sure how women could fit into this fellowship, while others stated openly that A.A. would not work for women.[176] Some in the latter group prophesied that the inclusion of women could threaten A.A.'s future. Some women entering A.A. were given rude treatment. The first alcoholic woman involved in the Cleveland group was "thrown out of A.A. by the wives."[177]

The primary fear regarding the involvement of women in A.A. was of the potential disruptiveness of the sexual dynamic that might emerge within the groups. This fear was sometimes legitimized by emotional upheavals—among individuals and within groups—over romantic involvement among some of these early members. Fear of the sexual dynamic imbedded itself within early A.A. folk sayings such as, "Under every skirt is a slip." New dangers were also brought to A.A. even where no such romantic relationships existed. Oscar W. recollected that the first Twelfth-Step casualty was an A.A. member who was killed by a jealous husband in upstate New York.

To manage this potential disruption during A.A.'s early years, women and men sat on different sides of A.A. meeting rooms, and the first women seeking help were often sponsored, not by A.A. members, but by their wives.[178] As more single and divorced women entered A.A., friction between these women and the wives of A.A. men increased. This led to the creation of "closed meetings," attended only by alcoholics, in addition to "open meetings," which were open to all.

When Bill Wilson penned Chapter Five of the Big Book in 1938, he introduced the Twelve Steps with the words "Here are the steps we took...." The "we" of that experience was almost exclusively male.[179] The "we" of that experience was also White. When critics say that A.A.'s program was designed primarily on the experience of White men, they are correct. But that fact, in and of itself, does not mean that A.A.'s program did not work for women and people of color who later entered A.A.

Indictments of A.A.'s response to women and people of color in the 1930s must be viewed within the historical and cultural context of this period of American history. It would be unfair to hold A.A. to a standard different than that of the whole culture of this period. Only a mere 15 years after women had won the right to vote, and at a time when "Whites Only" signs still decorated public accommodations in the South, it would have been unrealistic to expect a band of White alcoholic men struggling for their personal survival to respond more humanely to women and people of color than did White men within the larger culture. In A.A.'s early years, women and people of color encountered in A.A. exactly what they encountered within the culture as a whole, with one exception: there were several factors within A.A. (mutual identification as alcoholics, A.A.'s traditions, and the "group conscience" of A.A.) that slowly pushed this fellowship toward a higher standard.

Has A.A. adapted its program to address the special needs of women and people of color?

Women and people of color did become involved in A.A. groups relatively early in the organization's history. Special problems facing women in A.A. were acknowledged as early as 1945, when a *Grapevine* article[180] noted the isolation of alcoholic women and their propensity to be involved with pills as well as booze.[181] An article the following year—in spite of a disclaimer that it should not be read as a blanket indictment of women—was filled with perceptions of women that exemplified the kinds of stereotyping that women were likely to encounter in the A.A. of this period. The article made the following eleven points:

1) *The percentage of women who stay in A.A. is low.*
2) *Many women form attachments too intense—bordering on the emotional.*
3) *So many women want to run things.*
4) *Too many women don't like women.*
5) *Women talk too much.*
6) *Women are a questionable help working with men and vice versa.*
7) *Sooner or later, a woman-on-the-make sallies into a group, on the prowl for phone numbers and dates.*
8) *A lot of women are attention-demanders.*
9) *Few women can think in the abstract.*
10) *Women's feelings get hurt too often.*
11) *Far too many women A.A.'s cannot get along with the non-alcoholic wives of A.A. members.*[182]

In group after A.A. group, female pioneers fought their way through such attitudinal barriers to get what they needed from this FELLOWship. The experience of Hazel B.—Duluth, Minnesota's first female A.A. member—was not atypical. When she first arrived in A.A., Hazel was told that she wasn't an alcoholic —that they didn't have any women in their group.[183] Women were often refused sponsorship by the male members and were viewed as suspect due to their frequent concurrent addiction to "goofballs."[184] In some areas such as Houston, Texas, "split meetings" were held in which everyone shared an inspirational speech, after which the women were required to leave before the discussion started. It made no difference whether a woman was alcoholic or not; discussions were split by gender, not by qualification as an alcoholic.[185]

What is unique by today's standards is that concern about women joining A.A. focused not on the physical and psychological safety of women coming into A.A., but on the threats that such women were believed to pose to A.A. men. The typical view is expressed in Jack Alexander's 1950 article on A.A. in the *Saturday Evening Post,* in which he noted, "More than one group has been thrown into a maelstrom of gossip and disorder by a determined lady whose alcoholism was complicated by an aggressive romantic interest."[186] The attitude of early A.A. members toward women cannot be understood outside the context of the broader and incredibly intense fear that something was going to come along and destroy A.A. and, with it, themselves. This was, after all, not a social club, but a group of alcoholics fighting for their very lives.

Women did not destroy A.A., but they did change it. Female pioneers "toughed it out" and made things easier for the women who followed them. In addition, women's groups within A.A. began springing up during the early 1940s, in Cleveland and in other early A.A. strongholds. There, female A.A. members were free to talk about many issues (sexual abuse, intimate relationships, family problems, menstruation, abortion, menopause) that they would not have been comfortable addressing in mixed-gender meetings. But even meeting separately generated controversy and periodic accusations that the women attending all-female groups were lesbians.[187] The importance of this adaptation within A.A.—women-only meetings—is indicated by the stories of early women like Vi S., who spoke only at the women's meetings during their early years in the program. By the late 1940s and 1950s, announcements concerning the rise of special A.A. meetings for women regularly appeared in the *Grapevine*.[188]

The special stigma that female alcoholics faced in the 1940s and 1950s was reflected in some sensationalist treatment of early women in A.A. Newspaper articles about women in A.A. bore such titles as, "Women Drunkards, Pitiful Creatures, Get Helping Hand."[189] Perhaps most outlandish was a 1954 article on A.A. in *Confidential Magazine* entitled, "No Booze but Plenty of Babes." This public image of the female drinker no doubt kept many alcoholic women from seeking help and led to such other unusual events as Sunday drivers in Minnesota passing Dia Linn (Hazelden's treatment center for women) in hopes of seeing "wild woman drinkers."[190]

The role that women played in supporting A.A.'s life as an organization should also be noted. Women were the dominant force behind the *A.A. Grapevine* and did all of the early work of the General Service Office, as they continue to conduct much of that activity today.[191]

People of color also reached out to A.A. in the 1940s. The earliest African Americans seeking help from A.A. encountered the same ingrained prejudices reflected in the rest of society. The issue of inclusion of African Americans in A.A. was a subject of some controversy in the 1940s. Bill Wilson was criticized in 1940 for bringing two African-American alcoholics to a New York A.A. meeting. In some areas, African Americans were denied formal membership but were granted special status to attend the meetings as "visitors" or "observers." A separate group was sometimes created for early African Americans because existing groups would not accept them as members.[192] Bill Wilson identified a physician, Dr. Jim S., as the driving force behind the first A.A. group specifically for African Americans. That group was started in Washington D.C. in 1945.[193] African-American A.A. groups were also started in St. Louis, Missouri and Valdosta, Georgia in 1945. An integrated group met in Greenwich Village, New York in the mid-forties, and the first A.A. group in Harlem

(the St. Nicholas Group) started in 1947.[194]

In 1978, Mel B. interviewed a number of the first African Americans in the Michigan and Ohio A.A. groups. These interviews reveal a general acceptance of African Americans in A.A. in the late 1940s. These early members noted that Bill Wilson and Dr. Bob were particularly interested in getting Blacks involved in A.A. Jimmy F. told a particularly poignant story. When he met Bill Wilson at a Founders' meeting in Akron, Bill asked him what group he was affiliated with. Jimmy responded that he was a member of the "Interracial Group" in Ann Arbor. Bill wanted to know why it was called an interracial group, since the whole fellowship was interracial. Jimmy and his fellow local members were so struck by Bill's question that they subsequently changed the name of the group to the Ann Arbor Community Center Group.[195] The practice of designating certain A.A. groups as "interracial" seems to have died out because of that kind of growing consciousness among A.A. leaders.[196]

Trying to integrate A.A. within a culture that politically, economically and socially segregated the races was not easy. A.A. took the position of deferring the question of Black membership to each local group, to handle as it saw fit.[197] At the same time, A.A. publications took pride in the growth in African-American membership of A.A. A 1951 article in the *Grapevine* announced that Chicago's A.A. membership of 5,000 then included more than 300 African Americans.[198]

Several writers have taken the position that there are racial and class limitations to A.A.'s appeal and effectiveness.[199] Some texts on alcoholism among African Americans suggest that Blacks, particularly poor Blacks, drink as a coping mechanism in response to the harsh realities of discrimination and poverty, and that approaches that do not address these specific cultural and economic conditions will fail. The fact that A.A. had no such mechanism, as the argument goes, made the fellowship more effective with Whites than with Blacks.[200] Henry Hudson, on the other hand, suggests that these arguments lack an understanding of A.A. and its growth in the African-American community since the 1940s. He believes that A.A. is effective with African Americans because the strong group cohesion within the fellowship provides an antidote to the senses of powerlessness, isolation, and self-estrangement experienced so acutely by African-American alcoholics.[201] It could also be postulated that the spiritual approach of A.A. is quite compatible with the historical role of religion and spirituality within African-American culture.

Caetano's review of ethnic minority participation

in A.A. concluded the following: 1) A.A.'s view of alcoholism as an illness is shared by nearly all American ethnic communities,[202] 2) A.A. is the most frequently mentioned resource for problems related to alcohol within all ethnic groups, 3) A.A. exists within most ethnic communities in America, and 4) the style of A.A. (meeting format and rituals) has been adapted across a wide variety of cultural contexts.[203]

In a recent study comparing European-American and African-American participation in A.A., Humphreys and Woods found an equal percentage of Black and White clients participating in A.A. a year after treatment intake. They did, however, note that Whites and Blacks tended to attend groups in which they were members of the majority, with Whites attending predominately White groups and Blacks attending predominately Black groups. Humphreys and Woods contend that the level of participation in A.A. by people of color is grossly underestimated and that the notion that Blacks do not participate in Twelve-Step programs is primarily a function of the methods used in research on participation and the locations in which such research is conducted.[204] Researchers who attend A.A. meetings are often channeled to large suburban meetings and, based on their observations there, can conclude that "members of ethnic outgroups experience great difficulty in attempting to use A.A.,"[205] while very different conclusions might be drawn if the same study were conducted in urban communities with a higher concentration of African Americans.

Other ethnic groups were also entering A.A. during the 1940s. The first Spanish-speaking alcoholic entered A.A. in 1940 and translated the complete *Alcoholics Anonymous* into Spanish and presented it to Bill Wilson.[206]

The effort to relate A.A. to women, people of color, and other special populations of alcoholics is clearly evident in such A.A. pamphlets as: *A.A. for Women, Letter to a Woman Alcoholic, A.A. for the Native North American, A.A. for the Gay/Lesbian Alcoholic, Young People and A.A.*, and *Memo to an Inmate*.

What is the degree of participation of women and people of color in A.A.?

The percentage of women within the total membership of Alcoholics Anonymous has risen steadily since its founding. In 1955, A.A. reported that 15% of its members were women; by 1968 that percentage had risen to 22%; and in the 1989 and 1996 surveys of A.A. membership, women constituted 35% and 33%

of members respectively.[207] There are other countries in which women make up more than 40% of A.A. membership.[208]

One must be careful in assuming that, because women were not well represented within the early years when A.A.'s program of recovery was being formulated, this program is not inclusive enough to meet the needs of women, or that is has not evolved to meet the needs of women. Later studies, such as Laundergan's 1975 study of Hazelden graduates, found that, following treatment, more women than men were frequent attenders of A.A. (67% compared to 56%).[209] Feminist scholars who acknowledge approaching A.A. with some degree of negative bias often change their views after closer examination. Linda Beckman, for example, concluded her review of gender issues within A.A. with the following pronouncement: "I now believe that A.A., a fellowship originally designed by and composed primarily of men, appears to be equally or more effective for women than men."[210]

As for the representation of people of color within A.A. today, it is hard to speak definitively of trends because only the latest of A.A.'s four membership surveys asked respondents to identify their ethnic background. In the 1996 membership survey, 86% of members were White, 5% were Black, 4% were Hispanic, 4% were Native American, and 1% were Asian American and "Other." The degree of ethnic participation can also be identified by studies of special A.A. groups. Maxwell reported the presence of some 130 Native-American A.A. groups and 300 Spanish-speaking groups in the early 1980s.[211]

The contention that A.A. is a culturally bound phenomenon that attracts only White Protestants is further challenged by the dramatic growth of A.A. in Latin America, particularly in Mexico, where A.A. groups grew from zero in 1965 to 8,510 in 1986.[212] Kitano has also documented the existence of Japanese A.A. groups in Los Angeles. While some critics have suggested that A.A. has limited attraction for Native Americans because the concept of anonymity is alien within native cultures and Native Americans find the expectation of public confession repugnant, others have reported that A.A. has been successfully adapted to fit local tribal cultures.[213]

In my professional role during the past 30 years, I have observed women and people of color seeking entrance into A.A. It is my observation that the ability of A.A. in any one locality to attract large numbers of women and people of color depends on reaching critical mass of such involvement. Retention rates may be low until that critical mass is reached; after that, growth can be quite rapid. What occurs at this rapid-growth point is that the numbers achieve a level in which two things happen: 1) incoming women and people of color begin to experience greater psychological safety, and 2) the numbers of women and people of color become large enough that people begin to adapt A.A. for increased gender and cultural relevance. One's local view of the relevance of A.A. to women and people of color is often influenced by whether or not this critical mass has been achieved. In the end, A.A.'s "cell structure" allows members to sample and find meetings in which they can find people like themselves, or to create new meetings in concert with others who share similar characteristics and needs. This dynamic cell structure, by enhancing member identification, has contributed to A.A.'s growth and diversity. There is, however, as Klaus Makela has suggested, an unstated survival-of-the-fittest within these thousands of cells. Those groups that drift too far from the core program of A.A. experience failure and become extinct, with survivors drifting back into stronger cells.[214] This process allows for the achievement of diversification, but still sustains those aspects of the A.A. program most crucial to long-term sobriety.

This growing diversity in A.A. is one of the latest and most significant evolutions within A.A. It is doubtful that the earliest members of A.A. could have envisioned a day in which there would be specialty A.A. meetings for women, young people, gays and lesbians, doctors, those with "double troubles" (dual diagnoses), the poly-addicted, non-smokers, newcomers, pilots, old-timers, agnostics, and bikers. Such diversity gives one further pause about making sweeping generalizations about this fellowship.[215]

A.A.'s Place in History

We close this chapter on the A.A. program by briefly pausing to consider A.A.'s significance in the history of addiction and recovery in America—and perhaps its broader significance as an American cultural phenomenon.

A.A.'s legacies are many. First, A.A. constitutes the largest and most enduring mutual-aid society of recovered alcoholics in human history. It is the only addiction recovery mutual-aid society that has outlived its founding generation. A.A. also constitutes the most fully developed culture of recovery that has ever existed—a culture with its own history, mythology, values, language, rituals, symbols, and literature. As we shall see in the coming chapters, A.A. has also exerted an enormous influence on the evolution of

social policies related to alcohol and alcoholism, and on the evolution of alcoholism treatment. This influence is exerted—not institutionally, as A.A. traditions would prohibit—but through the personal advocacy of individual A.A. members whose beliefs about alcoholism and alcoholism recovery were shaped within A.A. Masked behind the veil of anonymity can be found A.A.'s influence on nearly every significant social-policy innovation related to alcoholism during the past 60 years. But A.A. has made an even broader contribution to American culture.

Kurtz believes that A.A. warrants a place in the history of ideas. Believing that "alcoholism replicates the essence of the human condition," Kurtz suggests that A.A.'s refutation of absolute control, its acceptance of limitation, its openness to dependence on resources outside and beyond the self, and its unique healing response to existential shame constitute a benchmark in the modern history of ideas.[216]

Harrison Trice and William Staudenmeier, Jr., note the precedent-setting manner in which A.A. survived the demise of its founders as a "stunning innovation in the politics of organizational life" and a unique "democratic solution to the succession problem inherent in charismatic leadership."[217] Robin Room echoed this area of unique innovation when he suggested that A.A. would merit mention in the history of the 20th century, not only for its work with alcoholics, but also for providing a unique organizational model that was "nonhierarchical, non-professionalized and flexible."[218]

If A.A. does not earn a place in the history of ideas or the history of organizational development, it will surely earn a place in the history of social institutions. The birth of A.A. marked the emergence of a new and seemingly enduring form of social affiliation that unfolded within the context of weakening nuclear family structures; decreased contact with extended families and kinship networks; the loss of socially stable, value-homogenous neighborhoods; and the growing impermanence of workplace affiliation. Here in A.A. were groups of people who were not relatives, neighbors, or co-workers; and who represented diverse social, political, and religious backgrounds. They represented different ages, genders, races, sexual orientations, and lifestyles. What bound them together into this association was a shared history of pain, psychological death, and resurrection. And in these small, intimate circles, alcoholics perhaps found an answer to a broader quest shared by alcoholic and non-alcoholic alike: the hunger for the experience of community.[219]

A.A. was the modern beginning of social affiliation based on shared experience. A.A. marks the apex of new voluntary spiritual communities that have increasingly taken over the functions of family, extended family, and neighborhood, as well as the social functions of the church and the workplace. A.A. marks the beginning of voluntary communities defined by psychological and spiritual boundaries rather than by the boundaries of blood, geography, faith, or profession. These voluntary communities are bonded together by what Kurtz has eloquently christened "the shared honesty of mutual vulnerability openly acknowledged."[220]

More than 400 groups have adapted the Twelve Steps and Twelve Traditions of A.A. to problems other than alcoholism.[221] A.A. and its emulators are clearly "providing some of the glue holding society together."[222] This broader cultural impact of A.A. is a story yet to be written. In the meantime, we will focus in the next chapter on the early relationships that developed between A.A. and mid-century alcoholism treatment programs and the unfolding of A.A.'s influence on modern addiction treatment in America.

Chapter Eighteen
A.A. and the Professional Care of Alcoholics: 1935-1960

The relationship between mutual-aid societies of recovered addicts and professionally directed addiction treatment is an enduring theme in the modern history of addiction treatment, and one that has taken on greater significance as the number and diversity of these societies has increased. The nature of this relationship has been overwhelmingly shaped by the interaction of Alcoholics Anonymous and alcoholism treatment programs. This chapter will describe the early (1935-1960) evolution of the relationship between A.A. and institutions that cared for alcoholics. We will conclude the chapter with a discussion of the differences between A.A. and professionally directed alcoholism treatment.[4]

Visions of A.A. Hospitals

A recently sober and impassioned Bill Wilson had a grandiose dream—a dream of alcoholism hospitals owned and operated by A.A., paid A.A. missionaries who would carry the message of recovery to the world, and a book that would tell the A.A. story and define its program for the still-suffering alcoholic. Bill later described the response of 18 A.A. members from Akron to the first presentation of these proposals.

The moment we were through [presenting the proposals], *those alcoholics really did work us over! They rejected the idea of missionaries. Paid workers, they said, would kill our good will with alcoholics....If we went into the hospital business, everybody would say it was a racket....Some turned thumbs down on pamphlets and books.*[223]

The Akron alcoholics were particularly hard on the idea of A.A.-owned and -operated hospitals, and even Dr. Bob had to confess that he thought the proposition a dubious one. But in the 1940s, the need for medical detoxification of alcoholics coming into A.A. kept alive the discussion of how this need could best be met. For A.A., it was a decade of experimentation, in which collective experience would dictate the final outcome of this issue.

Fleeting references to experiments with A.A. hospitals and A.A. homes appear in A.A. literature and in the alcoholism literature of the 1940s.[224] Bill Wilson revealed that A.A. had once been given a hospital, along with the donor's son as "principal patient and would-be manager." He later reflected that they had "tried A.A. hospitals," but that "they all bogged down" —the reasons for which he summarized in the aphorism, "too many busybody cooks spoil the broth."[225]

One of the strangest proposals in which A.A.'s name was involved was outlined in a 1946 article in the *Louisville Kentucky Times*. The article announced the "establishment of the first private-sponsored clinic for the treatment of alcoholics in the United States." The article claimed that the clinic was being jointly planned by "Norton Memorial Infirmary, Alcoholics Anony-

---

[4]I would like to acknowledge the assistance of Mitchell Klein, whose research into early relationships between A.A. and institutions in the Cleveland area, and whose willingness to share with me key materials from the papers of Clarence S., made an invaluable contribution to this chapter.

mous, and the distillery industry" in Louisville. Efforts to launch the clinic were to begin with a $6,000,000 building-fund drive. The paper announced that outside dignitaries, including Mrs. Marty Mann, were consulting on the project—Mann being described as "an executive of the National Committee for Education on Alcoholism and an A.A. member."[226] The clinic birthed from these efforts continues to operate in Louisville today as the Norton Psychiatric Clinic.

Whether any true A.A. hospitals actually became operational is open to question. According to this author's investigations, the closest A.A. came to operating a hospital was in Cleveland during the early 1940s. Cleveland faced a unique problem related to hospitalization. A series of articles in the *Cleveland Plain Dealer* brought an avalanche of requests for help and identified a desperate need for resources for detoxification. The A.A. Central Committee in Cleveland began plans to acquire and operate a hospital exclusively for the care of alcoholics and simultaneously began negotiating for detoxification services with several Cleveland-area health-care institutions. Fiscal management of the proposed hospital was to be handled by a board of non-alcoholic trustees, while operational aspects of the hospital—including staff selection and supervision—were to be guided by a five-person board of local A.A. members.[227] An A.A. Hospital Committee continued its planning and announced at the December 2, 1941 A.A. Central Committee Meeting that it was working with a Mr. Al Webster on plans for the hospital. The Hospital Committee reported that Mr. Webster had an option on an empty hospital building and had raised $15,000 from donors toward the purchase and operation of the hospital. The Committee had also identified a Dr. Nash, who had agreed to serve as the medical director of the new facility. It recommended that a final vote be taken by the local groups to proceed with opening of the hospital in early 1942.[228]

In the end, there were three major reasons for which A.A. did not get into the business of owning and operating alcoholism hospitals, even in Cleveland.

1. The Rockefeller Rejection: When A.A. requested financial support from John D. Rockefeller, Jr. in 1938, his staff report included the recommendation that Dr. Bob be provided finances to direct a small hospital for the treatment of alcoholics.[229] Rockefeller's overall conclusion that money could "spoil this thing" prevented that recommendation from being funded and kept A.A. out of the hospital business in the late 1930s. Had Rockefeller funding been forthcoming at such an early stage in A.A.'s

history, the evolution of the fellowship might have taken a very different turn. A.A. itself might have evolved into a chain of alcoholism hospitals.

2. Illness in Cleveland: The planned A.A. Hospital in Cleveland that came so close to fruition failed in the end by one of those serendipitous events that pervade A.A. history. The February 3, 1942 Cleveland A.A. Central Committee Minutes noted that Mr. Webster, the key figure collaborating with A.A. on plans for the hospital, had been ill during the past month and had been advised by his physician to stay out of the hospital business, at least for the imminent future. This saga ends with the Committee's regrettable conclusion: "At present, nothing will be done about the new hospital."[230] Had Al Webster not taken ill, A.A. might very well have launched itself into the hospital business in 1942.

3. The Group Conscience of A.A.: One thing that quickly became apparent within A.A. was that even discussions of A.A. involvement in owning or operating hospitals could generate enormous disruption within A.A. groups. By the mid-1940s, the group conscience of A.A. was beginning to articulate standards regarding the inadvisability of such ventures. There was a growing recognition of just how potentially destructive the forces of personal ambition, money, and property could be to the future of A.A. In 1946, A.A. Trustees concluded that A.A. must at all costs maintain its focus: "Better do one thing supremely well than two things badly!"[231] Six months later, this position was confirmed in clearer and bolder language:

> *Neither A.A. as a whole nor any A.A. Group ought to enter any other activity than straight A.A. As groups, we cannot endorse, finance, or form an alliance with any other cause, however good....But, if these projects are constructive and non-controversial in character, A.A. members are free to engage in them without criticism if they act as individuals only, and are careful of the A.A. name.*[232]

As for A.A. as an institution, it pledged itself to corporate poverty by declaring that "the A.A. group is a spiritual entity, not a business enterprise."[233] These sentiments, later codified in A.A.'s Twelve Traditions, closed the door on the vision of A.A. hospitals. A.A.'s focus would be on one thing—reaching the still-suffering alcoholic in a relationship that had no financial requirements—a not-unimportant characteristic in the years following America's worst depression.

During the time A.A. was continuing to consider

the prospect of owning and operating its own hospitals, very wet alcoholics were arriving daily at the organization's door. A.A. Committees and individual members reached out to local medical institutions and asked for their help in the medical detoxification of these alcoholics. To be clear and accurate in our coming depiction of A.A.'s growing role in the organization of community-based alcoholism services, we must understand the Knickerbocker paradox.

The Knickerbocker Paradox: Actions of A.A. Versus Actions of A.A. Members

An understanding of the relationship between A.A. and mid-century alcoholism treatment programs, like so many things about A.A., requires the understanding of yet another paradox. This paradox makes the fine distinction between actions taken by A.A. as an institution—that is, by the A.A. Foundation and local A.A. Intergroups and Central Committees—and actions performed individually or collectively outside the framework of "official" A.A. activity.

To introduce this paradox, let us consider the following example. An alcoholism treatment ward within a community hospital of the 1940s was planned almost exclusively through the efforts of A.A. members. Remodeling of the ward was completed through donations by A.A. members and through the volunteer labor of A.A. members drawn from the skilled trades. The ward was known as the "A.A. ward." Only A.A.-sponsored patients were admitted to the ward. A.A. sponsors signed or co-signed for financial responsibility for payment of each patient's treatment. Visitors to the ward were restricted to A.A. members. A.A. members worked assigned shifts as unpaid orderlies on the ward. As many as 15 A.A. members visited the ward daily to offer the patients encouragement and to explain their own personal perspectives on the A.A. program. The hospital claimed responsibility only for the patient's medical detoxification and for the treatment of any acute medical problems, leaving care of the patient's psychological and spiritual needs to A.A. And patients were discharged only in the presence of their A.A. sponsors, with the expectation that all continuing non-medical care would be provided by A.A. What might be rather shocking to the reader would be to run across a newspaper account of the unit in which an unnamed local A.A. representative was quoted as saying that A.A. had not been, was not, and would not be officially involved in any aspect of the operation of this alcoholism ward.

In spite of its obvious involvement in all phases of the planning and implementation of these units,

A.A. attempted to maintain a technical distance between itself and the operation of institutions that cared for alcoholics. Consider the following explanation of the relationship between A.A. and the alcoholic pavilion at Knickerbocker Hospital, as explained in a 1952 *A.A. Grapevine* article:

> ....though the work at Knickerbocker was started by A.A.'s, is carried on by A.A. efforts, has the full support of individual A.A.'s and all A.A. groups and is, indeed, one of A.A.'s outstanding achievements—it is still completely independent of A.A., as such.[234]

It has been through such fine distinctions, seemingly more linguistic ("not officially involved") than real, that A.A. shaped the nature of alcoholism treatment while denying this very role. This influence, and its lack of visibility to the casual observer, is not the product of some sinister plot, but rather the consequence of a singularly focused mission: carrying the message of recovery to the still-suffering alcoholic within the framework of A.A.'s Twelve Steps and Twelve Traditions.

Once A.A. decided to not operate its own hospitals, it had to find a way to fill the need for institutional treatment of alcoholics, while sustaining its own focused mission. The Knickerbocker Paradox was the answer. First, the newly defined stance of non-affiliation allowed A.A. to stay mission-focused and escape many potentially troublesome threats to the fellowship. Second, the principle of anonymity freed members to initiate or collaborate with efforts to organize alcoholism-related services, while protecting A.A. from any public acclaim or controversy surrounding such efforts. The elements that would come together to form a model for A.A. hospital relationships began in Akron, Ohio.

St. Thomas: The Beginning of a Model [235]

In 1938, Dr. Bob and the fledgling group of A.A. members in Akron were looking for an old house that could be used to sober up prospective A.A. members. The house was never found, and the task of sobering up alcoholics fell upon the shoulders of two Akron institutions, City Hospital and St. Thomas Hospital. Dr. Bob smuggled A.A. prospects into these hospitals for detoxification under the diagnosis of "acute gastritis" until 1939, when he began admitting the first patients under the diagnosis of "alcoholism."[236]

Formalized services to alcoholics at St. Thomas began in 1939, when Dr. Bob shared his own personal story of recovery from alcoholism with Sister Ignatia, the hospital's admitting clerk. Their discussions regarding the need for a place to treat alcoholics led Sister Ignatia to a unique solution to the problem of finding space for alcoholics in an already over-crowded hospital. She offered Dr. Bob the room where flowers were prepared for patients (and where deceased patients were kept until they could be picked up by a funeral home). In August 1939, St. Thomas' mission to alcoholics officially began. It expanded progressively from the flower room, to a two-bed room, to a four-bed room, to a six-bed ward, and then in 1944 to a newly remodeled eight-bed ward—all materials, labor, and furnishings for the new ward donated by local A.A. members.[237] Within five years, the treatment of alcoholics at St. Thomas moved from the status of a secret activity to one fully embraced by the hospital's administration and trustees.[238]

It did not take money to get into St. Thomas, but it did take commitment. Those admitted to the St. Thomas ward had to demonstrate "sincerity of pur-pose to get alcohol out of their life on a permanent basis."[239] This sincerity was assessed in an interview that included the patient, an A.A. sponsor, and an admitting clerk (usually Sister Ignatia). According to Sister Ignatia, the A.A. sponsor played a central role in the St. Thomas program:

The sponsor acts as a catalytic agent in combating all adverse forces. He tries to appease an exasperated wife, talks with the employer, landlord, creditors, and others. He explains the program, tells them that this is not simply another "sobering up pro-cess."[240]

A "no-repeater" admission policy rationed limited beds and prevented new patients from becoming disheartened about their prospects for recovery. (Occasional exceptions were made to this rule.) St. Thomas combined medical detoxification and care with A.A. indoctrination. Patients arriving on the unit were first oriented to the unit by other patients. The unit was staffed by a nurse's aide and an "A.A. employee," who was responsible primarily for heavy cleaning. Medical detoxification was achieved through administration of the "St. Thomas Cock-tail"—a mixture of alcohol and the sedative paraldehyde. Patients drank decreasing doses of this foul-smelling mixture until they were safely detoxi-fied. Patients with more severe withdrawal also received Chloral Hydrate or Tolserol. Dr. Bob made daily rounds to check on each patient—services that

he viewed as part of his A.A. work and never charged for.[241] The five-day, $75 program of recovery consisted of four basic elements: a commitment to total absti-nence, reliance on a Higher Power, involvement in A.A., and service to other alcoholics.[242]

As knowledge of St. Thomas spread, alcoholics came from many areas to receive the special care provided by Dr. Bob and Sister Ignatia. Each alcoholic remained in the hospital for the allotted five days and went through a phased treatment, each day of which was named for its goal. Day one was Reality and Reception—being admitted, oriented, and supported. A.A. sponsors and senior patients on the ward assumed major responsibility for welcoming and encouraging newly arriving patients. Day two was Realiza-tion—understanding that people can recover from alcoholism. During this day, A.A. members guided the alcoholic through the first three steps of A.A. Day three was Moral Inventory—assessing one's past and one's character. Day four was Resolution—reinforcing the reasons for which one could not take the first drink and asking those who had been harmed for forgiveness. The focus of day four was letting go of the past. Day five was Plans for the Future—developing a plan for living outside the hospital.[243]

The reading and talks that Sister Ignatia gave to the alcoholics at St. Thomas were filled with consistent themes about the aids to recovery: hope, prayer, humility, obedience, service, and silence. No visitors other than A.A. members were allowed, and patients were discouraged from superficial socializing. A.A. visitors—many of whom were former patients—filled the unit from noon until 10:00 P.M. No reading mat-erials were permitted that were not related to recovery from alcoholism. Treatment at St. Thomas was serious business.[244]

The final step in one's stay at St. Thomas was an interview with Sister Ignatia. She offered parting advice and presented each alcoholic with a personal-ized copy of Thomás Kempis' *The Imitation of Christ* or Margaret Colton's *A Thought from Saint Ignatius for Each Day of the Year*—a book similar to the daily meditation books commonly used today within Twelve-Step circles. Sister Ignatia also gave each departing alcoholic a Sacred Heart Medallion with the admonition that it be returned personally to her before the person took another drink. Many of the patients discharged from St. Thomas stayed with A.A. families in Akron until they had established a stable program of A.A. recovery and were back on their feet financially. It is quite possible that the seeds of the alcoholism halfway-house movement can be found in this linkage between St. Thomas and the homes of local A.A.

members.

The reader might wonder how the ward survived financially in an age of no public funding or private insurance coverage for alcoholism treatment. The ward was often strained financially. The Sisters of Charity of Saint Augustine absorbed some of the debt, and A.A. periodically raised funds to pay the debt when the future of the unit was threatened.

St. Thomas provided a successful model of alcoholism treatment that spread, first to New York and Cleveland, then on to many cities. As administrative and fiscal forces have dramatically shortened alcoholism treatment within today's hospitals, these institutions might profit from re-visiting the original brief-treatment model pioneered at St. Thomas.

Some key elements of the St. Thomas program that were imitated by many other early hospital-based units included:

1) *Personal A.A. sponsorship for all patients*: Sister Ignatia required that members visiting the unit had to have one year of continuous sobriety before they could assume sponsorship of an alcoholic treated at the hospital. She was the first to articulate standards for the use of A.A. volunteers in an alcoholism treatment unit.

2) *Step Work:* St. Thomas was the first hospital-based program that organized the Steps of A.A. into a structured program of rehabilitation.

3) *Bibliotherapy*: Literature played an important role in the St. Thomas experience. Patients were read to, were given assigned readings, and were given literature to take home with them.

4) *The use of slogans*: Several slogans still in use within recovery circles can be traced to St. Thomas. Dr. Bob's talks at St. Thomas were peppered with A.A.'s developing slogans: "Easy Does It" and "First Things First."

5) *The immediate involvement of patients in the care of other patients*: A senior patient on the ward, called "the Mayor," introduced all newcomers to other patients and helped orient patients to the unit. Patients were expected to support and care for one another, and treatment was defined as participation in a caring community.

6) *The use of tokens/chips*: The origins of the graduation ceremonies of many modern treatment institutions can be traced to Sister Ignatia's presentation of the Sacred Heart medallion to patients leaving St. Thomas.

7) *The use of the word "treatment"*: Sister Ignatia, under Dr. Bob's coaching, objected to patients'

references to taking the "cure." She always told them that there was no cure for alcoholism—that they were at St. Thomas for "treatment," not for a cure.

Model Evolution: A.A. Involvement with Public and Private Hospitals

Access to hospitals was extremely important to early A.A. As described by Dr. William Silkworth, A.A. in its first decade was "unanimous in its belief that hospitalization is desirable, even imperative, in most cases."[245] This belief stemmed primarily from A.A.'s propensity to attract "low-bottom" alcoholics during the 1930s and 1940s. Most were physically addicted to alcohol. What A.A. members knew and feared was that such alcoholics could experience delirium tremens ("DTs") and could die during withdrawal from alcohol.[246] The A.A. policy of working with alcoholics hospitalized for medical detoxification was such a crucial part of early A.A. that, as late as 1939, there was debate about whether someone could even be a member of A.A. who had *not* been hospitalized. The picture of A.A. members speaking to "the man on the bed" was an archetypal image of carrying the A.A. message.[247] Given these circumstances, A.A.'s future growth was extremely dependent upon access to scarce hospital beds.

Access to hospital beds for alcoholics was a critical problem. During the period under consideration (1935-1960), hospitals had five major reasons for resisting the provision of treatment to alcoholics.

1) Hospitals were overcrowded during this post-depression period, making it hard at times for anyone to get a hospital bed.

2) Alcoholics were viewed as moral degenerates, and their alcohol-induced physical problems were viewed more as stubbornness than sickness. The highly stigmatized alcoholic was viewed as potentially filling up a hospital bed that someone else who was "really sick" might need. Not surprisingly, people viewed as having legitimate illnesses or injuries were granted a greater moral right to scarce medical resources.[248]

3) Alcoholics were notorious for not paying their bills. No responsible administrator could be expected to seek out a class of patients whose presence compromised the fiscal integrity of the institution.

4) Alcoholics, particularly those in "DTs," were perceived to be a behavior-management problem that taxed the time and skills of staff and disturbed

the more reputable and more fiscally attractive patients.

5) The high frequency of re-admission of alcoholics for detoxification and treatment of drink-related trauma demoralized staff and made the treatment of alcoholics frustrating and seemingly futile.

Because A.A. members understood these barriers and found unique ways to overcome them, hospitals slowly began to open their doors to alcoholics in the 1940s. The contention that alcoholics were not "really sick" was met by arguments that defined alcoholism in terms of "illness" and "disease." Hospital concerns about non-payment of bills were addressed by A.A. sponsors, and A.A. Central Committees guaranteed payment of bills for people whose admissions they sponsored.[249] Concerns about the manageability of alcoholics in the hospital were addressed by creating separate wards for alcoholics and by bringing in A.A. volunteers to take over the direct management of such patients. As a result, these management problems disappeared completely or became exceptionally rare incidents. The problem of staff frustration with recidivism was handled in the early years by encouraging a policy through which "repeaters" could not be admitted to the alcoholism wards, and by A.A. members' demonstrating through their sustained sobriety the real potential for recovery from alcoholism.

In the stories that follow we will see that the primary incentive for hospitals to become involved in the treatment of alcoholism came from one primary source: unrelenting advocacy by local A.A. members. These members not only convinced hospital administrators that they *should* treat alcoholism, but also became involved in showing them *how* they could treat alcoholism without all the problems they had come to associate with the disorder.

The development of alcoholism wards within hospitals moved in tandem with A.A.'s growth in major population centers. As the burden of caring for alcoholics became too great at St. Thomas, similar arrangements were made with other Akron hospitals and sanataria: People's Hospital, Fair Oaks Villa, and Green Cross.[250] Collaborations between A.A. and several New York City hospitals were established, including Bellevue Hospital, St. John's Hospital in Brooklyn, and the Knickerbocker Hospital in Manhattan.[251] In Cleveland, where demands for beds were greatest, an A.A. Hospital Committee negotiated arrangements with ten local hospitals and sanataria for medical detoxification services. These facilities included St. Vincent's Charity Hospital, Deaconess

Hospital, St. John's Hospital, Post Shaker Sanitarium and the East Cleveland Clinic.[252]

There were several steps that local A.A. groups and committees took in encouraging the establishment of working relationships with local hospitals in the care of alcoholics.

Facility Selection and Recruitment: The way in which A.A. members persuaded Deaconess Hospital in Cleveland to commit beds to the care of alcoholics is typical of how the A.A./hospital relationship was built during the late 1930s and 1940s. Edna McD., a nurse whose husband was in A.A., suggested that, of all the local administrators, Dr. Kitterer, the administrator of Deaconess Hospital, might be most receptive to such an idea. Dr. Bob and another physician in A.A., Dr. Harry N., sold the idea of an alcoholic ward to Dr. Kitterer and the hospital board. Designated beds for alcoholics and A.A. visiting privileges were established, and the first patients were admitted in May, 1939.[253] A similar procedure was used in New York City in the 1940s. Two members from A.A.'s Manhattan Group, Al S. and George B., approached A.R. Monro, the President of Knickerbocker Hospital, with a proposal to open an A.A.-"sponsored" alcoholic ward within the hospital. After getting through the usual arguments that alcoholics would be disruptive to other patients and not pay their bills, the President was finally persuaded to establish an alcoholic ward. But he wanted a formal contractual agreement between A.A. and the hospital. Given A.A.'s growing stance of non-affiliation, a corporation ("Rehabilitation of Alcoholics of New York, Inc.") had to be formed by interested A.A. members so that agreements could be legally negotiated regarding the operation of the unit.[254] The first alcoholic patient was admitted to the 19-bed ward on Easter Sunday, 1945. Local A.A. committees pursued similar negotiations with hospitals in Philadelphia, Boston, and other major population centers.

Physician Recruitment: Once hospital administrators were persuaded to cooperate in the care of alcoholics, a physician had to be found who would take primary responsibility for the medical detoxification of alcoholics. Early doctors who worked with A.A. during this period are legendary in local A.A. lore. Among the many was Dr. William Silkworth, who worked with alcoholics at both the Charles B. Towns Hospital and the Knickerbocker Hospital in New York City. There was Dr. Nash in Cleveland and Drs. A. Wiese Hammer, C. Dudley Saul, William Turnbull, and John Stauffer, who worked with A.A. in Philadelphia. Such doctors were convinced by local A.A. committees that, if they would take medical responsibility for getting the alcoholic sober, A.A. members would provide a way to help the alcoholic stay sober.

Negotiation of Admission, Service, and Discharge Procedures: In their negotiations with hospital administrators and physicians, A.A. committees made sure that special A.A. guidelines would be followed in caring for alcoholics. These guidelines included admission criteria and procedures, service procedures that would be followed while the alcoholic was being detoxified, and discharge procedures. There were slight variations in these procedures from city to city, but most followed a general format that emerged out of the earliest experiences in Akron, New York, and Cleveland. Admission criteria demanded that each alcoholic patient be ambulatory, be agreeable to hospitalization, not have medical or psychiatric complications other than alcoholism, and "have a sincere desire to do something about his drinking problem." There was agreement in most cities that no "repeaters" (or "retroverts") would be admitted under A.A. auspices. Where exceptions to this rule were made, the relapsed patient was isolated from all other alcoholics undergoing treatment, to prevent the latter's demoralization.

The practice of granting admitting privileges to A.A. sponsors gained a strong footing at Knickerbocker Hospital and spread to other facilities. Even physicians wishing to admit a patient to the alcoholic ward did so through the A.A. Hospitalization Committee (A.A. Intergroup Headquarters), with final admission decisions being made, not by the physician, but by the A.A. sponsor. If the reader is wondering how an A.A. sponsor could be granted so much authority, the answer is a simple one. The A.A. sponsor who admitted the patient was responsible for the bill being paid in cash at the time of admission.[255]

The general guidelines for visitation, discharge, and participation in A.A. meetings are reflected in the procedures used in Cleveland in 1942, procedures that are well illustrated in the "Instructions to Hospitals" that appear on page 178.

Organization of Volunteers: The primary role of A.A. members on the alcoholism wards was to provide an intense indoctrination of patients in A.A. principles, primarily through the vehicle of personal stories, but in some settings (such as Knickerbocker Hospital) A.A. members performed even broader roles.

A.A. volunteers assist the hospital staff in nonprofessional chores. They report for duty on regular shifts throughout the day and night, helping as orderlies and providing companionship to patients during the lonely hours that mark the first stages of treatment.[256]

This voluntary workforce of A.A. members not only played a role in the alcoholic's recovery, but also played a significant role in persuading hospitals to enter into these collaborative agreements with A.A. In her efforts to promote alcoholism wards in general hospitals in the 1940s, Marty Mann often made the point that these units could operate with 75% fewer staff members than would be required for a medical-surgical ward.[257] This reduced cost came from the voluntary workforce provided by A.A.

The logistics of coordinating such a volunteer force were not easy. Twenty-two A.A. members per week (many of whom were ex-patients of the Knickerbocker alcoholism ward) were assigned to perform unpaid orderly duties on the Knickerbocker "A.A. Ward."[258]

Problem Solving and Establishment of Credibility: Once alcoholism units in local hospitals were opened, great care had to be taken to ensure that any problems arising within such units would not lead to the closure of the units. Regular meetings between A.A. Hospital Committees and these institutions were held to resolve such problems. Many factors led to the initial and enduring credibility of these units. The fact that some well-known A.A. members held professional status as physicians, nurses, social workers, and psychotherapists helped build A.A. credibility within the medical community in places like Akron, New York City, and Philadelphia.[259] The presence of recovered alcoholics such as Theresa ("Teddy") R. working as nurses at Knickerbocker served as a daily testament to the possibility of enduring recovery from alcoholism.[260]

It is unclear whether or not the treatment outcomes were monitored in these early alcoholism wards. There are only passing references to such figures, such as a 1950 article in the *A.A. Grapevine* noting that 60% of the 5,000 men and women treated in the alcoholism ward at the Knickerbocker Hospital in its first five years became permanent members of A.A.[261] Two things can be surmised from this period. The first is that the general rule of "no repeaters" prevented these units from deteriorating into drying-out stations for the chronically relapsing alcoholic. The second is that the large number of sober A.A. volunteers (many of them former patients) must have had an elevating effect on physicians and nurses in these hospitals and contributed to the credibility of these units. One can only imagine what effect it would have had on staff to see former alcoholic patients, sober and grateful, regularly visiting the hospital to convey a message of hope to newly admitted alcoholic patients.

Model Extension: A.A. and Private Hospitals, Sanitaria, and Psychiatric Institutions

The model of collaboration initially established by A.A. to work with public hospitals also was extended to private hospitals, sanataria, state and private psychiatric facilities, and prisons. By 1957, A.A. groups had been established with 265 public and private hospitals and 335 prisons.[262] Typical of these relationships was that established with Charles B. Towns Hospital.

The reader will recall that Charles B. Towns Hospital last entered our story when Bill Wilson was treated there in 1933 and 1934. Once sober, Bill was given permission to visit other alcoholics who were being treated at Towns, and it was there that he recruited men like Hank P. and Fitz M. into the first A.A. group in New York City.[263] The relationship between A.A. and the Towns Hospital continued through the 1940s and became more formalized in the 1950s. What made this relationship notable was the strong linkage between the local A.A. Central Committee and the hospital administration. The 1956 memo of agreement between the A.A. Intergroup Office of New York City and Towns Hospital included the following provisions:

1. *A patient is eligible to be hospitalized only once on the A.A. floor at Towns (no "retreads").*
2. *All patients are to be sponsored by members of Alcoholics Anonymous and all admissions are to be cleared through Intergroup.*
3. *All patients must be taken to the hospital by their A.A. sponsor.*
4. *Hospitalization shall be for five days.*
5. *The treatment by the hospital shall be primarily that of restoring the physical health of the patient with the psychological and spiritual job of restoring the patient to a normal and useful life reserved for Alcoholics Anonymous.*
6. *No patient shall be discharged until called for by his A.A. sponsor.*[264]

Other private alcoholism treatment hospitals with which A.A. worked closely in the 1950s included Brighton Hospital in Brighton, Michigan, and Willingway Hospital in Statesboro, Georgia.

Less formal relationships were maintained between A.A. and many private hospitals and sanataria whose names are sprinkled through early A.A. literature—names such as Overbrook Asylum,

Greystone Asylum, Minnesota Sanitarium, and Blythewood Sanitarium.[265] These relationships often consisted of the provision of A.A. literature to the facilities, visits to alcoholic patients, and arrangements for patients to attend A.A. meetings in neighboring communities.

At the time it was entering into relationships with community hospitals and sanataria, A.A. also began collaborating with psychiatric hospitals. In 1939, under the leadership of Dr. R.E. Blaisdell, the Rockland State Hospital in Orangeburg, New York became the first state psychiatric facility to enter into a "full-scale" collaborative relationship with A.A. The alcoholism treatment unit at Rockland hosted A.A. meetings, incorporated A.A. teachings into its treatment regimen, and used A.A. volunteers to transport alcoholic patients to outside A.A. meetings.[266] Blaisdell even arranged for Bill Wilson to speak at the hospital in 1939.[267] Similar relationships existed between A.A. and St. Elizabeth's Hospital in Washington D.C., the West Tennessee State Hospital at Bolivar, Creedmoor State Hospital and the Brooklyn State Hospital in New York, Longview State Hospital in Cincinnati, Ohio, the Dayton State Hospital in Dayton, Ohio, and Chicago State Hospital.[268]

In 1941, Dr. H. G. McMahan described the organization of an alcoholism program at Illinois' Manteno State Hospital. This program was inspired by the knowledge that former alcoholic patients treated at the hospital had achieved sustained sobriety through A.A. following their discharge. The new program consisted of three months of individual and group psychotherapy conducted by a psychiatrist and "group therapy" led by volunteer members of A.A. Of particular interest is the fact that orientation of patients to the Twelve Steps of A.A. was conducted, not by A.A. members, but by the hospital psychiatrists, who focused on how the Steps could be used by patients to develop a well-integrated personality. The major problem noted by Dr. McMahan was that A.A.'s rapid growth was making it difficult to obtain for their patients sponsors who had what the hospital judged to be adequate sobriety time.[269]

The collaboration between state psychiatric hospitals and A.A. reached its zenith in the early 1950s at Willmar State Hospital in Minnesota. This model incorporated much of A.A.'s view of alcoholism and recovery and integrated recovered A.A. members in paid service roles within a multidisciplinary alcoholism treatment service team. (The "Minnesota Model" would prove so influential to the future of alcoholism treatment that we will devote a forthcoming chapter to it.) By 1966, 74% of psychiatric hospitals with alcoholism units reported having "A.A. counselors" working in full- or part-time positions, and a 1970 survey would reveal that 77% of psychiatric hospitals involved A.A. in some form and that A.A. meetings were actually held within 43% of them.[270]

A.A. Members as Moral and Business Entrepreneurs

In the 1940s and 1950s, local A.A. groups were extending a hand of cooperation to a wide variety of institutions that could be of service to alcoholics. Where services to alcoholics through general hospitals, private hospitals and sanataria, and psychiatric hospitals were not available, a void was created that some A.A. groups and individual A.A. members were prompted to fill. They accomplished this in two ways. The first was for local A.A. groups to become involved in providing services such as detoxification. Most often they did so by adding a few beds to a local A.A. clubhouse for this purpose. As more "high-bottom" alcoholics began to enter A.A., some of these clubhouses became quite confident and casual about their ability to perform this function. But such direct involvement beyond the traditional boundaries of A.A. activities nearly always created problems, sometimes in unexpected ways. In Amarillo, Texas, for example, two A.A. members got drunk on purpose so they could be checked into the detox center above the local A.A. clubhouse. The impetus for these "slips" was the earlier admission of two very attractive women for detoxification.[271] The involvement of A.A. groups in such activities proved to be a source of internal dissension within A.A., even when the resulting stories were not as colorful or personally disastrous as the Amarillo story.

By far the most common and enduring way the void in local alcoholism services was filled was for individual A.A.s to take up the banner and advocate increased services, or to start such services themselves. Many alcoholism service programs were developed in the 1940s and 1950s that were not sponsored by A.A. but were created out of the actions of individual A.A. members, in the tradition of the Knickerbocker Paradox. A.A. members created, sat on, and in some cases dominated, state and local boards that planned, organized, and operated service programs for alcoholics. Alcan, West Virginia's first alcoholism treatment center opened in 1944. It provided a 5-day, $50, program staffed by A.A. members within a house owned by an A.A. member. The Twelfth Step House in New York City was founded by A.A. members in 1948 as a "prep school

for A.A." More office than house, the facility provided sober fellowship, and alcoholics obtained clean clothes and living accommodations. It also gave its "students" intense indoctrination in A.A. through "Twelfth Step Workshops."[272] During that same year, Chicago A.A. members were collaborating in opening an "A.A. ward" in the Chicago Washingtonian Home and supporting the newly created Portal House. Both of these facilities were actively supported by the Chicago Committee on Alcoholism, a group filled with many A.A. members.[273] When North Carolina established its first state-funded alcoholism services in 1949, it appointed a 15-member Alcoholic Advisory Committee that the state specifically required be filled with "all recovered alcoholics and workers in Alcoholics Anonymous."[274]

While advocacy and collaborative models like those described above worked in some areas, in other areas individual A.A. members took the financial risks in organizing their own service facilities—facilities that were often known as "A.A. farms," "A.A. rest homes," and "A.A. retreats," until consciousness of newly emerging A.A. traditions forced their rechristening.[275] There were A.A. member-spawned urban facilities such as 12 Step House and Friendly House in Los Angeles,[276] and there were more traditionally rural programs such as Beech Hill Farm, Alina Lodge, Bently Brook Farms, High Watch Farm, and Hazelden. Typical of these small operations was the 12th Step Retreat in Ann Arbor, Michigan.[5]

The 12th Step Retreat was opened in 1951 by Dean and Kay L. Although it was called an "Alcoholic Hospital," the facility was a large Victorian boarding house in which Dean and his family (wife and children) cared for some 12 alcoholics at a time. The seven-day program of medication-aided detoxification, vitamins, "metaphysical food," and immersion in A.A. philosophy cost $100 (the brochure proclaimed "Blue Cross Insurance honored"). The 12 Step Retreat was advertized as an "A.A. Hospital run by A.A.s and attended by A.A.s." After being operated by Dean and his family for three years, the home came under new ownership, moved to Williamston, and closed some four years later.

Dean L.'s sons' characterization of their father's zealousness gives some indication of the kinds of A.A. members who were launching such facilities. They describe Dean as "Captain Sobriety"—the ultimate A.A. salesman. Most of the facilities like the 12th Step

---

[5] I would like to acknowledge Mel B. For his assistance in finding materials on the 12th Step Retreat and for interviewing the sons of Dean L.

Retreat, whose names have been lost to history, lived short, precarious existences, but filled an important void in alcoholism services in the period between the prohibition-era collapse of alcoholism treatment and the rise of community-based alcoholism services in the 1960s and 1970s.

There were also partnerships between individual A.A. members and professionals to launch private alcoholism services. Between 1951-1953, Searcy W., in collaboration with E. M. Jellinek, opened alcoholism hospitals in Dallas, Texas (1950), Carlsbad, New Mexico (1951), and Houston, Texas (1951). Searcy describes the nature of the program.

> *Our focus was on physical detoxification. The staff was primarily medical doctors and nurses. We administered 1,000 cc of glucose every day and used the sedatives tolserol and toleseram to get people through the worst of it. We also used paraldehyde in the early days, and some of the more difficult cases were given sodium nembutal to sleep through the first few days. While our job was to get their bodies right, we emphasized that you had to go to A.A. to really get sober and stay sober. We got people out to meetings as quickly as we could, and there were A.A. members constantly in and out. There was very little formal sponsorship in those days—the whole A.A. group took on the alcoholics at the Clinics.*[277]

Those early A.A. entrepreneurs who initiated alcoholism-related business ventures did so at some personal and financial risk. Such people were often viewed with skepticism—if not outright derision—by mainstream health-care providers, and were also subjected to severe criticism from within A.A. An A.A. member of this era described the concern about A.A. members being hired to work in treatment centers.

> *We were all afraid something was going to screw up A.A., and we were particularly concerned about the idea of someone making money on A.A.*[278]

And yet Bill Wilson, A.A.'s co-founder, was quite supportive of most of these efforts. He visited some of these facilities and even sometimes arranged personally to have alcoholics admitted to such facilities. At a time when most hospitals would not admit alcoholics, Bill believed it was important that alcohol-ics be able to enter respectable places where they could sober up—places where people truly understood the alcoholic's condition.[279]

The Boundary Between Treatment and A.A.: The Story of High Watch

Although A.A. members in the late 1930s to mid-1940s were involved in starting, operating, and collaborating with a variety of institutions that cared for alcoholics, there remains a very real question as to whether or not such activities actually involved what has come to be called alcoholism "treatment." It is very important that we understand how the use of this term has evolved over time. It emerged first as a reaction to the word "cure"—a term that addictions professionals as diverse as Charles B. Towns and Sister Ignatia disliked. "Treatment" most often implied detoxification and medical stabilization rather than recovery from alcoholism itself. One could, for example, easily build the case that the models described in this chapter, from St. Thomas to the 12th Step Retreat, are nothing more than detoxification and A.A. immersion and do not constitute "treatment" as it is thought of today. As A.A. experiments with collaboration extended through the 1940s, A.A. members themselves began to seek clarification of the line between A.A. and the "treatment" of alcoholism. If there is one story in this era that can open our discussion of this line of demarcation, it is surely that of High Watch Farm.[6]

Beginnings: The earliest "retreat" or "rest house" operated on A.A. principles was known as High Watch Farm. High Watch evolved out of an earlier entity—Joy Farm—located in Kent, Connecticut. Joy Farm was founded in the mid-1920s by the Ministry of the High Watch, an organization devoted to promoting the teachings of Emma Curtis Thompson, a leader in the New Thought religious movement. The 200-acre Joy Farm served as a haven where the elderly and indigent could live and work in spiritual simplicity.[280] The farm's philanthropist and driving spirit was Etheldred Frances Folsom, known as Sister Francis because of her emulation of the life of St. Francis.[281] By 1939, Joy Farm was struggling financially, and the corporation that oversaw it was grappling to define a future use for the farm. There was even talk of closing the farm, when a Quaker group to whom the farm had been offered declined to assume its management. It

---

[6] I would like to acknowledge the pioneering work of Lyn Hartridge Harbaugh, whose work organizing the High Watch Archives and whose research and writings make possible the following synopsis.

was in this atmosphere that the history of Joy Farm and the history of A.A. intersected.

While Marty M. was in treatment at Blythewood Sanitarium, she met another alcoholic woman. Marty introduced Nona W. to A.A. and Nona, in turn, introduced Marty to a special place—Joy Farm —where she had briefly stayed in her search for sobriety. In the fall of 1939, Bill Wilson and Marty M. visited Sister Francis at Joy Farm. Bill was taken by the special spiritual presence that permeated the farm. For her part, Sister Francis was so taken by A.A.'s spiritual approach to the problem of alcoholism that she offered the use of High Watch as a retreat where A.A. members could initiate or strengthen their recovery from alcoholism. When Bill refused her suggestion that he personally "take over" the farm, they settled on the idea of creating a board to manage the facility. A small board composed mostly of A.A. members was set up in 1940 to oversee the newly christened High Watch Farm, and an A.A. member (Ray C.) who was also a "lay psychologist" was hired (at $50 per month) to manage the facility.[282]

The two goals of High Watch Farm as initially articulated were 1) to serve as a post-hospitalization retreat for alcoholics needing extended recuperation, and 2) to serve as a place of refreshment and renewal for A.A. members.[283]

Daily Life at High Watch: The "therapeutic" program first established by Ray C. for alcoholics seeking sobriety consisted of a series of eight talks and a prescribed program of reading. The lecture series included 1) a presentation on alcoholism as a disease, 2) an examination of negative personal qualities, 3) a discussion of how negative thoughts shape negative qualities, 4) a discussion of the power of conscious and unconscious thought, 5) a presentation on using substitution or sublimation to change thinking, 6) a demonstration of "affirmations (scientific prayer)" and methods of relaxation, 7) a discussion of the value of prayer, and 8) a spiritual workshop that focused on how to concentrate and meditate. This program was provided within a broader milieu in which newcomers were exposed to A.A. members visiting the Farm.

In its early years, High Watch could accommodate as many as 28 men and women in residence. In 1940, A.A. members who stayed at the Farm were charged $2 per day, and Ray C.'s "private patients" who stayed at the Farm were charged $30 per week. Referrals to High Watch came from A.A. members, and from alcoholism treatment programs that referred clients who they believed needed more extended time in treatment. A local physician in Kent supervised

detoxification and the physical recovery of guests. Daily life at High Watch consisted of vitamin injections, chapel, personal meditation, reading A.A. literature, shared work, common meals, exercise, and fellowship. Guests attended A.A. meetings in neighboring communities in Connecticut and New York, and in later years attended A.A. meetings organized on the Farm.

Conflicting Visions: Conflict quickly emerged over how High Watch could best achieve its goals. Minutes from board meetings during the years 1941-1943 reveal the kinds of tensions that surrounded efforts to shape the identity of High Watch. Ray, Sister Francis, and A.A. members on the board each had a somewhat different vision of how High Watch should be managed.[284] Ray envisioned a structured program of "treatment" provided within an environment with a central authority. Sister Francis envisioned a leaderless spiritual retreat where quiet reflection and fellowship could provide the seeds for recovery. She saw High Watch as "a place of refreshment, not a hospital." Speaking on behalf of A.A., Bill Wilson, while emphasizing A.A.'s desire to make the farm useful to as many alcoholics as possible, emphasized the separation between A.A. and the farm. He believed that having a therapist at the farm was fine as long as he was not an "A.A. therapist." He further noted that, "To A.A., the Farm is not an A.A. Farm, but a place where A.A.'s have special privileges."[285] Conflict over the future direction of High Watch reached a point of crisis during the summer of 1941, when Marty M. announced that she was resigning from the board on the grounds that she could "no longer endorse the principle" under which High Watch was being operated.

Both Marty M. And Sister Francis believed that Ray's program and his style of leadership was too psychological and authoritarian. Sister Francis declared that "the spirit of this place is being lost." The conflict was increasingly being framed as a strain between "Ray's therapy" and "A.A. principles."[286] Marty, in spite of her own positive experience with psychiatric treatment, believed that there was a fundamental distinction between psychiatry (and by inference, Ray's psychological approach to counseling alcoholics) and philosophies of New Thought and A.A. She believed that the former focused one's attention inward upon oneself, and the latter focused one's attention outward, toward others.[287]

Marty also believed that there was a fundamental difference between relationships that formed at High Watch under a system of lay psychology and relationships formed at a High Watch conceived as a spiritual retreat. When the facility was operated as a spiritual retreat, it was the freedom within the milieu in which "every individual had something to give" that made High Watch a special place. In contrast, Marty believed that Ray's activities in directing High Watch were imposing what Marty called the "one-man (or woman) idea, through which one individual—in trying to be THE one, alone giving help to all the others—inevitably becomes the sole arbiter of their thoughts and actions." Marty predicted that under such a system "....inevitably we get a doctor and his patient, a psychiatrist and his patients, or a lay psychologist and his patients."[288]

In her resignation letter, Marty went on to explain the difference, in her understanding, between High Watch and A.A. on the one hand, and treatment on the other:

> At Blythewood, a particular method of treatment, psychiatry, was used by one man, Dr. Tiebout, to help me get well. At the Farm, now, a particular method of treatment (the word is Ray's own: one might call it metaphysical psychology or psychological metaphysics perhaps) is being used by one man, Ray C_____, to help others get well. I repeat: I have nothing against either method of treatment. But they belong in one classification; and the Farm as it used to be, and A.A. as it is, belong in another....In my opinion the Farm contains enough within itself, IF its traditions are followed; and the A.A. steps and general principles contain enough within themselves, IF the alcoholic wishes to follow them, to make any further specialized treatment or teaching unnecessary....People who do not wish to avail themselves of what these two things have to offer need not stay at the Farm and should be no concern of ours.[289]

Marty ended her resignation letter by suggesting that, if the Farm were run on its original principles, what it needed was a person to provide administrative oversight, not someone to direct therapeutic activities. During the 1940s, Marty viewed alcoholism "treatment" as an adjunct to A.A. Treatment was something that medically stabilized the alcoholic and mentally prepared him or her for the "treatment of alcoholism itself" through A.A.[290] In her view, Ray was invading A.A. territory by introducing technology beyond the scope of A.A. to "treat" alcoholism.

Bill Wilson, who attended the meeting, tried to play the role of peacemaker by suggesting the possibility of middle ground: High Watch serving as a spiritual retreat with Ray's psychological services available on a voluntary rather than required basis. The board voted to attempt a compromise, and Marty agreed to withdraw her resignation until the annual meeting in October, 1941.

Ray C.'s responses to the objections of Marty and Sister Francis were recorded in the board minutes. He stated:

> That he would not wish to continue indefinitely as a manger. He feels there must be a "captain of the ship"—someone who takes care of people in trouble. This "captain" must in his opinion be more than a mere administrator—he must be an alcoholic, and must have control.

Ray discussed his desire to resign but was encouraged by other board members to try the compromise plan until it could be evaluated in October.

Following the July board meeting, Bill Wilson wrote Ray C. outlining the conclusions Bill had come to after further discussion with the board members. In the letter, Bill outlined Sister Francis' long involvement in the Farm, compared to the short involvement of A.A. in the Farm. He stated his realization that Sister Francis was "implacably opposed to anything that looks like therapy; that looks like the private aim of a single individual; that looks like the making of profit; that looks like conventional direction and management." Noting again Sister Francis' long involvement in the Farm and her current discomfort with the Farm's management, Bill noted that the other Board members had no alternative but to support Sister Francis. Bill, for his part, said that he had to "very reluctantly agree," and that in spite of his warm feelings for Ray, "the logic of the situation seems unanswerable."[291]

This struggle over the institutional identity of High Watch was temporarily resolved over the coming months through a series of actions: Bill W.'s assumption of the role of Honorary President of the Board; a vote by the board that the farm should be opened to older A.A.'s "for refreshment" while newer A.A. members should be encouraged to remain close to the clubhouses; and finally, in September, Ray C.'s resignation and the assumption of temporary financial management of High Watch by Sister Francis.[292]

With Ray's resignation, High Watch abandoned the integration of professionalized therapeutic services and focused instead on spiritual immersion in A.A. literature, stories, and rituals.

High Watch continued to struggle with the line between A.A. spirituality and professional-directed treatment. That controversy was even revisited in the modern era, when state authorities tried to hold High Watch accountable to licensing standards for alcoholism treatment programs while High Watch argued that what it did was not treatment.[293]

The Distinction Between A.A. and Treatment

Since the opening pages of this book, we have described many mutual-aid societies, and we have described many addiction treatment institutions and their methods. To enhance our understanding of both voluntary mutual-aid societies and professionally directed addiction treatment, we will close this chapter by comparing and contrasting A.A. with professionally directed alcoholism treatment. What we are looking for in this discussion is a clearer understanding of mutual-aid and treatment and the boundary that separates these two phenomena.

Differences between A.A. and alcoholism treatment could be drawn easily if the boundaries of both entities were clearly defined. While A.A.'s boundaries are defined to a great degree by the Twelve Steps and Twelve Traditions, the professional boundaries of what constitutes "alcoholism" and "alcoholism treatment" are much less clearly codified; they seem to be increasingly defined by professional and commercial interests, rather than by clinical science. In spite of these sometimes vacillating definitions, differences between A.A. and treatment can be noted in many areas. Linda Kurtz, in her sweeping 1997 review of self-help and support groups, captures much of the distinction between treatment and mutual-aid groups. She notes that the latter groups 1) focus on the mobilization of resources within the self and within the family and wider community, 2) are inherently personal, egalitarian, and anti-bureaucratic, and 3) eschew expert advice in lieu of personal and collective experience.[294] Listed below are elaborations of these points and additional reflections on the differences between A.A. and alcoholism treatment. They are offered as opening observations in what will be a continuing discussion of the historical delineation of mutual aid and professionally directed addiction treatment.

Organizational Context
Professionally directed treatment services take place within the context of a business environment; A.A.-directed recovery takes place within the context of a voluntary social and spiritual community. The field of addiction treatment is bound together by professional and institutional self-interest; A.A. is bound together by what Bill Wilson has called a "kinship of common suffering."[295]

Theory
The theoretical underpinnings of alcoholism treatment begin with different conceptions of the etiology of alcoholism and proceed from these conceptions to various derived intervention technologies; A.A. simply says to the alcoholic, "Stop drinking, and here's how to avoid taking the next drink." Treatment claims to be rooted in medicine and psychology; A.A. claims to be drawn from medicine and religion.

Focus
Treatment is depicted as a process of "getting into oneself." It is about self-exploration and self-healing. A.A. is about getting outside oneself through a focus on resources and relationships beyond the self. Treatment is about self-development; A.A. is about self-transcendence. Treatment is about discovery (initiating sobriety); A.A. is about recovery (sustaining sobriety).[296]

Locus of Control
In the face of any addiction treatment procedure, it is difficult for the "client" to control the degree of intimacy in the service relationship, due to the inherent inequality of this relationship. In contrast, each A.A. member, each day, decides if, when, where, for how long, and at what level of intensity A.A. contact will occur.

Degree of Invasiveness
A.A. culture, through such mechanisms as the discouragement of cross-talk and the admonition to avoid taking other people's "inventories," seeks to reduce the invasiveness of personal interactions. Treatment seeks a heightened degree of personal self-disclosure. A.A. asks for conclusions; treatment asks for the details. The story model in A.A. is a cognitive life *summary* couched in terms of psychological and social death and rebirth; the story model in treatment is an affective expression of the *particulars* of one's wounding.

Relationships
Addiction treatment is based on a professionally governed, fiduciary service relationship in which the treatment professional takes on a special ethical and legal duty and obligation for the care of the client. The treatment relationship is hierarchical, with an assumption that strength and control reside in the therapist and the therapeutic institution. A.A. relationships are equal

and reciprocal, with an assumption that strengths and vulnerabilities are shared by all members and that all are there because they need to be there. The treatment relationship is time-limited; A.A. relationships are open ended and potentially life-enduring. What one receives in addiction treatment is a service; what one receives in A.A. is membership in a recovering community.

Diagnosis

In alcoholism treatment, a diagnosis is made of the nature of the problems presented by the person seeking services. The diagnosis is made by one or more trained professionals with the awareness that errors in diagnosis can result in harm done to the client. The diagnosing professional possesses substantial power; the client being diagnosed brings significant vulnerability to the diagnostic event. A.A. places emphasis on self-diagnosis.

Credentials

In treatment, the credentials of the "experts" are measured in degrees, licences, and certifications awarded by governmental and private authorities. There is an assumption that the professional possesses special knowledge and skill that the "patient" lacks. In A.A., the experts are measured only by the credential of personal experience—one's sobriety today, one's sobriety date, and one's degree of actualization of A.A.'s aspirational values. Professionally credentialed members of A.A. must take off the professional "hat" when participating in A.A. As such, A.A. is a community of amateurs who relish rather than apologize for their amateur status. The lack of technical credentialing within A.A. reduces disparities in power and creates a foundation of universal vulnerability.

Money

Money, often in significant amounts, is paid by the alcoholic for treatment services (beyond room, board, and medical care). A.A. involvement calls for voluntary financial contributions—in small amounts—to the support of the group. Treatment involves an exchange of money for services. These fees (paid by the addict or someone else) reinforce the non-reciprocal character of the relationship and the inequality of power within the relationship. In A.A., token contributions are an optional ritual of membership.

Addiction-Specific Intervention Technology

Addiction treatment contains a core technology that distinguishes it from other branches of medical, psychological, or social intervention. Addiction treatment targets the craving and compulsion that drive addictive behavior, as well as the consequences of addiction. It is focused on the core of addiction AND its antecedents, consequences, co-morbidities, and obstacles to recovery. A.A. has but one focus: achieving sobriety one day at a time through a spiritual program of daily living. A.A. posits no claim of expertise on any issue other than that of its method of recovery from alcoholism.

Ethical & Legal Guidelines

Treatment relationships are guided by professional codes of ethics to which each individual practitioner is bound, and licensing and accreditation standards to which treatment institutions are bound; A.A. relationships are guided by "group conscience" and the historical experience of A.A. Specially conceived legal standards exist governing the delivery of addiction treatment services, because harm to the public might result from the delivery of fraudulent or incompetently delivered services. The invasive nature of addiction treatment interventions poses risks related to their misapplication. No such legal regulations govern A.A., because the public perceives no similar threat resulting from involvement in mutual-aid activity. Disclosures in treatment are confidential and legally protected; disclosures in A.A. are sacred and spiritually protected.

Records

Treatment programs maintain extensive records on those who seek their services; there are no individual records in A.A.

In comparing A.A. (mutual-aid) to alcoholism treatment, we are not comparing two types of treatment: we are comparing treatment and something else. A.A. is not a treatment for alcoholism. It is a spiritual community of shared experience—"a way of living and being."[297] The primary functional linkage between A.A. and alcoholism treatment is that both claim a mission of serving alcoholics. How and why these missions are achieved could not be more different. Putting alcoholism treatment and A.A. in the same basket misunderstands both. This is not a minor error of mistaking apples for oranges—two objects in the same family. It is instead analogous to comparing apples and automobiles.

Seeking to clarify the differences between A.A. and alcoholism treatment is not a meaningless exercise—the addictionologist's version of counting how many angels can dance on the head of a pin. The failure to recognize these distinctions or the loss of these distinctions has significant implications. Personal safety requires an understanding of and adherence to the principles and boundaries that govern personal and professional relationships. Physicians who abdicate their power and authority by offering friendship in place of their knowledge and skill are as dangerous as friends who assume an unearned power and authority by trying to play doctor. The issue is not: who is better, friends or doctors? The question—like the parallel question asked about A.A. and treatment—is unanswerable until one finds oneself in desperate need of one or the other.

If treatment turns itself into nothing but an undeclared A.A. meeting, it ceases to be treatment and becomes instead an unethical misrepresentation of itself. If it is deemed that an alcoholic might benefit from A.A., he or she should be referred to A.A. rather than charged fees for services that are neither professional nor services. To call Twelfth-Step work alcoholism counseling simultaneously violates A.A. traditions and the discipline of addiction counseling. A.A. itself attempted to assert this distinction in the 1940s and 1950s, in correspondence from the A.A. Central Office requesting that rehabilitation centers and halfway houses not link themselves with A.A. by using such names as "Twelfth Step House," and by later writing suggested guidelines for A.A. members working in the field.[298]

In a like manner, if A.A. transforms itself into a network of new-age therapy groups, it may meet some people's needs, but it will cease being A.A. It would be as devastating to turn A.A. over to professionals as it would be to turn the treatment of alcoholics over to amateurs. A lack of understanding of the differences between these two entities will inevitably result in the violation and corruption of both.[299]

A.A. and Alcoholism Treatment: A Synopsis

There were a wide range of ways in which A.A. as an institution and A.A. members related to alcoholism in the years between 1935 and 1960. A.A. made but then abandoned plans to create "A.A. hospitals" and "A.A. Rest Homes" and plans to send out field "missionaries" to carry the A.A. message to the far

corners of the earth. A.A. members served as advocates for the creation of local alcoholism treatment programs and served on national, state, and local alcoholism treatment advisory boards. Many state and national alcoholism efforts were pioneered almost exclusively by A.A. members. In many areas, A.A. emerged as a primary source of referral of alcoholics to treatment programs. There were also many alcoholism treatment programs in the 1940s and early 1950s in which A.A. sponsorship was a requirement for admission. A.A. members served as volunteers within alcoholism treatment programs—often in educational and "co-therapist" roles. A.A. members transported patients from hospitals, asylum, sanataria, rest homes, and prisons to A.A. meetings and facilitated A.A. meetings inside these same institutions. In the 1940s, A.A. members—acting as individuals rather than as representatives of A.A.—began organizing and working as paid staff within alcoholism education and treatment programs, a practice that forced A.A. and treatment institutions to begin a dialogue about the distinctions between A.A. and treatment. As treatment programs developed more formal patient-education programs, A.A. members were increasingly called upon to speak to patients about alcoholism, recovery, and A.A. And what is perhaps most significant is that A.A. became the primary sobriety-based support structure to which most alcoholic patients were referred upon their discharge from treatment.

What has been called the "modern alcoholism movement" rose in the 1940s to redefine America's view of alcoholism and the alcoholic. One of the legacies of this movement was a professionally directed model of alcoholism treatment that integrated A.A.'s philosophy and professionalized A.A. members within the new role of alcoholism counselor. In the next three chapters, we will tell this story, beginning with the movement and ending with a model that, more than any preceding it, made the boundary between mutual-aid and alcoholism treatment extremely difficult to draw.

---

*A*A*
INSTRUCTIONS TO HOSPITALS

1. Call a physician immediately.
2. The hospital shall make out a complete history.
3. The hospital will be furnished official A.A. Visitation Record, which must be kept for each patient.
4. No one excepting A.A. members will be permitted to visit patients, except at the discretion of attending physicians.
5. No visitors will be permitted after 11:00 P.M.
6. Patient will not be given street clothes until the last day, except on occasions when sponsor brings him to a meeting. Upon returning from the meeting, clothes are to be taken from patient.
7. All packages for the patient must be inspected by the person in charge.
8. Hospitals and Sanitariums will not permit more than two men to talk to any one patient at any one time.
9. Patients will not be permitted any outside contact, such as mail or telephone calls, except through his sponsor.
10. Hospitals will have patients available to visitors at all times, up to 11:00 P.M., except where it conflicts with hospital rules.
11. Hospitals and Sanitariums will be used for the purposes for which they are intended, and not as meeting places or club rooms, except at the Women's Hospital.
12. Under no circumstances may a patient in Hospital or Sanitarium be taken to a meeting, without the approval of his sponsor.
13. Wives or husbands of A.A. members will not be permitted to be present, when a patient is being contacted.
14. Hospitals and Sanitariums are not to make any reference to A.A. in their promotional or publicity programs.

Source: Attachment, A.A. Central Committee Minutes, July 7, 1942, Cleveland, Ohio (From Clarence S. Papers)

✠

Chapter Nineteen
The "Modern Alcoholism Movement": The Core

Between 1930 and 1955 a radical redefinition of the nature of alcohol problems in America was forged. Credit or blame (depending on one's perspective) for this change is regularly attributed to what has been called the "modern alcoholism movement."[300] This multifaceted movement, without a singular leader, unified strategy, or primary source of economic support, successfully initiated a remarkable revolution in American social thought.[1]

Within a period of 25 years, the modern alcoholism movement changed a century-old definition of America's alcohol problem and the entire language in which that problem was conceptualized. It shifted America's construction of alcohol-related problems from a religious and moral knowledge base to a secular one. It transformed the alcoholic from a morally deformed perpetrator of harm to a sick person worthy of sympathy and support. Within the American mind, it moved this diseased alcoholic from Skid Row into our own neighborhoods and our own families. The movement declared that this disease was treatable. It invited a new generation of scientists and doctors to investigate the disease. It incited average citizens, local and state governments, and wealthy philanthropists to invest their dollars to understand and treat those suffering from the disease. And it provided a bridge between A.A. spirituality and addiction medicine that profoundly influenced the modern evolution of alcoholism treatment. Quite an accomplishment for 25 years!

This chapter and the next tell how this movement came about: the individuals, the institutions, the ideas, and the unique economic and social conditions that nurtured it all. We will focus particularly on the "kinetic ideas" that led to the rebirth of addiction

---

[1] I would like to acknowledge the particular contributions Ron Roizen made to the development of chapters nineteen and twenty. His research and writings on this period and our ongoing correspondence about the context, institutions, and people of this period provided invaluable details and perspective.

medicine and the rise of private and state efforts toward alcoholism education and treatment. Most social movements have a core—the driving personalities and central institutions—and a periphery through which each movement extends its influence to touch major cultural institutions. This chapter will examine the overlapping and interacting histories of four organizations that formed the core of the modern alcoholism movement: the Research Council on Problems of Alcohol, The Yale (now Rutgers) University Center of Alcohol Studies, the National Committee for Education on Alcoholism, and Alcoholics Anonymous. We will also examine the relationships between these core institutions and the alcohol beverage industry.

The Context

What has been called the modern alcoholism movement advocated a cultural redefinition of the source of the alcohol problem from one rooted in the drug itself to one rooted in the unique vulnerability of a small percentage of alcoholic drinkers. In this shift from the temperance (demon rum) paradigm to the alcoholism (disease) paradigm, the perception of the etiology of alcohol problems shifted from the nature of the drink to the nature of the drinker.[301] At least three contextual factors influenced this problem redefinition: 1) the repeal of national alcohol prohibition, 2) the Great Depression, and 3) a rising public-health movement that drew national attention to the major diseases that threatened America citizens.

From the founding of the first temperance society to the passage and later repeal of the Eighteenth Amendment, America was polarized into warring camps on the alcohol question. Wets and Drys battled back and forth, producing cycles of prohibition and repeal initiatives at local and state levels. With this experience as a backdrop, there was nothing in the 1933 passage of the Twenty-First Amendment to the Constitution ensuring the permanence of repeal. America as a nation faced the prospect that its enduring ambivalence about alcohol might be played out in continuing cycles of national prohibition and repeal, as had occurred at local and state levels. This potential prompted Wet and Dry forces to monitor and, wherever possible, influence the policies of the organizations that were focused on alcohol-related problems.

Another legacy of prohibition and repeal was the damaged credibility of both Wets and Drys. Both camps had been guilty of propaganda excesses that had pushed the limits of public gullibility, tarnished the image of science, and corrupted the overall alcohol debate. The resulting public skepticism increased the likelihood that any new alcohol paradigm would have to be supported by a more rigorous and objective science perceived to be independent of Dry or Wet control. As Wets and Drys faced off in the post-repeal era, Americans were also growing exhausted from the sheer relentlessness of the alcohol issue. Ron Roizen has depicted this situation colorfully:

> *Like the two boxers taking counsel after a very lopsided round, Wets and Drys cautioned themselves with different warnings. In the Wet corner, the fighter with seemingly overwhelming advantage was cautioned against overconfidence and carelessness; in the Dry corner, the nearly-beaten fighter was told not to counter-attack right away but to hold on for the next round or two, stay out of range and regain strength. In the excitement of the fight, neither corner was immediately aware that most of the crowd—thinking the fight was over—had gone home.*[302]

In spite of their exhaustion, Americans needed some model of alcohol problem definition that provided an escape from the Wet-Dry dichotomy. Wets in post-repeal America were shopping for ideas through which their industry and their products could be de-stigmatized and promoted in a positive light. Drys were looking for new ways to crystallize and communicate the dangers of alcohol. And private citizens were seeking information to help buttress or redefine their own personal decisions about alcohol. In the marketplace of ideas about alcohol, any offering that opened a middle path between Wet and Dry would have great social utility; however, as we shall see, this middle ground was very treacherous political territory. The scientists and those concerned with alcoholic rehabilitation who entered this vacuum were inevitably viewed as simultaneously too wet and too dry.[303] This need did, however, create an opening for a new social construction of alcohol, alcohol problems, and alcoholism.

One also wonders how many alcoholics may have responded to the repeal of prohibition with a mixture of relief and celebration—as well as a sense of impending doom. Lord knows, prohibition didn't stop their drinking, but many must have had a sense of foreboding about what repeal would mean for their efforts to control or brake their drinking. If the history of A.A.'s earliest members is indicative, for many alcoholics, the speed with which alcoholism progressed accelerated after 1933. That collective self-acceleration may in and of itself have contributed to the cultural stew that nurtured the rise of a new approach to alcohol problems.

The Great Depression also served as much more than a mere backdrop for our current story. We shall see how the inability to raise funds from private and public sources sent organizations concerned with alcohol problems scurrying in search of ideas and approaches that could garner funds—a search that led them to a particular construction of the alcohol problem. What has been called the modern alcoholism movement was as much about a struggle for ideas that were saleable as it was for ideas that were scientifically "true." This is not to discount the "truth" of key ideas, but to reinforce that the emergence of these ideas had more to do with their viability in an economic market than with their validity in the arena of science.

Also shaping the broader context of the 1930s was a public-health movement that focused attention on such diseases as tuberculosis, cancer, poliomyelitis, and syphilis. New medical advancements in understanding and treating such diseases reduced the moral stigma that had been attached to them. A growing number of diseases were also being closely linked with alcoholism. This linkage, and the growing shift from moral to medical perspectives on health problems, left only a small conceptual step to a vantage point where alcoholism itself began to be seen as a disease. A review of public opinion regarding alcoholism as exemplified in popular U.S. literature revealed that, between 1900 and 1930, the amount of moral blame ascribed to those who were addicted to alcohol declined steadily.[304] As we enter the 1930s, we see that the American public was more open to a view of alcoholism that placed it beyond the personal control of the alcoholic. The roots of this view came, not only from the 19th-century professional inebriety literature, but also from a century of popular confessional literature that portrayed excessive drinking in medical and psychiatric, rather than moral, language. By the 1940s, public openness to a more medicalized definition of alcohol problems was about to receive a newly refined conception of alcoholism.

The Alcohol and Alcoholism Movements

The notion of a single coalition that orchestrated a radical change in America's perception of alcoholism and the alcoholic is a gross oversimplification. In truth, there was no modern alcoholism movement.

What existed were multiple movements—many institutions and leaders pursuing quite different agendas. The change in the way America defined her alcohol problems came more out of the dynamic of interaction among all of these interest groups than from a unified movement for social change. The movement—if it can be called that—was impromptu jazz. There was no prepared score—just people and institutions playing off one another. Synchrony dictated the players, the song, and its cultural effect. The modern alcoholism movement is a movement only in retrospect. Inside, as it was happening, it was a tumultuous mix of often-conflicting perspectives, personalities and interests.

These multiple movements can be catalogued briefly. There was the newly legal alcohol industry's multifactioned movement to sanitize its own image and the image of its product. There were the post-repeal Dry organizations that, while bruised and divided following national repeal, did sustain their efforts to stigmatize and suppress alcohol at the state and local levels. There was an alcoholism recovery movement led by a growing number of Peabody-inspired lay therapists and by Bill Wilson, Dr. Robert Smith, and the growing fellowship of Alcoholics Anonymous. There was an alcohol research movement centered in the Research Council on Problems of Alcohol. There was a movement for professional education on alcohol problems, led by Dr. Howard Haggard and E. M. Jellinek of the Yale Center of Alcohol Studies. There was a movement for public information and education on alcoholism, conceived by Dwight Anderson and led by Marty Mann and the National Committee for Education on Alcoholism. There was a movement to expand the availability of alcoholism detoxification and treatment programs, initiated by individual entrepreneurs and local health-care institutions. There was a movement to rethink alcoholism within America's premier medical and public health associations. There was a movement to establish and implement alcoholism intervention programs in the workplace. And there was a movement to involve state governments and private organizations in funding alcoholism education and alcoholism treatment efforts.

If anything resembling a single "alcoholism movement" arose, it could be found only in the collective and cumulative effects of these divergent initiatives. So we will speak of a "modern alcoholism movement" with an understanding of the divergent and sometimes conflicting interests collected under this linguistic umbrella.

The Volatility of the Post-Repeal Period

Historians are often fond of noting that the adage "to the victor belong the spoils" also includes the victor's power to write history. The history we have of the modern alcoholism movement is drawn primarily from the accounts of the organizations and individual leaders who successfully survived that period. There were, however, other organizations, individuals, and ideas whose accounts are all but lost to history. Before sharing the stories of those who survived to be regularly included in the history of the modern alcoholism movement, let us recount two tales from the 1930s that underscore the obstacles to success and survival during this period.

The Council for Moderation: In 1934, with the financial support of John D. Rockefeller, Jr., Everett Colby organized the Council for Moderation. The Council designed a campaign that was opposed, not to alcohol *per se*, but to the excessive use of alcohol. Colby's goal was to instill a new value of moderation in post-repeal America. It might be said that Colby was trying to go back a century and return "Demon Rum" to its "Good Creature of God" status, while promoting the temperate use of alcohol in its original meaning. While this focus on moderation would seem a logical middle ground between the Wet and Dry positions (in essence, a "Damp" movement), the Council for Moderation utterly failed in its efforts to garner financial support to sustain its work.

The Council's campaigns aimed at getting funds from a broad spectrum of wealthy philanthropists failed as badly as did its campaigns for general public contributions. Colby himself said of this failure: "The wets thought we were too dry and the drys thought we were too wet."[305] Alienating Drys with its moderation message and declining the many offers it received for financial support from alcohol beverage representatives, the Council for Moderation closed its doors 14 months after its founding.[306] If there was to be a middle path between Wet and Dry, it would not be simply a model of moderation.

Burning Science in Virginia: If Colby's failure reinforced the potential hazards of a moderation-based approach to alcohol problem resolution, events in Virginia underscored the idea that objective science was also not the safest of venues. Our Virginia episode begins in 1936, when the state legislature commissioned an investigation to provide the best scientific information on the effects of alcohol. The investigation was conducted by experts from the University of Virginia Medical Department and the Medical College of Virginia. The official findings

were authored by J.A. Waddell and H.B. Haag.

When it was released, the Waddell and Haag report came under such blistering public attack from Dry advocates that the legislature unanimously passed a joint resolution to guard the 1,000 copies of the Waddell-Haag report so they could be burned before they reached either the schools or the newspapers.[307]

The Virginia episode reinforced the fact that, while the country was hungry for objective information about alcohol, the venom of the Wet-Dry debate could still inflict injury on scientists who stumbled blindly into this arena. It also underscored public suspicion of science and scientists and a fundamental strain in the relationship between science and politics—a strain that could reach a breaking point when science conflicted with popular judgements about psychoactive drugs.

Although taking on any aspect of the alcohol question could be a high-risk area of scientific investigation, alcoholism was one of the safest topics of study within the alcohol problems arena. Roizen explains:

> *Drys could look with interest toward the phenomenon* [of alcohol addiction] *because, in their conceptual framework, addiction offered the weak link in Wet claims that moderate drinking was potentially unproblematic; Wets, on the other hand, could be drawn to alcohol addiction as a focus of interest because only in the presence of addiction was drinking, per se, likely to be problematic.*[308]

Alcoholism provided a window of opportunity through which scientists could seek broad financial support for alcohol-related research and—if they were careful—escape the wrath of both Wet and Dry political constituencies.

Research Council on Problems of Alcohol

During the early 1930s, Dr. Norman Jolliffe of the New York University College of Medicine initiated a series of studies on chronic alcoholism at Bellevue Hospital, at a time when the Hospital was admitting some 10,000 alcoholics per year for detoxification or treatment of alcohol-related medical problems. Jolliffe made many discoveries about the treatment of alcoholics, including the role that vitamin B_1 could play in the physical restoration of the alcoholic.[309]

However, Jolliffe became frustrated at the alcoholic's propensity to undermine these efforts at physical restoration by returning to excessive drinking following discharge. Jolliffe decided that studies of alcoholism must expand beyond the physical consequences of alcoholism to understand the process—the alcoholism itself—that created such destruction. According to his assistant Mark Keller, Jolliffe's shift of focus—from the consequences of excessive drinking to the etiology of the appetite that fueled excessive drinking—was the seminal event in the modern discovery of alcoholism.[310] It was Jolliffe's desire to understand the etiological mechanism at the root of alcoholism that led to his involvement in the Research Council on Problems of Alcohol (RCPA). The RCPA had been founded in 1937 and was linked to the prestigious American Association for the Advancement of Science.[311]

The RCPA was remarkably successful in bringing together some of the most renowned scientists in America concerned with alcohol-related problems. If there was a body in the 1930s whose reputation could stand up to the Wet-Dry scrutiny of any piece of alcohol-related research, it was surely the RCPA.

Both Wet and Dry forces recognized the damaged credibility that had emerged from their extended propaganda wars, and both took a calculated risk in supporting the general need for research on alcohol. The Wets were as thoroughly convinced that research would expose the exaggerated charges of the Drys as the Drys were convinced that research would prove alcohol's toxic effects. The public's desire for credible information—and particularly for post-repeal alcohol education in public schools—ensured that, if there was to be a new movement, it would at least have to appear scientific. The problem faced by the RCPA was not a lack of public or professional credibility; it was a lack of money.

The RCPA's entire history was one of a struggle to garner financial support. In the first two years of existence, the RCPA had not been successful at landing any significant philanthropic support.[312] Its first significant ($25,000) grant, received in May of 1939 from the Carnegie Foundation to study the effects of alcohol on the body, came with the clear message that no further support would be provided. The only quarters that seemed to be offering additional financial support to the RCPA were members of the alcohol beverage industry.

As long as the RCPA had a broadly focused research agenda concerning the problems of alcohol, it was clear that financing from the alcohol industry would undermine the credibility of its research findings. There was, however, a belief among RCPA leaders that this conflict would not necessarily apply to studies that focused on alcoholism. In the Fall of 1939, under the influence of Karl Bowman, the RCPA declared that it would focus its coming efforts on research specifically related to alcoholism and would not be studying broader alcohol-related issues. In what Ron Roizen has christened the "Bowman Compromise," the RCPA developed an alcoholism-focused agenda and opened the doors to financial support from the alcohol beverage industry.[313]

Events moved quickly during this period. Howard Haggard offered to provide (through Yale) a new journal—*The Quarterly Journal of Studies on Alcohol (QJSA)*—to disseminate the RCPA's research findings. The *QJSA* marked the first American alcohol/alcoholism specialty journal to be published since the demise of the *Journal of Inebriety* in 1914. Three individuals were hired to work on the Carnegie grant: E.M. ("Bunky") Jellinek, who had studied schizophrenia in his role of Chief Biometrician at Worcester State Hospital; Mark Keller, who had developed a reputation as an excellent writer and editor in his work with Dr. Norman Jolliffe; and Vera Efron, whose fluency in five languages proved invaluable in the world-wide literature reviews. All three went on to long and distinguished careers in the alcoholism field.

In the 1939 RCPA decision to focus on alcoholism, there was also a shift in the very character of the RCPA. Harry Moore, Director of the the RCPA at the time of the 1939 decision, noted that this action by the board placed the RCPA alongside other "public-health agencies now combating tuberculosis, syphilis, poliomyelitis, cancer, and other major disease."[314] Moore's comments are interesting in their shift of the RCPA from a research-based organization to an activist-based "public health" organization. There was within this shift, not only a movement in focus from alcohol to alcoholism, but also a movement from a research agenda (knowledge development) to an agenda of disease prevention and intervention.

As a result of this shift, the RCPA expanded its mission beyond its ambitious research agenda. Dwight Anderson, who served as a consultant to the RCPA and headed its Committee on Public Relations, recommended that long-term financial support for the RCPA hinge on two things: 1) changing the public's conception of alcoholism through portrayal of the disease nature of alcoholism, and 2) launching a program of practical services to treat alcoholism.[315] Anderson, who at the time served as the Public Relations Director of the New York State Medical Society, elaborated on this view by outlining four "kinetic ideas" that became the central tenets in the campaign to change the American public's view of alcoholism and the alcoholic.

1. *That the problem drinker is a sick man, exceptionally reactive to alcohol.*
2. *That he can be helped.*
3. *That he is worth helping.*
4. *That the problem is therefore a responsibility of the healing professions, as well as of the established health authorities and the public generally.*[316]

Partially through Anderson's influence, the RCPA broadened its scope with the presentation of a new plan. This plan included proposals to develop an alcoholism information center, model alcoholism clinics and hospitals, and a national network of organizations whose purpose would be the development of local alcoholism treatment services. When this plan was proposed in 1943, it was recommended that these programs be supported through an allocated portion of the excise taxes on alcohol and a 10% levy on the advertising budgets of the distillers and brewers.[317]

This visionary plan was never accomplished through the RCPA, but, as we shall see shortly, the ideas in the plan did not die. Other ideas generated in the RCPA would prove quite influential. In 1947, the RCPA articulated a set of principles regarding the medical treatment of alcoholism. The RCPA declared that responsibility for the care of the alcoholic should be moved from police authorities to public health authorities and that the focal points for the treatment of alcoholism should be local general hospitals, university-affiliated hospitals, and—for the most severe cases of alcoholism—psychiatric hospitals.[318]

The RCPA continued to struggle in its efforts to procure funds to implement its proposed programs. In the face of continued financial struggles, however, the RCPA disbanded in 1949. In his eulogy for the RCPA, Dwight Anderson suggested that it had for the first time "focused the interest of both science and the public on alcoholism as a No. 1 public-health problem."[319]

The Yale Center of Alcohol Studies

The story of the Yale School of Alcohol Studies begins with the 1923 organization of the Yale Laboratory of Applied Physiology, first under the leadership of Dr. Yandell Henderson, then headed by Dr. Howard Haggard. Under Haggard's direction, the Laboratory began studies on alcohol metabolism as early as 1930. While these studies answered numerous technical questions about what happened to alcohol in the body, they did not answer the questions about the etiology and treatment of alcoholism that had come into increasing prominence in RCPA discussions. As the RCPA's Carnegie grant drew to a close in 1941, Dr. Haggard recruited Jellinek, Keller, and Efron to come to Yale to complete their work on the literature review and to found a section of alcohol studies in the Laboratory of Applied Physiology. Under Haggard's and Jellinek's leadership, a Center of Alcohol Studies was formally established at Yale in 1943. Many of Jellinek's other proteges on the RCPA research team—Dr. Giorgi Lolli, Dr. Martin Gross, and Dr. Anne Roe—also followed him to Yale.[320]

The activities of the Center on Alcohol Studies were integrated within what came to be called the Yale Plan.[321]

1. Research: Research activities at Yale consisted of physiological, social, psychological, and historical studies on alcohol and alcoholism. Research activities emphasized extensive literature surveys and bibliographical and translation services. While Yale did continue some of the research activities of the RCPA, it focused primarily on a strategy of information collection, synthesis, and dissemination.[322]

2. Publications: The Center on Alcohol Studies published the *Quarterly Journal of Studies on Alcohol* (beginning in June, 1940) and a variety of books, pamphlets, and other educational materials on alcohol and alcoholism. By 1947, the Center's pamphlets had a circulation of some 100,000 each, and 69,000 copies of the Center's first book were in circulation.[323] The results of Jellinek's review of the scientific literature were published in the *QJSA* in 1940, and later in a series of books. Inheriting a century's worth of temperance education, the Center of Alcohol Studies created the modern field of alcohol education.

3. The Summer School of Alcohol Studies: In 1943, responding to increasing demands for alcoholism education, the Yale Center of Alcohol Studies founded the Summer School of Alcohol Studies—an intensive four-week alcoholism training program.[324] The school brought together an interdisciplinary faculty of physicians, physiologists, attorneys, clergy, and members of Alcoholics Anonymous to discuss alcohol- and alcoholism-related education, research, and treatment issues. The first Summer School consisted of three seminars, three public lectures, and eight courses. The courses included an introductory session and classes on physiology, personality, legis-

lative countermeasures, the prevention and treatment of alcoholism, and alcohol and traffic safety. Twenty-nine lectures from the 1944 Summer School were published in a book—*Alcohol, Science and Society*—which by the mid-1950s was in its sixth printing.

The Summer School drew physicians, nurses, ministers, teachers, social workers, probation officers, and students. The 1,168 people who attended the Summer School between 1943 and 1950 came from 47 states, the District of Columbia, nine Canadian provinces, and nine other countries.[325] Later innovations at the Summer School included specialized seminars or institutes for physicians, nurses, public-health specialists, and business representatives. Refresher courses were also added for students who had already attended the Summer School.

An enormous synergy of personalities and interests took place in the Summer Schools. The spread of the core ideas of the modern alcoholism movement can often be traced to the Summer Schools at Yale (and later at Rutgers).

4. The Yale Plan Clinics: Another innovation that emerged from the Yale Center of Alcohol Studies was the Yale Plan Clinics, which were initiated in 1944 under the direction of Dr. Giorgio Lolli and Raymond McCarthy. These clinics, developed in collaboration with the Connecticut State Prison Association, pioneered a new mid-century model of outpatient alcoholism counseling. The clinics' first tasks were to spread the idea that alcoholism was a disease until that concept was fully accepted and to develop local community resources that could be used to help rehabilitate alcoholics. Located in New Haven and Hartford, the clinics were originally designed to assess, diagnose, and refer alcoholics to treatment resources. However, the lack of available community services forced the clinics into providing treatment services.[326] The Yale Plan clinics were originally staffed by a part-time psychiatrist, two part-time internists, a consulting psychologist, a social field investigator, two psychiatric social workers, and two secretaries.

The operating philosophy of the clinics was based on a psychodynamic understanding of alcoholism. Jellinek believed that the goal of treatment at the clinic was to get each patient to "gradually recognize that his problem is not alcohol but that he is using alcohol as a remedy for a real problem the nature of which he must learn to understand."[327]

In his 1946 description of the Yale Clinics, McCarthy noted that "The approach to diagnosis and treatment of large numbers of unselected inebriates must be many-sided if it is to function on a sound and

practical basis." He emphasized his belief that there existed no "generalized treatment approach" or "single therapy" that would prove successful with the diverse populations of excessive drinkers.[328] He even went so far as to suggest the idea that "there is no alcoholic as such," only "thousands of individuals who persist in using alcohol after they have demonstrated that they cannot control its use."[329]

The Clinics utilized the following procedures. First, psychiatrists conducted an initial assessment of all alcoholics seeking services and screened out psychotics and psychopaths who would not be appropriate for clinic services. Those deemed appropriate were provided a combination of individual and group counseling. Clients participated in groups for approximately six months and were encouraged to participate simultaneously in A.A. meetings, although not all clinic patients were involved in A.A. Groups met weekly and ranged in size from nine to fifteen. The goals of the group were to stimulate the alcoholic's recognition of his problems through identification with others who shared those problems, and to hasten the alcoholic's social adjustment to sobriety. The format for group services involved a brief 15-to-25-minute talk by the group facilitator on some aspect of alcoholism or recovery, followed by extended group discussion. Topics ranged from the physiology of alcohol to psychological aspects of alcoholism presented under such titles as unconscious drives, feelings of inadequacy, emotional immaturity and instability, and sexual adjustment.

Ray McCarthy, who pioneered this group approach, noted that there were predictable stages that alcoholics went through during the course of their treatment, and that feedback and support from group members helped them anticipate and manage these stages. McCarthy viewed the alcoholic's isolation and his rigid defense structure as major barriers to recovery and believed that groups provided an opportunity to break through both of these barriers. McCarthy's articles articulating these stages constitute the beginning of modern interest in the developmental stages of alcoholism recovery.[330]

In the first six months, the Yale Clinics saw 145 men and 29 women. Referrals to the clinics came (in descending proportions) from the courts and probation departments, self-referrals, relatives, agencies, physicians and hospitals, and Alcoholics Anonymous. In 1946, McCarthy noted that the first 530 patients seen at the Yale Clinics ranged in age from 24 to 64, with most falling between the ages of 35 and 48. The male-to-female ratio was nearly 7 to 1. The patients represented diverse socioeconomic, cultural, and occupational backgrounds. The initial expectation was that the clinics would guide the rehabilitation of those late-stage alcoholics who were regularly filling the jails and hospitals, but the clinics instead reached higher-functioning alcoholics who were struggling to maintain their jobs and families.[331]

As exciting as the new treatment approaches were, the clinics were a significant financial drain on Yale's Center of Alcohol Studies. Even this problem was turned to an advantage for the field. Yale encouraged the Connecticut legislature to found the Connecticut Commission on Alcoholism—the first state-level department organized specifically to address alcoholism in the U.S. The operation of the Yale clinics was turned over to the Commission, and Dr. Lolli left Yale to become the Commission's first Medical Director.[332] Yale continued to consult with many states and local communities on the development of clinics based on its original model. Selden Bacon could boast in 1949 of outpatient clinics opening in Washington D.C.; Portland, Oregon; and Pittsburgh, Pennsylvania. By 1957, 34 states had set up clinics modeled on those developed at Yale.[333]

The Yale Clinics introduced a number of important features into the work of alcoholism counseling. In an era in which the institutional treatment of alcoholism was predominant, McCarthy declared that "There are a large number of alcoholics for whom the out-patient approach is feasible....," and Selden Bacon predicted that outpatient therapy would become "the basic unit of a rehabilitation service for alcoholics."[334] The Yale Clinics also introduced the use of multiple modalities in which efforts were made to match particular techniques to the needs of particular clients, a treatment model that placed great emphasis on group therapy, and the use of didactic information and discussion with groups of alcoholics.

The Yale Clinics also continued the Emmanuel Clinic's and the Peabody-Baylor's tradition of using "lay therapists" (recovered alcoholics) in the treatment of alcoholics. McCarthy predicted in 1946 that: "The ex-alcoholic, whose adjustment has come through intensive psychotherapy and who is trained psychiatrically so that he or she understands clearly his limitations and his potential contributions to the clinic program, may become a significant figure in working with the alcoholic."[335][336]

5. The National Committee for Education on Alcoholism: From 1944 to 1950, the National Committee for Education on Alcoholism operated as a division of the Yale Plan. Due to its separation from Yale, its operation as an independent organization, and its eventual significance to the field of alcoholism

treatment, the Committee's history will be told shortly in a separate section of this chapter.

6. Administration and Finance: One might reasonably ask how Yale could launch the extensive initiatives we have described while the RCPA was struggling for its very financial existence. While some of the costs of these initiatives were absorbed by the University and others, such as the Summer Schools, were in part offset by fees, other sources of financial support also contributed to these initiatives. When the Center opened, its leaders held up as a sign of its scientific objectivity and independence the fact that the Center had sought no outside financial contributions from any organization. Ron Roizen's research into this period has revealed that Yale did in fact receive outside private and corporate philanthropy and that a portion of those funds came directly from a representative of the brewing industry. These funds were used primarily to underwrite the Summer Schools, and there is no evidence of any liquor-interest intrusion into the Center's policies or research practices.[337]

The response of the broader Yale University community to the Center of Alcohol Studies was not a particularly warm one. As was typical of the overall stigma associated with alcoholism in this period, most Yale faculty saw the publicity surrounding the Center as distasteful and worried that Yale's image would be damaged by its association with such an unseemly subject.[338] The Center eventually was caught in the middle of shifting philosophies about the kinds of activities that should and should not be included in the University. Yale President, Whitney Griswold, eventually won a ten-year battle to eliminate the Center. In 1962, the Center for Alcohol Studies and the Summer School of Alcohol Studies moved from Yale to Rutgers University.[339] Most of the key staff from Yale transferred to Rutgers, with the exception of E.M. Jellinek, who had been ousted from Yale following a failed attempt to create a Yale Institute of Alcohol Studies in the Southwest.[340]

The National Committee for Education on Alcoholism

The National Committee for Education on Alcoholism grew out of a vision. That vision was one of a national organization and a national campaign to educate the public about alcoholism. The vision belonged to Marty Mann. This is the story of the woman and the organization she created.

Marty Mann spent the early 1940s—also the early years of her recovery from alcoholism—writing scripts for the American Society of Composers, Authors, and Publishers. While researching one of her assignments, she read Helen Marshall's biography of Dorthea Dix, the well-known crusader for the mentally ill. Mann began to ponder the possibility of a similar crusade on behalf of alcoholics and to question whether she had what it would take to be the "Dorthea Dix of alcoholism." She had already been encouraged by such notables as Grace Allen Bangs of the New York Herald Tribune to consider a career as a public speaker on alcoholism.[341]

One fateful night in February, 1944, Marty Mann worked into the night to refine her three-part strategy to change America's view of alcoholism and the alcoholic. The plan she envisioned was to : 1) establish an educational program on alcoholism for professionals, 2) establish local public-information centers to enhance community understanding of alcoholism, and 3) encourage local hospitals to care for alcoholics openly.[342] Her vision was to create a national organization with local branches that could work to destigmatize alcoholism in the way other national educational organizations had lessened the stigma associated with tuberculosis, cancer, polio, and heart disease.

Marty Mann first presented her vision to Bill Wilson, co-founder of A.A. Bill expressed concern that Marty might lack the scientific credentials to lead such a campaign of public education on alcoholism. He also feared that any direct A.A. involvement in such a campaign might serve as a distraction from A.A.'s focus on the suffering alcoholic. Marty next shared her vision with Harry Moore, Director of the RCPA. She was told that the RCPA had its own plan to do much of what Marty was proposing. Moore did offer Marty a part-time job to work on this effort, which Marty declined, partially out of growing concern about her lack of credentials.[343] Following her meetings with Bill Wilson and Harry Moore, Marty decided to approach Yale.[344]

E.M. Jellinek scheduled a meeting with Marty Mann the evening he received her proposal, and notified her the day after their meeting that Yale would financially support the new organization until it was on its feet. Ironically, Jellinek the scientist embraced the proposal and Marty's leadership in this new campaign where non-scientists had worried about her lack of scientific credentials. Jellinek, aware of the limitations of scientific knowledge of alcoholism, may have immediately recognized that this movement would be more about social values than scientific evidence.

Marty Mann moved to New Haven on April 1,

1944, to found the National Committee for Education on Alcoholism (NCEA). The NCEA offices initially resided at Yale, and Marty lived with the Jellineks during her early days in New Haven. After attending the 1944 Yale Summer School and saturating herself in alcoholism literature, Marty began to launch her program. Within six months, the NCEA moved into offices in the New York Academy of Medicine. The modern task of educating America about alcoholism had begun—on a $13,000 budget that covered Marty Mann, a secretary, and rent for the office.[345]

When Mann announced the opening of an NCEA office in New York City on October 1, 1944, she proclaimed that the goals of the NCEA would be to generate public understanding and support for five ideas drawn from Dwight Anderson's earlier-noted proposal:

   1. Alcoholism is a disease.
   2. The alcoholic, therefore, is a sick person.
   3. The alcoholic can be helped.
   4. The alcoholic is worth helping.
   5. Alcoholism is our No. 4 public health problem, and our public responsibility.[346]

Mann took a landmark step in expanding Anderson's four kinetic ideas to five. The fifth she added—and the first on her list—was to frame alcoholism as a "disease." She proclaimed that scientists had long known that alcoholism was a disease, but that this knowledge had remained an "unguarded secret."[347] In Mann's view, the NCEA's role would be to bridge that gap between scientific knowledge and public understanding. The difficulty that would emerge only decades into this movement was that, while many scientists were sympathetic to more enlightened treatment for alcoholics, in 1944 there was no scientific conclusion that alcoholism was a disease. The centerpiece of what Dwight Anderson called the "beginning of a new public health movement" to revolutionize how Americans viewed alcoholism and alcoholics was based, not on scientific evidence, but on proclamation.[348] While the NCEA cultivated the image of itself as the public information dissemination arm of a highly sophisticated research establishment, it operated quite independent of, and often in conflict with, the emerging scientists in the alcohol problems arena.

While Marty Mann did not have the scientific credentials that some suggested might be necessary to convey the core ideas of the NCEA credibly, she did have many assets. She was bright, articulate, and attractive. She had contacts in the major media outlets from her prior professional work. She had a personal story that exemplified the NCEA core ideas, and that riveted and deeply moved audiences. She was a fast learner, and—perhaps most of all—she had a lifetime of energy she was willing to devote to her goal of changing the way millions of people perceived alcoholics. Marty Mann spoke to an estimated 34,000 people in the nationwide lecture tour that marked the first 24 months of the NCEA's organizational efforts.[349]

The primary strategy of the NCEA was to establish local branches that would pursue a five-point program of 1) launching an intensive local public education campaign on alcoholism, 2) encouraging one or more local hospitals to admit alcoholics for acute detoxification, 3) establishing a local alcohol information center, 4) establishing a clinic for the diagnosis and treatment of alcoholism, and 5) establishing "rest centers" for the long-term care of alcoholics.[350] Local NCEA committee members were drawn primarily from recovered alcoholics and their family members and other local citizens who possessed special interest in and knowledge of alcoholism. Large numbers of these local committee members received what might be called their basic training at the Yale Summer School of Alcohol Studies.

In 1947, an assistant—Yvelin Gardner—was added to work with Marty Mann. Gardner, also a recovered alcoholic, supported himself on a small inheritance and accepted the position knowing that the organization's ability to pay his salary was questionable. He worked tirelessly on behalf of the NCEA for the next 25 years.[351] The NCEA's early years were ones of incredible financial struggle. When things looked most bleak, donors (many of them recovered alcoholics) seemed to come from nowhere to provide funds that kept the doors open and the message spreading across the country.

Although they collaborated in public, the NCEA and Yale experienced increasing tension that grew, in part, out of their different missions. Yale was in pursuit of knowledge; the NCEA was attempting to launch a cultural revolution in the public's conception of alcoholism and the alcoholic. Where the Yale

scientists were committed to a broad exploration of "alcohol studies," the NCEA's focus was exclusively on the issue of alcoholism and in securing help for the still-suffering alcoholic.[352]

The NCEA's early history is not one of unchecked progress. The organization struggled desperately for its own identity, then struggled to survive independently. In December, 1949, the Board of the NCEA passed a resolution that severed ties between the NCEA and Yale. The official announcement described this as an "amicable agreement between the two organizations." The announcement cited differing missions and problems that had arisen in fund-raising for both the NCEA and Yale during their union.[353]

As the NCEA emerged as an autonomous entity, its future was by no means secured. Marty said privately of this prospect: "All of us are well aware that we may not be able to do this, and that our demise may still come about in the Spring—but none of us believe it will."[354]

A year following the NCEA's separation from Yale, the board changed the name of the organization to the National Committee on Alcoholism, reflecting the organization's movement beyond the initial goal of public education. In 1954, the name was changed to the National Council on Alcoholism (NCA), which it remained until 1990, when it took on its current name, the National Council on Alcoholism and Drug Dependence (NCADD).

Marty Mann traveled the country for 35 years, speaking to more than 200 groups per year. She served as the Director of NCA from 1944 to 1968. Her speaking and writing exerted a profound influence on American attitudes toward alcoholism, and her political savvy and spellbinding oratory—like those of Dorthea Dix before her—coaxed many a legislature into formulating a public-health response to the problem of alcoholism. Marty Mann died July 22, 1980, having survived three of the most-often stigmatized health problems of the 20th century: alcoholism, tuberculosis, and cancer. She was unquestionably one of the most successful public-health reformers in American history.

✠

Chapter Twenty
The "Modern Alcoholism Movement": The Periphery

In the last chapter, we reviewed how three institutions—the Research Council on Problems of Alcohol, the Yale Center of Alcohol Studies, and the National Committee for Education on Alcoholism—spearheaded what has come to be called the "modern alcoholism movement." In this chapter we will see how that movement changed the alcoholism-related policies of medical and public-health institutions; spurred municipalities, states, and the federal government to launch model alcoholism treatment projects; inspired private philanthropists to subsidize alcoholism education and intervention; launched workplace initiatives to salvage alcohol-impaired employees; solicited the involvement of religious institutions in addressing alcohol problems; and recruited recovered alcoholics as local educators and alcoholism treatment advocates. We will close this chapter with some reflections regarding the enduring legacy of this movement.

Changing Medical Opinion on Alcoholics and Alcoholism

Within the broader umbrella of what we are calling the modern alcoholism movement was a more specialized movement to change how alcoholics and alcoholism were perceived and treated in American medicine. The years 1930-1956 set the stage for even more dramatic changes in medical views on alcoholism in the second half of the 20th century. Four milestones were critical: 1) a growing medical and popular consensus on replacement of the term "drunkenness" with the more medical term "alcoholism," 2) the growth of addiction medicine as a medical and psychiatric specialty, 3) the recognition of the alcoholic as a legitimate medical patient and the recognition of alcoholism as a disease, and 4) the development of specialized alcoholism treatment units in community hospitals.

The growing acceptance of the term "alcoholism"—to describe the condition commonly known as "drunkenness"—helped shift this problem from a moral arena to a medical arena. Federal public health officials like Lawrence Kolb used this new medicalized perspective as a foundation for their call to establish alcoholism treatment clinics throughout the country.[355]

The loss of inebriety specialists that accompanied the turn-of-the-century fall of the inebriate asylums was reversed in the 1930s by the re-involvement of mainstream physicians in clinical research and the clinical treatment of alcoholism. Addiction treatment as a specialty in medicine and psychiatry slowly re-emerged within the American medical community. Edward Strecker, William Silkworth, Harry Tiebout, Norman Jolliffe, Merrill Moore, and Robert Flemming were among a growing cadre of 1930s physicians who specialized in the treatment of alcoholism. In 1954, this mid-century rebirth of addiction as a medical specialty culminated in the founding of the New York City Medical Society on Alcoholism—a group that evolved into today's American Society of Addiction Medicine (ASAM).

A changing view of the alcoholic and alcoholism was also evident in the official policy statements of a growing number of health organizations. The World Health Organization's creation of an Expert Committee on Alcohol and Alcoholism, and its pronouncements on alcoholism in the 1950s, marked the first time a modern and statured medical organization advocated the idea that alcoholism was a disease. The American Medical Association (A.M.A.) defined alcoholism in 1952, and in 1956 passed a landmark resolution declaring that chronic alcoholism should not bar admission to a hospital and that the alcoholic should be viewed as a sick person. This resolution paved the way for a more unequivocal statement, issued eleven years later, that alcoholism was a disease. The NCEA lobbied heavily for the 1956 statement, and the statement itself was drafted by Selden Bacon of Yale and by Dr. Marvin Block, Chairman of the A.M.A.'s first-ever Committee on Alcoholism. Block also championed the resolution through the A.M.A.'s highly political resolution process.[356]

In a similar move, the American Hospital Association (AHA) in a series of resolutions taken in 1944, 1951, and 1957 declared that the best placement for alcoholism treatment services was in the local community general hospital. The AHA pronouncements take on significance when one considers that surveys as late as 1964 revealed a large percentage of hospitals still refusing to admit people with a primary diagnosis of alcoholism.[357] All of these landmark decisions laid the foundation for such later changes as the decriminalization of public intoxication, the extension of insurance coverage for alcoholism treatment, the public funding of alcoholism treatment and prevention efforts, and the rise in hospital-based alcoholism treatment units.

The Alcoholism Movement in the Workplace [358]

Three conditions set the stage for the infusion of the alcoholism movement into the American workplace in the early 1940s. The first was the repeal of alcohol prohibition and growing concern about how repeal would affect industrial efficiency. The second was the growing presence in the American workplace of A.A. members who began to propose alternative solutions to the problems posed by alcohol-impaired workers. The third influence was a lowering of employment standards during the Second World War, which forced employers to hire employees with histories of chronic alcoholism. Under the duress of wartime production demands, these companies became interested in ways of restoring and sustaining the productivity of alcoholic employees.[359]

Before the initiation of formal workplace intervention programs, the rehabilitation of alcoholic employees occurred in two diverse ways. The first was through the employees' discovery of A.A. or another source of outside assistance on their own, without company knowledge or assistance. The other was the "shape-up-or-ship-out" approach to alcohol-impaired employees. Both approaches sometimes evolved into informal programs of intervention. Many of these early industrial alcoholism programs were initiated by medical directors, supervisors, recovered alcoholic employees affiliated with A.A., and, later, union leaders working in concert to salvage the alcoholic employee whose performance was deteriorating.

The 1940s and early 1950s saw the rapid rise in industrial alcoholism programs. Eastman Kodak initiated a formal program as early as 1941, and E.I. du Pont de Nemours Company also launched a program during the early 1940s. Other early pioneers in the development of industrial alcoholism programs included Allis Chalmers, Consolidated Edison Co. of New York, Kennecott Copper Company, New England Electric, New England Telephone Company, North American Aviation, Standard Oil of New Jersey, Caterpillar Tractor Company, Chino Mines Division of Kennecott Copper, IBM, and the Great Northern Railroad Company.

The first step many companies took in imple-

menting a formal industrial alcoholism program was the employment of a recovered alcoholic (usually an A.A. member) whose role was specifically designated as one of counseling alcoholic employees. Some early pioneers in this role were David M. at Remington Arms and then DuPont (1940, 1942), Warren T. at Kaiser Shipyards (1943), and Earl S. at North American Aviation (1944). An A.A. member employed by the Maritime Commission in 1944 assisted in the recovery of more than 300 alcoholic employees in conjunction with the Welfare Department of the Permanente Hospital.[360] Medical Directors who played pioneering roles in the development of these early industrial alcoholism programs included Dr. Daniel Lynch of New England Telephone Company, Dr. John Norris of Eastman Kodak, Dr. George Gehrmann of DuPont, Dr. James Lloyd of North American Aviation, and Dr. Charles Franco of Consolidated Edison Co. of New York.[361]

The impetus for all of this activity to address alcoholism in the workplace can often be traced to the work of the NCEA and Yale. National coverage of E.M. Jellinek's 1946 speech to the Economic Club of Detroit, "What Shall We Do About Alcoholism?" stimulated discussion in business circles, particularly regarding his references to the 29,700,000 work days estimated to be lost each year to alcoholism-related problems, the increased health-care costs incurred by alcoholics, and the 1,500 fatal on-the-job accidents caused each year by the effects of alcoholism.[362] In 1947, Selden Bacon of Yale and Dr. John Norris organized the Industrial Physician's Committee on Alcoholism, which brought together many of the directors of early occupational alcoholism programs. In 1948, the first national conference on the problem of alcoholism in industry was sponsored by the Chicago Committee on Alcoholism (an NCEA affiliate) and the Chicago Association of Commerce and Industry. During the same year, articles with such titles as "Alcoholism Plagues Industry" and "Billion-Dollar Hangover" began to appear in the popular press. But all of these noteworthy influences paled in comparison with the efforts of Ralph ("Lefty") Henderson.

Henderson, first with the NCEA (1947-1949) and then as the Industrial Consultant for the Yale Center on Alcohol Studies for ten years, was relentless. The publication of his 1949 pamphlet "The Half Man" might be considered the launching of the mid-century industrial alcoholism movement. In this article, Henderson underscored the fact that the majority of alcoholic men and women in the workforce invisibly drained a billion dollars per year through absenteeism, accidents, errors in judgement, distraction, injury to equipment and products, irritation to fellow workers and consumers, and overall deterioration of morale.

Henderson spearheaded the Yale Plan for Business and Industry in 1950 and traveled throughout the United States promoting Yale's industrial alcoholism program model. The Yale Plan that Henderson promoted across America had five premises: 1) the majority of personnel problems are created by a small number of often-alcohol-impaired employees, 2) there is a means of discovering how many and which employees are so impaired, 3) there is a means of discovering which of these employees can be rehabilitated, 4) the means to rehabilitate these employees is now available, and 5) restoring an employee's health and productivity is more cost-effective than firing and replacing that employee. Henderson promised American business leaders that the problem drinker would come forward "if he knows that he will receive sympathetic understanding and that his case will be given consideration as a medical disorder"[363]

The Yale Plan, as outlined by Lefty Henderson and Seldon Bacon, consisted of nine implementation steps: 1) educating top management, 2) assigning program responsibility to an existing department, preferably the medical department, 3) selecting and training a coordinator to administer the program, 4) mobilizing internal intervention resources, 5) developing a company-wide policy outlining the relationship between treatment and discipline, 6) establishing linkages to alcoholism treatment services, 7) conducting supervisory training, 8) orienting and educating employees, and 9) periodically assessing (through surveys) the extent of the problem in the company. In 1953, Henderson and Bacon reported that companies that pursued these steps were experiencing recovery rates of between 40% and 80 percent.[364]

The number of formal occupational alcoholism programs in business and industry rose from a handful in 1945, to 50 in 1960, to more than 600 in 1975.[365] These occupational alcoholism programs replaced a longstanding policy of concealment and eventual extrusion of the alcoholic with a formal program of intervention, rehabilitation, and retention.

Occupational alcoholism programs were the direct application of the NCEA's core ideas in the workplace and were stimulated by many of the key organizations and personalities profiled in the last chapter. The workplace phase of the alcoholism movement was an essential step in changing public perceptions of the alcoholic and alcoholism. The challenge was then to create community resources that could help rehabilitate these alcoholic citizens.

Spurred by Yale and the NCEA, another cultural institution—the church—helped carry the banner of support for the creation of such resources.

The Alcoholism Movement in the Church

Clergy were among the first service professionals involved in the Yale Summer School of Alcohol Studies, and clergy often played key roles in many of the alcoholism education programs launched by the NCEA in local communities. Through such involvement a growing number of clergy began to see addressing alcohol related problems in their congregations and communities as part of the mission of the church, and as part of their own personal mission. Religious institutions—the bulwark of support for alcohol prohibition for more than 100 years—began to redefine the church's relationship to this problem in post-repeal America. How this new role was forged is illustrated in the creation of the National Clergy Council on Alcohol and Related Drug Problems and the North Conway Institute.

In 1949, the National Clergy Council on Alcoholism and Related Drug Problems (NCCA) was founded to provide education and consultation to the Catholic Church in America. NCCA members included priests, brothers, sisters, and lay members of the Catholic Church. NCCA activities focused on alcoholism education for clergy and laity and collaboration with alcoholism prevention and treatment agencies. The Council held annual conferences and published a proceedings called the *Blue Book,* which provided current information on addiction and its treatment.[366]

The North Conway Institute was founded by Reverend David Works in 1951 to encourage church ministry with alcoholics. Works' interest in alcoholism was spurred by his own recovery from alcoholism and his participation in the Yale Summer School of Alcohol Studies. His Institute held annual educational conferences on alcoholism for church leaders and issued "consensus statements" on a variety of alcohol-related issues. These statements received wide distribution through religious communities. The North Conway Institute encouraged the development of church policy statements on alcohol and alcoholism. It was instrumental in the National Council of Churches' 1958 proclamation on alcohol problems which called for 1) ministries to those afflicted by and those affected by alcoholism, 2) alcohol education in the church and the community, and 3) carefully planned legal control of alcohol.[367]

The rising concern with the church's role in preventing and responding to alcohol-related problems also produced momentum to address the problem of impaired clergy and members of faith communities.

Municipal, State, and Federal Responses to Alcoholism [368]

The grassroots momentum to redefine America's perception of and response to the alcoholic slowly reached the ears of local, state and national political figures during the 1940s and 1950s.

Even before prohibition was repealed, municipalities became involved in reducing the problems created by alcoholism. Initially, city jails and city hospitals bore the brunt of care for alcoholics, but as new models of intervention became known through the efforts of groups like Yale and the NCEA, cities experimented with these new program models out of their own funds or through funds generated by the pressure that was being exerted on state legislatures to support such efforts. For example, the City of Toledo, Ohio opened an alcoholism counseling clinic in 1948 with a $10,000 state grant, then passed a local ordinance requiring that everyone arrested for being drunk be screened for possible need of the clinic's services. [369]

In 1943, Oregon and Utah became the first states in several decades to legislatively establish state-level sponsorship of activities to address problems related to alcoholism. In 1944, the nationwide total expenditure by state alcoholism programs was $30,572. Alabama in 1945 created a Commission on Education with Respect to Alcoholism. With limited funds in its early years, the Commission restricted its activities to the distribution of pamphlets and the hosting of educational meetings. During the same year, New Jersey enacted legislation to provide for alcohol education and a rehabilitation program for alcoholics. [370]

In 1945, Connecticut became the first state to create a formal state-level division (within the department of mental health) to address the problem of alcoholism, but the failure to allocate funds delayed its implementation. The Connecticut Commission on Alcoholism was created in 1947 and supported through an allocation of 9% of the fees received from the state's Liquor Control Commission. The Connecticut program provided both public alcohol education and alcoholism treatment clinics.

The opening of the Connecticut clinics and similar services in Oregon, both in 1947, marked the mid-century rebirth of state-sponsored alcoholism treatment services, even though these clinics treated a small number of clients by today's standards. (During 1947, Connecticut treated 310 patients and Oregon treated 40 patients.) By 1952, Connecticut was operating a central 50-bed hospital and outpatient clinics in six communities. Each clinic received $22,000 per year to pay salaries and rent and purchase supplies. By 1954, 23 states were funding alcoholism treatment services that in that year treated more than 12,500 alcoholics. [371]

Most alcoholics treated in state-sponsored alcoholism programs in the mid-1950s were treated on an outpatient basis. Outpatient services were provided out of inpatient facilities, state-sponsored alcoholism clinics, and local health centers. [372] Inpatient services were provided in state psychiatric hospitals, state inebriate hospitals (such as Willmar State Hospital in Minnesota), local hospitals, local psychopathic hospitals, specialty institutions (such as the Blue Hills Hospital in Connecticut or the Wichita Recovery Center in Kansas), correctional facilities (such as the Workhouse Clinic in Virginia), private sanataria (such as the Brattleboro Retreat in Vermont), and special institutions for women (such as the House of Hope-Alcoholic Women's Residence in Utah). [373]

The combinations of forces that came together to initiate state responses to the problem of alcoholism are typified by activity that took place in Utah in the 1940s. An initial bill introduced by Senator June Kendall in 1943 opened the way for the Public Welfare Commission to use funds allocated for emergency relief to pay for the treatment of indigent alcoholics in private sanataria and hospitals. During the next four years, some 75 alcoholics were treated through this provision. In 1946, a number of A.A. members prepared a bill that was passed through the Utah legislature in 1947. This legislation provided $50,000 for both public education and the treatment of alcoholism. In addition to the A.A. members who contributed their work and influence, many staff from Yale and the NCEA—Bacon, Haggard, McCarthy, Mann—traveled to Utah to voice support for these early efforts. [374]

Bruce Johnson has unraveled some of the behind-the-scenes influences that spurred this expansion of alcoholism treatment services. In most cases, these initiatives can be traced to the national influence of the NCEA and Yale. The New Hampshire initiative is illustrative. The New Hampshire legislation was spurred on by three graduates of the 1944 Yale Summer School on Alcohol: Ernest Shepherd, James Reen, and Ernest Converse. All three were involved in drafting the legislation, and Shepherd went on to become head of the legislatively created Liquor Research Commission. Public and legislative support for this initiative was aided by detailed media coverage led by a state house reporter who was himself a recovering alcoholic.[375]

While states were beginning to respond to calls for a public-health response to the problem of alcoholism, the financial investments in these early experiments were still quite small. In a 1949 review of state efforts, Joseph Hirsch noted that the total of funds expended by all states in the area of alcoholism research, education, and treatment had not yet surpassed $1 million.[376] As more states initiated formal alcoholism prevention and treatment efforts, total state expenditure on these efforts rose to $3 million in 1955 and to $6 million in 1960.

What these dollars meant in terms of the number of clients served was significant. In 1948, 473 alcoholics were treated in state-sponsored treatment programs; in 1960, more than 26,000 were treated in such programs. Even where state efforts were horribly under-funded, the symbolic nature of recognizing alcoholism as a disease in statutory language served to destigmatize the disorder and laid a foundation upon which later state-supported treatment agencies and private treatment centers could and would be built.[377]

During the 1950s, most of the state responses to alcoholism were marked by instability and inconsistency. Commissions were formed and then disbanded—or launched, with great publicity but with only minimal funding to actually implement educational or treatment activities. Typical of these efforts was the California Alcoholic Rehabilitation Commission, created in 1954. The Commission survived only three years before its total appropriation was precipitously cut by the state legislature.[378] Texas also offers an interesting case study. While the 1876 Constitution for the State of Texas specifically noted that "the legislature may establish an inebriate asylum for the care of drunkenness and the reform of inebriates," it was not until 1951 that legislation was passed that made provisions for alcoholics to be treated in the state's psychiatric facilities, and not until 1953 that a state-level Commission on Alcoholism was created.[379] And yet, in 1956, the Commission was reported as "presently inactive in the field for want of funds."[380] All of these efforts were perhaps necessary false starts that prepared the ground for the explosive growth in alcoholism treatment during the 1960s and 1970s.

What can also be found in these early state efforts is a mirroring of those core elements of programming found at the NCEA and Yale. The national advocacy campaign was mirrored by local and state advocacy campaigns. Yale's clinic model is replicated in early state efforts. Even Yale's publishing function was

emulated. By 1952, the newly created state departments that addressed alcoholism began to distribute such publications as *Alcoholism—A Treatment Digest for Physicians* (New Jersey), *The Connecticut Review on Alcoholism*, *The Louisiana Bulletin on Alcoholism*, and the *Utah Alcoholism Review*.[381]

In 1949, representatives from the various state alcoholism programs came together to found the National States' Conference on Alcoholism, the organizational precursor to the Alcohol and Drug Problems Association of North America. The original objectives of the Conference were to provide a forum for sharing information on state alcoholism programming, to create standards for patient classification and patient care, to create standards for program evaluation, and to provide a central vehicle through which state alcoholism programs could coordinate their efforts at a national level with various voluntary agencies interested in the problem of alcoholism.[382]

There was little federal action on the alcoholism front in the 1940s. The primary piece of treatment-oriented federal legislation was a 1947 statute that established an alcoholism treatment and rehabilitation program in the District of Columbia. The primary significance of the law was its recognition that the alcoholic was a sick person in need of treatment—the first such recognition in a piece of federal legislation.[383]

We noted earlier that the inebriate asylum movement had failed in part because of its failure to garner stable public funding to support itself. The success of the alcoholism movement can be measured in part by the fact that three fourths of the states launched legislatively supported alcoholism initiatives in one ten-year period, 1945-1955. During this period the alcoholism movement laid a foundation for the dramatic increase in funding of community-based alcoholism treatment services in the 1970s. What financially sustained the movement itself in the interim introduces the next part of our story.

R. Brinkley Smithers: Private Philanthropy and the Alcoholism Movement [384]

R. Brinkley ("Brink") Smithers created a philanthropic foundation in 1952 named after his father, Christopher D. Smithers, one of the founders of IBM. After being successfully treated for alcoholism in 1954, Smithers became quite interested in the toll that alcoholism was taking upon the whole culture. Following Smithers' participation in the 1956 Yale Summer School of Alcohol Studies, the charter of the Christopher D. Smithers Foundation was amended, declaring its exclusive focus that of addressing alcoholism as a national public-health problem. Over the next 40 years, the Christopher D. Smithers Foundation allocated more than $12 million to alcoholism-related projects, and R. Brinkley Smithers provided more than $25 million in personal contributions to such projects. The strategic use of these resources, in addition to Smithers' personal leadership on alcoholism-related issues, provided enormous impetus to the modern alcoholism movement.

It can be said without exaggeration that the Smithers resources provided a life-sustaining bridge between the rise of the alcoholism movement in the 1940s and the government's significant entrance into the alcoholism arena in the 1970s. Brink Smithers and the Smithers Foundation:

- provided seed grants to launch more than 50 National Council on Alcoholism (NCA) affiliates in 36 states and the District of Columbia;
- subsidized Dr. Ruth Fox's salary as Medical Director of the NCA;
- funded the research and publication of E. M. Jellinek's *The Disease Concept of Alcoholism*;
- created publications and other mechanisms to educate the public, business and industry, police, clergy, and physicians on the problems of alcoholism;
- provided the financial support in 1961 to relocate the Center of Alcohol Studies from Yale to Rutgers;
- subsidized the move toward financial independence of the *Journal of Studies on Alcohol*;
- funded an alcoholism program at Trafalgar hospital in 1964 to demonstrate the feasibility of treating alcoholics in a general community hospital;
- allocated resources toward the establishment of a national Washington, D.C. office of the North American Association for Alcoholism Programs;
- helped organize support for passage of the Comprehensive Alcohol Abuse and Alcoholism Prevention, Treatment and Rehabilitation Act of 1970;
- provided the services of Harrison Trice to develop and implement model workplace alcoholism programs;
- provided a $10-million endowment to found the Alcoholism Treatment and Training Center at Roosevelt Hospital in New York City; and
- provided a $6.7-million endowment to Rutgers and Cornell Universities to establish the R. Brinkley Smithers Institute for Alcoholism Prevention and Workplace Problems.

Other activities funded by Brinkley Smithers or the Smithers foundations included student alcohol use surveys, public-opinion surveys on alcoholism, college alcohol education programs, alcoholism services for special populations, development and distribution of alcoholism treatment resource guides to more than 15,000 libraries, and research on the effects of parental alcoholism on children.

The Christopher D. Smithers Foundation provided a major impetus to the development of local alcoholism treatment and education efforts, to the rise of what is today known as the employee assistance field, to the early development of what came to be the American Society of Addiction Medicine, and to the development and professionalization of the treatment field as we know it today. It all began with one man's recovery and vision. Acts of philanthropy at critical times played an invaluable role in launching alcoholism education and treatment efforts in communities across the United States before the days of consistent public support for these services. Brink Smithers was not present at the birth of the modern alcoholism movement, but his financial resources and personal leadership breathed life back into that movement at times when its strength slackened, and he rescued components of that movement when they were in crisis and facing extinction.

While the philanthropy of Brink Smithers stands as a significant chapter in the story of the alcoholism movement, his was not the sole source of private philanthropy to the movement. Smaller acts of charity fed the initiation and spread of local alcoholism-related research, education and treatment initiatives.

The Role of A.A. and Recovered Alcoholics in the Alcoholism Movement

We have described the rise of these alcoholism-oriented agencies, with only peripheral references to the people who brought their own recovery from alcoholism into their investment in and support of these organizations. To ascertain their influence on the modern alcoholism movement, it may be well to pause and more specifically note their existence. There was first Dwight Anderson, whose sobriety began in 1932 at the Payne Whitney Clinic of the New York Hospital. Anderson served as the Director of Public Relations for the New York State Medical Society and used his public relations expertise to propose the need to change public perceptions of the alcoholic and to propose the strategies through which those attitudes could be changed. He is perhaps the most unheralded figure of this era, and undoubtedly the chief architect and behind-the-scenes prime mover of the events detailed in the past two chapters.

Next we have Dr. Robert Smith and Bill Wilson—A.A.'s co-founders. Bill and Dr. Bob were visibly associated with the NCEA at its inception, and remained involved until concern about issues of anonymity and A.A.'s policy of non-affiliation forced them to withdraw in 1945. Bill continued his behind-the-scenes involvement in the NCEA and lectured at Yale's Summer School on Alcohol Studies in 1943 and 1944. Next is Ray McCarthy, another early figure who became sober outside of A.A. and who brought the lay-therapist tradition of Peabody into the Yale Clinic model of alcoholism counseling. There was, of course, Marty Mann and her incomparable role in publicly challenging America's stereotypes about alcoholism. As noted above, there was Brinkley Smithers, whose philanthropy sustained and fueled the movement and who provided his own wisdom as a member and president of the NCEA's board. Perhaps most significant were the large numbers of unnamed recovered alcoholics who led and worked in the local NCEA chapters, who filled the first industrial alcoholism positions, and who worked as lay therapists in the newly opening mid-century alcoholism treatment programs.

The contributions of recovered alcoholics to the success of the modern alcoholism movement were often hidden behind masks of personal discretion or A.A. anonymity. Acts that pushed the movement forward were often performed by people not recognized as bringing personal passion to their contribution. In his history of the modern alcoholism movement, Bruce Johnson tells an anecdote that illustrates such hidden contributions. The New York *World Telegram* published a very well written feature article on the NCEA in November of 1944. The article, written by Douglas Gilbert, provided an in-depth presentation of the NCEA's key ideas and organizational objectives. It was, in total, a masterful piece of persuasive writing. What was missing from the public account of this story was the fact that Douglas Gilbert was himself a recovered alcoholic.[385]

It is hard to understand the modern alcoholism movement without understanding the hidden connections that have played such an important role in shaping the history of this field. During R. Brinkley Smithers' early days of sobriety, the person who was his most faithful source of support was Yvelin Gardner—Marty Mann's "alter-ego" at the NCEA.[386] Smithers' later financial contributions to the NCEA and other alcoholism-concerned organizations are legendary and may have, in one sense, reflected a

form of repayment for Yvelin Gardner's incomparable gift. The hidden hands of recovered alcoholics helped support and promote this movement in thousands of unseen ways—always with a very practical agenda concerning public education about alcoholism and the need for local resources for alcoholic detoxification and treatment. It was for many of them another way to carry the message of hope to the still-suffering alcoholic. It is noteworthy that a movement that purported to push the new science of alcoholism drew so much of its sustenance from those whose personal passion far exceeded their scientific interest or credentials.

The Role of the Alcohol Beverage Industry in the Alcoholism Movement

After the repeal of prohibition, representatives of the alcohol beverage industry were very much concerned with rehabilitating the image of their product and their industry. The industry was still left to the whim of states, counties, and municipalities—entities that had the power to ban or severely restrict the sale of alcohol. The entire future of the industry hinged on how American citizens viewed alcoholic beverages and the places in which they were sold and consumed. To that end, the industry sought a broad range of involvement to culturally cleanse the image of alcohol. That involvement included participation in discussions that focused on alcohol problems and alcoholism.

The story of the role of the alcohol beverage industry in the alcoholism movement is first and foremost an incomplete tale. There is much about the relationship between representatives of this industry and the major organizational torchbearers of the alcoholism movement that is not known. This makes interpreting what we do know all the more dangerous. And yet, this is a story that requires investigation because of its continued relevance. The strain in this relationship is not a historical artifact, but an ongoing ethical question in the prevention and treatment arena.

Those fledgling post-repeal organizations concerned with alcohol problems that did not accept money from the alcohol beverage industry became extinct. The three primary agencies profiled in this chapter—the RCPA, the Yale Center on Alcohol Studies, and the NCEA—all accepted contributions from the alcohol industry during at least part of their respective histories. What we do not know is the total amount of money that went directly or indirectly to each of these organizations; the timing of such contributions; and the effect of such contributions, if any, on the policies and programs of each organization. We also do not know the total non-monetary influence the alcohol industry exerted on these organizations during their early development.

We do know that alcohol representatives were ever present, monitoring and, where possible, participating in activities of the post-repeal organizations that focused on alcohol-related problems. For example, at the 1943 RCPA conference in New York City, at which the RCPA formulated its future program, the occupational distribution of those attending included only three representatives of temperance organizations—but eleven representatives of the liquor industry.[387]

John Burnham has articulated as clearly as anyone a rationale for the alcohol industry's concern about and involvement in the rising alcoholism movement. Burnham first suggests that the alcohol industry benefitted greatly from studies that focused on the vulnerability of the few (alcoholics) rather than on the broader social problems caused by alcohol. The industry saw Alcoholics Anonymous as a potential ally because the organization focused on a small percentage of late-stage drinkers and had little to say about the drinking habits of most Americans. In modern parlance, the organization was concerned about alcoholism, but not about alcohol use—or even alcohol abuse. Perhaps even more, A.A. located the problem of alcohol in the person, not in the bottle. In a similar manner, Burnham points out that the alcohol beverage industry sponsored some groups concerned with such issues as drinking and driving, because the focus of such groups was not on the harmfulness of drinking alcohol, but on the need for responsible drinking decisions.[388]

Alcohol representatives sat on national and local alcoholism councils across the country and provided financial support for educational programs designed to inform the public about alcoholism. Their presence helped to sustain a focus on the alcoholic as a biologically vulnerable individual, and to divert public attention from wider problems created by alcohol in the culture.

The capacity of the alcohol industry to provide financial support to fledgling organizations with few other options to support themselves ensured the industry's presence in the post-repeal alcoholism movement. However, this participation did not take place without conflict. This conflict is most evident in the history of the Research Council on Problems of Alcohol, which was supported in part by funds from the liquor industry. The RCPA history shows how the industry affected the policies of those agencies to which it contributed. Liquor-industry representatives

objected to what seemed to them to be the RCPA's constant references to "alcoholism." They didn't like a disorder named after their product. They went so far as to demand a ban on use of the term in the RCPA publications. The RCPA generally complied by substituting the industry's preferred language, "problem drinking."

The fact that the RCPA had liquor interests sitting on its Advisory Committee (e.g., Moreley Sturges, the Executive Director of the Distilled Spirits Institute) and received money from the liquor industry was not raised as an ethical concern by most RCPA members, but was questioned by some members of the public who were suspicious of this association. Yale's growing concern about this association led Haggard to sever connections between the RCPA and the *Quarterly Journal of Alcohol Studies,* but—as we saw—Yale had its own connection with the alcohol industry.

While those in the alcohol beverage industry may have had some shared interests, they by no means represented a unified movement. Beer, wine and distilled spirits manufacturers each had different political organizations—advocates who were not averse to promoting their individual interests over the collective interests of the whole industry. From what evidence is available, there does not appear to have been a unified strategy—no malign conspiracy—whereby the alcohol beverage industry sought to co-opt the alcoholism movement for its own purposes. The money donated by the alcohol industry that we know about does not seem to have dominated the institutions that received it, and the highly diversified alcohol beverage industry rarely "acted with one voice or checkbook."[389]

Part of the reason that ethical quandaries about industry money were not more intense was the fact that the total amount of these funds appears never to have been very large. Robin Room has suggested that the industry was never particularly interested in supporting the development of a large, powerful alcoholism movement. He characterizes the alcohol industry's involvement as "an ostentatious but minimal commitment to supporting alcoholism research, treatment or prevention programs."[390] From what we do know, the pattern of the industry's involvement might be more aptly depicted as haphazard than conspiratorial. It should be emphasized again, however, that what we know about the relationship between the alcohol industry and groups like the RCPA, Yale, and the NCEA in the 1940s is sketchy at best.

The most critical ethical issue seems not to be the simple issue of whether or not it was ethically justifiable to accept financial contributions from the alcohol industry. The RCPA made a fairly convincing case that an institution that focused itself narrowly on the study of alcoholism could accept support from all outside parties that shared an interest in this problem. It seems that the real ethical dilemma for the RCPA, Yale, and the NCEA lay in the secrecy with which they conducted their relationships with the alcohol industry. The lack of full disclosure—and the fact that this portion of the alcoholism movement's story can still not be fully told—is as much a concern in this history as is the question of the overall ethics of accepting money from the alcohol industry.

Questions concerning what might be called the ethics of affiliation were not fully resolved during this period. Controversies arose anew in the 1970s and 1980s about the role of alcohol representatives and alcohol industry dollars in alcoholism prevention and treatment activities—controversies that would lead groups like the NCEA to sever their connections with the alcohol beverage industry. Parallel fields are currently recapitulating this history, as state councils on problematic and compulsive gambling enter into intense debate regarding the ethics of accepting money from the gaming industry for gambling-related education and treatment activities.

The Legacies of the Alcoholism Movement

The first contribution of the modern alcoholism movement was in the arena of problem definition. The movement offered two problem-definition perspectives as alternatives to the temperance perspective, which had defined the problem of alcohol as one springing from the poisonous nature of the product. The first alternative, promoted by the RCPA and the NCEA, was an alcoholism-centered definition that shifted the locus of the problem from the bottle to a biologically vulnerable minority of drinkers. This perspective changed the debate from one about alcohol to one about who was and who was not vulnerable to alcoholism. The alcoholism paradigm blessed the drinking of the majority while it provided a rationale for radical abstinence by an alcoholic minority. The second, more encompassing problem definition, exemplified by the Yale Center of Alcohol Studies, shifted the question of "the alcohol problem" to a discussion of "alcohol problems." Where the former tended to focus on the status of the product, the latter suggested a problem of multiple dimensions that required diverse control and remediation measures. As Mark Keller summarized the shift, "We now were invited to consider not that alcohol was THE problem but that there were many problems in which alcohol was involved in a variety of ways."[391]

Although the alcoholism paradigm gained dominance in post-repeal America, it should be noted that these two alternative perspectives co-existed as replacements for the temperance paradigm and continue to compete as models for America's conceptualization of alcohol-related problems.

The alcoholism movement left many institutional legacies. There is the seminal work of the RCPA in bringing scientists back into the arena of alcohol and alcoholism research and in pioneering an alcohol science that could rise above the Wet-and-Dry propaganda wars. There are within the RCPA the "kinetic ideas" of Dwight Anderson, which provided the guiding ethos of the alcoholism movement and laid the cultural foundation for the rise of a modern alcoholism treatment system.

There are Yale's inestimable contributions: the Summer Schools, the Yale Clinics, the Yale Plan for addressing alcoholism in business and industry, the research and publishing activities (particularly the *Quarterly Journal of Studies on Alcohol)*, the creation of the Classified Abstract Archives of the Alcohol Literature, and technical breakthroughs such as Leon Greenberg's invention of the Alcometer to measure blood alcohol levels.[392] Yale, and later Rutgers, were the central institutions through which the foot soldiers of this new movement were educated and motivated to return to communities all over America and organize new responses to alcohol-related problems. The summer schools were an amalgam of science, spiritual renewal, and political and professional organizing—a petri dish in which the culture of this new movement could be kept growing. People returned for self-repair and rejuvenation and came together to organize broader initiatives. The National States Conference on Alcoholism, for example, was created at the 1949 Yale Summer School of Alcohol Studies. The Conference was renamed the North American Association of Alcoholism Programs in 1956, and renamed again in 1972 as the Alcohol and Drug Problems Association of North America (ADPA). ADPA played a significant role in lobbying at state and federal levels for expanded funding public for alcoholism treatment services—a contribution whose roots can be traced to Yale.

There are the NCEA's contributions and, in particular, the role of Marty Mann, who perhaps more than any other person is responsible for changing America's perception of alcoholism and the alcoholic. The existence of a national network of alcoholism treatment services would not have come about without the cultural groundwork and advocacy provided by Marty Mann and her NCEA colleagues.

There are the those in the World Health Organization, the American Medical Association, and other medical groups who pioneered more enlightened medical care for the alcoholic. There are those who first brought to the workplace the message that alcoholism was a treatable illness. There are the mid-century treatment pioneers, whom we will further explore in the following chapters. There are the mayors, city councils, and state legislatures that backed this new conception of alcoholism with funds that supported research, education, and treatment.

What was most remarkable about this movement as a whole is the way that it penetrated primary institutions to reframe our cultural view of alcohol problems and the alcoholic. This was a movement that profoundly affected our governmental bodies, our healthcare institutions, our professional associations, all of our major media channels, our churches, our workplaces and labor organizations, our schools, and our social clubs. This new alcoholism paradigm, which proclaimed through all of our social institutions that the alcoholic was a sick person worthy of treatment and able to be treated, was the primary legacy of the alcoholism movement.

There were, however, individuals left behind in the growing success of the new movement. One significant difference between this modern movement and the 19th-century movement that birthed the inebriate homes and asylums was that the modern movement was focused specifically on alcoholism, whereas the earlier movement had focused on addiction to all drugs. This split reflected the new post-repeal status of alcohol as a culturally celebrated drug for all but the small minority who were alcoholic drinkers. While the rehabilitation of alcohol as a product and the image of the alcoholic were championed by this movement, other drugs and drug users were being increasingly stigmatized and criminalized. This split ensured that the treatment of alcoholism and the treatment of other addictions would constitute separate worlds between 1945 and 1975. It would take the entire 30 years to rearticulate a model and a language—"chemical dependency," "substance abuse"—to conceptually re-unite the harmful use of all psychoactive drugs.

Origin of the Modern Disease Concept

While these two chapters have covered many of the ideas, institutions and key figures that made up what has been called the modern alcoholism movement, we are still left with one final question. Precisely when and where in all of these developments did the modern conceptualization of alcoholism as a disease begin? Let us track the evolution of this idea through the 1930s and 1940s.

One early thread leading to the idea of alcoholism as a disease came from William Silkworth's presentation of alcoholism as an "allergy," both to Bill Wilson and to the broader medical community. In spite of its lack of substantiating scientific evidence, Silkworth's concept of alcoholism as allergy was the first modern medical concept successfully used by large numbers of alcoholics as a metaphor to understand what happened to them and to explain why they could no longer drink. As suggestive and individually helpful as Silkworth's idea was, it still constituted no fully developed view of alcoholism as a primary, progressive disease.[393]

We next go to the formative years of A.A.: 1935-1939. If any institution has been given credit or blame for the disease concept, it is surely A.A. And yet William Miller and Ernest Kurtz have accurately pointed out that the origin of the disease concept of alcoholism is not to be found in A.A.[394] There are no references to alcoholism as a disease in the first 164 pages of the book that outlines A.A.'s basic program of recovery. While references to alcoholism's nature as an "allergy" or "illness" or to the alcoholic as a "sick" person occasionally appear in early A.A. literature, A.A.'s primary conceptualization of the etiology of alcoholism was one of emotional and spiritual maladjustment.[395] A.A. used these medically oriented terms primarily for their metaphoric value—more for sensemaking than for science.

In September of 1939, the announcement of the RCPA's shift in focus to alcoholism research included a single statement that said simply that alcoholism would be dealt with as a "disease" comparable in seriousness to cancer, tuberculosis, and other major disorders.[396] This is one of the earliest references to alcoholism as a disease in the institutions that were central to the modern alcoholism movement. This statement, however, stands as an isolated pronouncement rather than a central organizing motif for the RCPA's program efforts. We still have nothing comparable to a fully developed disease concept of alcoholism.

As we move to Yale in the early 1940s, we still find no disease concept. In fact, we find discomfort with the term "alcoholism" and a preference for an "alcohol problems" perspective. We see key scientists at Yale attacking elements of this emerging disease concept, as in Haggard's *Quarterly Journal of Studies on Alcohol* article pointing out the complete lack of scientific evidence to support Silkworth's allergy theory of alcoholism.[397] The conception of the etiology of alcoholism presented at the first Yale Summer Schools placed primary emphasis on personality configuration, rather than on biological vulnerability. Jellinek himself makes only brief mention of this idea of disease when he notes in passing that "It is justifiable to speak of all compulsive drinking as a disease, but it is not justifiable to say that all compulsive drinking originates in disease."[398] And in the Yale clinics we see a view of alcoholism, not as a primary disease, but as a symptom of underlying emotional maladjustment.

The first place we find the tenets that would eventually be refined into the modern disease concept of alcoholism is in Dwight Anderson's four kinetic ideas and their infusion into Marty Mann's national campaign to redefine perceptions of alcoholism and the alcoholic. Anderson seems to have been the seminal strategist, while Mann was the prime architect and energy source for the modern alcoholism movement. If the movement were portrayed graphically as concentric circles, with each circle representing the multiple personalities, constituencies, and interests involved, Anderson's and Mann's roles would warrant their placement in the inner-most core of these circles.

While this movement was launched with the aura of science, it is important to acknowledge that the critical ideas in the movement were not based on new scientific breakthroughs. These ideas were formulated and launched before Jellinek's first study of A.A. members documented the patterns and progression of alcoholism. From the NCEA's earliest days, Mann, wrapped in the reputation of Yale University, presented Anderson's kinetic ideas as scientific fact. This is not to say that the seminal ideas in the alcoholism movement were untrue, only that they were not based on established scientific evidence. There was no hidden intent to deceive here. What Anderson and Mann openly proposed and openly published was a view of alcoholism that was experientially true for both of them. The evidence of its truth was in their own transformed lives.

The emerging disease concept of the 1930s and early 1940s was an organizing metaphor that was useful both individually and culturally. The concept became what Robin Room has called a "governing image"—an image that provided a shorthand way of viewing alcohol-related problems and expressing the types of institutions that should have ownership of these problems.[399] On an individual basis, it provided a way for alcoholics to understand their vulnerability to addiction and their need for complete abstinence. For the American culture, it was a new way to talk about alcohol problems outside the stale Wet-Dry rhetoric. References to "illness," "sickness," and "disease" in speaking of alcoholism—indeed, even speaking of "alcoholism" rather than "drunkenness"—was a way of

signaling a break from an older cultural paradigm that viewed alcohol and drunkenness solely in terms of sin and moral degeneracy. The rise of a disease concept of alcoholism was based more on its metaphorical utility as a slogan than on its scientific validity. Its ascendence was more one of declaration than of scientific conclusion.

While recognizing this metaphorical utility, scientists were for their part always ambivalent about this disease conception. Jellinek himself continually expressed his fears regarding the dangers of extending the disease conception of alcoholism to all forms of excessive drinking. He even preferred limited use of the term "alcoholism" and advocated use of the term "inebriety" to encompass the broader spectrum of alcohol problems.[400] He believed the disease conception deserved narrow rather than broad application and spent most of his career trying to define which types of alcohol problems could and could not be so conceptualized.[401] Dr. Harry Tiebout, another influential advocate of the disease concept of alcoholism, acknowledged in 1955 that this disease concept emerged more as a slogan than as a scientifically validated concept. Tiebout shared his own doubts about the lack of scientific underpinnings of the alcoholism movement:

> *I cannot help but feel that the whole field of alcoholism is way out on a limb which any minute will crack and drop us all in a frightful mess. To change the metaphor, we have stuck our necks out and not one of us knows if he will be stepped on individually or collectively. I sometimes tremble to think of how little we have to back up our claims. We all are skating on pretty thin ice.[402]*

Other scientists shared Tiebout's concerns and predicted that "use of the (disease) concept as a slogan will come under criticism as alcoholism is subjected to more conceptual analysis."[403] As we shall see in forthcoming chapters, this is precisely what would occur.

To conclude that the concept of alcoholism as a disease in the 1930s and 1940s was more metaphor than fact takes nothing away from the social and personal utilities achieved by this view of alcoholism. In the next chapter of our story, we shall see how this cultural metaphor of alcoholism as a disease became refined and diffused as a philosophical framework for the treatment of alcoholics. For that story, we must leave New York and New Haven and venture to Minnesota.

Chapter Twenty-One
The Birth and Spread of the "Minnesota Model" [1]

This chapter will explore how the state of Minnesota came to be known as "The Land of Ten Thousand Treatment Centers"—a state that as early as 1981 had more than 3,800 residential beds for the treatment of alcoholism. But this story is not just a local one. In the late 1940s and early 1950s, a number of events coalesced to shape an approach to alcoholism treatment that was replicated widely throughout the United States and beyond. This is the story of the birth and spread of the "Minnesota Model" of "chemical dependency" treatment.[1]

Pre-A.A. History

During the 1870s, the attention of Minnesota—like that of many states—was drawn to the problem of alcoholic inebriety. In 1873, Dr. Charles Hewitt of the Minnesota Board of Health submitted a report to Governor Horace Austin entitled, *The Duty of the State in the Care and Cure of Inebriates*. This report called upon the state to officially declare:

> ....that inebriation is a disease; that it demands the same public facilities for its treatment as other diseases; that it is a curable disease under proper conditions; and that it is the duty of the State to care for this class of sufferers, even more than for almost any other, because the cause of their malady (alcohol as drink), is a source of national, state and municipal revenue.[2]

The report went on to call for the creation of inebriate asylums within the state of Minnesota. The state legislature passed a law providing a special tax on saloons, the proceeds of which were to go toward the erection and operation of a "treatment center for inebriates" in Rochester, Minnesota. Opposition to the tax was intense, and Rochester became a state

psychiatric hospital rather than an inebriate asylum.

In 1907, the Minnesota Legislature again turned its attention to the problem of alcoholism when it voted a two-percent tax on liquor licenses, with the revenue earmarked to build and operate a treatment facility for inebriates. Willmar State Hospital fulfilled this role until the tax lapsed just before the dawn of prohibition. Between 1920 and 1950, alcoholics were treated within several designated psychiatric facilities in Minnesota, using methods not unlike those we described in Chapter Eleven. But change was brewing—change sparked by the growth of A.A. in Minnesota and a growing disillusionment with traditional psychiatric approaches to the treatment of alcoholism.

The Story of Pat C. [3]

If the story of the Minnesota Model of chemical dependency treatment begins with one person, that person was surely Pat C. Pat drank his way through numerous careers before beginning his efforts to get sober. When Pat relapsed after taking the Keeley cure, a friend told him about something called the "Oxford Movement" in the East, which alcoholics were using to stay sober. He attended an Oxford Group meeting, concluded quickly that it was not for him, and used this temporary disillusionment as an excuse to get drunk.

Next came a series of serendipitous events that interrupted his raging alcoholism. After reading a review of the book *Alcoholics Anonymous* in *Time* magazine, Pat borrowed ten cents to check the book out of the public library. (There was a charge for checking a new book out in those days.) Pat's drinking slowed as he worked his way through this book: He didn't return it for two years. On August 9, 1940, Pat wrote to the Alcoholic Foundation in New York, inquiring whether there were any of their "Alumnae" in Minnesota. This letter, signed "Cynically yours," was forwarded to two Chicago A.A. members, who decided to visit Pat during a forthcoming trip to a football game in Minnesota. After the game, they barged in on Pat and his quart of Old Grandad, and—as fate would have it—stayed four days when one of those notorious Minnesota blizzards delayed their return to Chicago. On November 11, 1940, Pat C. had his last drink.

---

[1] This chapter was constructed using three excellent works: Forrest Richeson's 1978 history of AA in Minnesota, Damian McElrath's 1987 history of Hazelden, and Jerry Spicer's 1993 text on the Minnesota Model. This written material was supplemented by interviews with Dan Anderson, Gordon Grimm, Damian McElrath, Jean Rossi, and Jerry Spicer.

Pat C. was the beginning of A.A. in Minnesota and in many areas of the Midwest. When he died May 15, 1965, with 24 years of sobriety, more than 450 A.A. groups had been birthed directly or indirectly through his influence. His visits in the early 1940s to alcoholics "drying out" in the Minneapolis, Minnesota Sanitarium mark the first links between A.A. and institutions in Minnesota, and Pat also played a significant role in the emergence of Minnesota's alcoholism treatment system.[4]

Pioneer House

During the 1940s, those who administered the relief department of the city of Minneapolis, Minnesota developed a growing consciousness about the role that alcoholism played in the financial impoverishment of individuals and families served by the agency. The case of a family that had been on the relief rolls for a decade caught the department's attention when the case was closed due to the father's sudden support of his wife and four children. Upon investigation, they discovered that the father, a long-time alcoholic, had followed the example of his older brother and had sobered up in Alcoholics Anonymous. The welfare department became excited by the potential benefit of sobering up other alcoholics whose families burdened the city's relief roles. A one-year experiment spanning 1947 and 1948 was initiated, providing intensive social-work services to 29 families headed by alcoholic fathers. The project demonstrated that the welfare department could achieve substantial cost savings by providing specialized services to alcoholics. This discovery led to a proposal to create a special facility for the treatment of alcoholics.[5]

Plans for the opening of the new treatment center were delayed when the headlines that accompanied the purchase of the first facility ("City Buys a Dormitory for Drunks") triggered storms of neighborhood protest. It was then that Dr. William Paul, Superintendent of the Union City Mission, stepped forward and offered to locate the new treatment center on the property the Mission owned in Medicine Lake. The property was known as Mission Hills. The facility opened October 5, 1948, under the direction of Pat and John McDonnell. The fledgling program resided within a number of buildings at Mission Hills, which were known by such names as "the Ice House" and "Little Mother's Inn." They eventually obtained permanent quarters at a former potato warehouse, which was christened "Pioneer House."

In late 1948, Ole Pearson of the Division of Public Assistance of the Board of Welfare of the City of Minneapolis, Minnesota approached Pat C.—then eight years into his own recovery from alcoholism—to help launch this new alcoholism treatment center. Unsure of what the new role would mean in terms of his A.A. status, Pat traveled to New York to consult the Alcoholic Foundation, A.A.'s governing body. Bill Wilson and others encouraged Pat to consider this new role. They clarified the point that Pat would be paid as a social worker, not as an A.A. member, and that they saw no inherent conflict between his A.A. membership and the proposed job. In 1949, with support from New York, Pat shifted his role at Pioneer House from that of volunteer to that of counselor.

The program of treatment at Pioneer House had few precedents. While historical accounts of Pioneer House make reference to earlier models provided by Bridge House in New York and Portal House in Chicago, the primary influence that shaped Pioneer House was A.A. Pioneer House was the first alcoholism treatment program in Minnesota that based its two to three weeks of residential treatment primarily on the philosophy of Alcoholics Anonymous.

In its first 14 months of operation, Pioneer House treated 237 "guests," only 22 of whom were readmitted during this period. The bulk of referrals came (in descending proportions) from A.A., the welfare department, the municipal court, and the probation office. Pat could regularly be found in court trying to spot alcoholics he thought had a chance to make it in recovery. The average length of stay at Pioneer House was 29 days. The program was staffed by four counselors and a director.[6]

Treatment at Pioneer House might be called neo-Washingtonian. The emphasis was on flexibility, a minimum of rules and regimentation, and the importance of developing trust and confidence within the treatment community. A number of practices initiated within Pioneer House can be recognized for their enduring influence. Clients entering treatment at Pioneer House were given two books: *Alcoholics Anonymous* and *Twelve Steps and Twelve Traditions*. Lectures and discussions on the steps of A.A. were a core part of the program, and clients were expected to complete the first five steps before they left treatment. In those days, the Fifth-Step requirement at Pioneer House meant that the client either did the Steps or could "stay there forever."[7] The spiritual dimensions of recovery were emphasized from the earliest days of Pioneer House. Dr. Nelson Bradley later described how Pat C. was always searching for ways to open the alcoholic to the spiritual through the medium of meditation.

Pat's technique was to ask each of his clients to row by himself in a boat out into the middle of Medicine Lake, preferably just about sun-up. Whatever experience they had out there by themselves was his definition of meditation.[8]

Pioneer House made other interesting innovations during its early days. It used alumni meetings as a continuing support structure for clients leaving treatment—a practice that had not been fully developed since the collapse of the Keeley Leagues. Pioneer House was also the first program to create the position of the Minority Group Counselor within an addiction treatment program.[9]

While Pioneer House was getting off the ground, plans for another Minnesota treatment facility took root on a farm know as Hazelden.[10]

Hazelden: The Early Years [11]

The story of Hazelden is the story of a Minnesota farmhouse retreat that grew into an internationally recognized addiction treatment center. The original idea for Hazelden emerged in 1947 out of two divergent interests: 1) the creation of an alcoholism treatment center for priests and 2) the creation of an alcoholism treatment center for professionals (a group that would include priests). The key figures in this early dialogue were Austin Ripley, Father M., Lynn C., and Robert McGarvey.

Pledges of $5,000 from the Catholic diocese and $6,000 from Twin City business leaders provided seed money to explore the initial goal of creating a treatment center for priests. When this plan fell through, an alternate plan evolved to create such a facility for a broad spectrum of professionals. The goal of a specialized treatment center for priests continued on a separate track under the leadership of Austin Ripley and resulted in the eventual opening of Guest House in Lake Orion, Michigan.

Ripley's role in the original planning group was replaced by that of the banker, R.C. Lilly, who—as legend has it—became interested in alcoholism recovery after surviving a 120-foot drunken plunge in his car off a bridge onto a sand-filled barge on the Mississippi River. On December 29, 1948 the Coyle Foundation, which Lilly had been instrumental in founding, purchased the Powers' farm in Center City, Minnesota. The farm consisted of 217 acres, a 17-room farmhouse, a smaller tenant farmhouse, and two small cottages. The farm was known as "Hazelden" (named after Powers' wife, Hazel). The arrangement was that the property would be resold by the Coyle Foundation to a newly created entity, the Hazelden Foundation. The purpose of the latter was to operate a "sanitorium for curable alcoholics of the professional class." "Professional class" implied not so much social class distinctions as it did a desire to reach the alcoholic before he hit bottom on skid row, while he still had a family, a job, and some degree of social standing.[12]

The Hazelden Foundation was incorporated January 10, 1949. The incorporators were R.H. McGarvey, R.C. Lilly, Lynn C., John Kerwin and A.A. Heckman. Lilly became president of the foundation and its early driving force. Chuck Crewe's history of Hazelden notes that the incorporators "were dealing with a broad problem with little or no professional guidance from people familiar with the illness or its treatment." What they did know was that they wanted A.A. to form the foundation for treatment at Hazelden.[13]

Lynn C., a recovered alcoholic, was hired as the first general manager of Hazelden at a salary of $600 per month. His staff consisted of Ma Schnable, who cooked and nursed; Jimmy Malm, the grounds keeper; and a utility man. Hazelden officially opened May 1, 1949, although its first patient had been admitted on March 21.

In its first three years, Hazelden averaged between four and seven clients per day in residence, with each client staying approximately five days. In 1949, costs at the center were $100 for week one and $85 for each subsequent week. Hazelden struggled financially through its first two years, piling up debt and experiencing disappointments in its fund-rasing efforts. As Hazelden faced foreclosure in 1951, the Butler family purchased Hazelden and created a more stable financial footing for the center. Patrick Butler, who had himself been treated at Hazelden, became a central figure in shaping Hazelden's character and dramatic growth. In its early years, Hazelden did not achieve its goal of reaching alcoholics in the professional class. Most of the early residents were chronic alcoholics from Minneapolis and St. Paul whose stay at Hazelden was paid for by a grant from the Hill Foundation of St. Paul.[14] Everyone at Hazelden knew that early- and middle-stage alcoholics were out there; they just did not know how to get them to come to treatment. Dan Anderson would later reflect that "Hazelden started at the bottom and slowly worked its way to the top."[15]

The farmhouse was the center of all social and treatment activities. Forrest Richeson describes the simplicity of Hazelden's first Christmas.

Lynn C. and one patient were the only residents, and Lynn prepared the Christmas meal for the two of them.[16]

Patients during the earliest days stayed an average of five days, but this period was eventually extended to three weeks.

Counseling during the early years was provided by Lynn C.—a lawyer by training—and Otto Z., a banker, who started working as a part-time counselor in 1951. In 1954, Lon J., who had earlier gone through treatment at Hazelden, was hired as a full time counselor. Lon's hiring may mark the beginning of the modern practice of hiring recovered people as counselors in residential programs in which they themselves had been treated.[17]

Patients' daily life at Hazelden consisted of lectures, groups, constant informal "bull sessions," good food, and a smattering of recreational activities. The early Hazelden program was a simple one. According to Damian McElrath's account of this period, clients entering treatment were asked to do four things: "practice responsible behavior, attend the lectures on the Steps, associate and talk with the other patients, and make their beds."[18] Detox was "cold turkey" for most, with a few barbiturates prescribed for the most severe cases. Medical care was provided through the St. Croix Falls Clinic; there were no on-site medical services. The only routinely administered medications were vitamin B shots and yeast tablets, which were notorious for their propensity to create "black stools." The most frequently provided medication was a placebo that Otto Z. handed out when newcomers reported that they did not feel well.

There are brief historical references to some experiments with aversion treatment, but most of the emphasis was pure A.A. The men who came to Hazelden were given an intense indoctrination to the A.A. program. They were exposed to A.A. visitors and volunteers, A.A. literature, and a formal three-week cycle of lectures on alcoholism and the Steps of A.A. Hazelden's first decade saw the introduction of now-familiar rituals—the presentation of an A.A. pocket piece and a personalized coffee cup to each client and the introduction of a new mechanism of long-term support: the Center City Alumni Association.

Hazelden grew steadily, the average daily census rising to seven in 1951. Two needs emerged at Hazelden: the need for some kind of extended support facility and the need for services for women. In 1953, facing the circumstances of homeless and jobless men who were being discharged from treatment with no

place to go, Hazelden founded Fellowship House —Minnesota's first halfway house for alcoholics. After eight years of providing alcoholism treatment services only to men, Hazelden opened a women's program, called Dia Linn (Gaelic for "God be with us"), on a 300-acre estate near White Bear Lake in 1956. This remote location was chosen due to Lynn C.'s resistance to co-locating a women's facility on the Hazelden campus—and to community resistance to locating the facility in Minneapolis. Women were treated in a four-week program at Dia Linn—the longer period reflecting the belief that women were more difficult to treat. The cost of the four-week treatment in 1956 was $400. Dia Linn went through three directors in two years—a testament to the expectation that the director be on duty 24 hours a day. Early pioneer leaders of this facility included Dorothy Borden, Phoebe Brown, Hazel Taylor, and Jane Mill.

There was a special synergy among the new alcoholism treatment facilities that rose up in Minnesota in the late 1940s and early 1950s. Considerable interaction took place among Pioneer House, Hazelden, and a third institution, Willmar State Hospital.

Willmar State Hospital

Willmar State Hospital opened in 1912 as an inebriate asylum, but with the onset of prohibition, it shifted to the role of psychiatric asylum. In its early years as a designated treatment facility for alcoholics, Willmar was known as the "jag farm."[19] In the 1940s, Willmar State Hospital was one of seven state psychiatric hospitals in Minnesota that accepted chronic alcoholics for treatment. Some 150-200 alcoholics were usually in residence at Willmar during these years, each encouraged to stay for the four months that was then considered the ideal period for the treatment of alcoholism.[20] Willmar had been providing what was essentially custodial care of alcoholics for nearly 30 years when events unfolded that brought to the institution a radically new approach to the treatment of alcoholism.

Six key figures shaped the emergence of this new alcoholism treatment model at Willmar State Hospital. Ralph Rosen, Nelson Bradley, Dan Anderson, Jean Rossi, Fred E., and Mel B. Rosen, the Superintendent at Hastings State Hospital, brought a passion for cleaning up the "snake pits" that so many state psychiatric asylums had become. Bradley, a Canadian physician, encountered Rosen in 1947 at the University of Minnesota under unusual circumstances. Bradley had been on his way to a surgical residency in Michigan when his car broke down. Lack of transportation and a shortage of funds led him to consider a residency in Minnesota. Bradley accepted work with Rosen, first in the only opening Rosen had available—an R.N. position—and then as a staff physician at Hastings. Dan Anderson worked nights as an attendant at Hastings while he attended school during the day. It was at Hastings that he and Bradley struck up what became an enduring personal and professional relationship. Both were influenced by Rosen's passion to humanize and professionalize the care of psychiatric patients.

In 1950, Bradley was appointed Superintendent of Willmar State Hospital and asked Anderson to accompany him to Willmar. There, three other figures entered our story: Jean Rossi, Fred E. and Mel B. Rossi was a psychologist interested in closing the gap between clinical research on alcoholism and clinical practice. Fred E. was a recovered alcoholic who was working as Ralph Rosen's secretary at Hastings State Hospital. Bradley said of Fred, "His drinking episodes had been legendary and the miracle and caliber of his recovery made his arrested drinking habits also legendary."[21] In 1954, Bradley invited Fred and another recovered alcoholic, Mel B., to help launch a new approach to alcoholism treatment at Willmar. This approach will be described in some depth as Willmar was the first place in which all of the major elements of the Minnesota Model first came together.

Prior to the arrival of Bradley and Anderson at Willmar, alcoholics had been briefly detoxified and subjected to sustained institutional care on locked wards that often mixed alcoholics and the chronically mentally ill. Neither Bradley nor Anderson knew much about alcoholism when they arrived at Willmar. To educate themselves, the professional staff frequently attended A.A. meetings and built strong personal relationships within the A.A. community. Fred E. and the other recovered alcoholics who worked at Willmar during this seminal period, in addition to providing the bulk of direct patient services, provided "street education" to the professional staff about alcoholism. Bradley claimed that A.A. and A.A. members in Minnesota became "our model, our consultants and our advisory board."[22] A.A. members encouraged Bradley to look at the way Pioneer House and Hazelden were utilizing A.A. and its philosophy. Speaking at A.A.'s 40th Anniversary Convention in Denver in 1975, Bradley spoke of this influence.

We had two well-established A.A. inspired treatment programs already operational in the state. They became a source of inspiration and duplication. It was not until years

later that we were aware both Hazelden and Pioneer House had scarcely celebrated their first birthdays when we so blithely accepted them as models of experience and skill.[23]

Based on what they were learning, Bradley and Anderson took a number of key steps that incorporated and extended the approaches of Pioneer House and Hazelden. The process was a dynamic one guided by an openness to experimentation and a careful scrutiny of the accumulated lessons of their experience. We speak of this model of treatment today as if it had been implemented as a packaged formula, rather than as something that took more than a decade to formulate.[24]

Conceptualization of Alcoholism: Willmar staff first began to rethink the very nature of alcoholism. Dan Anderson describes this shift.

The only real clinical approach to alcoholism then was psychoanalysis—all that stuff about pre-genital oral fixations. Bradley and I were getting tired of psychoanalysis. It wasn't working for our alcoholic patents, and none of these patients could afford five years of intense psychotherapy. We realized that the primary condition we were treating was alcoholism—that all that alcoholic personality stuff was secondary. Through the influence of the A.A. members we were meeting, we developed the idea that alcoholism was multiply determined—that it had physical, psychological, social and spiritual dimensions. We decided we'd treat alcoholism by working on all of these areas, and that while working on all of those areas we would keep our focus on the addiction.[25]

They set about developing what was then a radical philosophy to guide their efforts. This philosophy recognized alcoholism, not as a symptom of underlying emotional problems, but as a primary, progressive disease. The philosophy shifted their focus from the etiology of the disease to a program of daily living that could produce sobriety. Dan Anderson described this philosophy as follows:

Our motto was: "Where it doesn't itch, don't scratch." We would deal directly with the addictive behavior. We would not look for other presumed underlying causes of the condition.[26]

Spirituality: What Bradley, Anderson and other key professional staff began to forge was a holistic approach that included—as a result of their A.A. tutelage—a deep respect for the power of spiritual experience as a driving force in alcoholism recovery. This was a bold and important move that went against mainstream psychiatric thinking in the 1950s. This openness to spirituality as a dimension of treatment was not something that the professional staff brought to Willmar. It was something that emerged out of their experience at Willmar.[27]

Multidisciplinary Team: Given the conceptualization of alcoholism as a multidimensional disorder, it made logical sense that treatment at Willmar had to be provided by a multidisciplinary team that represented diverse specialties. The interdisciplinary team created at Willmar was made up of physicians, nurses, psychologists, social workers, and clergy. The professional staff also decided that they needed counselors who were recovered alcoholics to work on this team. The team represented a fusion of medicine, clinical psychology, social work, and A.A. spirituality.

Recovered Alcoholics as Counselors: The first problem they encountered in including recovered alcoholics on the team was that there were no state job titles under which recovered alcoholics could be hired. They were first hired into "psychiatric aide" positions until 1954, when the Minnesota Civil Service Commission was finally persuaded to create a position —Counselor on Alcoholism—that allowed recovering alcoholics to be put on the payroll to work with alcoholics coming into treatment. Richeson reports that Governor Elmer Anderson was "laughed at" when he first asked for the creation of an "alcoholic counselor" position within the civil service system. The position required two years sobriety and a high school education.[28] Mel B. and Fred E. were the first two certified Counselors on Alcoholism in Minnesota.

Bradley effectively lobbied for salary levels that placed the recovered alcoholics at the same salary as a beginning social worker—a fact that triggered considerable resentment from the social workers. There was also resistance from the psychiatric aides and technicians, who perceived themselves as moving down the professional pecking order. The aides and technicians wondered how these people deserved such jobs. After all, they were just drunks![29] There was also some strain within the local A.A. community about Bradley's desire to hire recovered alcoholics. While they were delighted with the A.A. orientation that was developing within the Willmar program, many A.A. members were concerned that Bradley was asking A.A. members to do Twelfth-Step work for

pay. Several of the A.A. members corresponded with Bill Wilson about whether accepting such a position would violate any A.A. principles. Bill was generally supportive of members' accepting such roles.

Willmar pushed the earlier Hazelden and Pioneer House approaches to another level of development by placing these recovered alcoholics within a multi-disciplinary team. Dan Anderson later reflected on the challenge of integrating recovered alcoholics into Willmar's multidisciplinary treatment team.

Treatment is based on two kinds of knowing. You need the knowledge of science, but you also need the knowledge of wisdom and experience. The latter is where you get into the spiritual dimensions that recovered alcoholics bring to the mix. You have to mesh these two kinds of knowing together. The choices are a dynamic integration or a self-destructive polarization.[30]

The Employment of Recovered People in Professional Service Roles within Addiction Treatment

Something significant happened in Minnesota in 1954, and it was **not** simply the hiring of recovered alcoholics to carry the recovery message to other alcoholics. That had already been done. As we noted in earlier chapters, recovered alcoholics had worked as temperance organizers and as physicians, managers, and attendants within some of the 19th-century inebriate asylums and sanitaria. Recovered alcoholics like Courtenay Baylor and Richard Peabody had worked as lay therapists. During the 1940s, alcoholics—recovered and non-recovered—sometimes worked as "patient-employees" within state psychiatric hospitals.[31] All these preceded the events in Minnesota. Minnesota's innovation in the early 1950s—particularly the model at Willmar State Hospital—involved the following: 1) creating a means of preparing and credentialing (professionalizing) the recovered alcoholic to work in the field, 2) accepting the recovered counselor as a legitimate member of a multidisciplinary alcoholism treatment team, and 3) beginning the clarification of boundaries between a person's status and responsibilities as an A.A. member and his or her status and responsibilities as a professional alcoholism counselor.

Role of the Counselor: Each counselor was assigned three groups of ten alcoholic patients. These numbers slowly increased, and in the early 1960s, there were four counselors for the average population of 160 men.[32] The role of the alcoholism counselors at Willmar consisted primarily of serving as role models and teachers. For example, their primary focus in running groups was, not to do group therapy in the way psychiatrists and psychologists were being trained to do groups, but to facilitate group cohesion and sharing among patients on very specific aspects of the addiction and recovery experience. Counselors were encouraged to use their own self-disclosures as stimuli for such discussions. Topics were opened with, "This has been my experience related to this issue; How has your experience been similar or different?" Where psychoanalysis and psychotherapy had focused primarily upon the underlying inciting causes of alcoholism, the Willmar counselors focused on providing concrete guidance and support for the process of not drinking. What was infused into this counselor role was not psychology, but the core of A.A.'s philosophy of alcoholism recovery.

A.A. and Patient Volunteers: In addition to recovered alcoholics who worked as counselors, Willmar also involved A.A. volunteers in the treatment program and linked clients to A.A. as the primary means of continued support following discharge.

Another volunteer labor force at Willmar is worthy of mention. This force was made up of physicians and nurses who were sentenced to Willmar in lieu of losing their credentials or going to the narcotics hospital in Lexington, Kentucky. Most of the doctors who worked on the inebriate unit at Willmar were themselves there for treatment, and alcoholic R.N.s performed a wide variety of duties on the unit.[33]

Role of the Clergy: Willmar State Hospital, Pioneer House, and Hazelden all used clergy to assist alcoholic patients in taking A.A.'s Fifth Step. Willmar brought clergy into the interdisciplinary team as full-time, fully participating members.[34] Two clergy who played significant roles at Willmar were the Rev. John Keller and the Rev. Gordan Grimm. Both came to Willmar as part of their assignment from the American Lutheran Church. Keller describes how he was initially approached:

He [Fritz Norstad] said, "We have been looking around the country for a pastor to go full-time into specialized ministry in alcoholism and we think you are the guy." That statement made absolutely no sense.

My ministry in three congregations was marked by a lack of knowledge, no involvement with alcoholics, and total silence on alcoholism. The answer was "no."[35]

Keller finally agreed to a visit to Dr. Bradley at Willmar, and he walked out of Bradley's office agreeing to accept this mission. Norstad later explained that Keller had been chosen because he "had some rubber in him" and would be able to learn within the Willmar environment.[36] Grimm, for his part, accepted the job as full-time chaplain at Willmar after an internship that was part of his studies at the Lutheran Theological Seminary. His superiors chose him to go to Willmar because he had been open about his own father's struggle with alcoholism.

Unlocking the Doors: One of the most revolutionary steps Bradley and Anderson took at Willmar was to unlock the doors of the inebriety units. In spite of dire warning of the consequences, the doors were unlocked. The "escape rate" **dropped** from 22 % to 6 percent.

Treatment Modalities: The length of stay at Willmar during the early 1950s was 60 days. Dan Anderson reported that the hospital was often criticized for this length of stay on the grounds that no sustained therapeutic change could be accomplished in such a short time.[37] Treatment at Willmar focused on detoxification and education about alcoholism and an infusion of A.A. philosophy. Most of the treatment focused on one area: how to avoid the first drink. This message was conveyed in individual interviews with patients, in regular small-group discussions, and through a newly developing approach of teaching patients about their disorder.

Lectures: Two influences shaped the introduction of lectures at Willmar. The first was a series of articles by Ray McCarthy in the *Quarterly Journal of Alcohol Studies,* describing his use of lectures and discussions in group therapy with alcoholics. The second influence consisted of staff observation of the effects that A.A. speeches had on other alcoholics. McCarthy's lecture outlines were incorporated and later refined at Willmar. Anderson describes their process of learning that the lectures were having an impact.

We knew we were starting to get to people through the lectures. But the real test came with those relapsed clients who were returning for more treatment. Those alcoholics were so mad at us. They kept telling us, "You've ruined my drinking, so now you've

got to help me get something to replace it. "
We learned that with all the knowledge we
were giving them, they could no longer go
back and drink in the same little narrow
pattern they had before.[38]

What the recovered alcoholics first injected into these lectures was emotionally powerful but haphazardly organized. There was no consistent or formal presentation of the Steps of A.A.. Those counselors who worked the Steps tended to emphasize them; those who didn't work the steps tended to focus on other dimensions of A.A. and recovery. Each discipline, through trial and error, discovered the kinds of information that were most helpful in facilitating recovery. This openness to experimentation was essential to the discoveries that shaped the patient lecture series at Willmar. The series grew to 28 lectures on the physical and psychological progression of alcoholism and the process of recovery. It also conveyed an image of recovery that centered around the fellowship and Steps of A.A. A special series of five lectures was developed for female patients in 1959.[39]

A.A .Meetings: Willmar patients, in addition to being exposed to A.A.'s principles and practices through the recovered staff, were exposed to formal A.A. meetings. They were also expected to organize and manage their own A.A. meetings within the facility.

Motivation for Treatment: Nearly all of the professionally directed treatment programs that preceded Willmar explicitly noted the role that motivation played in alcoholism recovery. These programs emphasized that a motivation for sobriety was essential to recovery and sought to admit only those patients who could demonstrate such motivation. Bradley and his team discovered something that challenged this conventional wisdom. They discovered that the clients who were admitted under extreme duress and coercion did as well as those who presented themselves as "voluntary." What they discovered at Willmar was a principle that would have a great influence on the continued evolution of the Minnesota Model: a client's motivation or lack of motivation at intake was not a significant predictor of treatment outcome. They discovered that motivation for sobriety was something that emerged out of the treatment experience, not something to be set as a precondition for admission. They further discovered that what they had earlier perceived as motivation in a new voluntary patient often turned out to be superficial compliance.

Chemical Dependency: Because there were no specialty drug-addiction units in Minnesota in the 1950s, narcotic addicts were also being sent to Willmar and treated alongside alcoholics. As the pattern of cross-addiction and multiple drug use among these alcoholics and addicts became clear, the term *chemical dependency* was introduced to encompass this abuse of, and vulnerability to, multiple substances.

Reported Treatment Outcomes: The early recovery rate for alcoholics treated at Willmar was around 30%—a rate that improved as the population treated shifted from the skid-row alcoholic to the working class alcoholic. Jean Rossi, Alex Stach, and Dr. Nelson Bradley conducted an outcome study (published in 1963) of 208 alcoholics who had completed alcoholism treatment at Willmar. Thirty-two percent of Willmar graduates had achieved at least six months' abstinence, and 24% were rated as "improved" at follow-up. Thirty percent of graduates were drinking at follow-up, but drinking with "mild effects." (A one-year follow-up revealed that only 1 of the 45 men in the group had sustained this moderated drinking pattern.) Factors associated with positive treatment outcome were treatment intensity (measured by the number of days in the hospital) and participation in self-help groups following hospitalization.[40]

Aftercare: As aftercare became recognized as an extremely important part of treatment, Bradley asked Dan Anderson and Lucille Poor to organize a follow-up clinic to provide continuing care for discharged patients. Mel B. also provided a specialized follow-up service. He traveled the whole state, visiting alcoholics who had been through treatment at Willmar, and helped them link up with A.A. members in their areas.

Scattering of the Original Team: The early team that pioneered a new approach to alcoholism treatment at Willmar State Hospital stayed relatively intact through most of the 1950s. Three key figures at Willmar—Bradley, Rossi, and Anderson—took periods of respite to return to school and then go back to Willmar. In 1960, Bradley left to direct the alcoholism program at Lutheran General Hospital in Illinois. The impetus for this change was reportedly Bradley's chagrin that the state legislature in Minnesota was not providing sufficient support for alcoholism services. Rossi and Keller followed Bradley to Lutheran General Hospital. Dan Anderson—also ready for a new professional challenge—accepted a position at what at the time he thought would be a smaller and quieter place. He accepted the role of Vice President and Chief Executive Officer at Hazelden.

What had been created at Willmar was the modern multidisciplinary model for the treatment of alcoholism. In the 1960s, the institution that would best represent this model shifted from Willmar to Hazelden.

Hazelden: The Continuing Story

Because the ongoing events at Hazelden would play such an important role in defining the "Minnesota Model" of chemical dependency treatment—and in diffusing it throughout the United States and beyond—we will extend the Hazelden story into events that unfolded between 1960 and 1998.

Pat Butler had a vision for Hazelden—a vision of Hazelden as a model of alcoholism treatment that could be emulated and replicated around the country. But Hazelden first had to achieve that level of excellence. Butler had regularly visited Bradley at Willmar State Hospital and had carefully watched the changes implemented under Bradley's leadership. In the hopes of integrating the best of Willmar and the best of Hazelden, Butler recruited Dan Anderson to take over the leadership of Hazelden in 1961.

By 1964, the patient census on the main campus ran between 40 and 50 patients. Hazelden was busting at the seams. New units were planned that could carry Hazelden into the future. The first 22-bed unit, known today as Silkworth Hall, opened at the close of 1965. Other units followed, creating a campus whose buildings bore the names of well known contributors to the alcoholism field (Silkworth, Tiebout, Shoemaker, Ignatia) and names of people who played a significant role in Hazelden's history (Lilly). Other changes also occurred at the treatment center in the 1960s. A series of expansions and renovations at Dia Linn brought its capacity to 23 patients, and alumnae meetings brought as many as 50 former patients to Dia Linn on Friday afternoons. Dia Linn moved to Hazelden's main campus in Center City in 1966, but women continued to be segregated from men during the course of their treatment.[41] Treatment stays for all Hazelden patients were lengthened from three weeks to four weeks. Beneath the growth of this period is the story of a conflict whose resolution greatly influenced the evolution of the Minnesota Model.

A Period of Conflict: There was a strange synergy between Willmar and Hazelden. Hazelden significantly influenced the early development of the Willmar State Hospital Alcoholism Program, but the further innovations made at Willmar were in turn brought to Hazelden when Anderson was hired as Hazelden's Vice President and CEO in 1961. Consid-

erable tension surrounded Anderson's efforts to move Hazelden toward a professionalized, multidisciplinary model of treatment. The tension around these changes focused on a struggle between the recovered counselors and the new professionals coming to Hazelden. The conflict was most deeply personalized in the relationship between Dan Anderson and Lynn C.

Lynn C. was a lawyer whose alcoholism had destroyed his legal practice and taken him to the psychiatric ward of General Hospital in Minneapolis. He sought help from A.A. when he left the hospital, then went on to a distinguished career working with alcoholics. For years Lynn lived at Hazelden, serving as its only full-time counselor. He advocated the unadulterated application of A.A. principles in the treatment of alcoholism. He viewed the Step lectures that he had pioneered at Hazelden as the essential core of alcoholism treatment. He believed that the professionalization of treatment at Hazelden threatened the purity of the A.A. approach to recovery, and he resisted the integration of professional members and the ideas they brought. Tension between the old and new schools at Hazelden continued and escalated, resulting in Lynn C.'s departure from Hazelden in 1966.

Lynn C.'s exit confirmed the evolution of Hazelden's treatment regimen from "pure A.A." to one that integrated multiple disciplines and multiple treatment modalities, still bound together within an A.A.-oriented treatment philosophy. Out of this philosophical struggle in the early 1960s, treatment at Hazelden synthesized elements of the early Pioneer House and Hazelden experiences, many elements of the Willmar State Hospital design, and innovations that had not existed in any of these institutions. With Bradley, Anderson, Rossi, Grimm, and Keller all gone from Willmar, Hazelden became the institution most clearly responsible for carrying forward the Minnesota Model of chemical dependency treatment.

The purpose of this chapter is not to tell the complete story of Hazelden—a feat that has already been well accomplished by Damian McElrath—but to describe Hazelden's role in the creation and evolution of the Minnesota Model. While our resulting emphasis is on Hazelden's early history, it is important to add a brief postscript to this story. Hazelden's growth and continued success since the mid-1960s is part of the story of the successful spread of the Minnesota Model.

Chuck Crewe described Hazelden's milieu in 1968 as "Grand Central Station at Rush Hour." This characterization reflected the growing number of patients (1,420 in 1968), the growing number of staff

(165), and the daily deluge of professional visitors wanting to study Hazelden's treatment methods.[42] Daily patient census at Hazelden jumped from 45 in 1965 to 170 in 1975. In 1997, Hazelden facilities in Minnesota, Florida, Illinois and New York had a total daily residential capacity of 466 clients.

Major milestones since 1965 have included the initiation of the Pastoral Training Program by the Reverend Gordan Grimm (1965), the relocation of Dia Linn to Hazelden's Center City campus (1966), the initiation of Hazelden's counselor-training program by Eugene Wojtowicz (1966), the development of a special program for relapsed patients (1967), the opening of an extended-care program for clients needing more treatment time (1967), the initiation of Hazelden's three-day residential Family Program (1972), the initiation of Hazelden education and training services, the purchase of Pioneer House (1981), the initiation of prevention programs (1981), the opening of the Renewal Center (1984), the opening of the Hanley-Hazelden treatment facility in Palm Beach, Florida (1986) in cooperation with St. Mary's Hospital, the opening of the Fellowship Club (a halfway house) in New York (1991), and the opening of a Hazelden treatment facility in Chicago.

Through the 1970s and 1980s, Hazelden made many refinements in its approach to chemical dependency treatment. Greater emphasis was placed on the entire treatment community, in the belief that the essence of treatment was participation in a caring community, rather than something a counselor did to a client. The treatment day continued to consist of lectures, groups, individual interviews, films, readings, and informal discussions among patients. All these activities were integrated within a comprehensive rehabilitation plan developed for each patient. A new practice that evolved in the early 1970s was a confrontation technique known as the "hot seat." During this technique, a patient 10 to 14 days into his or her treatment was evaluated by the group in terms of positive and negative personality characteristics. Former patients often described this as one of their more memorable treatment experiences. An increased emphasis on involving the family in the treatment process also emerged during this period.

Hazelden also began to evaluate its treatment services formally in the 1970s.[43] Dan Anderson later summarized these studies by noting that, of the 85% of clients who completed treatment in Minnesota, 60-70% showed good-to-excellent recovery at two years following treatment. He believed that alcoholics treated within the Minnesota Model achieved an overall recovery rate of 55%—a figure he characterized as "deliberately conservative."[44]

In closing this brief synopsis of Hazelden, we would be remiss if we did not mention Hazelden's publishing activities and the role of these activities in spreading the Minnesota Model. In 1954, Pat Butler heard about a little book called *Twenty-Four Hours a Day*, written by an A.A. member in Florida. Pat contacted the author and arranged for Hazelden to publish the book, which over the past 43 years has sold more than seven million copies and continues to sell between 150,000 and 200,000 copies per year. *Twenty-Four Hours a Day* marked the beginning of Hazelden's entry into publishing books and other educational materials related to addiction recovery. From this auspicious beginning, Hazelden went on to become the largest publisher of self-help books and pamphlets in the world. In 1986, more than 12 million mailings were sent from Hazelden Publishing. Hazelden literature served as the primary vehicle through which the Minnesota Model of chemical dependency treatment was promoted throughout the world.

Further Minnesota Developments

The birth of the Minnesota Model did not stop with Pioneer House, Willmar State Hospital, and Hazelden. The 1960s also saw a significant expansion in hospital- and community-based treatment of alcoholism. Many programs influenced the continued evolution of Minnesota's approach to addiction treatment. St. Mary's and Northwestern Hospitals in Minneapolis and St. Luke's Hospital in St. Paul set the early model for alcoholism treatment units within general hospitals, even though during the early years some subterfuge (diagnoses of "nervous exhaustion") was used to facilitate such treatment.[45]

Minnesota was also at the center of the halfway-house movement of the late 1950s and 1960s. Early Minnesota pioneers in providing halfway services to alcoholics included Fellowship House, Nuway Houses, 180 Degrees, Freedom House, Progress Valley, Hope Haven, and the Howard H. Friese Memorial Halfway House. Granville House, Wayside House, and the Marty Mann Halfway House were early pioneers in offering halfway-house services to alcoholic women. These facilities established the halfway house as an integral part of the continuum of care within the Minnesota Model of chemical dependency treatment.

Other institutions such as the Johnson Institute, which played a significant role in the later evolution and dissemination of the Minnesota Model, are noted in later chapters.

Defining the Minnesota Model

The birth of the Minnesota Model of chemical dependency treatment can be traced first to the arrival and spread of Alcoholics Anonymous across Minnesota in the 1940s, then to three different treatment sites in Minnesota: Pioneer House, Willmar State Hospital, and Hazelden.

The philosophy of treatment that emerged and evolved within these three sites included the following 11 tenets:

1) Alcoholism is an involuntary, primary disease that is describable and diagnosable.
2) Alcoholism is a chronic and progressive disease; Barring intervention, the signs and symptoms of alcoholism self-accelerate.
3) Alcoholism is not curable, but the disease may be arrested.
4) The nature of the alcoholic's initial motivation for treatment—its presence or absence—is not a predictor of treatment outcome.
5) The treatment of alcoholism includes physical, psychological, social, and spiritual dimensions.
6) The successful treatment of alcoholism requires an environment in which the alcoholic is treated with dignity and respect.
7) Alcoholics and addicts are vulnerable to the abuse of a wide spectrum of mood-altering drugs. This whole cluster of mood-altering drugs can be addressed through treatment that defines the problem as one of *chemical dependency*.
8) Chemical dependency is best treated by a multidiscplinary team whose members develop close, less-formal relationships with their clients and whose activities are integrated within an individualized treatment plan developed for each client.
9) The focal point for implementing the treatment plan is an assigned primary counselor, usually recovered, of the same sex and age group as the client, who promotes an atmosphere that enhances emotional self-disclosure, mutual identification, and mutual support.
10) The most effective treatment for alcoholism includes an orientation to A.A., an expectation of "Step work," groups that combine confrontation and support, lectures, one-to-one counseling, and the creation of a dynamic "learning environment."
11) The most viable, ongoing, sobriety-based support structure for clients following treatment is A.A.[46]

While many of the above tenets mark a dramatic change in the conception and treatment of alcoholism, one is of particular historic note. An implicit element of the Minnesota Model is a treatment milieu within which the primary characteristic of the service relationship is one of respect. Jerry Spicer, who traced the emergence of these ideas in his book *The Minnesota Model*, rightly notes the importance of seeing this element within the historical context of the 1940s and 1950s. The Minnesota Model represented a radical shift from the prevailing view that alcoholism was both a hopeless condition and a reflection of moral inferiority. The Minnesota Model provided a marked contrast to the "degradation rituals" that alcoholics were subjected to within the psychiatric asylums of the mid-20th century and the mutual contempt that had long marked the relationship between alcoholics and professional helpers.[47]

While criticism later emerged regarding the rigidity of the Minnesota Model, during its early history the model was quite flexible and dynamic. The emphasis during this period was on the practical —a focus on discovering what approach would work with each client. Just as the program of A.A. was articulated in retrospect after it had been practiced for several years, the tenets of the Minnesota Model were similarly defined in retrospect. In the beginning, little time was spent on theory-building. The focus was placed on what was needed each day to move each client into an active recovery process. It was only when that question had been answered for hundreds of alcoholics that a model began to reveal itself.

Other programs also treated alcoholics across the country, but three institutions and a handful of people —all in Minnesota—played pivotal roles in the emergence of a model of alcoholism treatment that would first influence, then dominate, the treatment industry for the next 40 years.

Why Minnesota?

In reviewing this chapter, one is forced to ponder the inevitable question, "Why Minnesota?" What conditions existed at that time and in that place that contributed to the development of this unique model of alcoholism treatment? Dan Anderson attributed the birth of this model of treatment in part to the Scandinavian tradition of concern and innovation in the areas of education and social welfare issues.[48] Jerry Spicer, the current President of Hazelden, concurred with this cultural influence, but also noted other influences of time and place.

There was perhaps the serendipity of leadership—social entrepreneurs who brought great ideological or personal passion to the issue of alcoholism. I think you had a critical mass in the growth of Alcoholics Anonymous in the Midwest that created a medium within which a new approach to alcoholism treatment could flourish. There were key figures like Pat Butler, who spent time in Cleveland and New York, and who had a broad perspective of what was going on around the country. Those factors—plus the unique community-oriented culture within Minnesota and a general climate of social reform—all contributed to the rise of the Minnesota Model.[49]

Several people have noted the role that key individuals—"free spirits, gadflies, entrepreneurs"—played in launching the Minnesota Model.[50] Dan Anderson reflected on how this innovation emerged:

We could go against traditional models of thinking because we were on the fringe. Bradley could challenge mainstream thinking in psychiatry because at this point he wasn't a psychiatrist. It wasn't until 1956 and 1957 that we both went back to get our advanced education. Most of the innovations at Willmar occurred BEFORE we had those professional credentials.[51]

Bradley definitely broke the mold for psychiatrists. Gordy Grimm describes the reaction of clergy to Bradley.

I'll never forget that he was ambidextrous. When he'd lecture, he could draw with either hand. I remember one lecture he did for clergy. He would start by drawing on the board at the same time with both hands. It looked like he was doodling. Then he would turn, and say, "Well that's what I think most people in society think of alcoholics. And people would see that what he had drawn was a horse's ass. I'd have those clergy ask me, "Is that cuckoo for real?" What he brought was just so different than what people expected from a psychiatrist. Bradley was a brilliant innovator who never got the credit he deserved.[52]

The Spread of the Minnesota Model [53]

The Minnesota Model of chemical dependency treatment spread from Pioneer House, Hazelden, and Willmar State Hospital to other Minnesota sites, with many programs adding innovations to the model.

The growth of chemical dependency treatment programs in Minnesota was prolific. By 1977, 114 separate agencies provided alcohol information and referral that fed the state's 44 treatment centers and 54 halfway-house facilities.[54]

There were seven primary mechanisms for the diffusion of the Minnesota Model: 1) the A.A. network; 2) professional conferences, particularly the Yale-Rutgers Summer Schools; 3) the educational campaign of the National Council on Alcoholism; 4) former clients; 5) internship and training programs; 6) visitors to Willmar and Hazelden; and 7) former staff of Willmar and Hazelden.

Long before the Minnesota Model was recognized in professional circles, word of this new approach to alcoholism treatment was spreading through the informal A.A. communication networks around the country. It was doing so because the hiring of A.A. members as counselors within this model was a subject of great interest and considerable controversy within A.A. As A.A. members were pulled onto advisory committees and planning groups to launch new alcoholism treatment efforts, they steered these committees toward Minnesota as a point of initial investigation.

The second mechanism of diffusion of the Minnesota Model was through professional conferences. Lynn C., Dan Anderson, and John Keller spent considerable time traveling the alcoholism conference circuit, informing the field about this new model of treatment. Dan Anderson taught at Yale and then Rutgers from 1960 well into the 1990s, and Keller also served on the Yale-Rutgers faculty. People from all over the U.S. and beyond were exposed to the Minnesota Model as THE model of alcoholism treatment. These students formed personal relationships with Anderson and other key Minnesota Model advocates and brought these individuals into their own communities as consultants and trainers.

As National Council on Alcoholism chapters spread across the U.S., they also held up the Minnesota Model as a treatment approach that could be emulated by local communities. Pat Butler played a critical role in these methods of diffusion. He personally paid for Bradley's and Anderson's attendance at Yale, and he brought such people as Marty Mann, Selden Bacon, and Ray McCarthy in to give workshops in Minnesota. The interconnections among

Minnesota, Yale, Rutgers, and NCA were to a great extent the behind-the-scenes work of Pat Butler.

A hidden source of diffusion of the Minnesota Model was the growing number of clients who had gone through treatment in Minnesota programs. Given the sparsity of treatment before 1970, alcoholics from all over the U.S. made the sojourn to Minnesota for treatment. Many of these sober and grateful alcoholics joined local alcoholism advisory groups, and some became alcoholism counselors. All pointed to Minnesota as the fountain of knowledge on alcoholism treatment. The extent and power of this influence is noted in the growth of Hazelden's alumni association, which by 1986 had more than 5,000 members who were responsible for referring 60% of the new clients entering treatment at Hazelden.

The training programs launched at Willmar State Hospital and Hazelden also served to spread the Minnesota Model. As graduates of these programs assumed professional positions around the country, they brought with them the unique model of treatment practiced at Willmar and Hazelden. Hazelden staff were also being called upon to serve as consultants in establishing new alcoholism treatment programs around the country. When these demands became excessive, Hazelden increasingly relied upon converting such requests into invitations to visit Hazelden.

Professionals visited Willmar and Hazelden in great numbers. In 1960, Rossi and Bradley reported that professionals from 26 states, five Canadian provinces, and four European countries had visited Willmar to study the treatment methods used there.[55] An alcoholism treatment professional described his visit to Hazelden during this period as follows:

> I traveled to Hazelden in the early 1970s like a pilgrim going to Mecca. There I met Dan Anderson and Gordy Grimm and Harry Swift and absorbed everything I could about how they thought about alcoholism and how they treated alcoholism. Then, like thousands of others, I went back and replicated as close as I could what I'd seen and learned. The model got passed, not only because of Hazelden's reputation, but because of the infectious enthusiasm that permeated the place. There was no concern about giving away proprietary secrets: everything they had was yours for the asking. What you caught was the sense of being part of a social movement to spread alcoholism treatment. The movement was more important at that time than our indi-
> vidual institutional identities or interests.[56]

A final method of dissemination of the Minnesota Model involved the staff who worked at Willmar and Hazelden. Just as Willmar's multidisciplinary model had moved to Hazelden with Dan Anderson, the Minnesota Model was carried to remote outposts every time a trainee, intern, or staff member took a job in another program. Nelson Bradley, Jean Rossi, and John Keller took the Minnesota Model from Willmar State Hospital to Lutheran General Hospital, which eventually became Parkside Medical Services. Many generations of staff who worked at Hazelden went on to spread around the country all they had learned at Hazelden. Former staff spread Hazelden's treatment technology and continued to refer clients to Hazelden from their new locations.

During the rapid proliferation of treatment programs in the 1970s and 1980s, program staff were following the Minnesota Model who hadn't even heard of it. This happened through a long and rapid series of model replications, adaptations, and corruptions, in which the source of the original model was lost. It is hard to imagine how many people and institutions around the country took credit for innovations that had their origin in Minnesota. In a like manner, there may have been elements of the Minnesota Model whose sources could be traced to other people and institutions whose identities have been lost to history. The testament to the model's reach was its unconscious replication.

Further Contributions of the Minnesota Model

In addition to providing a replicable model of alcoholism treatment, the Minnesota Model legitimized the involvement of professional disciplines in the treatment of alcoholism. It not only reduced the contempt with which alcoholics had been viewed by professionals, but it also reduced the contempt with which professionals who chose to work with alcoholics and addicts had been viewed. Many of the most notable figures who pioneered the Minnesota Model began working with alcoholics at a time when no one else in their professions wanted to work with them. As Anderson notes of the professional climate of this period: "No self-respecting professional in their right mind wanted to work with alcoholics."[57] By the time these same figures ended their careers, work with alcoholics had become a legitimate professional specialty in psychiatry, psychology, social work, and counseling. The Minnesota Model contributed greatly to that achievement.

In 1915, Abraham Flexner defined the essential elements of a professional discipline. One of those elements was the possession of an "educationally communicable technique." The Minnesota Model not only conceptualized the role of the alcoholism counselor, but also provided within that role a body of knowledge and techniques that could be transmitted to those entering that new profession. This model provided a vehicle through which the earlier role of lay therapist could be mass-produced within the role of the alcoholism counselor.[58]

The Minnesota Model also represented a technical advancement. It provided a technology to integrate the philosophy of A.A. within a professionally directed regimen of alcoholism treatment. It introduced the application of spirituality into professional counseling. It added professional legitimacy to the premise that insight into the idiosyncratic cause of one's alcoholism was not an essential or even a helpful aspect of recovery from alcoholism. The Minnesota Model's concept of chemical dependency offered a framework that built a bridge between what had been separate worlds of alcoholism treatment and drug-addiction treatment. It provided a psychoeducational model for intervening in alcoholism and other behavioral-health disorders, with what was primarily an educational technology. The most significant contribution of the Minnesota Model to the treatment of alcoholism was that it provided a treatment scheme that focused on arresting alcoholism, rather than simply treating the medical, psychological, interpersonal, and financial consequences of alcoholism. The model's development was also well timed. It provided a model of community-oriented brief therapy—just as the backlash against custodial treatment in state psychiatric hospitals began the movement to "de-institutionalize" the treatment of psychiatric illness.

There is little question that the Minnesota Model made many specific contributions to the treatment of alcoholism. However, there is perhaps a broader contribution of the model that even transcends this special application. In reflecting on a career working within this model, Dan Anderson noted the following:

The most significant contribution of the Minnesota Model is that it affords a model of addressing chronic disease. That contribution carries far beyond what the model has meant to alcoholics. In the midst of all our acute-care interventions, the Minnesota Model provides a way to manage chronic diseases that have multiple etiological roots, multiple dimensions in their symptomatology, and which are characterized by episodes of remission and relapse. The model has the capacity to look at the whole person—and the whole person over time. The greatest health-care threat is the management of chronic illness, and the Minnesota Model offers a framework for managing such conditions. That, in the end, will likely be its greatest legacy.[59]

In evaluating the legacy of the Minnesota Model of chemical-dependency treatment, it is hard to separate the ideas and the methods from the people who helped introduce them and the impact these people had on the field of addiction treatment. Dr. Nelson Bradley and Dan Anderson clearly rank among the pioneers of 20th-century alcoholism treatment. Many other figures in the early development of the Minnesota Model, such as Jean Rossi, John Keller, and Gordan Grimm—to name only a few—went on to distinguished careers of service within the alcoholism treatment field. Many people working in the field today see themselves as carrying forth in the tradition of these pioneers.

While the Minnesota Model was germinating and evolving, many events were unfolding in the mid-century world of addiction treatment. In the next two chapters, we will find out what was going on in the rest of the country while this model was emerging.

Chapter Twenty-Two
Mid-Century Alcoholism Treatments

In the past few chapters, we have reviewed the rise of A.A. and a modern alcoholism movement that generated new alcoholism treatment initiatives across the United States. This chapter will outline the state of alcoholism treatment between 1945 and 1960. We will review alcoholism-related organizational activity during this period and the emergence of key concepts that influenced the treatment of alcoholism, and provide an overview of the types of organizational settings in which alcoholics were treated. We will also update the continued evolution of alcoholic mutual-aid societies and the rise of support structures for families of alcoholics.

Organizational Activity in the Alcoholism Field: 1950-1960

The state-sponsored alcoholism initiatives spawned by the modern alcoholism movement continued to be highly unstable during the 1950s. The only significant federal initiative was the 1956 modification of the Vocational Rehabilitation Act to render those suffering from alcoholism eligible for federally funded vocational rehabilitation services.[60] But there was a frenzy of grassroots activity at the local and state levels, which was triggering new local alcoholism treatment efforts and generating increased public interest in the subject of alcoholism. Every year, local alcoholism advocates were trained at Yale and returned to communities all across the country with new knowledge, organizational skills, and renewed motivation. Similarly, growing numbers of local National Committee for Education on Alcoholism (NCEA) affiliates were educating the public about alcoholism and nurturing local experiments with alcoholism treatment. There was also a growing cadre of professionals turning their skills toward the subject of alcoholism and a growing army of sober A.A. members exerting their own private influence upon the cultural perception of alcoholism and alcoholics. While treatment resources remained scant in many communities, attitudes were shifting in the opening years of the 1950s. By 1955, 38 states had officially recognized alcoholism as a public health problem. The decade of the 1950s generated new ideas about alcoholism, local treatment experiments, and an expanded network of mutual-aid resources for alcoholics and their families.

Expanding Knowledge and Ideas About Alcoholism

With Yale and NCEA acting as the fulcrum, the cultural perception of alcoholics was slowly changing, as was the professional understanding of alcoholism. During the 1940s and 1950s, Yale established a baseline of knowledge on alcoholism, which it disseminated through the *Quarterly Journal of Studies on Alcohol* and through its Summer School of Alcohol Studies. Yale was at the center of this new scientific approach to alcohol-related problems. Beginning with sweeping reviews of the alcoholism literature by Karl Bowman and E.M. Jellinek, activities at Yale stirred

discussions about alcoholism in professional and public arenas. The growing involvement of states in the problem of alcoholism also heightened these discussions. As early as 1952, newly created state alcoholism authorities were developing and distributing such publications as *Alcoholism—A Treatment Digest for Physicians* (New Jersey), *The Connecticut Review on Alcoholism*, *The Louisiana Bulletin on Alcoholism*, and the *Utah Alcoholism Review*.[61] In their study of alcoholism treatment literature between 1949 and 1972, Norman Giesbrecht and Kai Pernanen noted a virtual explosion of articles about alcoholism that took place between 1950 and 1954. It was as if, after a decade of sustained effort, the alcoholism movement had reached critical mass.[62]

In the 1940s and early 1950s, the most significant concentration of clinical discussion focused on questions of the etiology and proper classification of different patterns of alcohol-related pathology. Bowman and Jellinek catalogued the alcohol-related psychoses: pathological intoxication, delirium tremens, alcoholic melancholia, alcoholic paranoia, alcoholic hallucinosis, and Korsakoff's psychosis.[63] Then Jellinek, in a long series of contributions, pushed forward a series of classification systems that identified clinical subgroups within the total population experiencing alcohol-related problems. The assumption underlying this work was that a better scheme of classification would enhance diagnosis and the individualized treatment of alcoholism.

The reader will recall that the idea of multiple subpopulations of alcoholics and addicts dates to the earliest days of the inebriate asylum, and references to "species of inebriety" arose at least as early as 1909.[64] However, in the decades preceding Jellinek's work, alcoholism classification systems were reduced to broad generalizations. Robert Fleming, for example, suggested in 1937 that there were only two fundamental types of excessive drinking. The first, which he called *symptomatic drinking*, sprang from underlying physical or mental pathology and was directed toward the goal of alleviating the uncomfortable symptoms of such pathology. The second type, which Fleming called *true alcohol addiction*, was incited by a specific craving and was characterized by physical addiction. Fleming believed the latter should be viewed "as a disease, a separate clinical entity."[65]

Jellinek's first classification system derived from a sweeping review of the alcoholism literature and depicted fourteen overlapping "classes" of excessive drinkers.

Jellinek's 1942 Drinker Classification System

Drinking Class	Brief Description
True Addicts	People for whom alcohol has become a true need: includes the decadent, discordant, compensating, and poverty drinkers described below
Decadent Drinker	Drinking as a reflection of sensory excess and deficient moral discipline
Discordant Drinker	Schizoid personality who seeks relief through drinking
Compensating Drinker	People seeking to compensate for feelings of inferiority through drinking and self-aggrandizement
Poverty Drinker	Drinking to relieve misery from external conditions
Symptomatic Schizoid Drinker	Drinking as a vehicle to break out of social isolation
Early General Paresis	Drinking as an expression of grandiose personality
Manic-Depressive Drinking	Mania- and depression-fueled excessive drinking
Epileptic and Epileptoid Drinkers	Periodic binging by epileptics to counter dysphoria
True Dipsomania	People for whom an insatiable appetite for intoxicants results from neurological or biochemical causes
The Stupid Drinker	Drinking in the feeble-minded
The Stammtisch Drinker	Excessive drinking rooted in regular gregarious social interchanges

Occupational Drinker	Regular drinking as a function of one's occupational climate
Exuberant Drinker	Excessive drinking on special occasions as a sign of immaturity

Jellinek's continuing work stimulated much discussion and led others to propose their own classification systems. In 1960, Jellinek's *The Disease Concept of Alcoholism* described five major "species" of alcoholism, each of which he named after a letter from the Greek alphabet.

Jellinek's Species of Alcoholism

Alpha Alcoholism	Psychological dependence upon alcohol to relieve physical and/or emotional pain. Can develop into Gamma pattern, but generally exhibits no progression. No physical addiction.
Beta Alcoholism	Alcohol-related medical complications without physical or psychological addiction. Heavy-drinking cultural norms and poor nutrition.
Gamma Alcoholism	Psychological dependence upon alcohol which progresses to physical addiction. Characterized by loss of control and severe disruption of health and of occupational and interpersonal functioning. Dominant pattern of alcoholism in the U.S.
Delta Alcoholism	Steady, high-volume alcohol consumption which results in physical addiction. Inability to abstain from drinking but no evidence of loss of control.
Epsilon Alcoholism	Periodic bouts of explosive drinking interspersed with periods of sobriety.

Jellinek believed that only two of the five patterns—gamma and delta—qualified to be designated as diseases, because both involved addiction in the pharmacological and physiological sense. Much of the subtlety of Jellinek's work was lost in the years following publication of his landmark work. His notion of "alcoholisms," in particular, was reduced to an homogenous portrayal of alcoholism as one disorder—what Jellinek had called gamma-species alcoholism. *The Disease Concept of Alcoholism* remains one of the most frequently cited and least read books in the alcoholism field.

Changing Views of the Alcoholic: As a result of the alcoholic's placement under a clinical microscope in the 1950s, a profound shift began to occur in the image of the American alcoholic. The profile of the alcoholic emerging from alcoholism wards in hospitals, from the more than 100 Yale-type outpatient alcoholism clinics, and from the growing number of residential alcoholism programs suggested that America's view of the alcoholic was an extreme distortion. This traditional image depicted the (typically male) alcoholic as unmarried or estranged from wife, family, and stable friends. This image further portrayed the alcoholic as unemployed or at least occupationally unstable, in a state of extreme physical and moral degeneration, and moving toward—if not already on—one of America's Skid Rows.

Experience was confirming that this caricature accurately depicted only the smallest percentage of alcoholics in the latest stages of alcoholism. As treatment resources expanded, a much different profile emerged. Studies at the Yale clinics revealed that a majority of their alcoholic clients were married and living with their families. A 1947 study by Malzburg noted a sizable portion of alcoholics who exhibited a high degree of social and occupational stability. Wellman, Maxwell, and O'Hallaren conducted a study of more than 2,000 alcoholic patients who had been treated for alcoholism at the Shadel Hospital in Seattle between 1946 and 1954. They found that 75 % of the patients were living with their spouses and that the majority were still stable in their occupations.[66]

These studies confirmed that, during the early and middle stages of this disorder, the alcoholic looked remarkably like his or her non-alcoholic neighbors. Quite prophetically, Wellman, Maxwell, and O'Hallaren suggested that, if the majority of alcoholics were actually hidden within the culture, the entire focus of the alcoholism effort would have to be redirected toward efforts to intervene in the progression of alcoholism at the earliest possible point. They believed this could be achieved through educational efforts aimed at early-stage alcoholics and their families, and at parallel educational efforts with physicians, clergy, social workers, and educators. They further called for research that would reveal a much clearer picture of the earliest stages and symptoms of alcoholism, so that the prevailing conception of the typical alcoholic could be radically redefined.[67]

As the world of alcoholism treatment began to change, primarily through the continued growth of A.A. and the spread of the Minnesota Model of treatment, America's conception of alcoholism and of the people who were vulnerable to this disorder also changed. This change occurred in a remarkably short period of time. Within 20 years of Wellman's, Maxwell's, and O'Hallaren's proclamation of our need to redefine our cultural conception of the alcoholic, prominent alcoholics from all walks of life filled television screens and newspapers, boldly proclaiming their recovery from alcoholism. The changes that made those television images possible began in the 1940s and 1950s.

Changing Views of the Alcoholic Family: There was also renewed interest in the alcoholic family at mid-century, with a particular focus on the perceived pathology of the alcoholic's spouse. Dr. Merrill Moore and Mildred Gray, describing their work with alcoholics at Boston City Hospital, wrote of the need to educate the alcoholic's family and noted that "Often the person with the greatest need of psychiatric treatment is the marital partner who has *not* become alcoholic."[68] Alcoholics' wives were increasingly depicted as having chosen alcoholics in order to meet their own dependency needs. Two separately authored articles that appeared in the *Quarterly Journal of Studies on Alcohol* in 1953 illustrate this view.

In the first article, Samuel Futterman described the prototypical wife of an alcoholic as an inadequate woman who gains ego strength only in relationship to her husband's weakness. Futterman accused the alcoholic's wife of maintaining her "illusion of indispensability" at her husband's expense by inciting his drinking episodes. He noted that it was only through such behavior that the wife could escape the depression she experienced during the periods in which her husband was sober and adequately functioning.[69] In the second article, Thelma Whalen described the wives of alcoholics she counseled at a family service agency in Dallas, Texas. She mirrored Futterman's view that "the wife of the alcoholic has as poorly integrated a personality as her husband" and that the wife, as surely as the alcoholic, was responsible for creating the marriage and the "sordid sequence of marital misery" that followed. Whalen described alcoholics' wives as falling into one of four styles: 1) Suffering Susan, whose marriage and loyalty to the alcoholic was related to her need for self-punishment, 2) Controlling Catherine, who chose the alcoholic because of his inferiority and her own need to dominate, 3) Wavering Winnifred, who stayed with her alcoholic husband out of her need to be needed, and 4) Punishing Polly, whose relationship with her alcoholic husband was comparable to that of a "boa constrictor to a rabbit."[70] The general profile of the alcoholic wife depicted in this early literature was that of a woman who was neurotic, sexually repressed, dependent, man-hating, domineering, mothering, guilty and masochistic, and/or hostile and nagging.[71] The typical therapist's view of the wife of the alcoholic was generally one of, "I'd drink, too, if I were married to her."[72]

A second wave of studies began to shift from a focus on the alcoholic and the alcoholic's spouse as individuals to a focus on the alcoholic couple as a dynamic system. Of particular interest was the process through which the male alcoholic and his wife struck an "interpersonal bargain" to have their personal needs met and maintain some degree of balance in the marital relationship, all in the face of alcohol's assault on the marital relationship. Pioneering this emerging view was Joan Jackson and her seminal 1954 article, "The Adjustment of the Family to the Crisis of Alcoholism."[73] Jackson's sustained contributions focused on the ways in which alcoholism insulted the otherwise-healthy family as a whole and undermined the health of each individual family member.[74] While both views acknowledged the disruption in health of members within the alcoholic family system, there were marked differences as to whether this perceived pathology was a cause or a consequence of alcoholism.

At a practical level, alcoholism therapists—often noting the lack of cooperation and outright sabotage of the alcoholic's treatment by family members—vacillated between including and excluding family members from the treatment process. Therapists who did involve family members made interesting demands upon them by today's standards, including demands that members of the alcoholic's family also remain abstinent from alcohol.[75] While there was some mid-century interest in the alcoholic family in the alcoholism literature, it is still striking just how little attention was paid to the alcoholic family in the broader family systems literature and by mainstream alcoholism counselors. The most significant and sustained advocacy concerning the needs of the whole family of the alcoholic came, not from mainstream clinicians, but from a new organization of alcoholic family members, which we will shortly profile.

Mid-Century Alcoholism Treatment: An Overview

Where it was available, mid-century care for alcoholics occurred for the most part in general hospitals, state psychiatric hospitals, private sanitariums, and the newly arising free-standing alcoholism programs.

The shortage of hospital beds in the 1950s continued to make it difficult for alcoholics to be admitted for detoxification or treatment. Even those hospitals that would admit an alcoholic for detoxification on a psychiatric unit often maintained waiting lists for admission. Most alcoholics were lost before their names ever rose to the top of such lists. In spite of these limitations, the number of physicians and hospitals working with alcoholics, and the number of officially acknowledged "alcoholism wards" did increase during the 1950s and 1960s. The expansion of psychiatric units within general hospitals opened to many alcoholics the doors of admission that had been closed, as did the earlier-described A.A.-influenced hospital units. These units constituted pockets of hope in an otherwise bleak landscape—a landscape that would not change significantly until years later, when the growing number and size of hospitals created empty beds that these institutions discovered could be filled with alcoholics. To appreciate the challenges and obstacles to the mid-century care of alcoholics, one need only contemplate the fact that cities like San Francisco still had local ordinances that prohibited local hospitals from admitting alcoholics.[76]

State psychiatric hospitals continued to be a primary source of care for the late-stage alcoholic during the middle decades of the 20th century. These hospitals treated alcoholics who were experiencing psychotic states (organic brain syndromes) related to chronic alcoholism, and some treated non-psychotic people suffering from acute alcoholism. The state psychiatric hospital became a drying-out station for the younger, less deteriorated alcoholic—and a place where many older alcoholics entered, became institutionalized, and died. In 1946, the American Psychiatric Association, responding to exposés of the horrible conditions within many American state psychiatric hospitals, published a list of ten recommendations for improved management of psychiatric institutions. One of their recommendations called for every hospital that received alcoholics and addicts to provide a specialized unit for their care, and to provide adequate staffing levels for the administration of such specialized care.[77]

Some states, such as Illinois, New York, Minnesota, North Dakota, and Texas, did begin to formalize their approach to alcoholism treatment within their state psychiatric hospitals by developing specialized units for alcoholism treatment. However, the accessability of these psychiatric facilities to alcoholic patients varied widely. A 1961 survey of men's first-treatment admissions to state psychiatric hospitals conducted by Stanford University found the incidence of alcoholism diagnoses ranging from 1% to 46 percent.[78]

When Sidney Cahn surveyed the institutional treatment of alcoholism in 1963, this is what he found: Of the 85,000 admissions to private psychiatric hospitals in that year, 8,500 of the patients were diagnosed as alcoholic. Of the 300,000 patients discharged from psychiatric units of general hospitals, 40,000 were discharged with diagnoses of alcoholism. And of the 300,000 admissions to state psychiatric hospitals in that year, 45,000 patients were admitted for alcoholism. Cahn estimated that "three-fourths to four-fifths of all inpatient care for alcoholics takes place in state mental hospitals." The number of states that operated specialized wards or hospitals for alcoholism increased from one in 1946 to 30 in 1966. Cahn also estimated that specialized alcoholism clinics, general psychiatric clinics, and other counseling agencies treated approximately 20,000 alcoholics, 10,000 of whom were treated in the approximately 120 specialized alcoholism clinics in the country.[79]

The relationship between state psychiatric hospitals and alcoholics seems always to have been one of mutual ambivalence, if not outright hostility. This strain had several sources. There was first the problem of alcoholic recidivism. When Manteno State Hospital in Illinois launched a specialized treatment unit for alcoholic men in the 1940s, the first 146 patients admitted to this pilot program had among them 509 prior state hospital admissions.[80] This profile of repeated admissions flew in the face of another reality: the detoxified alcoholic's seemingly stable mental status compared to that of the more typical state hospital psychiatric patient. In spite of the alcoholic's general lack of psychosis, state hospital superintendents tended to frown on the admission of alcoholics, for one primary reason: "the average alcoholic, unless permanently insane, was a headache" to the staff of the psychiatric institution.[81] And alcoholics, for their part, regularly told tales of their maltreatment within these same institutions. Each saw the other as a source of personal abuse.

This situation had not changed by the time Moore and Buchanan conducted a survey of state psychiatric institutions in 1966. They found that the staff of state psychiatric hospitals resisted admitting alcoholics due

to a pessimistic view of their potential for change. On the other hand, alcoholics—particularly A.A. members—were equally ambivalent about the prospect of having alcoholics treated in psychiatric hospitals, because of the implication that the alcoholic was mentally ill. As Moore and Buchanan noted: "It was as if one side said the alcoholic was too good for the state hospital and the other side said he wasn't good enough."[82]

Some states tried to escape this mutual hostility between alcoholics and state psychiatric hospitals by creating specialized hospitals for the care of alcoholics. Connecticut's Blue Hills Hospital and Florida's Avon Park were two of the more notable of such specialized state-sponsored addiction treatment institutions in the 1950s.

Court Clinics also were established to test the proposition that alcoholics could be successfully diverted from the courts into treatment. One such program established through a district court in Massachusetts conducted a weekly clinic staffed by a psychiatrist, a physician, and a counselor. Clinic treatment methods included pharmacotherapy with vitamins, tranquilizers, sedatives, and Antabuse, as well as structured group therapy sessions and educational presentations from outside experts and A.A. members. New "members" attended the clinic classes for ten weeks and then returned every other week, then monthly. Half of those referred were reported to have made "better adjustments." As a result of this experience, clinic staff concluded that alcoholics could be helped even when their initial involvement in treatment was coerced.[83]

By far, the largest category of institutions caring for the alcoholic during the 1950s was made up of private sanataria, small "drying-out" facilities, small residential alcoholism treatment programs, and a growing number of outpatient alcoholism counseling clinics—many modeled on the earlier-profiled Yale Clinics.[84]

By the end of the 1950s, there were some 200 small private alcoholism treatment programs in the United States, and many of these programs had been birthed within the previous 15 years.[85] In the following discussion, we will provide a brief synopsis of nine free-standing alcoholism treatment programs, to illustrate the range of mid-century alcoholism treatment services. But first we will acknowledge those programs initiated before 1950 that continued to provide services into the modern era.

Continued Services of Existing Programs: Before we talk about alcoholism treatment innovations during the 1950s, we must, for the sake of historical continuity, note what treatment continued into the 1950s from earlier eras. There are many examples of such continuity in addition to the just-noted community and psychiatric hospital programs. The Washingtonian Homes of Chicago and Boston continued as viable institutions through the 1950s. The Chicago Washingtonian Home, a facility that had been treating alcoholics continuously since 1863, opened a 13-bed "A.A. Ward" during the 1950s.[86] The Keeley Institute in Dwight and the Charles B. Towns Hospital in New York City also continued their specialty treatment of alcohol and other drug addictions. The Keswick Colony of Mercy in New Jersey and the Salvation Army service centers across the country continued to provide religion-oriented recovery programs for alcoholics. The Menninger Foundation continued to provide psychoanalytically oriented hospital treatment for affluent alcoholics, and the Shadel Sanitarium in Washington continued to provide aversion therapy for the treatment of alcoholism. The Blythewood Sanitarium, where Dr. Harry Tiebout had treated Marty M., continued to care for other alcoholics. The Yale Clinics continued to operate under the auspices of the Connecticut Commission of Alcoholism and by 1957 had spawned similar clinics in more than 34 states.[87] There were continuing experiments with outpatient alcoholism treatment at medical institutions like the Institute of the Pennsylvania Hospital, John Hopkins Hospital, and Boston's Washingtonian Hospital. There were also a growing number of psychiatrists providing outpatient psychoanalytically oriented psychotherapy to alcoholics. Many of the "A.A. Farms" and "A.A. Retreats" continued to operate, although the use of such names declined during the 1950s. All of these institutions provided threads of service continuity for alcoholics into the 1950s. The following sketches reflect the types of facilities that were added to these existing institutions.

Mrs. Pink's Place: Because of the difficulty of being admitted to hospitals, many alcoholics who could not afford the Towns or Keeley institutions relied on small "drying-out" homes. One such home in Dallas, Texas, known as "Mrs. Pink's Place," was operated by a Mrs. Pilkington. Mrs. Pink's Place was an old two-story, ten-room wooden building in which, regularly, four to eight alcoholics could be found in varying stages of detoxification. For a fee of $125 paid in advance, alcoholics were detoxified through a regimen that included an ounce of whiskey every four hours, along with honey and milk to settle the stomach, and lots of encouragement from visiting A.A. members. The ounce of whiskey every four hours,

common in such homes, was sometimes referred to as the "St. Louis treatment."[88] Places like Mrs. Pink's continued to constitute an invisible system of care for alcoholics until the rise of professionally directed alcoholism treatment eventually put these places out of business.

Bridge House: One of the most widely known mid-century alcoholism treatment programs was Bridge House in New York City. It was opened in December, 1944 by the Bureau of Alcoholic Therapy in the New York City Welfare Department. The driving force behind Bridge House was the lawyer Edward J. McGoldrick, Jr., who modeled his treatment program after his own self-engineered recovery from alcoholism.

Bridge House had a residential capacity of 15 people and also operated an outpatient program, both staffed exclusively by recovered alcoholics. The treatment approach was primarily psychological—based on McGoldrick's 1954 book *Management of the Mind*. McGoldrick was critical of approaches to alcoholism treatment that presented alcoholism as a disease. He considered such a notion "pernicious" and an "excuse for excessive drinking." In McGoldrick's view, recovery involved getting down to the "basic frustration that led to it, and to find another, more satisfactory outlet." He viewed alcoholism as a regressive escape and treatment as a process of self-directed maturation.[89]

McGoldrick viewed alcoholism treatment at Bridge House as essentially an educational one: Residents were referred to as "students"; and treatment involved a four-week course of lectures, discussion groups, and written and oral examinations. The Bridge House treatment philosophy was based on 17 principles, samples of which include:

- *I know I must abstain from alcohol, not merely for the sake of others, but first and foremost for my own self-esteem. The solution of the problem rests primarily with me.*
- *I refuse to amuse others with my drinking escapades of the past. My abnormal drinking was pathetic, not funny. I know that fundamentally frustration was the cause of my abnormal drinking. I realize I was seeking to escape from the belief in my inability to express myself as I desired.*
- *I realize that it is necessary to abstain from alcohol, but my ultimate goal is to attain a peace of mind in an active, industrious and constructive life.*[90]

During Bridge House's first 20 years of operation, more than 8,500 alcoholics were treated there.[91]

Beech Hill Farm: With the financial backing of Dr. Lillian M. Mahoney, Johnny S. established Beech Hill Farm in Dublin, New Hampshire in 1948, as a "post-hospitalization rest home for recovering alcoholics." Alcoholics joined the family-like atmosphere and filled their days playing croquet, swimming, helping with the housework, and attending A.A. meetings in the communities of Jaffrey and Keene. Detoxification services were also provided at Beech Hill after its seven-bed infirmary was completed in 1951.

Alina Lodge: Ina T. fled Nazi Germany but could not escape her rapidly progressing alcoholism. Through the help of High Watch Farm and A.A., Ina gained sobriety and a burning desire to help other alcoholics. This passion to help others led her and three close friends, Al Silverman and Tom and Geraldine Delaney, to found Alina Lodge in Kenvil, New Jersey in 1951. Alina Lodge served as a retreat for alcoholics modeled on High Watch, a place that provided intense exposure to the principles of A.A. Under Ina's management and the later leadership of Geraldine Delaney, Alina Lodge was known for a "non-permissive approach" designed to instill discipline and a sense of self-responsibility in each alcoholic. Alcoholics and addicts in residents were called "students," emphasizing the concept that they were there for one thing: to learn about their disease and to learn how to live drug free. This intense, no-nonsense approach to treatment gave Alina Lodge a reputation as the place of last resort. Alina Lodge's treatment ingredients have been referred to as "tough love" for its boot-camp atmosphere, "tincture of time" for its expectation of extended stays, and "tincture of studied neglect" for its refusal to provide "empathy that feeds pathology."[92]

Beech Hill (now Beech Hill Hospital) and Alina Lodge (now Little Hill - Alina Lodge) are examples of the grassroots, heavily A.A.-influenced programs that arose in the 1950s and were later expanded, professionalized, and incorporated into a national network of alcoholism treatment programs.

Portal House: The Portal House of Chicago was founded in 1946 by the Chicago Department of Welfare, through assistance from the Chicago Committee on Alcoholism.[93] Portal House served both men and women (80 and 24 respectively in 1955) who were referred by physicians and hospitals, social service agencies, and Alcoholics Anonymous. The majority of people admitted for treatment in the 1950s were over 45 years of age, and more than 70% were married. During the 1950s, the facility operated on an annual budget that ranged between $40,000 and $60,000, most of which came from corporate contributions (93 separate contributors in 1953) and foundation grants.[94]

Brighton Hospital for Alcoholism: Brighton was established by Harry Henderson, a member of the Michigan State Liquor Commission, who "enticed" liquor dealers in his state to assist in soliciting funds from their patrons toward the support of a hospital for alcoholics. Operating under the slogan, "Give the price of a drink to the victim of drink," this campaign raised $30,000 toward the establishment of an alcoholism treatment hospital. An organization was created to launch the project, and in 1953, the organization located a large house in Brighton that would accommodate a six-bed ward for women and a six-bed ward for men. From this humble beginning, Brighton Hospital expanded over the years to its current inpatient capacity of 63 adults and 20 adolescents. In the 15 years following its opening, Brighton hospital treated more than 14,000 alcoholics. While Brighton's treatment approach emphasized A.A. and utilized recovered counselors, it was one of the more medically oriented of the programs started in the early 1950s.

The Georgian Clinic and Rehabilitation Center for Alcoholics: G. Elliott Hagan spearheaded legislation in 1951 that created the Georgia Commission on Alcoholism. The Commission opened an inpatient and outpatient alcoholism treatment clinic in Atlanta in 1953 and another outpatient clinic in Savannah in 1954. Under the leadership of Dr. Vernelle Fox, the clinics boasted a program based on three disciplines: religion, psychiatry, and medicine. Alcoholics seeking help from the clinics were medically detoxified, assigned a "religious counselor," and assigned to a group that met four times per week. The Georgian Clinic placed great emphasis on the use of an interdisciplinary team made up of physicians (internists), psychiatrists, clinical psychologists, pastoral psychologists, registered and practical nurses, an occupational therapist, and a lab technician. The focus was placed upon shaping these staff—and all the patients being treated—into a highly energized "therapeutic community." It is worth noting that this interdisciplinary model of alcoholism treatment in Georgia was unfolding during precisely the same years in which the Minnesota Model was being constructed. The Georgian model, in contrast to the Minnesota Model, relied primarily on an outpatient rather than an inpatient model, and relied primarily on psychiatrists and clergy rather than on recovered alcoholics to provide therapeutic services.[95]

The Georgian Clinics and Willingway Hospital in Statesboro were the two most significant alcoholism treatment resources in Georgia during the 1950s and early 1960s. The roots of the latter facility extend to 1959, when Dr. John Mooney and his wife Dot began caring for alcoholics in their home.

Chit Chat Foundation: When Richard Caron moved to Reading, Pennsylvania to take over a branch of his family's business, he and his wife Catherine began opening their home to alcoholics and family members in need of support during early recovery. Catherine referred to the bull sessions around the Caron kitchen table as "Chit Chat"—a name eventually used for a newsletter they published for those in recovery, and a name that would eventually be associated with a large alcoholism treatment complex.

As the numbers of people seeking help grew, the Carons became acutely aware of the need for a treatment facility on the East Coast similar to Hazelden, where Dick's own recovery from alcoholism had begun. In 1957, the Carons and some of their close friends established the Chit Chat Foundation and formally initiated treatment services by opening a halfway house for recovering alcoholics in Reading, Pennsylvania. Two years later, the Carons opened Chit Chat Farms in what had been a retreat hotel for wealthy vacationers in Wernersville, Pennsylvania. Using Hazelden as a model and a Smithers Foundation grant to expand its facilities in 1960, Caron guided the development of one of the East Coast's first modern alcoholism treatment facilities. Chit Chat was later rechristened the Caron Foundation.[96]

This review reflects several changes in the delivery of alcoholism services in the 1940s and 1950s. Three of the most significant of such changes were the overall increase in numbers of alcoholism treatment programs, the growing diversity of settings in which alcoholism treatment was being provided, and the emergence of professionally directed interdisciplinary alcoholism treatment teams. As these developments were underway, the network of addiction recovery mutual-aid groups was also expanding and diversifying.

A.A. and Mutual Aid: 1950-1971

In A.A., the decade of the 1950s opened on a sad note produced by the death of Dr. Bob, one of A.A.'s co-founders. That loss was softened by the growing awareness of what was happening to the fellowship that Dr. Bob had helped create. A.A. membership surpassed 90,000, and A.A. was recognized by the American Psychiatric Association. This honor was supplemented in 1951 by the Lasker Award for contributions to the field of public health, presented to A.A. by the American Public Health Association.

The Twelve Traditions that had been formulated in 1946 were formally adopted at A.A.'s 1950 International Convention in Cleveland, Ohio, and the book *Twelve Steps and Twelve Traditions* was published in 1953. Two years later, a second edition of *Alcoholics Anonymous* was released. The stories in the second edition reflected a membership that included more women, younger members, and members who were entering A.A. earlier in the progression of their alcoholism. *Alcoholics Anonymous Comes of Age*, A.A.'s first attempt to record its history, was published in 1957.

There were also changes in A.A.'s organizational structure during the 1950s. What had previously existed was a group of trustees linked to the membership through the two co-founders. In 1951, a General Service Conference of Alcoholics Anonymous composed of group representatives from across the United States and Canada was created, and A.A.'s trustees were made accountable to that Conference. With the co-founders removed from the middle of this relationship, A.A. members assumed responsibility for their own future. At A.A.'s 1955 International Convention, the organization celebrated its 20th birthday with Bill Wilson formally turning A.A. over to the conference and its trustees in the form of A.A.'s three legacies: Recovery, Unity, and Service. A.A. had "Come of Age." As the organization celebrated its 20-year anniversary, its membership reached 133,000.[97]

In 1956, a committee was set up to take over the public relations and correspondence previously conducted by Bill Wilson. In 1965, Bill asked the A.A. membership to assume a renewed pledge of personal responsibility for the still-suffering alcoholic: The pledge read: "I am responsible. When anyone, anywhere, reaches out for help, I want the hand of A.A. always to be there. And for that: I am responsible." He spoke to the A.A. membership for the last time at the Thirty-Fifth Anniversary Convention in 1970. Bill Wilson died January 24, 1971. His full name and picture appeared for the first time in the world press, accompanying the announcement of his death. The structures he had helped put in place ensured that Alcoholics Anonymous would continue to grow and serve in his absence.

The Al-Anon Movement: During the early years of A.A., alcoholics and their family members attended group meetings together. As these meetings grew larger, A.A. members made a decision to meet without family members present. As a result, the spouses of A.A. members were brought together in groups for the first time. This growth and separation occurred across the country. Meetings of family members evolved from a focus on their alcoholic spouses to a focus on their own emotional and spiritual health. As Lois W. noted:

> I suppose the seeds of Al-Anon actually germinated when the families of early AA members first felt the stirrings of their own regeneration, and began to do something about it.[98]

In the 1940s, wives (and later, wives and husbands) of A.A. members began to band together for mutual support in such places as Long, Beach California; Richmond, Virginia; and Chicago, Illinois. A close reading of early editions of the *A.A. Grapevine* reveals the considerable family activity that was underway. Family members of San Diego A.A. members organized themselves as "Alcoholics Anonymous Associates" in May of 1946. There began the practice of spouses' joining an A.A.-affiliated support group *before* their partners joined A.A. A May, 1947 article noted regular meetings of Family Groups in San Pedro and Sugar Hill, California. The former was noted to have held annual open meetings that were used to educate doctors, judges, and welfare workers. In July of the same year, an article noted the formation of a "Non-A.A. Group" (NAA) for family members in Austin Texas. A similar group, referring to itself as the "A.A. Auxiliary" (AAA), was formed in Rome, Georgia in July of 1947. The founding of another "Non-A.A. Group" in Rochester, New York was announced in July of 1948. The Rochester group was the first noted in the *Grapevine* to have adapted the Twelve Steps for use by the husbands and wives of alcoholics. Their first step read: "We admitted we were powerless to help the alcoholic." Formal groups of the wives of A.A. members began to spread, meeting under such other names as AA Helpmates, Al-Anon, Alono, and Onala.[99]

The growing number of these groups and their request to be listed in the A.A. Directory posed a growing question about the relationship between the family groups and A.A. itself.[100] To recognize this growing movement and to clarify its relationship to A.A., Lois Wilson and her friend Anne B. set up a service office in 1951 to support the groups. Their announced goals were:

1. To give cooperation and understanding to the

AA at home.
2. To live by the Twelve Steps ourselves in order to grow spiritually along with our AA.
3. To welcome and give comfort to the families of new AA.

They chose the name Al-Anon Family Groups and began responding to information requests from family members, requests that were arriving at A.A. headquarters. In the early days, they called themselves the Clearinghouse Committee, and in 1954, they incorporated as Al-Anon Family Group Headquarters, Inc. Just prior to incorporation, Henrietta S. became Al-Anon's first General Secretary/ Executive Director.[101] Responding to the need for more family-oriented literature, Lois began working on a pamphlet that, with the help of Bill Wilson and editorial assistance from Margaret D. and Ralph P., became the book, *The Al-Anon Family Groups*. The first mimeographed copy of this book made its appearance at the 1955 A.A. International Convention in St. Louis.

Like A.A.'s, Al-Anon's growth was spurred on by articles in such publications as the *Saturday Evening Post*, the *Christian Herald*, *Life Romances*, and *Life Today*, and by national television appearances. Ruth G., a San Francisco Al-Anon member, developed the idea of linking the newly forming groups in California with a newsletter. This newsletter, the *San Francisco Family Chronicle*—later renamed *The Family Forum*—was the forerunner of the newsletter by the same name used as the primary instrument of communication among the nation's Al-Anon groups.

Al-Anon shaped much of its character based on the early experience within A.A.—its organizational structure, its focus on the Twelve Steps, its construction of parallel traditions (written by Lois in 1952), and its incorporation of many A.A. slogans.

Al-Anon's explosive growth parallels that of A.A. Al-Anon grew from 145 registered groups in 1951 to 500 to 1954, and to 1,500 in 1963. Through its early developmental years, the general public knew little if anything about this budding support system for the families of alcoholics. The break into public consciousness occurred November 10, 1957, when the televised story of Al-Anon was featured on *The Loretta Young Show*. Later articles in *Time* and *Life* and Abigail Van Buren's positive treatment in her column "Dear Abby" enhanced public awareness of Al-Anon and brought many new members into the groups.

Al-Anon not only provided a sustained source of support to family members affected by alcoholism, but also brought together in one place a large enough pool of alcoholic wives to allow researchers to begin to test some of their propositions regarding these women's supposed pathology. By the early 1960s, objective studies began to call into question the 1950s portrayal of the alcoholic wife as having selected and remained with her husband out of her own deep emotional disturbance.[102]

As more and more women entered A.A., there was also increased concern within Al-Anon about the special needs of the husbands of alcoholic women. By 1960, this recognition was becoming apparent in a new genre of Al-Anon literature bearing such titles as, *The Stag Line, What's Next? Asks the Husband of an Alcoholic, My Wife is an Alcoholic,* and *Al-Anon IS for Men.*

By 1994, there would be more than 32,500 Al-Anon groups meeting in 12 countries and distributing literature published in 30 different languages. When once asked about the single most important lesson she had learned in Al-Anon, Lois Wilson stated simply:

> ....we cannot change another human be-
> ing—only ourselves. By living our own lives
> to the best of our ability, by loving deeply
> and not trying to mold another to our
> wishes, we can help not only ourselves but
> that other also.[103]

Alateen: Another significant milestone in the 1950s was the founding of Alateen in 1957. This was the first organization for children of alcoholics since the Junior Washingtonian Societies of the early 1840s. Alateen was started by a Pasadena, California adolescent whose parents were in A.A. and Al-Anon. Alateen provided a support-group structure for people ages 12 to 20 whose lives had been affected by the alcoholism of someone close to them, most often a parent. By 1963, there were more than 200 Alateen groups. Alateen later received national coverage in *Time, Seventeen, American Weekly,* and *Children's Family Digest.* This coverage stirred much interest in Alateen groups. The number of Alateen groups grew to 3,300 by the mid-1990s.

Other Mutual-Aid Societies: Alcoholics Victorious and the Calix Society

As A.A. grew in the 1950s and created new progeny (Al-Anon and Alateen), other mutual-aid societies of alcoholics were organized as alternatives and supplements to A.A. Except for Narcotics Anonymous, which we will discuss in a later chapter, most

of these societies were religious in orientation.

Several alcoholic mutual-aid groups emerged in the cauldron of the urban rescue missions. The most prominent and enduring of these groups was Alcoholics Victorious (A.V.). A.V. was founded in 1948 by Dr. William Seath of the Chicago Christian Industrial League. Seath's inspiration for A.V. was his sense that A.A. lacked the Christ-centered focus he believed was essential for the alcoholic's spiritual development. A.V. provides a haven for recovering alcoholics who recognize Jesus Christ as their "Higher Power." Most A.V. groups claim that their goal is not to replace A.A. or treatment, and many A.V. groups use both the Twelve Steps of A.A. and the A.V. Creed.

There are clear parallels between the processes of psychological transformation with A.V. and with A.A. Jerry Dunn, in his book *God is for the Alcoholic,* has even presented the Biblical equivalent of each of A.A. Twelve Steps.[104] A.V. uses a Biblical foundation for its advocacy of radical abstinence for the Christian alcoholic.

The goal of A.V. is to help recovering people "transfer dependence on their addictions to dependence on Christ." Many A.V. spokespeople claim that once "victory" has been achieved through "rebirth," there is no longer a need for the continued support offered by A.A.[105] "Sponsors" in A.V. are people from the wider Christian community who link the newly recovering alcoholic to a community church and provide ongoing support through early recovery.

The Alcoholics Victorious Creed

1. *I realize that I cannot overcome the drink habit by myself. I believe that the power of Jesus Christ is available to help me. I believe that through my acceptance of Him as my Savior, I am a new man.* (2Cor. 5:17)
2. *Because the presence of God is manifested through continued prayer, I will set aside two periods every day, morning and evening, for communion with my Heavenly Father. I realize my need for Daily Bible reading and use it as a guide for my daily living.* (Ps 27:1-5)
3. *I recognize my need of Christian fellowship and will, therefore, have fellowship with Christians through the church of my choice. I know that in order to be victorious, I must keep active in the service of Christ and His Church and I will help others to victory.*
4. *I do not partake of any beverage containing alcohol. I know it is the first drink that does the harm. Therefore, "I do not drink."*
5. *I can be victorious because I know that God's strength is sufficient to supply all my needs.*

Reprinted with Permission

A.V. spread slowly through city missions until its popularity was boosted by a recommendation in Jerry Dunn's 1965 book, *God is for the Alcoholic.* Dunn, a former rescue mission director, attributed his own recovery from alcoholism to his having picked up a Bible in a Texas jail cell.[106] Today, A.V. is an official program of the International Union of Gospel Missions—an association of some 250 rescue missions and inner-city ministries. A.V. meetings can be found in many rescue missions, Salvation Army Rehabilitation Centers, churches, and prisons. Another group similar to Alcoholics Victorious is Alcoholics for Christ.

Alcoholic mutual-aid groups that serve as supplements to A.A. also began to appear at mid-century. Sometimes referred to as "Eleventh-Step Programs," these groups are designed, not to help the alcoholic get sober, but to help the already sober alcoholic develop spiritually. These groups include Jewish Alcoholics, Chemically Dependent People and Significant Others (JACS) and the Calix Society. We will briefly profile the latter.

The Calix Society was founded in 1947 in Minneapolis, Minnesota by a group of five recovering men who met regularly for prayer and mutual support. These meetings grew out of an interest in finding a way to strengthen their sobriety and their spiritual development in the practice of A.A.'s Eleventh Step ("Sought through prayer and meditation to improve our conscious contact with God *as we understood Him,* praying only for knowledge of his will for us and the power to carry that out."). Members of the Calix Society see their fellowship as a way to pursue their search for spirituality and serenity as Catholic alcoholics in recovery. Calix—Latin for "chalice"—was a metaphoric substitution of the "cup that sanctifies for the cup that stupefies." As of 1992, the Calix Society had some 1,000 members in units scattered across the United States and Europe. Most Calix units hold a monthly meeting with a mass, breakfast, and speaker. Meetings are open to alcoholics and their family members and friends. The Calix Society sees itself offering something that is complementary to Twelve-Step Programs, rather than as an alternative or substitute for such programs. As their motto affirms, "Sobriety through AA—Sanctity through Calix."[107]

We have provided an overview of the changing contours of alcoholism treatment and alcoholism recovery mutual-aid societies during the 1950s. In the next chapter, we will discuss more specifically the approaches and techniques that were used to treat alcoholism during this period.

✠

Chapter Twenty-Three
Mid-Century Alcoholism Treatment: Treatment Methods

New methods of treating alcoholism emerged between 1940 and 1970. There was, as we noted in our depiction of the Minnesota Model, the first infusion of A.A. philosophy into alcoholism treatment and the beginning of the integration of recovered alcoholics into newly conceived roles within multi-disciplinary alcoholism treatment teams. There was the continuing rise of alcoholism clinics such as those in Georgia profiled in the last chapter, and of non-A.A.-oriented models of residential treatment such as Bridge House. There was a resurgence of the use of some turn-of-the-century psychological techniques, such as hypnosis, in the treatment of alcoholism. There were many new physical methods for treating alcoholism, particularly many new drug therapies. Finally, there were innovations in the kinds of psychosocial supports afforded alcoholics, the most significant of which was the emergence of the halfway house. This chapter will review some of these innovations in alcoholism treatment.

Hypnosis Revisited

The 19th-century advocacy of hypnosis by inebriate asylum specialists fell into disrepute in the early 20th century, rose as a primary method of treatment among the Peabody-trained lay therapists in the 1930s, faded in visibility in the 1940s, and returned in the 1950s. Robert Wallerstein's 1957 book *The Hospital Treatment of Alcoholism* listed hypnosis as one of four effective treatments for alcoholism (along with Antabuse treatment, conditioned-reflex treatment, and milieu therapy).

Hypnosis was used both as a general relaxation technique and to impart specific suggestions designed to help prevent relapse. In the latter use, the hypnotherapist implanted suggestions into the patient's mind to strengthen the desire for recovery and to instill an aversion to alcohol. Such suggestions included: "Your craving for alcohol is decreasing each day," "You have developed an allergy to alcohol," and

"You will experience a revulsion to alcohol in any form." Hypnotic suggestions were also used to strengthen the client's bond with the therapist or treatment group, to help the client visualize positive experiences that would come with sobriety, and to help patients prepare for specific situations that in the past had provoked drinking.[108]

Physical Methods of Alcoholism Treatment: An Overview

Physical methods dominated the mid-century treatment of alcoholism in most settings. First there were many of the so-called alcoholism therapies described in Chapter Eleven that extended into the 1940s and 1950s, methods that included the use of psychosurgery (prefrontal lobotomies) and shock therapies of both the insulin and electroconvulsive varieties. Mid-century treatments also continued to include what were earlier called "natural therapeutics." In the 1950s and 1960s, specialized nutritional therapies were advocated, and hydrotherapy techniques not unlike those in the 19th-century water-cure institutions were used on alcoholics in psychiatric hospitals throughout the country. But far and away the largest category of physical methods of alcoholism treatment was that of the drug interventions. The pharmacological arsenal assembled to do battle against alcoholism included drugs of incredible diversity: sedatives, tranquilizers, amphetamines, hallucinogens, hormones, and carbon dioxide.

Nutrition, Alcoholism, and Vitamin Therapy

The reader will recall that there were early suggestions of the link between malnutrition and alcoholism. Dr. Benjamin Rush reported an alcoholic patient cured by a vegetarian diet, specialized diets were the norm in the more exclusive 19th-century inebriate sanitariums, and the 1930s saw a recognition that alcoholism shared the same foundation of malnutrition as scurvy, pellagra, and beriberi. It was through this latter discovery that Dr. Norman Jolliffe and his colleagues introduced the use of thiamin in the treatment of Korsakoff's syndrome and made vitamin therapy a routine accompaniment to alcoholic detoxification.

Two decades following Jolliffe's discoveries, two English psychiatrists, Drs. Humphry Osmond and Abram Hoffer, reported positively on their experiments with the use of Vitamin B-3 (Niacin) in treating alcoholics who had not responded to traditional treatments. Bill Wilson, co-founder of A.A., became quite interested in the potential of vitamin B_3 to reach those who were not achieving or sustaining sobriety in A.A. He published three papers on the subject during the last years of his life and distributed them to physicians within A.A. Bill theorized that hidden emotional troubles were behind A.A. failures, chronic "slippees," and those sober but unhappy in A.A. In his communication to A.A. physicians, he claimed that Vitamin B-3 therapy had "promptly and radically relieved" "severe and long-standing emotional difficulties" in a third of A.A. members who had tried the treatment.[109]

Another central figure who aroused the alcoholism field's interest in nutrition was Dr. Roger Williams. Beginning with a 1947 article in the *Quarterly Journal of Studies on Alcohol*, Williams outlined his theory that alcoholism was caused by a genetically transmitted biochemical defect. According to Williams, those vulnerable to alcoholism possessed an increased need for vitamins and other nutritional elements not available in their regular diets. This deficiency in nutritional elements was proposed as the etiology of both the craving for alcohol and the alcoholic's abnormal response to alcohol. Williams' treatment recommendations, outlined in his book *Alcoholism: A Nutritional Approach*, focused on vitamin therapies that could alleviate these deficiencies.[110] Variations on Williams' theories and methods of treatment have continued to appear. A recent text by Dr. Bernard Ross reported that Individualized Replacement Therapy—the subcutaneous injection of small (5.0 milligrams or less) dosages of niacin —could consistently curb the craving for alcohol in confirmed alcoholics.[111]

ACTH: Alcoholism and Endocrine Dysfunction

Several physicians in the 1940s and 1950s set forth the proposition that a disorder of the endocrine system was the causative agent in alcoholism. Based on this theory, these physicians treated alcoholics with a variety of adrenal steroids and adrenocorticotropic hormones (ACTH). This so-called "thyroid treatment" involved injections of adrenal cortical extract—ACE. Early reports claimed that ACE provided rapid, safe detoxification and obliterated continued craving for alcohol.[112]

The Use of Tranquilizers, Anti-depressants, Mood Stabilizers, and Sedatives

One highly lauded breakthrough in the pharmacological treatment of alcoholism was the introduction

George Copway (Kah-ge-ga-gah-bowh)
Ojibway Temperance Reformer

Dr. Benjamin Rush, Father of the American
Disease Concept of Alcoholism

John Gough, Famed Temperance Organizer

FRANCIS MURPHY.

Francis Murphy, Founder—Blue Ribbon
Reform Clubs

**Dr. Edward Turner, Founder—First American
Inebriate Asylum**

DR. HENRY A. REYNOLDS.

**Dr. Henry Reynolds, Founder—Red Ribbon
Reform Clubs**

Early Washingtonians

A Temperance Progression Chart

**Dr. T.D. Crothers, Inebriate Asylum Pioneer
and Editor, Journal of Inebriety**

Boston Washingtonian Home

The Chicago Washingtonian Home

Chicago's Martha Washington Home, First Addiction Treatment Facility for Women

Chester Crest: An Early Inebriate Home

Walnut Lodge, Hartford, Connecticut

The New York State Inebriate Asylum

Keeley League No. 1 in Open Air Session, Dwight, Illinois

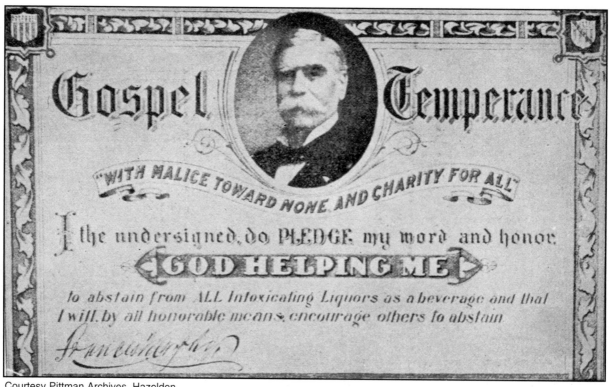

Francis Murphy Pledge Card

Keeley Institute Laboratory, Dwight, Illinois

Keeley Patients Standing in Line for their Injections

Courtesy Chicago Historical Society

The Ladies Home of the Keeley Institute, Dwight, Illinois

Courtesy James Oughton, Jr.

Label on Keeley Mail Order Bottle

Dr. Leslie Keeley

Keeley Patients Heading Home on the Train

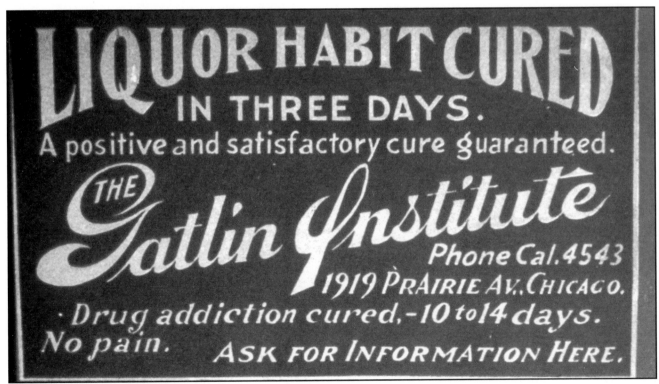

Gatlin Institute in Chicago

Geneva Gold Cure Institute,

GENEVA, N. Y.

DAVID W. ONDERDONK, M. D.,
Late Surgeon U. S. A.

GEORGE LESHER,
Supt. and Manager.

FOR THE TREATMENT OF

Liquor, Opium, Cocaine and Tobacco Habits,

Patients Treated Privately
When Desired. A CURE GUARANTEED.

ALL COMMUNICATIONS STRICTLY CONFIDENTIAL.

GENEVA GOLD CURE COMPANY,

Tompkins House. GENEVA, N. Y.

Geneva Cold Cure Institute

Neal Institute 3-Day Cure

Dr. Haines Golden Treatment

Advertisements Promoting "Secret Cures"

Mail Order Morphine Addiction Cure

Detox and Cure in 32 Bottles

Tobacco Cure Advertisement

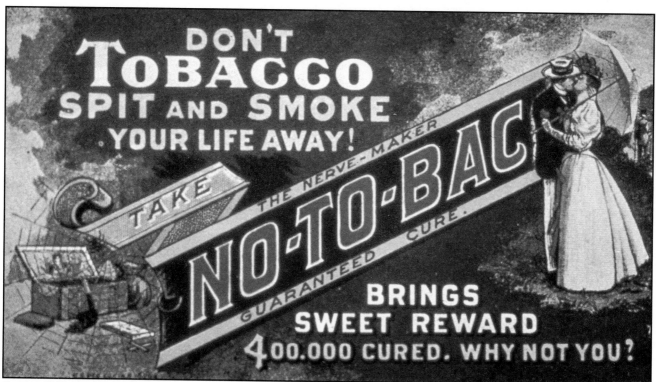

Tobacco Cure Advertisement

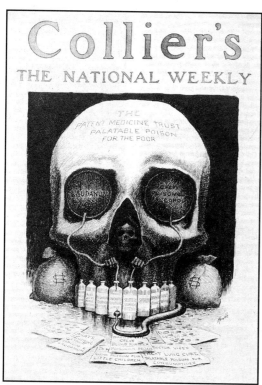

Collier's Expose of Fraudulent Cures

Jerry McAuley, Founder—Water Street Mission

William Booth, Founder-Salvation Army

**Salvation Army "Lassies" Carrying the
Message to the Bowery**

Bowery Men Seeking Services at the Salvation Army

Charles B. Towns

Charles B. Towns Hospital, New York City

Water Cure Postcard

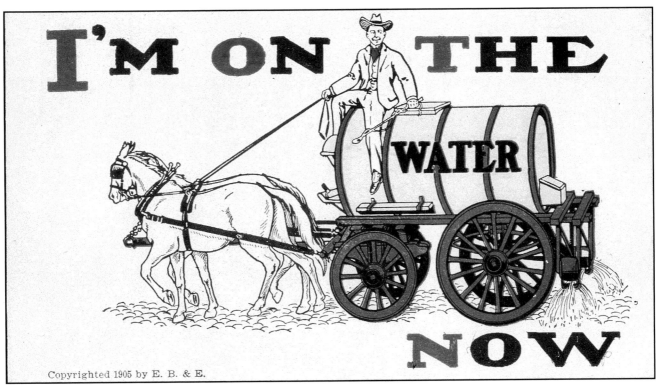

Water Cure Postcard

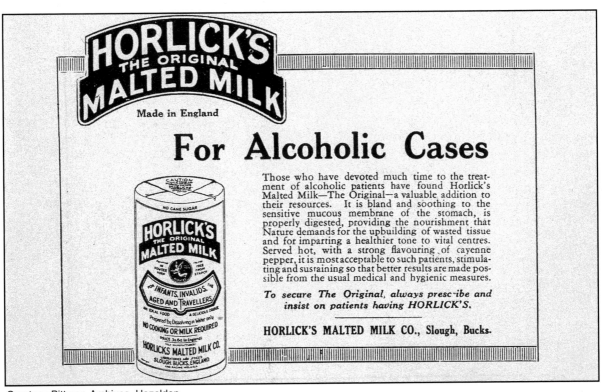

Horlick's Malted Milk for Alcoholics

Shadel Sanitarium, 1950s

U.S. PUBLIC HEALTH SERVICE HOSPITAL
LEXINGTON, KY.

Federal "Narcotics Farm," Lexington, Kentucky

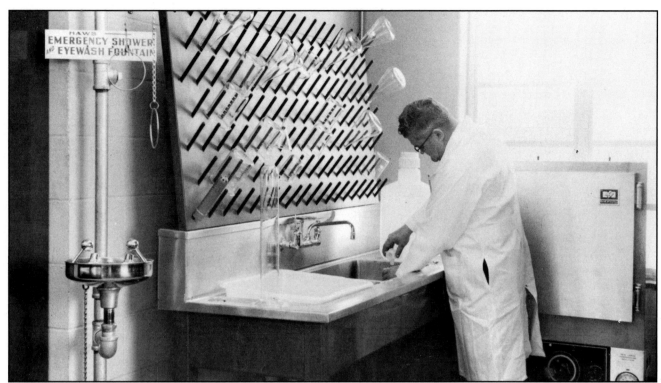

Medical Biologist Frank Pescor in the Laboratory of the Addiction Research Center

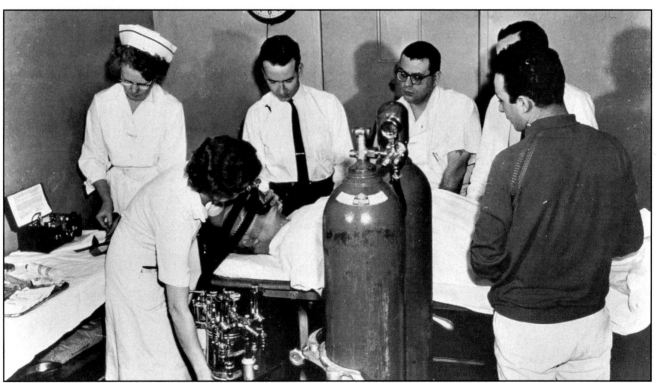

Addict Receiving Electroshock Treatment at Lexington

Dr. Robert Smith and Bill Wilson–A.A. Co-founders

**Dr. William Silkworth—
"The Little Doctor Who Loved Drunks"**

**Sister Ignatia—
"Angel of Alcoholics Anonymous"**

Early A.A. Members Practicing Anonymity at the Level of the Press

St. Thomas Hospital, Akron, Ohio

**Sacred Heart Medallion Given to Each Alcoholic
Discharged from St. Thomas**

AA-A Key

Dr. Harry Tielbout, Blythewood Sanitarium

High Watch Farm

Marty Mann and E. M. Jellinek (right) on Lecture Circuit

Ray McCarthy Lecturing

Dr. John Wittmer of Consolidated Edison Company Conferring with Selden Bacon

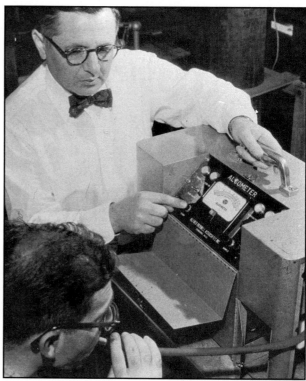

Yale's Dr. Leon Greenberg and his Alcometer

Hazelden, 1955

Willmar State Hospital, 1940s

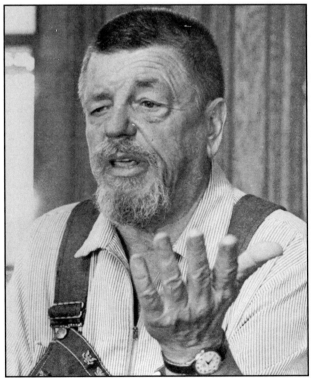

Charles Dederich—Founder, Synanon

**Dr. Vincent Dole and Dr. Marie Nyswander
Methadone Pioneers**

Courtesy Julianne Hughes

Harold E. Hughes

Courtesy Women for Sobriety

**Jean Kirkpatrick, Ph.D.—Founder,
Women For Sobriety**

of a new class of drugs: the tranquilizers. The first-generation tranquilizers—drugs like meprobamate (Miltown, Equinil), mephensin (Tolserol), chlorpromazine (Thorazine), and promazine (Sparine) were used to treat alcoholics in two ways. First, they were used to manage alcoholic intoxication and the period of acute alcoholic withdrawal. Second, they were given to alcoholics following hospitalization, in the belief that medicating the alcoholic's restlessness, hyperirritability, and anxiety might reduce the probability of relapse. In this view, excessive drinking was seen as the alcoholic's attempt to manage these same conditions. Tranquilizers were seen as a preferable and more effective substitute for alcohol. There was little recognition of the abuse potential of tranquilizers during the 1950s.[113]

A related and also highly lauded breakthrough in the pharmacological treatment of alcoholism was the introduction of the so-called "minor" tranquilizers. These drugs—mostly of the benzodiazepine family—proved highly effective as aids in the detoxification of alcoholics. There was also hope that these drugs would serve as an effective adjunct in treatment of alcoholism. Using the above-noted theory that excessive drinking was a failed effort at self-medication, anti-anxiety agents were prescribed as a substitute for alcohol. In spite of some controversy surrounding their use with alcoholics after detoxification, a 1972 survey of 15,000 physicians revealed that 65% of them prescribed tranquilizers in the post-detoxification treatment of alcoholism. The fact that many alcoholics abused and became addicted to these medications called this practice into question.[114]

Other types of new psychiatric medications for mood disorders also came into play in the treatment of alcoholism during the 1950s and 1960s. Lithium, a simple chemical used in the 1850s to treat gout and rheumatism, was discovered in 1949 by John Cade, an Austrian psychiatrist, to have psychoactive properties. Its use in the treatment of bi-polar disorder was later expanded by reports of its effectiveness as a treatment for alcoholism. New anti-depressant medications were also widely prescribed to alcoholics. These prescribing practices were again founded on the premise that drinking bouts were poorly chosen mechanisms of symptom management. Many alcoholics would later report that they went through multiple episodes of unsuccessful drug-aided treatment for depression before they finally focused on their recovery from alcoholism.[115]

Another category of drugs used in the mid-century treatment of alcoholism was that of the sedatives. Sedatives, bromides, chlorals, and paralde-

hydes came into common use in treating alcoholism in the 1930s, and paraldehyde continued to be used well into the 1960s before giving way to a preference for barbiturate and non-barbiturate sedatives. Treatment units that utilized paraldehyde were recognizable from some distance by the overpowering odor that was characteristic of the drug. An autobiographical account of the alcoholic ward at Bellevue Hospital in the 1950s described the use of paraldehyde in the treatment of acute alcoholic withdrawal:

> Bomber put a glass of paraldehyde to my lips. I gulped it knowing that a second convulsion, following immediately upon the first, might kill me...the paraldehyde was penetrating, warm, soothing.[116]

Like tranquilizers, the sedatives were used in the management of acute intoxication and withdrawal. They were also used to manage the alcoholic's disturbed sleep during and following alcohol withdrawal. One sedative, sodium amytal, was utilized by psychoanalysts to unlock the unconscious, and prolonged narcosis—drug-induced sleep therapy—became popular as a means of restoring the alcoholic patient's exhausted nervous system.

There was isolated recognition of the abuse potential of sedatives by alcoholics during the 1950s. In his 1957 review of the pharmacological management of alcoholism, Dr. Daniel Feldman noted:

> The temptation to use sedatives in ever-increasing amounts to control the disturbing manifestations of anxiety and tension [in alcoholic withdrawal] is a great one. Not infrequently sedatives have been abused in the treatment of alcoholism with resultant addictions and dependencies that are equally or more difficult to manage than alcoholism.[117]

William Miller, in a contemporary review of treatment-effectiveness literature, concluded that controlled research had supplied no evidence that anti-anxiety drugs had any post-detoxification value in the treatment of alcoholism. He further noted that, while antidepressant medications did play a role for some clients in treating sustained mood disorders, these drugs were not effective as an aid in establishing sobriety. Miller concluded his review of controlled research studies on the efficacy of drugs in treatment by declaring that "no psychotropic medication has yet been shown to produce reliable changes in drinking behavior."[118] But at mid-century, many physicians and psychiatrists thought that there must be a drug that had potential as a specific in the treatment of alcoholism. Three drugs, in particular, vied for this role: Benzedrine, Antabuse, and LSD.

Benzedrine in the Treatment of Alcoholism

The reader who has been surprised to find in this book reports of everything from morphine to barbiturates prescribed in the treatment of alcoholism may be equally surprised to find an amphetamine, Benzedrine, used to treat alcoholism in the 1940s and 1950s.

In 1939, Dr. Wilfred Bloomburg reported on the capacity of amphetamine sulfate to relieve "hangovers." He further reported that amphetamines, when consumed before or during drinking, allowed the drinker to consume larger quantities of alcohol without apparent signs of intoxication. Bloomburg was so struck with this effect that he experimented with what he called Benzedrine Replacement Therapy with 21 alcoholics. Bloomburg concluded that Benzedrine had great value in the treatment of chronic alcoholism.[119] During this same period, Dr. Edward Reifenstein and Dr. Eugene Davidoff described the effective use of Benzedrine to treat alcoholic stupor and alcoholic psychosis. They did, however, provide a warning of Benzedrine's abuse potential. Some of Reifenstein and Davidoff's alcoholic patients had discovered Benzedrine's euphorigenic effects—effects they referred to as a "cheap jag."[120]

By the mid-1940s, Benzedrine was showing up in various texts as a recommended treatment for nicotinism, morphine and codeine addiction, and alcoholism. The rationale for its use in the treatment of alcoholism was that it served to combat the depression, fatigue, and lethargy experienced by many alcoholics, and that the feelings of well-being that Benzedrine induced served to reduce the alcoholic's craving for alcohol. The use of Benzedrine was one experiment in a larger search to find a safe maintenance drug that could either alleviate conditions thought to incite binge drinking—such as anxiety or depression—or provide a safe substitute that could give the alcoholic a chemical "lift." In short, Benzedrine was considered a potentially safer substitute intoxicant.[121]

By 1957, in an alcoholism text written for general practitioners, Dr. Donald Hewitt was recommending to his colleagues that amphetamines never be utilized with alcoholics because of their abuse potential.[122] In spite of such warnings, stimulants continued to be recommended in the treatment of alcoholism, on the

theory that alcoholics suffered from a state of ego-deflation and that stimulants could boost energy and self-esteem, thus reducing the alcoholic's search for a chemical self-cure of this condition.[123] Benzedrine gradually fell from grace as a treatment for alcoholism. Like so many others, it had appeared as a panacea in the treatment of alcoholism and left as a drug that was viewed, not only as ineffective, but also as potentially harmful.

Antabuse and Other Antidipsotropics in the Treatment of Alcoholism

Thiram is a chemical ingredient used in the manufacture of synthetic rubber. It was common knowledge among those who worked in the rubber industry that people who drank alcohol after exposure to thiram could experience serious adverse reactions. E.E. Williams had noted this effect in a 1937 medical article, and had even suggested that thiram might have potential in the treatment of alcoholism. The article, however, incited no interest in the yet-to-be-reborn field of addiction medicine.[124]

In 1947, two Danish researchers, Erik Jacobsen and Jens Hald, were testing the potential of tetraethylthiuramdisulfide (a derivative of thiram later given the generic name "disulfram") in the treatment of worms. Jacobsen and Hald, unaware of rubber-industry folk wisdom, ingested small amounts of this substance to test its toxicity. There seemed to be little effect until they later drank alcohol and experienced profound discomfort.

As a result of this accidental discovery, Jacobsen and Hald speculated that disulfram might have potential in the treatment of alcoholism. In their initial report, they noted that 74 of 83 alcoholic patients treated with disulfram showed promising results.[125] In the late 1940s, through the protocol set forth by the two researchers, the drug became available as an adjunct in the treatment of alcoholism, most frequently under the trade name Antabuse.[126] Disulfram, and drugs with similar effects, were also sold under the trade names Abstinyl, Antiethyl, Aversan, Contralin, Esperal, Stopetyl, Refusal, Temposil, and Abstem.[127] Dr. Ruth Fox brought Antabuse to the United States in 1948, and Dr. Eric Glud's widely read review of Jacobsen and Hald's research helped introduce physicians in the United States to the potential role of Antabuse in the treatment of alcoholism.[128]

Antabuse works by interfering with the breakdown of alcohol in the body. Consumed alcohol first is broken down into acetaldehyde, which is quite toxic; and then is further broken down into acetic acid, water, and carbon dioxide. In that form it is expelled from the body through breath, sweat, and urine. Antabuse interferes with the breakdown of alcohol beyond the acetaldehyde stage. As acetaldehyde builds up in the body, it quickly (within five to ten minutes) produces flushing, sweating, increased pulse rate (heart-pounding), chest pain, nausea, vomiting, headache, breathing difficulties, weakness, and marked anxiety, including feelings of impending death. The intensity of the reaction is determined by both the dose of Antabuse and the quantity of alcohol consumed. Once a desired blood level of Antabuse is established, the alcoholic may not drink for a period ranging from four or five days up to two weeks without experiencing a toxic reaction.

The original goal of Antabuse was to provide a "pharmacological barrier" between the alcoholic and alcohol. The use of Antabuse as an adjunct in alcoholism treatment began with the administration of a daily dose of Antabuse to the patient for a period ranging from several days to two weeks. During the era of its introduction, researchers conducted a brief test of the effects of Antabuse by having the patient consume a small quantity of alcohol. The reactions, as described above, were uniformly unpleasant. Once the results of drinking were dramatically confirmed, a daily self-administration of Antabuse provided a powerful reason not to drink. Such demonstrations were later replaced by patient education on the drug's effects.

The use of Antabuse required close medical management, as there were people for whom Antabuse was contraindicated. There were particular concerns that, without medical management, an Antabuse reaction could be life-threatening to some people. Toxic reactions to Antabuse sometimes resulted from spouses' surreptitiously mixing Antabuse in with the alcoholics' food—a long tradition spawned by the alcoholism cures described in Chapter Eight.

Because of the medical risks involved in an Antabuse reaction, patients treated with Antabuse were usually given a card like the following:

```
+----------------------------------------------+
|                  WARNING                     |
|                                              |
| The bearer of this card _____, who    |
| resides at _____  |
| (Telephone _____) is taking Antabuse.   |
| When combined with alcohol, this medication  |
| can produce flushing, perspiration, breathing|
| difficulty, perspiration, vomiting, heart pal-|
| pitations, and low blood pressure. In the event|
| of a reaction, call Dr. _____ at the   |
| _____ Treatment Center (Tele-      |
| phone _____) for information regard-    |
| ing appropriate treatment.                   |
+----------------------------------------------+
```

When Antabuse was first introduced in the United States, there were many complaints of side-effects, but most of these resulted from the excessive dosages of the drug that were being prescribed. With the right protocol, side effects of Antabuse became mild and transitory for most patients, usually spontaneously disappearing within a few days of drug maintenance. Where mild side effects continued, patients were free to determine whether the potential threat of relapse posed more danger than the minor discomfort of such symptoms. The length of time alcoholics were maintained on Antabuse was for the most part left to the discretion of each patient and his or her physician. Dr. Ruth Fox, an early advocate of Antabuse, recommended its use for "as long as the patient needs it."[129]

Antabuse was not effective as a total program of treatment, but it was discovered to be a helpful adjunct in treatment with some clients. When it was combined with counseling and active group support, Antabuse proved an effective aid in reducing impulsive relapse and in reducing the alcoholic's preoccupation with alcohol during early recovery. Many successfully recovered alcoholics used Antabuse during their early recovery, as a consciously erected barrier between themselves and their first drink.[130] In a modern evaluation of the research on Antabuse, William Miller suggests that the therapeutic effects of Antabuse are produced by a "substantial placebo effect combined with a modest (at best) specific effect."[131]

In the years following the drug's introduction, the criminal justice system explored the potential of Antabuse as an aid in their efforts to treat and monitor alcoholic offenders. Some jurisdictions made Antabuse mandatory as a condition of probation or parole. Some criminal justice authorities even conducted clinics to supervise the daily administration of Antabuse.

One of the difficulties with Antabuse was clients' tendency to discontinue use of the drug and return to drinking. This raised interest, particularly within the criminal justice system, in a form of Antabuse that did not rely so heavily on the daily decision-making of the alcoholic. Subcutaneous implants of Antabuse were developed by Marie in France in the 1950s. The technique involved surgically implanting from three to 10 sterile disulfram tablets through a small incision in the lower abdomen. Disulfram implants were generally left in for about six months, then replaced with new tablets. In his review of Antabuse implants, Allan Wilson cited several practitioners who believed that the implants were, psychologically speaking, a more effective deterrent to drinking than the daily oral pill. The technique was not widely utilized because of such side-effects as subcutaneous abscesses and the finding that the implants did not provide a consistent Antabuse/alcohol reaction when alcohol was consumed. There were, however, isolated reports noting 60% "success rates" using implants with "hostile patients."[132]

LSD and the Treatment of Alcoholism [133]

Attempts to use hallucinogenic experience as a treatment for alcoholism date back to the introduction of the peyote ritual within the Native American Church. Commentators from anthropologist Thomas Hill to psychiatrist Karl Menninger have reported on the utility of the peyote experience in treating alcoholism among Native Peoples.[134] Some interest was again stirred by Erich Guttman and W.S. Maclay's 1936 report on the potential use of mescaline as a therapeutic agent in the treatment of certain psychiatric conditions.[135] But it was not until 1943—when Dr. Albert Hofmann of Sandoz Laboratories in Basel, Switzerland accidentally ingested and discovered the hallucinogenic properties of an ergot compound—that an agent emerged that would stir great interest in the use of hallucinogens in the treatment of alcoholism. Hofmann called his ergot compound LSD-25.

The first human experiments with LSD outside Sandoz Laboratories were conducted by Dr. Werner Stoll, the son of Arthur Stoll—co-developer of LSD-25. The young Stoll, a psychiatrist at the University of Zurich, discovered that, when low doses of LSD were consumed by humans, repressed thoughts and feelings became quickly accessible. When Stoll published his initial findings in 1947, the potential uses of LSD in psychotherapy seemed unlimited.

Between 1949 and 1966, LSD was employed by many researchers and psychotherapists in the treatment of alcoholism, childhood autism, obsessive and compulsive disorders, impotence and frigidity, neuroses, character disorders, anticipatory grief (of those facing death), and prolonged grief. Early reports of LSD's efficacy as a tool in psychiatric treatment included claims that the drug 1) loosened repressed contents of feeling and experience, 2) provided an opportunity to actually re-experience past events of personal importance, and 3) lowered resistance to psychotherapy.[136] It was found that, with careful patient selection and preparation and with adequate training and supervision of the therapist, the risk of adverse reactions to LSD psychotherapy was minimal.[137]

The two most important figures in the use of LSD in the treatment of alcoholism were Abram Hoffer and Humphry Osmond—the same researchers who had sparked Bill Wilson's interest in Vitamin B$_3$. It was LSD's psychosis-mimicking properties that first attracted Hoffer and Osmond to LSD's potential use with alcoholics. They described the earliest thinking about the use of LSD in the treatment of alcoholism in terms of LSD's potential to create a chemically induced experience of "hitting bottom."

We hoped that a frightful experience which modeled the worst symptoms in natural delirium tremens could persuade our alcoholic patients not to drink any more.[138]

Their first treatment of alcoholic patients with LSD occurred in 1953 at the Saskatchewan Hospital in Weyburn. In spite of the efforts to induce the "bad trip" that Hoffer described above, patients began escaping into pleasurable, enriching experiences that Osmond began to refer to as "psychedelic."[139] Hoffer's and Osmond's alcoholic patients began to improve on a number of treatment dimensions, but not for the reasons anticipated. It was thus more by accident than by intent that researchers discovered the way in which LSD would be used to enhance insight and behavioral change in alcoholics.

Where other researchers used small doses of LSD to bypass well-known alcoholic defenses, Hoffer and Osmond used high doses of LSD and guided clients through profound drug-induced experiences. Advocates of LSD psychotherapy with alcoholics began to speak of the potential of LSD to induce an "ego death" and "chemical conversion reaction"—experiences not unlike the conversion process described by William James and experienced by Bill Wilson at Charles Towns Hospital.

Two approaches to LSD therapy emerged: psycholytic therapy and psychedelic therapy. In psycholytic ("mind loosening") therapy, LSD was used to reduce alcoholic resistance, to "liquify" defenses, to retrieve repressed emotional material, to intensify emotional catharsis, and to deepen insight. In this approach, LSD was used to speed up the work of traditional psychotherapy. Small doses (25-150 micrograms) of LSD were used in repeated sessions. In the therapists' view, one disadvantage was that, even with these lower doses, alcoholic clients sometimes developed mystical insights that led some of them to conclude that they no longer needed therapy.

In *psychedelic* ("mind manifesting") therapy, large doses (300-1,000 micrograms) of LSD were used to create the same kinds of breakthroughs in perception and meaning that the psycholytic therapists were describing as a side effect. Psycholytic therapy viewed LSD as an adjunct to the psychotherapy experience; psychedelic therapy viewed psychotherapy as an adjunct to the identity-transforming LSD experience. While Hoffer and Osmond's early work with alcoholics was clearly in the category of psychedelic therapy, both modes of LSD therapy were used with alcoholics during the 1960s.[140]

During this period, a typical LSD treatment session involved the use of pleasant musical and visual backgrounds, along with instructions for the alcoholic patient under the influence of LSD to view and reflect on family pictures or to concentrate on a list of pre-selected questions concerning the patient's developmental history, current life problems, or future directions.[141] What was clear from both psycholytic and psychedelic therapy was that memories, emotions, and ideas experienced under the influence of LSD were received with a deep sense of validity. While the risks involved in LSD therapy could be minimized, the use of LSD in psychotherapy had many potential iatrogenic effects. It was discovered that the therapeutic use of LSD could be harmful for and was thus contraindicated in certain populations, e.g., people with paranoid or borderline personalities. In his 1976 review of LSD psychotherapy, Sidney Cohen also commented on the fact that a number of therapists had experienced psychotic breaks and other psychiatric disturbances as a result of their own LSD consumption.[142]

The early scientific literature on the use of LSD in psychotherapy with alcoholics was uniformly positive. Even medical specialists within the alcoholism field, such as Dr. Ruth Fox, the Medical Director of the National Council on Alcoholism, noted the potential of LSD.

LSD does seem to make the patient more willing to undertake the total program necessary for his recovery. After LSD most of the patients who formerly refused to cooperate were willing to take disulfram, attend group therapy and to affiliate with A.A.[143]

Many alcoholics reported new realizations and new perceptions that allowed them to achieve and sustain stable sobriety. Hoffer's and Osmond's patients reported new perceptions of themselves ("I was revolted by what I saw in myself.") and their surroundings ("I now find I understand the AA program," "I realized what I was doing to my wife.")[144]

By the 1960s, the drug's reported success rates in the treatment of alcoholism were ranging between 50 and 70 percent.[145] In 1968, Hoffer and Osmond proclaimed that "There is no longer any doubt that for the first time in history, a substance, LSD, and methods have been found to halt or control the drinking of the toughest alcoholics known."[146] While early success rates fired optimism for this new technique, all but two controlled studies revealed no particular advantages in the use of LSD in the treatment of alcoholism.[147]

While LSD-facilitated psychotherapeutic experiences could lead to breakthroughs in self-perception and awareness powerful enough to temporarily "unfreeze" compulsive patterns of addictive behavior, the weakness of this therapy was in the lack of any ongoing program of recovery that could sustain this emotional commitment to sobriety. One might recall similar emotional breakthroughs that alcoholics experienced in the Washingtonian Movement of the 1840s. As in that earlier era, many alcoholics who experienced LSD psychotherapy returned to active drinking in the absence of a daily program of long-term recovery. One of the more curious footnotes of history is the fact that two of the central figures in the emergence of addiction-focused mutual-aid societies in the 20th century—Bill Wilson and Charles Dederich—participated in LSD experiments.

Miscellaneous and Multiple Drug Therapies

Alcoholics in the 1940s were exposed to a wide assortment of agents thought to suppress the craving for alcohol, including bromides and tonic mixtures made up of quinine, gentian, and glycerine, sometimes combined with hypodermic injections of strychnine. The combination of atropine and strychnine was used in the treatment of alcoholism from the 1890s through the 1940s. Insulin, used at mid-century to induce what was perceived as a therapeutic coma in alcoholics, continued to be used into the 1960s in the treatment of alcoholism, although the rationale for its use shifted to that of stimulating the appetite during detoxification.[148]

Although we have catalogued a number of drugs used during the mid-20th century in the treatment of alcoholism, alcoholics rarely received a single type of medication. Because alcoholism presented such a broad and rapidly changing constellation of symptoms, alcoholics were often prescribed a complicated sequence of medications. Multiple-drug therapy, combined with the concurrent application of other treatment methods, characterized alcoholism treatment throughout the past century. An example of such multiple interventions comes from Dr. W.C. Ashworth, Medical Director of the Glenwood Park Sanitarium in Greensboro, North Carolina, who described in the *Virginia Medical Monthly* the treatment of alcoholism at Glenwood Park. Alcoholic refreshment was provided to all incoming patients in order to "establish confidence of the patient, and promote a feeling of well-being and good fellowship." Patients were then treated with trional and paraldehyde to induce sleep; given a saline laxative to clear the bowels; provided a tonic consisting of cinchoma, gentian, and nux vomica (strychnine); injected with pilocarpine and apomorphine to eliminate craving for alcohol; and administered "electrical and hydrotherapeutic measures."[149]

The Carbon Dioxide Treatment for Alcoholism

The purposeful induction of coma in a patient through the inhalation of carbon dioxide was first used as a treatment in psychiatry by Lovenhart in 1929. Its indicated uses included the treatment of psychosis, anxiety states, melancholy, and—in the 1950's—alcoholism. There were two different techniques of carbon dioxide therapy, both used on alcoholics. The first involved low doses (with less than 40% concentration of carbon dioxide) inhaled for 3 minutes, resulting in a brief loss of consciousness. The second technique involved high concentrations of carbon dioxide (40-80%), which could produce unconsciousness through a single inhalation. Carbon dioxide therapy was used periodically on alcoholics, in spite of a limited rationale for its use and poor results obtained in outcome studies.

A 1955 study of 47 alcoholics within a broader psychiatric population concluded that, of the various psychiatric populations treated with this method, alcoholics manifested the lowest level of reaction to carbon dioxide. Few alcoholics showed any improvement as a result of carbon dioxide treatment.[150] In a later study, Albert LaVerne reported on the use of carbon dioxide therapy in the treatment of addictive disorders. In his study of more than 300 alcoholics, LaVerne reported that more than half abstained from alcohol and that another 15% of relapsing clients maintained sobriety after they were put on weekly maintenance treatments of carbon dioxide.[151] [152]

Advances in Psychosocial Rehabilitation Technology

The mid-century also saw many advances in the rehabilitation of alcoholics that focused, not on their physiology, but on their psychosocial functioning, The emergence of the multidisciplinary team in Minnesota laid a foundation for new approaches to alcoholism treatment that would begin to treat the alcoholic as a whole person and incorporate psychological, social, and spiritual dimensions into the more traditional physical approaches to alcoholism treatment. There were the approaches of Bridge House and Portal House that we reviewed in the last chapter, which tended to focus on the social rehabilitation of the alcoholic. With the growing number of treatment facilities—particularly the growing number of acute-care hospitals and psychiatric hospitals that were developing alcoholism wards—one significant unmet need in the 1950s was that of a post-hospitalization setting in which the alcoholic could reconstruct his or her lifestyle in an environment that would support continued sobriety. A new institution was about to be born to fill this need.

The Halfway House Movement

Today's halfway house originated within different professional fields, evolved in unique directions, and then came together in the 1950s in a "halfway house movement." We will briefly trace the threads of the halfway house concept in allied fields, then provide a detailed account of the evolution of the halfway house within the addictions treatment field.

Background: The halfway house movement was by no means limited to the addictions treatment field. Professional arenas as diverse as psychiatry, criminal justice, child welfare, physical rehabilitation, and family violence each exerted an influence on the halfway house and its many variations: group foster care, group homes, reintegration centers, three-quarter-way houses, transitional living quarters, and shelters, to name just a few. The literature of each field depicts the halfway house as an innovation unique to itself.

Elements of what in the mid-20th century came to be called halfway houses can be found deep in history. The history of medicine in many cultures describes patients living with and becoming an extension of the physician's household. Oliver Keller and Benedict Alper trace the history of the use of halfway houses by the American criminal justice system to Massachusetts, New York, and Pennsylvania in the years 1820 to 1860. These states experimented with transitional living arrangements to enhance the effectiveness of two other innovations: prison and probation.[153]

Harold and Charlotte Raush cite 1953 as the entry of the term "halfway house" into modern mental health field. The term would signal the emerging movement to de-institutionalize the mentally ill in the United States.[154] Breakthroughs in the development of anti-psychotic medications—along with the new institutions called halfway houses, sheltered care homes, and group homes—made it possible to bring thousands of institutionalized, chronically mentally ill people back into American communities.[155]

Early Alcoholic Halfway Houses: In the addictions field, the term "halfway house" has come to mean a supportive, transitional residence where people live between inpatient addiction treatment or jail and independent living. But the use of such facilities actually predates residential treatment.

The creation of a stable residence to support alcoholics and addicts during early recovery has a long history. Alcoholics often stayed in almshouses and "county farms" in their efforts to sober up, and some of the facilities that pre-dated the inebriate asylums of the 19th century could be easily called halfway houses. There were the "temperance hotels." There were the "lodging rooms" above Washingtonian Hall in Boston. We can also find concern during the inebriate asylum era for patients who needed, not active treatment, but a home. In 1899, Thomas Holmes called for the state to provide a "halfway house" for those inebriates who "live in the borderland between sanity and insanity."[156] There were the later "treatment farms" of Durfee and others. There were the small "rest homes" and "retreats" that served as informal drying-out places for alcoholics who were not allowed admission to hospitals. All of these might be considered the ancestors of the modern halfway house for alcoholics.

The roots of the mid-20th-century halfway house movement can probably also be traced to the tendency

of early members of Alcoholics Anonymous to open up their homes to newcomers in A.A. Private residences, such as Dr. Bob and Anne Smith's and Bill and Lois Wilson's, were routinely turned into what today would be called halfway houses. The literature of A.A. is filled with stories of such experiments in support. Lois Wilson described the typical state of affairs at their home when Bill first became sober: "We had drunks all over the house; sometimes as many as five lived there at one time."[157] An early A.A. prospect who was staying with Bill and Lois Wilson killed himself while his hosts were on a visit to Maryland. Another oft-reported story is of the time Anne Smith was chased by a knife-wielding prospect who was staying in her and Dr. Bob's home.[158]

There were the small private sanataria that marked a halfway point for the alcoholic between acute medical and psychiatric hospitals and independent life in the community. There were the landladies who prided themselves on their ability to reform alcoholics and developed a specialty of caring for alcoholics within their boarding houses.

To a great extent, the halfway house movement was driven by concern for the male alcoholic who was homeless, alienated from family, socially isolated, rehabilitating himself from alcohol-related injuries, and jobless. The movement emerged out of a disillusionment with institutional approaches to personal reformation, and as such formed an alternative to traditional institutions.[159] Halfway houses were a means of keeping alcoholics from going to institutions as well as places for helping them make the transition out of such institutions. The movement had two roots: one that produced facilities that one might call "halfway in," the other that produced facilities that one could call "halfway out." Both can still be found in the addictions field.

While there is clearly a long history of providing supportive living for alcoholics as an alternative to institutionalization, or as transitional support on the way out of such institutions, three things of great significance occurred in the 1950s. First, there was a dramatic expansion in the number of these facilities. Second, there was a movement toward more formal organization of these facilities, including the integration of various therapeutic activities. Finally, there was an effort to link the halfway house to the broader continuum of care for alcoholics. Rather than standing as independent institutions, halfway houses became closely linked with hospitals, correctional facilities, and treatment programs.

There were two early efforts to organize halfway houses in the 1950s. The first, launched in 1952, was initiated by Joe Flynn. Flynn developed a network of halfway houses in Washington D.C. that were run on A.A. principles. These facilities became known as "Flynn Houses."[160] The second effort was the founding of Fellowship Club in Minnesota in 1953. This facility was started when it was recognized that alcoholics needed extended help following their brief treatment at Hazelden.[161]

Sponsorship and Structure: Earl Rubington's study of halfway houses revealed three patterns of financial sponsorship for halfway houses: private ownership, state funding, and church support.[162] The term "halfway house" embraced a wide variety of structures, and what we define as a halfway house also fell within a broader nomenclature that included such terms as work-camp, ranch, boarding home, rooming house, residential care facility, and transitional living facility. During the mid-20th century, there were also "quarterway houses," which provided supervised living and treatment activities that fell between the high intensity of the hospital or sanitarium and the less-structured living situations that existed in the halfway house. These were followed by even less-carefully supervised "group homes" or "recovery homes," where people in early recovery lived together for mutual support.

Mid-century halfway houses for alcoholics shared many common elements: 1) they provided a structured living situation with some meals; 2) they provided peer support and a modicum of professional staff support; and 3) they tended to focus primarily on lifestyle reconstruction—skills of daily living, obtaining and sustaining employment, developing a sobriety-based social network, and participating in drug-free recreation. Earl Rubington, in one of his many excellent articles on the halfway house movement, noted "four structural principles" upon which halfway houses for alcoholics were founded: 1) small size, 2) simple rules, 3) reduction of status differences between residents and staff, and 4) informality.[163]

One might legitimately ask in what ways the mid-century alcoholic halfway houses were different from the alcoholic treatment programs of the same era. Variations on both types of facilities were so numerous that the line between the two is quite indistinct. But a few generalizations might be made.

- Halfway houses tended to focus more on habilitation than rehabilitation.
- Halfway houses focused on sustaining rather than initiating sobriety.
- Halfway houses tended to focus more on social support than on "treatment."

- Halfway houses usually had less structure (rules, daily activities, limits on freedom of communication and movement) than did treatment programs.
- Halfway houses placed a major emphasis on employment—as much for the fees needed to support the facility as for the habilitation of the resident.
- Halfway houses often operated with only a small number of staff. The earliest homes often had only a "house manager" and a cook. The majority of staff were recovering alcoholics or recovering family members.[164]

One of the ways in which halfway houses were classified was by length of possible stay. The state of California classified recovery homes into three categories: primary recovery homes, in which clients were in residence from a few days to a month; supportive recovery homes, in which clients could stay in residence from a month to one year; and sustained recovery homes, in which clients could remain for an indefinite period of time.[165]

Mid-Century History and Status: In 1958, Edward Blacker and David Kantor conducted the first survey of hallway houses for alcoholics. Their review of resources in 49 states, the District of Columbia, US. Territories, and Canadian Provinces revealed the existence of 30 halfway houses which served alcoholics. The major characteristics of these programs included the following:

- The average duration of the homes' existence was four years, although one facility sponsored by the Salvation Army had operated for 55 years.
- The capacity of the 30 halfway houses averaged 25 beds and ranged from five to 150 beds.
- Sixty-eight percent of the facilities admitted only men.
- Fees charged to clients ranged from $7 to $110 weekly.
- The halfway houses were staffed with both paid and unpaid workers. The majority of workers and volunteers were recovered alcoholics, most affiliated with Alcoholics Anonymous.
- The perceived ideal length of stay ranged from five days to two years; the average actual length of stay was 90 days.
- The therapeutic programs of the surveyed facilities generally included combinations of the following four elements: 1) personal or religious counseling, 2) vocational counseling and supervised employment, 3) attendance at A.A. meetings, and 4) the use of Antabuse.[166]

In 1964, Robert Martinson described some 50 "recovery houses" for alcoholics, houses that had been initiated in California between the mid-1950s and the mid-1960s. He believed that the organizing principle of such homes was the introduction of the alcoholic to the concept and experience of a "sober community of ex-alcoholics." He noted that most of the California facilities served as a form of "sanctuary" or "retreat," in which the alcoholic could solidify his or her hold on recovery. In contrast to most residents of correctional or mental health halfway houses, most alcoholics were not coming into the community from institutional life, but were coming from relative freedom in the community to the more structured environment of the recovery homes. The recovery homes studied by Martinson were small (15 beds or less) and tended to be located in stable residential neighborhoods. During this era, the homes charged each resident an average of $20 per week. Nearly all staff working in the recovery homes surveyed by Martinson were themselves recovered alcoholics.[167]

In a later 1960s survey, David Pittman reviewed a wide variety of frameworks that provided transitional living or transitional support to the alcoholic. These frameworks included halfway houses, day hospitals, and outpatient clinics that were becoming visible components of the continuum of care for alcoholics. Pittman's list also contained other support mechanisms, such as: 1) traveling clinics which delivered support services to alcoholics in rural and other underserved areas, 2) community houses that provided long-term sheltered living for alcoholics suffering from organic brain syndromes, 3) foster homes that provided intimate supervised living situations for alcoholics in early recovery, and 4) social centers serving to replace the "tavern culture" that had been the center of social life for many alcoholics.[168]

Professionalization: In 1958, Margaret Rudolph —a pioneer leader in the halfway house movement—invited halfway houses from across the U.S. and Canada to a meeting in St. Paul, Minnesota. This meeting led to the creation of the Association of Halfway House Alcoholism Programs of North America (AHHAP).[169] A broader organization—the International Halfway House Association—was organized in 1964, and within a decade the association counted among its membership more than 1,300 halfway houses.[170]

The qualities that had made halfway houses successful, such as their small size and their informality, worked against the strength of these institutions as the broader field began to professionalize and industrialize. Challenges faced by halfway houses included obtaining and sustaining operational funds, managing controversies over their location in particular neighborhoods, recruiting and retaining staff, sustaining healthy staff-client relationships over time, managing the propensity of the halfway house to remain isolated from other community-service institutions, and systematizing the often-charismatic styles of institutional leadership.[171]

While new technologies were emerging in the treatment of alcoholism, quite dramatic changes were underway in the treatment of narcotic addiction.

Chapter Twenty-Four
Mid-Century Addiction Treatment: The Rise of New Approaches

This chapter will describe medical and psychiatric approaches to treatment for addiction to drugs other than alcohol that were first implemented in the 1950s and 1960s. We will discuss religion-sponsored addiction programs, the founding of Narcotics Anonymous, and the emergence of ex-addict-directed therapeutic communities.

The Legal Context

While few addiction treatment resources were available as the decade of the 1950s opened, awareness of the growing numbers of addicts—particularly juvenile addicts—sparked action in many communities to launch local efforts at addict rehabilitation. But before these efforts were underway, America embarked on a campaign to criminalize the status of addiction even further. America's urban communities responded to the rise in heroin use by organizing narcotics bureaus within their police departments and, in a few cases, by creating "narcotics courts."[172] But these local initiatives paled beside what was about to happen at the federal level.

Since the closing of the narcotics clinics in the early 1920s, America had defined narcotic addiction more as a problem of criminal deviance than as a disease. Legal interpretations of the Harrison Act and the enforcement policies of the Bureau of Narcotics pushed addicts deeper and deeper into subterranean cultures. In the early 1950s, hostility toward the issue of narcotic drugs intensified and led to the passage of two quite repressive measures. In 1951, Congress passed the Boggs Act—legislation that dramatically increased penalties for drug violations; introduced mandatory minimum sentences; and eliminated options of suspended sentences, probation, or parole for repeat drug offenders. In the aftermath of this action, President Dwight D. Eisenhower declared a "new war on narcotic addiction" and appointed a Cabinet Committee to lead the country into battle. Out of this crusade came the Narcotic Control Act of 1956—an Act that again increased penalties for drug offenses and, for the first time in American narcotic legislation history, introduced punishment that could include life imprisonment or the death penalty. The draconian nature of these measures would in time generate a backlash calling for more humane approaches to drug addiction, but their immediate effect was a chilling one. It was in the context of this hostility that some highly invasive and coercive methods of "treatment" emerged.

Medical and Psychiatric Context

When we left our story of the treatment of narcotic addiction in Chapter Fourteen, the federal narcotics hospitals at Lexington and Fort Worth stood as the primary—and nearly the only—sources of narcotic addiction treatment in the United States. While significant innovations were pioneered at these facilities, such as the use of methadone as a detoxification agent, few of these innovations found their way into mainstream medical or psychiatric practice. Between the 1930s and 1950s, most of the physical methods of treating narcotic addiction came as an afterthought of their use in the treatment of alcoholism. Most of the treatments for alcoholism that we reviewed in Chapter Eleven were experimentally applied to the treatment of narcotic addiction.

Insulin: In the 1930s, Dr. Fred Modern noted that insulin could suppress opiate-withdrawal symptoms and reduce the post-acute withdrawal cravings that were frequently associated with relapse.[173] Insulin-coma therapy was first discovered by Dr. Manfred Joshua Sakel of the Lichterfelde Sanatorium in Berlin and reported as a cure for drug addiction. The technique involved inducing a mild coma through injection of insulin, which was purported to reduce craving for morphine and other drugs. Dr. Sakel was invited to New York in 1937 to demonstrate this technique.[174]

"Shock" Therapy: Thigpen, Thigpen, and Cleckley reported the use of Electroconvulsive Therapy (ETC) in 1948 to "eliminate the adverse manifestations of withdrawal" in opiate-dependent patients. Their technique for the application of ECT was four treatments on the first day, three treatments the second day, and one treatment each following day, until withdrawal was complete. They reported that the confusion produced by the ECT was an effective antidote to the normal discomfort of withdrawal.[175]

Aversion Therapy: Aversion therapy was used experimentally in the treatment of morphine addiction. The primary aversive agents included apomorphine and succinyl choline, which were paired with self-administered morphine or heroin. The most vocal American advocate of this treatment was the writer William Burroughs, author of *Junkie*, who claimed he was cured of narcotic addiction through apomorphine treatment.

Psychosurgery: The peak period for the use of psychosurgery in the treatment of narcotic addiction spanned the years 1948 through 1952. Prefrontal lobotomies were performed on narcotic addicts in an effort to relieve withdrawal, reduce the experience of intractable pain, and reduce drug craving. At least nine cases of psychosurgical treatment of addiction appeared in the literature of this period. While initial reports praised the technique, there was no sustainable scientific evidence that such invasive procedures had any effect on drug cravings or on the drug-seeking behavior of addicts, in spite of claims to the contrary.[176]

Serum Therapy: The extent to which addicts were subjected to bizarre medical experiments is further indicated by the Colorado State Penitentiary's 1938 announcement of its discovery of an addiction cure. The procedure used at the Penitentiary involved raising blisters on the abdomen of the addict, withdrawing serum from the blisters with a hypodermic syringe, and then injecting the serum into the patient's arm. This procedure was repeated four to five times a day for a week to ten days in order to effect the "cure."[177]

Since the closing of the morphine maintenance clinics in the 1920s, narcotic addicts had found their way into both private and state-sponsored psychiatric hospitals. By 1960, 34 states provided some statutory allowance for the admission of addicts into state psychiatric hospitals.[178] Most "treatment" in these institutions involved rapid withdrawal and physical rehabilitation within the general psychiatric milieu of the state hospital. Few provided any specialized treatment regimen for addicts. If the psychiatric literature of the 1950s is any indication, the overall prospects for the treatment of narcotic addiction appeared grim, at best.

In 1951, Dr. Robert Knight and Dr. Curtis Prout reported on the treatment of 75 addicts at a hospital in Westchester, New York. Knight and Prout's study group was made up of 40 men and 35 women described as coming from "middle-class" homes blessed with cultural and educational advantages. The majority were addicted to morphine or other opiates. These patients began using drugs at an average age of 37 and entered the hospital at an average age of 43.8 years. Sixty-three of the 75 were married at the time of admission. Factors related to their use of narcotics were divided into two groups. Sixty-two of the patients reported endogenous factors such as physical illness, restlessness, or insomnia as factors in their drug use, and 16 patients reported such exogenous factors as family troubles or financial losses. Treatment consisted of progressive withdrawal, individual therapy, and phased re-entry into their home environments. The average length of stay in the hospital was 3.3 months. Follow-up interviews with these clients, who collectively should have had a good prognosis for recovery, revealed that only 20% of the patients were abstinent at the time of follow-up.[179]

Alfred Freedman described a hospital-based treatment program for narcotic addiction that began its operation at Metropolitan Hospital in New York City in 1959. The program was established within the hospital's Department of Psychiatry and emphasized the treatment of adult male patients who entered on a voluntary basis. The program consisted of two 25-bed units, in which the addicted patients remained for 28 days before being graduated to outpatient and aftercare services. In many ways, the Metropolitan units represented the state of the art in the psychiatric treatment of addiction. There were specialized units supported by medical school faculty and staff interested in both treatment and research. Patients were detoxified with methadone and provided psychological counseling and social support by an interdisciplinary team of psychiatrists, psychologists, social workers, vocational counselors, and recreational therapists. Patients received both individual and group psycho-

therapy from trained therapists. There was a strong effort to involve clients in aftercare services, which even included a social club designed to provide drug-free leisure for patients. In spite of these resources, the results of the program were meager. Only 66 of the first 490 adults treated sustained their involvement in aftercare services following discharge, and the relapse rate of treated patients was believed to be quite high. Freedman noted that the Metropolitan experience confirmed other studies suggesting that traditional psychotherapeutic approaches had only limited value in the treatment of addiction. Freedman also noted some difficulties that arose in the treatment of addicts in general community hospitals during this period. These difficulties included resistance from hospital staff and administration and community stigma associated with people and institutions that treated addiction.[180] A few mid-century addiction treatment hospitals under state sponsorship specialized in the treatment of addiction. These facilities included the Blue Hills Hospital in Connecticut and Avon Park in Florida.[181] One of the most significant local treatment experiments in the 1950s occurred at Riverside Hospital in New York City.

Juvenile Addiction: The Story of Riverside Hospital

In the early 1950s, New York City became alarmed by a rising incidence of adolescent heroin addiction. Addicts were being treated in the adolescent units of Bellevue Hospital or Kings County Hospital, but there was universal agreement on the need for a resource designed specifically to treat the problem of narcotic addiction among the very young. This recognition led to the opening of Riverside Hospital on July 1, 1952.

Riverside Hospital's 141-bed facility was divided into four wards, three for adolescent males and one for adolescent females. The facilities also included separate recreation and educational buildings, a chapel, and housing for staff who lived on the Island. The grounds contained tennis and handball courts, basketball courts, and a baseball diamond. The facility was staffed by 300 employees organized within a multi-disciplinary team approach that sought to integrate the technical knowledge of all team members in the treatment planning process.[182]

The program was initially designed on the assumption that clients would be voluntary and motivated to become drug-free, but adolescent addicts admitted to Riverside Hospital were almost always admitted under duress. Most of the adolescents treated at the hospital came from a small number of census tracts that were among the poorest and most crowded in New York City.[183]

Riverside should have worked. It had strong community support. It utilized a state-of-the-art theoretical framework to treat addiction. Patients were medically detoxified and offered the opportunity to remain for a six-month individualized rehabilitation program consisting of psychological therapy, educational classes, and structured leisure. The program was staffed by a multidisciplinary team of physicians, psychiatrists, psychologists, social workers, nurses, welfare case workers, teachers, clergy, and lay volunteers. Every effort was made to work with the families of the adolescents in treatment, and efforts were made to follow adolescents after treatment through a community clinic located in Manhattan. Riverside's program appeared to be the ideal model of treatment. It should have worked. But it did not. Riverside Hospital was closed in 1961, when a follow-up study of 247 former patients revealed that 97% of those treated had continued their addiction following treatment.[184]

Riverside was not alone in its efforts to provide hospital-based treatment of heroin addiction. Other early efforts at community hospital-based treatment in New York City included a detoxification unit at Manhattan State Hospital (55 beds) and detoxification services at Metropolitan Hospital (25 beds) and Manhattan General Hospital.[185] During the Riverside era, the primary resource for most addicts over age 21 was Rikers Island Penitentiary. Addicts were committed to Rikers for a 28-day "cold-turkey cure" until 1958, when the Corrections Commissioner closed the Rikers detoxification unit and banned the use of any correctional facility for detoxification. His rationale was that addicts in withdrawal should be treated in hospitals, not jails. The only problem was there were no hospitals willing to take on this task. It wasn't until the early 1960s that additional beds were allocated at Central Islip Hospital, Utica State Hospital, Buffalo State Hospital, Middletown State Hospital, and Pilgrim State Hospital for the treatment of addiction.[186]

Community-Based Support of Institutionalized Addicts

Another noteworthy addiction treatment project was started in 1957, a project whose goal was successful reintegration of addicts returning to New York City from the Public Health Hospital in Lexington. The New York Demonstration Center was funded by the National Institute of Mental Health to assess whether increased community supports (social casework) would lower the relapse rates of addicts returning home from institutional treatment. Efforts to support the continued abstinence of returning addicts were not particularly successful. A very frustrated staff attributed this failure to the addict's "dependency, passivity, narcissism, low frustration tolerance, suspiciousness, disregard for time, and irresponsibility."[187]

In the 1950s and early 1960s, some communities outside New York City tried combining short-term institutional detoxification with outpatient screening, counseling, and—where appropriate—referral to Lexington for more intensive treatment. Typical of these efforts was a program developed by the Department of Health in Detroit. Initiated in collaboration with the Mayor's Committee for Rehabilitation of Narcotic Addicts, this program combined detoxification at the Detroit Receiving Hospital with follow-up services at the Detroit Narcotic Clinic and referral to Lexington. The Detroit program was plagued by three major problems: 1) more than 80% of its patients failed to attend follow-up appointments after their detoxification, 2) patients refused to go for more intensive treatment in Lexington, and 3) most of the addicts who did voluntarily enter Lexington left shortly afterward against medical advice.

Chicago experimented with similar models. The first of these experiments was the establishment of three outpatient clinics funded by the Illinois Legislature in 1950. Perhaps most interesting among the descriptions of these clinics was the Northwestern Hospital clinic's reported goal of helping narcotic addicts "graduate" from drugs to alcohol.[188] In the later 1950s, Chicago treated its addicts through detoxification at Bridewell Hospital, probationary supervision, and referral for follow-up counseling at community clinics.[189]

The medical management of addicts in the 1950s and early 1960s often fell upon local general medical practitioners. These physicians treated overdoses, treated infections and sexually transmitted diseases, and also provided admission for inpatient detoxification on a limited basis. Some even began to experiment with new approaches to addiction treatment. During the mid-1960s, a number of physicians in San Francisco prescribed injectable amphetamines in the treatment of heroin addiction. This practice was driven both by profit motives and by the belief that amphetamine use was less physically and socially damaging than the use of heroin.[190] This medically sanctioned methamphetamine use opened the doors to the methamphetamine-injecting subculture that moved to center stage of the polydrug culture in 1968.

Religious Approaches to Addiction Recovery

As we noted in Chapter Nine, the use of religious experience as a framework for addiction recovery can be traced deep within American history. The 1950s and 1960s saw a revival in religious approaches to the treatment of narcotic addiction and polydrug abuse. Some of the more prominent of these early efforts included Saint Mark's Clinic, a Chicago program operated by Father Robert Jenks of Saint Mark's Episcopal Church from 1954 to 1959; the Addicts Rehabilitation Center (1957) in Manhattan, sponsored by the Christian Reformed Church; the Episcopalian-affiliated Astoria Consultation Service (1958) in Queens New York, later called the Samaritan Halfway Society; and Exodus House (1958), which was originally sponsored by New York City's East Harlem Protestant Parish.[191]

As early as 1950, members of the East Harlem Protestant Parish had begun ministering to addicts. In 1956, a Narcotics Committee was formed within the Parish to create a better-organized addiction ministry. The committee drew together people with many different religious views, including some community professionals, to address the growing problem of narcotic addiction. Their view of addiction and recovery was set forth in an unpublished paper by Norman Eddy:

> *We affirm that addiction to heroin is in the same category as other addictions, and that all represent varying degrees of rebellion against God...Spiritually, addicted people are empty, and they know that they are empty. After the first happy days of addiction are over, despair and meaninglessness press in upon them, offering them no hope. For a small number, rebirth in God has revolutionized their entire personalities, and they have found purpose in life without narcotics. These rebirths point to the possibility of all types of addicted people finding new life in giving their lives to God.*[192]

The Narcotics Committee of the East Harlem Protestant Parish established a storefront operation that provided outreach to addicts and delivered medical, psychiatric, and legal services.[193]

In his book *From Dope to Hope*, the story of the Samaritan Halfway Society in New York, Father Pitcaithly recounted the incredible array of obstacles encountered in initiating church-sponsored services to young drug users. The Astoria Consultation Service (ASC) was created in 1960 as a counseling service for drug-using youth. Organized under the skeptical eye of a local Episcopal Church, ASC offered individual and group counseling and a drop-in environment in which young addicts could arrive without appointment and spend time talking or playing cards. As the ASC grew and sought to expand its services by finding a facility that could handle its burgeoning clients, Father Pitcaithly encountered overwhelming community opposition that included incessant telephone threats, petition drives, marches protesting the program, repeated vandalism, and fires from Molotov cocktails. In spite of such resistance, a suitable location for the program was eventually found.[194]

While many of the above-described programs had religious sponsors, the counseling that they provided did not necessarily emphasize a religious dimension. Other churches, however, portrayed religion itself as an antidote to addiction. We will focus on two such religious organizations that have been visibly involved in addict rehabilitation: Teen Challenge and the Black Nation of Islam (formerly known as the Black Muslims).[195]

Teen Challenge: The story of the involvement of the Pentecostal (Assembly of God) Church in addict rehabilitation begins in 1958 with the Reverend David Wilkerson. Wilkerson, a Pentecostal Minister serving a rural parish in Philipsburg, Pennsylvania, opened a *Life* magazine article and was struck by the poignant faces of seven New York City teenagers on trial for the brutal murder of a 15-year-old youth. Touched by the story of their lives, Wilkerson visited New York City in an effort to see the seven youths.

Although he failed to meet the young men from the *Life* story, Wilkerson encountered many other street gang members and, through visits to the city over the next year, experienced a call to take the religious message to young delinquents and addicts. His vision was a sanctuary out of which street workers could carry the message to youth, and within which particularly troubled youth could live and be supported in their effort to change their lives. The center was to be designed for what Wilkerson called "open experiments in faith."[196] That vision became the seed for Teen-Age Evangelism and the eventual chain of Teen Challenge residential centers. Wilkerson's early efforts were recounted in the book, *The Cross and the Switchblade*, and in a 1971 movie of the same name.

Teen Challenge established itself in 1961 as a not-for-profit religious corporation, administered by an executive board of local clergy from the Assemblies of God and advised by a board of professional consultants. By 1972, Teen Challenge operated more than 40 programs around the country. Its residential programs, which began in New York and Pennsylvania, specialized in the treatment of delinquent and drug-addicted youth. Initially supported by 65 Spanish Assemblies, Wilkerson's efforts expanded to receive wide support from the Assemblies of God and other denominations, as well as donations from private philanthropists and small amounts of income that teen residents earned through part-time work.[197]

Pentecostal programs such as Teen Challenge view addiction in terms of sin and morality. The goal of the program is addiction recovery achieved through the medium of religious conversion. In this view, a true conversion experience is by its very definition transformative. The old sinful (addicted) self dies and a new (drug-free) self is born. It is in the context of this broader transformation that the drug and the addictive lifestyle are cast out and a new lifestyle embraced. Wilkerson saw the religious experience as a liberating substitute for drug addiction and believed that a power received through baptism could remove the addict's appetite for drugs.[198]

Many Teen Challenge programs utilize staff who are ex-addicts and who have completed treatment within the Teen Challenge program. The role of staff is to serve as a channel through which the Holy Spirit can reach the addict. In this view, it is not the worker or the addict that incites change, but the Holy Spirit working through and within each worker that is the source of healing.[199]

The primary admission requirement to enter Teen Challenge is the person's willingness to give up all drugs (including alcohol and tobacco) and homosexuality. Incoming clients are assigned a "Big Brother" from a sponsoring congregation. Teen Challenge Programs provide isolation and support within a residential milieu, both personal and religious counseling, and vocational counseling. The focus is on developing a personal relationship with Jesus Christ, developing self-respect for one's body, developing maturity and self-discipline, and carrying the message of religious salvation to others. When discharged, each client is placed within an individual church whose congregation takes responsibility for his or her ongoing spiritual support.

There is very little outcome data for Teen Challenge. Glascotte reported in 1972 that an estimated 22% of those admitted to Teen Challenge completed the program's three phases.[200] A 1995 seven-year follow-up study found that 18.3% of those admitted to Teen Challenge went on to complete the program and that 24% of those who completed never used narcotics following their graduation from Teen Challenge.[201]

The Black Nation of Islam:[202] Between 1910 and 1930, three million African Americans moved from the rural South to the North. The Nation of Islam was birthed in 1930, at the height of this Northern migration. The Nation was founded by Wallace Fard, but leadership of the Nation shortly passed to Elija (Poole) Muhammed, son of a Georgia sharecropper and Baptist minister. Organized in the tradition of Marcus Garvey's Universal Negro Improvement Association, the Nation called for black economic self-sufficiency, mutual support within the black community, and high standards of personal discipline and morality—including complete abstinence from alcohol and other drugs, including tobacco. The Nation sought its converts from among the outcasts of American society: criminals, convicts and former convicts, alcoholics and drug addicts, prostitutes, and the poorest and most destitute. Many individuals with prior histories of addiction were drawn to the Nation and used the Nation's brand of Islam as a framework for personal recovery. None was more widely known than Malcolm X.

The life of Malcolm X is a story of four identities, each marked by a significant personal transformation. First there was the child Malcolm Little, who would live through the torching of his home and the mysterious death of his politically active father. Then came the cocaine snorting, reefer-smoking, drug-dealing street hustler "Detroit Red," who in prison was known as the "the devil" because of his embittered rejection of all religion. Then came Malcolm X, the devoted follower of Elijah Muhammed and spokesperson for the Nation of Islam, and one of the most charismatic and controversial figures in American history. And then near the end of his life came his final identity as "El Hajj Malik el Shabazz."

The conversion experience that Malcolm X underwent in a prison cell in 1949 was no less transforming than the "hot flash" that Bill Wilson experienced in Towns Hospital in 1934. Out of these experiences, both men articulated ideologies that justified and glorified radical abstinence from alcohol and other drugs. Bill Wilson's rationale was quasi-medical—his understanding of Silkworth's declarations about the alcoholic's allergic hypersensitivity to alcohol. Malcolm's radical abstinence was based on rationales that were religious and political in nature. Each found a way to salvage a "spoiled identity." Each had remarkable leadership qualities, and each touched millions of lives through his words and the message exemplified in the conduct of his life.

Malcolm X demonstrated through his own life how passion and conviction could be used to transform oneself from a dope-peddling parasite to a person of honor and a servant of one's community and one's people. Many thousands of young African-American men have followed Malcolm's pathway in utilizing Islam—both the Afrocentric Nation of Islam and traditional Islam—as a religious pathway of addiction recovery.

The Nation of Islam experienced many tribulations and changes: charges of moral impropriety against Elijah Muhammed in 1963; Malcolm X's split from the movement in 1964; Malcolm X's assassination in 1965; continued violent clashes and ideological rifts within the Nation in the early 1970s; the death of Elija Muhammed in 1975; the collapse of the Nation of Islam and the creation of the World Community of al-Islam in the West by Elijah Muhammed's son, Wallace Muhammed, in 1976; and the revival of the Nation of Islam in 1978 under the leadership of Louis Farrakhan.[203]

What did not change through these many tribulations was the Nation's invitation to addicts to become part of its community. Some addicts continue to be drawn to the Nation and use its prohibition of drugs (including alcohol and tobacco), its moral code of conduct, and its demands for self-improvement as a framework for personal change. The Nation has been particularly influential in reaching addicts in prison. There are currently more than 140,000 Muslim inmates in state and federal prisons of the United States.[204]

<u>Religious Pathways to Recovery</u>: Religion-oriented programs of addiction recovery share many elements:

- the submission of individual will to a higher authority,
- isolation of the addict from the culture of addiction,
- an emphasis on conversion and rebirth,
- a clearly defined rationale for radical abstinence that generally involves two motifs: the sinfulness of intoxication/addiction and respect for the body as the temple of God,
- a reformulation of personal identity and a reconstruction of one's daily lifestyle and social world, and
- acts of service—carrying the message—to the unsaved.[205]

Religiously oriented therapeutic communities, like their secular counterparts, provide a closed world that buffers the newly recovering addict from re-exposure to the drug culture. These communities give the recovering neophyte a new identity, a new social world, food, shelter, clothing, employment, and a sense of participation in a meaningful cause. Critics of religious approaches to addiction recovery suggest that 1) religious ecstasy and all-encompassing religious affiliation can themselves have addictive qualities that prevent individual maturation and mainstream social functioning, that 2) the placement of people without histories of drug use in state-supported religious programs constitutes a misuse of public funds, and that 3) religious programs suffer from the lack of professionally trained staff and the lack of evaluation data to back up their claims of success.[206]

Narcotics Anonymous

The idea of the potential application of A.A.'s program of recovery to people addicted to drugs other than alcohol surfaced within A.A.'s first ten years. A physician interning at the federal narcotics hospital in Lexington wrote to the A.A. *Grapevine* in 1944, calling for a "Hopheads Corner" within A.A. While Bill Wilson warned A.A. members about the dangers of "goofballs" in a 1945 *Grapevine* article, in 1958 he cautioned A.A. membership about the need for A.A. to "avoid distractions and multi-purpose activity." Regarding the question of whether or not people addicted to drugs other than alcohol could become A.A. members, Bill stated clearly that "no non-alcoholic, whatever his affiliation, can be converted into an alcoholic A.A. member."[207] Although A.A.'s position excluded narcotics addicts without alcohol problems from participation in A.A., it left open the possibility of an adaptation of the A.A. program for people addicted to drugs other than alcohol.

<u>Beginnings</u>: Modern addiction texts variably place the date of the founding of Narcotics Anonymous (N.A.) between 1947 and 1953. The reason for this confusion is that there was more than one effort to organize A.A.-like support structures for addicts. The two most significant of these starts were in New York and California, but the origin story of N.A. begins, not on either coast, but in the South.

The story begins with Houston S., who got sober in A.A. in Montgomery, Alabama in 1944, then moved to the Lexington, Kentucky area three years later. Houston later sponsored a man who was addicted to alcohol and other drugs, and who eventually was sent to the federal narcotics hospital in Lexington. Houston called upon the medical director of the hospital, Dr. Victor Vogel, and suggested that initiating a group like A.A. specifically for addicts might prove a great benefit. With Vogel's approval, Houston volunteered to launch such a group inside the Lexington facility.

The first meeting of the new group was held on February 16, 1947. They called themselves Addicts Anonymous.[208] Many Addicts Anonymous members who left Lexington were successfully helped by local chapters of Alcoholics Anonymous in their various local communities.[209] Addicts Anonymous meetings continued at Lexington into the 1960s. Communication with members who had left Lexington came through an Addicts Anonymous newsletter, *The Key*. Addicts Anonymous groups also spread to the Ft. Worth public health hospital, as well as to other federal prisons. In 1949, the first organization called Narcotics Anonymous was officially begun in New York City by Danny C., following his eighth stay in Lexington. Danny C. had been exposed to Addicts Anonymous meetings while at Lexington, but chose to call his community-based group Narcotics Anonymous to avoid any confusion over the existence of two "A.A.s."

New York City's first N.A. meetings convened in the Salvation Army's Lowenstein's Cafeteria in Hell's Kitchen. Major Dorothy Berry of the Salvation Army was N.A.'s first patron, providing not only meeting space, but also N.A.'s first office. Jerome Ellison's 1954 *Saturday Evening Post* article reported that 90 members of N.A. had achieved stable, drug-free living since N.A.'s founding.[210] New York N.A. meetings continued under Danny's leadership until his death in 1956.[211] Following Danny's death, leadership within N.A. was provided by Rae L. and non-addicts like Father Dan Egan, who came to be known as the "Junkie Priest." The New York N.A. group remained very small, experienced little spread outside of New York City (with the exception of Cleveland), and dissipated in the early 1970s with the passage of harsh anti-drug laws and the death of Rae.

Meanwhile, on the west coast, another birth of N.A. had already taken place in what would mark the origin of N.A. as it exists today. Support groups for addicts in Los Angeles with names like Habit Forming Drugs (HFD) and Hypes and Alcoholics (HYAL) rose and fell in the early 1950s, until a group started in July, 1953 demonstrated its staying power. Among the participants in this group was Jimmy K.—widely considered to be the founder of N.A. as it exists today.[212]

There were significant differences between the modes of operation in New York and California N.A. groups. New York N.A. members, mostly heroin addicts, had little concern about alcohol and little contact with A.A. In contrast, three of the California founders of N.A. were dually addicted, brought in prior affiliations with A.A., and emphasized strict adherence to the steps and traditions adapted from the A.A. program. It took some 20 years for what would become the N.A. program to gel. Some groups were highly unstable during these early years, and group practices varied considerably. Some early meetings were called "Rabbit Meetings" because they jumped from site to site each week. While N.A. has always pledged its members to abstinence from all drugs including alcohol, that message was not consistently practiced in some early N.A. groups. There were even some reports of alcoholic beverages being consumed at N.A. meetings.[213]

After nearly dying in the late 1950s, N.A. slowly solidified its program of recovery and its operating structure. The details of this history have been recorded in excruciating detail by Bob Stone, former executive Director of the World Service Office of N.A., in his book, *My Years with Narcotics Anonymous*. N.A. was revived in 1960, beginning with four earlier N.A. members. It was often Jimmy K. and an assortment of sympathetic A.A. members who picked up the near-dying group and breathed life back into it again and again. Slowly, groups began to stabilize and grow from five meetings in 1964, to 38 meetings in 1971, to 225 meetings in 1976, to 2,966 meetings in 1984, to 7,638 meetings in 1987, to more than 15,000 by 1990. N.A. membership grew from 200 at the end of 1960 to more than 250,000 active members in 1990.[214]

A 1989 poll of more than 5,000 N.A. members provided a demographic profile of the organization's membership. The majority (48%) of N.A. members are between 30 and 45, 37% are between 20 and 30, 11% are under 20, and 4% are over 45. Of those surveyed, 64% were men and 36% were women. Fifty percent of surveyed members reported that they attend at least four N.A. meetings per week.[215]

N.A.'s structure and program mirror A.A.'s. The steps and traditions of N.A. are those of A.A., with only minor word changes. One subtlety in N.A.'s adaptation of the A.A. program is worthy of note. In N.A.'s first step, there is a declaration of powerlessness over addiction, rather than over a particular drug. This opened the door for the inclusion of all drugs, including alcohol, within N.A.'s definition of "clean and sober." Organizational structure, meeting formats, literature format, sponsorship rituals, and even slogans are similar between the two fellowships. Similarly, NarAnon and Families Anonymous are N.A.'s equivalent to Al-Anon.

N.A. faced many obstacles that were different from those faced by A.A., and these differences may account for the lack of parallel growth during N.A.'s early years. Duncan cites three early problems experienced by N.A.: 1) the problem of members getting high together after spending time in the meeting recounting episodes of drug use, 2) the presence of pushers and undercover agents at the meetings, and 3) the lack of sufficient personal sobriety and maturity to sustain the functioning of the group.[216]

Although N.A. later emerged as a significant resource for recovering addicts, during the 1950s this resource was not available to most addicts in the U.S. In fact, few resources of any kind were available to addicts in the 1950s. In 1957, Charles Winick alleged that not one addiction treatment program in the country integrated hospitalization, psychiatric treatment, and rehabilitation services.[217] That lack spawned some radical experiments in the treatment of drug addiction. The most remarkable of these experiments was Synanon.

Synanon: The Birth of Ex-Addict-Directed Therapeutic Communities

The roots of the idea of a "therapeutic community" can be traced from the "moral treatment" philosophy that pervaded the 19th-century inebriate and insane asylums to the pioneering work of Maxwell Jones in the early 1950s. Jones wrote about how the total resources of a psychiatric institution had to be organized into a therapeutic community. The therapeutic community's organizational antecedents could also be said to include the Oxford Groups and Alcoholics Anonymous.[218] But the history of therapeutic communities for the treatment of drug addiction begins with a man, Charles Dederich; and an institution, Synanon. The story of the man and the institution are inseparable—a fact that in itself is an important part of the story of the rise and fall of Synanon as a pioneering force in addiction treatment. As this story unfolded, no one could have imagined that Synanon would later be depicted as a paramilitary cult and that Charles Dederich would be charged with conspiracy to commit murder. Such are the twists and turns in the story of Synanon—the beginning of ex-addict-directed therapeutic communities.[219]

Charles Edwin Dederich was born in Toledo, Ohio in 1913, into a family that had known alcoholism on both its paternal and maternal sides. In 1944, he contracted meningitis, which resulted in a sustained partial paralysis of his face and hearing loss in one ear. Fearing that he might be dying, Dederich divorced his first wife and escaped to California, where he remarried and worked as a salesman and machinist. His drinking, which had worsened during the late 1940s and 1950s, took him through his second mar-

riage and out of a job at Douglas Aircraft.

Dederich's addiction to alcohol and Benzedrine led him to A.A. in 1956, where he became a self-described "frantic and fanatical Alcoholics Anonymous fellow."[220] The following year, Dederich took LSD as part of a University of California experiment on the use of LSD in the treatment of alcoholism. The LSD experience provoked an upheaval of emotions and a newfound confidence. A few months later, Chuck Dederich decided to make helping alcoholics his life mission.

Using the promise of a year's supply of unemployment checks, Dederich began to collect an assortment of down-and-out alcoholics, who stayed at or gathered at his home in Ocean Park, California for discussions. In addition to A.A. meetings, he began to experiment with a variety of group formats that ranged from discussions of Ralph Waldo Emerson's essay on self-reliance to confrontation tactics that used ridicule and profanity to batter away at the elaborate defense structures of just-sobered alcoholics. These meetings, held three times a week, were the beginnings of a new approach to treatment and recovery. Almost immediately, Chuck announced that something important was being discovered here—something that was going to make history. He became more convinced of this when the first addicts were drawn into the circle and actually stopped using drugs.

As the number of addicts increased, a power struggle ensued that resulted in his throwing out most of the "alkies" and severing ties with A.A. Synanon —a therapeutic commune—was born out of this struggle in 1958.

Synanon's first home was a storefront in Ocean Park, California. Chuck constantly told the fledgling membership that Synanon was going to become as famous as Coca-Cola. He was overweight, disfigured, and a failure at most everything he had tried. But he could hypnotize others through the sheer power of his personality and his voice. Later, asked how he had organized a thousand criminal addicts into a self-directed community, he replied simply, "It's all done with words."

Synanon: Early Days: This strange assortment of addicts led by an overweight, non-drinking alcoholic whose greatest desire was to be a "big man" and "make history" went through enormous ups and downs in its early struggle for existence.[221] The lack of any funding for this experiment made communal sharing of meager resources a necessity. As they grew, they faced great community resistance to their presence. Zoning wars raged and brought Synanon its first national publicity in *Time*, *The Nation*, and *Life*.

Because Synanon treated addicts, the organization's local opponents charged that it was operating a hospital without a license. Chuck ended up spending 25 days in jail for the offenses of operating a hospital without a license and failing to vacate the Synanon quarters. Dederich's and Synanon's struggles were portrayed gushingly in the press as a David-vs.-Goliath story. The popular press accounts of Synanon were followed by three praiseful books on the organization authored by Daniel Casriel, Guy Endore, and Lewis Yablonsky. Synanon was increasingly being recognized by the professional community. No less personages than Abraham Maslow were saying that Synanon would completely replace psychiatry within ten years.[222] By 1962, Yablonski would report that more than 19,000 guests had visited Synanon, most of them professionals who came to look at this "anti-criminal society" up close.[223]

The positive press masked some of the internal struggles that pushed the evolution of Synanon. Drug use and prostitution were still prevalent within Synanon until the June, 1958 "big cop-out"—the night the whole Synanon community came together to confess its continuing transgressions and to intensify its pledge toward abstinence and responsible living. Synanon members discarded the code of the streets and began to generate a fully developed culture of recovery. While these improvements were underway, Dederich's circumstances also changed. One of the early addicts drawn to Synanon was a woman named Betty Coleman, who became Chuck's third wife and an important influence on Chuck and Synanon.

The number of people living in Synanon grew to 500 in 1964, 800 in 1967, and 1,400 in 1969. Synanon facilities were added in San Diego and San Francisco, California; Reno, Nevada; Westport, Connecticut; Detroit, Michigan; and New York City. At the same time, Synanon-based experiments in the criminal justice system were initiated at the federal prison in Terminal Island and at the Nevada State Prison.

This was the era in which it seemed that Americans were searching for new experiences of self-awareness within what was broadly labeled the "human potential movement." Everyone seemed to be getting into group "experiences." In this climate, "squares" (non-addicts) were drawn to the emotional intensity, brutal honesty, and social cohesion of the Synanon "game" (groups) and the Synanon community. Synanon, in fact, was becoming something of a social phenomenon.

As the number of Synanon residents expanded, so did the businesses that members ran to support

Synanon. The community supported itself through "hustling" donations of materials and services and through the sale of advertising specialties—both achieved by holding out to the broader community the story of addict rehabilitation. All income came to the community, and the more responsible residents were issued small amounts of "WAM" (walk-around money).

What may have been a critical milestone in Synanon's history came when the organization turned down an offer of $380,000 from New York's Department of Health to treat addicts from New York. This decision reflected a fear of outside intrusion and control and a fear that such easy money would weaken Synanon's private business ventures—which were proving to be quite successful. Synanon leadership feared that compliance with all the "strings" that came with the money would turn Synanon into just another community agency. The policy of rejecting government funds and government scrutiny continued throughout Synanon's history.

Synanon II: By 1968, Charles Dederich—the "old man," as he was then affectionately called—had shifted his vision for Synanon from the goal of addict rehabilitation to the creation of an alternative community. Synanon was getting out of the "dope-fiend business." The community of Synanon and the process of restructuring one's character became more important than the publicly projected goal, rehabilitating and returning addicts to socially responsible positions in the community. Synanon was never able to return significant numbers of addicts to the outer community; only 26 people graduated during Synanon's first five years.[224]

In 1969, graduation for addicts was abolished. Addiction was recast as a "terminal disease" that could be arrested only by sustained participation within Synanon. The exit door of what Yablonsky had called the "tunnel back" had closed. "Synanon I," the drug rehabilitation program, gave way to "Synanon II," a utopian community. In this transition, the number of addicts in the community diminished. The name "Synanon," which in public had come to stand for a tough brand of addict rehabilitation, became something very different behind closed doors.

Synanon II introduced a greater degree of coercion and a series of loyalty tests that drove out all but the most committed members. In 1970, Synanon declared itself a tobacco-free community. Many ex-addicts who had kicked heroin "cold turkey" and had taken successful roles within Synanon left the organization over their failure to give up cigarettes. As more coercive methods of controlling behavior came into use, there were inevitable charges that Synanon was involved in a kind of brainwashing. In response to such charges, Synanon leaders simply responded that the brains that were coming into their community needed to be washed.

But Synanon was increasingly being redesigned for those not addicted. Some 3,400 "squares" in California, New York, and Detroit were paying cash to participate in Synanon games.[225] "Lifestylers" (non-addicts who paid Synanon to live within the community) were contributing $1.3 million per year to Synanon. Synanon continued to use its image in addict rehabilitation to promote its various business, but this function was diminishing. Synanon's sales of advertising gifts topped $1 million per year. (Annual sales would later approach $10 million.) Overall membership declined as financial assets of Synanon increased. As membership plummeted, there were failed attempts to revive the "dope-fiend business" and to initiate "Synanon Boot Camps" for young offenders.

From its beginning, life in Synanon revolved around Chuck Dederich. He was the father of Synanon and the center of its emotional life. His messianic complex, which would later have tragic dimensions, could also be a source of humor. One of many notorious "Chuck stories" within Synanon involved his request that a "hustling team" find him a suitable burial plot. When the hustling team explained to him that they had found no one willing to donate a plot but had found a suitable one for $30,000, Dederich is said to have exploded: "Ridiculous! Did you explain to them that I want it only for three days?"[226]

Synanon III: An incident in 1973 signaled another shift in Synanon. From its inception Synanon had two cardinal rules that were at the center of its community life: no use of drugs or alcohol in any form and no violence or threat of violence. In 1973, Chuck Dederich poured a Dad's Root Beer over the head of a resident who had interrupted him in a group. While this behavior might be viewed as a minor indiscretion by civilian standards, within the Synanon community any such act of aggression was absolutely taboo. The founder and chairman of Synanon had broken one of Synanon's cardinal rules. Some old timers in Synanon would say that this incident was the beginning of Synanon III.

In 1974, the Synanon Foundation, Inc. was chartered as a "religion." Synanon III unfolded in 1974 with a privatization of Synanon's wealth by the Dederich family, increased coercion of members, increased paranoia regarding outsiders, and the

emergence of paramilitary "defense" measures that included weapons purchases and martial arts training (Syn-Do). Daily life inside Synanon was filled with the sounds of taped games and the speeches of "the Founder" played on the "wire"—a cross between a radio and an intercom that linked all Synanon facilities. By 1977, Time magazine was referring to Synanon as a "Kooky cult."[227]

The exploitation of Synanon resources for personal gain was apparent from a number of changes within Synanon III. The Dederichs were housed in luxury and lavished with gourmet meals for themselves and their inner circle at Synanon's expense. They moved from place to place in Synanon vehicles and Synanon airplanes. Synanon increasingly became a Dederich family business. Dederich had personally taken almost $900,000 from the successful settlement of a libel suit. In 1977, he drew a "pre-retirement bonus" of $500,000; and in 1978, when he retired as Chairman of the Synanon Foundation, his salary was replaced by a guaranteed-for-life $100,000-per-year consulting contract. In addition, efforts were undertaken to transfer Synanon assets to another company, Home Place, Inc., which had been set up by Dederich. By the mid-1970s, Synanon's resources had become substantial. The organization had extensive property holdings, and in 1976-1977 its declared income was $13.7 million. A 1978 NBC series on Synanon referred to the organization's inquiries about how to convert its charitable assets into diamonds and foreign currency.[228]

New levels of member coercion included mandatory daily aerobics, a prohibition of sugar, mandatory diets, the shearing of the hair of all members, pressure for women to get abortions, and mandatory vasectomies for all men who had been in Synanon community more than five years. (Dederich exempted himself from this last requirement.) This coercion reached the extreme in October of 1977, when all Synanon couples were pressured to go through a "separation ceremony" and choose new intimate partners. David Deitch and Joan Zweben have suggested that the growing emotional disorganization of Dederich was projected onto the entire community during this period. Dederich's own struggles with smoking and weight, and his own grief at the death of his wife Betty in 1977, all were acted out within the community as a whole. Individual and collective experience was driven by the daily vacillations in the health of Synanon's founder and leader.[229] The loyalty tests in Synanon III pushed all but the most committed members out of the Synanon community. Increased coercion was also reflected in reports of physical abuse of and by the "Punk Squad"—a group of difficult-to-manage delinquent boys diverted to Synanon from the juvenile justice system.

Synanon's new militaristic posture was indicated by the procurement of weapons ($60,000 worth) and violent confrontations with Synanon's neighbors and local citizens. A Synanon security force was trained, and increased security procedures were initiated at all Synanon facilities. Synanon was also fighting in the courts. Using its in-house lawyers, Synanon attacked any who dared to print negative reports about the community. The organization filed multi-million-dollar libel suits against *Time*, ABC, the *San Francisco Examiner*, a public health official, and the county supervisors and grand jurors who had been called to investigate Synanon. Through this tactic Synanon collected millions in out-of-court settlements, including $1.6 million from the Hearst Corporation.

There were reports that Dederich was getting increasingly paranoid about the existence of conspiracies to imprison and kill him. In the midst of one such episode, Dederich quickly left for Europe, where reports surfaced that he was drunk much of the time—a violation of one of Synanon's cardinal rules. Synanon's paranoia and aggressiveness reached a climax on October 11, 1978 when Paul Morantz—a lawyer who three weeks earlier had won a $300,000 lawsuit against Synanon—reached into his mailbox and was bitten by a four-and-one-half-foot rattlesnake, with its rattles removed to prevent his being warned of its presence. A neighbor had seen two men place something in the box and had noted their car's license number. It was later traced to Synanon. Two Synanon residents were arrested, and on December 2, 1978, Charles Dederich was arrested in Lake Havasu City, Arizona, on the charge of conspiracy to commit murder. Film crews captured Charles Dederich being carried off to jail on a stretcher. He was intoxicated with alcohol at the time of his arrest. Dederich later pleaded *nolo contendere* and was fined $10,000 and placed on five years probation. During this time, Synanon's membership dropped and then stabilized at about 700. Synanon as an organization continued an isolated existence for some time but played no significant continuing role in the treatment of addiction. Charles Dederich died in March, 1997, at the age of 83.

Synanon's Legacy: Synanon marked a unique turn in the evolution of addiction-focused mutual-aid movements detailed in this book. Synanon was the first such movement that was imbedded within a closed, sustained residential community. Synanon stripped the religious and spiritual trappings from its predecessors and offered in their place the possibility of a secular-psychological rebirth—a conversion that could be as emotionally intense and transformative as its religious counterpart. Synanon also differed in its therapeutic technology. Where its predecessors had focused on experience-sharing in groups—sequential monologues with a strong discouragement of "cross talk"—Synanon went to the other extreme by making the centerpiece of the therapeutic experience an intimacy born in the heat of mutual confrontation.

Although the first therapeutic community in the United States evolved into an alternative community and then a religious cult, its history serves as more than a bizarre artifact in the history of substance abuse treatment. Synanon I made a number of lasting contributions to the addictions treatment field.

1) Synanon marked the modern introduction of "ex-addicts" as counselors within the addictions field. While lay therapy had a long history in alcoholism treatment, this was not the case in the treatment of addiction to drugs other than alcohol. As a result of this innovation, the Federal facilities at Lexington and Forth Worth, and many emerging community-based facilities, began recruiting and training recovering addicts to work as addiction counselors.[230]

2) Synanon introduced a new technology of addiction treatment that would be refined by second-generation therapeutic communities across the United States. Although they were castigated as non-people in the Synanon community, key individuals who left Synanon adapted Synanon's therapeutic technology to diverse populations and settings. Of particular note are John Maher, who founded Delancey Street; and David Deitch, who provided early leadership to Daytop Village.

3) Synanon, more than any previous treatment modality, had the ability to strip the culture of addiction from an addict and replace it with a fully developed culture of recovery. Language, dress, values, rituals, and symbols were all taken and then replaced. The strength of this culture is indicated by the author's need to revert to "Synanese" in describing the Synanon life. Synanon demonstrated that addicts could be taken from a deviant drug culture and enmeshed within a tightly organized community that could at least temporarily alter their behavior and values. Its only flaw in this regard was the inability to transfer that culture and that learning into the broader community.

The history of Charles Dederich and Synanon also offers a cautionary tale for substance abuse organizations and their leaders. It is a tale about the potential for abuse of power and exploitation of clients in treatment institutions that fail to contain service relationships within clearly defined ethical boundaries. Endore's casual report that a senior Synanon staffer was making sexual advances to a woman lying in heroin withdrawal sends a warning that, in the absence of such boundaries, exploitation can become extreme and systemic.[231]

Synanon offers a cautionary tale about helping institutions' potential to become what this author has described as "closed, incestuous systems," and about the vulnerability of such systems to cult-like abuses and eventual implosion.[232]

Synanon also offers a cautionary tale about the potential destructiveness that can unfold from the unchecked ego of an organizational leader. In bold contrast to the anonymity and decentralization of power within A.A., Synanon offers a warning about what can happen when power is centralized in one person and that person becomes more important than the institution or its mission.

Finally, Synanon offers a cautionary tale about how easily addiction treatment programs can be diverted from their historical missions. When the alcoholics were driven out of Synanon in its earliest days, it was only a matter of time before the addicts would be driven out as well. Having cut itself off from its historical mission, Synanon became vulnerable to all manner of distortions and mutations. When the alcoholics and addicts were replaced by "Lifestylers" within Synanon, its destiny was set. Lacking the group conscience and traditions of A.A., it imploded.

The Therapeutic Community Movement

Although Synanon III verged off on its own unique organizational history, Synanon I provided a foundation for later generations of therapeutic communities (TCs). The story of the spread of the therapeutic community movement begins with Jesse Pratt, a recovering heroin addict who used his years of experience within Synanon to found Tuum Est in Venice, California. Early therapeutic communities modeled on Synanon included the Delancey Street Foundation, founded by John Maher; and Amity of Tucson, founded by Naya Arbiter, Betty Fleishman, and Rod Mullen. Many others followed: Daytop Village in New York City; Topic House in Long Island, New York; The Family (at Mendocino State Hospital in California); Phoenix House in New York City; Gaudenzia House in Philadelphia; Gateway House in Chicago; Integrity House in Newark; Archway House in St. Louis; and Marathon House in Coventry, Rhode Island—to name a few—all started

in the 1960s. Most of the early therapeutic communities spread through the use of graduates of earlier therapeutic communities, or through personality conflicts and philosophical schisms. By 1975, there were an estimated 500 drug-free residential programs modeled upon the Synanon-type therapeutic community.[233] These early therapeutic communities were linked through two organizations: the Therapeutic Communities of America and the World Federation of Therapeutic Communities.[234]

The second- and third-generation therapeutic communities differed from Synanon in at least three fundamental ways: 1) They sustained a goal of returning addicts to productive roles in society; 2) They accepted public funds and accompanying federal and state guidelines and monitoring; and 3) They integrated professional staff into the therapeutic community and emphasized the importance of training ex-addicts to enhance their therapeutic skills.[235]

The story of Daytop Village illustrates the character of the second- and third-generation therapeutic communities.

Daytop Village:[236] Daytop was initially sponsored by the Probation Department of the Kings County Supreme Court of New York. Daytop is an acronym of varying attribution. It was first an approximate acronym for "Drug Addicts Treated on Probation," but later reports claim that it stood for "Drug Addicts Yield to Persuasion." Early impetus to launch Daytop came from a $390,000 five-year research grant from the National Institute of Mental Health. Key movers in launching this project were Joseph Shelly, a chief probation officer; Dr. Alexander Bassin and Dr. Daniel Casriel, both clinicians; and Herbert Bloch, a criminologist. They recognized Synanon as a revolutionary new approach to the treatment of addiction and utilized Synanon as a model for Daytop.

The lack of a centralized figure such as Charles Dederich created great difficulty in replicating the Synanon model in Daytop. The first two resident managers fled under the "strain and anguish" of the work, and the third left to run a charm school for airline hostesses.[237] Through most of 1963 and 1964, Daytop more closely resembled a loosely controlled halfway house than a tightly run therapeutic community. After several early changes in leadership, David Deitch and Ronald Brancato were brought to Daytop to adapt structures and concepts they had acquired in Synanon to the Daytop setting. Their entry in October 1964 marked the beginning of Daytop as a therapeutic community. Deitch provided the sparkplug that was needed. He was charismatic, eloquent, and the ultimate taskmaster.

Daytop grew rapidly under Deitch's leadership. In 1965, the name Daytop Lodge was changed to Daytop Village. This was spurred by the acquisition of new quarters and the organization of Daytop as an independent corporation outside the direct control of the Probation Department. This change allowed Daytop to treat people, particularly women, who were not involved in the criminal justice system. Increased demands for addiction treatment resources led Daytop to open a facility at Swan Lake in upstate New York in 1966 and another New York City facility in Manhattan in 1968—expansions that pushed Daytop's total treatment capacity close to 400.[238] The driving force on the board at this time was Monsignor William O'Brien.

In 1968, conflict escalated between the board and staff leadership. The board feared that Daytop was moving in the retreatist, cult-like direction taken by Synanon. At the same time, the board expressed concern about Daytop's staff leaders' active collaboration with radical political groups like the Black Panther Party and the Young Lords. Conflict escalated between Deitch and such key members of the board as Dr. Casriel and Monsignor O'Brien.[239]

Deitch fired seven staff members who failed to back him, then turned in his resignation. Sixty-one staff members also simultaneously submitted their resignations. All refused to leave the Daytop facilities. On December 2, 1968, residents and staff of all three Daytop facilities were forcibly evicted. Many sought shelter in other East Coast therapeutic communities that Daytop had been instrumental in starting. There were hopes that they could all be later reunited as a community—an event that never came to fruition. During this period, some 450 clients left Daytop.[240] Reflecting on this schism, Frederick Glaser noted:

> Given their fundamentalist and absolutist approach, therapeutic communities are prone to be tempted into extreme political positions. They do so at their own peril. The peril arises because it tends to submerge the primary purpose of the organization—that of therapeutic intervention.[241]

Following the 1968 split, a "new" Daytop was slowly built by the board and remaining staff. Dr. Daniel Casriel assumed the position of Executive Director of Daytop during this period.

This early history of Daytop typifies the early struggles to replicate the Synanon model. Those TCs that couldn't find a charismatic leader did poorly, while those that could find such a leader often had to

survive the long-term effects of this leadership style. It was all part of the experiment in shaping therapeutic communities that could sustain themselves. What the second- and third-generation TCs were able to do was to reclaim Synanon's early focus on addict rehabilitation. Most fully embraced the goal of returning addicts to socially appropriate roles in the community as rapidly as was clinically feasible.

The Therapeutic Community: Treatment Methods

This section describes the philosophies and treatment methods that typified Synanon I and the second- and third-generation therapeutic communities. Many of these elements have obviously changed as TCs have increasingly been integrated into the mainstream addictions treatment field.

Etiology: Early TCs viewed addiction, not as a primary disorder, but as a symptom of underlying characterological disturbance: "At Reality House the emotional problems are primary and drug use is the secondary problem."[242] Drug addiction was viewed as a socially (society and family) induced character disorder in which "chemicals become a substitute for human feelings."[243] In the TC clinical paradigm, the addict's feelings of "shithood" are masked behind a veneer of grandiosity, narcissism, and hedonism. In the TC addiction paradigm, the grown addict is pictured as an infant: immature, irresponsible, stupid, impulsive, and incapable of empathy with others. Treatment is conceptualized as a process of emotional maturation achieved through heightened self-awareness and self-discipline. This view is implicit in the shared philosophy of Daytop and Gateway:

> We are here because there is no refuge, finally, from ourselves. Until a person confronts himself in the eyes and hearts of others, he is running. Until he suffers them to share his secrets, he has no safety from them. Afraid to be known, he can know neither himself nor any other—he will be alone. Where else but in our common ground can we find such a mirror? Here, together a person can at last appear clearly to himself, not as the giant of his dreams or the dwarf of his fears, but as a man—part of a whole, with his share in its purpose. In this ground, we can each take root and grow, not alone any more, as in death, but alive to ourselves and to others.

The essence of recovery within the early TC was

viewed as nothing short of a fundamental reconstruction of personality, interpersonal relationships, and personal lifestyle.

Treatment Goal: The goal of the second- and third-generation TCs was to help their members remain completely abstinent from drugs—but there was considerable hedging on what was included within this category. Heavy smoking was the norm in early TCs, and then there was the interesting question of alcohol. In light of the fact that the therapeutic community was the creation of a recovering alcoholic, it is somewhat surprising that it took the therapeutic community so long to recognize alcohol as a drug. Although Synanon banned the use of alcohol, there was a softening of this position in many second-generation therapeutic communities. In the late 1960s and early 1970s, programs like Daytop and Gateway permitted and ritualized social drinking by senior residents as part of their re-entry into the social life of the broader community. Residents in these therapeutic communities looked forward to earning "drinking privileges" as a sign of their progress in treatment. While some managed their relationship with alcohol without difficulty, a significant number of former clients (and ex-addict staff) developed serious problems with alcohol and later entered treatment for alcoholism. The alcohol policy in most TCs changed as a result of these casualties.

Client Intake: In places like Daytop and Gateway, potential residents had to "claw" their way into treatment. Many early TCs utilized the "prospect chair." There an individual applicant sat quietly for hours to observe the TC milieu and to think about what decisions he or she needed to make about his or her life. This all occurred before the client even had an intake interview. Intake interviews were provocative, sarcastic, and hostile. Interviewers were confrontational and required that an addict admit three things: "I am a baby," "I am stupid," and "I need help." Rather than selling their program to the addict, they made the addict fight his or her way into the program. While some early therapeutic communities such as Phoenix House were involved in outreach, these were the exception.

Length of Stay: Residents of early therapeutic communities often remained in residence from 18 months to three years. Treatment usually proceeded in three phases: 1) complete sequestration in treatment, 2) living in the facility while working outside it, and 3) living and working outside the community while returning for support activities.

Staffing: The bulk of staff working within early TCs were ex-addicts ("ex-hypes"), most of whom had been through treatment in the programs in which they later worked. They were intended to be a living antidote to the myth: "once an addict, always an addict." In the 1970s, the percentage of ex-addict staff decreased as an increasing number of roles within the therapeutic community were filled by professionals who had no personal histories of recovery from addiction.

The Milieu: The second- and third-generation TCs resembled a paternalistic, authoritarian family. They were organized into caste systems with elaborate pecking orders. One moved up the hierarchy by adhering to system norms for appropriate behavior, and one was demoted for violations of those norms. Theoretically, one could move from the "dishpan," to line worker, to "ramrod" of a department, to "expediter," to department head, to coordinator-trainee, to coordinator, and to house director. The entire system was set up on what Yablonsky has described as "an achievable status system."[244]

The elaborate system of rewards and punishments within the TC milieu served as a powerful vehicle of resocialization. One had total responsibility for one's behavior—and constant feedback. It was through sustained interaction in this feedback-rich environment that the addict's basic character was re-shaped. Acts of immaturity, irresponsibility, unawareness, and insensitivity were immediately confronted through such rituals of feedback and discipline as "pull-ups" or "haircuts." Periodic calls for a "tight house" helped pull the milieu back to a high level of intensity and afforded regular opportunities for residents to recommit themselves to the process of change. These sessions also served as a kind of pressure cooker that cleared out "dead wood"—residents who were doing nothing for themselves and who were pulling down the whole community. Those resisting this resocialization process were put on the "prospect chair" to think about why they were in treatment, and were forced to fight for the privilege of staying. Resistant members were also subjected to "general meetings," in which the entire community was brought together to confront their behavior.

The early therapeutic communities were closed cultures with their own elaborate argot—language that was itself part of the technology of personal transformation. A client in the TC could be confronted for "tipping out" (developing exclusive relationships), "stuffing" (not motivating oneself), "punching holes" (complaining), or "selling wolf tickets" (threatening violence); or could be congratulated for "showing your ass" (revealing one's true self) or "growing balls" (standing up to people). One had to learn the language even to exist in such a community, and in learning the language, one changed. To master this new culture, incoming residents were prohibited from talking to one another but were instead encouraged to relate to the "strength" (old-timers) within the facility.

Treatment Methods: TCs criticized the traditional methods of insight-oriented therapies as "psychological masturbation" and introduced techniques of much greater intensity. In the view of most TCs, the addict's "encapsulating shell" had to be removed if the addict was to grow up.[245] The central catalyst for such growth was the "Game." The game was a synergy of leaderless group therapy, confrontational theater, verbal riot, group confessional, and improvisational comedy. Dederich himself characterized the game as "a full unfettered expression of the most intimate and innermost thoughts, feelings, fears, ambitions, obsessions, convictions, hatreds, prejudices, joys, and hopes."[246] Members learned the techniques of game interaction: "indictment," "backing someone's play," "rat-packing," exaggeration and caricature, and "turning the game." There were also extended games, called "probes," "reaches," "stews," "trips," or "marathons" that went on for anywhere from eight to 48 hours.

The rationale for the game was: "Dump your emotional garbage in the circle and you will be happy outside it."[247] In the TC, one was expected to communicate gut-level emotion while remaining in total control of one's behavior. The goal was to get clients to stop "acting off their belly" and grow up.[248][249]

Most TCs were quite behavioral in their management of the milieu. Discipline and emotional control were developed by teaching the dichotomy between "in the game" and "out of the game." While there was an emphasis on affective expression inside the game, there was also a total focus on responsibility for one's behavior outside the game. When people reported that they didn't feel like doing this or that, they were challenged to "act as if"—a concept that reinforced the TC philosophy that behavior shaped emotion. The admonition of the TC was clear and unrelenting: Act as if you're mature. Act as if you're confident. Act as if you're well. Act as if you feel good. Act as if you were the person you aspire to be.

Humiliation was commonly used as a "learning experience" in the early TCs. Gross violation of community norms could result in such sanctions as being required to have one's head shaved; wear a sign such as "I am a baby. Please Help me grow up!"; or wear a costume (such as a diaper). "Splitees" (residents who left, relapsed, and returned) in particular were subjected to such "hard contracts." Gregory Johnson suggests that these humiliation techniques served a two-stage process of mortification and absolution

through which addicts shed an addiction-based identity and embraced a new recovery-based identity.[250]

Other therapeutic mechanisms utilized in the early TCs included:

- *Image work:* The TCs tried to strip superficial images to create a kind of psychological nakedness. They believed that, by stripping such images, they could open opportunities for maturity and authenticity.
- *"Running data":* In the TC, new-client indoctrination occurred through a constant peer-oriented teaching process. Like A.A., the TC relied heavily upon slogans to reinforce key elements of its philosophy.
- *"Story Hour":* Clients in treatment long enough to construct their personal stories were asked to share their stories with the entire treatment community.
- *"Concept Sessions":* Clients met in group discussions to explore ideas or events, in order to enhance their ability to think and communicate.

Treatment Outcome: The person most responsible for pioneering evaluation studies of therapeutic communities was George DeLeon of Phoenix House in New York City. DeLeon's major findings, set forth in a 1984 NIDA Monograph, were that the TC had a therapeutic effect that increased with the amount of time spent in treatment and that dose-related positive effects of treatment accrued even to those who failed to complete treatment. The minimum dose of treatment found to generate positive changes fell between 120 and 180 days.

Criticisms of The Therapeutic Community: The following were among the most frequently expressed criticisms of TCs during the first two decades of their operation. They are offered here, as were those of A.A., without extensive analysis or discussion as to the degree of their legitimacy.

1. *The therapeutic community has been unable to sustain the voluntary involvement of most addicts.* The majority of clients in TCs were there by legal mandate, and even under such duress they did not often stay through all phases of treatment. The oft-quoted statement that 90% of those who graduate from TCs remain drug free belies the fact that only a very small percentage of those admitted graduate. Only a portion (some as low as 20%) of clients screened for admission are accepted into TCs. Of those accepted, as many as half leave the program against staff advice within the first year.[251]

2. *The therapeutic community's bias toward long-*

term residential treatment reflects a "one-size-fits-all" approach to treatment that may not be appropriate for all clients. Many therapeutic communities reflect biases of race, social class, and drug choice in whom they admit and who successfully completes treatment. The therapeutic community is generally thought to be more successful with youthful polydrug users than with confirmed narcotic addicts.[252] Some suggested that the early TCs worked best for those with middle- and upper-class backgrounds, and there was some evidence of such selection bias.[253]

3. The therapeutic community cultivates the dependence of its members and inhibits rather than promotes their autonomous functioning in the community. Because early TCs recruited staff members from within their own pools of clients, some critics suggested that there was an inherent conflict between the goal of returning addicts drug free to the wider community and the need to keep the best and brightest clients inside the system to support the on going operation and expansion of the TC. Gregory Johnson conceptualized this as a conflict between the goal of client rehabilitation and the goal of organizational self-preservation. Johnson charged that "therapeutic conversion" was being used, not to support the goal of individual rehabilitation, but to support the human resource needs of the therapeutic community.[254] Larry Hart similarly criticized the TC on the grounds that the professional ex-addict subculture made up of former clients is really an extended drug culture that nurtures continued emotional dependency.[255]

4. The exclusive use of nonprofessional, ex-addict staff in the TC poses the risk of misdiagnosis and an increased risk of iatrogenic effects of treatment. This criticism was spawned by the failure of TCs to screen out people with serious psychiatric illnesses, and other people who might not only fail to respond to the TC environment and methods, but also be emotionally injured by those methods.

5. Therapeutic communities have weak ties to broader community life and fail to adequately transfer support systems for graduating clients into the wider community. This criticism was particularly apt during the years in which TCs had few, if any, links to other community-based support structures such as A.A. and N.A.

6. The organization of most TCs around a single charismatic figure makes the health of the program contingent upon the physical and emotional health of the leader. Critics suggest that this extreme dependency upon a charismatic leader may render the TC inherently unstable as an organization.

7. The concentration of power in a few roles

within the therapeutic community makes the TC vulnerable to abuses of power.* The abuse of institutional resources for personal gain and the abuse and exploitation of clients were not uncommon during the first two decades in which TCs operated in the U.S. The TC was also accused of being a self-perpetuating system that could easily be diverted from its mission of rehabilitation.[256]

8. The cost per treatment episode in the therapeutic community would make broad application of this modality financially prohibitive. As federal and state policy makers began to consider how best to allocate dollars toward the goal of addict rehabilitation, they were confronted with high demands for treatment, limited resources, and the following comparison. In 1968, three clients could be maintained on methadone or provided outpatient drug-free counseling for a year for what it cost to maintain one client in residence at a therapeutic community.

9. The status hierarchy that is essential for the successful operation of any TC requires continued expansion for the model to work. David Deitch —himself a pioneer in TC programming—observed that, when TC growth diminishes and there are no more opportunities for vertical movement in the hierarchy, the most significant motivator within the TC milieu is lost. His answer to this inherent weakness was for the TC to expand outward into community activism to address root cause of addiction—a move that would expand the number of potential roles that maturing addicts could fill.[257]

Recent Innovations: Most therapeutic communities first resisted and then responded to critics by implementing changes in their operations. Beginning in the 1970s, therapeutic communities began to evolve beyond the early Synanon model to meet the changing characteristics of their clients and to establish the TC as a professionally legitimate modality within the total continuum of addiction treatment services. Changes in the original Synanon model included a shortened length of stay; a greater use of professionally trained staff; a greater emphasis on professional education and training of ex-addict staff; the elimination or softening of methods of coercion (signs, shaved heads); and a greater focus on the needs of women, adolescents, and other special populations. Many TCs also expanded their services into the criminal justice system, particularly providing treatment units inside jails and penitentiaries. Most have also expanded their services to include outpatient clinics.[258] TCs also explored alternatives to the autocratic and charismatic leadership that typified early TCs and led to many serious organizational problems and abuses of power.

Chapter Twenty-Five
Mid-Century Addiction Treatment: Part Two

While the therapeutic community was emerging as a major modality in the treatment of addiction, other significant changes were also underway in the America's emerging addiction treatment system. First, several states created new laws that provided procedures for the involuntary commitment of addicts to treatment. Second, new psychopharmacological and policy breakthroughs widened the span of options available for the treatment of narcotic addiction. All of these new approaches were integrated into experiments with multimodality addiction treatment programming. These breakthroughs spawned the rise of community-based systems of addiction treatment and signaled the end of the federal narcotics hospitals in Lexington and Fort Worth.

Civil Commitments[259]

As the problem of narcotic addiction rose in the late 1950s and early 1960s, the portrayal of the addict was dominated by two perceptions. The first perception was that the majority of addicts were not motivated to change their lifestyles and would not voluntarily seek or remain in treatment long enough for it to have a reasonable chance of positive results. Family members and friends of addicts saw no means of effectively intervening in the lives of their addicted loved ones. The second perception was that addiction was contagious and that the primary carrier of this social disease was the addict. Lee Speer, the Field Supervisor of the Federal Bureau of Narcotics, stated this view quite clearly in 1958.

> *The fact that addicts create addicts is axiomatic and means that removing one addict from society not only saves another person from becoming addicted, it saves a geometric progression of possible addicts.*[260]

These perceptions generated two central questions: 1) how do we get people who do not want treatment into treatment? and 2) how do we stop addicts from transmitting addiction to other people? The answers seemed to be mandatory treatment and quarantine of addicts. The program that achieved both of these goals was called "civil commitment."

Readers will recall that the civil commitment of addicts to compulsory treatment was first used in Connecticut in 1874 and later used in the early part of the 20th century in states such as New York, Massachusetts, and Iowa.[261] Civil commitment was a legal proceeding through which addicts were remanded to institutional care within a state psychiatric facility for a specified period of time. Civil commitment became a way of diverting addict offenders out of the criminal justice system and into a treatment system, while simultaneously protecting the community from the addict. It also allowed addicts in crisis to seek their own commitment voluntarily or be committed on the testimony of family and examination by a physician.

In states with large addict populations, such as California, New York, and Illinois, the civil commitment programs initiated in the 1960s brought large numbers of addicts into state psychiatric facilities, where they were committed for periods of one to three years. Unfortunately, they were met by staff who were ill-trained and ill-equipped to care for addicts. Addicts were detoxified, physically rehabilitated, emotionally encouraged, and eventually discharged to outpatient programs that provided supervision and counseling in their home communities. Civil commitment programs eventually became available in most states in the U.S.

The California Civil Commitment Program was enacted in 1961 and expanded legislatively in 1963 and 1965. It included a legal framework for the nonvoluntary commitment of addicts "not of bad repute or character" and people who were "in imminent danger of becoming addicted."[262] The program also provided funding for the California Rehabilitation Center (CRC), mandated aftercare programming and drug testing, and, for some addicts, residence in halfway houses. By the early 1970s, the CRC at Corona housed 1,700 men, with the overflow going to a second facility in Tehachapi. Beginning in 1969, female addicts were committed to a separate program on the grounds of Patton State Hospital. The women's program had a capacity of 350.

The basic treatment regimen was a 60-person dormitory that operated as a "modified therapeutic community" under the supervision of a staff team. This milieu-oriented treatment was supplemented by individual and group counseling provided by psychologists and psychiatrists. There was also considerable emphasis on education and vocational services. Classes were provided through the high-school level, and fourteen different vocational training tracks were offered.[263] While there was a strong drug-free bias within the civil commitment program, a Supreme Court decision (*Alice Walker and Richard Marks v. the Narcotic Addict Evaluation Authority*) led to changes in the program in 1970, changes that included the option of methadone maintenance. The Department of Corrections later operated a methadone maintenance clinic in Los Angeles with a capacity of 200 clients.

People discharged from these facilities who failed to meet standards for community living—those who relapsed, failed to find employment, or broke one of numerous rules for daily living—lost their "clean time" and were re-incarcerated. Decisions regarding release and return were made by a four-person Narcotic Addict Evaluation Authority.[264] By 1973, more than 18,000 addicts were admitted for treatment within the civil commitment program.[265]

The most adamant critic of civil commitment programs was Dr. John Kramer, a psychiatrist who directed research activities at Corona during the period in which the civil commitment program was implemented. Of the first 120 people released from Corona during the years 1962 through 1964, only 17% eventually succeeded in achieving three continuous years of drug abstinence. According to Dr. Kramer, the civil commitment program "failed to rehabilitate more than a modest proportion of those drug users delivered to its care."[266] [267] Reasons for this failure include poorly developed and culturally insensitive inpatient treatment designs, a lack of adequate community treatment resources to support re-entry, and a lack of sustained academic and vocational alternatives for people returning to the community. In his critique of the New York Civil Commitment program, James Inciardi suggests that the program was doomed to failure for four reasons: 1) it was founded on faulty research findings regarding the effectiveness of compulsory treatment, 2) treatment was housed in former prisons that proved to be an unsuitable milieu to support behavioral change, 3) the program was led by political appointees who had little administrative or clinical expertise, and 4) the program suffered from a weak aftercare program.[268]

Amidst the calls for civil commitment laws were sweeping recommendations that intractable addicts be placed under extended quarantine within self-supporting addict colonies—some suggested the use of an island—where they could be made to work, and where their addiction would not spread to others.[269] While

this rebirth of proposals for inebriate colonies struck a few responsive ears, new pharmacological technology and new social and political circumstances led to a variation on an older strategy for managing narcotic addiction.

Methadone and Modern Narcotic Maintenance

While the advent of therapeutic communities and civil commitment programs marked significant milestones in modern addiction treatment, the most significant milestone in terms of number of addicts affected was the introduction of methadone maintenance.

Methadone: The Early Story: In 1946, U.S. intelligence teams combing through records of German industries after VE day came across a description of a drug called Dolophine at I.G. Farbenindustrie. This long-acting synthetic narcotic had been developed in Germany in 1943 as an alternative to morphine. The discovery of its existence by the Americans resulted in its eventual release in the U.S. by Eli Lilly, Inc., under such names as "AM148," "Ammidon," and "Methodon." It became available in the U.S. in 1947 and became the drug of choice in the detoxification of narcotic addicts who entered the U.S. Public Health Hospitals in Lexington and Ft. Worth.[270]

The Context for Renewed Experiments with Addict Maintenance: When the ambulatory treatment of addicts by drug maintenance was banished with the closing of the last morphine maintenance clinics in 1923-1925, isolated critics continued to condemn this unforseen consequence of the Harrison Act. Dr. Henry Smith Williams, for example, published a torrid criticism of policies that he believed left the interpretation of medical practice to juries of citizens who knew nothing about medicine or addiction. Williams proclaimed:

> *When Cotton Mather hanged witches, and along with them a clergyman whose crime was that he denied the existence of witches or witchcraft, he forecast exactly, the action of the modern prosecutor who would imprison the victim of drug addiction and the physician who dares to pronounce drug addiction a disease.*[271]

Williams mistakenly predicted that the opening of the new federal narcotics hospital in 1935 signaled an end to the superstitious scapegoating of addicts and the beginning of a revitalized medical approach to drug addiction disease. Williams' pointed remarks were followed by only isolated voices that sustained the refrain of this criticism. However, in the 1950s and early 1960s, a number of events opened the way for renewed experiments in the medical management of narcotic addiction.

The increased penalties for drug offenses produced by the Boggs Act of 1952 led the American Bar Association to establish a Standing Committee on Narcotics and Alcohol. In 1955, this Committee recommended that it collaborate with the American Medical Association on an investigation of the narcotics problem. An Interim Report issued by this group recommended softer penalties and the development of increased treatment resources. While this report came under heavy attack from the Bureau of Narcotics, Anslinger's efforts to suppress the report findings failed.

The final 1961 ABA/AMA report, *Drug Addiction: Crime or Disease?* recommended the establishment of an experimental facility to treat addicts in the local community rather than in institutional settings. The Joint Committee Report went on to recommend that

> ....if the clinic does not succeed in taking and keeping the addict patient off drugs after a period of intensive treatment, its personnel should then consider supplying the addict with sufficient drugs for his needs, so that he does not have to patronize the illicit peddler.

Bureau of Narcotics efforts to suppress and discredit this final report also failed. While other AMA committees disagreed with this recommendation, the Joint Committee Report of the ABA and the AMA signaled a window of opportunity to re-evaluate America's 60-year ban on the medical maintenance of addicts.

Another report exerted a similar influence. The final report of the Advisory Commission on Narcotics and Drug Abuse was submitted to John F. Kennedy just three weeks before his assassination. While much of the report dealt with the consolidation of drug-enforcement activities, it also recommended that doctors' prescription of drugs to addicts should be a matter of medical discretion guided by professional standards rather than by legal prohibitions. The report concluded that "good-faith" medical care of addicts should be defined within the medical community rather than within the law-enforcement community.

The Supreme Court also paved the way for broadened experiments in treating narcotics addicts when it struck down a California law that made addiction to narcotics a crime punishable by incarceration ranging from 90 days to one year. In the 1962 *Robinson v. California* decision, the Court reverted to the position it had taken in the *Linder* case in 1925, when it had declared addiction a disease worthy of medical treatment.

The Court suggested that compelling addicts to undergo treatment was a preferable alternative to incarceration and that punitive sanctions should be used only when addicts refused to enter treatment. The re-conceptualization of narcotic addiction as a disease was gaining momentum. The publication of *Drug Addiction: A Medical Problem*, authored by highly respected addiction expert Lawrence Kolb, called for a more treatment-focused social policy to address illicit drug use. Kolb's text was published in 1962, the same year in which Harry Anslinger, the godfather of American narcotic enforcement policy, was retired as head of Bureau of Narcotics. Kolb's work was followed in 1965 by another influential text, *The Addict and the Law*, authored by Alfred Lindesmith, one of the foremost modern critics of American narcotic-control policy. Lindesmith's book called into question many of the assumptions upon which American drug policies were based and documented some of the damaging effects of these policies.

There was also a growing body of scientific literature that set the stage for new approaches to the treatment of narcotic addiction. The overwhelming conclusion conveyed in this literature—decades of follow-up studies of public and private narcotic treatment programs—was that sustained abstinence was not a realizable goal for most narcotic addicts.[272] The failure of so many abstinence-based programs, from Lexington to Riverside Hospital to the most exclusive private psychiatric hospitals, added momentum to the search for a medically administered heroin substitute that could be used with large numbers of addicts.[273] The advent of methadone maintenance marked the first time in 40 years that a treatment intervention was launched which articulated a goal other than the immediate and enduring abstinence of the addict. Methadone provided both a new rationale for treatment and a new technology of treatment.

The Birth of Methadone Treatment: Two people now enter our story who dramatically altered the treatment of narcotic addiction in the U.S. Dr. Marie Nyswander, a psychiatrist, and Dr. Vincent Dole, an endocrinologist, began a professional and personal collaboration in 1963 (they were later married), experimenting with the use of methadone in the treatment of heroin addiction.

Nyswander and Dole boldly proclaimed that heroin addiction was a chronic biological condition characterized by relapse, that large numbers of addicts were biologically incapable of enduring abstinence, and that some form of narcotic maintenance was the only viable treatment option for large numbers of addicts. They further contended that what was being called the "addict personality" represented, not pre-existing and enduring personality traits, but biological and social adaptations resulting from addiction to an illicit narcotic. Using a "disease concept" of heroin addiction, Nyswander and Dole theorized that the incredibly high relapse rate of heroin addicts was attributable to enduring metabolic changes that accompanied heroin addiction. In this view, addicts needed narcotics the way diabetics needed insulin: to achieve normal metabolic functioning. They advocated the use of a suitable narcotic for daily maintenance as a way to stabilize this metabolic condition and allow the addict to begin a process of social rehabilitation.

Dole and Nyswander began their work with the premise that prior efforts at addict maintenance had failed partially because the wrong drugs had been used. Their efforts to find a suitable maintenance agent were initiated in a pilot program on the metabolic disease ward at Rockefeller University Hospital in New York City. Their experiments with older drugs such as morphine and heroin, and several new synthetic narcotics, all failed because of their inability to find a dosage plateau of stable functioning between the two extremes of narcotic sedation and narcotic withdrawal. At that point, the prospect of modern maintenance did not look good.

Then, in 1964, there occurred one of those quirks of serendipity that often accompanies scientific discoveries. The research subjects, because of their involvement in previous tests, had developed exceptionally high tolerance for narcotics. As a result, high dosages were required when the drug methadone was tested. To their surprise, patients were able to function for extended periods on stable doses of methadone, without experiencing either the euphoria of acute intoxication or the dysphoria of withdrawal.[274] At appropriate dosages, methadone also seemed to block the effects of illicit narcotic drugs and suppress the sensation-seeking and risk-taking behavior usually exhibited by addicts. Buoyed by these initial observations, Dole and Nyswander expanded their experimental trial of methadone maintenance to a ward of the Manhattan General Hospital (a hospital later absorbed into Beth Israel Medical Center) and, with the support of Ray Trussell of the New York City Health Department, began to extend and evaluate their work.[275]

The major obstacle to Dole and Nyswander's continued investigations during this period came from agents of the Bureau of Narcotics, who threatened the two doctors and tried to suppress the pilot program by infiltrating the clinics, stealing records, spreading false rumors, and encouraging public attacks on methadone. Nyswander and Dole were not to be deterred. At one point, Dole even challenged the agents to arrest him so that the matter could be determined in the courts. The Bureau backed off. A new era of narcotic-addiction treatment had begun. Methadone maintenance emerged in 1965 as a new and controversial component of the addiction treatment landscape. Its arrival was announced in an article detailing Dole and Nyswander's approach to addiction treatment, published in the *Journal of the American Medical Association*.

Two models of methadone maintenance developed. The first, pioneered by Nyswander and Dole, sustained addicts on high doses (50-120 milligrams per day) of methadone. Called "Blockade Treatment," this method used methadone both to forestall withdrawal sickness and to block the euphorigenic effects of any supplemental heroin use. Drs. Nyswander and Dole believed this form of treatment would reduce supplementary and secondary drug use by people being treated. The second model of methadone maintenance stabilized the addicted client on 30 milligrams or less of methadone per day. Arguments over the relative effectiveness of high-dose versus low-dose protocol have continued for more than 25 years.[276]

Studies of methadone maintenance listed the advantages of this treatment as follows:

1. Methadone, in contrast to heroin, is a long-acting narcotic which can suppress narcotic withdrawal for 24 hours with a single oral maintenance dose.
2. Methadone's ability to suppress narcotic hunger significantly reduces drug-seeking behavior.
3. Methadone at therapeutic doses produces no "high"; clients can function in their work and social lives without cognitive, affective, or psychomotor impairment.
4. For most clients, methadone produces minimal side effects.
5. Methadone is the only opiate treatment modality in which a high percentage of addicts voluntarily enter and remain involved in treatment.
6. Clients on methadone maintenance show increased social productivity, as measured by

educational and occupational involvement.

An independent evaluation of the first 4,000 addicts involved in the Dole and Nyswander program revealed that 80% had remained in the program and improved their social functioning.[277] Numerous evaluations of methadone maintenance corroborated Dole and Nyswander's initial findings.[278]

Before we continue our history, we should emphasize that the early programs pioneered by Dole and Nyswander were very different from the programs that were destined to become widely available. The pilot was an intense, inpatient "methadone-assisted rehabilitation" model that employed intensive addiction counseling, vocational counseling, and aftercare case management, whereas the widely diffused model relied almost exclusively on outpatient methadone pharmacotherapy.[279] We will elaborate on this difference and its implications shortly.

Other drugs explored for their potential as maintenance agents included Darvon, LAAM (levo-alpha-acetylmethadol) and PN (propoxphene napsylate).[280]

The Methadone Critics

There were severe criticisms of methadone in professional, political and lay circles. The most frequent of these criticisms included the following:

1. *"Methadone simply replaces one drug addiction for another."* This criticism was often buttressed by anecdotal reports from addicts claiming that it was harder to get off methadone than it was to get off heroin. Methadone proponents met this criticism by suggesting that methadone's addictive qualities (combined with the ability to establish non-sedating doses) were precisely why it worked so well as a maintenance agent.

2. *Methadone ignores the underlying dynamics of addiction: disordered personalities, family dysfunction, and the squalor of impoverished neighborhoods.* This criticism posited that the management of an addict's cellular hunger for narcotics would not resolve those factors that initiated and sustained drug addiction.

3. *Take-home policies for methadone pose threats to the community.* Critics cited the adverse reactions and deaths that resulted from the accidental ingestion of methadone by children of addicts. (Early take-home methadone was often mixed with orange drink and easily mistaken for orange juice.) There were also reports that methadone was being diverted to the illicit market from take-home methadone given to clients at methadone clinics.

4. *The milieu of the methadone clinic sustains the addict-client's involvement in a culture of addiction.* This criticism focused, not on methadone, but on the lack of control of the milieu of the methadone clinic and, more specifically, the sparsity of rehabilitative services linked to methadone maintenance.

5. *Private methadone clinics constitute legalized drug dealing by profiteering physicians.* This criticism, often appearing in local newspaper exposés, was usually accompanied by anecdotes of physicians making excessive profits from their reputation for distributing high doses of methadone with a minimum of hassle.

6. *Methadone is a strategy of control and pacification of African-American and Latino communities.* Activists in African-American and Latino communities were quick to point out the existence of prevention and drug-free initiatives in White communities and the overwhelming preponderance of methadone programs in communities of color.

In response to criticisms like the above, Dole and Nyswander continued to affirm what methadone could and could not achieve.

> *No program (maintenance or drug free) that has treated addicts of comparable severity and followed them for three years or more after discharge has presented any evidence of better long-term results. Although a minority of subjects with a history of serious addiction can remain abstinent after discharge from treatment (or become so without treatment), most cannot. For the majority continued maintenance is needed for normal functioning.*[281]

It is hard to develop a perspective on methadone without distinguishing between methadone maintenance as a clinical model of treatment and methadone as it was used as a social and political strategy. Our continuing story focuses on just such a perspective.

Methadone, Watergate, and Federal Narcotics Control [282]

Although methadone was introduced into addiction treatment in the mid-1960s, it is an irony of history that the person who would have the greatest influence on the spread of methadone maintenance would be President Richard Nixon. Between 1971 and 1973, the number of people enrolled in federal- and state-sponsored methadone programs exploded. By October of 1973, 80,000 addicts were registered in methadone programs. The story of this increase is a fascinating one that influenced the very nature of methadone treatment and its perception within professional and lay communities.

Elected in 1968 on a "law-and-order" platform, Richard Nixon was very much concerned about the rise in urban crime following his rise to the presidency. Egil Krogh and Jeffrey Donfeld's Domestic Council was asked to develop a solution. Two addiction experts brought in as consultants—Dr. Jerome Jaffe and Dr. Robert DuPont—suggested that there was only one way to reduce urban crime in 24 months (the time-span before the next presidential election), and that was the massive infusion of methadone maintenance in America's inner cities. In 1970, the Domestic Council provided a paper that summarized the options and concluded:

> *In 1972, citizens will be looking at crime statistics across the nation in order to see whether expectations raised in 1968 have been met. The federal government has only one economical and effective technique for reducing crime in the streets—methadone maintenance.*[283]

White House figures Egil Krogh and John Erlichman expressed concern about the "morality and wisdom" of narcotic maintenance, but tentative evidence that methadone could produce a precipitous drop in drug-related crime tipped the scales toward political expediency. The Nixon White House could not tolerate the continued rise in heroin-related urban crime, and there were growing concerns about reports of heroin-addicted soldiers returning from Vietnam. The creation of a national network of methadone programs seemed to be the answer to the twin goals of lowering urban crime and quickly and increasing treatment capacity for heroin addicts without great expense.[284]

Whatever the reader thinks and feels about methadone maintenance, it is important to understand that methadone maintenance as a social policy was designed and targeted first as an intervention into urban crime, and only secondarily as a new medical treatment for drug addiction. From the beginning, the tension was evident between this policy intent and the doctors, nurses, and counselors working in methadone programs who attempted to emphasize individual medical and social rehabilitation.

Dr. Vincent Dole—one of the co-developers of methadone maintenance—criticized the rapid expansion of this form of treatment for two reasons. First, the growth was so explosive that program expansion moved faster than the development of medical competence to initiate and administer such programs. Abuses surrounding methadone programs in the early 1970s often reflected this lack of basic competence. A second criticism was that methadone was increasingly being used for detoxification rather than maintenance, which in Dole's view surrendered the goal of rehabilitation to the idealistic but mostly unachievable goal of total abstinence. As it was being mainstreamed, methadone treatment was often not based on the model whose success Dole and Nyswander had demonstrated. Dr. Stephen Kandall would later reflect that:

> *Political forces reduced methadone to an inexpensive, stripped down way to "control" a generation of addicts without having to provide essential rehabilitative services....*[285]

In the early 1970s, methadone clinics rapidly sprang up in urban environments. Addicted clients seeking services were given physicals, provided a urine drop to verify addiction, and started on a daily dosage of methadone. Clients came to the clinic each day and drank their methadone dosage. After a period of stability, clients could also earn the right to take-home medication that required that they visit the clinic only three times per week. Clients could enroll in a clinic and be rapidly or slowly detoxified through progressively decreasing dosages of methadone, or they could be stabilized and then maintained on that dosage for indefinite periods of time. Those clients in the latter category were assessed by a physician every two years to justify continued maintenance. Rehabilitation services accompanying methadone programs consisted of individual and group counseling provided primarily by ex-addict staff, some of whom were themselves being maintained on methadone.

There continued to be isolated reports of methadone diversion into the illicit market, adverse reactions from children accidentally drinking methadone, the lack of rehabilitation services at methadone clinics, and financial mismanagement of methadone programs. In an effort to reduce abuses within methadone programs, the Narcotic Addict Treatment Act of 1974 implemented stringent guidelines governing the operation of methadone detoxification and maintenance clinics.

One interesting side-story in the rise of methadone maintenance in the United States was the advent of private for-profit methadone clinics. These clinics catered to a more affluent addict population, but they sometimes came under attack for their use of exceptionally high methadone doses, their loose standards for take-home medication, and what many considered to be excessive profits—up to $2-3 million per year.[286]

Having reviewed the story of the introduction of methadone maintenance into American addiction treatment, we will now explore another medical breakthrough that for a period held out great promise.

Narcotic Antagonists

A narcotic antagonist is a drug that, through its ability to bind to opiate receptors in the body, reduces or completely blocks the effects of narcotics. If a person who is addicted to narcotics is given a narcotic antagonist, the latter drug will induce withdrawal symptoms.

Nalline (nalorphine), a semi-synthetic derivative of morphine with narcotic antagonist properties, was first synthesized in 1941. It was followed by the development of other antagonist drugs: naloxone, cyclazocine, pentazocine, naltrexone and buprenorphine.[287] The discovery of the narcotic antagonist nalorphine introduced a new treatment of opiate overdose, and a test for opiate use that came to be called the Nalline challenge. Under this latter procedure, people on probation or parole who had histories of addiction were required to undergo periodic injections of Nalline, which, if they were currently addicted, would precipitate immediate physical symptoms of withdrawal, such as pupillary dilation. Similar procedures were used with the narcotic antagonist naloxone hydrochloride, marketed under the trade name Narcan.[288]

There were many objections to the Nalline challenge. Critics cited its invasiveness, its unreliability (false negatives and false positives), and its potential risks (side effects).[289] Some critics even suggested that exposure to the hypodermic injection and the effect of Nalline itself triggered drug-seeking behavior in addicts who were remaining abstinent.[290] A particular problem with the Nalline challenge was its indiscriminate use with people who had violated drug laws. Young people on probation or parole for marijuana violations were subjected to Nalline injections—giving them their first narcotic-like intoxication.[291] In spite of such objections, Nalline was widely used, particularly in states like California, where there were large addict populations in the criminal justice system.

The use of narcotic antagonists as an adjunct in treatment was first introduced by William Martin and Abram Winkler in the early 1960s. This technique utilized daily administration of an antagonist at doses high enough to block the euphorigenic effects of narcotics. The rationale was that drug-seeking behavior could be extinguished if the effects of narcotics

could be chemically neutralized. By blocking the effect of any subsequent narcotic use, the antagonist provides a kind of chemical shield to help the recovering addict avoid the momentary temptation to get high. In a review by Senay and Renault, the problems encountered in early clinical trials with such antagonists as cyclazocine and naloxone included unpleasant side effects, severe withdrawal following regular use, and the expense and short supply of these drugs. Antagonist therapy also required a highly motivated client willing to self-administer the antagonist drug on a daily basis.[292] Although the mainstream addict population rarely shows this level of motivation, such populations do exist. Washton, Gold, and Pottash have reported on the effective use of naltrexone in the treatment of opiate-addicted business executives and physicians. More than 80% of these clients treated with naltrexone had successfully completed treatment and had not relapsed at 12-18 month follow-up.[293]

Vincent Dole, co-originator of methadone maintenance, criticized the use of antagonists in treatment, based on his belief that narcotic addiction stems from opiate receptor dysfunction. Dole noted:

> *Antagonist drugs block the action of natural ligands as well as that of illicit narcotics. If the basic problem leading to relapse is a failure of the modulating system to return to normal function after withdrawal of narcotic, then antagonist treatment adds to the problem.[294]*

The search for a long-acting narcotic antagonist that has no addiction liability and no untoward side effects—but which is capable of blocking the effects of opiates and opiate substitutes—is still a major research goal. The introduction of narcotic antagonists as adjuncts in treatment in the 1970s was part of the rapid advancement in pharmacological approaches to the treatment of narcotic addiction. By 1972, there was even discussion of an anti-heroin vaccine. The development of such a vaccine would eliminate addiction to heroin by safely neutralizing the physical and euphorigenic effects of the drug.[295] Heroin maintenance was also under consideration and had some advocates during this period. Perhaps the most unusual pharmacotherapy for narcotic addiction involved the combined use of psychotherapy and high doses (300-450 micrograms) of LSD.[296] As new treatment technologies evolved, the challenge was to integrate these new methods into a comprehensive treatment system. Some states attempted to do just that.

Multimodality Treatment Systems: The Story of the Illinois Drug-Abuse Program[297]

Many states with large addict populations—California, New York, Illinois, Massachusetts—launched their own programs in the late 1950s and 1960s. By the late 1960s, a multimodality model of organizing addiction treatment services emerged.

Dr. Effren Ramirez pioneered an addiction intervention model in Puerto Rico, then brought his model to New York City in 1966. The Ramirez model emphasized street outreach, multiple treatment modalities, levels of care within each modality geared to the client's level of maturity, and collaboration among professional and ex-addict staff.[298] The Illinois Drug Abuse Program in Chicago and the Drug Dependence Unit of the Connecticut Mental Health Center in New Haven became similarly known for their systematic use of multiple modalities to respond to heroin addiction. The Connecticut and Illinois programs were founded on the belief that different modalities worked for different individuals, and that a single individual might need different modalities at different stages of his or her addiction career. In both Illinois and Connecticut, the question of which addiction treatment modality was best was reframed as "best for whom" and "best at what point in time."[299] The New Haven program, under the leadership of Dr. Herbert Kleber, began in 1968 as a National Institute of Mental Health demonstration project. The Illinois program was initiated the same year under the administrative authority of the Illinois Department of Mental Health. We will explore the evolution of the Illinois system in some detail.

Background:[300] In the mid-1960s there were very few treatment services for addicts in Chicago. Most addicts had one of four choices: 1) brief detoxification at Cermak Hospital for those addicts entering the Chicago House of Corrections, 2) involvement in St. Leonard's House, a small private treatment program in Chicago, 3) commitment to a state psychiatric facility, or 4) treatment at the federal narcotics hospital in Lexington, Kentucky. In 1965, one quarter of those in Illinois prisons were there for drug or drug-related offenses. The Illinois Drug Abuse Program (IDAP) grew out of the efforts of the Council for Understanding and Rehabilitation of Addicts (CURA), a grass-roots group of judges and clergy whose advocacy led to legislation creating the Illinois Narcotic Advisory Council. This latter Council included representatives from the state legislature, state medical society, judiciary, and other concerned professionals and citizens. Dr. Jerome Jaffe, then of New York's Albert Einstein School of Medicine, served as an expert consultant to the Council. IDAP was created to implement the Council's recommendation that the state initiate specialized treatment services for addicts. It began as a demonstration project of the Illinois Department of Mental Health and was administered under the leadership of Dr. Daniel Freedman of the Department of Psychiatry at the University of Chicago.

Organization and Funding: With the infusion of state and federal funds from the National Institute of Mental Health, the Illinois Drug Abuse Program opened its first addiction treatment clinic in 1968. Alcoholism services during this period were provided within another division of the Department of Mental Health, with little interaction between the alcoholism division and IDAP. In 1968, in Illinois—as in most of the country—treatment of alcoholism and treatment of narcotic addiction represented two separate political and professional worlds. IDAP continued to serve as the primary source of state-supported addiction treatment services until 1974, when all drug-abuse prevention and treatment services were moved to a newly created state department, The Illinois Dangerous Drugs Commission.

The financial resources that were committed to the provision of treatment services are interesting by today's standards. IDAP began in 1968 with a budget of $185,000. During the early 1970s, therapeutic communities were being reimbursed $8.50 per day for first-year residents and $4.50 a day for second-year residents. Fifty-bed therapeutic communities operated with only two or three paid staff per facility. Methadone clinics were paid $15 per patient per week during this same period.[301]

Scope: Between 1968 and 1973, IDAP grew from one office in the University of Chicago's Billings Hospital to a network of 55 community-based programs serving more than 5,000 clients. Service capacity grew rapidly in response to demand and available resources. The first clinic had a capacity of 75 clients. Within three months of the first clinic's opening, there was a list of 2,000 people waiting for treatment services. This demand forced IDAP to create "holding clinics" that could support clients with a minimal baseline of services until treatment slots opened for them. As IDAP expanded, efforts were made to de-centralize the clinic system by areas of the city. This occurred as a result of the hesitancy or outright refusal of clients to cross racial, ethnic, and geographical boundaries within the city.

The scope of IDAP's early activities was reflected in its five departments: administration, clinical services, research and evaluation, community organization and training, and public information and education.

Philosophy: The overriding philosophy of IDAP was shaped by the Narcotics Advisory Council, which set the following project parameters:

- the primary target of IDAP's rehabilitative efforts should be narcotic addiction;
- the program should utilize many different treatment modalities, which could then be tested to determine their relative effectiveness; and
- the goal of all programs should be to "help all compulsive narcotics users become law-abiding, productive, drug-free, and emotionally mature members of society who require no additional medical or social support to maintain this ideal status."[302]

Modalities: As IDAP grew to a statewide network of contracted treatment services, a full range of modalities were included: hospital-based methadone detoxification, methadone maintenance, residential methadone maintenance, residential drug-free therapeutic communities, outpatient drug-free counseling clinics, and multi-modality residential facilities that integrated heroin addicts and polydrug users into a mixture of drug-free and methadone-based treatment services. A special treatment unit cared for pregnant addicts, addicts with severe alcohol problems, and addicts who also suffered from severe psychiatric illness.

What made IDAP unique was the integration of people and programs of widely differing philosophies under a single administrative structure. The way the structure worked was that clients were channeled through a central intake unit, where they were medically screened, diagnosed, and then referred for treatment to a particular program based on an assessment of their individual needs. The motto of IDAP was "Different strokes for different folks"—a motto that reflected the belief that heroin addicts were not a homogenous group, and therefore required individualized assessment and treatment planning.[303]

About 10% of addicts entering IDAP wanted immediate detoxification, 10% wanted admission to a therapeutic community, and about 80% preferred enrollment in a methadone maintenance program.[304] Cost also played a role in this client-placement process. In the early 1970s, a client could be maintained on methadone for a year for $1,500 to $2,000, whereas treatment of the same client in a therapeutic community would cost between $5,000 and $6,000.

Client Profile: Of the 7,448 people admitted for addiction treatment in IDAP between 1968 and 1972, 84% were narcotic users and 16% were polydrug users. Men made up more than 78% of narcotic users and 69% of polydrug users. Sixty-eight percent of the narcotic users were Black, and 75% of polydrug users were White. The age of clients decreased in the first five years of IDAP's operation. Although no narcotic users under age 20 were admitted in 1968, 39% of narcotic users admitted to treatment in 1972 were less than 20 years of age. Between 80 and 90% of clients entering treatment did so under legal duress or in the hope that treatment involvement would help resolve pending criminal cases.[305]

Where most mainstream health and human service institutions had erected every manner of barrier to exclude addicts, the overriding goal at IDAP was to include all of the diverse subpopulations of addicts within its treatment units. Dr Ed Senay, who provided clinical leadership within IDAP for many years, described this approach.

We wanted to take everybody we could. We didn't want to exclude people because they were severely mentally ill and heroin addicted, or pregnant and heroin addicted, or alcoholic and heroin addicted. We wanted to do something about the public health problem presented by ALL heroin addicts.[306]

To attempt to treat all addicts, IDAP had to find a way to handle deviants within its own system—addicts who defied rules by carrying guns, threatening violence, or selling drugs or themselves on the clinic grounds. IDAP's answer was to create what internally was known as the "losers clinic." This clinic accepted those clients who had been expelled from IDAP's mainstream programs for rule violations. Senay describes how the losers clinic came to be a success.

We put Superman in charge of the "losers clinic." Superman was one of the most streetwise people that ever came to IDAP. He was tough and he could communicate. He was the best natural reader of people I have seen in 37 years in psychiatry. All the deviants got sent to Superman. He didn't take any bullshit, but he really worked with those people. It turned out that patients at his clinic did better than clients at most of the line clinics. With a multi-modality model, we could seek alternatives for clients who had gotten in trouble within a particular clinic without excluding them from the whole system.[307]

Staffing: The bulk of IDAP staff (440 out of 500) were ex-addicts, particularly those who provided front-line counseling in the various treatment units. Ex-addicts were part of an "affiliational model" of addiction treatment utilized within IDAP. Ed Senay explains:

The recruitment from patient ranks of ex-addicts who then became ex-addict counselors provided a vital chain for the program that linked the program with the pool of addicts in the street in a manner that could never have been effected with professional programming.[308]

The state faced great difficulty in trying to figure out how to screen and hire these individuals. There was initially a "patient-employee status" that allowed some recovering addicts to be paid on contract, with no job security or benefits. A rehabilitation counselor position was created, with an oral exam that focused primarily on screening for knowledge about addicts and the addict's culture. This position was later changed to a series of addiction specialist job titles. While most ex-addict counselors were drug free, some were being maintained on methadone.[309] Potential drug-abuse problems among staff members were monitored through the drug testing of all staff, from top to bottom.

A typical staffing pattern at a methadone clinic consisted of a part-time physician, two nurses, one to three ex-addict counselors, and a chief counselor. Each counselor was assigned 30-50 clients. Training programs were implemented to provide staff the rudimentary training in addiction counseling and to enhance their ability to communicate outside the drug cultures within which they themselves had been enmeshed.

The Milieu: The experience of putting addiction treatment programs together in the earliest days of IDAP is difficult to describe. First, there was a frenzy of development going on—the organization of more than 50 separate programs and the rapid engagement of more than 5,000 addicts. There were no established clinical ground rules for addiction treatment—no texts, no papers, no clinical protocol. All these were developed out of the trial and error of the service process. And if the addicts were not difficult enough, the political climate was one of incredible turbulence.

Dr. Senay reports of this period:

We seemed to face off against everyone. The Black Panthers wanted a clinic. Some of the street gangs wanted a clinic. Representatives from Students for a Democratic Society and Hispanic and African-American groups angrily denounced our use of methadone. Some people wanted to kill us for using methadone, and others threatened to kill us if we didn't get them on methadone. My life was threatened on almost a daily basis for a period of two to three years, until things settled down. I knew the Chicago Bomb Squad on a first-name basis.[310]

And then there was the conflict among staff, who were split into ideological camps, each believing that addicts were a homogenous group that responded best to their particular method of treatment.

Jerry (Jaffe) had group therapists come in to try to get us to work together because there was so much hostility between the methadone clinic staff and the staff from the therapeutic communities. It took a lot of work to pull people from those different backgrounds and different philosophies into a working system.[311]

And in the midst of organizational challenges, client challenges, community challenges, and staff challenges, there were the visitors: some 10,000 of them from all over the world, who arrived between 1969 and 1973 to study the organization and operation of a multi-modality addiction treatment system.

Evaluation: A five-year evaluation of IDAP was published in 1973, covering the first 8,564 treatment admissions.

Fifty-two percent of opioid users were retained in treatment for at least one year; employment rates improved; at least half of all weeks in treatment were free of illicit drug use and criminality appeared to decrease sharply during treatment.[312]

The evaluation study noted a direct relationship between treatment outcome and length of treatment. Those clients with the longest periods of treatment engagement had the best treatment outcomes.

Legacy: IDAP was one of the first large-scale multi-modality addiction treatment programs in the

United States. It treated large numbers of addicts, trained visitors from around the country and around the world, and generated considerable research on the nature of narcotic addiction and its treatment. Many individuals who worked within IDAP went on to further distinguish themselves in the addictions field. Jerome Jaffe went on to serve as Director of the White House Special Action Office for Drug Abuse Prevention, and the research literature on addiction is filled with the names of other noted contributors who worked within IDAP—Edward Senay, John Chappel, Patrick Hughes, and Pierre Renault, to mention only a few. Some of the front-line counselors who began their careers during the IDAP days continue more than a quarter of a century later to work within Illinois' addiction treatment programs.

Lexington and Fort Worth: The Twilight Years

We would be remiss in recounting the story of mid-20th-century addiction treatment if we did not bring to a close the story of the federal narcotic hospitals at Lexington and Fort Worth. With the passage of the Narcotics Addict Rehabilitation Act of 1966 (NARA), Lexington stopped taking voluntary clients and prisoners already serving time, and instead treated addicts who had been sentenced to Lexington for six months. In 1967, the Lexington and Ft. Worth facilities were designated as Clinical Research Centers and placed under the National Institute of Mental Health. This change signaled that the role of these two facilities would be more one of clinical research and training than one of primary treatment. As a result of this change, these facilities became more open to experimenting with new models of treatment.

Treatment at Lexington seemed to change with the times. The Lexington facility became particularly interested in the therapeutic community movement, and set up its own therapeutic community called Matrix House, modeled on Synanon and funded by the National Institute of Mental Health.[313] Matrix House was initially housed as a somewhat autonomous unit within the larger Lexington complex. It was first known as "Lighthouse," until a split within the group resulted in the emergence of what came to be Matrix House.

The Lighthouse II faction took over a three story, 100-bed facility and launched itself as a Synanon-style therapeutic community. For the first time in American history, four ex-addicts were hired by the Federal government to manage an addiction treatment program. The Matrix program was launched amidst many misgivings on the part of the traditional institutional

staff. The response from the broader patient community was also not a warm one, as few were attracted to the rigorous work schedule and emotional intensity of the groups in the Matrix unit.[314]

Matrix was dominated by two inmate authority figures and a second echelon of five department heads. In 1971, rumors began to abound concerning various patient abuses, including allegations of homosexual activity between key leaders and patients. There was also significant conflict among the different personalities and echelons regarding how the community should be run. Both of these factors led to growing isolation within the hospital community. The hospital responded in early 1972 by giving Matrix six months to relocate itself off the grounds of the hospital. Matters worsened amidst FBI reports that Matrix was channeling money to revolutionary political groups. On March 16, 1972, the members of Matrix House were given two hours to collect their belongings and leave the hospital grounds. In the aftermath of the closing, a grand jury was impaneled to investigate reports of patient abuses and the presence of drugs and weapons within the Matrix facility. The director of Matrix was later sentenced to 36½ years in prison, on charges ranging from sexual exploitation of patients to assault and possession of firearms. The first full-blown therapeutic community experiment inside the Lexington facility had ended in an ignominious fashion.[315]

The failure of Matrix House was a minor one compared to two much more fundamental forces that were affecting the Lexington and Forth Worth facilities. The first force was the growing loss of confidence in the effectiveness of institutional treatment of narcotic addiction. Follow-up study after follow-up study confirmed that the majority of addicts leaving the Lexington and Forth Worth facilities quickly returned to narcotic use. These outcome studies increased the momentum for more community-based treatment and for different approaches to addiction treatment. The second force—the rapid development of local- and state-funded and -operated addiction treatment programs—seemed to make obsolete the two federal narcotics hospitals that had stood as the primary sources of addiction treatment in America for more than 30 years.

In the 1970s, methadone programs, therapeutic communities, and other community-based treatment efforts replaced the federal treatment programs. The Fort Worth program was closed in 1971, and Lexington was closed in 1974. Both facilities were transferred to the Bureau of Prisons.

Those with long tenure at the two public-health

hospitals had watched addiction change through the evolving characteristics of those admitted. When the facilities opened, addicts were primarily Chinese, Orthodox Jews, and White Southern males. In the 1930's, Chinese inmates filled a whole ward; in 1973, there were no Chinese inmates. The first-generation addicts at Lexington and Fort Worth were followed by a second generation of European immigrants and by a third wave of African-Americans and those of Puerto Rican and Mexican ancestry who had migrated into Northern cities.[316] At the time of their closure, the two facilities had treated more than 60,000 addicts.[317] When Lexington closed in 1974, more addicts were being treated in community-based treatment agencies that year than had been treated by the Lexington and Fort Worth facilities in all their years of operation.

One of the unique observations about the role of the Federal Narcotics Hospitals was offered by Earl Simrell in 1970. He noted that the original legislation that created the hospitals set forth four goals: 1) providing treatment to addicts convicted of federal offenses, 2) providing treatment to addicts on a voluntary basis as a strategy of crime prevention, 3) conducting addiction-related research and training, and 4) assisting states and local communities in the development of community-based addiction treatment services. Simrell suggested that the creation of two federal treatment institutions and the failure to actively provide community assistance actually slowed the development of a community-based treatment system. States and communities relied on these institutions for more than 30 years before developing state and local addiction treatment services.[318]

Many new approaches to addiction treatment were developed during the mid-20th century, but as this period came to a close, Harris Isbell, the noted addiction specialist, decried the lack of research on treatment effectiveness and concluded that "we still do not know whether our present system of managing addicts is useful, or possibly even harmful."[319] This unevaluated treatment technology was about to be further challenged by a youthful polydrug epidemic the likes of which the nation had never seen.

Section Seven

✠

Chapter Twenty-Six
The Modern Evolution of Addiction Treatment

The history of the rise and evolution of the modern system of addiction treatment in America is a complex one. It should be told, not in a chapter—or even a book—but in a series of books capable of analyzing its many dimensions. For myself, I have chosen to tell this story in three ways. First, this chapter will briefly recount the history of the treatment field as a "system" and as an evolving professional discipline between 1965 and 1998. The next chapter will then detail two aspects of this broader story: the history of the most seminal and controversial ideas within the field and the changes in treatment technology that were implemented during this period. Finally, Chapter Twenty-eight will tell the story of one treatment system—Parkside—whose birth, rise, and fall exemplifies the ecstasies and agonies experienced in the field during this period.[1]

Reaching Critical Mass

A certain critical mass had to be reached before a community-based system of addiction treatment could be established in America.[1] There had to be a cultural perception of alcoholism and other drug-related troubles as problems worthy of public sympathy and attention. Several factors helped establish that climate. First, the National Council on Alcoholism succeeded in its sustained campaign to implant the idea that the alcoholic was a sick person, worthy of help, who could be helped, and that alcoholism was a public-health problem toward which public resources should be allocated. Second, the explosive growth of A.A. brought the real potential for addiction recovery within the mainstream experience of American citizens. There was a growing professional and public

perception that alcoholism was a "primary disease" requiring "primary treatment" within a specially designated "continuum of care."[2] Third, the growing involvement of middle-class children in drug experimentation reconstructed the "drug problem" as one that could touch any community and any family. In the 1950s, joint committees of the American Medical Association and the American Bar Association had advocated that the problems of alcoholism and drug addiction be increasingly moved from the criminal justice system into the arena of medicine and public health. Experiments with more medically oriented interventions into these problems were already underway in 1962, when the Supreme Court, in the case of *Robinson v. California*, declared that drug addiction was a disease and that punishing the addict for his or her status of being an addict was unconstitutional. Momentum for change was building. In the 1960s, there was also a broader activist agenda, which launched numerous social reform movements in such areas as mental health, public health, child welfare, and criminal justice. The addiction treatment industry was born within this reform atmosphere. The economic resources needed to launch a national network of alcohol and drug treatment programs became available when a young, charismatic president came to the White House in 1960 with a personal passion for mental health services. John F. Kennedy pushed mental health to a high national priority in a way that profoundly influenced the emergence of treatment services for alcoholism and drug addiction. Lyndon Johnson, who would carry forward Kennedy's mental health initiatives, had himself been a member of the National Council on Alcoholism since 1948. Political leadership for alcoholism-specific legislation was also provided by a growing number of prominent recovered alcoholics who advocated for alcoholism legislation. Some of these recovered alcoholics were themselves members of state legislatures and members of Congress.

To create a funding stream that would birth new addiction treatment agencies across America required a treatment model that was replicable. Minnesota's model of residential treatment, Yale's and Georgia's outpatient clinic models, the halfway house for alcoholics, the ex-addict-directed therapeutic community, methadone maintenance, and a new cadre of

---

[1]I would like to express my appreciation for the work of Laura Schmidt and Constance Weisner of the Alcohol Research Group in Berkeley, California. Their meticulous research on the modern evolution of alcoholism treatment laid a foundation for my own exploration of this era. Helpful background interviews for this chapter were also conducted with Dr. Ed Senay, Dr. LeClair Bissell, Dr. Edgar Nace, and Terence T. Gorski. Mark Godley, Susan Godley, Russell Hagen, Dave Sharar, Al Sodetz, and Randall Webber provided thoughtful critiques of early drafts of this chapter.

outpatient drug-free counseling clinics all seemed to meet this requirement of replicability. There also *appeared* to be a growing number of professionals with interest and expertise in alcoholism and other addictions to help launch this nationwide movement. The cultural, economic, political, legal, and professional climate was ripe for massive infusion of alcohol and drug treatment agencies into American communities. What was needed was a plan for legislative action that would guide this new-found will.

The Cooperative Commission on the Study of Alcoholism

If there was a single event that set the stage for legislative action in the alcoholism arena, it was the creation of the Cooperative Commission on the Study of Alcoholism in 1961. The Commission was formed by a five-year National Institute on Mental Health grant to the North American Association of Alcoholism Programs (NAAAP). The purpose of the grant, which grew out of a series of alcoholism conferences, was to create a research organization that could evaluate federal, state, and local alcoholism-intervention activities and make recommendations for the future. In 1967, the Commission published its final report: *Alcohol Problems: A Report to the Nation.* The report documented the nature of the alcohol problem and made sweeping recommendations related to society's best response to this problem.

The report noted that 40 states had established some type of designated alcoholism program, although it was acknowledged that the budgets to support these programs were quite small. The picture of the current state of alcoholism treatment presented in the report was, in fact, a bleak one. The commission reported that detoxification of the alcoholic most often occurred in jails and that few community-based treatment services were available. In the 1960s, the most common treatment intervention for alcoholism was the involuntary admission of the alcoholic to a state psychiatric hospital, many of which provided no specialized treatment for alcoholism. The Commission found that only a very small percentage of alcoholics—mostly the affluent—received treatment in special alcoholism facilities or private psychiatric hospitals.[3]

In response to this situation, the Cooperative Commission outlined a program of national action that provided a blueprint for policy makers and the alcoholism treatment field. The Commission recommended:

- the establishment of a national center on alcohol-

ism that would provide federal leadership in the development of alcoholism public policy and in the promotion of community-based alcoholism prevention and treatment programs;

- the initiation of a national program of basic research on alcoholism;
- the initiation of a national program of alcohol education, to include the integration of alcohol education into all driver-education courses;
- the designation of state and local agencies responsible for the planning and delivery of alcoholism prevention and treatment services;
- the shift from a legal/criminal to a medical/social approach to the chronic public inebriate;
- the development of a comprehensive continuum of locally delivered alcoholism treatment services, to be implemented through a series of funding grants that would provide for service planning, facility construction, and service initiation and maintenance;
- the development of training programs for health and human service personnel, to prepare them to intervene with alcoholics and their families;
- the development of business and union policies aimed at the detection, referral, and treatment of alcoholic employees; and
- the inclusion of alcoholism treatment as an insurable benefit by the major insurance carriers.[4]

The Commission's work foreshadowed and contributed to the creation of the National Institute on Alcohol Abuse and Alcoholism, the decriminalization of public intoxication, the coverage of alcoholism treatment within the insurance industry, the emergence of occupational alcoholism programs, and the development of a community-based approach to the prevention and treatment of alcoholism. President Kennedy's Advisory Commission on Narcotics and Drug Abuse made parallel recommendations for the medicalization of drug addiction via the expansion of drug-treatment services.

A Deluge of Addiction Treatment Legislation

The cumulative effect of 20 years of public education on alcoholism—and growing concerns about youthful alcohol and other drug use—bore legislative fruit in the 1963 and 1965 acts funding comprehensive community mental health centers (CMHCs). Each federally funded CMHC was mandated to include services for those suffering from alcoholism and drug abuse. In many communities this set the stage for the initiation of outpatient alcoholism counseling services and for the planning of detoxification and residential treatment centers.

The next milestone was the Economic Opportunity Amendment of 1966, which provided more than $10 million to support the development of local alcoholism treatment programs and to give alcoholics and addicts legal advice on alternatives to incarceration. This legislation, championed by Organization for Economic Opportunity (OEO) administrator Matt Rose, was unique in that it specifically initiated the hiring and training of recovered alcoholics to work as alcoholism counselors within more than 200 local OEO programs.[5] The Law Enforcement Assistance Administration (LEAA) similarly began to fund local projects designed to divert alcoholics and drug-using juvenile offenders from the criminal justice system to newly funded alcoholism detoxification and treatment centers and youth service bureaus.

In September, 1965, the first Congressional hearings on alcoholism since prohibition were held to consider the Hagan Bill—a measure that declared alcoholism to be an illness and public health problem warranting federal intervention. The bill was introduced by C. Elliot Hagan, who as early as 1951 had introduced legislation supporting alcoholism rehabilitation programs in his home state, Georgia.[6] Hagan's efforts gave impetus to a growing willingness to allow federal involvement in the issue of alcoholism treatment. Such willingness was being reflected at the highest levels of government. In a 1966 address to Congress, President Lyndon Johnson declared that "The alcoholic suffers from a disease which will yield eventually to scientific research and adequate treatment." For the first time in history, an American President had addressed the country about the problem of alcoholism. Added evidence of federal involvement in alcoholism treatment was passage of the District of Columbia Alcoholic Rehabilitation Act (1967).[7]

In 1966, Congress passed the Narcotic Addict Rehabilitation Act (NARA). The Act included provisions for civil commitment, through which certain addict offenders could be diverted legally from the criminal justice system to treatment, or placed in treatment at the voluntary request of the addict or his or her family members. Limited funds were also provided for the Public Health Service to contract for local outpatient services and to encourage the development of local addiction treatment programs. In 1968, Congress passed the Alcoholic and Narcotic Addict Rehabilitation Act, which provided funds specifically for the construction of community-based treatment facilities. A survey conducted that year identified only 183 drug-addiction treatment programs in the entire country—most of which had recently been opened—and underscored the need for such funding.[8] By July, 1971, 50 community-based treatment programs were being funded through NARA.[9]

After decades with no significant legislative action in support of addiction treatment, no less than 13 separate pieces of federal legislation passed between 1963 and 1974 addressed the need for treatment service for people who were addicted to alcohol and other drugs. By the early 1970s, more than 30 separate agencies and subagencies of the Federal Government were involved in some aspect of addiction treatment. Addiction treatment services were being supported by the National Institute on Mental Health, the Office of Economic Opportunity, the Veterans Administration, the Department of Justice, the Department of Defense, Model Cities, and the U.S. Office of Education.[10] The Federal Government's financial investment in drug-addiction treatment rose from $28 million in 1969 to $386 million in 1973.[11]

During the 1960s, alcoholism/drug abuse was also slowly gaining institutional autonomy within the federal NIMH bureaucracy. First, an "alcohol desk" was created within NIMH to coordinate activities within the alcoholism arena. Then, in 1961, the Cooperative Commission on the Study of Alcoholism initiative began. Two years later, Anthony J. Celebrezze, Secretary of HEW, hosted a National Conference on Alcoholism and created a National Advisory Committee on Alcoholism. The following year, Celebrezze created within NIMH a "Section on Alcoholism and Drug Abuse," first staffed by Carl Anderson and Edward Sands. In 1966, The National Center for Prevention and Control of Alcoholism was created within NIMH, with Jack Mendelson as its first Director. The Center was elevated to divisional status in 1970, paving the way for its evolution into the National Institute on Alcohol Abuse and Alcoholism.[12]

If there was a single piece of legislation that birthed today's system of addiction treatment, it was unquestionably the 1970 Comprehensive Alcoholism Prevention and Treatment Act (the Hughes Act). In 1968, Iowa's three-term Governor Harold Hughes was elected to the U.S. Senate. As a self-declared recovered alcoholic, Hughes was a natural selection in 1969 to chair the Senate's Subcommittee on Alcoholism and Narcotics. The public hearings that his committee conducted did much to generate political momentum for federal support for the treatment of alcoholism as a public-health problem. Those testifying before the Subcommittee included Marty Mann of NCA and Bill

Wilson, co-founder of A.A. One of the more interesting moments in those hearings was the appearance of the Academy Award-winning actress Mercedes McCambridge to testify about her own recovery from alcoholism. Hughes and his staff, with broad input from alcoholism treatment advocates, crafted the Comprehensive Alcoholism Prevention and Treatment Act of 1970. The Act passed both houses of Congress and, following last-minute lobbying to avert a Presidential veto, was signed into law by Richard Nixon on December 31, 1970.[13]

This statute, which came to be known as the Hughes Act, followed the Cooperative Commission's recommendations by creating a National Institute on Alcohol Abuse and Alcoholism (NIAAA). The act charged NIAAA with the responsibility of creating a program of alcoholism research, education, and training, and of establishing a national network of alcoholism prevention and treatment centers. Leadership for this challenge fell to Dr. Morris Chafetz, the first Director of NIAAA. The creation of NIAAA marked the growing political power of the alcoholism constituencies that had rebelled against the placement of alcoholism within the bureaucratic umbrella of mental health. Their efforts pushed alcoholism into a category of its own. The political recognition of alcoholism as a disease and public-health problem in its own right had arrived. The passage of the Hughes Act marked the political coming-of-age of the invisible army of recovering and non-recovering people who had toiled as the foot soldiers of the "modern alcoholism movement." When fully mobilized, the numbers and political power of this group were impressive. The Hughes Act transformed this social movement into a new industry, which Hughes himself later referred to as an "alcoholism and drug abuse industrial complex." The flurry of federal alcoholism initiatives was spawned, in part, by an invisible network of recovered alcoholics who worked in tandem across political parties, branches of government, and governmental agencies to forge a new national response to alcoholism.[14]

Dan Anderson, who helped formulate the Minnesota Model of alcoholism treatment, noted the tremendous boost that the Hughes Act provided to the availability and quality of alcoholism treatment during this period:

In 1973, we had perhaps around 500 alcoholism treatment programs in the United States. By 1977, there were around 2400 programs. By the end of NIAAA's first decade, it had provided more than $468
million in grants to the states and $654 million in project grants. And these grants provided treatment resources in many areas of the country where none had existed before or they upgraded and modernized many other programs.[15]

The growth of alcoholism treatment programs was almost explosive in its intensity. In 1978, 250,000 alcoholics were admitted to federally supported alcoholism treatment.[16] An NIAAA survey in 1980 identified 4,219 treatment units in the United States, whose total expenditures were $795 million, only about 6-7% of which came from NIAAA grant funds. The federal seed money had helped create a system that was now being supported by a broad mix of local, state, federal and private resources.[17] In contrast, the reader will recall that the total national expenditure on alcoholism treatment in 1960 was $6 million.

While the modern alcoholism treatment field was being funded expansively, developments were also underway to expand the nation's treatment resources for those addicted to drugs other than alcohol. The rise in youthful polydrug abuse—and concern about drug use among soldiers in Vietnam—reached a political boiling point in 1971, forcing President Richard Nixon to declare drug abuse "America's Public Enemy Number One." The Drug Abuse Treatment Act of 1972 created the Special Action Office for Drug Abuse Prevention (SAODAP) and brought Dr. Jerome Jaffe of the University of Chicago to Washington D.C. to coordinate the federal response to drug abuse. Jaffe's mandate was to replicate on a national scale the multi-modality treatment system he had overseen in Illinois. The law also established the National Institute on Drug Abuse (NIDA), an institute that joined NIAAA and NIMH within the Alcohol, Drug Abuse and Mental Health Administration of the Department of Health, Education and Welfare. NIDA's first director was Dr. Robert Dupont, a Washington, D.C. psychiatrist. Between mid-1971 and early 1973, the number of communities with federally funded drug-abuse treatment programs increased from 54 to 214, and the treatment capacity of these units jumped from 20,608 to 63,382.[18] By 1975, there were more than 1,800 drug treatment programs in the country.[19]

Another milestone in the development of an addictions treatment "system" during this period was the 1972 funding of Treatment Alternatives to Street Crime (TASC). This Law Enforcement Assistance Administration (LEAA)-funded pilot project eventually expanded to 185 programs operating within 24 states and two U.S. territories. TASC screened drug-involved offenders, linked them to appropriate treatment services, then served as a case-management and monitoring bridge among the client, the criminal justice system, and the treatment system.[20]

While many alcoholism treatment advocates viewed this sudden infusion of federal money as a godsend, some—such as Peter Hutt, an activist lawyer involved in many of the landmark legal decisions affecting alcoholism in the 1960s—warned of the potential long-term effects of such money. Hutt went so far as to claim that the treatment field was becoming "addicted to federal dollars as the alcoholic is addicted to alcohol."[21] But voices such as Hutt's were isolated ones in the midst of the field's euphoria at having won a decades-long struggle to birth a national network of community-based addiction treatment resources.

Addiction services had existed in America before the 1970s, but there had never been a national *system* of addiction treatment. The creation of NIAAA and NIDA created such a system. This system involved a partnership, in which each state and territory created a designated state agency responsible for alcohol and drug treatment services. These agencies, in collaboration with NIAAA and NIDA, planned, funded, constructed, monitored, and evaluated local alcoholism and drug-abuse prevention and treatment programs. Federal and state authorities also shared responsibility for the training, technical assistance, and research activities that supported these local efforts. The system provided a means by which federal policies and federal funds could filter through the states to local communities, while providing incentives for states and local communities to invest their own resources in the expansion of services to alcoholics and addicts. This partnership created a geographically decentralized and highly diversified system of treatment.

Local Sponsorship and Organization

While the federal and state administrative authority for the planning and funding of addiction treatment services was being defined in the early 1970s, there was little rhyme or reason to the organization of addiction treatment services at the local community level. As the visibility of alcohol and other drug problems moved to center stage in each community, both existing and newly emerging institutions struggled to define their relationship to these problems. In some communities, these institutions competed for

local ownership of the addiction problem and the community resources that would be devoted to it. In other communities, none of the existing institutions wanted this problem, and these institutions actively repelled efforts to enlist their involvement. New institutions rose up to fill this service void.

Service variability was the rule. A cursory survey would find one state providing services in state psychiatric hospitals; another operating state-run specialized addiction treatment units; and still another contracting for the delivery of addiction treatment services from a patchwork of hospitals, mental health centers, public health departments, youth agencies, free-standing not-for-profit addiction treatment agencies, "counter-culture institutions," and even police departments. Many alcoholism and drug-abuse programs birthed earlier—the Washingtonian Homes, the federal narcotic hospitals, Minnesota-Model residential programs, Yale- and Georgia-modeled outpatient clinics, ex-addict-directed therapeutic communities, religiously oriented programs—all became part of this growing patchwork of community-based programs. Recently created innovations such as the alcoholic halfway house also spread rapidly, with the number of such facilities increasing nationally from 107 in 1970 to 597 in 1973.[22] Youthful polydrug experimentation also spurred a host of new community institutions: crisis hotlines, drop-in centers, free clinics (most modeled on the Haight-Ashbury Free Medical Clinic), "crash pads," "acid rescue," street-drug analysis programs, outpatient drug counseling programs, police counselors in local schools, and the beginnings of what would evolve into student assistance programs. In spite of considerable outside technical assistance, many of these well intended programs did not survive the 1960s and 1970s, due to their poor organizational infrastructures—weak boards, weak or predatory leaders, inadequate systems for recruiting and training staff, and poorly developed systems of fiscal and information management. But other programs survived their birthing and early developmental crises to emerge as mature service organizations. What is perhaps most strange about this evolving smorgasbord of addiction treatment agencies is the fact that they were carefully delineated by the drug choice of their clients.

Two Worlds: Alcoholism and Drug Abuse

In communities across America, the treatment of alcohol problems and the treatment of problems with drugs other than alcohol constituted separate worlds in the 1960s and early 1970s. Alcoholism and drug-abuse treatment services were provided in different agencies and by different types of staff, utilized very different models of treatment, and served clients with different demographic and clinical characteristics. The alcoholism field consisted of alcoholism units within large psychiatric institutions, halfway houses, the early community-based alcoholism programs, a smattering of hospital-based detoxification and rehabilitation programs, occupational alcoholism programs (the forerunners of employee assistance programs), and programs targeting the drunk driver. The drug-abuse field consisted of methadone programs, long-term residential therapeutic communities, a growing number of community-based counseling programs targeting young polydrug abusers, and a smattering of prevention and early intervention programs. The two fields believed that their respective clients suffered from different disorders that sprang from different etiologies and required substantially different treatment philosophies and techniques. What separated these two worlds was an almost unchallengeable belief: alcoholics and addicts cannot be mixed within the same treatment program.

The isolation of the two fields created treatment protocols that would be unthinkable today. During this period, residential drug-abuse programs, particularly the therapeutic communities, not only failed to address problems of alcoholism, but sometimes actually integrated drinking into the later phases of treatment. Since part of one's rehabilitation as a drug addict was viewed as learning the appropriate use of alcohol, clients were rewarded for their progress in treatment with the privilege of access to alcohol. Since clients were not followed well after discharge, the first indication of trouble with this failure to address alcohol as a treatment issue was the increasing number of ex-addict staff members who were being fired or quietly sent away for alcoholism treatment.[23] The alcoholism field similarly was plagued by alcoholics "chewing their booze"—a euphemism for alcoholics' propensity to abuse sedatives, tranquilizers, and other prescribed psychoactive drugs. Over time, awareness of the problem of cross-addiction grew in both fields, and public-policy makers began to explore ways of bringing together both the administrative and clinical structures of care of the two fields. Within professional circles, the proposition of integrating alcoholism and drug abuse treatment within the same facilities—merging what were often separate state alcohol- and drug-abuse funding agencies, merging separate worker credentialing systems, and merging or broadening the scope of professional associations—triggered debates of great emotional

intensity. But year by year, more and more of these structures began to come together into their present configurations.

At the clinical level, the debate over "combined treatment" raged. Staff from programs like Eagleville Hospital and Rehabilitation Center in Pennsylvania made presentations at conference after conference in the 1970s, advocating the integration of these two fields at the direct-service level. If there was a single person at the front of this integration movement, it was surely Dr. Donald Ottenberg of Eagleville. While these debates were quite contentious in the 1970s, the movement away from "alcohol-only" and "drug-only" treatment units spread rapidly during the 1980s. In national surveys of alcoholism and drug-addiction treatment units, the percentage of alcohol-only treatment units dropped from 51% of the total in 1982 to 13% of the total in 1990.[24] This trend toward integration was further reflected in the field's growing use of terms such as "addiction," "substance abuse," "chemical dependency," and "alcohol, tobacco, and other drugs" (ATOD). System integration was also evident in the trend toward merging what had often been separate state alcohol and drug authorities, and in the integration of alcohol and other drug concerns in the creation of new federal agencies such as the Center for Substance Abuse Treatment and the Office of Substance Abuse Prevention.

Early Programs: What Was it Like?

Working in early community-based programs was as exciting as it was chaotic. There were excessive demands for time and emotional energy and salaries that rarely reached five figures for line workers. It was a difficult period for those solo workers who were attempting to organize local addiction services. A "streetworker" of the late 1960s explains:

Those were crazy times. I got hate mail from both ends of the spectrum. The county sheriff thought I was on drugs and dealing drugs. Paranoid speed freaks thought I was a narcotics agent. Left-wing radicals thought I was working undercover to investigate them, and right-wing radicals thought I was a communist. Many of my fellow professionals saw my long hair and the way I dressed as a lack of professionalism and evidence that I'd "crossed over." I had one high school who wanted me there full time and another who wouldn't let me in the building. I was like a man with no country until I finally established my credibility.

There was in these early days a sense of mission that was remarkably clear: Change the community's perception of alcoholism and addiction and open doors of service for alcoholics and addicts. Those of us who chose to take on such an upstream battle often brought more commitment than competence, and, as a result, we created work milieus more typical of a social movement than of a service agency. Staff understood little about professional boundaries, and many saw themselves more as "hip" older brothers/sisters/friends to their clients than as professional counselors. Staff and clients came together to form a recovering community that had few of the institutional trappings typical of today's agencies. Alcoholics and addicts walked in off the streets and could be in a group a few minutes later, without going through today's army of gatekeepers and pounds of paperwork. Formal procedures were few, and clinical records were not much more elaborate than a recipe-card file of whom to notify in case of death. Training came on the job, and supervision came more by osmosis than by design. Treatment programs were plagued by meager and unpredictable funding, weak leadership, and poor organization. Entire programs were supported by a single grant, and at the end of the grant year, staff and clients alike were not sure on Friday whether or not the program would exist on Monday.

There was also a closeness-to-death that was ever-present within these early programs. A worker from this era explains:

> *Because alcoholics and addicts entered treatment in such late stages of addiction, we had an acute sense of the importance of what we were doing. This was a time when alcoholics were hanging themselves in jail cells and dying from withdrawal because they couldn't get adequate medical care. This was an era where every staff member had come face-to-face with alcoholic seizures and had stood over the bed of a dying alcoholic. We knew beyond a shadow of a doubt that, if what we were doing didn't work, the death of many of our clients was not only possible but imminent. There was a clarity of purpose and a rawness of emotion that is missing in the almost antiseptic atmosphere of many of today's treatment programs.*

Few other agencies wanted to work with alcoholics or addicts, so competition was minimal in those days. But in communities across the country where one could not get an alcoholic admitted to a hospital for acute head trauma, let alone detoxification or treatment, fundamental changes were unfolding that would alter the entire complexion of addiction treatment in America. Changes in the circumstances of American hospitals and the insurance industry's stance toward alcoholism were setting the stage for alcoholism/addiction units within local hospitals and a new generation of private addiction treatment programs that would take their place alongside the newly arising publicly funded programs.

Alcoholism: An Insurable Illness [2]

If there is a critical center upon which the entire modern industry of addiction treatment has turned, it is surely the evolving policies of the insurance industry toward the reimbursement of addiction treatment services. Given the profound impact of these evolving policies, we will try to place these changes in brief historical perspective. Insurance companies began to grow interested in alcoholism during the era of scientific temperance. Life insurance companies conducted research which concluded that, by dying at unexpectedly early ages, alcoholics defied the odds upon which their profits were based.[25] During the early 20th century, every effort was made to identify, exclude, or subsequently extrude alcoholics from coverage on the grounds of intemperance. Companies like Equitable Life and Security Mutual Life promised lower rates to customers who were total abstainers from alcohol.[26] Alcoholics who had "taken the cure" had to wait five years and verify their uninterrupted sobriety and present health before they could obtain life insurance.[27] Attitudes of the insurance industry toward alcoholics had not substantially changed by mid-century, when a 1949 survey of 282 insurance companies revealed that insurance companies denied policies to known alcoholics between 70% and 100% of the time, even if the applicants' health met the medical standard for such policies.[28]

For most of the 20th century, known alcoholics were denied life insurance and disability insurance, and the insurance industry refused to provide—or

---

[2] Information provided in an interview with James S. Kemper, Jr. and the source documents provided by Mary Ellen Kane and David Folkes of Kemper National Insurance Companies were essential to the construction of this section.

severely restricted—payments for alcoholism treatment under their health-care policies. Two things contributed to this policy stance. First, the consequences of alcoholism were viewed by the general public and the insurance industry as self-inflicted —products of willful misconduct. Second, it was believed that providing alcoholism treatment benefits could lead to escalating costs that would hurt industry profits and increase costs for all policy holders.[29]

For insurance companies to consider coverage for alcoholism, they first had to understand it. This understanding began when many of these companies began developing internal alcoholism intervention programs for their own employees. One of the first insurance companies to launch a formal internal alcoholism program was the Equitable Life Assurance Society of the United States. This program was initiated in 1956 under the leadership of Drs. Norvin Kiefer and Luther Cloud, both of whom served on the Board of Directors of the National Council on Alcoholism.[30] Within the culture and within the insurance industry, the growing recognition of alcoholism as a treatable disease laid the groundwork for change, but it would take some brave pioneers in the industry to demonstrate the financial feasibility of an alcoholism treatment benefit.

One of the pioneers in this area was James Kemper, Jr. of Kemper Insurance Companies. Kemper brought a special interest and understanding, based on his own recovery from alcoholism. After establishing an internal alcoholism program for Kemper Insurance Company employees in 1962, he added alcoholism coverage to the group insurance plans offered by the Kemper company two years later. Kemper's motivation in establishing this benefit was to provide a financial incentive for identifying and treating alcoholism at an early stage, in order to avoid the expensive medical costs that would accumulate in later stages of the disease. Kemper described the insurance industry's response to this initiative:

> *The response of the rest of the industry was skepticism, particularly when we added alcoholism treatment coverage at no extra cost to our policy holders. But two things happened. First, Prudential and a number of other insurance companies followed our lead in offering this benefit. Second, we showed we could offer this benefit and stay competitive. It took the industry a while to recognize that it was already paying for the consequences of alcoholism and to recognize that what we were proposing was to*

reduce those costs by treating the disease itself.[31]

This unprecedented stand had a significant influence on the willingness of other companies to consider similar coverage.

Insurance companies that were slowly beginning to perceive alcoholism as a disease similar to other illnesses in their purview went through several stages in their approach to this disorder. The first stage provided reimbursement for inpatient treatment of alcoholism in accredited hospitals. Early (1964-1974) providers of this coverage included Kemper Insurance, Blue Cross Association, the Prudential Company, Wausau, Hartford Insurance Group, Blue Cross of Maryland, and Capitol Blue Cross of Harrisburg, Pennsylvania. The majority of insurance companies did not provide these benefits until the early 1980s.

The second stage involved the extension of benefits to include reimbursement for alcoholism treatment provided in alcoholism treatment facilities that were not located in or affiliated with accredited hospitals. Insurance companies that were the pioneers (1972-1974) in the extension of these benefits included Prudential Insurance, Kemper Insurance, and Hartford Insurance Group. These companies demonstrated that the financial liability of these new benefits could be managed effectively through such mechanisms as requiring physician certification of the need for admission, requiring treatment at a company-approved treatment facility, setting a limit on days of treatment, requiring pre-approval for all length-of-stay extensions, setting quality standards for both the treatment agency and treatment personnel, and setting conditions related to re-admission.[32] Again, it was more than a decade before such innovations became widespread in the insurance industry.

A third milestone was the extension of alcoholism treatment benefits to include outpatient services. Early (1973-1975) pioneers providing reimbursement for outpatient alcoholism treatment services included Kemper Insurance, the Hartford Insurance Group, and Blue Cross of Maryland. Once they had reached this stage, many companies expanded the language of their policies to extend alcoholism treatment benefits to include treatment of people addicted to drugs other than alcohol.[33]

Another factor that contributed to the insurance industry's move into coverage for alcoholism treatment was action by an increasing number of state legislatures. By 1974, nine states had passed legislation that required insurance companies operating within their boundaries to provide reimbursement for alcoholism treatment.[34] Some of the states, such as Illinois, prohibited the exclusion of hospital treatment of alcoholism; other states, such as Massachusetts, mandated minimum coverage, e.g., 30 days of inpatient treatment and up to $500 in outpatient counseling per calendar year. The National Council on Alcoholism also provided sustained advocacy for an alcoholism health-care benefit, and NIAAA played a crucial role by supporting the development of alcoholism accreditation standards, promoting efforts to credential and certify alcoholism treatment personnel, offering management training to upgrade the administration of alcoholism treatment facilities, and funding pilot programs to explore the financial consequences of alcoholism coverage.[35]

The creation of an alcoholism treatment benefit was a significant step in de-stigmatizing addictive disorders, paving the way for explosive growth in the treatment industry during the 1970s and 1980s.

Program Accreditation and Licensure

Several concerns made the insurance industry wary of expanding coverage for the treatment of alcoholism. Among the more significant of these barriers were the lack of accepted diagnostic criteria for alcoholism and the lack of an acceptable set of standards to determine which institutions and which professional workers were qualified to treat the alcoholic. The first problem was addressed in 1972 with the National Council on Alcoholism's release of its *Criteria for the Diagnosis of Alcoholism*. These criteria ensured some degree of minimal clinical specificity in defining the diagnostic boundaries of the disorder, and in defining the services that should be reimbursed under the diagnosis of alcoholism. The problem of institutional and service-provider qualifications was addressed by creating program accreditation and licensing standards and by developing counselor credentialing, certification, and licensing programs.

The development of voluntary accreditation standards for addiction treatment programs gave insurance companies and other third-party carriers a mechanism for determining which programs met high enough standards of quality to warrant approval of treatment costs as a reimbursable health-care benefit. That step was a major milestone in the legitimization of alcoholism treatment in the health insurance industry and the health-care industry. Early work on addiction treatment standards dates to the 19th-century inebriate asylums, and modern work on standards goes at least as far back as the 1955 work of the Committee on Standards and Program Evaluation of the North American Association of Alcoholism Programs.[36] But in 1972 the Joint Commission on Accreditation of Hospitals (JCAH) developed accreditation standards that granted alcoholism and other addiction treatment programs probationary entry into the mainstream health-care system.

Programs across the country scrambled to come into compliance with JCAH standards, with the dream that reimbursement by the insurance industry would put their programs on a stable financial foundation. Later, standards for state licensure of publicly funded addiction treatment programs were heavily influenced by the JCAH standards, as were Medicaid standards for reimbursement of addiction treatment services. The evolving JCAH standards exerted a profound influence in moving addiction treatment agencies from folk institutions to formal organizations modeled after the community hospital.

The move from informal to formal organizational structures was not without its growing pains. Among other things, staff began to complain that the process of treatment (documenting service activity) seemed to be growing more important than the service goal (recovery).

Three Worlds: Public, Private, and Military

The circumstances of community hospitals had changed dramatically since the 1940s, when the beds in overcrowded hospitals were carefully rationed and denied to alcoholics. The over-bedding of the American health-care system—and the resulting competition—triggered a search for billable diagnoses that could fill empty beds and enhance corporate viability and profit. The recognition of alcoholism as a legitimate illness, the availability of replicable hospital-based alcoholism treatment models, JCAH accreditation standards for alcoholism units, and the growing willingness of insurance companies to pay for the treatment of alcoholism all set the stage for an explosive growth in the number of alcoholism treatment units operating in community hospitals. The sudden profitability of alcoholism treatment also led to the rapid growth of free-standing, non-hospital-affiliated private alcoholism treatment programs.

In this climate, America saw the revival of its first addiction treatment franchise since the earlier closure of the Keeley, Neal, Gatlin, and Empire Institutes. The new private franchises bore names like Comprehensive Care Corporation, Charter Medical Corporation, Life-Mark Corporation, Parkside Medical Services Corporation, Psychiatric Institutes of

America, Raleigh Hills (American Medical International, Inc.), Addiction Recovery Centers, and Horizon Health Corporation, to name just a few.[37] By the early 1980s, the American system of addiction treatment was organized into three fairly distinct worlds. There was the growing world of public addiction treatment agencies supported by federal, state, and local funds. These agencies served a predominately indigent and working-class clientele. There was the world of private addiction treatment programs, operating out of hospitals and newly constructed free-standing facilities which served the more affluent—or at least, insured—alcoholic and addict. And there was a rarely acknowledged but growing system of addiction treatment that cared for active and discharged military personnel and their families. This system, spawned out of growing concern about alcohol problems and dramatically enlarged in response to concerns about drug use in Vietnam, grew from a few isolated experiments in the 1950s and 1960s to a worldwide network in the 1980s. By 1981, the military was spending $45 million a year—in 54 residential and 420 outpatient programs that employed more than 2,500 military and civilian personnel—to treat more than 50,000 military personnel for alcohol- and other drug-related problems.[38]

The Veterans Health Administration (VA), the largest health care delivery system in the U.S., also treated a large number of alcoholics and addicts through its hospitals and outpatient service centers. Between the initiation of specialized alcoholism treatment in the VA in 1957 and 1986, the VA developed 172 alcohol-dependence treatment units. The VA also opened some 75 drug-addiction treatment programs in the early 1970s, which by 1975 were treating more than 8,500 veterans a year. By 1986, the VA's specialized units were treating more than 53,000 individuals for alcohol and/or drug addiction, while an additional 44,000 veterans were treated in medical and psychiatric units for alcohol-related problems. The VA also contracted with community-based addiction treatment providers to place veterans in community halfway houses.[39]

By the 1980s, the standard treatment design in the private and military addiction treatment programs was a mix of medical and sub-acute detoxification, group-oriented outpatient counseling, A.A.-oriented 21-to-28-day inpatient/residential treatment, and a short regimen of aftercare counseling.

There was some overlap in the public and private systems—some agencies that seemed to have a foot in each world. Many public programs chased the dream

of private insurance reimbursement. They upgraded treatment protocol and staff credentials. They built modern, attractive facilities; they became accredited; and they launched marketing programs to attract paying clients. But only a small percentage of programs would ever manage to obtain the majority of their funding through insurance reimbursement. The growth in public dollars (federal, state, and local) committed to addiction treatment offset their failure to win private funds. By 1982, both the private and public treatment sectors were positioned for explosive growth.

Before we continue our story of the evolving treatment system, we need to pause to discuss the evolving nature of the addiction treatment workforce. One of the first outcomes of the growing number of public and private dollars supporting addiction treatment was the return of physicians to this field and the establishment of addiction medicine as a recognized specialty.

The Rebirth of Addiction Medicine

When America criminalized alcohol and other drugs of abuse in the early 20th century, the responsibility for the care of alcoholics and addicts passed from physicians and hospitals to police and jails. With the subsequent closing of the inebriate asylums and the demise of the American Medical Society for the Study of Alcohol and other Narcotics, physicians *as a group* left the field of addiction medicine and did not return for almost half a century. While individual physicians continued to reach out to care for the addicted, no organized medical specialty focused on the treatment of addiction until the New York Medical Society on Alcoholism was founded by Dr. Ruth Fox in 1954. In 1967, this Society expanded its scope to that of a national organization and re-christened itself the American Society on Alcoholism. As the treatment field expanded in the 1970s and 1980s, other organizational efforts were also underway. NIDA and NIAAA created a Career Teacher Program for Medical School Faculty. The Kroc Foundation provided national support for improved addiction-related medical education. State medical societies explored ways in which they could provide support for physicians who were practicing primarily in the area of addiction medicine. Particularly influential was the work of the California Society for the Treatment of Alcoholism and Other Drug Dependencies, which in 1981 and 1982 defined the knowledge components of addiction medicine and developed an exam to test physicians on their mastery of this core knowledge.

Other organizations, such as the American Academy of Addictionology and the American Medical Association, were also actively involved in addiction-related physician education. In 1982, the House of Delegates of the American Medical Association called for the creation of one national organization that would represent the addiction medicine specialty. With support from the Kroc Foundation, a number of meetings were held that in 1983 paved the way for the creation of the American Society on Alcoholism and Other Drug Dependencies, subsequently re-christened the American Society of Addiction Medicine (ASAM). ASAM played a major role in professionalizing the field of addiction medicine as a board-certified physician specialty, and in providing physician education in addiction medicine throughout the country. ASAM organized state chapters and went on to certify more than 2,700 physicians in addiction medicine, to increase its own membership to more than 3,000 physicians, and to publish the *Journal of Addictive Disease.* Other indications of the growing professionalization of addiction medicine included the development of various addiction-focused workgroups and task forces in the American Psychiatric Association and the 1985 establishment of the American Academy of Psychiatrists in Alcoholism and Addiction (later re-christened The American Academy of Addiction Psychiatry).[40]

In 1991, more than 9,000 physicians were employed in addiction treatment programs in the United States.[41]

An Evolving Workforce

When America declared war on alcoholism and drug addiction in the 1960s and early 1970s, it did so without an army to wage this war. There were quite simply no foot soldiers to fill the front-line positions of service delivery. A workforce had to be created —and created quickly. At what seemed like the cutting edge of the field were the Minnesota Model alcoholism programs that used recovered alcoholics and the therapeutic communities that used ex-addict counselors and managers. As the field expanded, there was an enormous market for recovered people willing to work in the expanding network of addiction service programs. They were referred to as "paraprofessionals" or—more benignly—as "professionals by experience." Although the use of recovered people in service activity had a long history, it was also influenced by a contemporary community mental health movement that experimented with the training and deployment of indigenous workers who had no formal academic credentials.[42]

Those who worked in the alcoholism field in these early programs were mostly middle-aged white men, recovered alcoholics with strong A.A. backgrounds. Few had relevant formal education or supervised clinical training, and most were hired, not because of their skills, but because of certain traits that were thought to be useful in work with alcoholics: flexibility, humor, warmth, and creativity.[43] Most of the first "ex-addicts" drawn into this burgeoning field were ethnically diverse, and most brought a past history of heroin addiction, and—not uncommonly—had more prior contact with penal institutions than with educational institutions. An incredible variety of people began working as alcoholism and drug-abuse counselors without regard to their education, their training, or the stability of their personal recovery from addiction.[44] Many were hired first as non-therapeutic aides, but they soon evolved into counselors when it became apparent that they could quickly establish deep rapport with and influence upon clients.[45]

The professionals who worked in the addictions field in the 1960s and 1970s were an interesting mix. In its earliest days, the field served as both a dumping ground and an oasis, drawing some of the lowest- and highest-functioning professionals from allied human service fields. At a time in which choosing to work with alcoholics and addicts was itself viewed as a professional kiss of death, professionals who risked entry into the addiction treatment field did so either because they had few choices or out of a special attraction to the field. The field attracted those with their own personal or family-related addiction issues and those who were drawn to a frontier profession that valued creativity and innovation. Others were swept into the addictions field from their participation in what was being christened "the counterculture." Melvyn Kalb and Morton Popper observed in 1976 that those professionals who were staying in the field were "likely to be the best and the worst."[46] It was out of this stew of backgrounds, personalities, and circumstances that the fates of the early programs and their clients were shaped.

Controversy accompanied the very birth of community-based treatment, and no controversy was more heated than the question of whether or not one had to have experienced addiction and recovery in order to work effectively with addicts. In 1963, two Michigan psychiatrists, Dr. Henry Krystal and Dr. Robert Moore, entered into a debate in the *Quarterly Journal of Alcohol Studies* on the question: "Who is Qualified to Treat the Alcoholic?" Krystal took the position that alcoholism was a complex emotional disorder accompanied by "transferences and counter-transferences" of such a strong nature that only professionally trained psychiatrists, psychologists, and social workers were qualified to treat the alcoholic. Krystal illustrated the subtleties of working with alcoholics by suggesting that, without truly understanding the alcoholic, an untrained person's "pat on the back" could throw an alcoholic patient into a "homosexual panic," just as an untrained person's "swift kick in the pants" could "precipitate irreversible self-destructive behavior." Krystal suggested that the professionally trained therapist who had no experience with alcoholics was superior to the untrained recovered alcoholic who had not "worked through his own emotional problems." Moore, for his part, cited studies suggesting that psychiatrists were not particularly effective with alcoholics and that individual psychotherapy delivered by anyone was not the treatment of choice for alcoholism. Moore argued that the 80% of alcoholics who constitute the category "addictive drinkers" were being treated effectively in institutions and clinics by recovered people who were not trained in psychotherapy, and that such people had a significant role to play in the treatment of alcoholism. The Krystal-Moore debate stirred much continuing discussion and focused attention on the emerging role of the alcoholism counselor.[47]

What this debate missed was the fact that the casualty rate—people leaving the field due to the emotional distress of the work—was high during this period for both the professional by education and the professional by experience. There were, however, some special problems related to the ways in which recovered people were used, problems that have not been fully revealed in the professional literature.

A Hidden Story: The Exploitation and Relapse of Recovering Alcoholics and Addicts

It is remarkable by today's standards that alcoholics and addicts fresh from the throes of their addiction could—just a few months later—be working as full-time paid helpers in newly arising addiction treatment programs. While support groups for workers were advocated and sporadically implemented, these quickly evolved into formats that focused more on training than on caregiver support.[48]

During the period of rapid expansion in the number and size of addiction treatment programs, there was no pool of educated and trained people willing or available to fill all the newly created positions. The answer to this dilemma was often the recruitment and cursory training of recovering people to work as outreach workers, house managers, detox technicians, "patient counselors," "senior alcoholic patients," "A.A. counselors," rehabilitation aides, or community educators. All such roles focused on the ability of the recovering alcoholic to establish rapport with incoming alcoholic patients and to serve as a stimulus for hope and a source of instruction. Some treatment centers also hired A.A. members during this period as an appeasement tactic, to mollify the community group most responsible for referrals.[49] In such programs, the recovering alcoholic hired as counselor was expected to be a walking tape recording of the A.A. recovery message and to assume responsibility for the behavior management of alcoholics in the treatment milieu. It was not unusual in the 1960s and 1970s to have clients still in treatment recruited into entry-level employment. One day someone was a client in treatment; the next day he or she was employed in the same program. Such clients-promoted-to-staff often worked excessive hours with little pay and even less supervision. At times, their employers even posed obstacles to their continued recovery, such as the assignment of a work shift that precluded A.A. participation.[50] Such practices were the results, not of conscious intent to inflict harm, but of insensitivity and managerial incompetence.

The field simply grew so rapidly that few quality-control standards existed to guide the selection, training and utilization of recovering and recovered people. Staff barely knew how to treat addicts, let alone how to manage complex organizations and supervise professionally untrained and personally vulnerable staff. One of the unfortunate consequences was relapse, and these relapses tended to be dramatic and severe in their consequence. This author personally knew many such people whose fall from grace (relapse) was followed by great debility or death by overdose, addiction-related diseases, or suicide. These relapses were shrouded in silence for many years before we as a field began to establish general standards related to the hiring and supervision of recovered people. Surveys as late as 1983 and 1986 continued to underscore the prevalence of relapse among recovering people working in the field and to cite factors that contributed to such relapses.[51] A 1987 survey cited the top three causes of counselor relapse to be failure to maintain a personal recovery program, a lack of detachment from the work situation, and an over-commitment to work.[52] Programs eventually established standards requiring a specified period of sobriety (usually between two and five years) before one could be hired as a counselor. What is perhaps most remarkable is that many recovering people who entered the field during this period so full of demands and so devoid of support went on to establish solid programs of personal recovery and to make significant professional contributions—in spite of the field's lack of understanding of their true assets and vulnerabilities.[53]

Professionalization: Training, Credentialing, and Worker Certification

The coming of age of addiction treatment agencies—and of addiction counseling as a distinct discipline—was marked by the emergence of a formal professional infrastructure. This infrastructure had six major elements: 1) national and state treatment advocacy organizations through which treatment agency directors could protect and advance the interests of the field; 2) standards for the licensing and accreditation of addiction treatment programs; 3) national and state alcohol and drug counselor associations; 4) the creation of academic and non-academic counselor-training programs; 5) the development of systems for credentialing, certifying, and licensing alcohol and drug counselors; and 6) ancillary support institutions that generated addiction-related research and addiction-related professional literature (books, journals, newsletters, magazines, pamphlets).

State alcoholism counselor associations grew in number in the 1960s and 1970s, and a national counselors' association evolved out of several developmental stages: the OEO alcoholism training centers, the National Association of Alcoholism Counselors and Trainers (NAACT,1972), the National Association of Alcoholism Counselors (NAAC,1974), and finally the National Association of Alcoholism and Drug Abuse Counselors (NAADAC,1982).[54]

In 1970, the challenge for the alcoholism and drug abuse counselor training field was nothing short of the creation and legitimization of a new profession. Only six training programs in the entire country were designed to prepare recovered alcoholics for the role of lay counselor.[55] Both NIAAA and NIDA launched major worker-training initiatives. In the mid-1970s, they each established national training centers (The National Center for Alcohol Education and the National Drug Abuse Training Center) and regional training centers and subsidized the creation of state and territorial alcoholism and drug-abuse counselor training programs. These efforts generated training courses and a cadre of trainers who could deliver those courses to the people who worked on the front lines of addiction treatment. NIDA and NIAAA also

funded special projects aimed at credentialing recovered alcoholics and addicts and preparing women and minorities for leadership positions in the field. The task was a daunting one: to prepare a new field of more than 40,000 workers who came to their roles with almost no relevant academic experience.[56] Out of the collective efforts of the state and national counselor associations, the two national institutes, and state addiction agencies, a professional field and a professional role came into being. There were several significant milestones in this professionalization process. In 1974, Roy Littlejohn Associates released its NIAAA-contracted report on model standards to be used by states in licensing or certifying alcoholism counselors. The report recommended minimum requirements for certification that included 1) a minimum of two years without alcohol or drug misuse, 2) completion of a certified training program of basic alcoholism counseling competencies, 3) one year of alcoholism counseling experience, and 4) passage of a test on basic knowledge of alcoholism and alcoholism counseling.[57] Three years later, an Alcohol, Drug Abuse and Mental Health Administration expert panel issued the "Finger Report," in which it recommended the creation of a national credential for alcoholism counseling.

Building on this work, a Birch and Davis Associates, Inc. report later defined 12 core functions of drug-dependency counseling, which included assessment; treatment planning; counseling and education of individuals, families, and groups; crisis intervention; record keeping; and client-oriented consultation with other agencies. The Littlejohn and Birch and Davis reports helped many states create standards for the certification of alcoholism and drug-abuse counselors. In 1981, the Certification Reciprocity Consortium/Alcohol and Other Drug Abuse (CRC/AODA) was created. It became the National Certification Reciprocity Consortium (NCRC) in 1989. This consortium linked the activities of more than 40 state alcohol-and-drug counselor-certification boards and provided a procedure for reciprocal certification of counselors who moved from state to state. The period from the mid-1980s to the early 1990s was marked by considerable controversy over certification, as states tried to merge separate alcoholism counselor and drug-abuse counselor credentialing systems, and as no less than three organizations—The American Academy of Health Care Providers in Addictive Disorders, NCRC, and NAADAC—offered national addictions counselor credentials.[58]

By 1991, more than 160,000 people were

employed in substance abuse treatment programs in the U.S., and more than 87,000 of them filled direct-care roles.[59]

Explosive Growth

Blessed by new access to reimbursement for alcoholism treatment, and by an expanding workforce, hospital-based and free-standing private addiction treatment units grew explosively. The number of such units actually doubled between 1982 and 1990. The number of for-profit alcoholism programs alone increased by 48% between 1979 and 1982.[60] A 1987 survey by the American Hospital Association revealed the existence of 58 addiction specialty hospitals and another 874 general hospitals and 165 psychiatric hospitals that contained designated addiction treatment units.[61] [62] In a national survey sponsored by NIAAA and NIDA, private for-profit alcoholism treatment units increased from 295 in 1982 to 1401 in 1990. In October, 1987, a NIDA/NIAAA survey identified 5,791 treatment units, which at the time had 350,613 clients enrolled in treatment. Sixteen percent of the units surveyed were private for-profit programs, and 66 % were private not-for-profit programs. More than 2,000 of these units were outpatient facilities that were treating 50% of the total clients in treatment during the survey.[63] National surveys of clients in substance-abuse treatment reveal that the percentage of clients treated in free-standing outpatient facilities increased from 40% in 1980 to 53% in 1993. In 1993, 87% of clients in all substance abuse treatment settings were treated as outpatients.[64] At the same time (1982-1990), the number of public programs actually decreased, although the sizes of many of these units were growing larger.[65]

These numbers tell the story of an increasing number of private entrepreneurs who were being drawn to the provision of alcoholism treatment services as a profit-making venture. Growth of the overall field was staggering. The modern treatment industry grew from a handful of programs in the 1950s, to 2,400 programs in 1977, to 6,800 in 1987, and to 9,057 in 1991.[66] The number of clients served annually by these institutions rose from 289,933 in 1982 to 1.8 million in 1991.[67] Some states' annual prevention and treatment budgets grew from a few million dollars in the 1970s to more than $200 million in the 1990s.[68] This growth accelerated changes in the characteristics of the addiction treatment workforce. Addiction counseling curricula were installed in colleges and universities and offered through independent training programs, to prepare people to work

in these new and expanding addiction treatment agencies. Surveys of addiction treatment counselors conducted in the 1990s profiled an addiction counseling workforce that was becoming younger, more diversified in gender and ethnicity, more tenured (number of years' prior experience in the field), more educated, and more likely to be working in private and public practice than in any previous period.[69] The addictions counselor role had evolved from that of a "paraprofessional" working within a more highly credentialed multidisciplinary team to that of a professional who could operate independently. This change reflected, not so much that the "paraprofessional" had achieved legitimacy, but that the role of addictions counselor was being increasingly filled by professionals trained in psychology, counseling, social work, nursing, and the newly created addictions counseling specialty. The number of "professionals by experience" declined as the field experienced rapid growth and professional legitimization.[70] During this transition, the use of the term "paraprofessional" dropped from common usage in the field.[71]

The interests of this growing body of private institutions and this newly professionalized workforce came together in the 1980s to form powerful new strategies of early intervention into alcohol and other drug problems.

Early Intervention Programs

Addiction specialists had long lamented that they seemed to see addicts only in the latest stage of addiction and that much better prognoses could be expected if they could find a way to reach the alcoholic/addict earlier. The involvement of such specialists in the creation of an early intervention technology came out of a genuine desire to prevent the devastation of late-stage addiction. Where the traditional addiction specialist wanted to intervene early to enhance the prospects of recovery, the new business entrepreneur saw early intervention technologies as engines that could generate the raw materials (patients) to sustain and increase profits. An unplanned synergy between these two groups resulted in incredible breakthroughs in intervention technology—as well as the abuse of that technology.

The 1970s saw a series of new intervention techniques, some of which will be detailed in the next chapter. The growing presence of employee assistance programs (EAPs) in business and industry in the 1970s collided with workplace drug testing in the 1980s to force a much more diverse population of alcohol and drug users into the addiction treatment system. Mandatory drug testing and the near-automatic referral to treatment of employees who tested positive for drugs all but obliterated the line between drug use and drug addiction. Treatment agencies became involved in providing EAP services, primarily for the anticipated referrals that such contracts would bring. Mandatory clinical evaluations of people arrested for drunk and drugged driving—also often provided by treatment agencies—forced an equally recalcitrant group of alcohol and drug users into the confines of treatment. Family intervention technologies that were pioneered by Vernon Johnson in Minnesota began to be offered as a "free" service by treatment programs. As the "adolescent business" picked up, increasing numbers of treatment agencies operated, or sought close relationships with, a growing network of student assistance programs (SAPs) that operated in public and private school systems. Similar intervention programs were launched via "first-offender" programs in the criminal justice system and specialized programs in the child welfare system aimed at substance-using mothers.

These new intervention services were usually framed simply as a means of extending badly needed services to difficult-to-reach and underserved populations. But the use of such technologies also reflected a shift from treatment as a voluntary enterprise focused on personal recovery to treatment as a coerced experience whose primary goal was social control and institutional profit. Throughout history, addicts have often entered treatment under the coercive influences of family and community—and even their own fear of insanity or death. Three differences distinguish this modern period. First, coercive influences were brought to bear at much earlier stages in the development of alcohol- and drug-related problems. Second, there were a greater number of such coercive agents, often working in tandem. And finally, the primary goals of such coercion had shifted toward cultural and institutional gains and away from the more restricted focus on personal reformation. While these changes reflected a less benevolent side of the evolving treatment industry, there was also a growing number of grateful people whose lives were profoundly changed by addiction treatment.

Recovery as a Cultural Phenomenon

What we earlier described as the "Modern Alcoholism Movement" had achieved many of its goals by the mid-1970s. Most of the public had come to view the alcoholic as a sick person, and there had been broad public support for legislation that was creating a national network of alcoholism treatment programs. The next developmental stage in this now-quite-successful movement included a full redefinition of the public image of the alcoholic—and a shifting of that image from Skid Row to the house next door.

During the mid-1970s, the National Council on Alcoholism launched a campaign to decrease the stigma associated with alcoholism and enhance people's willingness to seek treatment. One such strategy, called "Operation Understanding," was the brain-child of Walter Murphy. On May 8, 1976, in Washington, D.C., 52 prominent citizens from all walks of life publicly proclaimed their recovery from alcoholism. Operation Understanding—both the first program and a second in 1977—broke the cultural silence that accompanied alcoholism and set the stage for large numbers of public figures to follow suit. Another highly publicized event that occurred shortly after the first Operation Understanding meeting was Freedom Fest '76—a gathering of 26,000 people in Bloomington, Minnesota to celebrate their freedom from chemical dependency. During this same period, NIAAA media campaigns further reinforced the view that alcoholism crossed all boundaries of age, gender, race and social class, and that the Skid-Row alcoholic constituted less than five percent of America's total alcoholic population. The image of the alcoholic as a Skid-Row bum rapidly broke down under this media assault. "Drunk" jokes that had been an American staple quickly fell out of cultural favor.

A seemingly unending progression of notable figures were announcing their entry into addiction treatment or their recovery status. There were noted political figures and their family members, actors and actresses, well known athletes, Rock stars, and other public figures. During the late 1970s and early 1980s, going to treatment and participating in some type of Twelve-Step recovery program became something of a fad. Programs like the Palm Beach Institute, Betty Ford Center, Hazelden, Edgehill-Newport, Fair Oaks Hospital, Regent Hospital, and Sierra-Tucson found themselves catering to the addicted rich and famous, whose entrance and ongoing status in treatment was regularly reported in newspapers, popular magazines, and the tabloids. The reach of such programs was quite remarkable. The Betty Ford Center, for example, treated more than 33,000 people from all 50 states and more than 30 foreign countries.[72]

Addiction recovery had gone from the shameful to the "chic"—something Dr. Klaus Makela referred to as more of a "lifestyle choice than the only way out of intolerable pain." Evidence of this "chicness" seemed to be everywhere. Addiction treatment and recovery were prominent in popular fiction (such as Peter Benchley's *Rummies*) and cinema (such as *Clean and Sober*). Television shows prominently featured recovered alcoholics, and there was even a televised portrayal of the life of Bill Wilson, called "My Name is Bill W." "Easy Does it," "A Friend of Bill's," "Protected by Smith and Wilson," and other A.A.-themed bumper stickers dotted American highways. Book stores across the land were filled with racks and racks of newly minted recovery literature, and recovery paraphernalia turned into a multi-million dollar industry.[73] There were recovery magazines, recovery newspapers, recovery retreats, recovery bowling leagues and softball teams, and recovery cruises. There was even a U.S. stamp with an alcoholism recovery theme. Between 1978 and 1985, Twelve-Step recovery became nothing short of a phenomenon of American pop culture. Like other such phenomena, it was popularized, commodified, and commercialized.[74] And yet there was something quite superficial about this growing cultural acceptance of the alcoholic—a social veneer reflecting an intellectual acceptance of the idea of alcoholism as a disease, which served to hide the enduring emotional stigma attached to alcoholism and the alcoholic. This undercurrent of continuing stigma was even more prevalent in relationship to drugs other than alcohol. But for a brief moment, it looked as if the battle to destigmatize addiction was being won.

As might be expected, this period witnessed the expansion, distortion, and diversification of addiction-recovery mutual-aid societies.

Expansion and Diversification of Mutual-Aid Societies

The rapid expansion of early intervention and addiction treatment programs—and the broader cultural infatuation with Twelve-Step recovery—had a profound impact on A.A. In the decade of explosive growth of private- and public-sector treatment programs (1978-1988), membership in Alcoholics Anonymous grew from 750,000 to 1.6 million, with a growing number of these members coming to A.A. directly upon the advice of treatment agencies.[75] Some local A.A. groups began to be overrun by groups of alcoholism treatment center patients arriving by bus, or by a growing assortment of sullen, recalcitrant men and women mandated to attend A.A. meetings by their employers, judges, and probation and parole officers. In some areas, the number of coerced attendees might surpass the number of core A.A. members two- or three-to-one on a given night. In spite of the fact that

some of these resistant attendees actually became sober, concerns began to be raised about the effects that coerced attendance had on A.A. culture and practices.

This was all part of a broader discussion of the effects that alcoholism treatment was having upon A.A. Old-timers in particular were noting the diminished Twelfth-Step activity—a function that seemed to have been increasingly taken over by (or turned over to) treatment centers. There was also a growing concern that treatment centers were becoming a source of corruption to A.A. In earlier periods, we noted how A.A. language had permeated some treatment milieus via references to "A.A. counselors," depictions of programs being "A.A.-oriented," and the infusion of A.A. concepts and slogans. In the 1980s, there was a reversal of this process. Treatment language began to filter into A.A., and the line between what happened in a group in a treatment center and what happened in an A.A. meeting became increasingly blurred.

When old-time A.A. members were asked to describe how this new infusion of treatment-enmeshed clients had affected A.A., they would inevitably lament the loss of "real A.A." and "real drunks." Some observed that new therapeutic buzzwords and psychobabble were replacing A.A. slogans, that A.A. story styles were shifting to a focus on affective pain, and that A.A. laughter was being replaced by angst—trends that were turning the usual celebratory atmosphere of A.A. into an increasingly somber one. A.A. traditionalists began to refer to the burgeoning mountains of commercialized literature, tapes, and paraphernalia as "recovery porn."

In this climate, it should not be surprising that there were attempts by long-time observers of A.A. to delineate the essence of A.A. from its more superficial imitators. Ernest Kurtz, in his efforts to delineate the historical A.A.—the "real A.A."—from meetings that had taken on the flavor of treatment groups, proposed that the former was distinguished by five elements: 1) the use of A.A. vernacular (e.g., defects of character, self-inventory, Higher Power); 2) the presence of humor to reflect the recognition of mutual experience and to deal with incongruity and paradox; 3) a story style that shares experience, strength, and hope while respecting privacy; 4) faithfulness to A.A. traditions; and 5) a conviction by those present that they are there because they NEED to be there, rather than because they WANT to be there.[76]

What was remarkable about this period was the virtual explosion in adaptations of the A.A. program to problems other than alcoholism. There were what might be called traditional adaptations, such as the founding of Potsmokers Anonymous in 1968, Pills Anonymous in 1975, and Cocaine Anonymous (C.A.) in 1982. C.A.'s birth, like N.A.'s, was heavily influenced by an A.A. member, in this case Tom K., who suggested the idea of such a meeting and provided continued support to the first Hollywood, California group. C.A. grew to thirty meetings within six months and spread to several other states during its first year.

It looked for a while as if everyone was going to get into some kind of Twelve-Step group, as hundreds upon hundreds of A.A. adaptations spread across the land. A 1988 article on A.A.'s 60th anniversary lamented this rise of Twelve-Step variations for everyone from shoplifters to Edsel owners, and expressed a growing fear that the meaning of the Steps—particularly the Twelfth Step—was getting lost "amid an incessant whine about the injured self."[77] Only time and retrospect will tell whether A.A. itself was helped or hurt during this period. Another trend was the growing number of other mutual-aid societies that defined themselves, not as adaptations of, but as alternatives to A.A. There had long been alternatives to A.A. outside the United States, and many of these alternatives had been profoundly influenced by A.A.[78] But from 1935 to 1975, A.A. existed almost unchallenged as THE mutual-aid society for recovered alcoholics. However, between 1975 and 1985, in the midst of the explosive growth of the addiction treatment industry, new addiction-recovery mutual-aid societies sprang up as alternatives to A.A.

One of the first major alternatives to A.A., Women for Sobriety (WFS), was founded in 1975 by sociologist Jean Kirkpatrick out of her own experience of addiction and struggle to recover in A.A. WFS was organized on the premise that the etiology, progression, and recovery from alcoholism were fundamentally different experiences for women than they were for men. In this view, women not only needed to be with other alcoholic women, but also needed a program of recovery designed specifically for alcoholic women.[79] The WFS principles of recovery are set forth in the program's Thirteen Statements of Acceptance and elaborated in a series of books authored by its founder.[80]

While many elements of WFS are drawn from A.A. (their emphasis on abstinence, the role of spirituality in recovery, the practice of daily meditation), Kirkpatrick believed that what helped men in A.A. could even be harmful to women. In her view, women did not need ego-deflation; they needed to build self-esteem. In the WFS framework, this self-esteem came

through an experience of empowerment, rather than through a focus on powerlessness and surrender. WFS shortened A.A.'s expectation of life-long meeting attendance. WFS members attend as long as they feel the need for support, then leave with the addiction chapter of their lives closed. Anonymity is a choice in WFS, rather than a mandate. Cross-talk (direct feedback and advice) at meetings is encouraged rather than discouraged, and WFS meetings are remarkably free of the sloganeering that is pervasive at many A.A. meetings.

Lee Ann Kaskutukas' studies of WFS reveal a membership that is predominately White, educated, affluent, middle-aged, married with children, and likely to have been addicted to drugs in addition to alcohol. Most WFS members (89%) have also received professional help, and about one third attend A.A. as well as WFS meetings.[81] In her studies of WFS, Kaskutukas notes that women-only groups like WFS seem to be particularly appropriate for women whose drinking stems from problems related to sexuality issues, gender conflicts, family problems, and poor self-esteem.[82] There were 325 registered WFS groups in 1997.

Women For Sobriety: Thirteen Statements of Acceptance

1. I have a life-threatening problem that once had me.
2. Negative thoughts destroy only myself.
3. Happiness is a habit I will develop.
4. Problems bother me only to the degree I permit them to.
5. I am what I think.
6. Life can be ordinary or it can be great.
7. Love can change the course of my world.
8. The fundamental object of life is emotional and spiritual growth.
9. The past is gone forever.
10. All love given returns.
11. Enthusiasm is my daily exercise.
12. I am a competent woman and have much to give life.
13. I am responsible for myself and my actions.

Source: Women for Sobriety, Reprinted with permission.

A.A.'s perceived religious orientation posed an obstacle to some alcoholics and gave rise to alternative support structures. While there were a few early efforts to forge an A.A. alternative for such individuals, such as the American Atheists Addiction Recovery Groups, two major "rational" frameworks of recovery emerged as alternatives to A.A. in the mid-1980s. The first, Secular Sobriety Groups—later renamed Secular Organization for Sobriety—Save Our Selves (SOS)— was organized in 1985 by James Christopher, an alcoholic who had achieved sobriety in spite of his frustrations with A.A.'s perceived religious trappings. When he wrote an article on his struggles as an atheist in A.A., he received responses that convinced him that thousands of alcoholics desired a non-spiritual alternative to A.A. There is much in SOS that bears a striking resemblance to A.A. If one imagined support groups that operate much like A.A., but without references to Higher Power, God, or prayer, one would be very close to a picture of the SOS milieu. SOS places emphasis on the "sobriety priority," "not drinking no matter what," and on maintaining perpetual vigilance to keep from awakening the "sleeping giant" of addiction. SOS rejects A.A.'s requirement of personal anonymity at the public level, A.A.'s emphasis on helping other alcoholics as a means of staying sober, and A.A.'s practice of sponsorship. The SOS program has been laid out in a series of contributions by its founder, James Christopher.[83]

An SOS membership survey reveals a membership that is overwhelmingly White, predominately male, middle-aged, unmarried or divorced, highly educated, and affluent. Nearly two thirds of SOS members have abused drugs in addition to alcohol.[84] There were more than 1,000 SOS groups meeting in the U.S. in 1995.[85]

The second "rational" alternative to A.A., Rational Recovery (RR), was founded by Jack Trimpey in 1986. RR provides a non-religious, non-spiritual approach to alcoholism recovery that focuses on the use of reason and rational self-interest to solve alcohol-related problems. RR's program of recovery is based on the belief in an individual's power of personal self-control. RR, like A.A., begins with an acknowledgment of one's status as an addict and posits complete abstinence from alcohol as essential for personal health and happiness. RR recovery focuses on making an irrevocable sobriety decision, creating a plan to achieve sobriety, and developing techniques to battle the "Beast" (the irrational ideas that can lead to relapse). RR focuses on the ability to build a fulfilling life free from dependency on alcohol or on alcoholism-related support groups.

Like A.A., RR is based on participation in mutual-aid groups, but it differs from A.A. in that these groups often have a professional sponsor— usually a Rational Emotive Therapist—and are viewed as being necessary for only a limited period of time.

RR's program of recovery was outlined in a 1989 book by Jack Trimpey entitled—with tongue in cheek—*The Small Book.*[86] There were 600 registered RR groups in the U.S. in 1995.[87] Both SOS and RR were heavily influenced by the ideas of psychologist Albert Ellis.

Religious as well as non-religious alternatives to A.A. arose in the closing decades of the 20th century. Added to Alcoholics Victorious and other such religiously oriented addiction recovery groups was Overcomers Outreach (OO). OO was started in 1977 by Bob and Pauline B. in Whittier, California. OO members practice the Steps and Traditions of A.A./N.A./C.A., but name Jesus Christ as their "Higher Power." The focus of the organization is on applying Christian teachings to achieve a deeper understanding of the process of Twelve-Step recovery. It lists groups in 49 states.[88] Other contemporary groups similar in orientation to OO include Liontamers Anonymous and the National Association of Christian Recovery.

There were also a growing number of alternatives to A.A. for non-addicted drinkers who sought to moderate rather than end their drinking careers. These programs—some mutual-aid societies and others packaged educational counseling programs—included Moderation Management, DrinkWise, SMART (Self-Management and Recovery Training), and Drink Watchers.[89]

The proliferation of Twelve-Step adaptations and alternatives not only widened the choice for people seeking mutual-help experiences, but also resulted in many people's choice to be simultaneously or sequentially involved in multiple programs. This "program juggling" was not without its critics, who suggested that the "program tripper" often ended up more confused than helped, and that the failure to commit to a single program represented "shopping for recovery," rather than a commitment to recovery.

This proliferation of recovery programs had little direct impact on treatment agencies, which continued for the most part to embrace the mainstream Twelve-Step programs. But as these alternatives grew over time, treatment agencies were forced to investigate them and to explore how such programs might be used for certain clients. Some began to offer a menu of ideas and support structures within the treatment milieu and to link clients with those structures that seemed best suited to their individual needs. In other treatment programs, however, any divergence from traditional A.A. concepts was viewed as heresy.

While all this growth was underway, addiction treatment as a system was threatened—not by outside forces—but by itself. An industry that had moved from the status of a fledgling social movement to an accepted component of the American health-care system was about to face unanticipated threats to its very existence.

Competition, Profit, and Profiteering

As more public and private entrepreneurs entered the addiction treatment arena, several things changed. First, communities that used to have a single addiction treatment provider found themselves with several competing resources—particularly competition between publicly funded programs and hospital-based and private programs. As the non-public programs encountered difficulty filling inpatient beds and outpatient treatment slots, they launched marketing wars and expanded their geographical territory, bringing them into collision with other addiction treatment service providers. This sparked growing competition and conflict between different branches of the addiction treatment field. While the public programs continued to sustain a high level of service delivery (and often maintained waiting lists for services), the private programs, in order to survive, had to find better ways to "capture" and retain clients. In the words of one administrator:

> For the director of an addictions unit in the 1980s, there was one overriding preoccupation: DAILY CENSUS! There was never any doubt in my mind that my primary, if not my exclusive area of accountability was filling beds in the hospital. In the four years I spent at one hospital, I was never asked one question by my superiors about the relative success of our efforts to treat addictions.

Publicly funded agencies faced similar pressures as federal and state funders of addiction treatment shifted from grants to reimbursement for units of service delivered. As a result, the public programs —like their private counterparts—needed to sustain levels of service delivery in order to survive. This challenge intensified with the increased proliferation of programs. This would become the era of the marketer and the business manager.

In the 1980s, addiction treatment programs shifted their identities from those of service agencies to those of businesses. A growing number of for-profit companies that measured success in terms of profit and quarterly dividends—rather than treatment outcomes—entered the field. At the same time, the

character of many not-for-profit agencies underwent a similar change. These agencies had been told for years that their survival hinged on their ability to incorporate the management, fiscal, marketing, and public relations technologies of private industry. There is little question that most public-sector programs needed significant improvement in many of these areas. Caught up in the economic frenzy of the 1980s, many not-for-profits actually achieved this goal of increased organizational sophistication.

Agencies expanded dramatically, built beautiful buildings, dressed up the credentials and images of their staff, launched sophisticated and aggressive marketing campaigns, and became quite successful businesses. And many public programs used this increased sophistication to enhance their service mission to their local or regional communities. What was hidden amidst these changes, however, was the accumulation of wealth by many programs whose profit was not turned back into expanded or upgraded client services, but instead contributed to an escalation of salary and benefits accruing to organizational leaders. Their self-images shifted from those of public servants to those of health-care entrepreneurs. For a time, a predatory mentality became so pervasive that it affected even some of the most service-oriented institutions. In this climate, alcoholics and addicts became less people in need of treatment and more a crop to be harvested for their financial value. This evolving shift in the character of the field left in its wake innumerable excesses that tarnished the public image of the field and set in motion a financial back-lash that would lead to fundamental changes in the primary treatment modalities available to addicts and their families. While abuses in private-sector addiction treatment were among the most egregious and visible, there were parallel but different types of abuses occurring in the public sector.

Ethical Context and Breaches of Ethical Conduct

A critical stage in the development of any profession is the articulation of standards of competency and standards of ethical practice. Both are intended to protect the public from the power to do harm—as well as good—that is an inherent part of the professional role. The addictions treatment field was very slow in its development of ethical standards of professional conduct. Even when professional associations, certification bodies, and individual agencies developed codes of ethical conduct, these codes often represented little more than vaguely worded aspirational values, rather than explicit codes of professional conduct. In the professional literature, similarly scant attention was directed to ethical issues, and by 1985 there was still not a single text on ethical issues in addiction treatment. On the front lines of service agencies, ethics consisted of two inconsistently followed maxims: "be careful about confidentiality," and "don't have sex with your clients—at least not while they're 'clients'." Entering the mid-1980s, the field had poorly developed ethical sensitivities, a weak foundation of ethical standards, no universally accepted model of ethical decision-making, and rare utilization of ethics-related disciplinary processes. Moreover, the entire issue of ethics as conceived in the field's early development focused on clinical ethics. It was virtually silent on ethical issues related to the business practices of treatment agencies. Those vulnerabilities would prove to be the field's Achilles Heel.

The ethical abuses that unfolded in the face of intensified competition were widespread and severe: unethical marketing practices, financially motivated and clinically inappropriate admissions, excessive lengths of stay, inappropriate re-admissions, excessive fees, and the precipitous abandonment of clients when they reached the limits of their financial resources. Treatment programs with plummeting numbers of patients began to operate EAP, SAP, and drunk-driver evaluation services that—while posing as sources of independent and objective clinical assessment —actually served as feeder systems for financially lucrative inpatient treatment. Treatment itself took on a more coercive quality, with a growing number of clients entering treatment under duress from courts, employers, schools, and families. As competition tightened, some programs moved into questionable areas of specialized service, in an effort to sustain or increase patient census. Aggressively marketed "Women's Programs," "Dual-Diagnosis Programs," and "Cocaine Treatment Programs" often masked the lack of any significant expertise to conduct such services. Some programs' migration beyond the boundaries of their education, training, and experience was further evidenced in their practice of embracing an ever-widening range of disorders under the addiction service umbrella—conditions that ranged from codependency to eating disorders to sexual addiction. As the insurance companies' share of the cost of alcoholism treatment rose rapidly, insurance industry representatives began to focus closer scrutiny on the services they were paying for and the differences in costs between programs. Dan Anderson, former President of Hazelden, describes their conclusions:

Those paying for alcoholism treatment

looked at programs whose costs ranged from $35 a day to $2,000 a day, and on paper it looked like they were providing the same treatment. People began to ask, "My god, what kind of professional field is this?"[90]

Efforts were made to respond to these growing breaches in ethical conduct. As early as 1982, the National Association of Alcoholism Treatment Programs issued guidelines for promoting more ethical and responsible advertising of alcoholism programs. These guidelines called upon programs to refrain from criticizing alternative approaches, exaggerating success rates, and using advertisements that made recovery appear to be an easy process. There were also early voices of warning. By 1986, traditional treatment advocates such as James Kemper, Jr., were challenging the treatment industry to "get its act together." Kemper warned that the rapid proliferation of treatment programs was creating a climate ripe for "fringe operators" and "grifters and thieves" who could do great harm to the integrity of the addiction treatment industry.[91] Alarms also came in the form of the field's first two texts on ethics: LeClair Bissell and James Royce's *Ethics for Addiction Professionals* and William White's *Critical Incidents: Ethical Issues in Substance Abuse Prevention and Treatment.* By 1990, 50 out of 57 of the nation's addiction counselor credentialing boards specifically prescribed a code of professional ethics.[92] Under the sponsorship of NAADAC and state counselor certification bodies, ethics training increased—sometimes initiated in the aftermath of ethical explosions that placed local agencies and the field itself on the front pages of newspapers. In 1988 and 1989, a growing number of voices at professional conferences began making dire predictions about the future of addiction treatment institutions, and the addiction treatment profession, if the field could not be clinically and ethically re-centered.

In the 1980s, it was very difficult for the field to heed such warnings. A field birthed in virtual poverty found itself addicted to its own success. Whispered voices of self-confrontation began to suggest that maybe the addiction field itself needed treatment. The field was ripe for a wake up call. That call came in two forms: a financial backlash and an ideological backlash.

The Financial Backlash

The most significant responses to ethical abuses

in the addiction treatment field (and the larger health-care field) came from the insurance industry and private employers who were seeking to reduce their health-care benefit costs—particularly their rapidly escalating behavioral-health costs. Under their influence, institutions involved in funding, licensing, and accrediting treatment facilities began to closely monitor admission, length-of-stay, and re-admission decision-making processes.

Payors of addiction treatment services responded initially by requiring substance abuse treatment programs to develop formal utilization review (UR) and quality assurance (QA) programs. UR programs necessitated the development of admission, continued-stay, and discharge criteria for all modalities, along with a formal mechanism of case review to ensure the appropriateness of client placement. When internal UR procedures failed to curtail abuses—many programs simply manipulated their criteria and case documentation to justify the continuation of their existing practices—insurance companies and self-insured employers began requiring external utilization review of addiction treatment programs, by their own people or by independent consultants. Over time, this review function evolved into an approval (precertification) function—companies would not pay for services for their insured customers/employees without independent verification of medical necessity, both of admission and of the intensity and duration of services. During the mid-1980s, abuses in health-care organizations and in addiction treatment programs spawned the birth of a whole new industry to perform this monitoring and verification function.

QA programs were intended to ensure that programs charging for addiction treatment services were identifying and resolving problems related to quality of care. JCAH-influenced quality assurance programs went through a number of stages. In the 1970s, most of the focus was on establishing quality-assurance structures. Treatment programs were required to establish quality-assurance committees and quality-assurance record-keeping systems. Monitoring focused more on the presence and regular utilization of these structures than on whether or not these structures were actually resulting in improved service quality. During the 1980s, the focus shifted to problem identification and problem resolution. Programs were expected to track service volume data and quality-of-care indicators, in order to identify and resolve problems. In the early 1990s, there was a marked shift from quality assurance to total quality improvement. This shift in philosophy moved the focus away from the identification of problems in quality of care to the creation of processes through which quality of care could be constantly refined and improved.

In a further effort to control costs and ensure quality, some businesses established preferred provider organizations (PPOs), which would provide all of the addiction treatment services needed by any of the company's employees at special negotiated rates. Individual employees were free to choose another treatment site, but the company would pay full benefits only for services delivered by the PPO. Treatment programs competed intensely for such PPO designations. This was also the era of "carve-outs"—the creation of managed systems of mental health and chemical dependency treatment services organized by insurance companies or by business and industry. Programs competed intensely for inclusion in these systems. Just as PPOs were coming into prominence, insurance benefits for addiction treatment began to erode in many ways. The restrictions on coverage mirrored the areas of abuse by the treatment industry. In response to inappropriate admissions, pre-admission approval by an independent assessor was now required. In response to the field's inpatient bias, some insurance companies required prior failure (or a designated number of failures) in outpatient treatment as a criterion for inpatient admission. In response to treatment programs' practice of recycling chronically relapsing clients again and again, companies set limits on the number of days or dollars that could be expended for addiction treatment in a year, or in a lifetime. In response to excessive lengths of stay and multiple admissions of adolescents, companies began to place special restrictions on adolescent substance abuse and psychiatric benefits.

All of these steps were stages in the emergence of a system of "managed care," through which external gatekeepers (private companies) came to control what occurred inside treatment institutions. These gatekeepers evolved from internal health-benefits specialists to external consultants to a growing number of for-profit, investor-owned behavioral-health companies that earn their profits by tightly managing behavioral health-care utilization—and by lowering service costs by forcing local service agencies to compete with one another for their business.

At its best, managed care is an assertive approach to ensuring that each client receives the most appropriate, the highest-quality and the most cost-effective treatment services. At its worst, it is an aggressive approach that reduces costs to employers (and garners profits for managed-care firms and insurance companies) by denying or minimizing people's access to health-care services. At its worst, managed care replaces abuses of inclusion with abuses of exclusion. Whatever one's view of managed care, its consequences to the addiction treatment field were, and are, profound. The financial backlash that birthed managed care was not the only legacy of the 1980s. The addiction treatment field also faced an ideological and cultural backlash that challenged some of its most basic assumptions.

The Ideological and Cultural Backlash

The climate for an ideological and cultural backlash against addiction treatment was in some ways set when President Ronald Reagan ushered in an era of federal drug-control policy that dramatically shifted the public emphasis from treatment and research to law enforcement. It was in this broader de-valuation of treatment, "zero tolerance" of drug users, and re-criminalization of addiction that more specific attacks on the conceptual foundation of treatment occurred.

The modern system of treatment had been built on a series of premises about the nature of alcoholism, alcoholism treatment, and alcoholism recovery. These premises, presented to the public as scientific conclusions, had paved the way for more enlightened views of the alcoholic, generated public support for alcoholism treatment services, and drawn other addictions in under this medicalized banner. But in the 1970s and 1980s, evidence was accumulating that challenged many of the premises of the modern alcoholism movement. It is perhaps ironic that the very vehicle that the pioneers of the modern alcoholism movement used to launch their movement in the 1940s —science—subsequently gave birth to the most serious challenges to that movement's most basic declarations about alcoholism.[93]

By the 1980s, professional debate had moved to the level of popular culture, through a deluge of articles and books aimed at the general public. Herbert Fingarette's 1989 book *The Myth of Alcoholism as a Disease* and Stanton Peele's 1989 book *The Diseasing Of America* declared that everything the popular culture had come to believe about alcoholism was a collection of myths unsupported by scientific evidence.[94] These backlash writings declared that:

- There was no clearly definable and diagnosable disease of alcoholism.[95]
- Claims that alcoholism is due to biological or genetic vulnerability are at best overstated, and at

worst patently false.[96]
- The concepts of "loss of control" (the belief that alcoholics cannot control how much alcohol they will consume once they begin drinking) and "craving" (the belief that alcoholics experience overwhelming physical cravings that drive them to drink) are myths unsupported by scientific research.[97]
- Alcohol problems do not inevitably self-accelerate into advanced stages of alcoholism. Approximately one third of people with alcohol problems experience a lessening or complete diminishment of such problems. As a result, treatment programs claim success for what is often a natural recovery process.[98]
- A.A. is not effective with the "general population of alcoholics."[99]
- "It has been remarkably hard to find systematic proof that treatment for alcoholism and other addictions *accomplishes anything at all*."[100]

These authors not only attacked the scientific foundation of the disease concept of alcoholism, but further noted that this concept had proved injurious. According to these critics, the disease concept stigmatizes, infantilizes, and socially isolates the alcoholic, while mislabeling as alcoholics and addicts those with minor and transient problems in their relationship with alcohol and other drugs.[101] The issue for this chapter is not truth or falsehood of such claims, but the acknowledgment that these highly publicized charges received considerable public press and triggered a more critical evaluation of the treatment industry and its pronouncements. Such re-evaluation was evident in a growing number of court decisions upholding the denial of benefits on the grounds that alcoholism resulted, not from a disease, but from "willful misconduct"; and decisions declaring that legally mandated attendance at A.A. meetings was an unconstitutional violation of the First-Amendment separation of Church and State.

The knowledge of ethical abuses in the addiction treatment field and the growing debate about the field's conceptual foundations were relatively well contained in professional circles until the 1980s, when they began to break into the broader culture. Television exposés were added to the popular books and articles that attacked both the dominant treatment approaches being used in the U.S. and the conceptualization of alcoholism as a disease. These exposés vividly portrayed what were characterized as exploitive practices in certain addiction treatment programs. As early as November 1981, station KUTV in Salt Lake City, Utah, conducted an exposé of the Raleigh Hills program and its parent company, Advanced Health Systems, charging ethically questionable practices related to management, patient billing, and patient care. Various newspapers and the national networks ran similar exposés of other programs.[102] The financial, ideological, and cultural backlash reached a peak in the late 1980s and early 1990s.

The Crash

In the late 1980s and early 1990s, aggressive gatekeeping by managed-care companies and health-maintenance organizations dramatically eroded inpatient and residential treatment. Approved reimbursement for inpatient addiction treatment had dropped from 28 days to 18-21 days, to 14 days, to 5-7 days, and then to a few days of detoxification. The entire managed-care industry and the companies it represented seemed to make a simultaneous decision: future benefits for addiction treatment, where they existed, would be offered almost exclusively for outpatient rather than inpatient or residential services. As the field struggled to defend its bias toward extended residential treatment, it found itself facing research studies concluding that inpatient treatment offered no significant advantages over outpatient treatment, as measured by controlled studies of treatment outcomes.[103]

To accommodate this shift, inpatient programs across the country scrambled to establish outpatient and intensive outpatient programs. The difficulties involved in this transition were many. First, these units were much less valuable as providers of outpatient services than they had been when they were filling unoccupied beds in community hospitals. Outpatient services generated far less income for these institutions and decreased the units' ability to support the overhead for other areas of the hospital that always lost money. Second, hospitals that had operated successfully as regional addiction treatment centers, drawing patients from a wide geographical area, could not sustain that role when services moved from an inpatient to an outpatient basis. Third, program personnel learned that it was much harder to sustain continued client involvement in outpatient programs than it was in inpatient programs. Many programs had problems recruiting and retaining alcoholics and addicts in outpatient programs. These factors, along with the diminished income from inpatient services, meant that—just to survive—programs had to generate a much larger number of clients and services than they ever had in their histories. For many, this proved

an impossible task.

Occupancy rates for private (insurance-supported) inpatient addiction treatment programs eroded between 1989 and 1990, then plummeted between 1991 and 1993. Even treatment centers such as Hazelden, which had traditionally maintained close to 100% occupancy, found themselves with empty beds and no waiting lists.[104] Large and exclusive "campuses"—where the affluent addicted had once paid upwards of $650 a day for treatment—contracted in size, collapsed, or redefined their purposes.[105] In response to plummeting census figures, many hospitals merged their psychiatric and addiction treatment units, marking a reversal of the progressive three-decade separation of these two fields. Some of these mergers could be more aptly described as devourings. Rather than integrating the best of the clinical technologies and professional assets from both units, psychiatry usually won out in these quite primitive power struggles. What was sometimes left was an on-paper version of addiction services, with no sustained core technology of addiction treatment. Many counselors lost jobs in this era of program closures and downsizing.

While hospital-based units closed or sat underutilized, waiting lists for treatment in publicly funded residential programs grew unconscionably long. While service demands on these programs were escalating, experiments with managed care of public-sector health-care expenditures raised serious questions about the future accessibility, duration, and intensity of addiction treatment in the U.S. While treatment leaders drew some solace and hope from exposés of profiteering and zealous service exclusion by managed-care companies, the managed-care industry proved itself highly adaptable and resilient in the face of such charges.

What did provide a balm for the publicly funded programs was an infusion of federal "War-on-Drugs" money between 1986 and 1990. Growing media coverage of cocaine-generated crime and violence, cocaine-exposed infants, the cocaine-related deaths of sports and entertainment celebrities, and drug-related HIV/AIDS transmission all generated increased dollars for treatment. The requirements that came with these dollars brought the treatment system into much closer collaboration with America's public-health, criminal-justice, and child-protection systems.

A critical shift in values occurred in the field over the course of its growth, crisis, and crash periods. When one asked how a particular program was doing, one was not referring to the number or percentage of clients that program was successfully rehabilitating.

Success was measured by budget, facility count, head count (number of staff), and occupancy rate. During the crash of the early 1990s, these numbers declined for many addiction treatment institutions. There were sporadic efforts to revive the grassroots movement to counter these backlashes, but these attempts were almost universally ineffective. Those who survived this period remained in a state of shock, trying to make sense of precisely what had happened and anxiously speculating about what fate the future would bring.

Harold Hughes died in October, 1996, his passing little noted by the front lines of the field he had played such a crucial role in creating. What he had once called an alcohol- and drug-abuse industrial complex was in a state of considerable crisis at the time of his death.

A Panicked Field In Search of Its Soul and Its Future

The 1990s was a sobering decade for the addiction treatment industry. In the wake of program closings, the survivors entered a period of re-assessment and embarked on a flurry of activity designed to protect their future. Several trends emerged.

First, as other facilities closed, demands for services increased at some of the better-known programs. In facilities like the Betty Ford Center and Hazelden, service demands increased, as did the percentage of self-paying clients. This latter trend raised the specter that the classic three-to-four-week program would continue to be available, but only for America's most affluent citizens. What seems to be re-emerging is a multi-tiered system of care in which the nature of one's treatment is shaped, not by the nature or intensity of one's alcohol- or other drug-related problems, but by social class.

Second, the growing sense that "ma and pa shops" in the field would not survive led to a frenzy of voluntary mergers and sometimes less-than-cordial acquisitions that resulted in fewer, but larger, treatment agencies. In many states, the bulk of addiction treatment services are being increasingly provided by a small number of ever-growing agencies. Outright mergers are also being accompanied by a long list of affiliations, consortia, and joint business ventures that link addiction treatment agencies with one another and with other health-care and human-service institutions. This is being sparked in part by the growing allocation of addiction treatment dollars through large "capitated" contracts, in which networks of agencies agree to provide all addiction treatment services for a

total population of "covered lives" for a fixed cost per person. The large geographical areas covered by such contracts require the formal organization of "managed care networks," in which service agencies join together to create a provider-owned network of services sharing a single point of access, clinical criteria for placement in various levels of care, care management, and a management information system. Through such networks, agencies can jointly sell their services directly to purchasers of health care. Underlying all of this activity is the implicit assumption that bigger is better—and safer. Time and experience will reveal the wisdom or foolishness of that assumption. We have yet to determine whether provider networks will be able to achieve a fair pre-paid price and still deliver the levels of services needed by the clients being served by member agencies.

As the addiction treatment field was weakened in the early 1990s, it was also caught up in a broader wave of human-service integration. Addiction-specific state agencies were absorbed into large human-service departments, just as new waves of local service integration moved addiction treatment from a categorically segregated arena into "integrated behavioral-health systems." Such moves toward integration left the field struggling to protect its identity, its philosophy, and its treatment technology.

In the face of such threats, the field is experiencing a strange phenomenon. As the core of the addiction treatment field shrinks, the field is growing at the periphery. Where the total amount allocated to residential and inpatient addiction treatment services is shrinking, the number of providers of outpatient services is actually increasing, as is a growing number of new specialty programs that extend addiction treatment services into allied fields. The growth zone of the addiction treatment industry is not at the traditional core but in the delivery of addiction treatment services into the criminal justice system, the public-health system (particularly AIDS-related projects), the child-welfare system, the mental-health system, and the public-welfare system. What is emerging at the core of the field are attempts to enhance the stewardship of treatment dollars: central intake units, case-management projects, outreach projects, and special tracks for multiple-problem clients—particularly those co-presenting with substance use and psychiatric impairment. Emerging on the periphery of the field are criminal justice case-management systems, drug court initiatives, treatment inside jails and penitentiaries, treatment programs designed for substance-using women with histories of abuse and neglect of their children (particularly those who are pregnant or have delivered drug-exposed infants), and treatment interventions designed to help move individuals off SSI disability and welfare rolls. If one looks at these trends as a whole, what is emerging in the 1990s is a treatment system less focused on the goal of long-term personal recovery than on social control of the addict. The explosive growth in "case management" is indicative of a system more focused on managing people than on treating people. The goal of this evolving system is moving from a focus on the personal outcome of treatment to an assurance that the alcoholic and addict will not bother us and will cost us as little as possible.

Voices from every quarter are describing a field in crisis. Signs of that crisis are evident in program cutbacks and closings, deteriorating morale, the exit of tenured staff from the field, and a growing sense among those leaving and those remaining that something of great value has been lost in the field. This crisis can be depicted in many ways. Given the field's obsession with the topic of managed care and its consequences, this crisis might be—and most often is—defined as a financial one. It might be defined as a crisis of leadership—the loss of statured figures like Marty Mann and Harold Hughes to champion alcoholism and addiction services at the social-policy level. It might be defined as a social or cultural crisis, given the erosion of support for service programs and the

seeming re-stigmatization and re-criminalization of addiction. While all of these factors are part of the unfolding story, my own bias leads me to depict this developmental period of the field as one of spiritual crisis—a crisis of values. Only time will tell whether this crisis will mark a call for renewal and recommitment, or whether it will mark a stage in the death of the field as it is currently constituted. In Chapter Four, we identified nine factors that led to the fall of the inebriate-asylum movement. While many of those factors are replicated within our current environment, it may be premature to project the demise of the late-20th-century addiction treatment field. The field has been wounded but is still very much alive. There remains a large network of addiction treatment institutions and a large pool of committed and talented treatment professionals. The fate of the field will be determined by its ability to redefine its niche in an increasingly turbulent health-care and social-service ecosystem. That fate will also be dictated by more fundamental issues—the ability of the field to: 1) reconnect with the passion for service out of which it was born; 2) re-center itself clinically and ethically; 3) forge new service technologies in response to new knowledge and the changing characteristics of clients, families, and communities; and 4) the ability of the field to address the problem of leadership development and succession.

✠

Chapter Twenty-Seven
Modern Addiction Treatment:
Seminal Ideas and Evolving Treatment Technology

This chapter undertakes two formidable and somewhat dangerous tasks: briefly outlining the most seminal and controversial ideas within the arena of addiction treatment and reviewing new treatment technologies that emerged during the last decades of the 20th century.[3]

Eleven Seminal/Controversial Ideas

1. The Concept of Inebriety Reborn

When the concept of inebriety dropped from

professional and public use in the early 20th century, American social policies and treatment strategies began to be split into those that addressed good drugs (so good, they were declassified as "drugs") and those that addressed bad drugs. For most of the 20th century, no conceptual umbrella existed to help the field understand and intervene in the destructive use of all psychoactive drugs. The most seminal event in the modern era of addiction treatment was the reformulation of terms analogous to the earlier concept of inebriety, terms that could help organize the field's thinking and service activities. While debate continues to rage over which term should become the organizing fulcrum of the field—*addiction; chemical dependency; substance abuse; alcohol, tobacco, and other drug (ATOD abuse)*—what the emergence of

---

[3]I would like to acknowledge the following people for their thoughtful critiques of this chapter: Michael Dennis, Mark Godley, Susan Harrington Godley, and Randall Webber.

these terms did collectively was to launch a process of integration in the field's organization, theory-building, and clinical technologies. The culture's more temperate relationship with alcohol and its growing rejection of tobacco, as well as the modern rebirth of addiction medicine, were born out of this conceptual shift.

2. From a Single- to a Multiple-Pathway Model of Addiction and Recovery

If there is an overarching shift in addiction treatment paradigms in the modern era, it is surely the movement from single-pathway models to multiple-pathway models of understanding addiction and recovery.

The model of alcoholism that became codified within the mid-century emergence of alcoholism treatment posited that alcoholism was a singular disease. This disease was described as springing from unique biological vulnerabilities that clearly distinguished alcoholics from non-alcoholics. Alcoholism was proclaimed to be diagnosable by a highly consistent cluster of symptoms that unfolded within predictable, self-accelerating stages. Those who had the disease responded to a relatively narrow approach to treatment—generally defined as the Minnesota Model of chemical-dependency treatment. And finally, the model posited only one legitimate long-term pathway of recovery—lifelong abstinence from alcohol and other mood-altering drugs and lifelong affiliation with a Twelve-Step recovery program.[106] Agencies that operated drug treatment modalities—from therapeutic communities to methadone maintenance programs—had in a parallel fashion created quite narrow views on the etiology, progression, and treatment of, and long-term recovery from, addiction to drugs other than alcohol.

Growing numbers of studies began to erode the premises of these single-pathway models. The contention that the alcoholic was predisposed to alcoholism was challenged by studies that failed to find sustainable evidence of a single predisposing biological source of alcoholism and failed to verify the existence of a pre-drinking "alcoholic personality."[107] Concepts like *progression,* which were central to the field's characterization of alcoholism, were challenged by research revealing that many people move in and out of the pool of problem drinkers over time—most without any professional intervention or mutual-aid involvement. The concepts of *craving* (cellular hunger for alcohol) and *loss of control* (the inability to limit the amount of alcohol consumed once drinking started) were similarly challenged in studies that failed to validate either

the clear existence or the universality of these phenomena in alcoholics. Even the belief that the only option for alcoholics was complete abstinence from all alcohol was challenged in a series of studies revealing that at least a small percentage of alcoholics eventually achieved a state of sustained non-problematic drinking.[108]

Clinical research and cumulative clinical experience began to suggest an alternative view of alcohol-related problems—one in which there were perhaps multiple "alcoholisms" and other populations of people with transient alcohol-related problems. This emerging model further suggested that: 1) there were multiple etiological pathways out of which these conditions emerged; 2) there were multiple clinical subpopulations, whose characteristics and treatment needs were very different one from the other; and 3) there were multiple long-term pathways of recovery from these problems, some of which did not involve lifelong abstinence and lifelong affiliation with a Twelve-Step recovery program.[109] A growing number of studies called for genuinely different treatment choices to which individuals could be carefully matched.[110]

While many in the treatment field regarded multiple-pathway models as heretical, there was actually some mustiness to these "new" models. The reader will recall the existence of multiple-pathway models within the inebriate-asylum era, and these new models echoed Bowman and Jellinek's writings of the early 1940s and Jellinek's later work, which referred to "alcoholisms" and depicted multiple "species" of alcohol-related problems.[111] It is quite possible that a single-pathway model of alcoholism was essential to launch the modern alcoholism movement at both cultural and professional levels, but that, once the movement was launched, more sophisticated models were required to move the field of addiction treatment into professional maturity.

While some addiction treatment practitioners defensively rejected all that was implied in the new models, and others embraced the new models with the passion of the newly converted, most addiction service providers moved slowly toward the conceptualization of addiction as a complex, multi-determined "biopsychosocial" disorder requiring careful assessment and highly individualized treatment approaches. This stance allowed clinicians to achieve a new eclecticism that integrated what seemed worthwhile from old and emerging treatment models.

3. The Biology of Addiction

Interest in the role of biological factors in the etiology of addiction gained momentum in the closing decades of the 20th century, in the wake of growing interest in the role of genes in a whole spectrum of human characteristics and problems. Lectures to clients in treatment programs were regularly filled with genetic and neurochemical explanations of the cause of addiction to alcohol and other drugs. Where such explanations were not presented as accomplished facts of science, patients were told that a breakthrough was imminent that would confirm the biological foundations of addiction. There was tremendous interest in research that could undergird such beliefs. What everyone was waiting and hoping for was THE study that would unlock the biological key to alcoholism. To the disappointment of many, the evolving evidence was far more humble than the proclamations made to clients. But some discoveries did offer great promise for the future understanding and treatment of addiction.

One of the most remarkable stories of modern science unfolded in the 1970s with the discovery that all vertebrates produce substances (neurotransmitters) that mirror the effects of narcotics and other psychoactive drugs. In 1973, Candace Pert and Solomon Snyder of John Hopkins University, Eric Simon of New York University Medical Center, and Lars Terenius from Sweden co-discovered the existence of opiate receptors within human nerve tissue. Shortly afterwards, John Hughes and Hans Kosterlitz isolated the naturally occurring opiate peptides—later christened "endorphins"—that interacted with those receptor sites. Researchers such as Avram Goldstein quickly began to explore what this discovery might mean to the understanding and treatment of addiction. New theories suggested that endorphin-deficient individuals were at high risk of alcoholism and other addiction and that their drug-taking behavior was a way to self-medicate physical and emotional discomfort and to normalize their metabolic functions. It was further speculated that sustained drug use, particularly narcotic use, disrupted the opiate-receptor system, further depleting endorphin levels and increasing the likelihood of continued drug use.[112] Speculations abounded about future medical treatments that would correct the operation of this system in order to prevent or treat addiction. It was predicted that endorphin research would quickly produce amazing breakthroughs in the treatment of addiction, mental illness, and pain.[113]

Unfortunately, this system turned out to be an extremely complex system of highly specialized receptor sites that interact with multiple types of endogenous opiate peptides and exogenous opiate and non-opiate drugs. While research on this system continues to unravel new understanding of addiction, the hope of a quick and singular breakthrough cure for addiction did not materialize.

Another branch of biomedical research explored the potential role of genetics as a cause of alcoholism. Key contributors to this genetic view of alcoholism were Drs. Robert Cloninger, Donald Goodwin, Mark Schuckit, and Kenneth Blum. Cloninger and Goodwin's twin studies and Schuckit's study of alcoholic offspring supported the view that alcoholism could be genetically influenced.[114] While this view was presented to the public as established fact,[115] the question of genetic influences on the transmission of alcoholism continued to be heavily debated in scientific circles. This debate intensified in 1990, when Drs. Kenneth Blum and Ernest Noble announced in the *Journal of the American Medical Association* the discovery that the presence of A1 allele of the D_2 receptor gene increased one's risk of alcoholism. In their view, alcoholics self-medicated with alcohol to compensate for dopamine depletion and to stimulate increased dopamine production.[116] It appeared for a brief period that the long-promised biological breakthrough in finding THE cause of alcoholism had arrived, and such was the impression conveyed by the popular media's coverage of the Blum-Noble article. But Blum and Noble's findings could not be consistently replicated and came under considerable challenge.

Highly reputable scientists have continued to disagree on the role of genetics in the etiology of alcoholism. In his review of the evidence of a genetic link to alcoholism, David Lester concluded that there was no sustainable evidence of a genetic role in alcoholism and that researchers seeking such a link were "pursuing a scientific will-o'-the-wisp."[117] David Goldman, in a separate review, concluded that genetic determinants play a significant role in alcoholism and that first-degree relatives of alcoholics face a seven-fold increase in their risk of alcoholism, compared to first-degree relatives of non-alcoholics.[118] Most responsible researchers and clinicians took the position that alcoholism and other addictions are complex, multiply determined disorders in which biological and environmental factors interact to enhance personal vulnerability. Alcoholism policy leaders continue to hold out promise that genetic research on alcoholism will help identify individuals at high risk of alcoholism, prevent alcoholism, intervene early in the development of alcoholism, and lead to new treatments for alcoholism.[119]

A related area of biological research sought to identify biological or developmental markers that could predict adult alcoholism. Research on biological markers of vulnerability for alcoholism focused on such factors as color blindness, abnormalities in blood platelet enzymes and serum hormone levels, atypical alcohol metabolism and tolerance, and abnormal EEG (alpha-wave) patterns.[120] Attempts to identify developmental/behavioral markers indicating risk of adult alcoholism focused on the diagnosis of attention deficit hyperactivity disorder and mild characterological disturbances in latency and early adolescence. Some researchers predicted the development of a mass-screening device that would be administered to grade-school children to detect the risk of adult alcoholism.[121] Even the discussion of that possibility drew heated debate about the potential abuses of such technology if and when it were developed.

4. Toward a Developmental Model of Alcoholism Recovery

Since its inception, the core experience of addiction treatment professionals has been with alcoholics and addicts in the latest stages of addiction and the earliest stages of recovery. The field has known very little about the early stages of addiction and even less about the process of long-term recovery. What was needed was a clinically useful, research-validated developmental model of recovery.

John Wallace opened this area of study in 1974, when he outlined a three-part paradox that characterized the alcoholic's shift from active alcoholism to sustained recovery. Wallace first acknowledged the propensity of the alcoholic to develop an elaborate cognitive defense structure that helped rationalize drinking and minimize the consequences of excessive drinking. The elements of this defense structure included denial, minimization, projection of blame, rigidity, black-and-white thinking, avoidance, rationalization, narcissism, and obsessive thinking. While Wallace contended that the elements of this defense structure had to be given up specifically as they related to alcoholism, he argued that many of the elements of this defense structure were essential in getting the alcoholic through the earliest challenges of recovery. The task of the therapist, according to Wallace, was not one of confronting, uncovering and eliminating this defense structure. It was rather one of skillfully switching the use of these mechanisms to support sobriety. In this view, therapeutic interventions that

prematurely weakened this defense structure undermined rather than supported recovery. Wallace then pointed out that the defense structure that supported active alcoholism and early recovery eventually had to be given up to achieve long-term recovery. Failure to make this last transition left the alcoholic either frozen at an infantile stage of recovery or facing increased risk of relapse.[122] Others such as Stephanie Brown followed Wallace's essay with developmental models of recovery whose research bases were stronger, but Wallace's work was pivotal in underscoring the common assumptions of these models:

- Addiction and recovery are developmental processes characterized by generally predictable stages and milestones.
- There are developmental windows of opportunity in which the potential for initiating a process of addiction recovery is increased.
- Skills and perspectives must be mastered at each stage of recovery before one can move to the next stage.
- Completion of some stages, and some tasks within those stages, is time-dependent. One cannot move from one stage to the next until a point of developmental readiness has been reached.
- These stages can differ across various clinical subpopulations of addicted clients.
- Failure in treatment often results from asking clients to do something that they are incapable of performing or sustaining at that time.
- Treatment interventions that are highly appropriate at one stage may prove ineffective or even harmful at another stage.

5. Addiction as a Chronic Disease

The recognition of recovery as a developmental process was also accompanied by the further conceptualization of addiction as a *chronic* disease characterized in most people by episodes of remission and relapse.[123] This view suggested that addiction recovery required, not only primary treatment, but also a monitoring of the mechanisms that were keeping the disease in remission and, when necessary, strategic re-intervention. Addiction in this emerging view became analogous to hypertension or diabetes—a chronic, relapsing condition that is confounded by co-occurring personal and environmental problems, and that for many people is likely to require interventions at multiple points in time.[124] The recognition that recovery was a long-term process, and that the needs of recovering people and their families evolved through the various stages of this process, forced the most progressive programs to explore how they could serve clients more effectively over this extended period. Hazelden even went so far as to rechristen its primary service orientation, changing its name from "treatment services" to "recovery services," in order to acknowledge this much broader span of time and need.

6. The Continuum-of-Care Concept

Although treatment programs have existed in the United States for nearly 150 years, it is only in the past 30 years that widespread attention has been given to organizing these services within local continua of care. The concept of *continuum of care* reflected the understanding that services to addicts must reflect the heterogeneity of needs experienced by addicts during different developmental stages of their recovery. What grew out of this concept was a shift from the provision of a single addiction treatment modality, offered by one or more local agencies, to an attempt to create integrated local service networks. These networks would offer a menu of comprehensive services organized in a number of levels of care, with no gaps between levels. The concept of the continuum of care linked traditionally competing service modalities and expanded the range of addiction treatment modalities to encompass pre-treatment services, early intervention services, and formally organized post-treatment services (continuing care, recovery homes, renewal centers). The levels of care pioneered by the American Society of Addiction Medicine moved programs from fixed lengths of participation in a particular modality to highly individualized placement and lengths of stay in one or more modalities, based on preliminary and continuing assessment of client needs and responses to intervention. Once the many elements of these continua of care were in full operation, prospective clients sometimes found themselves confused about the best ways of getting what they needed from the expanded service menus. This in turn spawned specialized assessment services, central intake units, and the growing use of case managers, who provided support and assistance in moving addicts and their families through these menu selections.

7. Rethinking the Question of Motivation: Pain Versus Hope

During the second half of the 20th century, the field of addiction treatment has experienced four overlapping stages in its view of the role of addict motivation in addiction recovery. The baseline position was the belief that no one could recover who did not have a sincere desire to get sober, and that this desire came almost exclusively out of the pain of "hitting bottom." The second-stage view was an understanding that the reason it took addicts so long to reach this crisis was their ability to manipulate people in their environment into protecting them from the consequences (pain) of their drug use. This understanding suggested the possibility that, if well-meaning people in their lives were taught not to perform such rescues, addicts would experience this change-inducing crisis earlier. The third stage, emerging from industrial alcoholism programs and the work of Vernon Johnson in Minnesota,[125] suggested that the bottom could be brought up to meet the addict through a caring confrontation of the individual by employer and/or family members. This method gained public awareness when it was used by Betty Ford's family to motivate her to seek treatment. Formal intervention services used in the workplace and in the family marked an enormous breakthrough in addiction treatment technology, but this approach still relied on a view of pain as the principle motivating force in addiction recovery. The fourth stage, currently emerging within the field, has developed primarily out of work with disempowered addicts whose failure to enter recovery is based, not on an absence of pain in their lives, but on an absence of hope. This approach posits that motivation is something that should emerge out of empowering relationships within the treatment milieu, rather than be a precondition for admission into treatment. Growing numbers of programs have initiated "pre-treatment" services that, through such mechanisms as outreach services, build relationships with treatment-resistant addicts and enhance their readiness for treatment and recovery. Such projects are experimenting with what might be called "treatment priming"—a pre-behavioral stage of recovery that occurs at cognitive, emotional, and spiritual levels.[126] Such approaches are buttressed by the research of James Prochaska, John Norcross, and Carlo DiClemente, who pioneered a *transtheoretical* model of understanding the stages of change. Prochaska and his colleagues discovered that critical stages of internal change must be completed before the more action-oriented change demanded by most addiction treatment programs can take place. Their work suggests that helping interventions must be carefully selected and matched for appropriateness to each client's stage of readiness for change.[127]

8. Needle Exchanges: A Harm-Reduction Case Study

The idea of "harm reduction" is posited on the belief that some alcoholics and addicts are for some extended periods of their lives incapable of sustained sobriety, and that no viable intervention technology exists that can immediately alter this condition. Therefore, intervention strategies are recommended that enhance the quality of life for addicts while reducing the personal and social costs of addiction. Harm-reduction strategies in the modern era have included recommendations for public funding of "wet hotels," where chronic inebriates could be supervised minimally, in order to reduce their disruptiveness and cost to the community, and the provision of drug information that would help drug users achieve lower-risk methods of use. By far the most controversial of recent proposals were the provision of information on safer methods of drug injection and the provision of sterile needles to addicts.

Individual activists, and then organized programs, have sought to alter the high-risk behaviors (needle-sharing and unprotected sexual contact) that were spreading HIV/AIDS from infected drug users to others. The methods utilized have included education via street outreach, HIV testing and counseling, bleach (for cleaning injection equipment) and condom distribution, syringe- and needle-exchange programs, and linkage to treatment and other health and human services.

Needle-exchange programs emerged as acts of resistance within communities hard hit by drug use and AIDS. Needle distribution started in November, 1986, when Jon Parker, a student studying public health at Yale, began distributing needles to drug injectors on the streets of New Haven, Connecticut and Boston, Massachusetts. Parker was eventually arrested in eight states as a result of his challenge of laws restricting needle and syringe availability. More formally organized programs followed in Tacoma, New York City, San Francisco, Portland, Seattle, and Chicago. By 1992, more than 20 needle-exchange programs had been started. Some operated in open defiance of the law, while others operated with tacit or formal support from local public-health and law-enforcement officials.[128] Over time, many public health officials came to support the harm-reduction strategies implicit in needle-exchange programs. Some states passed legislation allowing legal distribution of sterile injection equipment by public-health service agencies.

Proponents of needle-exchange programs argued that their programs could 1) reduce the transmission of HIV, hepatitis, and other diseases among injection-drug users and their sexual partners; 2) build a relationship through which workers could influence safer drug use and safer sexual practices; 3) provide a link between active drug injectors and addiction treatment; and 4) provide a means of detection and early intervention for HIV infection. Opponents argued that: 1) needle-exchange programs would send a mixed message of acceptance or encouragement of drug use; 2) needle-exchange programs would result in heightened drug use, including an increase in the number of young drug injectors; 3) needle-exchange programs would reduce the number of addicts seeking treatment; and 4) drug injectors were uneducable—they would continue to share contaminated injection equipment even if sterile alternatives were available.

Research studies on needle-exchange programs concluded that such programs reduced risk-taking behavior among program participants, reduced the incidence of new HIV infections by as much as one third, reduced the incidence of Hepatitis B, and reduced the number of contaminated needles discarded in public places. Also noteworthy were the findings that no new increases in numbers of drug injectors had resulted from the initiation of needle-exchange programs, and that the needle exchanges themselves had emerged as a significant vehicle for referring addicts to treatment.[129] In response to the accumulation of such studies, groups like the American Public Health Association began to recommend reversal of the current policy banning the use of federal funds to support needle-exchange programs.

The cultural debate about harm-reduction programs—and needle-exchange programs in particular—continues as this book goes to press. The debate within the treatment field focuses on the question: "What is the field's responsibility, if any, to serve individuals committed to continued drug use?" In response to this debate, there are growing numbers of experiments in "low-threshold" service designs: minimal admission requirements, home-based and neighborhood-based service delivery, no-fee services, and service menus based on client-defined (versus agency-defined) needs. Needle exchange and other harm-reduction strategies force the professional field, communities, and the culture as a whole to confront the following question directly: Should the prevention of the personal and social costs of drug addiction, including the spread of life-threatening disease, take precedence over—or at least be considered alongside—the prevention of drug use? As of June 30, 1997, the Centers for Disease Control had received reports of 154,664 cases of AIDS in which the primary risk factor was injection-drug use.

9. Natural Recovery, Spontaneous Remission, and Maturing Out

Natural Recovery, spontaneous remission, and *maturing out* are terms that have been given to the process through which some alcoholics and addicts stop addictive patterns of alcohol or other drug use without benefit of treatment or involvement in a mutual-aid society. This possibility has long been noted. Dr. George Beard wrote in 1871 that such cases of spontaneous and permanent recovery, while rare, did exist.[130] In 1876, Dr. T.D. Crothers suggested that addiction was a "self-limiting disease" for some people. Dr. Joseph Parrish noted in 1884: "It is well known that there are some drunkards who 'recover naturally,' that is, of their own unaided efforts."[131] He believed that a small number of inebriates "worked out their own salvation" in this manner.[132] Such reports continued,[133] but no one actually calculated the prevalence of natural recovery until Frederic Lemere analyzed the life histories of 500 deceased alcoholics in 1953. Lemere concluded that:

> *Approximately 28% of all alcoholics will drink themselves to death, 7% will regain partial control of their drinking, 3% will be able to drink moderately again, and 29% will continue to have the problem of drinking throughout their lifetime. Twenty-two percent will stop drinking during a terminal illness and 11% will quit drinking exclusive of terminal illness.*[134]

Lemere noted that most alcoholics who quit drinking completely did so without any kind of professional assistance, most through spiritual conversion.[135]

Don Cahalan and Robin Room's 1974 study, *Problem Drinking Among American Men,* found a similar pattern of "maturing out." Cahalan's data challenged the notion that alcohol problems inevitably self-accelerated by finding that the majority of alcohol problems were concentrated in 21-24 year old men.[136] A 1976 review of research on spontaneous remission in alcoholics concluded that this phenomenon occurred in rates ranging from 10% to 42%. Studies of spontaneous recovery found such recovery associated with aging; an alcohol-related illness, accident, or financial or legal problem; religious conversion; a change in job, marital situation, or residence; the resolution of a developmental crisis; intervention by

family or friends; the alcohol-related death of a close friend or family member; acquisition of information on alcoholism; or a personally humiliating experience.[137]

Several studies have suggested that similar processes operate with heroin addicts. Charles Winick introduced the concept of maturing out to explain the decline of heroin addiction with age and life experience. His studies indicated that as many as one third of heroin addicts stopped using heroin in this manner during their thirties and forties. Patrick Biernacki noted two styles of maturing out, one in which a new identity emerged to replace the addict identity, and another where an older, pre-addiction identity was resumed. Many addicts in Biernacki's study reached a kind of existential crisis in which they re-evaluated their drug use as part of a re-evaluation of the direction their whole lives were taking. Heroin was shed, not so much from hitting bottom as from a desire to reclaim something positive out of life.[138] Biernacki's studies, along with the work of Winick and others, are important for their confirmation of a number of provocative findings.

- Addicts are not a homogenous group: Not all people who use heroin become physically addicted to it, addicts may or may not be involved in drug-related criminal activity, and addicts may or may not show a pattern of self-accelerating drug use.
- Some addicts move from active addiction to self-initiated and self-sustained recovery without benefit of treatment or mutual aid.
- Some addicts stop using, not as a climactic emotional decision, but as something that just happens—through the serendipity of a new relationship or a new opportunity.

Natural-recovery research raises the question of how brief therapeutic interventions might be used to capitalize on such developmental windows of opportunity for positive change. The use of brief "motivational interviewing" that provides clear advice and positive encouragement[139] and the growing presence of "do-it-yourself" addiction recovery manuals may both be capitalizing on the propensity of many people with alcohol and other drug problems to reach a stage of heightened readiness for "natural recovery."[140]

10. The Question of Controlled Drinking and Drug Use

Since the days of Benjamin Rush, medical opinion has been almost universal in its suggestion that the only recourse for the alcoholic was complete abstinence from all alcoholic products. Cracks in this position began to appear in the 1950s, first with the earlier-noted study by Lemere, and then with James Shea's 1954 report of a confirmed alcoholic who, after quitting his decade-long quart-a-day whiskey habit after repeated hospitalizations, remained abstinent for five years, then for the following five years consumed an average of two beers or two glasses of wine per day without episodes of drunkenness and without the resurgence of the prior alcohol-related medical disorders. Shea presented this case as an exception to the rule and suggested that the number of alcoholics who could achieve such a feat "must surely be infinitesimal."[141] Similar accounts appeared in 1957 in Drs. Melvin Selzer's and William Holloway's follow-up study of alcoholic patients treated at Ypsilanti State Hospital in Michigan. Selzer and Holloway called for "a second look at the long-cherished theory that no alcoholic can ever become a moderate drinker."[142] While these early reports generated little professional response, debate was aroused in 1962, when D.L. Davies of the Maudsley Hospital Institute of Psychiatry in London published an account of seven alcoholics who returned to non-problematic relationships with alcohol. Davies concluded that:

> *such cases are more common than has hitherto been recognized, and that the generally accepted view that no alcohol addict can ever again drink normally should be modified, although all patients should be advised to aim for abstinence.*[143]

The research literature was slowly acknowledging the existence of some alcoholics practicing what Reinhart and Bowen in 1968 christened "controlled drinking."[144]

One of the first modern attempts to provide an alcoholism therapy whose espoused outcome was moderate drinking was that of Arthur Cain in his 1964 book, *The Cured Alcoholic*. Cain believed that there was no such scientific entity as alcoholism and that loss of control over drinking was a reversible state of mind rather than an irreversible state of physiology. Cain claimed that:

> *....there is not a single alcoholic in the world today who could not learn to live normally without worrying in any way about alcohol and even learn to drink normally if he so desired.*[145]

Cain's vaguely described treatment method set off a brief storm of professional and public protest.

In 1976, the issue of controlled drinking by alcoholics broke into heated controversy again with the publication of a Rand Corporation study commissioned by NIAAA to evaluate its treatment programs. The study, published under the title *Alcoholism and Treatment* but generally known as "The Rand Report," incited controversy through such statements as the following.

> *For some alcoholics, moderate drinking is not necessarily a prelude to relapse.*
>
> *....it appears that some alcoholics do return to normal drinking with no greater likelihood of relapse than alcoholics who choose permanent abstention....it [study evidence] does support a definition of remission that allows for drinking in normal or moderate amounts.*

The report was attacked on methodological grounds and branded as dangerous and irresponsible by many alcoholism treatment professionals. The controversy sparked a second study, published in January of 1980, which softened many of the conclusions of the initial report.

Two psychologists, Mark and Linda Sobell, moved to the eye of this storm with the publication of outcome studies of groups of alcoholics treated at California's Patton State Hospital, some in abstinence-based treatment and others in treatment that sought to help patients moderate their drinking. These reports claimed that those alcoholics who were treated with individualized behavioral therapy that sought to inculcate moderate drinking skills had better treatment outcomes than those who were coached toward abstinence. The controversy sparked by these findings prompted another group, led by Mary Pendery, to criticize the Sobells' research methodology and to reassess the status of the Sobells' controlled-drinking subjects. Pendery and her group reported that they found most of these subjects continuing their excessive drinking patterns, dead, or abstinent. Only one of the subjects in Pendery's follow-up had managed to sustain a moderate drinking pattern, but Pendery argued that this patient was not a true (gamma-species) alcoholic. The Pendery group, however, failed to note that the alcoholics in the abstinence-oriented control group had even worse outcomes than those coached in moderate drinking. The Sobell-Pendery debate escalated to charges and counter-charges of ethical misconduct, patient lawsuits, and untold attention in the popular print and television media.[146]

The controlled-drinking controversy played itself out primarily at the academic and leadership levels of the field, with most front-line treatment practitioners continuing to concur with the advice that Francis Hare offered to alcoholic patients at the beginning of the 20th century:

> *I think it is expedient that the last word of the medical superintendent should be — "Never forget for a single instant the vital necessity of avoiding the first drink."*[147]

Paralleling the controlled-drinking controversy were reports on the mysterious phenomenon of controlled heroin use. Buried in studies by such renowned addiction researchers as Isador Chein were references to people who used heroin socially without developing addiction.

> *We have reason to believe that individuals differ in their susceptibility to dependence, and we know of individuals who go on using a drug like heroin for several years on a more or less regular weekend basis and then, apparently without difficulty, quit.*[148]

Chein's observations of controlled heroin use were not the first in the professional literature. Reports of prolonged, non-addictive, non-injurious use of opiates extend back at least to Kane's 1882 treatise on opium-smoking.[149] Richard Jacobson and Norman Zinberg studied controlled heroin users in the 1970s and found that the mechanisms of control involved:

- sustaining social relationships in which one's primary identity was not that of a compulsive drug user;
- limiting use to particular environments, situations, and times;
- keeping drug use as a peripheral rather than a central activity (rendering drug use secondary to work, school, and intimate relationships); and
- developing and adhering to codes that strictly govern which drugs will be used, when (not daily) and where use will occur, and how use will occur (method of ingestion).[150]

Why some people can use these mechanisms of control and others progress to compulsive use is a question that will be carried into the new century.

As this book goes to press, professional and public discussions of controlled drinking by those who have been diagnosed with alcoholism continue to generate more heat than illumination.[151]

11. Codependency: Popularization and Backlash

One of the most controversial concepts within the modern addictions field has been that of *codependency*. It emerged out of a natural evolution of the field's growing attention to the ways in which individual family members—and the family as a dynamic system—adapted to the deteriorating role performance of an addicted family member. Codependency had several conceptual precursors. The first was the idea that parental alcoholism inflicted emotional injury upon children.[152] The second was the emergence of the concept of *enabling* to depict many of the well intended behaviors of others—behaviors that inadvertently helped the alcoholic sustain his or her drinking. The next steps were the conceptualization of alcoholism as a "family disease" and the labeling of the negative effects of being enmeshed with an alcoholic as "co-alcoholism" or "para-alcoholism."[153] There was also a growing body of work on the general subject of dependency, including writings of Karen Horney, Erich Fromm, and other psychologists, work that was about to be swept into this new concept.[154]

During the early to middle 1980s, the work of Claudia Black and Sharon Wegsheider-Cruse graphically depicted the psychological and developmental consequences of parental alcoholism on children and catalogued how these consequences continued to affect children of alcoholics in their adult lives.[155] This marked a significant shift, in which the alcoholic's family members were viewed, not simply as sources of support for the alcoholic's recovery, but as patients in their own right, who suffered from a condition that required treatment and support services. This transition gave rise to a new clinical specialty within the psychotherapy and addictions fields—counseling children and adult children of alcoholics—and gave rise to a broader social-support movement. Adult Children of Alcoholics (ACOA) groups were formed within Al-Anon—some 1,100 by 1986—and the National Association for Children of Alcoholics (NACoA) organized more than 1,500 local groups between its founding in 1983 and 1990.[156][157]

As this movement took off, the extension of these findings to children and adult children who had been raised in other types of dysfunctional families marked a transition between the concept of co-alcoholism and the newly emerging concept of "codependence." In a series of published works in the mid-1980s, Dr.

Timmen Cermak conceptualized codependency as a "disease," proposed criteria for its medical diagnosis, and advocated that the treatment of this disease be paid for by major insurance carriers.[158] Addiction treatment programs began offering codependency treatment tracks and extending stays of alcoholics and addicts in treatment because of their "ACOA issues" or "codependency issues."

Melodie Beattie launched a veritable social phenomenon with the 1987 publication of her book *Codependent No More*. Adding fuel to this movement was the publication the following year of John Bradshaw's *Healing the Shame That Binds You* and his highly popular PBS television series that was based on the book. A whole nation seemed to be riveted on the exploration of the "dysfunctional family" and on the extension of this concept to the workplace, and to society as a whole. This new movement also spawned its own Twelve-Step adaptation, Co-Dependents Anonymous, which by 1990 had more that 1,600 registered groups.[159]

The ACOA/codependency movements left many legacies. For the first time, children and adult children of alcoholics were admitted as primary patients and given a primary diagnosis as well as their own individualized treatment. These movements culturally mainstreamed their premise that childhood trauma altered one's developmental trajectory into adult life, producing emotional turmoil, disorders of perception and thought, and self-destructive behavior. And these movements gave many people a heightened understanding of their own family-of-origin experiences. However, the codependency movement did bear unanticipated fruit: ideological and financial backlashes that hurt the movement itself and the broader addiction treatment community from which it had been spawned. Ideological attacks on the concept of codependency included the following charges.

1.   *The definitions of codependency are so inclusive as to lack any clinical utility.*
2.   *The symptomatology of codependency inordinately targets characteristics that women have been raised to cultivate. Codependency turns social pathology into psychopathology, directing personal energy toward inner healing rather than toward social and political change.*
3.   *Defining the problem of "women who love too much" as psychopathology fails to hold abusive men accountable for their neglectful, demeaning, and violent behavior.*
4.   *The codependency movement creates a milieu in which women bond with each other out of their*

weakness rather than their strength.
5.   *The codependency movement infantalizes its members ("Adult Children") and traps them at an immature stage of development.*[160]

Insurance companies, observing the ever-widening net of this concept, reasonably concluded that it would be financial suicide to provide coverage for a disease that apparently almost everyone had. Insurance companies backed away from coverage of codependency treatment during the same period in which they began to impose severe restrictions on coverage for alcoholism and other addictions.

Treatment of Special Populations and Treatment in Special Settings

As addiction treatment programs expanded, new populations of clients brought in unique problems and needs that surpassed the knowledge base and capabilities of most programs. Over time, the treatment industry came to recognize that innumerable "special populations" of clientele presented with different needs and obstacles to their recovery. These special populations included: women; pregnant women; adolescents; seniors; people of color; gay men and lesbian women; people with concurrent medical, psychiatric, or developmental problems; people with visual and hearing impairments; runaway youth; homeless people; clients living in rural areas; and addicted criminal offenders. Certain occupational groups (from physicians to prostitutes) also came to be regarded as special populations, and even the rich achieved this designation. There were also treatment tracks designed for people whose addiction to a particular drug was thought to require specialized services. This was particularly true of cocaine. Nationwide, the number of clients whose primary drug of choice was cocaine rose from 9,000 (4.1% of clients) in 1979 to 261,000 (43.3% of clients) in 1993.[161] Rising cocaine use led to the founding of Cocaine Anonymous in 1983 and the creation of a national cocaine hotline that received three million calls between 1986 and 1990.

While the addiction treatment field was expanding between 1975 and 1990, it was also undergoing intense specialization. Programs were being designed and implemented for all of the just-described "special populations," as were training programs designed to enhance the ability of addiction treatment professionals to address the special needs of these clients. The premise behind special-population programming was that these identified client characteristics affected the etiology of addiction, obstacles to treatment engagement, the course and prognosis of treatment, stages and styles of recovery, and vulnerability to relapse.

Special-population programs generally shared a number of elements: the segregation of clients into a homogenous treatment milieu; the use of indigenous healers and institutions; specialized staff training; population-specific client literature, population-sensitive services; the elimination of potentially offensive mainstream treatment language and rituals; and the generation of new population-specific ideas, language, and rituals within the treatment milieu. The modern addiction treatment system's responses to eleven "special populations" are briefly outlined below.

The Public Inebriate

Several studies in the 1950s—particularly David Pittman's and C. Wayne Gordon's 1958 *The Revolving Door*—captured the plight of chronic alcoholics in the criminal justice system. These studies demonstrated that incarceration did little either to rehabilitate the public inebriate or to reduce the prevalence of public drunkenness. In the 1960s, leaders in the alcoholism field and representatives from the American Civil Liberties Union pushed legal appeals that challenged the repetitious incarceration of the chronic public inebriate. During that decade, three court decisions—*Easter v. District of Columbia*, *Driver v. Hinnant*, and *Powell v. Texas*—addressed the special problem of the indigent public inebriate.

DeWitt Easter was by anyone's definition a chronic alcoholic. His excessive drinking spanned more than 30 years and 70 convictions for public intoxication. On behalf of the American Civil Liberties Union, Peter Hutt prepared a defense that claimed Easter was a victim of chronic alcoholism, and that his public intoxication was an involuntary consequence of his disease. Easter's local conviction was reversed in 1966, when a U.S. Court of Appeals panel agreed with Hutt's argument.

Joe Driver was arrested four times within a month following his release from jail for his 203rd conviction for public drunkenness. Although Driver's conviction was upheld by the U.S. District Court, the U.S. Court of Appeals reversed Driver's conviction on the grounds that he was a sick person not in voluntary control of his behavior and to punish him would be a violation of the Eighth Amendment's "cruel and unusual punishment" provisions.[162]

Leroy Powell was a chronic alcoholic arrested for public intoxication in Austin, Texas in 1966. Powell appealed his conviction and $20 fine all the way to the Supreme Court, on the grounds that public intoxication was an inevitable consequence of the chronic alcoholism over which he had no control, and that therefore his intoxication could not be considered voluntary criminal conduct. The Supreme Court voted 5 to 4 to uphold Powell's conviction. Whether or not Powell's behavior was voluntary was not under debate. The Court feared that most communities did not have alternatives to incarceration for the public inebriate, and that hospitals would be turned into drunk tanks.[163]

These cases generated momentum to divert the chronic alcoholic from the criminal justice system. In addition, two crime commissions appointed by President Johnson independently concluded that the criminal justice system's response to the chronic alcoholic was ineffective and inhumane, and that such people should be diverted to treatment.[164] The recommendations of these commissions were further solidified by two of the most definitive works ever written on the transformative power of the culture of skid row: Samuel Wallace's *Skid Row as a Way of Life* and James Spradley's *You Owe Yourself a Drunk*.[165] Momentum for the shift from a criminal-justice to a public-health response to the chronic alcoholic had reached a critical turning point.

In 1971, the National Conference of Commissioners on Uniform State Laws adopted the Uniform Alcoholism and Intoxication Act. This model law set the stage for the decriminalization of public intoxication by encouraging alternatives to jail, such as detoxification and treatment programs, and by encouraging an aggressive program of community outreach and education about alcoholism.[166]

Special detoxification centers began to spring up within America's larger cities, beginning in St. Louis, Washington, D.C., and New York City.[167] These early programs were based on a model called "social-setting detoxification," which had been pioneered by the Addiction Research Foundation of Canada. Social-setting detoxification was found to be a safe and cost-effective method of managing public drunkenness at the local community level, but the model was not without its problems.

Challenges facing the more than 1,000 detox centers that existed by 1980 were intensified by fundamental changes in America's Skid Rows. While urban renewal was reducing the number of such areas and the populations within them—from 150 areas with 750,000 people in 1940 to 35 areas with 135,000 people in 1980—there was a greater concentration of alcoholics within the Skid Row population, and they were increasingly being joined by addicts and people with severe mental illnesses. The intensity and chronicity of the problems that these individuals presented to alcoholism treatment programs were at times overwhelming.[168]

While there was great hope that chronic alcoholics could be moved into long-term recovery, most of these clients did not enter treatment following detox. The newly created detox centers not only failed to stop the "revolving door" of apprehension/release/re-apprehension, but also created a "spinning door" that placed the alcoholic on the street more quickly than did the drunk tanks they replaced.[169] The shortcomings of these facilities, however, were offset by the memory of all the alcoholics who in earlier eras had died in jail cells, and by the occasional chronic alcoholic whose movement into long-term recovery began through entry into a detox center. Medical and social-setting detoxification became essential elements in the evolving addiction treatment system.

Changing Responses to the Drunk Driver

As early as 1904, medical journals noted the risks involved when alcohol-impaired people drove "motor wagons." These journals called for laws restricting the operation of motorized vehicles to total abstainers.[170] Although the National Safety Council introduced a campaign against drunk driving—and judges in some cities sentenced drunk drivers to "safety schools" in the 1930s—during the 30 years following the repeal of prohibition, there was, by today's standards, remarkable cultural silence on the threat posed by drunk drivers.[171] This began to change in the early 1960s, when pioneers like Mary Ross of the Monterey Peninsula Committee on Alcoholism established classes that served to educate drunk drivers and link those with clearly identifiable problems to alcoholism treatment.[172] Between 1960 and 1980, the climate of toleration changed dramatically through the efforts of the courts, local alcoholism councils, and newly emerging citizen action groups. Penalties for drunk driving increased, enforcement intensified, and a national model (the Alcohol Safety Action Program) emerged to divert drunk drivers for evaluation of potential alcohol problems, for remedial education, and for treatment services. The impetus for much of this increased focus often came from those whose lives had been forever changed by the actions of drunk drivers.

Candy Lightner's 13-year-old daughter was killed by a drunk driver in 1980. To her horror, Lightner discovered that drunk drivers—including

those who killed—rarely ever went to jail and often found ways to manipulate the system and keep their driving privileges. Lightner channeled her grief and her rage into the creation of a support and advocacy group—Mothers Against Drunk Driving (MADD). A growing number of MADD chapters took on the role of heightening public awareness, in order to change America's silent acceptance of drunk driving.[173] MADD was joined by other groups such as SADD (Students Against Driving Drunk), RID (Remove Intoxicated Drivers), AAIM (Alliance Against Intoxicated Motorists), and BACCHUS (Boost Alcohol Consciousness Concerning the Health of University Students).[174]

The citizen action groups that took on the issue of drunk driving were exceptionally effective in their ability to mobilize the country's media resources to wage campaigns against drinking and driving. Their lobbying generated Presidential Commissions, an increase in the legal drinking age, a trend toward lowering of the blood-alcohol concentration in legal definitions of impaired driving, toughened penalties and enforcement, and—most important for the treatment industry—the movement toward mandatory clinical evaluation of all people arrested for drunk driving. This last trend quite literally created a sub-industry within the addictions field that specialized in the evaluation, education, and treatment of drunk drivers.

Through the 1960s and 1970s, the prevailing view was that most drunk drivers were social drinkers who made a horrible and isolated error in judgement. The twin tasks of the evaluator during this period were to educate these social drinkers through a series of remedial-education classes on the effects of drinking on driving, and to find the small percentage of alcoholics mixed in with this larger pool of social drinkers. Research evidence and accumulated clinical and judicial experience challenged this view and suggested that the vast majority of drunk drivers either had, were developing, or would develop serious problems in their relationship with alcohol.[175] This changing view brought increased numbers of drunk drivers into America's expanding system of alcoholism treatment. Those working in the public-safety arena also focused on the issue of drug-impaired driving and the need for special policies and strategies to manage the drunk-driving recidivist.

Gender-Specific Treatment

Impetus for the development of treatment approaches for addicted women came from three sources. The first source was made up of women in recovery and women who were filling a growing variety of roles within the addictions field. When women like Marty Mann, Lillian Roth, Mercedes McCambridge, Jan Clayton, Elizabeth Taylor, Kitty Dukakis, and, most significantly, Betty Ford shared the stories of their recoveries, there were inevitable concerns about the numbers of less well known women who failed to seek treatment because of the special stigma attached to addicted women.

A second influence was the growing concern about the effects of maternal alcohol and other drug use on fetal and child development. The modern rediscovery of fetal alcohol syndrome (FAS) and increasing concerns about the effects of prenatal drug exposure exerted a profound influence on the evolution of modern addiction treatment services for women. This concern came in two waves. The first was triggered by reports in the 1960s of neonatal narcotic addiction, preliminary reports of harmful effects of marijuana and LSD on fetal development, and Drs. Kenneth Jones and David Smith's re-documentation in 1973 of alcohol-related birth defects.[176] The verification of severe alcohol-related birth defects (FAS) and milder alcohol-related damage (Fetal Alcohol Effects) focused attention on the problem of alcoholism in women. A second wave of concern about addiction in women was sparked in the mid-1980s by exaggerated reports of the enduring effects of prenatal cocaine exposure. Hysterical claims that "crack babies" constituted a "lost generation" and a "biological underclass" sparked a skyrocketing of child neglect and abuse reports (from 1.1 million in 1980 to 2.4 million in 1990), parallel rises in foster-home placements, the criminal prosecution of more than 200 women (by 1994) for delivering drugs to their infants through the vehicle of pregnancy, and—between 1980 and 1992—a tripling of the number of women incarcerated.[177] In the early 1990s, a number of professionals challenged the validity of early reports on cocaine exposure and offered warnings about the harmful effects of labeling cocaine-exposed children.[178] Many, like Dr. Barry Zuckerman, proclaimed that those labeled "Crack Babies" were not a lost generation and that prenatal exposure to cocaine "creates a biological vulnerability....which may be completely or in part compensated by the brain itself and by competent caretaking."[179] The latest and largest study of cocaine-exposed infants reported only "subtle, nuanced effects in some babies"–a far cry from the reports in the 1980s that provided a rationale for massive intervention into the lives of cocaine-using women and their children.[180]

One effect of the concern about FAS and drug-exposed infants was an infusion of money for services specifically targeting alcohol- and drug-addicted women and their children.

The third impetus in the development of specialized addiction services for women was a growing body of research suggesting several clinically relevant differences between addicted women and addicted men: different biological effects of drugs, different etiological influences, different patterns of use, different obstacles to entering and completing treatment, different treatment issues, and differences in styles of recovery.[181]

Both federal (NIAAA and NIDA) and state responses to these issues included increased funding for women's services. These funding tracks resulted in a tripling of the number of women-only addiction treatment units between 1982 and 1992.[182] In 1993, the Center for Substance Abuse Treatment further expanded this capacity by funding more than 65 demonstration projects that focused on serving addicted women and their children. What made women's programs different from mainstream programs were such elements as the following: 1) special strategies of engagement (media campaigns, outreach services) designed to overcome stigma-induced resistance to treatment; 2) ancillary services to minimize barriers to participation (case management, child care, transportation); 3) coordination with specialized services (women's health centers, domestic-violence programs); 4) special attention to issues of physical and psychological safety; 5) focus on issues of particular importance to addicted women (sexual abuse, rape, relationships, parenting, menopause); 6) services that enhanced mother-child relationships (parenting training and family therapy); and 7) linkage of clients with mutual-aid societies for women. As experiences treating addicted women accumulated during the 1990s, new resources were developed and widely distributed to enhance the quality of services to women.[183] In September, 1991, 213,681 women—27% of all clients in treatment—were enrolled in addiction treatment in the U.S.[184]

Adolescent Treatment

The development of specialized services for drug-using youth in the second half of the 20th century grew out of several significant changes: the growing variety and potency of psychoactive drugs, the decreased price-per-unit of certain illicit drugs, the increased accessibility of drugs to youth, the lowered age of onset of alcohol and other drug exposure, and the resulting increases in alcohol- and drug-related casualties via role impairment, arrest, and death. Youth-oriented treatment services began with efforts to stem juvenile narcotic addiction in the 1950s, expanded dramatically to respond to the youthful polydrug use of the 1960s and 1970s, and became institutionalized in private and public adolescent addiction treatment programs in the 1980s and 1990s. The number and types of settings offering counseling to adolescent alcohol and other drug users has grown, but, according to Dr. Yifrah Kaminer, adolescent treatment has been handicapped by the lack of organizations that specialize in adolescents (less than 5% of all programs) and offer services by staff who have in-depth training in child and adolescent development.[185]

While some programs minimally modified their adult addiction services for applicability to adolescents, others took the position that problematic alcohol and other drug use by adolescents stemmed from different etiologies and required substantially different treatment. There was, in particular, a recognition that some patterns of adolescent alcohol and drug-abuse were not necessarily chronic and progressive in nature and therefore required more expansive and flexible models of treatment than those used with adult alcoholics and addicts. These models included adaptations of Twelve-Step models, specialized family therapies, behavioral and cognitive-behavioral therapies, new psychopharmacological adjuncts to treatment, and the development of lapse management and relapse prevention techniques designed specifically for adolescents.[186] These adaptations occurred in outpatient, intensive outpatient, residential, and therapeutic community settings. Between 1965 and 1998, the treatment technologies utilized in adolescent programs became increasingly differentiated from those used in adult programs. What made adolescent programs different from the mainstream programs was their: 1) focus on habilitation rather than rehabilitation; 2) emphasis on the short-term rather than the long-term benefits of treatment/sobriety; 3) almost universal provision of educational and recreational services; 4) heightened intensity of family involvement and family therapy; 5) recognition of the seemingly ubiquitous co-occurring emotional and behavioral problems; 6) understanding of the enormous role of peer social support on treatment outcome; 7) recognition of special legal and ethical concerns related to such issues as confidentiality, informed consent, and the potential iatrogenic effects of labeling; and 8) recognition of the special vulnerabilities that adolescents face in their risk of exposure to HIV infection.[187]

The Employed Alcoholic/Addict [4]

During the modern era, efforts to intervene with alcohol- and drug-impaired employees have evolved through four overlapping stages. The first stage involved the organization of programs specifically designed to identify and rehabilitate alcoholic employees. These formal alcoholism-intervention programs within business and industry grew from a handful in the mid-1940s to more than 600 programs by 1975—growth spurred in part by employee recovery rates as high as 80%.[188] A key milestone in the professionalization of those working in the arena of industrial alcoholism occurred in 1971, with the formation of the Association of Labor-Management Administrators and Consultants on Alcoholism (ALMACA).[189] Another pivotal event in this first stage was the establishment of an Occupational Programs Branch within NIAAA and the creation of a panel to advise NIAAA on occupational alcoholism issues. This panel successfully lobbied NIAAA to fund two Occupational Program Consultants within each state to organize occupational alcoholism programs in business and industry. More than 300 programs were initiated during the first year of this effort.[190] By 1979, 59% of Fortune 500 companies had established formal alcoholism intervention programs, and estimates of the number of American companies with such programs at the end of the 1970s ranged from 2,500 to 4,000.[191]

A second stage emerged during the 1970s, a stage marked by a shift from the focus on alcohol-impaired employees to a "broad-brush" concern with the whole range of problems that could affect employee health and performance. While there was significant resistance to this change, the shift in identity from "occupational alcoholism" to "employee assistance" was all but complete by the late 1970s.[192] This expanded identity was marked by a new wave of professionalization. By the end of the 1970s there were some 3,000 people working within a profession in which, a decade earlier, fewer than 20 people had been employed.[193] The field's increasing numbers spawned professional organizations—ALMACA's transformation to Employee Assistance Professionals Association, Inc. (EAPA) and the Employee Assistance Society of North America (EASNA)—new EAP-credentialing efforts, and the proliferation of new newsletters and journals—including the *EAP Digest,* the *EAPA Association Exchange,* the *Employee Assis-*

---

[4]I would like to acknowledge the assistance of Brenda Blair, who provided a helpful critique of a very early draft of this section.

tance Quarterly, and the *Journal of Employee Assistance Research*.

This shift from alcoholism intervention to employee assistance was accompanied, first by a movement of the EAP function from company medical departments to personnel departments, and then toward contracting EAP services from external vendors. While estimates of the number of companies with formal EAPs climbed to 12,000 by 1985, the nature of those who provided these services was also changing.[194] The professionalization of the EAP field pushed many recovered alcoholics out of EAP roles, in a process similar to what was occurring in the addiction treatment field as a whole.

The second stage opened up company-sponsored support services to a broad range of employees and their dependents while diluting the focus on, and expertise to intervene with, alcoholic employees.[195] Jim Wrich, whose book *The Employee Assistance Program* helped spark the transition from stage one to stage two, recently looked back on these changes.

> *As a systematic endeavor, workplace interventions with alcoholic employees have gone through several stages. In the first stage of occupational alcoholism programs, there was a low identification rate (about ½ of 1% of employees each year), but good recovery rates. During the early broadbrush approach of EAPs, there was high penetration (about 3-4% annual utilization) with 40-50% of these contacts involving a substance use disorder—a significant increase in addiction intervention. Today, with a deterioration in addiction expertise among EAP practitioners, only 10% of first-time contacts to EAPs are diagnosed with a substance use disorder. This is the same unacceptably low level of identification that created the demand for a new approach we called employee assistance in 1972.*[196]

A third stage in response to alcohol- and drug-impaired employees was triggered by the movement of the war on drugs into the workplace. During the 1980s the government, private companies, and professional EAP organizations shifted much of their attention toward problems related to drugs other than alcohol. This shift was sparked in great part by President Reagan's 1986 Executive Order calling for the creation of drug-free workplaces in all federal installations and the testing of all federal employees in sensitive positions. Following this lead, companies across America developed formal drug-free workplace policies, established fitness-for-duty and drug-testing policies, established or refined EAP services for drug users, trained supervisors, and educated employees. Drug testing had a significant effect on EAPs and addiction treatment agencies. Most important, it shifted the definition of who needed treatment from those employees who were *addicted* to drugs to those employees who *used* drugs—a shift that injected a new level of invasiveness and coerciveness into the EAP and treatment arenas.

A fourth stage in the evolution of workplace programs emerged when companies became alarmed at their escalating health-care benefit costs. While employee assistance programs claimed that they paid for themselves through enhanced productivity and the lower costs incurred by rehabilitated employees, the rising prices of addiction and psychiatric treatments forced many companies to take a closer look at their management of health-care benefit costs in general, and the cost-effectiveness of EAPs in particular. Some EAP contractors expanded their services to manage such costs. EAP contractors took on more active roles in screening and selecting behavioral-health providers, negotiating rates for services, handling pre-certification for treatment, monitoring and approving lengths of stay, and providing intense case management of the entire process—from pre-treatment to post-treatment. Some companies even asked their EAP contractors to provide all needed behavioral-health services for a fixed rate—arrangements called "carve-outs" that turned what had been an assessment-and-referral function into a primary treatment and managed-care function. During the 1990s, an increasing number of EAPs absorbed managed-care functions, were bought out by managed-care companies, or spent much of their existence fighting with managed-care companies to secure services for employees whom they had assessed to be in need of services. This book goes to press with an EAP field as much in search of its soul and identity as is the addiction treatment industry with which it has been so closely linked.

Treating Impaired Professionals

One special population of employed addicts that has garnered considerable attention during the modern era of addiction treatment includes those who have been called the "pedestal professionals"—individuals working in professions that historically have been held to very high standards of personal conduct.[197] There is an extensive body of earlier literature on such groups. In his famous essay on ardent spirits,

Benjamin Rush noted that people "who follow professions, which require constant exercise of the faculties of their minds, are very apt to seek relief, by the use of ardent spirits, from the fatigue which succeeds great mental exertions."[198] During the inebriate asylum era, T.D. Crothers, William Cobbe, George Pettey, and Franklin Clum spoke of the vulnerability of clergy, physicians, lawyers, editors, and students; and Dr. John Snowden, an early 20th-century addiction expert, noted that doctors made the "most troublesome, hardest to manage, and most unsatisfactory patients."[199] In the modern era, Dr. LeClaire Bissell, Dr. George Talbot, and Dr. Dan Angres were among the pioneers in calling attention to the special needs of addicted professionals.

What emerged in this modern period was the growth of a body of professional literature on the treatment of addicted professionals, the development of specialized intervention and treatment programs for particular professions (clergy, lawyers, and physicians in particular), and the development of special sobriety-based support structures for particular professional groups. The intervention programs were most often organized by national or statewide professional associations, and they could be used both on a voluntary basis and as a dimension of disciplinary action taken against an alcohol- or drug-impaired professional. As in the EAP arena just discussed, many intervention programs for impaired professionals began with a focus on alcoholism, then expanded to a wide spectrum of problems that could affect professional functioning. These programs trained volunteer intervenors (often in addiction recovery themselves) to handle hotline calls from impaired professionals and their family members or professional associates. The intervenors also staged formal interventions with impaired professionals and provided linkage to treatment and ongoing support.[200]

Factors that often complicate treatment for esteemed professionals include culturally reinforced patterns of grandiosity and denial, fear of being disbarred or losing one's license to practice, fear of the loss of public trust, and the difficulty that solo practitioners experience in trying to cover their practices while participating in treatment. There are also several dimensions of professional training and lifestyle that can become barriers to treatment and recovery: intellectualization and repression of feelings, excessive workloads, poor nutritional and sleeping habits, emotionally aloof social and intimate relationships, ease of access to drugs, and a ready supply of enablers willing to protect the impaired health-care professional, cleric, or lawyer.[201] A

recognition of these factors led to the development of some treatment programs that exclusively serve particular professions. One of the oldest of such facilities, Guest House, was founded by Austin Ripley. Guest House has operated facilities in Lake Orion, Michigan and Rochester, Minnesota since the 1950s; these facilities have treated clergy and other members of communities of faith.

Special networks of support for recovering professionals have been well catalogued in the professional literature.[202] These groups are often a port of entry for professionals who are hypersensitive and fearful that knowledge of their addiction will hurt their reputation and their business. During the 1980s and 1990s, members of a variety of high-status professions, along with a broader class of the "rich and famous," became "special populations" served by a cadre of niched programs vying for their business.

Treatment in the Military

The story of addiction treatment in the military, like those of many aspects of treatment covered in this chapter, deserves to be told at a depth beyond what is possible in this book. We can, however, note the events that led to the modern rise of addiction treatment in the U.S. military.

In the 1960s, there was a growing recognition of alcohol- and other drug-related problems within the military. Alcohol-related admissions to Veterans Administration hospitals doubled during the decade, and a number of surveys underscored the growing scope of such problems. Efforts began to move alcohol and other drug problems in the military from the status of personal misconduct to that of a treatable illness.[203] The military approached this change quite tentatively with fledgling experiments in treatment at the Long Beach Naval Station in California, Fort Benning in Georgia, and the Wright-Patterson Air Force Base in Ohio, but events in 1971 precipitated a rapid change in military thinking on this issue. The earlier policy of prompt discharge of identified drug users had to be abandoned when the surprise drug-testing of soldiers in Vietnam revealed that as many as 20% tested positive for opiate drug use.[204] Under newly created policies, soldiers who tested positive for drugs were provided detoxification and counseling within a network of military treatment centers.

In 1971, the U.S. Army initiated an Alcohol and Drug Abuse Prevention and Control Program. The Army provided 30-60 days of rehabilitative effort, at the end of which a determination was made of the soldier's level of functioning and continued treatment needs. Those who had responded to treatment and established acceptable levels of performance were continued on active duty. Those whose continued substance use led to failed performance standards were separated from the Army and referred to the Veterans Administration for continued treatment as civilians. The primary mechanism for the delivery of treatment services was a rehabilitative team of both military and non-military personnel established within each base. Specific approaches varied from team to team but generally involved individual and group counseling, exposure to Alcoholics Anonymous groups, pastoral counseling, and such pharmacological adjuncts as Antabuse and tranquilizers.[205]

The Air Force's response to alcohol-related problems began in the 1950s with the establishment of an alcoholism program at Lackland Air Force Base in San Antonio, Texas. Alcoholics hospitalized in the base hospital received one or more of the following: a high-dose vitamin regime, adrenal cortical extract (ACE) injections, Antabuse, Thorazine, individual and group psychotherapy, marriage counseling, and exposure to Alcoholics Anonymous. Educational and counseling services were provided by a non-commissioned officer with more than five years' sobriety in A.A.[206] The Air Force opened regional detox centers in 1969 and three years later established alcohol-abuse control programs at 140 Air Force installations around the world.

A centerpiece in the Navy's response to alcoholism was the establishment of the Alcohol Rehabilitation Service within the Naval Hospital in Long Beach, California. This service grew out of the efforts of a recovered retired Commander, Dick J., to initiate A.A. meetings at the Long Beach Naval Station. Dick J. initiated "A.A. Drydock One" in February, 1965. The group grew to some 30 regular members in the next 18 months. In 1967, Dick received permission to launch an informal treatment program that consisted of daily group discussions and lectures and weekly A.A. meetings. Capt. Joseph Pursch describes the status of the program within the naval station during the early years.

Housed in a dilapidated World War II barracks, it [the Alcoholic Rehabilitation Center] *remained essentially a bootleg operation, its product more and more widely known but its location and means of production shrouded in a sinister, illicit fog, like a whiskey still in a dry county.*[207]

By the mid-1970s, the treatment program at Long Beach involved 6 to 8 weeks of detoxification, vitamins and Antabuse, rigorous physical-fitness training, group counseling, educational lectures, weekly psychodrama sessions, and A.A. participation. The milieu was a mix of intense support and intense confrontation.[208] Jim Baxter took over leadership of the Navy's Alcohol Abuse Control Program and oversaw its dramatic expansion. Alcohol Rehabilitation Centers were opened in Norfolk, Virginia; Great Lakes, Illinois; San Diego, California; and Jacksonville, Florida. Smaller treatment clinics were set up in an additional 14 Naval hospitals, and "Drydocks" (outpatient support groups) were set up around the world.[209] By 1980, the Navy had developed the capacity to treat up to 20,000 alcohol- and drug-addicted service personnel per year.

The biggest surprise in the military's assault against drug use in the 1970s occurred in response to drug use by soldiers in Vietnam. In preparation for what was feared to be an epidemic of heroin addiction among returning Vietnam veterans, the Veterans Administration set up large-scale treatment programs. While these programs did treat more than 26,000 veterans, by 1974 many of the programs had been closed due to lack of utilization.[210] The answer for such low utilization was revealed in a study conducted by Lee Robbins. Robbins discovered that less than 15% of those who used heroin in Vietnam continued the practice upon their return to the U.S. Vietnam demonstrated that a pattern of drug use could emerge in response to a particular environment and that spontaneous remission could occur when the environment was changed.[211]

Treatment efforts in the military achieved much less visibility in the 1980s and 1990s, as surveys of illicit drug use in the U.S. military plummeted from a high of 27% in 1980 to 9% in 1985. However, heavy alcohol use continued to be reported by 12% to 14% of military personnel surveyed during this period.[212]

The rise of treatment for alcoholism and other addictions provided by the Veterans Administration, briefly described in the last chapter, continued in the 1980s and 1990s. In 1990, the Department of Veterans Affairs operated 175 inpatient substance-abuse programs that operated out of 130 VA medical centers, in addition to an extensive network of outpatient clinics. In 1990, the average inpatient unit had 30 beds, discharged 384 patients, employed 17 full-time staff (18% of whom were recovered), and had an annual budget of more than $750,000.[213]

Culture-Specific and Culturally Competent Treatment

As people from diverse racial, ethnic, and cultural groups were swept into an expanding system of addiction treatment, concerns were quickly raised about the need to adapt treatment to fit the special needs of these groups. Just how ill-prepared the field was to face this challenge was illustrated in a 1976 literature review that found that only 77 of the 16,000 articles on alcoholism published in the previous 30 years specifically addressed the issue of alcohol problems among African Americans, and only 11 of those articles were written exclusively on this topic.[214] Funding of programs for alcohol and drug addiction in communities of color emerged as NIAAA and NIDA funding priorities in the 1970s; and Native American alcoholism programs evolved through targeted funding from the Office of Economic Opportunity, NIAAA, and the eventual transfer of most of these programs to the Indian Health Service. Native American alcoholism programs were also supported by state and tribal resources.[215] During the 1990s, the Center for Substance Abuse Treatment sustained federal support of demonstration projects aimed at developing methods of enhancing cultural competence in the delivery of addiction treatment services.

Many themes emerged as African-American, Asian-American, Hispanic, and Native American communities sought to create culturally relevant responses to alcohol- and other drug-related problems, and as majority programs altered their policies and procedures to improve their responsiveness to clients of color. While the definition of culturally competent treatment varied greatly as one traveled throughout the U.S., these emerging approaches generally emphasized the recognition of: 1) the diversity of interpersonal styles among and within various ethnic groups; 2) the importance of viewing cultural differences as strengths rather than deficits; 3) the role of economic, political, and social disempowerment as an etiological factor in addiction and as an obstacle to recovery; 4) the massive promotion of licit and illicit drugs in disempowered communities; 5) the potential role of indigenous healers, indigenous institutions, and indigenous methods of healing in addiction recovery; 6) the importance of including culturally relevant stories, metaphors, and rituals in the recovery process; and 7) the potential for varying styles of recovery and the viability of diverse sobriety-based support structures. Culturally competent addiction treatment programs actively cultivated cultural diversity among their board members, staff, and volunteers, and built and sustained close ties with their communities.

One culture-specific addiction treatment process was launched in the late 1980s by the Reverend Cecil Williams of the Glide Memorial United Methodist Church in San Francisco. Williams had grown increasingly frustrated by the growing epidemic of crack cocaine use and the failure of his efforts to get poor cocaine addicts into traditional treatment and Twelve-Step recovery programs. Recognizing that these programs were not meeting the needs of his people, Williams sought a way to "define our troubles that took seriously our culture, our history, and our ways of relating to one another."[216] The recovery program forged at Glide involved four core acts: recognition, self-definition, rebirth, and community. These were elaborated within the Ten Acts of Resistance that served as guidelines for personal recovery. These Acts called for assertion of personal control, honesty, self-acceptance, forgiveness, feeling, and acts of love. Glide's programs included support groups for recovering addicts (designated First Generation, Second Generation....), larger support groups (called Placenta Groups) whose role was to support those in recovery, and specialized groups for women (Women on the Move) and men (Men in Motion).

Williams used Afrocentric metaphors (slavery, genocide) to conceptualize addiction, called upon individuals to discover the power within themselves, reframed religious/spiritual concepts (rebirth, resurrection) to support addiction recovery, and strengthened and expanded the traditional extended family and kinship network within the Black community to support addiction recovery.[217]

There have also been appeals to addicts of color based on political consciousness—appeals that conceptualized drugs as a tool of colonial pacification and exhorted addicts to cast off the chains of addiction.[218] What these appeals from religious and political organizations provide is a well articulated rationale for total abstinence, a means of redeeming a "spoiled identity," loyalty to a cause greater than oneself, a radical reconstruction of daily lifestyle, and a sobriety-based social network. This position might be summarized as follows.

Alcohol and other intoxicating drugs disempower African-American men and women, undermine the African-American family, and drain energy and resources from the African-American community. Alcohol and other drugs serve as tools of suppression and oppression by anesthetizing Black rage and replacing political action with personal self-destruction. Alcohol and other drug use contributes to the systematic incarceration of young Black men. Alcohol and other drugs are tools of genocide that destroy Black lives through suicide, homicide, accident and disease. Addiction recovery is a political act—an act of cultural as well as personal survival.

When one compares traditional treatment milieus with those milieus that treat historically disempowered clients, one is struck by the contrast in organizing metaphors. In the latter, there is more talk of empowerment than powerlessness, more talk of pride than humility. There is a focus on power within oneself in addition to the traditional emphasis on power beyond and greater than the self. There are different rationales for understanding one's addiction, just as there are different rationales for radical sobriety. There is less talk of doing one thing only—not drinking—and more talk of putting it (a whole life) all together in ways that make sense individually and collectively. There is a greater presence of political and religious metaphors and less emphasis on medical metaphors.[219]

The Addicted Offender

The number of people entering the criminal justice system exploded in the 1980s and 1990s as the Federal drug-control budget rose from $1.5 billion in 1981 to $13.2 billion in 1995. Under the influence of increased enforcement and new mandatory sentencing laws, the number of alcohol- and drug-involved offenders going to prison rose from 19 out of every 1,000 arrested in 1980 to 104 out of every 1,000 arrested in 1992. By 1994, there were more than a million men and women incarcerated in U.S. prisons, and new prison construction continued at an unprecedented pace and cost. A National Institute of Justice study of arrestees in 23 U.S. cities revealed positive drug screens ranging from 54% to 81%. The percentage of drug offenders among inmates sentenced to federal prisons rose from 25% in 1980 to 61% in 1993.[220] In the face of such dramatic changes, the criminal justice system began experimenting with new linkages with addiction treatment providers.

Collaborative efforts between the criminal justice system and local addiction treatment agencies strove to balance the former's role in punishing and preventing injury to the community with the latter's concern for the individual rehabilitation of the addict. Treatment personnel working with alcohol- and drug-involved offenders were required to learn more about criminality and public safety issues, while judges, prosecutors, public defenders, probation officers, and corrections personnel were required to enhance their knowledge about addiction, treatment, and recovery.

Programs initiated during the last three decades of the 20th century included pre-arrest diversion of the addict to detoxification or counseling; post-arrest diversion to detoxification; treatment as a court-mandated condition of pre-trial release; treatment inside jail while awaiting trial; treatment outside a criminal justice facility while waiting trial; treatment as an alternative to prosecution; treatment as a required component of suspended sentence, conditional discharge, or probation; treatment inside county jails and state and federal prisons; and treatment as a requirement of parole.

The major trends in working with addicted offenders include the widespread use of screening and case management services (in TASC), the widespread use of drug testing as a monitoring tool for offenders being supervised in the community, and the emergence of specialized mechanisms inside the criminal justice system to enhance the effectiveness of intervention with addict-offenders.[221] The last of these includes the use of drug courts, the use of specially trained probation officers, the use of specialized intensive supervised probation, treatment groups in day reporting centers, treatment combined with home confinement, "boot camp" programs, and the integration of addiction treatment services into jails and prisons. Prison-based treatment, particularly the use of self-contained therapeutic communities for addict-offenders, has been evaluated quite positively in terms of its effects on post-discharge drug use and arrest rates.[222]

Although the development of specialized drug courts is a relatively recent innovation, these courts have generated considerable interest within a criminal justice community that has been bending under the weight of its drug-related caseload.[223] Drug Courts involve collaborative efforts by the judiciary, prosecution, defense, and local addiction treatment providers to divert and rehabilitate non-violent drug-involved offenders. Drug courts often combine rigorous judicial case review, explicitly defined behavioral contracts for participation, intense case-management services, specialized treatment that looks at criminality as well as addiction, graduated penalties that provide consequences short of program expulsion, closely supervised aftercare, and—where needed—re-intervention. Federal legislation in late 1994 allocated $1.8 billion to support local experiments with drug courts.[224]

While many counselors contended that coerced

treatment was neither effective nor appropriate, studies during this era confirmed that clients legally coerced into treatment had outcomes comparable to or better than those clients who entered treatment voluntarily.[225]

Treating Addicts With HIV/AIDS

The response of addiction treatment programs to the AIDS epidemic was not uniform. Early responses included the development of more rigorous confidentiality standards and infection-control procedures, establishment of protocol and procedures for AIDS testing, training of staff on the management of HIV/AIDS-related clinical issues, the integration of formalized programs of HIV/AIDS prevention into the treatment curriculum, and the development of special treatment or support groups for clients with HIV/AIDS. Much of this effort was driven by the fact that the movement of federal substance abuse treatment dollars to the states was tied to the presence of HIV/ AIDS prevention efforts, access to testing and counseling services, and referral for specialized services.

One of the earliest and most difficult aspects of the addiction treatment community's response to the AIDS epidemic was the clinical management of countertransference that arose in relationships between treatment personnel and clients with HIV/ AIDS. HIV and AIDS brought new and intense agendas into treatment programs, as it did into many arenas of health care: fear of contagion, fear of dying and of others' death, managing anticipatory grief and losses from AIDS-related deaths, guilt over one's own relative health, and anger over the slow national response to the epidemic. HIV and AIDS heightened old issues as well: feelings about homosexuality, the risk of detaching from or over-identifying with clients, fears about personal shortcomings, and the ever-pervasive confrontation with clients' pain.[226]

Services to people with HIV/AIDS improved as community-based AIDS service organizations were created and AIDS case-management services became more widely available. Services to addicts with HIV/AIDS also improved as a body of clinical technology emerged and special support groups developed for recovering people affected by HIV/AIDS. HIV had been spreading for almost a decade before the 1988 publication of the first text that specifically addressed AIDS and substance abuse.[227] Since that time, the American Society of Addiction Medicine, the Center for Substance Abuse Treatment, and many state chemical dependency agencies have generated clinical protocol to improve responsiveness to the needs of people with HIV/AIDS seeking addiction treatment services.

As more people with HIV/AIDS moved into substance abuse recovery, the knowledge base about their special needs grew. A body of literature emerged in the 1990s conveying the addiction recovery stories of people living with HIV/AIDS.[228] What these stories revealed was that the diagnosis of HIV could be, not a death sentence, but what some clients came to recognize as "a defining moment." This author interviewed a number of recovering people with HIV/AIDS who defined their diagnosis, not as their problem, but as their solution—a breakthrough experience that allowed them to move from self-destruction to positive living. As one client said:

HIV was like a fork in the road. I felt I had the opportunity to either give up and die or make something of myself. I felt I could walk into that spotlight and make a choice. Today I have meaning in my life. If I didn't have HIV in my life, where would I be?[229]

A national survey of substance-abuse treatment programs reported 29,343 HIV-positive clients in treatment on September 30, 1991.[230] As the number of addicted people with AIDS becomes a larger proportion of the total number of AIDS cases in the U.S., the addictions field will continue to be called upon to increase its responsiveness to the needs of these men, women, and children.

The Multiple-Problem Client

One of the enduring preoccupations of addiction treatment personnel during the 1980s and 1990s was the issue of "dual diagnosis"—a term used to designate clients who presented with both addiction and emotional/psychiatric problems.[231] While this concern generated its own body of literature, training, and specially designed programs, it was only part of a more fundamental shift in the characteristics of clients entering addiction treatment: the emergence of multiple-problem clients and families. The problems of these clients, particularly in the publicly funded programs, were characterized by great chronicity and intensity and were often being transmitted inter-generationally. The problems presented by these clients crossed all the categorical service boundaries within which modern health and human service agencies were organized. Growing numbers of clients presented with a multitude of concurrent issues related to addiction, criminality, gang involvement, physical health (from AIDS to tuberculosis), mental health, domestic violence, child neglect and abuse, housing, transportation, school failure, and unemployment, to name just a few.

Many of these clients had long histories of involvement with human-service agencies-involvement so extensive that one was forced to ask whether these agencies, working together or in isolation, had done anything to influence the quality of life or level of functioning of these clients. Client histories with these agencies were marked by periodic service exclusion; service extrusions (administrative discharges for failure to comply with various program rules); premature service disengagement; the delivery of inappropriate, ineffective, and at times even harmful services; and a pattern of chronic relapse related to nearly all major problem areas. Post-mortems of each failed service design revealed a repetitious assessment of only one narrow arena of the client's life. They revealed patterns in which a single agency and a single professional discipline had intervened with limited resources, usually during a period of crisis in the life of the client. They revealed agencies working with clients who had lost or destroyed their family and social networks, leaving providers who historically worked with a client's family in the position of having to function as the client's family—a change that contained profound implications that few agencies grasped.

What clearly emerged in the addictions field, and in allied fields of health and human services, was a collision between changing client characteristics that indicated the need for greater intensity and doses of treatment and fiscal and administrative trends that dictated diminished intensity and doses of treatment. Both clients and staff caught in this systemic double-bind found themselves overwhelmed and demoralized.

When it became apparent that multiple-problem clients/families could not be treated effectively in a categorically segregated service system, programs began to experiment with new models of intervention. The emerging models, many evaluated in federally funded demonstration projects, were characterized by some themes that have already been touched on in this chapter. These models consisted almost exclusively of multi-agency, interdisciplinary (and cross-trained) teams that utilized outreach and case-management services to enhance motivation for service involvement and to manage personal and environmental obstacles to recovery. The models involved gender- and culture-specific approaches to overcoming chronic self-defeating patterns of behavior. The models combined resources from multiple agencies, in order to increase the intensity and duration of service involvement. They focused on building a recovering community that included indigenous healers and indigenous institutions. They focused on a fundamental reconstruction of identity and lifestyle. Such models brought addiction treatment programs into integrated teams with probation departments, child welfare agencies, psychiatric units, domestic violence programs, community-action groups, AIDS case-management agencies, mutual-aid societies, and a plethora of other community institutions. These were dynamic models, but difficult ones to implement—not just because of the clients' difficulties, but because of issues of ego, ideology, professional turf, and budgetary concerns that had to be overcome if these models were going to work.

The emergence of multiple-problem clients is the Achilles heel of the entire health and human service system. While this problem is not unique to the addictions field, how the problem is resolved within the larger umbrella of human services may very well determine the fate of those individuals and agencies which deliver services to people with addictions.

Modern Addiction Treatment Technologies

A comprehensive review of modern addiction treatment technology is beyond the scope of this historical review, but it is important at least to note some of the advances that occurred in the closing decades of the 20th century.

Family-based intervention technologies pioneered by Vernon Johnson, and parallel intervention techniques refined in the workplace, in schools and in the criminal justice system, brought growing numbers of people into addiction treatment at earlier stages of addiction than at any time in American history. New outreach and case management techniques were also developed that engaged many multiple-problem, treatment-resistant clients on a voluntary basis.[232]

Another innovation that held out promise of expanding the range of people coming into treatment was what William Miller christened "warm turkey." Miller suggested that the immediate demand for all clients to become immediately and forever abstinent ("cold turkey") might actually constitute an obstacle to some people's achievement of abstinence. As an alternative to the "abstinence-now-or-nothing" stance of most treatment programs, Miller proposed such methods as "sobriety sampling" (short-term experiments in sobriety), tapering down, and monitored trials of moderated drinking for clients who strongly resisted the demand for immediate abstinence. Miller advocated Behavioral Self-Control Training—an approach that included setting general guidelines for personal drinking behavior (frequency of drinking, number of drinks, manner of consuming each drink, time between drinks), active self-monitoring of drinking behavior, analysis of situational cues that incite higher alcohol consumption, the use of specific reduction techniques (drinking beverages with lower alcohol content, taking smaller sips), self-reinforcement, and the development of alternatives to drinking—believing that this approach might prove effective in reducing alcohol-related problems among people who were not addicted to alcohol.[233] According to Miller, demand for immediate abstinence was not the only, nor necessarily the best, strategy for promoting long-term sobriety for all clients.[234] Strategies like those suggested by Miller offered a new technology of intervention for people who were developing drinking problems but were not alcohol dependent. They also provided a structured way to speed up some alcoholics' recognition that continued efforts to control their drinking were futile.

Individuals suspected of having alcohol- and other drug-related problems were assessed using a new arsenal of quick screening, assessment devices, and interview protocol. These included such instruments as the Michigan Alcoholism Screening Test (MAST), the Drug Abuse Screening Test (DAST) the four-question CAGE, the Alcohol Use Inventory, the Addiction Severity Index (ASI), the McAndrews Scale of the MMPI, the Adolescent Problem Severity Index, the Adolescent Drinking Index (ADI), the Adolescent Diagnostic Interview (ADI), the Adolescent Drug Diagnosis, and the Diagnostic Interview Schedule for DSM-IV. Some of these devices were used by allied health professionals, child protection specialists, criminal justice personnel, and employee assistance counselors to identify individuals who needed to be referred to addiction treatment agencies.

Treatment approaches through the 1970s and 1980s were clustered within the categories of therapeutic community, methadone maintenance, Minnesota Model inpatient and intensive outpatient treatment, and the broad category of outpatient drug-free treatment. The boundaries between these modalities shifted in the 1990s, as more programs organized a comprehensive range of services and moved clients through multiple levels and types of care. This transition marked a fundamental shift in the century-long practice of organizing each treatment agency around a single treatment modality and level of care. The move to multi-dimensional and multi-tiered treatment was accompanied by more sophisticated processes of clinical assessment and treatment planning, dramati-

cally enhanced systems of clinical documentation, increased use of urine testing, and the delivery of formal case-management services.

While the core philosophies that birthed the therapeutic communities and methadone maintenance programs are still recognizable in their current applications, outpatient drug-free treatment evolved through a variety of theoretical frameworks and dominant techniques. Generations of alcoholics and addicts were exposed to an unusual and evolving eclecticism that used psychodrama, transactional analysis, Gestalt therapy, Reichian orgone therapy, Janov's primal scream therapy, Lowen's bioenergetics, and Glasser's reality therapy. Nearly all of these approaches, with the possible exception of reality therapy, were based on psychodynamic conceptualizations of addiction as a symptomatic manifestation of underlying emotional distress. More recently, outpatient drug-free counseling was heavily influenced by brief strategic therapy and cognitive/behavioral approaches to addiction counseling. Brief therapies usually involved concise communication with the client regarding the results of assessment data, clear verbal and written advice for change, an emphasis on the client's responsibility for initiating and sustaining change, development of a menu of strategies for reducing substance use, and the expression of optimism regarding the client's ability to change.

One of the most positively evaluated but least frequently utilized outpatient models of alcoholism treatment in past decades was the Community Reinforcement Approach (CRA). This approach emerged out of studies in the 1970s and early 1980s that suggested that CRA was superior to traditional inpatient and outpatient treatments.[235] The CRA systematically rewarded sobriety while progressively extinguishing drinking behavior through a behaviorally managed Antabuse protocol, social-skills training, drink-refusal training, problem-solving training, marriage counseling, job-procurement training, the use of a "buddy system," and participation in a non-drinking social club.[236]

Family-oriented treatment evolved through several overlapping stages in the modern era: referral of wives to Al-Anon, groups for wives of alcoholics, conjoint marital therapy, residential or outpatient family education, and primary treatment for family members that focused on their individual recovery. The research of Drs. Stephanie Brown and Virginia Lewis challenged the prevailing expectation that families should move rapidly toward health with the initiation of the client's alcoholism recovery. Brown and Lewis discovered that the emotional turbulence that addiction produced in the family continued well into the first three to five years of recovery, and that the risk of family disintegration was high if family members were not supported through this transition period.[237] Family therapy emerged as a more legitimate primary mode of treatment for addiction disorders during the modern era and was explored particularly for its utility in intervening in the substance abuse of adolescents.[238]

Another nuance that emerged in family programming in addiction treatment programs in the past 20 years was the effort to break intergenerational patterns of alcohol- and other drug-related problems. These efforts, particularly those that emerged in programs designed to treat addicted women with histories of child neglect and child abuse, began with simultaneous but separate interventions with addicted mothers and their children, then focused attention on enhancing the health of the family as a unit. Combining treatment services for parents and children, parenting training, and family therapy, they sought to decrease the likelihood that the children of today's clients would recapitulate these problems as they moved into their own adolescence and adulthood.

The oft-predicted definitive breakthrough in the pharmacological treatment of addiction did not materialize in the second half of the 20th century. Antabuse continued to be available but not routinely utilized in the treatment of primary alcoholism. Where Antabuse was used, its effectiveness was found to be positively related to high motivation to take the drug, supervised administration of the drug, and participation in ancillary treatment activities.[239] Antipsychotic drugs, anti-anxiety drugs, and anti-depressant drugs, while valuable as treatments for co-occurring psychiatric conditions, proved to have no significant value in the post-detoxification rehabilitation of the primary alcoholic or addict. Mood stabilizers such as Lithium, considered for a while to be a breakthrough in the treatment of alcoholism, proved effective only as an adjunct in the treatment of those alcoholics who were also manic-depressive or who suffered extended bouts of depression.[240] In reviewing ten years of progress in alcoholism treatment, Edward Gottheil concluded in 1993 that: "Despite a great deal of research, new agents such as buprenorphine, buspirone, clonidine, and fluoxetine, and many advances in neurobiology, there have been no major breakthroughs in the pharmacological treatment of alcohol and other substance dependencies."[241] The closest thing to a pharmacological breakthrough in the treatment of alcoholism came from a most unexpected source: naltrexone—a narcotic antagonist used in the treatment of opiate addiction. Studies beginning in 1992 suggested that daily

consumption of 50 milligrams of naltrexone reduced alcoholic relapse. Naltrexone, by elevating beta-endorphin levels and reducing the reinforcing properties of alcohol, lowered the frequency and intensity of cravings for alcohol and, perhaps most dramatically, prevented acts of drinking from becoming full-blown relapses. Subjects treated with naltrexone reported fewer and milder cravings, fewer post-treatment drinking days, lower relapse rates, and fewer alcohol-related problems than alcoholics who had been given placebos.[242] As a result of this newfound use for naltrexone, the drug was renamed ReVia and heavily marketed to the treatment industry by its manufacturer, DuPont Merck.

Research also continued in the search for more effective adjuncts in the treatment of addiction to drugs other than alcohol. Methadone continued its preeminence as the primary tool in the management of narcotic addiction, with more than 95,000 clients per year receiving methadone in the U.S.[243] Levo-alpha-acetylmethadol (LAAM), methadone and clonidine combinations, ibogaine, and new methods of rapid detoxification were also advocated in the treatment of narcotic addiction. Combinations of buprenorphine and methadone were used to treat clients addicted to both opiates and cocaine. Tryptophan, amantadine, bromocriptine, desipramine, imipramine, Lithium, and Ritalin were also tried in the treatment of cocaine, but no chemical magic bullet was found that consistently reduced relapse for cocaine addicts.[244] One of the more positively evaluated adjuncts in the treatment of cocaine addiction was, quite surprisingly, Antabuse. Antabuse was found to lower cocaine relapse by eliminating alcohol-induced impulsivity and impairment of judgement. Pharmacological treatments were sometimes supplemented with other physical treatments, such as acupuncture, to facilitate drug withdrawal and reduce post-acute withdrawal cravings.[245]

One of the most dramatic changes in addiction treatment in the past 20 years was the changing perception of and response to nicotine. Coming to grips with staff and client addiction to nicotine was one of the most professionally controversial and personally difficult challenges of this era. Meeting this challenge brought the field full circle. Nineteenth and early 20th-century inebriety specialists such as T.D Crothers, Leslie Keeley, John Kellogg, Charles Towns, and Alexander Lambert waged a consistent attack on tobacco as a harmful and addictive substance and viewed smoking as a contributing factor in alcoholic and narcotic relapse.[246] Modern addiction specialists took on the issue of tobacco only when the evidence of the harmfulness of smoking and the addictiveness of nicotine had become overwhelming. As the addictions field began to confront the issue of smoking, it faced a question that addiction experts had been asking for more than a century: Is there a relationship between alcoholism and nicotine addiction? Thomas Bien and Roann Burge reviewed the research on this question in 1990 and reported the following findings.

• An overwhelming number (over 90%) of alcoholics smoke.

• Alcoholics smoke more cigarettes per day (98% smoke more than one pack per day) than do non-alcoholic smokers, make up almost the entire group of smokers who consume more than 40 cigarettes per day, and are more likely to smoke mentholated cigarettes.

• Smoking and drinking have a biphasic quality; people use them both for stimulation and for relaxation.

• The number of cigarettes consumed rises in tandem with volume of alcohol consumed, adding to the significant health risks related to heavy alcohol consumption.

• There is no research support for the contention that alcoholics should not try to quit smoking at the same time they are attempting to quit drinking. In fact, the research more closely supports the view that "smoking and drinking are correlated behaviors, anything causing a reduction in one may be associated with a reduction in the other."[247]

By the late 1980s the addiction treatment field was going through a rather painful process of self-examination and self-confrontation related to its response to the nicotine addiction of the majority of its workforce and clients. There were growing calls to look at the issue of smoking as an ethical as well as a clinical issue.[248] Growing numbers of programs went smoke free and began to state explicitly that they would hire only non-smoking staff. Programs also began to combine treatment for smoking with the treatment for alcoholism and other drug addiction, and conduct these simultaneously.[249] This last process was helped by new pharmacological aids to smoking cessation: smoke-free nicotine-delivery systems (nicotine chewing gum, transdermal nicotine patches, and experimental nicotine sprays and inhalers) that could be used to minimize the discomfort of physical withdrawal from nicotine and reduce relapse by systematically reducing nicotine levels. Special support groups like Nicotine Anonymous (Nic-A) and

Smokers Anonymous also emerged to apply Twelve-Step recovery principles to recovery from nicotine addiction.

As focus shifted toward the construction of comprehensive local continua of care for the addicted, greater attention was given to the post-treatment adjustment of clients. The first evidence of this concern was in the re-emergence of what in modern parlance came to be called relapse prevention. Treatment protocol specifically designed to reduce relapse in treated alcoholics and addicts dates back to the 19th century. In his 1883 work *Alcoholic Inebriety,* Dr. Joseph Parrish noted:

> *Frequently there are well marked premonitory signs, which introduce a paroxysm of intoxication, such as restlessness, irritability, general malaise, or it may be, the occurrence of an injury....The paroxysms may be arrested, prevented, or controlled, by becoming familiar with the prodromic symptoms, and by giving timely heed to their admonitions by the use of remedial measures.[250]*

Friedrich Erlenmeyer included an entire chapter entitled "Prevention of Relapse" in his 1889 book on the treatment of morphine addiction. What was new in the late 20th century was the emergence of research data that allowed increased precision in the development of clinical techniques of relapse prevention that could be applied in systematic ways. This work was pioneered and popularized by a number of researchers and clinicians: Alan Marlatt, Judith Gordon, Terence Gorski, Merlene Miller, and Dennis Daley. Their collective strategies involved teaching clients coping skills, new patterns of thinking, and new drug-free lifestyles.[251] Relapse prevention and intervention technologies were widely applied in addiction treatment programs during the 1980s and 1990s and represented a significant advancement in the core technology of addiction treatment. As early as the 1960s, some programs, such as Hazelden, created specialty tracks for treating clients who had been treated and then relapsed. However, the efforts of Marlatt and the others were the first systematic attempts to reduce the number, duration, and severity of relapses experienced by alcoholics and addicts following primary treatment.[252]

A second indication of concern regarding post-treatment adjustment was the rise of what came to be called the recovery-home movement. Alcoholics have long chosen to live together for mutual support during early recovery, from the 19th-century temperance hotels and reform clubs to Bill Wilson's stay with Dr. Robert Smith, sharing quarters during the earliest months of A.A.'s birth. In the middle of the 20th century, supportive living via the "halfway house" model had always involved paid staff operating as central authority figures. What emerged in the 1970s and 1980s was a new kind of "recovery home" that utilized no paid staff, was financially self-supporting, and operated as a communal democracy. While variations on this recovery-home concept sprang up in many places, the epicenter of the movement can be traced to Silver Spring, Maryland in 1975. When Montgomery County, Maryland closed its alcoholic halfway house due to lack of funding, the residents who lived in the facility were challenged by the owner of the facility (an A.A. member) to operate the facility themselves without paid professional staff. That challenge was the beginning of what came to be a chain of 14 recovery homes operating from Washington D.C. to Bethlehem, Pennsylvania by 1988. Known as Oxford Houses, these facilities provided a communal living situation for alcoholics in the early stages of recovery. Each house was run by group discussion and democratic decision-making, with very few rules—among the most fundamental of which was the immediate expulsion of any member who relapsed. If there was any internal motto that captured the essence of the recovery-home movement, it was "Just don't drink and pay the rent!" The Drug Abuse Act of 1989 mandated that each state establish a fund to lend money to groups seeking to create recovery homes on the Oxford House model. This led to a dramatic increase in the numbers (more than 300) and geographical dispersion (more than 28 states) of such homes. Many programs attempted to combine the recovery home with intensive outpatient treatment, to approximate the level of support previously provided by inpatient or residential treatment.[253]

Treatment Evaluation Research

Modern efforts to measure the relative effect of addiction treatment have focused on two primary areas: 1) evaluation research that sought to measure the effects of various interventions on post-intervention substance use and related measures of personal and social functioning, and 2) experimental research that sought to manipulate various variables to test the relative superiority of various interventions in highly controlled (efficacy studies) and naturalistic (effectiveness studies) settings.[254] Randomized controlled trials—the most scientifically rigorous test of treatment interventions—were not conducted in the addiction

treatment field until quite recently. Methodological problems such as the focus on soft outcomes (retention rates, discharge status, counselor ratings of client progress), grossly inadequate follow-up rates, short periods of follow-up, and failure to control for case-mix (to name just a few) have limited what can be scientifically stated about the effectiveness of modern addiction treatment.[255] Evaluation research in the addictions field has progressed from naturalistic single-site follow-up studies to large multi-site experimental studies. Research evaluating addiction treatment has also moved from a narrow focus on post-treatment abstinence rates to the evaluation of many dimensions of post-treatment functioning and the broader evaluation of the cost-effectiveness of treatment.

Some of the largest-scale evaluations of addiction treatment between 1969 and 1995 included the Drug Abuse Reporting Project (DARP), the Treatment Outcome Perspective Study (TOPS), the Drug Abuse Treatment Outcome Study (DATOS), and the National Treatment Improvement Evaluation Study (NTIES).[256] The number of clients included in these large-scale studies ranged between 5,300 and 44,000. There were also privately operated treatment-evaluation services such as the Comprehensive Assessment and Treatment Outcome Research (CATOR) and Drug Outcome Monitoring Systems (DOMS).

Looking at the variable outcomes of different treatment interventions, early researchers quickly migrated toward the issue of treatment dose as a predictor of treatment outcome. Treatment dose was conceptualized at three levels: 1) a minimal dose, below which no positive outcome can likely be expected, 2) an optimum dose, at which clients can be expected to experience a positive outcome, and 3) an excessive dose, at which positive treatment outcomes deteriorate into iatrogenic effects, e.g., increased institutionalization and dependency. The early DARP and TOPS studies found that even the outcome of clients who dropped out of addiction treatment was determined by how much treatment they had received before leaving. Treatment outcome became viewed primarily as a function of the intensity and duration of treatment intervention.[257] But this conclusion, drawn primarily from clients who were being treated for addiction to drugs other than alcohol, was not always supported by alcoholism treatment studies. William Miller, in a 1986 review of controlled studies on alcoholism treatment effectiveness, came to three conclusions: 1) in studies that evaluated the effect of length of inpatient treatment on treatment outcome, there was no study that concluded that longer stays produced better treatment outcomes; 2) in controlled studies that compared the outcome of residential treatment versus that of non-residential alternatives, not a single study concluded that residential treatment was more effective than the outpatient alternatives; and 3) those treatments with the best demonstrated outcomes in controlled studies (social-skills training, stress-management training, marriage and family counseling, and the community reinforcement model that combines several such interventions) were not part of the mainstream treatment system in the United States. Controlled studies, challenging the prevailing view that treatment improved as the intensity (inpatient versus outpatient) and duration of treatment increased, sped the shift from inpatient to outpatient treatment of alcohol- and drug-related problems in the U.S.[258]

A synopsis of 30 years of treatment-evaluation research published in 1997 by the Substance Abuse and Mental Health Administration drew several conclusions. First, methadone maintenance, therapeutic communities, traditional "Minnesota Model" chemical dependency treatment, and outpatient drug-free treatment were associated with enhanced psychosocial health of treated clients. Methadone maintenance and therapeutic communities were further associated with decreased criminal activity and improved social and vocational functioning. Methadone and the Minnesota Model programs were also associated with improvements in physical health, with methadone having specific effects in reducing needle sharing and lowering HIV infection and transmission rates. Those methadone programs that utilized higher daily methadone dosages (60 mg or higher) had the best outcomes in terms of retention and reduction of illicit drug use. Comparing outcomes across inpatient, residential, outpatient, and intensive outpatient settings, the review did not find one setting superior to others in generating positive outcomes for the general population of addicts. There was evidence that clients with more severe patterns of alcohol and other drug use, more severe psychiatric impairment, and fewer social supports were more likely to be placed in inpatient treatment, and that they did better in inpatient treatment than in outpatient treatment.[259] The emerging view that alcoholics were a heterogenous population and that treatment effectiveness would be enhanced by a process of matching unique client needs to specialized treatments has recently been challenged in the findings of NIAAA's Project Match. In this study, 1,726 patients were evaluated and then randomly assigned to one of three treatments: Twelve-Step Facilitation, Cognitive/ Behavioral Ther-

apy, or Motivational Enhancement Therapy. The study then sought to determine whether patients with particular characteristics did better in a particular modality. This preliminary study drew the highly unexpected conclusion that patient-treatment matching added little to enhance treatment outcome.[260]

Studies evaluating the cost-effectiveness of treatment have indicated that the costs of treatment are recouped in reductions in other social costs.[261] One study found that approximately half of the cost of treatment was offset within a year by reductions in the health-care costs of the addict and his or her family.[262] A recent study conducted by the California Department of Alcohol and Drug Programs concluded that every dollar invested in addiction treatment generated a societal reduction of $7.14 in future social costs, most of which was achieved by reductions in post-treatment criminal activity.[263] Recent national studies have noted similar patterns of cost-offset.[264]

The general effects of the treatment interventions evaluated in recent decades—reduced alcohol and other drug use, improved health, reduced risk of HIV infection/transmission, decreased criminal activity, decreased homelessness, improved family and occupational functioning, and reduced addiction-related social costs—were sufficient for policy makers to conclude that "treatment works."[265] However, the story of treatment effectiveness proved much more complex than a simple evaluation and comparison of the impact of various treatment interventions at a particular point in time. Mike Dennis, a long-time treatment-evaluation specialist, explains:

> *The early studies consistently demonstrated that treatment was producing effects in terms of reduced drug use, reduced illegal activity, increased employment, and increased health, but the results were always mixed. This research demonstrated most of all that addicts were not a homogenous population. We found that nothing worked perfectly with all clients, or even with the same clients at different points in time. The outcomes in many ways mirrored people's experience with diets. A small percentage of people diet, lose weight, and keep the weight off. But most people fail the first times they diet, and many will experience periods of success and periods of relapse in effectively managing weight problems. That's the very nature of a chronic condition. We are just beginning to fully appreciate the nature of addiction as this kind of chronic condition. The evalua-*

tion of modern addiction treatment focused primarily on the effects of single episodes of treatment on post-treatment substance-use patterns. This focus has continued in spite of the reality that most clients present with multiple personal and environmental problems that can confound treatment outcome, and undergo multiple and sometimes quite varied treatments over the course of their addiction and recovery careers.

When asked to summarize the implications of this emerging view, Dennis offered the following conclusion:

Our treatment-evaluation research tells us that certain interventions work with certain people at particular points in their lives. The most significant implication of this finding is

not that we need to match treatments to particular clients at particular times, but that we must monitor responses to such interventions and re-intervene strategically to shorten the intensity and duration of relapse and to minimize the personal and social costs of relapse. The best predictor of long-term positive outcomes is the monitoring of client responses to treatment and early reintervention.[266]

In the past two chapters, we have explored the modern evolution of addiction treatment in the United States. In the next chapter, we will portray this story through the experience of one institution whose story, perhaps more than any other, portrays the strengths and vulnerabilities of addiction treatment in the second half of the 20th century.

✠

Chapter Twenty-Eight:
Parkside: A Rich Legacy and a Cautionary Tale

Earlier references have been made to the development of addiction treatment franchises in the 19th and early 20th centuries: the Gatlin Institutes, the Neal Institutes, the Empire Institutes and the well-known Keeley Institutes. The attempt to franchise particular models of addiction treatment re-emerged in the 1980s, as companies like CompCare, Raleigh Hills, Psychiatric Institutes of America, Charter, Parkview, Horizon, and Koala franchised their treatment models regionally or nationally. The largest of such franchises was known as "Parkside."

Parkside was unique among the modern treatment franchise companies because of its deep roots in the refinement and diffusion of the "Minnesota Model" of alcoholism treatment. Parkside grew from a single program to the largest network of free-standing addiction treatment programs in the United States—and then collapsed as an organization. If the rise and fall of Parkside were idiosyncratic to place or personality—if it were the story of only one organization—it would not warrant inclusion in this book. But the Parkside story elicits themes that illuminate both the strengths and vulnerabilities of addiction treatment programs in the last half of the 20th century. Much of what Parkside experienced—the best and the worst—was replicated on a smaller and less dramatic scale in programs across the country. The rise and fall

of Parkside reveals the forces that both shaped and threatened the field of addiction treatment in the second half of the 20th century.

The Birth[5]

The early threads of this story lead from Minnesota to Illinois. Dr. Fredric (Fritz) Norstad, the Director of Chaplaincy Services at Lutheran Services of Minnesota, conducted a clinical pastoral education program at Willmar State Hospital in Minnesota in the 1950s. At Willmar, Dr. Norstad began to explore with Dr. Nelson Bradley, the hospital superintendent, the church's need to become more deeply involved in the problem of alcoholism. Dr. Naurice Nesset, a top

---

[5] Most of this history was constructed from interviews with former Parkside employees, including Rev. Carl Anderson, Miles Conway, William Filstead, David Folkes, Sister Therese Golden, Kathy Hennessy, Kathy Leck, Orville McElfresh, Rosemary McKinney, Jim M., Gina Priestley, William Priestley, Betty Reddy, Jean Rossi, John Small, and Randall Webber. I am also indebted to the work of John Keller, whose various papers were invaluable in constructing the accurate chronology of this story. The Rev. Carl Anderson and the Rev. John Keller provided particularly meticulous and helpful reviews of an early draft of this chapter.

executive at Baxter Labs and an active Lutheran Layman, served as President of the Board of Trustees of Chicago Deaconess Hospital when a decision was made to build Lutheran General Hospital in Park Ridge, Illinois. Nesset recruited Dr. Norstad to assist with the development of the new hospital. When the decision was made to include an alcoholism treatment unit, Nesset and Norstad sought the one person they both believed was committed to an alcoholism treatment approach that treated the whole person and who was comfortable incorporating spirituality into the alcoholism treatment process. The person they sought was Dr. Nelson Bradley, who had pioneered such an approach to alcoholism treatment in Minnesota.

Nelson Bradley was recruited by Lutheran General shortly before the hospital opened on December 24, 1959. Two years later, Bradley recruited Dr. Jean Rossi, the psychologist who had worked with him at Willmar State Hospital in Minnesota, to join him in private practice and to help develop alcoholism services at Lutheran General. In the earliest days, Bradley admitted alcoholics for detoxification in the psychiatric unit and worked with Rossi to provide alcoholism counseling services. Rossi describes this period as follows:

We segregated our alcoholic clients at one end of the psych unit to conduct lectures and groups. This open format, particularly the lectures, attracted the attention of other patients on the psych unit and physicians who were coming through the unit. Other patients on the unit began to ask their physicians if they could join our groups. The doctors' opportunity to casually observe this no nonsense approach to alcoholism treatment contributed to an early positive reputation in the hospital.[267]

As a result of this early success, a decision was made to build a 102-bed alcoholism treatment, research, and training center on the grounds of the hospital. In 1963, Rev. John Keller—who had been a staff member in training with Bradley and Rossi at Willmar while on assignment from the American Lutheran Church—was brought to Lutheran General to help raise the funds for this new facility and to recruit the rest of the team that would operate the center. Dr. Vincent Pisani, a clinical psychologist, was also hired as a consultant to the treatment center.

Funds for the new center were raised through a combination of federal grants and philanthropic donations. Lutheran General was the first hospital in the country to receive federal Hill-Burton funds for the express purpose of building an alcoholism-treatment facility. In addition to this $300,000 grant, $1.7 million was donated by foundations, corporations, and individuals to build the Alcoholism Rehabilitation Center (ARC).[268]

The first person Keller hired was Jim M., who brought personal recovery from alcoholism, social work training, and prior alcoholism counseling experience. Jim would play a profound role in professionalizing the role of alcoholism counselor at Lutheran General and on a national level.[269] His primary responsibility included:

1) inclusion of A.A. within the program, in accordance with treatment concepts and A.A. traditions, 2) development of qualifications and standards for the hiring of alcoholism counselors who were recovering in A.A., 3) building bridges of cooperation between the ARC and the A.A. community, and 4) developing an A.A. volunteer program.[270]

Alcoholism treatment services at the hospital increased during the planning and construction of the new facility. In 1966, an eight-bed detoxification unit was established on the eighth floor of the main hospital. This unit provided inpatient treatment services until the rehabilitation center was opened on St. Patrick's Day, 1969. The hospital unit continued to serve as a detoxification and intake unit after the ARC was opened. The newly christened Alcoholism Treatment Center (ATC) opened with 30 beds, was expanded to 50 beds, and then grew to 74 beds, all during the first year. It expanded to 94 beds in 1978, at the same time a new detox unit was opened that allowed patients to be admitted directly to the ATC.

Early Influences

Four distinct influences shaped the early evolution of alcoholism treatment at Lutheran General Hospital. The first influence was the American Lutheran Church's exploration of its mission in serving those injured by alcoholism. At the staff level, Drs. Norstad and Nesset, and Lutheran clergy such as Rev. John Keller and Rev. Carl Anderson, helped evolve and actualize a philosophy of "human ecology" that shaped the treatment of the alcoholic as a whole person in relationship with God, family, and society. The second influence was the rich Minnesota experience of Bradley, Rossi, and Keller. The imprint of Willmar State Hospital, Hazelden, and Pioneer House are all evident in what unfolded in Park Ridge. A third influence was that of Jim M., who brought deep roots in A.A., East-coast treatment experience, and experience working in Canada with the likes of E.M. Jellinek and Milton Maxwell. A fourth influence was the incorporation of people with Al-Anon experience into the treatment milieu—a move that both shaped the treatment of the alcoholic and ensured increasing acknowledgment of the needs of the family members surrounding the alcoholic. This unique mixture of influences unfolding in the environment of an acute care hospital were destined to speed the dissemination and evolution of the Minnesota Model of alcoholism treatment.

The Early Program

All clients were admitted to the hospital unit for detoxification and evaluation. During this stay, family members, friends, and employers were assembled to diminish the alcoholic's denial of his or her problem and to encourage the alcoholic to pursue extended treatment. Most clients went directly from this unit to a 28-day stay in the Alcoholism Treatment Center.

The goal of the team was to get each patient to accept four premises of alcoholism recovery: 1) "I have a problem with alcohol," 2) "My problem requires total abstinence from alcohol," 3) "I will need an ongoing program of help and support following treatment," and 4) "Help and support can best be found in Alcoholics Anonymous." All treatment activities were directed toward the infusion of these beliefs.

The residential treatment community was organized into treatment teams, each made up of approximately 24 patients and six staff members. The typical treatment day consisted of a morning community meeting (team meeting), two 30-minute lectures, one small-group therapy session per day, individual counseling, and assigned reading. A meeting of the entire treatment community was also held each Wednesday.[271] The lectures focused on concepts of recovery—but stopped short of being formal lectures on A.A.'s Twelve Steps. (This was to help distinguish the treatment experience from the A.A. experience.)

Patients also attended A.A. meetings and participated in informal discussions in the evening with A.A. volunteers. Three A.A. meetings per week were held on the grounds of the hospital facilities. A family conference was held at least once, and usually weekly. Prior to discharge, there was also an employer confer-

ence attended by the client and the client's workplace supervisor, employee assistance program (EAP) representative, and counselor. In this meeting, the client's prior performance problems were identified, information about alcoholism and recovery was provided, and mutual expectations were set regarding the client's return to work.

A system of overnight passes was used to phase the patient back into life outside the hospital—eight hours the first weekend, 12 hours the second weekend, and an overnight pass during the third weekend. Before leaving for the overnight pass, each client called the A.A. Central Office in Chicago and requested a Twelve-Step call during the time in which he or she would be home. This practice of home visits was stopped when insurance companies began to argue that, if patients were healthy enough to go on home visits, they were healthy enough to be discharged.

Recommendations for post-treatment support activities differed from client to client. During the early years, some clients were referred only to A.A. Most clients (and later, all clients) were expected to participate in weekly aftercare support groups led by staff members. The spouses of patients were also encouraged to attend these groups. After participating in three months of aftercare groups, patients were invited to participate in a "Bridge Group," to share their experiences with other patients and families who were currently in treatment.

In 1969, the program introduced the weekly Bridge Group, which brought together patients, family members, A.A. members, employee assistance counselors, and company supervisors. The large numbers of people arriving for Bridge Group were quickly sorted out to ensure a diverse mixture by gender, age, and recovery background. Each Bridge Group was led by a counselor. As many as nine groups at a time met simultaneously on Friday afternoons. Jim M. explained the origin of this innovation and the kind of dynamic experimentation that went on during these years.

> Bridge Group was a necessity. The demands for our time were so great and there were so few of us, we had to find a way to respond. We decided to bring them all together in this therapeutic stew....[272] What was needed was a vehicle to get more commitment in the areas most affected: home and work. Then, why not just families, employers, patients and staff? This was very good, but still not comprehensive

*enough. Why not former patients to tell
what it's like to live dry in a wet world?
Why not A.A. and Al-Anon, too? Both of
these have the highest track records! But
ALL of this mixed together? Impossible!
Madness! Who could possibly support that?
Why, it's like a circus! It will be a fiasco!
O.K., let's try it and see.*[273]

Referrals to Lutheran General came from a growing cadre of A.A. volunteers, from an ever-expanding group of grateful former patients, and from growing numbers of employee assistance professionals working in business and industry. Companies like Caterpillar constituted a virtual pipeline through which alcoholic employees were sent to Lutheran General. The center was always full, with a waiting list for admission that held up to 100 names.

The cost of treatment during this early period was $69 a day—a cost that a growing number of insurance companies were covering, first under a psychiatric diagnosis and later under the diagnosis of alcoholism.

While the centerpiece of Lutheran General's treatment of alcoholism was its 28-day rehabilitation program, there was an early effort to develop outpatient services. An attempt to initiate an intensive outpatient (IOP) treatment model in the late 1970s was met with interesting resistance in light of more recent history. When Lutheran General first tried to sell the IOP model of treatment to EAP representatives from business and industry (many of whom had themselves been treated for alcoholism in an inpatient setting), the hospital encountered almost uniform opposition. EAP representatives at this time feared that the IOP model was "watering down" treatment in ways that were likely to lower success rates. There was also an almost uniform financial bias against outpatient treatment. At that time insurance companies would pay 100% of inpatient, but only 50% of outpatient treatment. The bias toward inpatient services was both internally and externally reinforced.

Contrasts Between Lutheran General and Hazelden

There was a considerable cross-fertilization of ideas and methods among some of the early programs in the Midwest during the 1960s, particularly among Lutheran General, Hazelden, and the DePaul Rehabilitation Center in Milwaukee. There was also periodic contact with Eagleville and Chit Chat on the East Coast, Martha Washington and Grant Hospitals in Chicago, and the Keeley Institute in Dwight. But there was a very special relationship between Lutheran General and Hazelden. Lutheran General and Hazelden held annual meetings of key staff to exchange ideas and had a formal program of staff exchange, through which individual staff members from one facility worked for a period of time at the other. These exchanges contributed to the evolution of both programs and to many shared characteristics. However, there were some differences between the two programs during the 1960s and early 1970s. The following discussion depicts how those differences were perceived by those working at Lutheran General.

Lutheran General was committed to hospital-based, medically oriented alcoholism treatment, believing that the long-range solution to alcoholism was its treatment by physicians in the mainstream health-care system. Nelson Bradley's position was clear: Alcoholism is a disease and its treatment should be in the mainstream of medical and psychiatric care. As a result, the Lutheran General team had a distinctly medical orientation. Alcoholics admitted to treatment were called "patients," and physicians, nurses, and nurse-clinicians played central roles in the interdisciplinary team. In contrast, Hazelden's staff was quite non-medical in its orientation. While both programs embraced the importance of A.A. spirituality in the recovery process, Lutheran General strove to complement this dimension with concepts and practices from medicine and psychiatry.

While both programs utilized recovered people as counselors, Lutheran General pioneered the additional role of "nurse clinician"—a synthesis of medicine and counseling. Where Hazelden advocated a multidisciplinary team (multiple disciplines with clearly defined roles), Lutheran General utilized an "interdisciplinary team" (multiple disciplines with a high degree of interchangeability of roles and a flattening of the traditional professional "pecking order"). Hazelden counselors were all recovered, with chaplains, social workers, and psychologists serving as specialist consultants to the counselor teams. The counselors at Lutheran General Hospital included people who were and were not in personal recovery from alcoholism, with chaplains and social workers serving as counselors first and specialists second.

Where Hazelden at this time was adamantly opposed to co-ed treatment, Lutheran General advocated treating men and women together. Where the role of alcoholism counselor at Hazelden focused on the sharing of one's story and on A.A. indoctrination, the role at Lutheran General was "professionalized," with discouragement of counselor self-disclosure as the primary medium of client education. The expectation to complete A.A.'s Fourth and Fifth Steps before discharge was almost inviolate at Hazelden, whereas Lutheran General took a more voluntary approach to Step work and emphasized that the Fourth and Fifth Steps had to be done within the framework of A.A., rather than in the framework of treatment. Where Hazelden's use of a clinical technique called the "hot seat" was almost legendary among patients, Lutheran General eschewed use of this particular technique. Where Hazelden had a clear anti-medication bias, Bradley advocated the selective use of anti-depressants, Lithium, and anti-psychotic medications.

In spite of differences that evolved, the relationship between Hazelden and Lutheran General during the 1960s and 1970s was one of mutual respect and support. As one former Lutheran General staffer noted:

> *There was little sense of competition in those early years. There was real affection for one another and a sense of shared mission. The move toward isolation and competition didn't arrive until the 1980s.*

This cooperation did not diminish the feeling in Lutheran General that treatment as a "professional" venture was being born and pushed into maturity in Illinois. The combination of hospital-based treatment; a medically based interdisciplinary team; the professionalization of the role of the alcoholism counselor; the integration of psychologists, social workers, and clergy; and the formal organization of A.A. and Al-Anon volunteers all contributed to a sense that something original and special was unfolding at Lutheran General—and that everyone had an important role to play in it.

The Treatment Team

At Lutheran General, mixing traditional medical professions and non-traditional (non-degreed alcoholism counselor) roles was not without its strains. There was much early posturing between "professionals" and "paraprofessionals"—the latter a term that Jim M. considered a derogatory slur. Everyone had to get used to the new role expectations in this team concept. One nurse noted of this period:

> *I was absolutely floored! Coming from psychiatry, I was particularly struck by the flattening of the usual hospital hierarchy. Seeing recovering alcoholics relate as equals to psychiatrists was a shock to someone like myself trained within the traditional medical hierarchy.*

Several interdisciplinary teams were assigned to work with subgroups of the 74-94 patients who were in residence at any point in time. Each team consisted of a team leader (who could be drawn from any discipline), a nurse, a nurse clinician, a counselor/pastor, and an alcoholism counselor. All teams usually represented a mix of people with and without personal alcoholism recovery experience. Each patient was assigned a primary counselor, and each patient was staffed by the whole team at least twice during his or her stay.

The Role of the Alcoholism Counselor

The role of the alcoholism counselor became more fully professionalized through the influence of many people, but Jim M. exerted a profound influence on how this role was defined at Lutheran General. He extended this influence nationally through his presentations at Rutgers and the other summer schools for alcoholism counselors and through his professional writing. He was particularly concerned about what were then called "two-hat" issues—the clear delineation between one's personal recovery activities in a Twelve-Step program and one's professional activities as an alcoholism counselor. In his view, the clear delineation of these two roles served to protect the client AND the counselor. Jim described the potential for strain in this dual affiliation as follows.

> *While there is a real need for AA members on treatment teams, they have to take care not to use their AA affiliation to foster their professional career lest their AA membership suffer. On the other hand, to safeguard their professional career, they must not use it to enhance their AA status.*[274]

Jim M. consistently posited that there were differences between what he called "bread-and-butter counseling" and Twelfth-Step work. It was his position that alcoholism counselors were hired as professional counselors, rather than as professional mouthpieces of A.A. philosophy. Treatment programs and their staff, in this view, should never perform A.A. functions. One counselor who worked under Jim M. remembers his pointedly declaring:

> *This hospital is paying you for your counseling skills—not your A.A. work. Your A.A. work is not for sale—patients can have that*

for free—but only within the framework of A.A. Professional counseling is not 12-Step work and if it is, you are violating the canons of counseling and the traditions of A.A.[275]

Personal self-disclosure by the alcoholism counselor was not prohibited, but it was discouraged, especially when the counselor was new or in training, because it usually indicated a shift in "hats"—a shift thought likely to indicate more about the insecurities of the counselor than about the immediate needs of the patient. Self-disclosure was viewed as an effective tool, but a tool that required an increased level of clinical sophistication. Jim M., noting how this position later became a rigid prohibition on counselor self-disclosure, reflected back on his stance on this issue.

I wasn't trying to prohibit self-disclosure; I was merely trying to influence the clinical circumstances under which it should occur. My position was simple and clear: disclose only if it serves a purpose with the client.[276]

Counselors and other staff took great pride in the fact that clients could not figure out which counselors were recovered and which were not. Perhaps they took equal pride in the fact that alcoholism counselors—recovered and non-recovered—were paid on the same salary scale.[277]

The parity of salary was accompanied by high standards for those coming out of recovery backgrounds into alcoholism counseling. Where other programs were organizing training and internship programs that could be entered directly following completion of one's treatment, Lutheran General required five years' stable recovery as a qualification for being hired.

My position was clear and inflexible. I didn't want counselors working out their personal problems on my payroll. I wanted at least five years of sobriety, regardless of how much education they had. They had to have enough maturity to grasp the spiritual nature of recovery and to assure that the focus would stay on the client and not shift to themselves.[278]

Senior staff at Lutheran General were sticklers for counselor supervision and self-care. All alcoholism counselors were expected to attend weekly Twelve-Step meetings—A.A. for those who were

recovering and open A.A. and Al-Anon meetings for those individuals who were not in alcoholism recovery. During the early years, recovered counselors also met together twice a week for training and supervision, as did separate groups of social workers and staff with Al-Anon backgrounds. Many former staffers report that the most intense training and supervision they received in their entire career occurred during these sessions.

The A.A./Treatment Center Relationship

Jim M. had a unique vision of the relationship between A.A. and what he intuitively knew was going to become a treatment "industry." He worked to construct that relationship in a way that eliminated competition and strengthened both treatment and A.A. He used two key methods in actualizing that vision: the extensive involvement of A.A. members in the treatment milieu and the professionalization of the role of alcoholism counselor.

When I first came to Chicago, there was great hostility within the A.A. community toward anyone in the program who was working professionally in the field. I had to find ways to bring them in to see what treatment was really all about. We did this through recruitment of A.A. members into our volunteer programs and our open invitation for A.A. members to attend our Bridge Groups. We converted a lot of die-hard disbelievers in treatment through these activities.[279]

Initially, building a relationship between the new treatment center and the A.A. community was fraught with obstacles, most springing from the alcoholic's historical exclusion from hospital care and the common feeling among A.A. members that their own care had often been mishandled by psychiatrists. These obstacles were overcome by visibly showcasing the A.A.-friendly nature of the Center's treatment philosophy and by heavily involving A.A. members in the treatment process.

There was an extensive use of A.A. volunteers. Volunteers were rigorously screened for length of sobriety (1 year required), knowledge of A.A. literature, and indicators of an active program of personal recovery—meeting attendance, sponsorship, and completion of Fourth and Fifth Steps. Three A.A. volunteers were present each night, and two stayed over at the facility. A.A. volunteers were an essential element in the chemistry of this milieu. These volunteers were also used to transport clients to outside A.A. meetings. By 1974, more than 200 A.A. volunteers were providing almost 10,000 hours of service per year at Lutheran General.[280] By using only volunteers with well established sobriety and mainstream A.A. involvement, and by having each client make direct contact with A.A. to solicit a Twelfth-Step call, Lutheran General legitimized A.A. and built a strong working partnership with A.A.

Al-Anon and Family Programming

An original goal was to have family members live in apartments above Lutheran General's ATC so that they could fully participate in treatment, but these plans were abandoned when insurance companies refused to pay for the extra expense that would have been incurred. In spite of this setback, efforts to increase family involvement in treatment at Lutheran General continued through the early years.

An early "family night" program consisted of a lecture/discussion group. In 1978, a half-day Saturday program using Al-Anon volunteers was added, and in 1979 a formal Family Treatment Program was implemented, consisting of a three-day off-site residential retreat. Later iterations included a residential weekend model. Lutheran General's response to the families of alcoholics had two phases. The first phase was to seek family involvement because of the ways in which they could enrich the alcoholic's treatment experience. The second phase, which began to emerge in the mid-1970s, was the recognition that family members needed and deserved treatment and support services in their own right.

A key source of family advocacy was the staff hired to work in the ATC who had extensive prior Al-Anon experience. The initiation of a formal alcoholism counselor-training program increased the involvement of Al-Anon members in the ATC. A.A. and Al-Anon members, many of them volunteers, enrolled in the training program and formed a pool from which new counselors could be hired. Of the recovered people (A.A. and Al-Anon) whom Lutheran General considered for this training program, only those whose recovery was judged to be active and enduring were accepted.

As the number of people with Al-Anon experience and a family-oriented perspective on alcoholism recovery increased at Lutheran General, these perspectives became integrated into Lutheran General's clinical, training, and public education programs.

Early Diversification

During the 1970s, Lutheran General's ATC diversified its offered services. The new services were perceived as logical extensions of the ATC's focus on alcoholism treatment. The earlier-noted alcoholism counselor-training program was initiated in 1971. This program involved students in a full-time (40 hours per week), 9-12-month program of classes and supervised clinical work, all of which took place in the milieu of the treatment unit. In the ATC's 12 years of operation, more than 120 people from more than ten states and six countries were trained in this program. A formal community alcoholism-education program was also initiated in 1976 under a three-year grant to Lutheran General from private foundations.

Employee assistance services were initiated for companies that referred employees to the treatment center. These services, initiated by Betty Reddy, were the embryo of an EAP division, later headed by Dr. Jack Clairno. EAP services grew out of Lutheran General's practice of attempting to involve every alcoholic's workplace supervisor in his or her treatment. The growing relationship between the hospital and the major employers in the Midwest led to efforts to help these companies formalize their efforts to intervene with alcohol-impaired employees.

Other early innovations included the development of an independent living program established through the acquisition of two 12-unit apartment buildings and the development of specialized screening services for people arrested for driving under the influence. A formal Clinical Pastoral Education program, through which ministers could learn about alcoholism as part of their pastoral counseling training, was also initiated during the early years. What characterized all of these areas of expansion was that they were natural outgrowths of the Center's specialized expertise on alcoholism. And they grew out of four areas of activity that were visualized when the ATC building opened in 1969: Alcoholism treatment, research, education and training.

Evaluation Research

A review of the early history of alcoholism treatment at Lutheran General Hospital would be incomplete without some reference to the role of research. Dr. Jean Rossi believed that clinical research should drive the evolution of the ATC's alcoholism treatment protocol. To that end, he hired Dr. William Filstead in 1969 to conduct treatment outcome studies for Lutheran General. The overall goals of the research services were to determine how and why people developed addiction problems, to delineate the clinical subpopulations of clients seeking treatment, to determine what types of services were effective with these subpopulations, and to elucidate the process of long-term addiction recovery.[281] Filstead's client follow-up studies confirmed, among other things, that clients who followed residential treatment with outpatient counseling and A.A. affiliation were much more likely to be abstinent at follow-up than clients who completed residential treatment but pursued no ongoing sobriety-based support structures.[282]

Model Dissemination

During the 1970s Lutheran General played a significant role in the refinement, evolution, and dissemination of the Minnesota Model of alcoholism treatment throughout the United States. Prior to the formation of Parkside and the creation of a national system of treatment centers, the mechanisms for this dissemination were many. First, Lutheran General established a three-to-four-day residential observer program, through which people wishing to organize or improve treatment services could get a detailed indoctrination into Lutheran General's philosophy and treatment methods. Alcoholism professionals from all over the United States who were planning to open alcoholism treatment programs came to Park Ridge (as they did to Center City, Minnesota) and studied the treatment methods being used. Two consulting teams (Bradley and Jim M., and Rossi and Keller) were also organized to provide on-site consultation for new programs.

Other mechanisms by which Lutheran General's methods of treating alcoholism were disseminated included the formal training program; the involvement of Lutheran General staff in regional and national addiction conferences; and the authorship of many pamphlets and professional papers and three books that contained descriptions of the ATC: *The Therapeutic Community* (1973), *Alcohol and Alcohol Problems: New Thinking and New Directions* (1976), and *Perspectives on the Treatment of Alcoholism* (1978). Other texts, authored by John Keller, were written to help pastors counsel alcoholics and their family members. A less visible but equally significant form of diffusion was the spread of the Lutheran General approach to alcoholism treatment through informal communications shared by staff and former patients at regional and national A.A. conferences.

Model-dissemination activities at Lutheran General Hospital in the 1970s were marked by an almost religiously fervent belief, a sense of pioneering uniqueness, and a deep appreciation for the spiritual nature of the work that was being carried forward. The clear sense of mission and interpersonal chemistry in the ATC during the 1970s generated a feeling of excitement that could infect the most jaded professional and the most resistant clients. Former employees speak in glowing terms of the warm camaraderie and sense of destiny that permeated the organizational atmosphere during those early years.

Those years were not without growing pains. There were periods of strain and conflict even before the period of rapid expansion. And there were key changes in personnel that set the stage for even more significant changes. Bradley, Rossi, Keller, and Jim M. all left Lutheran General in the 1970s. New directions were perhaps inevitable.

Explosive Growth

Two entrepreneurial spirits, George Caldwell and Bill Mueller, influenced Lutheran General's shift from a local to a national alcoholism treatment vision. Caldwell assumed leadership of Lutheran General Hospital in 1979, believing that church-affiliated hospitals could not survive the coming decades without expansion, diversification, and increased clinical sophistication. In 1980, Bill Mueller brought to Lutheran General a marketing and business perspective honed in his years as a head of the International Division of the Arthur Anderson consulting firm. Together, Caldwell and Mueller forged a vision of taking what had been learned at Lutheran General's Alcoholism Treatment Center and franchising it throughout the United States The vehicle that was to drive this expansion was a new corporate entity: Parkside Management Services (PMS). PMS was established in July, 1980 as a for-profit corporation affiliated with Lutheran General Health Care System. Another entity, the Parkside Foundation, was created to oversee the management of PMS. The rationale for this change in status to for-profit was that Parkside would be able to operate across state lines and generate profits that would support Lutheran General Hospital.[283]

While PMS began to pursue its expansionist vision, the original treatment unit in Park Ridge, Illinois continued to operate as a not-for-profit corporation under the name Lutheran Center for Substance Abuse (LCSA). Bill Mueller headed PMS, John Keller was recruited back to serve as President of the

Lutheran Center for Substance Abuse, and Orville McElfresh served as Vice President of Clinical Services of LCSA. Then in 1981, Parkside Management Services changed its name to Parkside Medical Services Corporation—a change that reflected its intent to own as well as manage treatment units. The seed money to launch this move into the national arena came from a loan from Lutheran General Health Care System.

In order to replicate itself, Parkside had to define its model of treatment precisely—had to define the Parkside "product." As in most treatment programs of that era, most of the knowledge about how treatment was really accomplished existed primarily as oral history. Bill Mueller created a franchisable model of treatment by persuading key staff, under the direction of Kathy Leck, to put the philosophy of human ecology and every idea, every technique, every policy, and every procedure down on paper. These documents became the vehicles that made rapid replication of the model possible.

In 1981, Parkside purchased a facility in Mundelein, Illinois and started a free-standing residential program that included treatment services for youth. Management contracts, through which Parkside operated inpatient alcoholism units inside general hospitals, began with the first such unit in Hoisington, Kansas. As these contracts increased in number, a new approach to system expansion was added in 1982 and 1983, an approach that came to dominate Parkside's approach to growth.

The new vision was clear. Parkside would not just manage treatment units; it would own them. The expansion became intoxicating in its speed. Parkside first purchased treatment programs in Wisconsin and Colorado, and then in 1986 purchased Brookwood Recovery Centers—a chain of 11 addiction treatment facilities operating in Texas, Alabama, Georgia, Florida, and Ohio. With this purchase, Parkside owned and operated more free-standing addiction treatment facilities than anyone in the country. The buying continued. Parkside purchased the Phoenix Company—a chain of 12 treatment programs in California—in 1987. This was followed by the purchase of 30 program-management contracts from CompCare, and the 1988 purchase of Monarch Health Systems' chain of 20 psychiatric programs. Somewhere in this buying frenzy, Parkside also paid $1 million for a smoking-cessation program and purchased the Cokeenders program.

In the midst of these expansions, the original ATC (now the LCSA), while technically retaining its independence, increasingly came under the control of Bill Mueller and PMS. LCSA went through several transitions in leadership: John Keller from 1980 to 1983, Orville McElfresh from 1983 to 1984, and Carl Anderson from 1984 to 1986. In 1986, LCSA changed its name to Parkside Lutheran Hospital, reflecting its full incorporation into the Parkside System.

At the beginning of the expansionist phase (1980), Lutheran General operated a treatment system with a static treatment capacity of 94 beds. A decade later, Parkside Medical Services Corporation had a static treatment capacity of more than 2,000 beds. It owned more than 30 programs, had management contracts to operate 40 others, and delivered addiction treatment services in more than 100 sites scattered across 20 states. In the peak years of 1985 through 1989, annual revenues exceeded $220 million. The company had evolved from a small core staff at Lutheran General Hospital to a corporation that employed more than 2,500 employees.

An expanding administrative structure was required to support the growing Parkside empire. This structure included corporate offices in Illinois, Massachusetts, and California; trainers to indoctrinate staff hired at new sites; "float counselors" who could move from location to location, filling in temporary vacancies; and marketing staff to ensure a high utilization of services. Corporate staff grew from a handful of people to more than 125. At the organization's peak, more than 75 full-time marketing staff worked for Parkside. As this structure grew, overhead costs escalated, and the low daily rates that had been a hallmark of the early program began to rise.

Parkside took particular care in instructing staff from newly acquired programs in the Parkside philosophy. All such staff were brought to "Mecca" (Park Ridge) for seven days of Parkside indoctrination and team building, and some stayed on for three months before returning to assume their new roles.

> *It was like a week-long pep rally for Parkside. You left feeling like the luckiest person on earth to be working for Parkside. You caught the bug—the passion, the commitment. It was the most well-orchestrated process of team building I've experienced in all my career.*

As expansion speeded up, the original three-month training period for key staff from the new sites was reduced to six weeks. Eventually four training sites were established in Illinois, Colorado, Texas, and Connecticut.

While there was a recognition at the highest levels that there would be trade-offs in trying to franchise nationally a highly successful local treatment program, every effort was made to maintain the integrity of the original as it was replicated. Some of these efforts at quality assurance were quite unique.

We did everything we could to make sure that our clinical philosophy and our focus on the patient permeated the programs we acquired. We hired a cadre of program consultants that we used to infuse the Parkside philosophy into new treatment sites. These clinical experts—first two and eventually 13—generated no income. Their whole focus was to make sure the patient came first—to carry our highest clinical standards throughout the Parkside system. We performed semi-annual audits of the philosophy and clinical services in every treatment facility and program.

Parkside's growth did not stop at the borders of the United States. Bill Mueller believed that there existed great potential in the franchising of alcoholism treatment internationally, if a European ally could be found to help market such services. The foundation for such a project was laid through a joint-ventured treatment effort involving Parkside and a Swedish program, Provita. Parkside consultants helped Provita set up a clinical program that is still operating successfully today.

This period of explosive growth seemed natural in the overall business climate of the 1980s. Parkside operated in a broader economic environment caught up in a frenzy of leveraged buy-outs, mergers, sales and acquisitions, and the successful franchising of nearly every conceivable product and service. Parkside also operated in an arena of private addiction treatment that during the early expansion was also characterized by great success and profitability. In fact, Parkside viewed its own business strategy as rather conservative in comparison to that of its primary competitor during this period, CompCare.

Later Diversification

Parkside's initial growth involved the geographical expansion of its historical mission of providing alcoholism treatment. By the mid-1980s, Parkside had extended its service focus to encompass other drug addictions via cocaine-specific treatment programs and smoking-cessation programs. It had expanded its area of claimed expertise to the provision of addiction treatment services for special populations (adolescents, women, the elderly, gays and lesbians, people with dual diagnoses, and impaired professionals). And it had initiated specialized tracks for codependency treatment and for treatment of adult children of alcoholics.

During the 1980s Parkside expanded its activities in research, EAP, training, community education, family intervention, and the development of intervention teams in religious congregations. A particularly innovative approach to working with churches was developed during this period. Sister Therese Golden and Rev. Jerry Wagenknecht traveled throughout the United States organizing and training intervention teams in congregations and religious communities. This process involved training pastors, recruiting and training core alcoholism intervention teams in congregations, developing congregation covenant statements (pledging "God's loving compassion to all who are wounded by alcohol and drug addiction."), and linking impaired church members with treatment and self-help resources.

Parkside also expanded beyond the provision of treatment services. One such area of expansion involved its emergence as a publisher. In 1986, John Small was recruited into Parkside to head a newly created publishing division. The primary focus of this division was to publish and distribute literature and tapes for recovering people and their family members. The first mail-order catalogue was distributed in 1987, and the publishing of original works began in 1988. During the peak years of 1990 and 1991, annual publication sales approached $1 million.

While many of these activities seemed a natural step in the evolution of the Lutheran ATC's original mission, they showed a progressive extension of Parkside's boundaries of expertise beyond the arena of alcoholism treatment. During the 1980s, diversification moved Parkside into the operation of psychiatric and eating- disorder programs.

The Demise

The earliest sign of trouble in Parkside's long-term investment in residential and inpatient services appeared in the area of adolescent services. By 1986, Parkside was having difficulty filling its adolescent beds, in the face of growing competition from newly created adolescent psychiatric and addiction treatment programs. Managed care was also beginning to erode the daily census in many Parkside facilities, and this effect intensified during 1989. Daily census in Parkside units dropped as admissions were denied, treatment stays were shortened, and more patients were forcibly channeled into outpatient treatment. Parkside opened 19 outpatient clinics in one year in order to stay abreast of this trend, but problems of income generation caused many of those clinics to close.

In the meantime, as the frenzied acquisition of inpatient programs continued and revenues declined, debt management became a problem of nightmarish proportions. Declining income from inpatient services and new fledgling outpatient programs could not support corporate overhead.   Yet the expansion continued. Some attribute this continuation to the forceful personality of Bill Mueller and his assertion that good programs would survive, and others cite collective denial in the Parkside management culture.

As incredible as it may sound, there were continuing commitments to build or buy new units during this same period. There was incredible denial of what was unfolding. We really believed that managed care was going to be a passing phase and that Parkside would emerge as the dominant survivor.

Parkside continued to invest in inpatient and residential beds at a time in which managed care was pushing the whole treatment field toward outpatient modalities—something we now know in retrospect. While minority voices offered warnings about Parkside's continued acquisition of beds, these voices were not heeded. As lengths of stay began to shorten and patient census at Parkside facilities plummeted (as they did in other hospital-based and private programs across the country), Parkside became particularly reliant on key referral sources that sustained their margin of profitability. For some time, the Canadian government had paid to have many Canadian alcoholics treated in the U.S. Parkside had an arrangement with Crossroads, a Canadian broker in Toronto, which screened patients, arranged for transportation and customs clearance to fly them to Parkside facilities, then conducted aftercare on patients after they returned to Canada. By the summer of 1990, Canadian patients made up as much as 50% of clients in treatment at some Parkside facilities. But in 1991, the Canadian government changed its reimbursement policy, bringing about a precipitous drop in census at Parkside treatment facilities. The Canadian decision was described by one staffer as "one more nail in the coffin."

The closing of smaller, poorly performing units in the Parkside system began in 1988. Staff at these local sites were offered positions in other Parkside facilities, and no corporate staff cuts occurred during this first phase of downsizing. Some other units, such as Chicago's Lincoln Park unit, were closed when the financially strapped hospitals in which they were located closed. As the treatment units shrank in size and number, the corporate resources needed to support these units also declined. In the Fall of 1989, the first major staff layoff affected more than half of Parkside's clinical consultants to local programs. Later layoffs in 1992 and 1993 touched all corporate locations and divisions.

Bill Mueller and George Caldwell, the driving forces behind the expansionist period at Parkside, both left in 1989. Other changes in key positions also took place during this period.   Parkside's Mundelein program went through three executive directors in three years, and some long-term staff chose to leave. Staff layoffs, the voluntary exit of key staff, and the daily erosion of patient census in Parkside facilities all signaled that something had gone wrong with the Parkside dream.   There was a growing sense of impending doom.

We were losing status in the eyes of our patrons: the larger hospital and the Lutheran Church. We were no longer money-makers and a unit that brought great recognition. New leaders who had not been part of our historical mission became dissatisfied and impatient and saw us as a drain rather than a resource.

By 1993, the relationship between Parkside and the Lutheran General Health Care System had become a quite ambivalent one. On one hand, Lutheran Health Care wanted Parkside to survive because alcoholism treatment had been such a visible part of the hospital's historical mission. But then there was Parkside's deteriorating financial condition. Parkside had gone from a profitable cost center, to a center with a blank check for expansion, to a cost center plagued by debt and declining revenues.

While this decline was unfolding, a new CEO of Lutheran Health Care launched a visioning process in which Lutheran Health Care redefined its niche from that of a national to a regional health-care provider. Under this new vision, cost centers that were doing national work were held to a greater level of accountability. Such cost centers had to justify how their work would enhance rather than drain resources away from this regional vision. It became progressively evident that Lutheran Health Care could no longer support Parkside. The Board decided to draw back into a Chicago-regional niche. This position was based on the board's view that, with the advent of managed care, substance-abuse treatment—and behavioral-health care in general—had a very bleak future. As financial problems worsened ($13 million in operating losses reported in FY 1990), Parkside announced in November, 1990 that 11 of the 22 centers it owned and operated would be closed.[284] This was followed by a later announcement that all of the out-of-state programs owned by Parkside would be sold and that the Chicago-area treatment services—as well as the contracts to manage other treatment units and research and publishing operations—would be continued under the auspices of Lutheran General Behavioral Health. By the Winter of 1993, most of the out-of-state properties had been sold.

These public announcements further escalated problems by discouraging referral sources and creating for potential buyers the image of a corporation bailing out of a rapidly eroding industry. The selling price of addiction treatment units plummeted to the point where some programs around the country were sold for half of their construction costs.

Wholesale layoffs occurred in 1993, and by the end of the year the Parkside Medical Services Corporation had ceased to exist. Parkside's primary asset—the management contracts to operate treatment units—was sold to a former employee, Mike McCarthy. With the aid of two other former senior Parkside managers, David Cushing and Bob Clapp, McCarthy took over existing contracts to operate hospital-based treatment units. Along with the rights to these contracts came continued use of the Parkside name. In 1995, "The Parkside Company" sold its contracts to operate addiction and psychiatric programs to another company, which was in turn sold to Horizon in 1996. Although it continues to exist, that company is not involved in the provision of addiction treatment services.

What had been the national network of Parkside treatment programs was now collapsed into Lutheran General Behavioral Health—an organizational entity created in 1992 to refocus the Chicago-based addiction services. Within this new entity, there was a struggle over whether the historical Parkside personnel or the psychiatry department would take the lead in directing local behavioral-health services. The hospital's decision was to place the original treatment facility under the direction of the Department of Psychiatry. Today, outpatient alcoholism counseling and recovery-home services are still offered at the West Pavilion in Park Ridge. This facility, which used to house the 94-bed residential alcoholism treatment center, is now the primary home of a Cancer Care unit. Detoxification services were moved back to the main hospital. At the Mundelein facility, residential services were phased out and replaced by outpatient youth and adult services. That facility was sold in the summer of 1995. Mundelein's outpatient services were first moved to Vernon Hills, then closed in 1996. Parkside's DuPage facility was given a year to make it on its own and was then closed and sold. Parkside's publishing division, which had risen to the second largest publisher of alcoholism-related materials, was also kept in the Lutheran system for a year, then sold to Hazelden. Internal activities of the research division of Parkside Medical Services decreased with the downsizing of the treatment system, and in the fall of 1993 Bill Filstead left, effectively ending the research activities of the Parkside Corporation.

Lessons and Legacies

The Parkside story is surely one pregnant with lessons for the addictions treatment field, yet we may find ourselves still too close to extract such lessons accurately. To bring this most remarkable story to closure, I have chosen to rely primarily upon the lessons claimed by people who experienced the Parkside story from the inside. Outlined below are the most prominent responses that former Parkside staff gave to my questions: 1) "How do you explain what happened to Parkside?" and 2) "What are the lessons and legacies of Parkside?" There is no claim that what follows is objective history, but as Churchill has suggested, sometimes we must begin to tell the tale even if all we have is rumor. I will leave it to the reader to sort through the differences between the objective realities and the subjective, or perceived, realities contained in these reports. When key individuals who participated in the Lutheran General/Parkside history were prodded to extract from their experience lessons for the field, they were unanimous in organizing their comments by different time-periods of this history. All spoke glowingly of the early history, and all began with the core philosophy.

> *The Lutheran/Parkside legacy is the miracle of personal transformation that can unfold within a therapeutic milieu—this challenging, magical, wonderful, spiritual mystery through which deformed bodies and spirits enter this milieu and emerge with the potential for wellness and wholeness. The first legacy is about the transformative power*

that can be generated when the diverse elements of this milieu get intensely focused on suffering alcoholics and their family members.

The emotionally effusive praise for what the clinical program of Lutheran General-Parkside was able to achieve made the subsequent organizational problems even more painful to bear. As one staff person noted:

Parkside's legacy is bittersweet. First, there is the incredible legacy of what the "wounded healers"—the recovering alcoholics and recovering family members—were able to bring to this program. There is the sheer enthusiasm and raw optimism about recovery that permeated Parkside's early history. There are the thousands of patients and their families whose lives were touched by this program and an untold number of counselors still practicing today who continue to use elements of this treatment approach. The bitter part of the legacy is that an institution that was so instrumental in birthing the modern treatment movement got side-tracked and lost. The knowledge that what remains of this empire is a small unit under the wing of the Department of Psychiatry is almost more than my heart can bear. I hope we can figure out how to extract the lessons from this tragedy.

When informants were pushed to extract lessons from the Lutheran-Parkside history, they offered highly contradictory perceptions of the organization and its decline. Such perceptions were often determined by the part of the system in which the individual worked.   Such discrepancies reveal that two cultures existed: a Parkside corporate culture and the culture of the treatment units themselves. The reader should keep the existence of these two worlds in mind in reviewing some of the following staff comments, which sometimes read like descriptions of two radically different organizations.

Most of those interviewed by the author attributed the demise of Parkside to a combination of three factors.

The first and most significant set of factors that contributed to Parkside's demise as a national treatment system was composed of the company's business practices. Former Parkside staff, interviewed between 1995 and 1997, noted errors in judgement related to an expansion strategy that focused on the acquisition of beds, errors in the selection of programs, and errors in the exorbitant prices paid for some acquisitions. Nearly all of the people interviewed commented on the flaws in an expansionist strategy tied to the acquisition and centralized management of existing inpatient programs. Carl Anderson offered the following perspective.

A fatally flawed business plan was implemented in the early 80's that was based on the belief in a national market for a high-quality uniform approach to addiction treatment. This never materialized to any significant extent.   Referrals remained almost totally a local relationship....The horrendously expensive corporate overhead, and the corporate culture which emphasized centralized control and decision making, without a national market, simply added cost and, in some cases, sluggishness of response to local markets....Corporate restructuring was too little too late to change this problem significantly.

A second factor, the strategy of purchasing residential programs, was equally flawed. Anderson explained the error in that strategy:

The planned overinvestment in property and "beds" that had little value except as treatment centers was a grievous error. When these properties were devalued in the late 80's (some as much as 50% of the original purchase price), there simply was not enough cash flow to finance the debt.

The purchase of inpatient facilities continued, even while the census in inpatient program across the country eroded under the influence of managed care. This aggressive program of expansion was not atypical of the ways in which many businesses responded to the financial crises in the turbulent economic markets of the 1980s. But the strategy of aggressive acquisition that did work for some companies in the 1980s did not work for Parkside. This portion of our story has wide application. It reinforces the stakes that are involved in the financial strategies which support or fail to support addiction treatment agencies operating in an increasingly turbulent business and health-care environment. In the years surrounding Parkside's demise, some 40% of private treatment programs closed their doors. What made Parkside unique was that it was the largest and one of the oldest.

And finally, the internal redirection of the mission of Lutheran General Health Center from a national to a regional/local focus left Parkside without parental support for its mission of creating a national network of treatment centers. This, perhaps more than any other change, marked the end of the earlier vision of extending the local achievements in alcoholism treatment to a national level. While this could be considered a local story unique to Parkside and its relationship with Lutheran General Health Center, the changing philosophy of the latter reflected the diminished status of alcoholism treatment in the general health-care industry and within the broader culture.

When staff asked themselves how such fatal decisions could have been made, they were forced to reflect on aspects of the corporate culture of Parkside that might have contributed to its demise. There were internal changes in the organizational culture that undermined Parkside's resiliency. Comments from former staff sound a warning about the dangers that can accompany success. The problems that they articulated are presented here, not as a kind of organizational Fifth Step for Parkside, but as a way of illustrating the forces that were pervasive in addiction treatment organizations during this period. Most, but by no means all, of the former staff interviewed generally agreed that the following conditions may have helped set the stage for Parkside's later demise.

Dilution: A critical lesson in the Parkside history is that explosive growth can threaten the clinical integrity and success of a treatment program. This would seem an unlikely lesson to come from Parkside. Hundreds of programs have gone through dramatic growth, but few have ever approached such expansion as systematically as did Parkside. And yet respondents expressed concern about the dilution of the original Lutheran General treatment technology as it was widely disseminated through the Parkside expansion.

There just wasn't enough of our best and brightest to spread over that many programs. The whole thing became like soup watered down 20 times.

There is perhaps only a limited degree to which certain aspects of addiction treatment can be replicated. The chemistry of the original Lutheran General team was clearly not easy to replicate. The problem of dilution seems to have been exacerbated by:

- purchasing programs and retaining existing personnel whose treatment philosophies were incompatible with the Parkside philosophy;
- lowering standards for the hiring of counselors;
- staff turnover, particularly the exit of tenured staff; and
- role mismatches through which people with clinical training were making business decisions and people with business backgrounds were making clinical decisions.

Grandiosity: Former staff depicted a kind of elitism and "mania" that periodically permeated the corporate center of Parkside. At its best in the treatment units, it was a period of healthy pride and exhilaration. At its worst in the corporate culture of Parkside, it was a period of grandiosity that made it hard for those inside to question anything from Parkside's business philosophy to its internal policies and procedures. There was an almost euphoric feeling of destiny that Parkside would serve as the vehicle to spread the Lutheran General model of alcoholism treatment across the country.

It was a wonderful period in which it seemed we could do no wrong. People were getting well and everyone was praising what we were doing. We were always full, with a long waiting list of people waiting for admission. We just assumed this incredible foundation of success would be replicated all over the country.

The grandiosity that fueled the expansionist vision was the belief that we were the true disciples, that we alone possessed the secret of treatment, and that no one else was capable of doing it like we could. The demise began in the switch from "Let's search for the truth" to "We've got THE truth." It is hard to acknowledge that each of us got caught up in the elitism.

This grandiosity led to an unusual form of isolation. On one hand, the open collaboration that had marked the early years seemed to reverse itself during the expansion years. Replacing the mission to "give it away" was a preoccupation with not divulging Parkside's "proprietary technology." On the other hand, staff members were encouraged to serve as experts in their encounters with personnel from other programs. As one staffer described it:

It wasn't isolation in the usual sense: We were going to conferences and serving on committees and visiting other programs. It was isolation in the sense that our collaboration tended to be one way: What we could teach others, rather than what we could learn from others.

Other staff members offered a slightly different slant on this theme.

I don't feel grandiosity was a characteristic of the units, but certainly was a corporate culture characteristic. Many staff who were "promoted" to corporate status became quite impressed with their new "national" status, the traveling, and the business aura. But, this was not much different than other behavioral health companies of the '80s. In fact, I felt Parkside tempered theirs quite a bit with some healthy spiritual perspective.

The incredible success that Lutheran General had experienced in its alcoholism treatment efforts led to the belief that there was an unlimited number of areas to which this treatment technology could be successfully applied. Several staff members believed that this collective grandiosity contributed to a diversification into new areas—diversification that turned out to be a dilution of and a diversion from the Lutheran General ATC's historical mission.

The unrelenting optimism and passion that had been such a crucial element of Parkside's success in the arena of clinical operations became the Achilles heel of its business operations. One would assume that the early closing of some Parkside units would have stirred a major internal re-evaluation of Parkside's future, but several informants noted that these events were all explained away as temporary aberrations. Program failures were attributed to the idiosyncracies of locations or personnel, rather than recognized as symptoms of a flawed national strategy.

Distraction: In interviews with former Parkside employees, the resounding theme is that of the lost Parkside vision.

We became addicted to making the deal. We got caught up in the economic frenzy that was the 1980s. It was growth by acquisition of capacity, rather than by building utilization in response to real need. It was growth for growth's sake, with no market research to gauge whether the growth was

sustainable. We implicitly operated on the premises, "Residential treatment is needed; we provide it better than anyone; the business will always be there." The ego-fix of making the deal and growing as a company became more important than our product.

In these interviews, former staff could not help but suggest that Parkside had perhaps taken on some characteristics of its clients.

Once the acquisitions started, it became a kind of binge behavior that couldn't be brought back under conscious control. Given our addiction expertise, you would have thought we could have recognized this pattern.

We kept doing what was failing. It was like a repetition compulsion. It was pure addictive behavior. We got so caught up in the trappings of business that we forgot our mission.

Some former Parkside staff reported that the general atmosphere in Parkside slowly and subtly shifted from a clinical orientation to a business orientation, but others disagreed with this position. It seems that certain pockets (programs/individuals) maintained their clinical focus while, in the overall Parkside system, this clinical orientation was weakened by a new business orientation. Some of those interviewed believed that the emphasis on the individual client had shifted to an emphasis on the institutional client —responsiveness to the various referral sources that referred individuals to Parkside.

Insulation: Many former Parkside staff report that Parkside became insulated in a way that prevented market and clinical data from being utilized for self-correction of Parkside's management strategy. There seems to have been a fatal character flaw that did not allow Parkside to utilize either external or internal feedback regarding its business strategy. Warnings about this strategy were difficult to sound or to hear in the internal communications at Parkside.

When we asked, "Is this [flurry of acquisitions] crazy?" we were told that we didn't understand the big picture. People at the top didn't want to hear bad news. When the messengers started getting killed, no one told the truth.

Many of us [corporate staff] *who disagreed strongly with these decisions (especially during 1989-1991) could not do so publicly, and maybe we appeared to be supportive....I discovered when talking with LGH leadership in 1993 that many of us were seen by them as supporting a business plan and philosophy that we strongly disagreed with.*

A Lasting Legacy

There are many ways in which the fall of Parkside could be told. Parkside could be depicted as an innocent victim of shifting markets. Parkside could be depicted as a victim of poor business decisions by its leaders. Or the story of Parkside's fall could be told—as former staff tended to tell it—in terms of character defects that emerged in its own organizational culture. Some of the themes we have touched on in this are not unique to Parkside. They can be traced from the rise of the earliest treatment institutions into the present. Lutheran General/Parkside provided a rich vein of knowledge and experience that continues to be felt in many areas of the field today. As one former employee noted:

The company may be gone, but the best of that system—the core of its treatment—is not gone. Our people are everywhere, taking the best of what was Parkside to the far corners of the treatment industry. In spite of what happened to Parkside as a company, the simple message of Twelve-Step recovery continues to live among the former Parkside clients and staff.

As I constructed the dramatic growth of Parkside in the 1980s and the crises of the 1990s, it was impossible not to think of A.A. in the 1940s and the crises that sprang from a similar period of explosive growth. There was a recognition in the 1940s that issues of money, property, and personality could destroy A.A., and the Twelve Traditions were created as a means of ensuring the future of the fellowship. These traditions articulated a set of values and principles that came to guide the organizational life of A.A. in the same manner that the Twelve Steps had guided the personal recovery of A.A. members. What is striking about the Parkside story is that, after almost 150 years, the field of addiction treatment still has no counterpart to A.A.'s Twelve Traditions, and that some of the best programs in the field continue to self-destruct. The fall of Parkside, as much as any modern milestone in the field, underscores the field's need for a core set of values and principles that can help its organizations and individual practitioners focus on its primary mission. If that focus cannot be sustained, if the field cannot forge a set of core values and principles to guide its business and clinical practices, many other programs—and even the field itself—might share Parkside's fate.

Chapter Twenty-Nine:
Some Closing Reflections on the Lessons of History

My goal in this final chapter is to guide the reader beyond the details of this history we have shared, to an exploration of some of its meanings. There are many levels at which lessons can be extracted from this history, and each reader will need to draw his or her own conclusions about what this has all meant. For myself, I have chosen to bring this work to closure by focusing primarily upon the forces that have contributed to the cyclical birth, development, decay, death, and rebirth of addiction treatment in America.

Approaching History

The Dangers of History

We will need to steer our way through three dangers in our approach to this final task. The first is revealed in George Santayana's oft-noted observation that those who have no memory of history are doomed to repeat it. This danger is a failure to recognize the pendulum swings and cycles that lie within the rhythms of human history. An opposite danger is to over-interpret history, so that all we see in the present and anticipate in the future is the unfolding repetition of old dramas. This is the danger that we might blind ourselves to that which is fundamentally new in what is unfolding before our eyes. A third danger is the temptation to use isolated artifacts of this history as a platform for moralizing. While these dangers call for caution in our approach to this exercise, in the end each of us must stake his or her claim on the meanings we choose to take from these pages. What follows are merely a few of my own.

The Immediacy of History

The history we are reviewing lives through its lasting influence. It is at once a looking glass pointed backward and forward and a mirror of the present moment. When William Green writes to us so eloquently of the psychological and cultural wounds inflicted by slavery and the extension of that legacy into patterns of destructive drug use in the African-American community today, we must consider that the past has a long reach.[285] We must consider the possibility that, when a White counselor and an African-American addict face one another, the ghosts of slave and slave master shimmer in the air until that history is buried in each developmental stage of their relationship. We must consider that, when an African-American counselor first meets an African-American addict, the ghosts of the house slave and the field slave are there with them until an authentic, present-oriented relationship is forged. We must consider that the emotional memory of this history lives even where the detailed knowledge of this history has been lost to its current participants. We must consider the possibility that the strengths and flaws of character in those drawn to this field a century ago continue in our own era. And we must consider the possibility that those forces that dictated the fate of the 19th-century inebriate asylum movement may very well define the fate of the current system of addiction treatment. To consider all of these possibilities, we must look to history as a window to the present and a tool that can help us face the future with expanded choices.

Recovery

Pathways of Recovery

This history has catalogued three overlapping pathways of addiction recovery. The first is highly personal and involves a reorganization of identity in the face of sudden crisis or cumulative maturation. This pathway is embraced within what we have earlier referred to as natural recovery, spontaneous remission, and maturing out. The second pathway is highly social and involves the use of informal community resources that provide a sobriety-based framework in which one can stop drinking and sustain sobriety. This pathway, called "indigenous therapy" by Andrew Gordon, includes culturally proscribed rationales for radical abstinence, mutual-aid groups, religious institutions, and personal recovery guided by indigenous healers/elders.[286] The third pathway—formal, professional, and institutional—involves the guided movement into recovery via the mechanism of "treatment." What is most striking in this American history of addiction recovery is the incredible diversity of styles and media through which people have resolved their problematic relationships with alcohol and other drugs. Science is confirming Bill Wilson's 1944 observation that there are many roads to recovery.[287]

Addiction Science

Clinical Research and Clinical Practice

Astute observers of the addictions field have noted that the field's core concepts emerged, not through the articulation and testing of theory, but by proclamation and sloganeering. Some have even suggested that the concepts that drive mainstream clinical practice in addiction treatment exist, not because of research, but in spite of it.[288]

While a gap between research and clinical practice exists in every arena of health and human services, this gap might more aptly be called a chasm in the field of addiction treatment. Government-funded academic studies all too often generate reports whose implications are absorbed into bureaucratic black holes without ever reaching treatment practitioners. While research activity creates the illusion that the field is operating on a scientific basis, research and treatment constitute separate industries that have little awareness of, contact with, or regard for one another.

While few would challenge the contention that the addiction treatment field rests on a poor scientific foundation, such observations sometimes reveal a lack of awareness of two very different ways of knowing in the field. Where the scientist is searching for empirical truth, the alcoholic and addict are searching for a workable answer to their painful entrapment. The objectivity and detachment of the scientist stand in stark contrast to the passionate belief and commitment that marks most avenues of addiction recovery. A.A.'s program of recovery, for example, boasts—not that it is true—but that it works. While the scientist seeks objective truth, the addicts and those who work with them seek a truth that has the metaphorical power to incite change. The dialogue between these two worlds is hampered by these different ways of knowing. Each side tends to perceive the other with a degree of blissful arrogance and condescension. While calls for cooperation and synergy between these two very separate worlds have become commonplace, science is not likely to become the driving force in addiction treatment until it moves beyond contributing to our knowledge of addiction, to a replicable technology of human transformation.

The Perceived Causes of Addiction

While addiction has long been defined as evil, the source of this evil alternately has been pointed toward the drug, the person, and—more rarely—the social, political, and economic environment in which addiction unfolds. When the focus shifts to the individual, quite different explanations are offered as to the source of personal vulnerability to addiction. These explanations, heavily influenced by the broader social climate, vacillate between theories that posit the source of addiction as biological, psychological, spiritual, moral, and criminal.

During periods in which alcohol and other drug addictions are medicalized, we view only a small percentage of the population as physiologically or psychologically vulnerable to addiction. During periods in which addiction is being criminalized, the entire population is portrayed as vulnerable to addiction. These vacillating views are not so much about the evolution of addiction science as they are about cultural sense-making. Science tends to be more the mirror than the mediator of cultural belief about addiction and recovery.

The Abuse of Technology

The real and imagined advances of science have a potentially malevolent side. In reviewing a history that includes the sterilizing, electroshocking, lobotomizing, and relentless drugging of alcoholics and addicts, we must pause to consider the potential abuses inherent in current and future addiction treatment technologies. We must similarly consider the potential that unintended harmful consequences might grow out of our broader approaches toward solving alcohol- and other drug-related problems.

The Disease Concept

What is most remarkable about the "disease concept" of alcoholism and other addictive disorders is the concept's sheer survivability. This concept has survived more than 200 years of attacks from theologians, philosophers, reformers, psychiatrists, psychologists, and sociologists, and yet continues to survive. This suggests that, as a people, we have both an individual and a collective need for this concept to be "true," regardless of its scientific status. This truth may be more metaphorical than scientific. Science is unlikely to destroy the popularity of the disease concept, but a better metaphor could.

The history of the disease concept may tell us something about the history of ideas. Michael Agar has suggested that what can appear to be radical changes in a professional field can, more often than not, be merely a cosmetic alteration of traditional ideas and practices held together with newly formulated "political cement." Conversely, the introduction of a change labeled as a minor refinement may constitute the touchstone of a radical shift in philosophy and practice.[289] The introduction of the disease concept of alcoholism into 19th-century medicine, and some of the concept's most recent refinements, may illustrate both Agar's principle and its corollary.

Misuse Versus Addiction

Throughout history, efforts have been made to reduce the plethora of personal and social problems created by drug consumption into a single theoretical mold. We have yet to produce a conceptual umbrella under which all of these problems will fit comfortably. In particular, we have failed to create an umbrella that facilitates differential diagnosis and the true individualization of treatment for the many variations of alcohol- and other drug-related problems experienced by American citizens. We will never address these problems effectively by forcing them into an addiction paradigm and enticing or coercing all people suffering from such problems into narrow approaches to treatment—and an equally narrow pathway of long-term recovery. The emergence of "multiple-pathway models" opens up the potential to distinguish between alcohol problems and alcoholism and to develop menus of intervention that will allow highly individualized approaches to the resolution of quite varied alcohol- and other drug-related problems.

Patient Classification Systems

The creation of taxonomies of addicts and addictive disorders has been an enduring pastime of American addictionologists and is an essential step in the true individualization of addiction treatment. These classifications have been based on perceived etiological roots of addiction, patterns of addiction, and personality differences of addicts (to name just a few). But masked behind the illusion of scientific precision lurk moral judgements which declare some people worthy and others unworthy of treatment. Diagnoses can delineate whom we like and whom we do not like—in the name of delineating one disorder from another.

Toward a Core Addiction Treatment Technology

Every health-care profession and every health-care institution must establish a core technology—a consistently applied body of knowledge and technique. Throughout the health-care system there are technologies of assessment and diagnosis, models of clinical decision-making, established service procedures and techniques, and methods of systematic follow-up to monitor and increase patient compliance with continuing-care protocol.

In each era of addiction treatment, the central innovation has been the shift from treating the consequences of addiction to a focus on treating the addiction itself. This innovation has been discovered, lost, rediscovered, and lost again in what seems to be an unending cycle. For the addiction treatment field to sustain itself, we must find ways to develop and refine that core technology, to infuse that technology into the field's institutions, and to transmit that technology to new generations of workers. If it turns out that we have no such technology, then there is no long-term rationale for the field's existence.

On Blaming

Harold Hughes, the political Godfather of the modern alcoholism treatment system, often noted that alcoholism was the only disorder in which the patient was blamed when treatment failed.[290] Alcoholics and other addicts have suffered, not only as a result of poorly developed and at times harmful treatment technology, but also through being blamed for their failure to respond to such technology. For decades many addicts have been subjected to treatment interventions that had almost no likelihood of success; And when that success has indeed failed to materialize, the source of that failure has been attributed, not to the intervention, but to the addicts' recalcitrance and lack of motivation. The issue is, not just that such mismatches do not work, but that such mismatches generate their own iatrogenic effects via increased client passivity, helplessness, hopelessness, and

dependence. Blaming protects the service provider and the service institution at the expense of the addicted client and his or her family. Defining failure at the personal level can also mask broader failures of social policy.

The Rise of Treatment Institutions and Mutual-Aid Societies

The Cultural Context of Addiction Treatment

Addiction treatment was birthed in a larger arena of cultural, legal, moral, and scientific thought; And this treatment—how it is conceived, what it involves, where and by whom it is delivered, and to whom it is provided—continues to evolve in tandem with advancements and regressions in the larger cultural ecosystem.[291] This society's willingness to invest resources in the addiction treatment enterprise has been extended and withdrawn in cyclical patterns of moralization, criminalization, medicalization, and demedicalization. These broader cultural rhythms dictate whether treatment resources exist, the nature of those resources, who has access to such resources, and the goals toward which this thing called "treatment" is directed.

Addiction treatment as a social movement must serve multiple personal and social utilities. It must serve its individual and institutional clients—and the community and culture in which it is nested—in both real and symbolic ways. The allocation of public resources toward addiction treatment, along with the diversion of addicts from the criminal justice system to the health-care system, serves as a symbolic act through which we collectively define ourselves as our brother's keeper. During this stage, the act of providing treatment meets broader needs of the culture that are unrelated to the actual effectiveness of the treatment offered.

When the culture demands rigorous evaluation to prove the effectiveness of treatment, such demands usually reflect that the treatment industry is failing to meet those larger social utilities. This usually occurs when broad social forces redefine one's "brother" as "perpetrator" and redefine "keeper" as "warden." Prisons serve similar symbolic functions that have little to do with their actual capacity to punish, protect, or rehabilitate. Caretaking and punishment are venues through which the culture expiates its most powerful emotions. The acts of caring and punishing are more about ourselves than about the consequences of those acts on the addict. The images of the addict that we create can alternately evoke empathy or disdain, and it is through these images that we define, not the addict, but ourselves.

The Birth of Mutual-Aid Groups: Ecological Influences

While the stories of the rise of mutual-aid movements often focus on the roles of individuals, these movements are nurtured within a much broader social and economic climate. The rise of most alcoholism-related mutual-aid groups emerged during periods characterized by a decline in overall alcohol consumption. Three of the periods in which alcoholism-related mutual-aid recovery movements arose in America followed declines in per-capita alcohol consumption. The Washingtonians emerged after a decade (1830-1840) that saw per-capita alcohol consumption decline from four gallons to two gallons of per-capita alcohol consumption.[292] A.A. emerged following America's experiment with national prohibition, which had also produced significant decreases in alcohol consumption. The third period (1975-1985), in which Women for Sobriety (WFS), Secular Organization for Sobriety (SOS), Rational Recovery (RR), and other alternative mutual-aid recovery groups flourished, was marked by what some observers were calling a new era of temperance. Mutual-aid movements seem to rise when casualties have accumulated from a period of excessive use, but when the majority seems to be moving toward more temperate patterns of alcohol or drug use. Left in the lurch and unable to make such a transition by themselves, these casualties reach out to one another for support in reclaiming their injured bodies and stained identities.

Mutual-aid groups also seem to share a formal or informal function of mutual economic support. It may well be that shared economic hardship is a pre-condition for the rise of such movements. Mutual-aid movements are likely to arise following periods of widespread or pocketed economic depression or recession. Economic hardship creates a climate of increased cooperation and mutual-aid, and the focus on personal recovery from alcoholism may also serve metaphorically and practically as a framework for personal economic recovery.

In their explosive growth in the second half of the 20th century, mutual-aid groups emerged as surrogate family structures and as voluntary spiritual communities. Their cultural significance and future may have more to do with meeting these broader cultural needs than with their discovery of various programs of recovery for alcoholism.

Destigmatization and Professional Status

The movement to destigmatize addiction and addicts has been as much about enhancing the prestige of service providers as it has been about reducing the stigma on consumers of addiction treatment services. Destigmatization required a medicalized language and an altered image of the target population—from skid-row alcoholic to next-door neighbor. Marginalized clients were pushed out of the system to make room for more attractive clients, just as many marginalized staff were pushed out of the way to make room for a more socially attractive staff. The professionalization of addiction treatment required attractive and articulate clients and staff.[293]

Mutual-Aid Societies and the Rise of Addiction Treatment Institutions

Addiction treatment systems seem to rise out of the energy generated by mutual-aid movements. Treatment systems begin as an adjunct to mutual-aid societies, but as these systems acquire professional power, they turn mutual-aid societies into adjuncts of themselves. Professionalized addiction treatment is birthed to broaden the gate of entry into personal recovery, then enters a period of demise when it begins to conceive of itself as the power that initiates personal recovery.

A History of Contempt

Contempt, often mutual, is an enduring and troubling theme in the historical relationship between helping professionals and addicts. The addiction treatment industry as a specialized field grew out of the contempt in which other helping systems regarded alcoholics and addicts. For generations, physicians, nurses, social workers, psychologists, welfare workers, and other service professionals barely masked their contempt for the alcoholic and addict. Beneath the veneer of professional discourse about addicts during the past century lies a pervasive undertone: Most professionals simply do not like alcoholics and addicts.

The term "countertransference" has long been used to connote the feelings elicited in the therapist toward a particular patient. The history of the relationship between professional helpers and alcoholics and addicts is, to a very real extent, a story of countertransference gone awry. Addicts and professional helpers have maintained through much of American history a mutual disregard and a mutual avoidance of one another. The ways in which contempt has influenced the evolution of treatment for addiction is a subject worthy of extended investigation. Many of the coercive and invasive "treatments" detailed in this book could have occurred only in a climate of such contempt. Alcoholics and addicts are uncanny in their ability to sense the most carefully disguised contempt—and even more adept at retaliating in kind.

It is clear from this history that alcoholics and addicts do not fare well in service relationships in which one party claims moral superiority over the other. It was this understanding that, more than 50 years ago, led Drs. C.E. Howard and H.M. Hurdam to suggest that therapists working with alcoholics should practice abstinence. It was their belief that the drinking therapist inevitably communicated a stance of psychological and moral superiority over his or her alcoholic patients.[294] It was not the drinking that stood in the way of clinical effectiveness, but the moral superiority that their ability to drink conveyed.

The delivery of effective services to addicts begins with the transcendence of contempt. We can learn much from some of the real pioneers in this field. What recovered people brought to this field was, first and foremost, a capacity for moral equality and authenticity. But what of those pioneers in our field who did not bring histories of addiction and recovery—Dr. Silkworth, Sister Ignatia, Sam Shoemaker, Willard Richardson, Frank Amos, Dr. Harry Tiebout, and Father Ed Dowling, to name only a few? Here's how Ernie Kurtz characterized these individuals.

> They were not alcoholic, but they did all have something in common: each, in his or her own way, had experienced tragedy in their lives. They had all known *kenosis*; they had been emptied out; they had hit bottom....whatever vocabulary you want. They had stared into the abyss. They had lived through a dark night of the soul. Each had encountered and survived tragedy.[295]

There are ways in which the "kinship of common suffering" can transcend such labels as "alcoholic" and "non-alcoholic." While the mechanism of identification between alcoholic and alcoholic and between addict and addict is crucial in the mutual-aid arena, what may be important in the professional arena is, not only technical knowledge and skill, but also a similar authenticity of emotional contact. Such authenticity transcends the issue of one's recovery status and provides a means of escaping the mutual

contempt that has haunted the addict-professional relationship for more than a century.

The Segregation-Integration Pendulum

American history is replete with failed efforts to integrate the care of alcoholics and addicts into other helping systems. These failed experiments are followed by efforts to move such care into a categorically segregated system that, once achieved, is followed with renewed proposals for service integration. After fighting for 40 years to be born as an autonomous field of service, addiction treatment is once again in the throes of service-integration mania. This cyclical evolution in the organization of addiction treatment services seems to be part of two broader pendulum swings in the broader culture, between specialization and generalization and between centralization and decentralization. Once we have destroyed most of the categorically segregated addiction treatment institutions in America, a grassroots movement will likely arise again to recreate them. When the 21st century once again gives birth to specialized addiction treatment, perhaps this "new" institution will be given a colorful name fitted to its form and function—perhaps something like *inebriate asylum*.

Observations on the Treatment Field

Treatment as Religion, Social Movement, Science, and Business

The history of addiction treatment involves the synergy of religion, science (medicine), social movement, and business. The earliest treatment system in the U.S. was made up of four overlapping branches: the temperance movement, religiously influenced inebriate homes, medically oriented inebriate asylums, and the business-oriented cures of the private sanataria and the patent-medicine industry. The threads of these four branches have existed in the field since the 1870s, with each branch periodically rising and receding in influence.

Each branch represents a form of potential excess: reform zealotry that promises to eliminate drug problems by eliminating the drug, religious zealotry that appeals to only the smallest percentage of the addicted, medical experimentation whose alleged cure has sometimes proved quite injurious, and the unconscionable financial exploitation of addicted people and their families. The addictions-treatment field has operated at its highest levels during periods in which a reasonable balance existed that reined in the potential excesses of each of these branches. The field has deteriorated when one of these elements has taken dominance over the others. If there is "truth" to be found in this field, it is probably not in the dogma of the true believers residing within each of these spheres, but in the questions raised by the synthesizers who operate across the boundaries of all of these spheres.

Defining Treatment

A definition of alcoholism/addiction treatment should be able, at a minimum, to: 1) distinguish between addiction treatment and other interventions of a medical, psychological, social or religious nature, and 2) distinguish between the activities of addiction treatment agencies and voluntary mutual-aid societies. We shall attempt such a definition, which might guide our continued observations.

Alcoholism/addiction treatment is the delivery of professionally directed services to the alcoholic or addict, with the primary goal of altering his or her problematic relationship with alcohol and/or other drugs.

"Real" alcoholism or addiction treatment services are characterized by at least five elements: 1) Services are professionally directed in the context of a contractual, fiduciary relationship. One party has taken on professional responsibility for the care of the other; 2) The focus of the services is on the addiction itself, and not merely on the neurobiological, psychological, social, economic, and legal consequences of addiction; 3) There is a core technology of addiction treatment that is replicable; it can be articulated, codified, and taught to other caregivers. That technology outlines what is to be done (service protocol) and why (theory); 4) The relationship is governed by a set of legal and ethical standards designed to protect the client, the service provider, the institution, the profession, and the public. These standards include the definition of boundaries of what is and is not appropriate in the service relationship; 5) The assessment, diagnosis, clinical decision-making, interventions, and client responses to those interventions are carefully recorded and subject to peer, supervisory, and administrative review.

According to this definition, interventions that focus solely on resolving the problems created by and co-existing alongside addiction are not in and of themselves addiction treatment. Detoxification and medical stabilization may be provided in a treatment

institution and may be valuable, essential services, but by themselves they do not constitute addiction treatment as defined above. Ernest Bishop understood this in 1920, when he insisted that the care of the addict had to be focused, not on the mechanics of drug detoxification, but on the actual "mechanism of narcotic drug addiction-disease."[296] Removing the drug from an addict's body is not the same as treating addiction—a truism reinforced throughout this history.

Based on this definition, we could say unequivocally that the mutual-aid groups described in this book—the Washingtonians, the fraternal temperance societies, the reform clubs, the Oxford Group, A.A./N.A./C.A., WFS, and SOS—do not constitute addiction "treatment," though individuals may use these frameworks to move from the status of addiction to the status of stable recovery. Many other institutions—"drying-out" places, some halfway houses, and nearly all recovery homes—similarly do not constitute treatment. So when did addiction treatment begin?

Defining the Birth of Treatment

The problem with defining precisely when alcoholism and addiction treatment began in the United States is complicated by the fact that the term "treatment" was not used routinely in the 19th century, and that its meaning has evolved throughout the 20th century. One's opinion regarding the time addiction treatment began will vary by one's definition of treatment. Here are my own conclusions, based on the just-offered definition.

Alcoholism treatment began in the United States when the first patient asked a physician to treat, not the physical ravages of drinking, but the compulsion to drink. Benjamin Rush, if not the first, was clearly one of the first to make this transition. Addiction treatment began when the first doctor went beyond tapering a patient off of morphine to attempting to remove the patient's continued cravings. Many 19th-century physicians made this transition before the first inebriate asylum was built. Providing housing for alcoholics over a temperance hall did not constitute treatment. Institution-based treatment began the first time the alcoholic (or someone else) began to pay for services directed at the permanent elimination of addiction. When the focus of the help shifted from the need for detoxification, housing, food, and employment and focused on the appetite for drink itself, treatment began.

The nominees for American "firsts" in the arena

of addiction treatment and recovery include the following. Samson Occom, Handsome Lake, Kah-ge-ga-gah-bowh, and William Apess were among the earliest Native Americans who, having recognized their own self-injury by alcohol, led local or regional temperance campaigns between 1770 and 1830. J.P. Coffin, J.F. Pollard, W.E. Wright, Jesses Vickers, Jesses Small, John Hawkins, and John Gough were among the most noted recovered alcoholics working to reform alcoholics in the temperance movement of the 1830s and 1840s. The earliest specialized home for inebriates was Washingtonian Hall, opened briefly in 1841 and re-opened in 1857. The first medically oriented institution specializing in the treatment of inebriety was the New York State Inebriate Asylum in Binghampton, New York, opened in 1864. The first mutual-support group birthed in a treatment institution was the Ollapod Club, founded at the New York State facility in 1869. The first specialized institution for inebriate women was the Martha Washington Home in Chicago, opened in 1869. One of the earliest institutions that specialized in the treatment of narcotic and cocaine addiction was the Brooklyn Home for Habitués, opened in 1891. There are three early candidates for the delivery of specialized outpatient services: The Keeley Institutes, beginning in 1879, set the model for what today would be called intensive outpatient or day treatment services; the Massachusetts Hospital for Dipsomaniacs and Inebriates operated 29 outpatient offices in the early 20th century; and the Emmanuel Clinic of Boston was among the first to deliver outpatient alcoholism counseling services out of a local community-based clinic, beginning in 1906. Courtenay Baylor was the first recovered alcoholic to work in a paid role as an alcoholism counselor (beginning in 1913), and his protégé Richard Peabody was one of the first alcoholism counselors to work in a solo private counseling practice (in the mid-1920s). All of these firsts predate the founding of A.A. and the rise of the modern alcoholism treatment system.

Who is the Client?

Each era of addiction treatment opens with a vision of addicts voluntarily entering treatment and closes when such treatment results almost exclusively from coercion. The "client" whom treatment institutions serve cyclically vacillates between the individual addict and community social and economic institutions. Addiction treatment swings back and forth between a technology of personal transformation and a technology of coercion. When the latter dominates,

counselors become, not helpers, but behavioral police. The fact that today's treatment institutions often serve more than one master has created the ethical dilemma of "double agentry," wherein treatment staff profess allegiance to the interests of the individual client, while those very interests may be compromised by the interests of other parties to whom the institution has pledged its loyalty.[297]

Motivation, Treatment, and Pretreatment

The history of addiction as experienced by America's addicts is a history of ambivalence. Addicts simultaneously want—more than anything—both to maintain an uninterrupted relationship with their drug of choice and to break free of the drug. Behaviorally, this paradox is evidenced both in the incredible lengths to which the addict will go to sustain a relationship with the drug and in his or her repeated efforts to exert control over the drug and sever his or her relationship with it.

Views over the past century have varied considerably regarding the role of initial motivation in the addict's long-term prospect of recovery. Friedrich Erlenmeyer expressed the traditional view in 1899, when he asserted that the morphinist's desire for cure was essential to successful treatment.[298] But one of the constant rediscoveries in this history is that espoused motivation to be drug free at the time of admission to treatment is not a predictor of positive treatment outcome. This "discovery" was announced in the inebriate asylums; by Bradley and Anderson at the Willmar State Hospital in the 1950s; and by a long series of studies in the second half of the 20th century.[299] There has been a growing recognition that motivation is best viewed, not as a precondition of treatment, but as something that emerges out of an effective treatment process. Motivation is increasingly being viewed, not as something inside the client, but as something that emerges out of the interaction of the client, the client's intimate social network, the therapist and the broader treatment milieu.[300]

The Cyclical Nature of Treatment Fads

Ideas and approaches in addiction treatment do seem to recur in cycles, almost as if certain strains of thought and action in the field re-occurred every other generation in some inexplicable mechanism of professional heredity. There are also predictable life cycles for each new proclaimed cure—announcement, dissemination, institutionalization, decay and loss of faith, hibernation, and revival. These periodic cycles of renewal suggest that treatment outcome is influenced in part by the infusion of hope surrounding each new treatment.

The profuse praise and promise heaped on treatment innovations have, to-date, slowly dissipated under the sober judgement of controlled studies and prolonged clinical experience. A century of specifics—from the gold cures to LSD, from spinal drainage to hypnosis, and from psychosurgery to psychotherapies with endless names—have offered promise and then disappointment. Each has been hailed as a breakthrough. Each promise in itself represented a jockeying for problem ownership and professional status.

What our sweeping review of addiction treatment tells us is that almost any treatment—be it drinking wine in which eels have been suffocated, taking the latest medication, or joining the latest group-therapy fad—will produce some successful outcomes. Any new intervention technology will produce cases in which cure can be claimed. Addicts make numerous attempts at aborting active addiction, and success and failure are all too often measured by a single intervention rather than combined or cumulative interventions. It is always the last attempt that is judged to be successful when, in fact, what may have proved the crucial factor was time, experience, maturity, the sudden opening of some developmental window-of-opportunity for change, or the cumulative effect of numerous interventions. What history tells us is that the early reports of such breakthroughs in the understanding and treatment of addiction are notoriously unreliable and should be treated with great caution and skepticism.

The Challenges of Model Replication

David Deitch, an early pioneer in the therapeutic-community movement, and Dr. Vincent Dole, the co-developer of methadone maintenance, have both suggested that many elements of model treatment programs may not be easily replicated without losing efficacy.[301] I would further add that the highest quality of treatment involves, not merely choosing the right program for the right client, but choosing the right program at the right time—that unique period in the developmental history of an organization when it is at its optimum effectiveness. Some aspects of the best treatment cannot even be sustained in the program in which that treatment was birthed, let alone replicated and mainstreamed within the larger treatment system.

The Therapeutic Underground

A mysterious element seems to be at work in the arena of addiction treatment—and perhaps also in the arena of addiction recovery mutual-aid groups. Each breakthrough in addiction treatment offers some formula for recovery that seems to have its followers and success stories. So perhaps there are some common threads that all of these approaches—lay and professional, spiritual and rational, medical and non-medical, altruistic and predatory—have in common. This therapeutic underground offers a rich field of investigation. We tend to strive to define what *within* a particular approach makes it uniquely successful. Perhaps we should also search for the common ground of experience that *crosses* all of these approaches. What affects positive treatment outcomes may be related, not to the treatment itself, but to unrecognized elements in the client, the client's environment, or the treatment milieu. As we suggested earlier, the most effective element of the Keeley cure may not have been the medicine, but what happened among the Keeley patients while they were standing in line four times a day waiting for their injections. No doubt similarly unrecognized influences operate in today's treatment environments.

Recovery as a Social Process

Alcoholics and addicts whose alcohol and other drug use is enmeshed in drug-using social institutions such as the saloon have always needed an alternative social structure to support their new-found sobriety. This need has given rise to lodging houses, patient-run temperance societies, temperance libraries and inns, coffeehouses, the Jacoby Club of the Emmanuel Clinic, A.A. clubhouses, halfway houses, and self-directed recovery homes. Those recovery frameworks that have been successful over time have had a deep understanding of the social ecology of alcoholism and have mirrored it.

Priests and Shaman

The noted mythologist Joseph Campbell often made distinctions between the roles of priests and shaman across different cultures. According to Campbell, priests were social functionaries who derived their legitimacy from social institutions and in turn supported the social order. In contrast, the shaman's legitimacy sprang from his or her passage through emotional death and rebirth. Where the priest had been prepared by the social order, the shaman was prepared by his or her own personal experience.[302] "Professionals by education" and "professionals by experience" represent the priests and shaman of the addiction treatment field. For more than 100 years, tension has reigned in the relationship between our field's priests and shaman. That tension stems, in part, from two very different types of knowledge: the knowing of the mind and the knowing of the heart. The former involves the mastery of externally validated truth, while the latter springs from within one's own experiential truth.

On rare occasions (and that rarity is itself significant), someone raises the question of the future of recovered people in the addiction treatment field. The question has been rendered obsolete by three decades in which shaman were either pushed out of the field or turned into priests. If shaman are denied expression of that which distinguishes them from priests, then the question of the future of recovered people working in professional roles in the field is rendered irrelevant. The field at its best was energized by a unique synergy between the priests and the shaman, but we have lost, silenced, or transformed most of our shaman. The issue is not which is the more effective of these two groups. Treatment outcome has not been shown to be consistently related to counselor type.[303]

It is quite likely that clients need different experiences and perspectives at different developmental stages of their recovery, and that these diverse experiences can best be provided in a multidisciplinary team that brings a great diversity of professional, cultural, and personal backgrounds. Efforts to professionalize (such as credentialing and certification) may have inadvertently homogenized these differences and diluted the power of what a treatment team could bring to each alcoholic and addict. Credentialing, by focusing on that knowledge which could be codified and transferred to others, implicitly pushed the recovered counselor to emphasize physical and psychological, rather than spiritual, dimensions of the recovery process. Recovered and recovering people brought passion and energy to the treatment milieu. They brought a focus on direct service and a deep faith in the possibility of change derived from their own recovery and their participation in a community of recovered and recovering people. In the wake of their declining numbers, the presence of that hope in the field seems to be diminishing.

Programs Versus Systems of Care

The mental-health and public-health fields have been much more adept at organizing themselves into integrated and coordinated "systems of care" than has the addictions field. We still exist in relative isolation, whether as "freestanding programs" or as encapsulated units within broader service organizations. That isolation has historically been our greatest strength and our greatest vulnerability.

Treatment in Relationship to Community and Society

Dynamic Interactions: A Problem, a Profession, and a Society

One can often gauge the health of a field by observing its management of the boundary that separates it from other professional fields and the larger society. When that boundary is drawn too tightly, addiction treatment programs can become therapeutic cults. When the boundaries of competence become ill-defined and over-extended, the potential for loss of identity and mission is great.

Professional fields are always in dynamic relationship with the society in which they are nested. Born out of the needs of that society, they in turn shape the evolution of that society. Birthed to respond to one need, they must inevitably meet other societal needs in order to sustain their existence. Reciprocal adaptations occur at the boundary between the professional field and the society. It is through its success or failure to adapt to these larger economic, social, and political rhythms that a field evolves or becomes extinct.

The modern system of addiction treatment grew out of the broader medicalization of personal and social problems, and might fall victim to the current de-medicalization of such problems.[304] The reframing of personal problems in moral and characterological terms—along with a restructuring of responses to social problems that focuses more on managing their economic costs than on their personal outcomes —poses a significant threat to the future of the addiction treatment field, in terms of both the field's existence and its essential character.

Overselling Treatment

There has always been a propensity to oversell what treatment could achieve, both personally and socially. While such promises can help generate funding, they also create unrealistically high expectations of what treatment should achieve on a broad scale.

Jim Baumohl, in his review of the inebriate-asylum era, pointed out the danger of suggesting addiction treatment as a panacea for the cure of complex social problems.[305] The overselling of the ways in which addiction treatment could benefit the home, the workplace, the school, the criminal justice system, and the broader community during the 1970s and 1980s sparked a subsequent backlash. When time—the ultimate leveler—began to expose the fact that these benefits were not forthcoming at the level promised, a rising pessimism fueled the shift toward increased criminalization of addiction. This recent history has underscored an enduring lesson: successful short-term strategies for generating public support for the funding of addiction treatment can have unanticipated and harmful long-term consequences.

Rhythms of Despair and Hope

The experiences of despair and hope that can move in and out of the lives of addicts and those close to them are replicated in the larger social responses to addiction. Despair over—and hope for—the addict co-exist throughout most of the history we have reviewed, but there clearly have been periods in which one emotion has dominated the other. When hope dominates, alcoholics and addicts are pulled into the rubric of "we" and cared for in medical and religious institutions. When despair and fear prevail, addicts and alcoholics become "they" and are controlled by police, courts, and prisons. In the transition between these two cycles, we can see addiction counselors who serve as therapeutic police—and judges and probation officers who serve as social workers. When despair and hope co-exist, gender, race, and social class operate to define who will be treated and who will be punished.

Alcoholism Treatment and the Alcohol Industry

The alcohol industry has, according to Alex Wodak, attempted to reframe what were being called "alcohol-related problems" as "alcohol misuse or abuse." In Wodak's view, such "liquorspeak" has served to shift the focus of the problem from the nature of the product to the nature of the drinker.[306] Since the days of the inebriate asylums, the treatment industry conducted itself in ways that prevented it from becoming a target of the alcohol industry. Both the conceptualization of inebriety as a disease and the disease conceptualization of alcoholism that followed it several decades later placed the focus on the personal vulnerability of the alcoholic, rather than on the "evilness" of alcohol as a product.

In 1983, Robin Room, in his classic essay "Sociological Aspects of the Disease Concept of Alcoholism," suggested that the "tacit coalition" that had existed between the alcoholism movement and the alcohol beverage industry was rapidly disintegrating. The cause of this change was a shift from "alcoholism" as the field's conceptual centerpiece to a broader "alcohol problems" perspective.[307] This shift produced a greater focus on alcohol as a drug and the practices of the industry that manufactures and promotes it.

As treatment expanded beyond its alcoholism focus to an alcohol-problems focus, two things occurred. First, ethical issues were raised regarding alcohol and drug prevention and treatment agencies' practice of accepting financial contributions from the alcohol industry. Second, there was a growing sense that the treatment field needed to "take on" the alcohol beverage industry—that this industry was "the enemy." This shift has brought the alcohol beverage industry and the alcoholism treatment industry into increasing conflict. While some would suggest that such tension is long overdue, others express concern about the long-term consequences of an already weakened addictions field's movement into an adversarial position with such a powerful enemy.

Issues surrounding the alcohol industry are part of a broader emerging question: What role should addictionologists—that whole host of people who work in the arena of addiction research, prevention, and treatment—play in the broader discourse on alcohol and other drug problems in this culture?

The Fall of Treatment Institutions and Mutual-Aid Societies

Seeds of Decline

Sometimes the seeds of demise are sown in the early success of a new treatment venture. Those institutions that discover something quite workable in the midst of their experiments in treating alcoholics and other addicts can sustain themselves over long periods of time without knowing precisely what it is that is producing these positive outcomes. Unable to identify the exact nature of their strength, they become inherently superstitious and resistant to change—a stance that sometimes squeezes the breath out of the very thing they are trying to protect.

Problem Ownership and Treatment System Instability

Joseph Gusfield has described how certain social

or professional groups emerge to "own" a social problem.[308] How alcohol and other drug problems are constructed is not merely a theoretical issue debated by academics. Whether we define alcoholism as a sin, a crime, a disease, a social problem, or a product of economic deprivation determines whether this society assigns that problem to the care of the priest, police officer, doctor, addiction counselor, social worker, urban planner, or community activist.[309] The model chosen will determine the fate of untold numbers of alcoholics and addicts and untold numbers of social institutions and professional careers.

The existence of a "treatment industry" and its "ownership" of the problem of addiction should not be taken for granted. Sweeping shifts in values and changes in the alignment of major social institutions might pass ownership of this problem to another group. Robin Room suggests that the institutional ownership of an intractable problem such as alcoholism is inherently unstable. Because so many aspects of the problem are not fully resolvable, new proposals with unknown outcomes always look more promising than the highly visible shortcomings of present practices.[310] What is required to unseat an existing model of response to an intractable problem is sometimes only a dynamic articulation of the existing model's failures and the expression of an alternative vision. This unseating can occur at the local community level or at the societal level.

The Fall of Treatment and Mutual-Aid Movements

Overlapping factors contribute to the fall of treatment as a system, of individual treatment institutions, and of mutual-aid societies.

The factors most likely to contribute to the fall of addiction treatment institutions include: 1) the image of such institutions as drying-out havens for the irresponsible—particularly the irresponsible rich, 2) ethical breaches that wound the field in the eyes of potential service consumers and the public, 3) poorly developed clinical technology, 4) ideological conflicts in the field and between the field and allied disciplines, 5) economic or social disruptions that trigger a shift toward de-medicalization or criminalization, 6) the failure to achieve or sustain public funding, and 7) the failure of the field to address problems of leadership development and leadership succession.

The factors that contribute to the fall of mutual-aid societies include 1) organization of the movement around a single charismatic figure, 2) failure to develop or sustain an exclusionary membership that ensures addict-to-addict identification, 3) conflicts

over money and status, 4) ideological splintering, 5) diversion of purpose to broader social, political, or religious agendas, 6) failure to create a codified program of recovery, 7) failure to create standards of group life that can enhance organizational resiliency, and 8) professionalization.

Three of the most significant threats to treatment and recovery movements as a whole, and to individual treatment and recovery organizations, are the processes of implosion, diffusion, and diversion.

Implosion and Inversion

Addiction treatment programs, like other institutions charged with the care of historically stigmatized individuals, have a propensity to become closed, incestuous systems that cloister themselves socially and professionally and then die through a process of internal stagnation. Taking on the tenor of therapeutic cults, these systems migrate toward ideological extremism, then implode through the actions of their charismatic leaders; through ideological splits, coups or purges; or through the progressive physical and emotional depletion of institutional members. Implosion intensifies flaws of character and magnifies the best and the worst in interpersonal relationships. The result is a legacy of conflicting ideologies and personalities that have left many a treatment program in shambles. From the conflict between Dr. Edward Turner and Dr. Willard Parker that led to the demise of the first inebriate asylum in America, we can trace this thread through the Hargreaves-Keeley disputes, and on forward to a 20th century filled with such conflict. This turmoil is by no means unique to addiction treatment organizations, but there may be certain characteristics about these organizations that make them particularly vulnerable to the forces of implosion.

Implosion can also incite a process of inversion—an intense focusing on the personal and interpersonal problems of staff. There is a dangerous propensity for the energy of a treatment milieu to become directed inward toward staff self-exploration and self-healing, rather than outward in service to clients. There is danger that we—those professional helpers with and without addiction histories—treat ourselves in the name of treating others. There is a danger that we ourselves become intoxicated with the subject of intoxication, that we sublimate our own desire for excess into our work with those who have suffered from excess. This dynamic leaves the field as a whole and each individual agency vulnerable to a shift in focus regarding whose needs will drive clinical decision making—our own or those of the clients we are pledged to serve.[311]

Diffusion and Diversion

Diffusion and diversion constitute two of the most pervasive threats in the history of addiction treatment institutions and mutual-aid societies. Diffusion is the dissipation of an organization's core values and identity, most often as a result of rapid expansion and diversification. Diffusion creates a porous organization (or field) that is vulnerable to corruption and consumption by people and institutions in its operating environment. Diversion occurs when an organization follows what appears to be an opportunity, only to discover in retrospect that this venture propelled the organization away from its primary mission.

The current absorption of addiction treatment into the broader identity of behavioral health is an example of a diffusion process that might replicate two earlier periods—the absorption of inebriate asylums into insane asylums and the integration of alcoholism and drug-abuse counseling into community mental health centers in the 1960s. This diffusion-by-integration has generally led to two undesirable consequences: 1) the erosion of core addiction treatment technologies, and 2) the diversion of financial and human resources earmarked to support addiction treatment into other problem arenas.

The Price of Profiteering

From the patent-medicine vendors, the exclusive drying-out hospitals and sanatoria, the private methadone clinics, and the private addiction treatment programs of the 1980s and 1990s, addiction has long been viewed as an entrepreneurial opportunity. The histories of profit-driven treatments present a pattern of hit and run. They fill a void; extract financial resources from addicts, families, third party payors, and communities; then flee to other, more profitable ventures, leaving institutions and professional helpers whose commitment to addiction treatment is more enduring to weather the backlash from the profiteers' excesses. The failure to define and enforce clear ethical standards governing our business practices has long rendered the addiction treatment field a predator's paradise. The price the field could pay for that failure might be the loss of its own future.

The Impermanence of Treatment Innovation

In the sweep of this history we have shared, there is a marked lack of permanence in the innovations pioneered within a single institution. Most of the institutions chronicled in this text were able to make great breakthroughs, but were unable to sustain that edge of vitality. One of the collective lessons drawn from all the programs we have profiled must surely be that treatment programs evolve dynamically through stages of expansion and contraction: stages of birth, growth spurts, plateaus, decay, and renewal or death. They span generations of clients and staff who each carry forward, re-interpret, or change the institution's core philosophy. They experience critical turning points—some that are easily recognizable and others that are visible only in retrospect. What is most clear from stories reaching from Keeley and Lexington to Synanon and Parkside is that no treatment institution is invulnerable, regardless of the intelligence and commitment of its staff or the sophistication and effectiveness of its treatment technology.

What are we to make of this impermanence? I think there are two possible conclusions. One is that the meaning in the life of an institution is the experience of one period of peak performance in which that institution makes its contribution to the larger whole. Perhaps what matters in the long run is not that the innovation at Willmar State Hospital was able to be sustained for 50 years, but that such innovation once existed and enriched an entire professional field. The second possible conclusion is that there are no lasting institutional legacies, that the only legacy possible is in the continuing lives of those who are briefly touched by an institution. Enduring careers and enduring personal recoveries often outlive the institutions in which they were birthed. Both staff and clients often carry the knowledge that their lives are forever different because of one brief period in the life of such an institution.

The Future of Treatment and Mutual Aid

Trend Summary

Trends in treatment have involved cyclical shifts between: medical and religious/psychological models; inpatient and outpatient settings; social sequestration and social integration; voluntary and involuntary engagement; public and private treatment agencies; delivery of addiction treatment services by generalists and the emergence of addiction specialists; and between the organization of services by drug choice and the organization of services by age, gender, culture, geography, social class, or clinical sub-classification. Trends in mutual-aid have involved shifts from inclusive to exclusive membership, from the large-group meeting to the small-group meeting as the basic unit of organization, from multi-purpose to single-purpose groups, from culturally homogenous to heterogenous groups, and from groups that focus on initiating sobriety to groups that focus on sustaining sobriety.

The Future of Treatment

As this book goes to press, America is caught in a transition between two addiction paradigms: one that views addiction as a diseased condition emanating from biopsychosocial vulnerability, and the other that views addiction as willful and criminal behavior emanating from flaws of personal character. In a shift that began in the early 1980s, America is moving addiction once again from the arena of public health to the arena of public morality.

If this trend continues, it is likely that addiction will be de-medicalized and increasingly criminalized for all but the most affluent of our citizens. During the next decade more addiction programs will close, and many more will be integrated into larger behavioral-health organizations and networks. The field will continue to be buffeted in a highly turbulent operating environment, and many programs will risk losing their focus on personal recovery. There is considerable danger that much of the core technology of addiction treatment will be lost in the coming decade, eroding the field's ability to further develop that technology. In many communities, waiting lists for inadequate doses of specialized addiction treatment will—where they already have not—lengthen to the ridiculous. Alcoholics and addicts will once again drift to or be captured by other institutions: the jail cell, the prison cell, the hospital emergency room, the local psychiatric unit, the state psychiatric hospital, the urban mission, or the domestic-violence shelter.

Addiction treatment from 1965 to 1985 was characterized by increased accessibility, intensity, and duration; Addiction treatment from 1985 to 1998 has been characterized by decreasing accessibility, intensity, and duration. As we approach the 21st century, we have begun the wholesale movement of addicts —particularly poor addicts of color—from treatment programs to the criminal justice system. This reverses the trend toward integrating the treatment of addiction into local communities and re-initiates a pattern of isolation, sequestration, and punishment.

How much of the current system of addiction treatment will survive and be recognizable a decade from now is open to question, but one thing is certain. The movement to generate and sustain support systems for recovering alcoholics and addicts in this country has been, and will continue to be, unstoppable. Every time formal systems of treatment collapse, new grassroots movements rise up to rebuild or replace those systems. Hopefully the wheat of this last era can be threshed from the chaff and used to sow the seeds of a revitalized system of addiction treatment.

The Future Redefinition of Treatment

During the past 150 years, "treatment" in the addictions field has been viewed as something that occurs inside an institution—a medical, psychological, and spiritual sanctuary isolated from the community at large. In the future, this locus will be moved from the institution to the community itself. Treatment will be viewed as something that happens in indigenous networks of recovering people that exist within the broader community. The shift will be from the emotional and cognitive processes of the client to the client's relationships in a social environment. With this shift will come an expansion of the role of clinician to encompass skills in community organization. Such a transition does not deny the importance of the reconstruction of personal identity and other cognitive and emotional processes—or of the physical processes of healing—in addiction recovery. But it does recognize that such processes unfold within a social ecosystem and that this ecosystem, as much as the risk and resiliency factors in the individual, tips the scales toward recovery or continued self-destruction.

As these new community organizers extend their activities beyond the boundaries of traditional inpatient and outpatient treatment, they will need to be careful that they do not undermine the natural indigenous systems of support that exist in the community. The worst scenario would be that we would move into the lives of communities and—rather than help nurture the growth of indigenous supports—replace these natural, reciprocal relationships with ones that are professionalized, hierarchical, and commercialized.

Final Words

History as a Lesson in Humility

As a culture, we have heaped pleas, profanity, prayers, punishment, and all manner of professional manipulations on the alcoholic and addict, often with little result. With our two centuries of accumulated knowledge and the best available treatments, there still exists no cure for addiction, and only a minority of addicted clients achieve sustained recovery following our intervention in their lives. There is no universally successful cure for addiction—no treatment specific. In 200 years of addiction treatment history, the most significant breakthroughs have existed alongside the most ill-conceived. Some of the most passionately claimed truths and best championed interventions have proven wrong, ineffective, and at times harmful. It is easy for us to smugly condemn the past imbecility of treating morphine addiction with cocaine, or to be outraged at the cruelty of sterilizing and lobotomizing alcoholics and addicts, but it would be the ultimate in arrogance and blindness for us to deny that such errors in understanding and judgement are likely present in our own era. Given this perspective, addiction professionals who claim universal superiority for their treatment disqualify themselves as scientists and healers by the very grandiosity of that claim. The meager results of our best efforts—along with our history of doing harm in the name of good—calls for us to approach each client, family, and community with respect, humility, and a devotion to the ultimate principle of ethical practice: "First, do no harm."

Keeping Our Eyes on the Prize

So what does this history tell us about how to conduct one's life in this most unusual of professions? I think the lessons from those who have gone before us are very simple ones. Respect the struggles of those who have delivered the field into your hands. Respect yourself and your limits. Respect the addicts and family members who seek your help. Respect (with a hopeful but healthy scepticism) the emerging addiction science. And respect the power of forces you cannot fully understand to be present in the treatment process. Above all, recognize that what addiction professionals have done for more than a century and a half is to create a setting and an opening in which the addicted can transform their identity and redefine every relationship in their lives, including their relationship with alcohol and other drugs. What we are professionally responsible for is creating a milieu of opportunity, choice and hope. What hap-

pens with that opportunity is up to the addict and his or her god. We can own neither the addiction nor the recovery, only the clarity of the presented choice, the best clinical technology we can muster, and our faith in the potential for human rebirth.

Slaying the Dragon

I have enmeshed myself in this history for the past ten years, and the most profound message that I have drawn from this work is the power of one individual and a single institution to change the future, often in the face of insurmountable odds. I think we can draw sustenance from many of these heroes and heroines, and extract important values and lessons from their lives to help keep us focused during the turbulent days ahead. I think we must ask these pioneers to help us keep our eyes on the prize, ask them to help us when we doubt ourselves, ask them to help us stay focused. I look back on 30 years of working with alcoholics and addicts with few illusions about this incredibly imperfect instrument we call "treatment," but still believing that, at its best, it has the power to heal bodies, touch hearts and transform lives. I would bid those of you who will carry this history forward to align yourselves as closely as possible with that power. When you strip away all the pomp and paper and procedures, it is that power that has and will continue to be the beacon of hope for us all. If the external structures of the field one day collapse, it is that power that will rise again in the future. The privilege to participate in this process of rebirth is the most sacred thing in our field. It is a prize worth protecting.

Slaying the dragon—for our clients and for ourselves—begins with waging war against our flawed selves and ends with the capacity to move forward through the acceptance and transcendence of our own imperfection. In this transition exists recovery, service, and life for us all. To those of you who choose to toil in the treatment of alcoholics and addicts, let me say that generations of humanly flawed but highly committed individuals have delivered this field to your care. You must write with your own lives the future chapters of this history. In accepting such a challenge, you must find a way to respect and learn from this history without getting trapped within it. I wish you Godspeed on your journey into that future.

ENDNOTES

Each citation used more than once in the same Section appears first as a full citation and thereafter as author, year of publication, and page number(s).

Abbreviations for Frequently cited Journals

AHRW–Alcohol Health and Research World
ATQ-Alcoholism Treatment Quarterly
BON–Bulletin on Narcotics
CDP–Contemporary Drug Problems
JAMA–Journal of the American Medical Association
JI–Journal of Inebriety
JSA–Journal of Studies on Alcohol
MR–Medical Record
QJI–Quarterly Journal of Inebriety
STJ-Scientific Temperance Journal

AJP-American Journal of Psychiatry
BJA–British Journal on Addictions
BMSJ–Boston Medical and Surgical Journal
IJA–International Journal of the Addictions
JDI–Journal of Drug Issues
JPD–Journal of Psychedelic (Psychoactive) Drugs
JSAT–Journal of Substance Abuse Treatment
NEJM–New England Journal of Medicine
QJSA–Quarterly Journal of Studies on Alcohol
TC–The Counselor

Other Abbreviations

GPO-Government Printing Office
NIAAA-National Institute on Alcohol Abuse and Alcoholism
NIDA-National Institute on Drug Abuse
SAMHSA-Substance Abuse and Mental Health Services Administration

PROLOGUE

1. This *prologue* is abstracted from: White, W. (1997). The Lessons of Language: Historical Perspectives on the Rhetoric of Addiction. Presented at Historical Perspectives on Alcohol and Drug Use in American Society, 1800-1997, The College of Physicians of Philadelphia, May 9-11. **2.** Watts, T. (1981). The Uneasy Triumph of a Concept: The 'Disease' Conception of Alcoholism *JDI* 11(Fall):p. 451. **3.** Levine, H. (1978). The Discovery of Addiction: Changing Conceptions of Habitual Drunkenness in America. *JSA*, 39(2):143-174. **4.** Rush, B. *An Inquiry into the Effect of Ardent Spirits upon the Human Body and Mind, with an Account of the Means of Preventing and of the Remedies for Curing Them* 8th rev. ed. (1814) Brookfield: E. Merriam & Co. **5.** Baker, J. (1844). The Washingtonian Reform: An Address Delivered Before the Hingham Total Abstinence Society June 16, 1844. Published by the Society, pp.1-20; Wilkerson, A. (1966). *A History of the Concept of Alcoholism as a Disease*. DSW Dissertation, University of Pennsylvania, p. 90. **6.** Lucia, S. (1963). The Antiquity of Alcohol in Diet and Medicine. In: Lucia, S. Ed. *Alcohol and Civilization*. New York: McGraw-Hill Book Company, Inc., p. 171. **7.** Sournia, J. (1990). *A History of Alcoholism*. Cambridge, MA: Basil Blackwell, Inc. **8.** Levine, H. (1981). The Vocabulary of Drunkenness. *JSA* 42(11):1046. **9.** Wilkerson, A. (1966). *A History of the Concept of Alcoholism as a Disease*, DSW Dissertation, University of Pennsylvania, pp. 65-66. **10.** Johnson, B. (1973). *The Alcoholism Movement in America: A Study in Cultural Innovation*. Urbana, Illinois: University of Illinois Ph.D. Dissertation, p. 473. **11.** Bynum, W. (1968). Chronic Alcoholism in the First Half of the 19th Century. *Bulletin of the History of Medicine*, 42:161. **12.** Abraham, K. (1927). *Selected Papers on Psychoanalysis*. London: Hogarth Press. **13.** Peabody, R. (1930). Psychotherapeutic Procedure in the Treatment of Chronic Alcoholism. *Mental Hygiene*, 14:109-128; Peabody, R. (1930). Psychotherapy for Alcoholics. *NEJM*, 202:1195-1202; Towns, C. (1915, 1920). *Habits that Handicap: The Menace of Opium, Alcohol, Tobacco, and the Remedy*. New York: Funk & Wagnalls Company. **14.** Durfee, C. (1937). *To Drink or Not to Drink*. Boston: Longmans, Green; Durfee, C. (1938). Re-Education of the Problem Drinker. *Journal of the Connecticut Medical Society* 2:486. **15.** Strecker, E. and Chambers, F. (1938). *Alcohol: One Man's Meat*. New York: The MacMillan Company, p. 21. **16.** Johnson, 1973, pp. 243, 293. **17.** Bacon, S. (1949). The Administration of Alcoholism Rehabilitation Programs *QJSA* 10(1):8; Keller, M. (1982). On Defining Alcoholism: With Comment on Some Other Relevant Words In: Gomberg, L., White, H. and Carpenter, J. *Alcohol, Science and Society Revisited*. Ann Arbor: The University of Michigan Press, p. 123. **18.** Jellinek, E.M. (1960). *The Disease Concept of Alcoholism*. Highland Park, New Jersey: Hillhouse. **19.** Plaut, T. (1967). *Alcohol Problems: A Report to the Nation by the Cooperative Commission on the Study of Alcoholism*. New York: Oxford University Press. **20.** Jellinek's Disease. (1974). *AA Grapevine* 31(4):42 (September); Fitzgerald, K. (1983). Living with Jellinek's Disease. *Newsweek* (October 17), p. 22. **21.** Keller, M (1982). On Defining Alcoholism: With Comment on Some Other Relevant Words. In: Gomberg, White, and Carpenter, pp. 129-130. **22.** American Psychiatric Association (1994). *Diagnostic and Statistical Manual of Mental Disorders*

(Fourth Edition): Washington, D.C., pp. 175-272; see also: Schuckit, M., Nathan, P., Helzer, J., Woody, G. and Crowley, T. (1991). Evolution of The DSM Diagnostic Criteria for Alcoholism. *AHRW* 15(4):278-283. **23.** Crothers, T.D. (1902). *Morphinism and Narcomanias from other Drugs.* Philadelphia: W.B. Saunders & Company. **24.** Remarks on Cocaine and the So-Called Cocaine Habit. (1886). *Journal of Nervous and Mental Disease*, 13:754-759; Mattison, J. (1883). Opium Addicts Among Medical Men. *Medical Record*, 23:621-623; Rogers, A. (1913). Some Observations During Eighteen Years Experience With Drug and Liquor Habitués. *Wisconsin Medical Journal*, 12:43 (July). **25.** Origin and Meaning of the Word Addiction. (1936). *STJ*, Spring, p. 9. Mark Lender, in his research on the colonial management of drunkenness, discovered Puritan references to persons "addicted to" alcohol. Lender, 1973, p. 357. The first known appearance of the term "dope fiend" was in an 1896 article in the *New York Sun*. Hess, A. (1971). Deviance Theory and the History of Opiates. *IJA* (4):593. **26.** Ayto, J. (1990). *Dictionary of Word Origins.* New York: Arcade Publishing, p. 226. **27.** Hickman, T. (1997). The Double Meaning of Addiction: Habitual Narcotic Use and the Logic of Professionalizing Medical Authority in the United States, 1900-1920. Presented at Historical Perspectives on Drug and Alcohol Use in American Society, 1800-1997 College of Physicians of Philadelphia, May 9-11, p. 6. **28.** Fishbein, M. (1932). *Fads and Quackery in Healing.* New York: Blue Ribbon Books, p. 285. **29.** Greenleaf, J. (1983). Co-Alcoholic...Para-Alcoholic...Who's Who...and What's the Difference. *Alcoholism: The National Magazine* May-June, pp. 24-25. **30.** A very animated debate continues over the terms recovered and recovering. While *recovering* conveys the dynamic, developmental process of addiction recovery, *recovered* provides a means of designating those who have achieved stable sobriety and better conveys the real hope of for a permanent resolution of addiction. Blume, S. (1977). Role of the Recovered Alcoholic in the Treatment of Alcoholism. In: Kissin, B. and Beglieter, H. Eds. *The Biology of Alcoholism, Vol. 5, Treatment and Rehabilitation of the Chronic Alcoholic*, p. 546, New York: Plenum Press. James Royce criticized the use of "recovering" in 1986 on the grounds that the term implied that the alcoholic was still sick. He believed "recovering" should be used to designate only the earliest stages of alcoholism remission. Royce, J. (1986). Recovered Vs. Recovering: What's the Difference? *The U.S. Journal,* March, p.7. Testimony to just how far back this concern over language goes can be found in Harrison's 1860 report that the Washingtonian Society of Boston "fitted up rooms under their hall for the temporary accommodation of reformed, or rather, reforming, men." Harrison, D. (1860). *A Voice From the Washingtonian Home.* Boston: Redding & Company. **31.** *A History of Alcoholics Anonymous in Oregon: 1943-1983.* Portland, Oregon: The Oregon Area General Service Committee of Alcoholics Anonymous, p. 39. **32.** Several of these have interesting histories. *Cure,* derived from the Latin *cura,* came to mean "care" or "looking after." *Treat* and *treatment* came to imply "dealing with something by discussion," and "counsel" referred to the act of discussing or consulting. Ayto, 1990 pp. 133, 150, 527. **33.** White, 1997.

Section 1
Chapter One: The Seeds of Addiction Medicine and Personal Recovery Movements

1. MacAndrew, C. and Edgerton, R. (1969). *Drunken Comportment.* Chicago: Aldine Publishing Company, pp. 113-114. **2.** For a detailed account of the role of alcohol in the period of contact between old- and new-world peoples, see Mancall, P. (1995). *Deadly Medicine: Indians and Alcohol in Early America.* Ithaca, NY: Cornell University Press. **3.** Herd, D. (1985). We Cannot Stagger to Freedom: A History of Blacks and Alcohol in American Politics. In: Brill, L. and Winick, C. *The Yearbook of Substance Use and Abuse: Volume III.* NY: Human Sciences Press, Inc., pp. 152-153. **4.** Larkins, J. (1965). *Alcohol and the Negro: Explosive Issues.* Zebulon, NC: Recod Publishing, p. 19. **5.** For an excellent review of this period, see Lender, M. and Martin, J. (1982). *Drinking in America.* NY: The Free Press. **6.** Steinsapir, C. (1983). The Ante-Bellum Temperance Movement at the Local Level: A Case Study of Schenectady, New York Ph.D. Dissertation: Rutgers University, p. 72. **7.** Cherrington, E. (1920). *The Evolution of Prohibition in the United States.* Westerville, Ohio: The American Issue Press, p.41. **8.** Bynum, W. (1968). Chronic Alcoholism in the First Half of the 19th Century. *Bulletin of the History of Medicine,* 42:160-185, p. 163. **9.** Quoted in Wilkerson, A. (1966). *A History of the Concept of Alcoholism as a Disease.* DSW Dissertation, University of Pennsylvania, p. 1. **10.** Jessica Warner's research suggests that viewing alcoholism as a primary disease characterized by loss of control, and whose treatment required lifelong abstinence, originated not with Rush and Trotter but with the religious oratory and writings of clergy in early 17th-century England. Warner, J. (1993). "Resolv'd to Drink No More": Addiction as a Pre-industrial Construct. *JSA,* November, pp. 685-691. **11.** Dacus, J. (1877). *Battling with the Demon: The Progress of Temperance.* Saint Louis, MO: Scammell & Company, p. 122. **12.** Rush, B. (1814). *An Inquiry into the Effect of Ardent Spirits upon the Human Body and Mind, with an Account of the Means of Preventing and of the Remedies for Curing Them.* 8th rev. ed. Brookfield: E. Merriam & Co. (Reprinted in Grob, G. Ed. *Nineteenth-Century Medical Attitudes Toward Alcoholic Addiction* NY: Arno Press, 1981), p. 13. **13.** Wilkerson, 1966, p. 57. **14.** Armstrong, D. and Armstrong, E. (1991). *The Great American Medicine Show.* NY: Prentice Hall, p. 5. **15.** Katcher, B. (1993). Benjamin Rush's Educational Campaign Against Hard Drinking. *American Journal of Public Health*, 83(2):277. **16.** Rush, 1814, pp. 35-36. **17.** Rush, B. (1810). Plan for an Asylum for Drunkards to be Called the Sober House, reprinted in: Corner, G. Ed. (1948). *The Autobiography of Benjamin Rush.* Princeton: Princeton University Press, pp. 354-355. **18.** Cherrington, 1920; Rorabaugh, W. (1979). *The Alcoholic Republic: An American Tradition.* Oxford: Oxford University Press, p. 233. **19.** Rorabaugh, 1979, p. 108. **20.** McCarthy,

R. and Douglas, E. (1949). *Alcohol and Social Responsibility.* NY: Thomas Y. Crowell Company and Yale Plan Clinic, pp. 16-17. **21.** Dorchester, D. (1884). *The Liquor Problem In All Ages.* NY: Phillips & Hunt, p. 260. **22.** Daniels, W. (1877). *The Temperance Reform and Its Great Reformers.* NY: Nelson and Phillips, p. 60. **23.** Steinsapir, 1983, p. 236. **24.** Dorchester, 1884, pp. 219-220. **25.** Steinsapir, 1983, pp. 5, 28, 102. **26.** Cherrington, 1920, pp. 104, 113. **27.** Baumohl, J. and Room, R. (1987). Inebriety, Doctors, and the State: Alcoholism Treatment Institutions Before 1940. In: Galanter, M. Ed. *Recent Developments in Alcoholism*: Volume Five NY: Plenum Publishing, p. 138. **28.** Mancall, 1995, pp. 111-112. **29.** Apess, W. (1992). *On Our Own Ground: The Complete Writings of William Apess, a Pequot.* O'Connell. B. Ed. Amherst: The University of Massachusetts Press; Mancall, 1995, p. 175. **30.** Steinsapir, 1983, pp. 236-268. **31.** Alexander, R. (1988). "We Are Engaged as A Band of Sisters: Class and Domesticity in the Washingtonian Temperance Movement, 1840-1850. *Journal of American History,* p. 766; Bordin, R. (1990). *Women and Temperance.* New Brunswick: Rutgers University Press, p. 161. **32.** Benson, L. (1879). *Fifteen Years in Hell: An Autobiography.* Indianapolis: Douglas & Carlon, pp. 128-129. **33.** Benson, 1879, p. 148. **34.** Benson, 1879, pp. 145-146. **35.** Benson, 1879, p. 134.

Chapter Two: The Washingtonian Revival

36. General references for this chapter include: Cherrington, 1920; Conley, P. and Sorensen, A. (1971). *The Staggering Steeple: The Story of Alcoholism and the Churches.* Philadelphia: The Pilgrim Press.; McPeek, F. (1944). The Role of Religious Bodies in the Treatment of Inebriety in the United States. In Haggard, D. and Jellinek, E., Eds. *Alcohol, Science and Society.* New Haven: QJSA.; Maxwell, M. (1950). The Washingtonian Movement. *QJSA,* 2:410-451; Blumberg, L. with Pittman, W. (1991). *Beware the First Drink!* Seattle: WA: Glen Abbey Books. **37.** Krout, J. (1925). *The Origins of Prohibition.* NY: Alfred A. Knopf, p.161. **38.** Tyrell, I. (1979). *Sobering Up.* Westport, Connecticut: Greenwood Press, pp. 160-167. **39.** Some sources report that the speaker was Elder Jacob Knapp. **40.** The Society was named after George Washington–an unusual choice in light of the fact that Washington was a distiller and a known drinker of alcoholic beverages. The choice of name reflected the founders' admiration of Washington's character, rather than a desire to emulate Washington's drinking and distilling habits. **41.** Fehlandt, A. (1904). *A Century of Drink Reform.* Cincinnati: Jennings and Graham, p. 88. **42.** Tyrell, 1979, p. 173. **43.** Dorchester, 1884, p. 270. **44.** Anonymous (1842). *The Foundation, Progress and Principles of the Washington Temperance Society.* Baltimore: John D. Toy. **45.** Tyrell, 1979, p. 162. **46.** Cited in Maxwell, 1950, p. 419. **47.** Lincoln, A. (1904). *Letters and Addresses of Abraham Lincoln.* NY: Howard Wilford Bell, pp. 32-40. **48.** Quoted in Zimmerman, J. (1992). Dethroning King Alcohol: The Washingtonians in Baltimore, 1840-1845. *Maryland Historical Magazine,* 87(4):379 (Winter). **49.** Anonymous, 1842. **50.** Krout, 1925, pp. 189-190. **51.** Maxwell, 1950, p. 414. **52.** Alexander, 1988, pp. 770, 772. **53.** Blumberg, L. with Pittman, W. (1991). *Beware the First Drink!* Seattle: WA: Glen Abbey Books, pp. 184, 86. **54.** Blumberg & Pittman, 1991, p. 155. **55.** Tyrell, 1979, pp. 178-179; Blocker, J. (1989). *American Temperance Movements: Cycles of Reform.* Boston: Twayne Publishers, p. 44. **56.** Dorchester, 1884, p. 269. **57.** Martyn, C. (1893). *John Gough: The Apostle of Cold Water.* NY: Funk & Wagnalls Company, pp. 92-93. **58.** Gough, J. (1870). *Autobiography and Personal Recollections of John B. Gough.* Springfield, MA: Bill, Nichols & Company, pp. 203-206; Furnas, J. (1965). *The Life and Times of the Late Demon Rum.* London: W.H. Allen, pp. 152-153. **59.** Gough, unlike Hawkins, did not get sober within the Washingtonian Movement but had great sympathy for the movement and promoted the work of the Washingtonians through his speaking tours. **60.** The Rev. John Marsh later wrote a book--*Hannah Hawkins: the Reformed Drunkard's Daughter*--commemorating Hannah's role in her father's reformation. **61.** Martyn, 1893, p. 108. **62.** Daniels, 1877. **63.** Maxwell, 1950, p. 425. **64.** Martyn, 1893, p. 91. **65.** Martyn, 1893, p. 91. **66.** Blumberg and Pittman, 1991, p. 152. **67.** Quoted in Zimmerman, 1992, p. 380. **68.** Blumberg and Pittman, 1991, p. 175. **69.** Baker, J. (1844). The Washingtonian Reform: An Address Delivered Before the Hingham Total Abstinence Society June 16, 1844. Published by the Society, p. 17. **70.** Zimmerman, 1992, p. 375. **71.** Blumberg and Pittman, 1991, p. 137. **72.** Clinebell, H. (1956). *Understanding and Counseling the Alcoholic.* NY: Abingdon Press. **73.** Baker, 1844, p. 10. **74.** Maxwell, 1950, p. 443; Blumberg, L. (1978). The Institutional Phase of the Washingtonian Total Abstinence Movement: A Research Note. *JSA,* 39:1593; Blumberg and Pittman, 1991, p. 73. **75.** Blumberg and Pittman, 1991, p. 91. **76.** Blocker, 1989, p. 47. **77.** The same cultural phenomenon would affect the addiction treatment and recovery movement in the mid-1980s, with some of the same results that had occurred 140 years earlier. **78.** Maxwell, 1950.

Chapter Three: Fraternal Temperance Societies and Reform Clubs

79. Fahey, D. (1996). *Temperance and Racism: John Bull, Johnny Reb, and the Good Templars.* Lexington: University Press of Kentucky, p. 11. **80.** Tyrell, 1979, p. 210. **81.** Tyrell, 1979, p. 212; Blocker, 1989, p. 48. **82.** Temple, R. (1886). *A Brief History of the Order of the Sons of Temperance.* NY: The National Temperance Society and Publication House, p. 429. **83.** Beattie, D. (1966). *Sons of Temperance: Pioneers in Total Abstinence and "Constitutional" Prohibition.* Ph.D. Dissertation: Boston University, p. 88. **84.** Temple, 1886, pp. 492-503. **85.** Brown, J. (1966). *Early American Beverages.* Rutland, Vermont: Charles E. Tuttle Company, p. 79. **86.** Beattie, 1966, p. 21. **87.** Tracy, S. (1992). *The Foxborough Experiment: Medicalizing Inebriety at the Massachusetts Hospital for Dipsomaniacs and Inebriates.* Ph.D. Dissertation. University of

Pennsylvania, pp. 20-21. **88.** Fahey, 1996, p. 20. **89.** Levine, H. (1984). The Alcohol Problem in America: From Temperance to Alcoholism, *BJA*, 79:112. **90.** Baumhol & Room, 1987, p.143. **91.** Sibley, F. (1888). 2nd Edition *Templar at Work: What Good Templary Is, What it Does and How to do it.* Mauston, Wisconsin. **92.** Blumberg and Pittman, 1991, pp. 161-163. **93.** Krout, 1925, pp. 211-212. **94.** Alexander, 1988, pp. 776-777. **95.** Fahey, 1996. pp. 38, 105. **96.** Dacus, 1877, pp. 370-371. **97.** Arthur, T.S. (1877). *Strong Drink: the Curse and the Cure.* Philadelphia: Hubbard., p. 606. **98.** Dorchester, 1884, p. 410. **99.** Cherrington, E. (1925-1930). Ed. *Standard Encyclopedia of the Alcohol Problem.* (Six Volumes). Westerville, Ohio, American Issue Publishing Company. pp. 2258, 2268-69. **100.** Daniels, 1877, p. 392. **101.** Dacus, 1877, p. 380. **102.** Daniels, 1877, p. 421. **103.** Ferris, G. (1878). *The Life and Work of Francis Murphy and Dr. Henry A. Reynolds.* NY: Henry S. Goodspeed & Company, p. 828. **104.** Ferris, 1878, p. 582. **105.** Dacus, 1877, p. 400. **106.** Furnas, 1965, p. 177. **107.** Ferris, 1878, p. 587. **108.** Daniels, 1877, p. 505. **109.** Ferris, 1878, p. 829. **110.** Daniels, 1877, p. 387. **111.** Dorchester, 1884, pp. 412-413. **112.** Cherrington, 1925-1930, Volume 4, p. 1798.

Section 2
Chapter Four: The Rise and Fall of Inebriate Homes and Asylums

1. Sources used to construct this chapter that deserve special acknowledgment include Jim Baumohl's and Sarah Tracy's seminal work on the early inebriate asylums. Their respective dissertations and many subsequent papers provided the foundation of scholarship for this chapter. Their ground-breaking research; their critiques of early drafts of Chapters Four, Five, and Six; and their sustained encouragement of my work on this book are gratefully acknowledged. **2.** Woodward, S. (1838). *Essays on Asylums for Inebriates.* Worcester, MA. (Reprinted in Grob, G. Ed. *Nineteenth-Century Medical Attitudes Toward Alcoholic Addiction.* NY: Arno Press, 1981), p. 29. **3.** Crothers, T.D. (1893). *The Disease of Inebriety from Alcohol, Opium and Other Narcotic Drugs: Its Etiology, Pathology, Treatment and Medico-legal Relations.* NY: E.B. Treat, Publisher, pp. 17-18; Cherrington, E. (1925-1926). Ed. *Standard Encyclopedia of the Alcohol Problem,* (Six Volumes). Westerville, Ohio, American Issue Publishing Company. **4.** Crothers, T.D. (1912). A Review of the History and Literature of Inebriety, The First Journal and its Work to Present. *JI,* 33:139-151, 1912; Pittman, B. (1988). *AA: The Way It Began.* Seattle, Washington: Glen Abbey Books; Dorchester, D. (1884). *The Liquor Problem In All Ages.* NY: Phillips & Hunt; Tracy, S. (1992). *The Foxborough Experiment: Medicalizing Inebriety at the Massachusetts Hospital for Dipsomaniacs and Inebriates.* Ph.D. Dissertation. University of Pennsylvania, pp. 10-53. **5.** Woodward, 1838, p. 1. **6.** Grindrod, R. (1886). *Bacchus: An Essay on the Nature, Causes, Effects and Cure of Intemperance.* Columbus: J & H Miller, Publisher. (Reprint of the 1840 edition), pp. 497-498. **7.** Rorabaugh, W. (1979). *The Alcoholic Republic: An American Tradition.* Oxford: Oxford University Press, p. 38. **8.** Wilkerson, A. (1966). *A History of the Concept of Alcoholism as a Disease*, DSW dissertation, University of Pennsylvania, pp. 98. **9.** Romano, J. (1941). Early Contributions to the Study of Delirum Tremens. *Annals of Medical History*, 3:128-139. **10.** Wilkerson, 1966, p. 283. **11.** Bynum, W. (1968). Chronic Alcoholism in the First Half of the 19th Century. *Bulletin of the History of Medicine,* 42:163. **12.** Tyler, A. (1944). *Freedom's Ferment.* NY: Harper and Row, p. 331. **13.** Oliver, J. (1936). Spontaneous Combustion. *Bulletin of Medical History,* 4: 559-572. **14.** MacNish, R. (1835). *Anatomy of Drunkenness.* NY: William Pearson & Co., p. 83. **15.** Furnas, J. (1965). *The Life and Times of the Late Demon Rum.* London: W.H. Allen, p. 190. **16.** Rothman, D. (1971). *The Discovery of the Asylum: Social Order and Disorder in the New Republic.* Boston: Little, Brown and Company. **17.** Day, A. (1867). *Methomania: A Treatise on Alcoholic Poisoning.* Boston: James Campbell (Reprinted in Grob, G. Ed. *Nineteenth-Century Medical Attitudes Toward Alcoholic Addiction.* NY: Arno Press, 1981), p. 213; Crothers, T.D. (1902). *Morphinism and Narcomainias from other Drugs.* Philadelphia: W.B. Saunders & Company, p. 101. **18.** Jaffe, A. (1978). Reform in American Medical Science: The Inebriety Movement and the Origins of the Psychological Disease Theory of Addiction, 1870-1920. *British Journal of Addiction to Alcohol and Other Drugs* 77:139-147. (June); Baumohl, J and Room, R. (1987). Inebriety, Doctors, and the State: Alcoholism Treatment Institutions Before 1940. In: Galanter, M. Ed. *Recent Developments in Alcoholism*: Volume Five NY: Plenum Publishing. This number does not include the many proprietary institutions. **19.** Jaffe, A. (1976). *Addiction Reform in the Progressive Age: Scientific and Social Responses to Drug Dependence in the United States, 1870-1930.* Ph.D. Dissertation, University of Kentucky. **20.** Brown, E. (1985). What shall we do with the Inebriate? Asylum Treatment and the Disease Concept of Alcoholism in the Late Nineteenth Century. *Journal of the History of the Behavioral Sciences,* 21:48-59. **21.** Jaffe, 1976, pp. 68-69; Corwin and Cunningham, 1944, p. 17; Tracy 1992. **22.** Baumohl, J. (1993). Inebriate Institutions in North America, 1840-1920. In: Warsh, C. Ed. *Drink in Canada: Historical Essays.* Montreal: McGill-Queens University Press, pp. 92-114. **23.** Mattison, J. (1891). Cannabis Indica as an Anodyne and Hypnotic. *St. Louis Medical and Surgical Journal*, 61:266. **24.** Tracy, 1992, pp. 167-168, 194; Baumohl, 1993, p. 231. **25.** Crothers, 1893, p. 200. **26.** *Chicago Washingtonian Home, Sixth Annual Report,* 1870, p. 27. **27.** Cherrington, 1926, p. 1322. **28.** Sarah Tracy, Personal Communication, October 25, 1997. **29.** Jim Baumohl, Personal Communication, September, 1996. **30.** Dodge, D. (1877). Inebriate Asylums and Their Management. *QJI,* I:126-144. (June). **31.** Baumohl, 1993, p. 227. **32.** Crother, 1893, p. 25. **33.** Corwin and Cunningham, 1944, p. 15; Clum, F. (1888). *Inebriety: Its Causes, Its Results, Its Remedy.* Philadelphia: Lippincott, p. 191. **34.** *Proceedings 1870-1875, American Association for the Cure of Inebriates.* (1981). NY: Arno Press, p.

100. **35.** Baumohl, J. (1991). Administering the Pledge: Episodes in San Francisco's Management of Drunken Public Employees, 1858-1920. *JDI,* 21(4):825-838. **36.** Parish, J. (1883). *Alcoholic Inebriety: From a Medical Standpoint.* Philadelphia: P. Blakiston, Son & Company. **37.** Deutsch, 1949; Grob, G. (1983). *Mental Illness and American Society, 1875-1940.* Princeton, NJ: Princeton University Press; Novick, R. (1941). The Problem of Alcoholism in State Hospitals. *Illinois Medical Journal* 80: 414-419; Noble, D. (1858). On the Use of Opium in the Treatment of Insanity. *Journal of Mental Science* 4:111-118. **38.** Geller, J. and Harris, M. (1994). *Women of the Asylum: Voices From Behind the Walls, 1840-1945.* NY: Doubleday. **39.** Jaffe, 1978, pp. 140-141. **40.** Parish, J. (1888). Historical Sketch of the American Association for the Cure of Inebriety. *JI,* 10:189-193. **41.** Proceedings (AACI), 1870, p. 8. **42.** Crothers, T.D. (1893). *The Disease of Inebriety from Alcohol, Opium and Other Narcotic Drugs: Its Etiology, Pathology, Treatment and Medico-legal Relations.* NY: E.B. Treat, Publisher. **43.** Proceedings, (AACI), 1874, p. 80. **44.** Mercadante, L. (1996). *Victims and Sinners: Spiritual Roots of Addiction and Recovery.* Louisville, KY: Westminster John Knox Press. **45.** Calkins, A. (1871). *Opium and the Opium Appetite.* Philadelphia: Lippincott. **46.** Jaffe, 1976, p. 50. **47.** Jaffe, 1978, p. 143. **48.** Keeley, L. (1881). *The Morphine Eater, or From Bondage to Freedom.* Dwight, Illinois: C. L. Palmer Co. **49.** *JI,* 1900, 22:483. **50.** Douglas, C. (1900). Historical Notes on the Sanatorium Treatment of Alcoholism. *Medical Record,* 57: 410-411. **51.** Crothers, 1893, p. 24. **52.** Pollock, H. and Furbush, E. (1917). Insane, Feebleminded, Epileptics and Inebriates in Institutions in the United States. *Mental Hygiene.* 99:548-566. **53.** Stoddard, C. (1922). What of the Drink Cures? *STJ.* September, pp. 55-64. **54.** Blumberg, L. (1978). The American Association for the Study and Cure of Inebriety. *Alcoholism: Clinical and Experimental Research,* 2:234-240. **55.** Cherrington, 1925, Vol I, 155-156. **56.** Ozarin, L. (1973). Moral Treatment and the Mental Hospital In: Rossi, J. and Filstead, W. (1973). *The Therapeutic Community.* NY: Behavioral Publications, p. 34. **57.** Baumohl, 1993; Baumohl, J. And Tracy, S. (1994). Building Systems to Manage Inebriates: The Divergent Pathways of California and Massachusetts, 1891-1920. *CDP,* 21: 557-597. **58.** Rothman, D. (1971, 1990). *The Discovery of the Asylum: Social Order and Disorder in the New Republic,* Boston: Little, Brown and Company. **59.** Porter R. (1989). *The Social History of Madness* NY: E.P. Dutton, pp. 19-20. **60.** Rothman, 1971, 1990, p. 238. **61.** Hall, H. (1982). *Professionalism, Psychology, and Alcoholism: The Association for the Study of Inebriety, A Case Study.* Psy.D. Dissertation Rutgers University. The State University of New Jersey, p. 47. **62.** Tracy, 1992. **63.** Baumohl, J. (1986b). On asylums, homes, and moral treatment: The Case of the San Francisco Home for the Care of Inebriates, 1859-1870. *CDP,* 13: 395-445. **64.** Tracy, 1992. **65.** Terry, C. and Pellens, M. (1928). *The Opium Problem.* Montclair, New Jersey: Patterson Smith, p. 89. **66.** Tracy, 1992, pp. 95-138. **67.** Editorial: The Charges Against Foxborough Asylum. (1894). *QJI* 16:191-193. **68.** Editorial: The Charges Against Foxborough Asylum. (1894), p. 191. **69.** Hall, 1982, p. 48.

Chapter Five: Inebriate Homes and Asylums: Treatment Philosophies, Methods, and Outcomes
70. Parton, J. (1868). Inebriate Asylums, and A Visit to One. *The Atlantic Monthly,* 22:385-404. (October). **71.** Tracy, 1992, p. 39. **72.** *Proceedings 1870-1875, American Association for the Cure of Inebriates.* (1981). NY: Arno Press. **73.** Tracy, 1992; Baumohl and Tracy, 1994. **74.** Baumohl and Tracy, 1994, p. 579. **75.** Tracy, 1992, pp. 70, 162-164, 211, 246. **76.** Crothers, T.D. (1897). Reformed Men as Asylum Managers. *QJI,* 1897, 19:79-81. **77.** Crothers, T. (1897). p. 80; Crothers, T.D. (1902). Morphinism and Narcomainias from other Drugs. Philadelphia: W.B. Saunders & Company, p. 130. **78.** Kerr, N. (1894). *Inebriety or Narcomania: It's Etiology, Pathology, Treatment and Jurisprudence.* NY: J. Selwin Tait & Sons. Third Edition. pp. 402-405. **79.** Grob, G. (1983). *Mental Illness and American Society, 1875-1940.* Princeton, NJ: Princeton University Press; Novick, 1941, p. 21; Rothman, D. (1980). *Conscience and Convenience: The Asylum and Its Alternatives in Progressive America.* Boston: Little, Brown & Company, pp. 354-355. **80.** Proceedings (AACI), 1872, p. 61. **81.** Turner, J. (1888). *History of the First Inebriate Asylum in the World.* NY: (Privately printed). **82.** Crothers, 1893, p. 125; Baumohl and Room, 1987. **83.** References to problems of alcoholism experienced by African Americans before 1890 come, not from the asylums, but from the prisons. Proceedings, 1874, p. 40. **84.** For example, a Dr. Edwards of Richmond, Virginia noted in an 1893 report that, while African Americans drank, they rarely became drunkards. T.D. Crothers confirmed this by noting that he had not seen a single case of African-American alcohol inebriety during his quarter-century of practice as an inebriety specialist. Crothers, 1893, p. 124. **85.** Arthur, T.S. (1877). *Strong Drink: the Curse and the Cure.* Philadelphia: Hubbard, F. (1881). *The Opium Habit and Alcoholism.* NY: A.S. Barnes & Co., p. 560. **86.** Tracy, 1992, pp. 232-233. **87.** Crothers, 1893, p. 127. **88.** *Proceedings (AACI),* 1871, p. 19. **89.** *Proceedings (AACI),* 1871, pp. 662-670; Wright, T. (1885). *Inebriism: Pathological and Psychological Study.* Columbus, Ohio: William G. Hubbard, p. 34; Crothers, 1893; Palmer, C. (1898). *Inebriety: Its Source, Prevention, and Cure.* Philadelphia: Union Press, pp. 97-105. **90.** Tracy, 1992, p. 63. **91.** Crothers, 1893, pp. 27-28; Crothers, T. D. (1911). *Inebriety: A Clinical Treatise on the Etiology, Symptomatology, Neurosis, Psychosis and Treatment.* Cincinnati, Ohio: Harvey Publishing Company; Keller, M. (1986). **92.** Baumohl, J. (1990). Inebriate Institutions in North America, 1840-1920. *BJA* 85:1187-1204. **93.** Osborn, W. (1907). State Care and Treatment of Inebriates. *Bulletin of Iowa Institutions,* 9: 8-9. **94.** Arthur, 1877, p. 547. **95.** Baumohl, J. (1986a). *Dashaways and Doctors: The Treatment of Habitual Drunkards in San Francisco from the Gold Rush to Prohibition.* Doctoral Dissertation, Berkeley, CA: University of California; Baumohl, 1993, p. 105. **96.** *Proceedings (AACI),* 1871, p. 98. **97.** Crothers, 1893. **98.** *Proceedings (AACI),* 1871, p. 5. **99.** Dorchester, D.

(1884). *The Liquor Problem In All Ages.* NY: Phillips & Hunt, p. 553. **100.** Baumohl, 1990, p. 1194; Beard, G. (1871). *Stimulants and Narcotics.* NY: G.P. Putnam and Sons. **101.** MacNish, R. (1835). *Anatomy of Drunkenness.* NY: William Pearson & Co., p. 61. **102.** Grinrod, R. (1886). Bacchus: An Essay on the Nature, Causes, Effects and Cure of Intemperance. Columbus, OH: J&H Miller, Publisher, (Reprint of 1840 Edition), p. 181. **103.** Anstie, F. (1865). *Stimulants and Narcotics: Their Mutual Relations.* Philadelphia: Lindsay and Blakiston **104.** Clum, F. (1888). *Inebriety: Its Causes, Its Results, Its Remedy.* Philadelphia: Lippincott, p. 69. **105.** Day, A. (1877). Abstract of the Nineteenth Report of the Washingtonian Home for Inebriates, Boston, 1877. *QJI* I (September), 222; Day, A. (1891). Causations of Alcoholic Inebriety. *QJI,* 13 (April).127; Proceedings, 1875, p. 29. **106.** Kane, H. (1881). *Drugs That Enslave.* Philadelphia: Preseley Blakiston. **107.** Palmer, 1898. **108.** Crothers, T.D. (1891). Are Inebriates Curable? *JAMA* 17:923-927; Crothers, T.D. (1902). The Drug Habits and Their Treatment. Chicago: G.P. Englehard & Company. **109.** Proceedings, 1874, p. 52. **110.** Kerr, 1894, p. 197-202. **111.** Crothers, 1902, p. 60. **112.** Grob, G. Ed., (1981). *The Medical Profession and Drug Addiction.* NY: Arno Press, p. 33. **113.** Clum, F. (1888). *Inebriety: Its Causes, Its Results, Its Remedy.* Philadelphia: Lippincott, p. 204. **114.** Clum, 1988, p. 63. **115.** Tracy, 1992, p. 6. **116.** Dana, C. (1891). Inebriety: A Study of its Causes, Duration, Prophylaxis, and Management. *QJI,* 23:469-479. **117.** Kane, H. (1881). *Drugs That Enslave.* Philadelphia: Preseley Blakiston , p. 145. **118.** Clum, 1888, p. 187. **119.** Dodge, 1877, p. 128. **120.** *Proceedings (AACI),* 1874, p. 54. **121.** Clum, 1888, p. 161. **122.** Kerr, 1894, p. 316. **123.** Crothers, T.D. (1902). The Drug Habits and Their Treatment. Chicago: G.P. Englehard & Company, p. 46. **124.** Dodge, D. (1877). Inebriate Asylums and Their Management. *QJI,* I:142. (June). **125.** Kerr, 1894, p. 704. **126.** Crothers, 1902, p. 57. **127.** Crothers, T.D. (1902). *Morphinism and Narcomanias from other Drugs.* Philadelphia: W.B. Saunders & Company , pp. 343-344. **128.** Tracy, S. (1997). Therapeutic and Civic Ideals in the Rehabilitation of Inebriates: The Evolution of State Hospital Care for Habitual Drunkards in Massachusetts, 1890-1920. Presented at Historical Perspectives on Drug and Alcohol Use in American Society, 1800-1997. College of Physicians of Philadelphia, May 9-11, p. 14. **129.** Wilkerson, 1966, p. 145. **130.** MacKenzie, D. (1875). *The Appleton Temporary Home: A Record of Work.* Boston: T.R. Marvin & Sons, p. 17. **131.** This term came from the characteristic "gooseflesh" that characterized the addict's skin during opiate withdrawal. **132.** Dodge, 1877, p. 140. **133.** An Inmate of the New York State Asylum, (1869). Our Inebriates, Harbored and Helped. *Atlantic Monthly* 24:112. (July). **134.** An Inmate, 1869, p. 115. **135.** Arthur, 1877, p. 550. **136.** Tracy, 1992. **137.** Parton, 1868, p. 395. **138.** Clum, 1988, p. 199. **139.** *Proceedings (AACI),* 1872, p. 60. **140.** Crother, 1902, pp. 52, 70. **141.** Ludlow, F. "What Shall They Do to Be Saved? *Harper's Magazine,* 35: 377-387. (Also in Day, 1868. 250-284). **142.** Kane, 1881, p. 130. **143.** *First Annual Report of the Board of Managers of the Washingtonian Home of Chicago* (1865). Chicago: Jameson & Morse, Printers, p. 12. **144.** Dodge, 1877, pp. 141-143.**145.** Arthur, 1877, pp. 515-517. **146.** An Inmate...1869, p. 116. **147.** Kane, 1881, p. 116. **148.** Palmer, C. (1896). *Inebriety: Its Source, Prevention, and Cure.* Philadelphia: Union Press, p. 42. **149.** Cutten, G. (1907). *The Psychology of Alcoholism.* NY: Charles Scribner's Sons, p. 325. **150.** McKelvey, B. (1977). *American Prisons: A History of Good Intentions.* Montclair, New Jersey: Patterson Smith, p. 59. **151.** Ford, 1910, p. 53. **152.** Parton, 1868, p. 401. **153.** Tracy, 1992, p. 257. **154.** *Sixth Annual Report of the Board of Managers of the Washingtonian Home of Chicago* (1870). Chicago, Illinois: Press of Jameson & Morse, p. 7. **155.** Tracy, 1997, p. 35. **156.** Proceedings (1870), p. 75-77. **157.** Parish, J. (1883). *Alcoholic Inebriety: From a Medical Standpoint.* Philadelphia: P. Blakiston, Son & Company , p. 121. **158.** Crothers, 1893, p. 220. **159.** *Proceedings (AACI),* 1870, p. 78. **160.** Chamberlain, H. (1891). Modern Methods of Treating Inebriety. *Chautaquan* 13:494-499. (July). **161.** Crothers, 1893, p. 128. **162.** Tracy, 1992, pp. 76, 82, 194. **163.** Day, 1877, p. 222. **164.** Davis, N. (1877). Inebriate Asylums: The Principles that should Govern us in the Treatment of Inebriates and the Institutions Needed to Aid their Restoration. *JI,* 2:80-88. **165.** Steele, J. (1888). *Hygienic Physiology with Special Reference to the Use of Alcoholic Drinks and Narcotics.* NY: American Book Company, p. 223; Crothers, 1902, pp. 78-79; Simonton, T. (1903). The Increase of the Use of Cocaine among the Laity in Pittsburg. *Philadelphia Medical Journal* 11:556-560; Pettey, G. (1913). *Narcotic Drug Diseases and Allied Ailments.* Philadelphia: F.A. Davis Co., p. 431. **166.** Ellsworth, V. (1897). The First Home for Inebriates and Its Work. *QJI,* 19:278-283. **167.** Crothers, T.D. (1898). Gold Cures in Inebriety. *JAMA,* 3:756 **168.** Tracy, 1992, p. 76. **169.** *Proceedings (AACI),* 1874, pp. 44-45. **170.** Geller and Harris, 1994, pp. 11-30, 87-105. **171.** Myerlet, A. in Grob, G. Ed., (1981). *The Medical Profession and Drug Addiction,* p. 24. **172.** Terry and Pellens, 1928. **173.** Noble, 1858. **174.** Geller and Harris, 1994, p. 25. **175.** Clum, 1888, p. 239. **176.** Kelley, M. (1899). Women and the Drink Problem. *The Catholic World,* 69:678-687. **177.** Proceedings, 1874, p. 39. **178.** Kelley, 1899, p. 679. **179.** Kelley, 1899, p. 683. **180.** MacNish, 1835. **181.** Beard, 1871, p. 51. **182.** *Proceedings (AACI),* 1874, pp. 56-57. **183.** *Proceedings (AACI),* 1874, p. 27. **184.** Crothers, T.D. (1878). Inebriety in Women. *QJI,* 2:247-248. **185.** Hubbard, F. (1881). *The Opium Habit and Alcoholism.* NY: A.S. Barnes & Co., pp. 17-19. **186.** Hall, L. (1888). Inebriety in Women: Its Causes and Results. *QJI,* 5:223-224; Peterson, F. (1893). The Treatment of Alcoholic Inebriety. *JAMA,* 20:408-411. **187.** Kerr, 1894, p. 44. **188.** Kerr, 1894, p. 232. **189.** Sparks, A. (1898). Alcoholism in Women: Its Causes, Consequence, and Cure, *QJI,* 20 (1898): 31-37. **190.** Smith, H. (1901). Alcohol in Relation to Women. *QJI,* 23: 190-193. **191.** Partridge, G. (1912). *Studies in the Psychology of Intemperance.* NY: Sturgis & Walton Company, p. 59. **192.** Doner. T. (1878). *Eleven Years a Drunkard: The Life of Thomas Doner.* Sycamore, IL: Arnold Brothers, pp. 19-20. **193.** Johnson, L. (1843). *Martha Washingtonianism: A History of the Ladies' Temperance*

Benevolent Societies. Boston: Saxton, Peirce & Company. **194.** Baumohl, 1986, p. 440. **195.** Bordin, R. (1990). *Women and Temperance.* New Brunswick: Rutgers University Press, p. 161. **196.** Baumohl. 1993, p. 99. **197.** Turner, 1888, p. 166. **198.** McKelvey, 1977, pp. 165-166; Grob, 1983, p. 65; Freedman, E. (1974). Their Sisters' Keepers: An Historical Perspective on Female Correctional Institutions in the United States, 1870-1900. *Feminist Studies,* 2:82-86. **199.** Blumberg, L. (1978). The Institutional Phase of the Washingtonian Total Abstinence Movement: A Research Note. *JSA,* 39:1591-1606; Kerr, 1894, p. 437; Peterson, 1893, p. 408. **200.** Lender, M. (1981). Women Alcoholics: Prevalence Estimates and their Problems as Reflected in Turn-of-the-Century Institutional Data. *IJA,* 16(3): 443-448. **201.** Kerr, 1894, p. 706. **202.** Crothers, 1879; Mattison, J. (1898). Morphinism In Women. *QJI,* 20:202-208; Sparks, A. (1897). Alcoholism in Women. *MR,* 1898, 52: 699-701. **203.** Sparks, 1897, pp. 699-701; Crothers, 1879, pp. 247-248.

Chapter Six: Four Institutional Histories

204. The New York State Inebriate Asylum is often credited with being the first specialized institution for the treatment of inebriety, in spite of the fact that the Washingtonian homes in Boston and Chicago predate the opening of the New York facility. This may be attributable to Dr. Turner's early (1846) advocacy role in the asylum movement and to distinctions between an inebriate "home" and an inebriate "asylum." **205.** Turner, 1888, pp. 19, 56. **206.** Turner, 1888, p. 45. **207.** Cassedy, J. (1976). An Early American Hangover: The Medical Professional and Intemperance. *Bulletin of the History of Medicine,* 50:3, 405-413. **208.** Turner, 1888, p. 55. **209.** Crothers, 1912, p. 142. **210.** Turner, 1888, p. 439. **211.** Voegtlin, W. and Lemere, F. (1942). The Treatment of Alcohol Addiction: A Review of the Literature. *QJSA,* 2:717-803. **212.** Brown, 1985, p. 51. **213.** Crothers, T.D. (1914). The Pioneer Founder of America's Inebriate State Hospital. *Alienist and Neurologist,* 35:40-60. **214.** Jewitt, C. (1849). *Speeches, Poems, and Miscellaneous Writing on Subjects Connected with Temperance and the Liquor Traffic.* Boston: Joyn P. Jewitt. **215.** *Proceedings (AACI),* 1870, p. 50; Harrison, D. (1860). *A Voice from the Washingtonian Home.* Boston: Redding & Company, pp. 103, 113. **216.** Ellsworth, 1897, p. 280. **217.** Harrison, 1860, pp. 305-306. **218.** Howard, G. (1941-1942). Alcoholism: Its Treatment at the Washingtonian Hospital. *STJ,* 49(3-4): 57-60,74-76,91-95. **219.** Blumberg, 1978, pp. 1597-1598. **220.** Martha Washington Alcoholic Treatment Center Relieves Suffering--with AA Help, Here's How. (1971). 22(6):1,5 (July-August). **221.** *QJI,* (1884) 6(4):249. (October). **222.** *Proceedings (AACI),* 1871, p. 107. **223.** *Martha Washington Hospital: 1863-1988* (1988). Chicago: Martha Washington Hospital. **224.** Baumohl, J. (1986a). *Dashaways and Doctors: The Treatment of Habitual Drunkards in San Francisco from the Gold Rush to Prohibition.* Doctoral Dissertation, Berkeley, CA: University of California. p. 103. **225.** Baumohl, 1986b, p. 418. **226.** Baumohl, 1986a, p. 132. **227.** Baumohl, 1986b, p. 431. **228.** Baumohl, 1986a, p. 152. **229.** Baumohl, 1986b, p. 435.

Chapter Seven: Franchising Addiction Treatment: The Keeley Institutes

230. The work constructing the history of the Keeley Institute was enriched by discussions with James Oughton, Jr. and Mrs. Anne Withrow, and by three unpublished manuscripts by Ben Scott, Paul Weitz, and Mary Sigler. Paul was a bubbling fountain of information and resources on Keeley, and his help is gratefully acknowledged. **231.** All of these cures are mentioned in the early (1890's) correspondence of Dr. Leslie Keeley–Illinois State Historical Librarry, Letterpress Volume K4. **232.** James Oughton, Jr. Interview, July 11, 1995. **233.** Inside the History of The Keeley Cure. (1907). *JAMA,* 49:1861-1864, 1941-51. **234.** Inside the Keeley Institute (1960). *The Magazine of Livingston County,* pp. 6-11. **235.** Morgan, H. (1989). "No, Thank You. I've Been to Dwight": Reflections on the Keeley Cure for Alcoholism. *Illinois Historical Journal* 82(3):147-166. **236.** Clark, C. (1893). The Perfect Keeley Cure; Incidents at Dwight and "Through the Valley of the Shadow" into the Perfect Light. Milwaukee: Clark, p. 112; Scott, B. (1974). *Keeleyism: A History of Dr. Leslie Keeley's Gold Cure for Alcoholism.* Normal, IL: Illinois State University, Unpublished Master's Thesis, pp. 4-5. **237.** Barclay, G. (1964). The Keeley League. *Journal of the Illinois State Historical Society,* 57:341-365. **238.** Scott, 1974, p. 13. **239.** Barclay, 1964, pp. 356-357. **240.** Scott, 1974, pp. 216-225. **241.** Morgan, 1989, p. 156. **242.** Hargreaves, F. (1880). *Gold as a Cure for Drunkenness! Being an Account of the Double Chloride of Gold Discovery Recently Made by Dr. L.E. Keeley of Dwight, Illinois.* Dwight, Illinois: Keeley, Institute, p. 6; Keeley, L. (1892). Drunkenness, a Curable Disease. *American Journal of Politics,* 1:27-43. **243.** Keeley, L. (1893). *Drunkenness and Heredity* and *The Inebriety of Childhood.* Dwight, IL: Keeley Institute, p. 12. **244.** Keeley, L. (1882). *An Essay upon the Morphine and Opium Habit* (Pamphlet). Dwight, IL: The Keeley Institute, p. 6. **245.** Keeley, L. (1896). *The Non-Heredity of Inebriety.* Chicago: S.C. Griggs & Company, pp. 344-345. **246.** Sigler, M. (1993). *A Sobering Trip To Dwight.* Unpublished manuscript, p. 25; Speed, J. (1891). Dr. Keeley's Treatment for Drunkenness. *Harper's Weekly* 35:755-756. **247.** Keeley Archives, Bound Volume 286. **248.** Keeley Archives, Advertising Pamphlets, Box 57. **249.** Sagendorph, K. (1940). The Keeley Cure. *Coronet,* December, pp.13-18. **250.** Keeley Archives, Box 76, File "Source of Patients." **251.** Calhoun, 1892, p. 179. **252.** Warsh, C. (1988). Adventures in Maritime Quackery: The Leslie E. Keeley Gold Cure Institute of Fredericton, N.B. *Accedences* 17(2): 129 (Spring). **253.** Crothers, 1897, p. 79. **254.** Keeley Archives, The Leslie E. Keeley Company Physician's Record, Bound Volume 267. **255.** Instructions to Attendants (ND). Dwight, Illinois: The Keeley Institute.

256. Rules, Regulations and Instructions (ND). Dwight, Illinois: The Keeley Institute. **257.** Mrs. Anne Withrow, Personal Interview, August 25, 1995. **258.** James Oughton, Jr., Personal Interviews, July 11, 1995, January 29, 1996. **259.** Barclay, 1964, p. 357. **260.** Calhoun, 1892, p. 118. **261.** Keeley, L. (1897). *Opium: Its Use, Abuse and Cure.* Dwight, Illinois: Banner of Gold Company. **262.** To the Keeley Graduate (ND). Dwight, Illinois: The Keeley Institute. **263.** Clark, 1893. **264.** Keeley Archives, Bound Volume 152, p. 38. **265.** Keeley Archives, Bound Volume 152, p. 100. **266.** Keeley Archives, Bound Volume 152. **267.** Hargreaves, No Date. **268.** Keeley Archives, Letterpress, Volume K4. **269.** Calhoun, 1892, p. 134. **270.** Calhoun, 1892, p. 220. **271.** Weitz, P. (1989). *The Keeley Treatment: A Description and Analysis.* Unpublished Master's Thesis Park Forest, Illinois: Governors State University, p. 15. **272.** Flinn, J. (1892). The Keeley League and Its Purpose. *American Journal of Politics,* 1 (December): 654-666. **273.** Barclay, 1964. **274.** The horseshoe symbol was chosen because the first meeting of what came to be the Keeley League was held in a blacksmith shop. Flinn, 1892, pp. 656-657. **275.** Barclay, 1964, p. 361. **276.** Weitz, 1989, pp. 22-23. **277.** Scott, 1974, p. 45. **278.** "Account of an Interview with John Kelly", Box 23 Keeley Institute Records, Illinois State Historical Library. **279.** Scott, 1974, p. 72. **280.** The Neal contract is in the William Helfand Collection. **281.** Hargreaves, 1880, p. 6. **282.** For other Keeley outcome reports, see: Keeley, L. (1891). My Gold Cure. *North American Review,* 153 (December) 759-761; Speed, J. (1891). Dr. Keeley's Treatment for Drunkenness. *Harper's Weekly* 35:755; Haskell, W. (1896). Keeley Cure for Inebriety. *The Arena,* 16 (July):222-227. **283.** Keeley, 1892, pp. 10-11, Pamphlet. **284.** Keeley, 1897, p. 128. **285.** Scott, 1974, p. 82; Helfand, W. (1996). Selling Addiction Cures. *Transactions & Studies of the College of Physicians of Philadelphia Series* V, 43 (December), pp. 85-108; William Helfand Collection. **286.** Key, B. (Circa 1894). Good Advice and Practical Hints Relative to the Opium, Morphine, Chloral, Whiskey, Cocaine and Kindred Habits (or Diseases) and Their Treatment and Cure. Chattanooga, Tennessee: Dr. Bailey P. Key (Advertising Pamphlet). **287.** Morgan, 1989, p. 148. **288.** Keeley, 1892, pp. 39-40. **289.** Kerr, N. (1892). Secret Specifics for Inebriety. *QJI* 14:350-351. **290.** Clark, 1893, p. 117. **291.** Keeley's practice of keeping his formula secret was typical of the addiction institute cures and mail order cures. The Gatlin Institute sued Dr. Benjamin Neal, a one-time employee, for stealing their formula and starting his own chain of addiction cure institutes. Dr Neal, for his part, maintained that he kept his formula secret because it required special competence to administer. The Modern Method for Treatment of Alcoholism, AMA Archives, Box 0033-13. **292.** Evans, B. (1893). Keeleyism and Keeley Methods, with Some Statistics. *Medical News,* 62:477-484. **293.** Crothers, 1898, pp. 755-757. **294.** Chapman, C. (1893). The Bichloride of Gold Treatment for Dipsomania. *Chicago Medical Recorder,* 4:104-111; Evans, 1893, p. 484. **295.** Speed, 1891, pp. 755-756. **296.** Scott, 1974; Weitz, 1989. **297.** Mines, J. (1891). Drunkenness is Curable. *The North American Review,* 153:442-449. **298.** Buckley, 1895, article without journal designation, Keeley Archives. **299.** Keeley, 1897, p. 115. **300.** Inside the History of the Keeley Cure. (1907). *JAMA,* 49:1861-1864, **301.** Dewey, R. (1892). Insanity Following the Keeley Treatment for Inebriety. *International Medical Magazine,* pp.1142-1152. **302.** Weitz, 1989. **303.** Weitz, 1989. **304.** Keeley Institute Building is Used by Bootleggers, *Los Angeles Times,* August 5, 1920, p. 3. **305.** Ruff, C. (1972). The Keeley Institute. *Illinois History* 8:193-194. **306.** Sigler, 1993, p. 28. **307.** Weitz, 1989, p. 37. **308.** Personal Interview, James Oughton, Jr., July 11, 1995 and January 29, 1996. **309.** Personal Interviews, James Oughton, Jr. and Mrs. Anne Winthrow, 1995. **310.** Spreng, R. (1948). Alcoholism and the Keeley Treatment Presented at the North Central Illinois Medical Association, November 11, Princeton, Illinois. **311.** Inside the Keeley Institute (1960). *The Magazine of Livingston County,* pp. 6-11; Weitz, 1989. **312.** Peterson, in an 1893 article in the *Journal of the American Medical Association* reported: "The so-called gold cure of Keeley, upon analysis, was found to contain about 1/32 of a grain of muriate of ammonia, 1/16 grain of aloin, and 45 minims of compound tincture of cinchoma. His hypodermic injection was ascertained to be composed of sulphate of strychnia, atropia, and boric acid." Peterson, 1893, p. 408. **313.** Keeley, 1893, p. 412. **314.** Symptoms included dilated pupils, blurred vision, dryness of the mouth and throat, skin rash, short-term memory loss, mild confusion, dizziness, weakness, and temporary loss of sexual libido. **315.** It is perhaps a touch of irony that Keeley himself discussed atropine in his 1897 book,*Opium: Its Use, Abuse, and Cure,* and described symptoms of its use that precisely matched the symptoms his patients described experiencing during their first week of Double Chloride of Gold treatments. Keeley, 1897, p. 68-73. **316.** An 1893 report critical of the Keeley method attributed this lost appetite for alcohol to the nausea-inducing injections of apomorphine. Apomorphine emerged in the twentieth century as a nauseant drug used in aversion therapy. Chapman, 1893, p.109. **317.** Bannister, H. (1892). The Bichloride of Gold Cure for Inebriety. *American Journal of Insanity,* 48:470-475 (June). **318.** Baumohl, 1993, p. 100; Warsh, 1988, p. 129.

Chapter Eight: Miracle Cures of Alcoholism and Other Addictions

319. Rogers, A. (1913). Some Observations During Eighteen Years Experience With Drug and Liquor Habitués. *Wisconsin Medical Journal,* 12:40-43 (July). **320.** DeCorse, C. (1984). Elixirs, Nerve Tonics, and Panaceas: The Medicine Trade in Nineteenth-Century New Hampshire. *Historical New Hampshire* 39:1-23. **321.** Furnas, J. (1965). *The Life and Times of the Late Demon Rum.* London: W.H. Allen; Cherrington, 1926; Holbrook, S. (1959). *The Golden Age of Quackery.* NY: Macmillan Co. **322.** Clum, F. (1888). *Inebriety: Its Causes, Its Results, Its Remedy.* Philadelphia: Lippincott, p. 914. **323.** The general references for the products listed in this section include Nostrums & Quackery, 1910, 170-178; Cramp, 1921; AMA

Archives 9 Boxes, Headings Alcoholism and Substance Abuse, Call Numbers 0030-09/0035-12 and 0822-04/0824-11. **324.** AMA Archives, Box 0035-07. **325.** Century-Old 'Cure.' (1970). AA *Grapevine,* 26(12)40. (May). **326.** Advertising Flyer, Pittman Archives. **327.** Nyswander, M. (1956). *The Addict as a Patient.* NY: Gruene & Stratton, p. 9. **328.** Brown, H. (1872). An Opium Cure. In: Grob, G. Ed., (1981). *American Perspectives on Drug Addiction.* NY: Arno Press, p. 41. **329.** Holbrook, 1959, pp. 87, 174; Nostrums and Quackery, 2nd ed., 1912, Chicago: AMA; Drugs to Curb The Tobacco Habit (1963). *The Medical Letter on Drug Therapeutics,* 5(10):1-2; AMA Archives, Files 0030-09, 0031-01, 0031-02, 0031-4. **330.** Fobes, W. (1895). The Alcohol, Tobacco and Opium Habits: Their Effect on Body and Mind and the Means of Cure. In: Grob, G. Ed., (1981). *American Perspectives on Drug Addiction.* NY: Arno Press, p. 1. **331.** Mason, L. (1903). Patent and Proprietary Medicines as the Cause of the Alcoholic and Opium Habit or Other Forms of Narcomania: With Some Suggestions as to How the Evil May Be Remedied. *QJI,* 25:1-13. (January). **332.** Advertising pamphlet, Circa 1890, IASI Collection. **333.** Directions for the Use of Denarco, AMA Archives, Box 0823-07. **334.** AMA Archives, Advertising Pamphlet, Box 0035-05. **335.** AMA Archives, Box 0823-03. **336.** William Helfand Collection. **337.** White Cross Anti-Liquor Society Correspondence, AMA Archives, Box 0035-11. **338.** AMA Archives, Report from Post Office Department, p. 3, Box 0030-10. **339.** Helfand, 1996, p. 92. **340.** AMA Archives, Box 0824-06. **341.** AMA Archives, Box 0033-13. **342.** Bradner, N. (1890). Report of the Committee on Nostrums, Proprietary Medicines, and New Drugs. *QJI,* 12:25,36-38. (January). **343.** Bradner, 1890, pp. 36-37. **344.** Peterson, F. (1893). The Treatment of Alcoholic Inebriety. *JAMA,* 20:408-411. **345.** Mattison, J. (1886-1887). Cocaine Dosage and Cocaine Addiction. *Peoria Medical Monthly,* 7:568-579; Jaffe, 1976, p. 73. **346.** Musto, D. (1973). *The American Disease: Origins of Narcotic Controls.* New Haven: Yale University Press, pp. 79-81, 88-90. **347.** Dykstra, D. (1955). The Medical Profession and the Patent and Proprietary Medicines during the Nineteenth Century. *Bulletin of the History of Medicine* 29:401-419. **348.** Gilbert, S. (1989). *Medical Fakes and Frauds.* NY: Chelsea House Publications, p. 38. **349.** Holbrook, 1959, p. 21. **350.** Towns, C. (NDa). The Habit That Destroys--How To Destroy It. NY: Charles B. Towns Hospital (Promotional Article/Brochure); Towns, C. (NDb). *Special Information for Physicians Concerning the Organization and Work of the Charles B. Towns Hospital, 293 Central Park West, New York (Promotional Brochure).* **351**. Young, J. (1961). *The Toadstool Millionaires: A Social History of Patent Medicines in America before Federal Regulation.* Princeton, New Jersey: Princeton University Press, p. 132. **352.** Young, 1961, p. 243. **353.** Towns, C. (1915). *Alcohol and Tobacco, and the Remedy.* **354.** Cures for Liquor and Drug Habits, National Better Business Bureau, Inc., pp. 1-5, AMA Archives, Box 0031-02. **355.** Masters, W. (1931). *The Alcohol Habit and Its Treatment.* London: H.K. Lewis & Co.; Jellinek, E.M., Ed. (1942). *Alcohol Addiction and Chronic Alcoholism.* New Haven: Yale University Press, p. 57. **356.** Rx Medicinal Spirits; the Peculiar Claims for "Nonintoxicating" Whiskey. (1939). *JAMA,* 112:351. **357.** Rx, 1939, p. 351. **358.** The promotion of so-called "non-intoxicating" liquors as remedies for the alcohol habit goes back at least to 1902, when the product Whiskol (28.2% alcohol) was widely advertised as a "non-intoxicating stimulant." (The Alcohol in Secret Nostrums, 1904, *Medical World,* 22:228). **359.** Anderson, D. (1950). *The Other Side of the Bottle.* NY: A.A. Wyn, Inc., pp. 106-118. **360.** AMA Archives, Box, 0823-11. **361.** Federal Trade Commission Press Release, August 14, 1941, AMA Archives, Box 0031-03. **362.** FTC Press Release, AMA Archives, Box 0035-01. **363.** Kane, 1881, p. 220. **364.** Kane, H. (1882). *Opium-Smoking in America and China.* NY: G.P. Putnam & Sons. **365.** Crothers, T.D. (1892). Specifics for the Cure of Inebriety. *The Popular Science Monthly,* 41:732-739; Crothers, 1902, p. 48. **366.** Benton, G. (1914). State Control and Inspection of Public and Private Institutions. *JI,* 35(5), 210-212. **367.** Towns, 1915, p. 178. **368.** Helfand, 1996, p. 91.

Chapter Nine: Religious Conversion as a Remedy for Alcoholism

369. General references for this chapter include Conley, P. and Sorensen, A. (1971). *The Staggering Steeple: The Story of Alcoholism and the Churches.* Philadelphia: The Pilgrim Press. **370.** Tyler, A. (1944). *Freedom's Ferment.* NY: Harper and Row, p. 319. **371.** Chavigny, K. (1997). Reforming Drunkards in Nineteenth-Century America: A Popular Religious Therapeutic Tradition Presented at Historical Perspectives on Drug and Alcohol Use in American Society, 1800-1997 College of Physicians of Philadelphia, May 9-11. **372.** Chavigny, 1997. **373.** Abel, E. (1987). *Alcohol: Wordlore and Folklore.* Buffalo. NY: Prometheus Books, p. 130; Fleming, A. (1975). *Alcohol: The Delightful Poison.* NY: Delacorte Press, pp. 35-36; Levinson, D. (1974). The Etiology of Skid Rows in the United States. *International Journal of Social Psychiatry,* 20:25-33. **374.** This section has been constructed primarily from Arthur Bonner's 1967 account of Jerry McAuley and the Water Street Mission. **375.** Bonner, A. (1967). *Jerry McAuley and His Mission.* Neptune, NJ: Loizeaux Brothers, p. 22. **376.** Bonner, 1967, p. 35. **377.** Bonner, 1967, pp. 41-44. **378.** Bonner, 1967, p. 87. **379.** Bonner, 1967, p. 67. **380.** Bonner, 1967, p. 39. **381.** Bonner, 1967, p. 78. **382.** B., Mel (1991). *New Wine: The Spiritual Roots of the Twelve Step Miracle.* Center City, MN: Hazelden Pittman Archives Press, p. 52. **383.** Dunn, Rev. J. (1877). *Moody's Talks on Temperance.* NY: National Temperance Society and Publication House. **384.** Boyer, P. (1978). *Urban Masses and Moral Order in America, 1820-1920.* Cambridge, MA: Harvard University Press, p. 136. **385.** Boyer, 1978, p. 140. **386.** Boyer, 1978, p. 140; Mckinley, E. (1986). *Somebody's Brother: A History of the Salvation Army Men's Social Service Department, 1891-1985.* Lewiston, NY: The Edwin Mellen Press. **387.** McKinley, 1986, p. 131. **388.** McKinley, 1986, pp. 178-179. **389.** Stoil, M. (1987). Salvation and Sobriety.

AHRW 2(3):14-17. **390.** Raws, W. (1996a). History of America's Keswick (unpublished manuscript provided by the Keswick Colony of Mercy, Whiteing, New Jersey); Raws, W. (1996b). Our Story, His Story Keswick Today: *The Newsletter of America's Keswick* (Fall), pp. 1,5; Personal Interview with William Raws, November 11, 1996. **391.** Included among these facilities are Bethel Colony of Mercy in Lenoir, NC; the Dunklin Memorial Camp in Okeechobee, FL; the Friends of Alcoholics in Pocahontas, MS; Hebron Colony and Grace Home in Boone, SC; the Home of Grace in Vancleave, MS; and Mission Acres in Pleasant View, TN). **392.** Bannister, 1892, p. 475. **393.** Leuba, J. (1896). A Study in the Psychology of Religious Phenomenon. *American Journal of Psychology*, 7:309-385. **394.** Cutten, 1907, pp. 285-287. **395.** Starbuck, E. (1897). A Study of Conversion. *American Journal of Psychology.* 8:268-308; Starbuck, E. (1901). *The Psychology of Religion.* NY: Walter Charles Scribner's Sons. **396.** Monroe, H. (1914). *Twice-Born Men in America.* Philadelphia, PA: The Lutheran Publication Society. **397.** James, W. (1902). *The Varieties of Religious Experience.* NY: Penguin Books (1985 Penguin Classic Edition). **398.** James, 1902, p. 196. **399.** James, 1902, p. 210, 196. **400.** James, 1902, p. 237. **401.** Partridge, 1912, p. 259. **402.** Fleming, R. (1937). The Treatment of Chronic Alcoholism. *NEJM,* 217:779-783. (November). **403.** Anderson, 1950, p. 134. **404.** Willet, J. (Rev.). (1877). *The Drunkard's Diseased Appetite: What is It? If Curable, How? By Miraculous Agency or Physical Means--Which?* Fort Hamilton, NY: Inebriates Home, Fort Hamilton, Kings County, New York, p. 13. **405.** Bacon, S. and Roth, F. (1943). *Drunkenness in Wartime Connecticut.* Hartford: Connecticut War Council, pp. 39-41.

Section 3
Chapter Ten: Alcoholism Treatment Settings: 1900-1940

1. Anderson, V. (1916). The Alcoholic as Seen in Court. *BMSJ,* 74:492-495. **2.** General references for this section include Mason, L. (1909). The Relation of the Pauper Inebriate to the State from an Economic Point of View. In: *The Alcohol Problem and Its Practical Relations to Life* (Paper read at the American Society for the Study of Alcohol and Other Drug Narcotics, Washington, DC, March 17-19, Washington: GPO, pp. 74-84.; Lawrence, A. (1909). The Medico-legal Care of Alcoholic Defectives In: *The Alcohol Problem and Its Practical Relations to Life.* Paper read at the American Society for the Study of Alcohol and Other Drug Narcotics, Washington, DC, March 17-19, Washington: GPO, pp. 71-73; Latimer, D. and Goldberg, J. (1981). *Flowers in the Blood: The Story of Opium.* NY: Franklin Watts; Pittman, B. (1988). *AA: The Way It Began.* Seattle, Washington: Glen Abbey Books. **3.** Crothers, T.D. (1891). Are Inebriates Curable? *JAMA,* 17:923-927. **4.** Crothers, T.D. (1893). *The Disease of Inebriety from Alcohol, Opium and Other Narcotic Drugs: Its Etiology, Pathology, Treatment and Medico-legal Relations.* NY: E.B. Treat, Publisher. **5.** Crothers, T.D. (1902). The Drug Habits and Their Treatment. Chicago: G.P. Englehard & Company. **6.** Ford, J. (1910). The First Farm Colony for Inebriates and Its Work. *Survey,* 25:46-55. **7.** Peterson, F. (1893). The Treatment of Alcoholic Inebriety. *JAMA,* 20:408-411. **8.** Cohen, M. and Kern, J. (1983). The Influence of Morality on Alcoholism Treatment: An Historical Analysis. *Journal of Psychiatric Treatment Evaluation,* 5:269-276. **9.** Medicolegal Notes: The Commitment of Alcoholics to Medical Institutions (1940). *QJSA,* 1(2):372-387; Corwin, E. and Cunningham, E. (1944). Institutional Facilities for the Treatment of Alcoholism. *QJSA,* 5(1)36. **10.** The First City Farm for Inebriates (1912). *The Survey* (November 16):209-211. **11.** Samson, C. (1913-14). The Care and Treatment of Inebriates in New York. *British JI,* 11:27-29. **12.** Cohen and Kearn, 1983; Burritt, B. (1910). The Habitual Drunkard. *Survey,* 36 (October) p.31. **13.** Baumohl, J. (1986a). *Dashaways and Doctors: The Treatment of Habitual Drunkards in San Francisco from the Gold Rush to Prohibition.* Doctoral Dissertation, Berkeley, CA: University of California. **14.** McCormick, 1941, pp. 243, 251. **15.** Moore, M. and Gray, M. (1937). The Problem of Alcoholism as the Boston City Hospital. *NEJM,* 217:388. **16.** Deutsch, A. (1937, 1949). *The Mentally Ill in America: A History of Their Care and Treatment from Colonial Times.* NY: Columbia University Press. **17.** Dana, C. (1890). A Study of Alcoholism as it Occurs in the Belleville Hospital Cells. *N.Y. Medical Journal,* 51:564-647. **18.** Dana, C. (1891). Inebriety: A Study of its Causes, Duration, Prophylaxis, and Management. *QJI,* 23:469-479; Meyer, A. (1932). Alcohol as a Psychiatric Problem. In: Emerson, H. Ed. *Alcohol and Man: The Effects of Alcohol on Man in Health and Disease.* NY: The MacMillan Company; Parkhurst, G. (1938). Drinking and Alcoholism. *Harper's Magazine,* 177:468-469 (July). **19.** Voegtlin, W. and Lemere, F. (1942). The Treatment of Alcohol Addiction: A Review of the Literature. *QJSA,* 2:717-803. **20.** Flemming, R. (1937). Management of Chronic Alcoholism in England, Scandinavia and Central Europe. *NEJM,* 216:279-289. (February 18). **21.** Wiebe, R. (1967). *The Search for Order: 1877-1920.* NY: Hill and Wang. **22.** Osborn, W. (1907). State Care and Treatment of Inebriates. *Bulletin of Iowa Institutions,* p 6. **23.** Pollock, H. and Furbush, E. (1917). Insane, Feebleminded, Epileptics and Inebriates in Institutions in the United States. *Mental Hygiene,* 99: 548-566 (January 1). **24.** Corwin and Cunningham, 1944, p. 43, 48-49. **25.** Baumohl, J. (1992). The "Dope Fiend's Paradise" Revisited: Notes on Research in Progress on Drug Law Enforcement in San Francisco, 1875-1915. *The Surveyor* 24:3-16. **26.** Baumohl, J. And Tracy, S. (1994). Building Systems to Manage Inebriates: The Divergent Pathways of California and Massachusetts, 1891-1920. *CDP,* 21: 557-597. **27.** Grob, G. (1983). *Mental Illness and American Society, 1875-*

1940. Princeton, NJ: Princeton University Press; Novick, R. (1941). The Problem of Alcoholism in State Hospitals. *Illinois Medical Journal* 80: 414-419. **28.** These gloomy reports of treatment outcome in the 1940s are in marked contrast to Dr. Alexander Lambert's 1912 reports of studies in Massachusetts and Iowa, showing 49% and 42% of alcoholic patients remaining sober or greatly improved following their treatment at these institutions. Lambert, A. (1912). Care and Control of the Alcoholic. *BMSJ,* 166:615-620. **29.** Pollock, H. (1932). The Prevalence of Mental Disease Due to Alcoholism. In: Emerson, H. Ed. *Alcohol and Man: The Effects of Alcohol on Man in Health and Disease.* NY: The MacMillan Company. **30.** Advertising flyer, Pittman Archives, Hazelden. **31.** Corwin and Cunningham, 1944, pp. 54-55. **32.** Seabrook, W. (1935). *Asylum.* NY: Harcourt, Brace and Company, Inc. **33.** More detailed information on William Seabrook can be found in his own work, *Asylum,* and in the book *The Strange World of Willie Seabrook.* (1966). NY:Harcourt, Brace & World, Inc. by Marjorie Worthington (Seabrook's second wife). **34.** Cabot, R. (1911). The Towns-Lambert Treatment for Morphinism and Alcoholism. *BMSJ,* 164:676-77 (May 11). **35.** Merwin, S. (1912). Fighting the Deadly Habits. *American Magazine,* 74:708-717. (October). **36.** It is impossible not to consider the possibility that this "country doctor" was Dr. Leslie Keeley and that the Towns treatment was an adaptation of the Keeley cure. **37.** Merwin, 1912, p. 716. **38.** Macfarlane, P. (1913). The "White Hope" for Drug Victims. *Collier's,* November 29, pp. 16-17, 29-30. **39.** Macfarlane, 1913, p. 16. **40.** Lambert, 1912; Cabot, 1911. **41.** Towns, C. (1914). *The Physician's Guide for the Treatment of the Drug Habit and Alcoholism.* (8 page pamphlet). **42.** Towns, C. (1922). *Hospital Treatment for Alcohol and Drug Addiction.* (Promotional brochure targeting physicians, 27 pages). **43.** Towns, 1914, p. 7. **44.** Towns, 1914, p. 8. **45.** Towns, C. (1928). *The Medical Treatment of Alcohol and Drug Addictions by Modern Hospital Methods.* New York City: Charles B. Towns Hospital (Promotional Pamphlet). **46.** Towns, 1928, p. 8. **47.** Towns, C. (1912). Help for the Hard Drinker. *Century Magazine,* June (Reprint) p. 4; Towns, C. (1917). Successful Medical Treatment in Chronic Alcoholism. *The Modern Hospital,* 8 (1):10. **48.** Towns, C. (1917). The Present and Future of Narcotive Pathology. *Medical Review of Reviews, N.Y.,* 23:35-37, 113-119, 195-201. **49.** Towns, 1917, p. 115. **50.** Towns, 1917, p. 103. **51.** Towns, 1916, p. 10. **52.** Lambert, A. (1912). Care and Control of the Alcoholic. *BMSJ,* 166:615-621. **53.** Lambert, A. (1909). The Obliteration of the Craving for Narcotics. *JAMA,* 53(13): 985-989. (September 25). **54.** Towns, 1922, p. 7-8. **55.** Towns, 1928, p. 8. **56.** Towns, C. (ND). The Habit That Destroys--How To Destroy It. NY: Charles B. Towns Hospital (Promotional Article/Brochure); Towns, 1914, p. 7; Musto, D. (1973). *The American Disease: Origins of Narcotic Controls.* New Haven: Yale University Press, pp. 79-81, 88-90. **57.** Lambert, 1912, p. 619. **58.** Colonel Ed Towns, (Towns Hospital, NY: City) (1960). 25th A.A. International Convention, Long Beach, CA. (Audiotape). **59.** White, J. (1955). *Ward N-1.* NY: A.A. Wyn, Inc. **60.** Towns, C. (1912). The Peril of the Drug Habit and the Need for Restrictive Legislation. *Century Magazine,* 84:580-587. **61.** Towns, C. (1917). The Sociological Aspect of the Treatment of Alcoholism. *The Modern Hospital,* 8(2):103-106; Merwin, 1912, p. 717.

Chapter Eleven: Physical Methods of Treatment and Containment

62. Rosenberg, C. (1976). *No Other Gods: On Science and American Social Thought.* Baltimore: John Hopkins University Press. **63.** Clum, F. (1888). *Inebriety: Its Causes, Its Results, Its Remedy.* Philadelphia: Lippincott; Steele, J. (1888). *Hygienic Physiology with Special Reference to the Use of Alcoholic Drinks and Narcotics.* NY: American Book Company. **64.** Crothers, T.D. (1902). *Morphinism and Narcomanias from other Drugs.* Philadelphia: W.B. Saunders & Company; Grob, G. Ed., (1981). *The Medical Profession and Drug Addiction.* NY: Arno Press. **65.** Quoted in Wilkerson, 1966, p. 222. **66.** Kevles, D. (1985). *In the Name of Eugenics: Genetics and the Uses of Human Heredity.* NY: Alfred A. Knopf. **67.** Kevles, 1985, p. 47. **68.** Sparks, A. (1898). Alcoholism in Women: Its Causes, Consequence, and Cure. *QJI,* 20:31-37. **69.** Quoted in Parmelee, M. (1909). *Inebriety In Boston.* Ph.D. Thesis. NY: Columbia University, p. 65. **70.** Reilly, P. (1991). *The Surgical Solution: A History of Involuntary Sterilization in the United States.* Baltimore: The Johns Hopkins University Press; Sinclair, A. (1962). *Era of Excess: A Social History of the Prohibition Movement.* NY: Harper & Row Publishers. **71.** Pittman, B. (1988). *AA: The Way It Began.* Seattle, Washington: Glen Abbey Books. **72.** Vines, S. (1899). The Prevention of Alcoholism. *Lancet* 2:1125. **73.** Boody, G. (1903). *Acute and Chronic Alcoholism.* Sioux City: Iowa State Medical Society; These proposals continued well into the 1930s and 1940s. The following recommendation appeared in 1935 in the *STJ:* "The best measure to prevent parenthood of the "degenerate" drunkards would be early and, if possible, voluntary sterilization. . . .Considering that the alcoholics in question all come from families with many hereditary defects, sterilization is justified by general eugenic considerations." Gachot, H. (1935). Alcohol and Eugenics. *STJ,* Spring, pp. 12-16. **74.** Quoted in Reilly, 1991, p. 53. **75.** Kevles, 1985. **76.** Reilly, 1991. **77.** Gachot, in a 1935 article on alcohol and Eugenics, reported that 23 alcoholics who had been admitted to the California State Asylum for alcoholic psychosis were sterilized during years 1910-1912. (Gachot, 1925, p. 16) Baumohl, who reviewed data on sterilization of alcoholics in California's state psychiatric hospitals, noted that less than 10% of those sterilized had alcoholism-related diagnoses. Baumohl, J. (1986a). *Dashaways and Doctors: The Treatment of Habitual Drunkards in San Francisco from the Gold Rush to Prohibition.* Doctoral Dissertation, Berkeley, CA: University of California, p. 349. **78.** Fahrenkrug, H. (1991). Alcohol and the State in Nazi Germany: 1933-1945. In: Barrows, S. and Room, R. Eds. *Drinking Behavior and Belief in Modern History.* Berkeley: University of California Press, pp. 315-334.; Kevles, 1985; Rafter, N. (1988). *White Trash: The Eugenic Family Studies 1877-1919.* Boston: Northeastern University Press; Fahrenkrug, 1991, pp. 315-334. **79.** Lindlahr, H. (1919). *Practice of Natural Therapeutics.* Chicago: Lindlahr Publishing Company. **80.** Editorial: New Methods of Treatment of Inebriety. (1898). *QJI*, 20:119-120. **81.** McBride, C. (1910). *The Modern Treatment of Alcoholism and Drug Narcotism.* London: Rebman Limited. **82.** Pettey, G. (1913). *Narcotic Drug Diseases and Allied Ailments.* Philadelphia: F.A. Davis Co.. **83.** Wall, J. (1937). A Study of Alcoholism in Women. *The AJP,* 93:943-952. **84.** Cayleff, S. (1987). *Wash and Be Healed: The Water-Cure Movement and Women's Health.* Philadelphia, PA: Temple University Press. **85.** Cayleff, 1987, p. 3. **86.** Tyler, A. (1944). *Freedom's Ferment.* NY: Harper and Row. **87.** Buchman, D. (1979). *The Complete Book of Water Therapy.* NY: E.P. Dutton. **88.** Katcher, 1993, p. 278. **89.** Longmate, N. (1968). *The Waterdrinkers: A History of Temperance.* NY: Hamish Hamilton. **90.** Cayleff, 1987, p. 123; Shephard, C. (1909). The Turkish Baths in Inebriety In: *The Alcohol Problem and Its Practical Relations to Life.* (Paper read at the American Society for the Study of Alcohol and Other Drug Narcotics, Washington D.C., March 17-19, Washington: GPO, pp. 170-176. **91.** Weiss, H. and Kemble, H. (1967). *The Great American Water-cure Craze: A History of Hydropathy in the United States.* Trenton: The Past Times Press. **92.** Kellogg, J. (1898). A New and Successful Method of Treatment for the Opium Habit and Other Forms of Drug Addiction. *Modern Medicine and Bacteriological Review,* 7:125-132 (June); Kellogg, J. (1903). The Treatment of Drug Addiction. *QJI,* 25:30–43 (January); Kellogg, J. (1915). *Neurasthenia.* Battle Creek, Michigan: Good Health Publishing Co. **93.** Gehman, J. (1943). *Smoke Over America.* East Aurora, NY: Roycrafters. **94.** Marcet, J. (1868). *On Chronic Alcoholic Intoxication: With an Inquiry into the Influence of the Abuse of Alcohol as a Predisposing Cause of Disease.* NY: Moorhead, Simpson and Bond. **95.** Gallavardin, D. (1890). *The Homeopathic Treatment of Alcoholism.* Philadelphia: Hahnemann Publishing House. **96.** Sournia, J. (1990). *A History of Alcoholism.* Cambridge, MA: Basil Blackwell, Inc; Pittman, 1988, p. 62. **97.** Black, J. (1889). Advantages of Substituting the Morphia Habit for the Incurably Alcoholic. *The Cincinnati Lancet--Clinic,* 22:540. **98.** McBride, 1910. **99.** Greer, J., Albright, I., and Smith, D. (1915). *Tragedies of the Opium Trade.* Chicago: J. Regan & Company. **100.** Scott, J. (1918). Drug Addiction. *Medical Clinics of North America,* 2:607-615. **101.** Kellogg, 1989, p. 128. **102.** DeRopp, R. (1957). *Drugs and the Mind.* NY: Grove Press, Inc. **103.** Voegtlin and Lemere, 1942, p. 775 **104.** General References for this section include Kolb, (1959). *Narcotic Drug Problems: Proceedings of the Symposium on the History of Narcotic Drug Addiction Problems, March 27-28, 1958, Bethesda, MD.* Bethesda, MD: National Institute of Mental Health.; Rodgers, J. (1992). *Psychosurgery.* NY: Harper Collins Publishers.; Sergeant, W. (1967). *The Unquiet Mind: The Autobiography of a Physician in Psychological Medicine.* (Quoted in Porter, R. (1991). *The Faber Book of Madness* London: faber and faber); Vallenstein, E. (1986). *Great and Desperate Cures: The Rise and Decline of Psycho Surgery and Other Radical Treatments for Mental Illness.* NY: Basic Books; and Wikler, A., Pescor, M., Kalbaugh, E., and Angelucci, R. (1952). Effects of Frontal Lobotomy on the Morphine-abstinence Syndrome in Man. *A.M.A. Archives of Neurological Psychiatry,* 71:510-521. **105.** Rodebaugh, H. (1903). The Value of Surgery in Certain Cases of Inebriety. *QJI,* 25:115-121. **106.** Valenstein, 1986. **107.** Sergeant, 1967. **108.** Talbot, B., Bellis, E. And Greenblatt, M. (1951). Alcoholism and Lobotomy. *QJSA, 12(3):386-394.* **109.** Vallenstein, E., Ed. (1980). *The Psychosurgery Debate: Scientific, Legal and Ethical Perspectives* San Francisco: W. H. Freeman. **110.** "The Solution: Surgery." (1976). *AA Grapevine,* 33(6):45. (November). **111.** Ashworth, W. (1932). Rambling Thoughts About Whiskey and Drug Addiction. *Virginia Medical Monographs,* 58:678; Voegtlin, W. and Lemere, F. (1942), p. 772; Corwin and Cunningham, 1944, pp. 11-85. **112.** Gonorrhea, A Cure for Inebriety (1900). *Canadian Practice,* 25:170.

Chapter Twelve: Psychological Approaches to Alcoholism and Addiction Treatment

113. Abraham, K. (1908, 1926). The Psychological Relations Between Sexuality and Alcoholism. *International Journal of Psycho-Analysis,* 7:2-10. (January). **114.** Abraham, 1908, 1926, pp. 4,7 **115.** Brill, L, (1977). Historical Evolution of the Current Drug Treatment Perspective. In: Schecter, A. *Rehabilitation Aspects of Drug Dependence.* Cleveland, OH: CRC Press; Blum, E. (1966). Psychoanalytic Views on Alcoholism *QJSA,* 27(2): 259-299; Voegtlin and Lemere, 1942, p. 766; Jellinek, E.M., Ed. (1942). *Alcohol Addiction and Chronic Alcoholism* New Haven: Yale University Press. **116.** Blum. E., 1966, p. 263. **117.** Wurmser, L. (1978). *The Hidden Dimension: Psychodynamics in Compulsive Drug Use.* NY: Jason Aronson. **118.** Chafetz, M. and Demone, H. (1964). Alcoholism: Causes and Treatment. In: McCarthy, R. Ed. *Alcohol Education for Classroom and Community.* NY: McGraw-Hill Book Company. **119.** Steckel, W. (1924). *Peculiarities of Behavior: Wandering Manias, Dipsomania, Kleptomania, Pyromania and Allied Impulsive Acts.* NY: Liveright Publishing Corporation, p. 201. **120.** Stekel, 1924, pp. 212,227 **121.** Simmel, E. (1929). Psycho-analytic Treatment in a Sanatorium. *International Journal of Psycho-Analysis,* 10:70-89. **122.** Rado, S. (1933). The Psychoanalysis of Pharmacothymia. *Psychoanalytic Quarterly,* 2:1-23. **123.** Menninger, K. (1966). *Man Against Himself.* NY: Harcourt, Brace & World, Inc. **124.** Menninger, 1966, pp. 140-161. **125.** Bacon, S. and Roth, F. (1943). *Drunkenness in Wartime Connecticut.* Hartford: Connecticut War Council. **126.** Wurmser, 1978, p.163. **127.** Knight, R. (1938). The Psychoanalytic Treatment in a Sanatorium of Chronic Addiction to Alcohol. *JAMA,* 111: 1443-1446. **128.** Blum, E. and Blum R. (1967). *Alcoholism: Modern Psychological Approaches to Treatment.* San Francisco: Jossey-Bass Inc. **129.** Voegtlin, 1942, p. 765. **130.** Blum, 1966, p. 281. **131.** Knight, 1938, p. 1447. **132.** Tiebout, H. (1951a). The Role of Psychiatry in the Field of Alcoholism; With Comment on the Current Concept of Alcoholism as Symptom and as

Disease. *QJSA,* 12:52-57 (March). **133.** Tiebout, H. (1956a). Why Psychiatrists Fail with Alcoholics. *A.A. Grapevine,* 13(4):8. **134.** Brill, 1977, p. 17. **135.** Karpman, B. (1956). *The Alcoholic Woman: Case Studies in the Psychodynamics of Alcoholism.* Washington DC: The Linacre Press. **136.** Zimberg, S., Wallace, J., and Blume, S. (1978). *Practical Approaches to Alcoholism Psychotherapy.* NY: Plenum Press. **137.** Tiebout, H. (1955a). The Pink Cloud and After . *A.A..Grapevine,* 12(4):2.; Johnson, B. (1973). *The Alcoholism Movement in America: A Study in Cultural Innovation.* Ph.D. Dissertation. University of Illinois, p. 197 **138.** Hall, H.R. (1982). *Professionalism, Psychology, and Alcoholism: The Association for the Study of Inebriety, A Case Study.* Psy.D. Dissertation Rutgers University. The State University of New Jersey. **139.** Hall, 1982, p. 7. **140.** General references for this section include: Worcester, E. (1908). *Religion and Medicine, The Moral Control of Nervous Disorders.* NY: Moffatt, Yard and Co.; Boyd, T. (1909). *The How and Why of the Emanuel Movement, A Handbook on Psycho-Therapeutics.* San Francisco: The Emanuel Institute of Health.; Baylor, C. (1919). *Remaking a Man.* NY: Moffat, Yard & Company; Worcester, E. and McComb, S. (1931). *Body, Mind and Spirit.* Boston: Marshall Jones Company; Strecker, E. and Chambers, F. (1938). *Alcohol: One Man's Meat.* NY: The MacMillan Company; Anderson, D. (1944). Committee for Education on Alcoholism Historic Event. *AA Grapevine,* 1(5):1; Bishop, J. (1945). *The Glass Crutch: The Biographical Novel of William Wynne Wister.* NY: Doubleday, Doran & Co., Inc.; Clinebell, H. (1956). *Understanding and Counseling the Alcoholic.* NY: Abingdon Press; and McCarthy, K. (1984). Early Alcoholism Treatment: The Emmanuel Movement and Richard Peabody. *JSA,* 45(1):59-74. **141.** McComb, S. (1909). The Religio-Medical Movements--A Reply. *North American Review,* (March), pp. 445-454. **142.** McComb, 1909; Hale, N. (1971). *Freud and the Americans: The Beginnings of Psychoanalysis in the United States,* 1876-1917. NY: Oxford University Press. **143.** Peabody, R. (1936). The Danger Line of Drink. *Scribner's Magazine* (June), pp. 370-372. **144.** Purrington, W. (1909). The Church's Attitude Towards Mental Healing. *North American Review* 189:(642):719-730. **145.** One other obscure thread of historical continuity is the fact that the first regular A.A. meeting in Boston began at the Jacoby Club in 1941, along with the fact that an A.A. group now regularly meets in the old parish house where, 70 years earlier, alcoholics attended the classes taught by Worcester and McComb. P., Wally (1995). *But, For the Grace of God...: How Intergroups & Central Offices Carried the Message of Alcoholics Anonymous in the 1940s.* Wheeling, WV: The Bishop of Books, p. 51. **146.** McCarthy, 1984, p. 62. **147.** Mann, M. (1950). *Primer on Alcoholism.* NY: Rinehart and Company, p. 139. **148.** Baylor, 1919, p. 35. **149.** Baylor, 1919, p. 35. **150.** McCarthy, 1984, p. 60. **151.** Free, J. (1955). *Just One More: Concerning the Problem Drinker.* NY: Coward-McCann. **152.** Peabody, R. (1936). *The Common Sense of Drinking.* Boston: Little, Brown, and Company. **153.** Voegtlin, 1942, p. 747. **154.** Bramwell, J. (1903). On the Treatment of Dipsomania and Chronic Alcoholism by Hypnotic Suggestion. *JI,* 25:122. **155.** Quackenbos, J. (1908). Treatment of Inebriety by Hypnotic Suggestion. *JI,* 30(2):143-156. **156.** Peabody, R. (1930). Psychotherapeutic Procedure in the Treatment of Chronic Alcoholism. *Mental Hygiene,* 14:109-128. **157.** Peabody, 1930, pp. 124-125 **158** McCarthy, 1984, p. 60-61. **159.** Strecker, E. (1937). Some Thoughts Concerning the Psychology and Therapy of Alcoholism. *Journal of Nervous and Mental Disorders,* 86:191. **160.** Chambers, F. (1937). A Psychological Approach in Certain Cases of Alcoholism. *Mental Hygiene,* 21:67. **161.** Strecker and Chambers, 1938, p. 35. **162.** Strecker, 1937, p. 196; Chambers, F. (1968). *The Drinker's Addiction: Its Nature and Practical Treatment.* Springfield, Illinois: Charles C. Thomas, p. xii, 7, 73. **163.** Chambers, 1937, p. 74. **164.** Chambers, 1937, p. 76-77. **165.** Strecker and Chambers, 1938, pp. 190-191. **166.** Chambers, 1968, p. 87; Strecker and Chambers, 1938, p. 201. **167.** Chambers, 1968, pp. 127-135. **168.** Anderson, D. (1950). *The Other Side of the Bottle.* NY: A.A. Wyn, Inc.; Anderson, 1959, p. 161. **169.** Anderson, 1950. **170.** Strecker and Chambers, 1938, pp. 160-161. **171.** Anderson, D. (1944). The Place of the Lay Therapist in the Treatment of Alcoholics. *QJSA,* (September), pp. 257-266. **172.** Clapp, C. (1942). *Drunks Are Square Pegs.* NY: Island Press. **173.** Clapp, 1942, p. 94. **174.** If Drunks are Square Pegs, A.A. is My Square Hole, (1946). *AA Grapevine,* 2(9):6. **175.** Durfee, C. (1937). *To Drink or Not to Drink.* Boston: Longmans, Green; Durfee, C. (1938). Re-Education of the Problem Drinker. *Journal of the Connecticut Medical Society,* 2:486. **176.** Durfee, 1938, p. 486. **177.** Durfee, 1937, p. 75. **178.** MacNish, R. (1835). *Anatomy of Drunkenness.* NY: William Pearson & Co.; Rush, 1814; Crothers, T. D. (1911). *Inebriety: A Clinical Treatise on the Etiology, Symptomatology, Neurosis, Psychosis and Treatment.* Cincinnati, Ohio: Harvey Publishing Company; Keller, M. (1986). The Old and the New in the Treatment of Alcoholism. In: Strug, D.; Priyadarsini, S.; and Hyman, M., Eds., (1986). *Alcohol Interventions: Historical and Sociocultural Approaches.* NY: The Haworth Press. **179.** Rolleston, J. (1941). The Folklore of Alcoholism. *British JI* 39:30-36; Thimann, J. (1946). The Conditioned Reflex Treatment for Alcoholics. In: Glueck, B. Ed. *Current Therapies of Personality Disorders.* NY: Grune and Stratton. **180.** Sansweet, S. (1975). *The Punishment Cure.* NY: Mason/Charter. **181.** Shadel, C. (1944). Aversion Treatment of Alcohol Addiction. *QJSA,* 5 (2):216-228. **182.** Anderson, 1950, pp. 127-127. **183.** Shadel, 1944, p. 224. **184.** Shadel, 1944, pp. 227-228. **185.** O'Halloren, P. And Lemere, F. (1948). Conditioned-Reflex Treatment of Chronic Alcoholism: Results Obtained in 2,323 Net Cases from 3,125 Admissions Over a Period of Ten and a Half Years. *NEJM,* 139:331-333. **186.** Sansweet, 1975. **187.** Thimann, 1946, p. 104; Wallerstein, R. (1957). *Hospital Treatment of Alcoholism.* NY: Basic Books. **188.** Corwin and Cunnigham, 1944, pp. 30, 51. **189.** Thimann, 1946, p. 111. **190.** Sanderson, R., Campbell, D, and Laverty, S. (1963). An Investigation of a New Aversion Conditioning Treatment for Alcoholism. *QJSA,* 24:261-275; Madill, M, Campbell, D., Laverty, S., Vandewater, S. (1965). Aversion Treatment of Alcoholics by Succinylcholine-induced Apneic

Paralysis: An Analysis of Early Changes in Drinking Behavior. *QJSA*, 26:684-685; Sansweet, 1975. **191.** Holzinger, R., Mortimer, R. and Van Dusen, W. (1967). Aversion Conditioning Treatment of Alcoholism. *AJP*, 124(2):150-151. **192.** Hsu, J. (1965). Electro conditioning Therapy of Alcoholics: A Preliminary Report. *QJSA*, 26:449-59. **193.** For a review of the modern Schick's Shadel treatment methods and reported treatment outcomes, see Smith, J. and Frawley, J. (1993). Treatment Outcome of 600 Chemically Dependent Patients Treated in a Multimodality Inpatient Program Including Aversion Therapy and Pentathal Interviews. *JSAT*, 10:359-369. Shick's method of treating cocaine addiction is also described in Frawley, P. and Smith, J. (1990) Chemical Aversion in the Treatment of Cocaine Dependence as Part of a Multimodal Treatment Program: Treatment Outcome. *JSAT* 7(1):21-29. **194.** Portland Pioneer Continues Four-Decade Tradition (Raleigh Hills Celebrates 40th Anniversary). (1982). *Alcoholism Magazine.* (August) pp. 55-58.

Section 4
Chapter Thirteen: The Treatment of Addiction to Narcotics and Other Drugs: 1880-1925

1. Bentley, W. (1880). Erthroxylon Coca in the Opium and Alcohol Habits. *Detroit Therapeutic Gazette* 1:253-254. **2.** Bentley, 1880, p. 254. **3.** Estes, J. (1988). The Pharmacology of Nineteenth Century Patent Medicines. *Pharmacy in History*, 30:3-18; Huse, E. (1880). Coca-Erthoxylon–A New Cure for the Opium Habit. *The Therapeutic Gazette*, pp. 256-257. **4.** Whittaker, J. (1885). Cocaine for the Opium Habit. *Medical and Surgical Reporter*, 53:177-178. **5.** The practice of injecting a mixture of narcotic and cocaine solution may have actually come from this recommendation of using cocaine to treat opiate addiction. Dr. J.T. Whitaker recommended mixing cocaine and opium together as part of his treatment. Whittaker, J. (1885). Cocaine in the Treatment of the Opium Habit. *Medical News*, 47:144-149. (August 8). **6.** Musto, D. (1968). A Study of Cocaine: Holmes and Freud. *JAMA*, 204(1):27-32. **7.** Erlenmeyer, A. (1889). *On the Treatment of the Morphine Habit.* Detroit, Michigan: George S. Davis. (Translated from the German). **8.** Penfield, W. (1969). Halsted of John Hopkins: The Man and His Problem as Described in the Secret Records of William Osler. *JAMA,* 210:2214-18; Nuland, S. (1988). *Doctors: The Biography of Medicine.* NY: Vintage Books, pp. 386-421; Brecher, E. (1972). *Licit and Illicit Drugs.* Boston: Little, Brown and Company. **9.** Schneck, J. (1988). Cocaine Addiction and Dr. William S. Halsted. *Journal of Clinical Psychiatry* 49:503-504. **10.** Quoted in Penfield, 1969, p. 2216. **11.** Crothers, 1893. **12.** Morgan, H. (1981). *Drugs in America: A Social History 1800-1980.* Syracuse University Press. **13.** Prentice, A. (1921). The Problem of the Narcotic Drug Addict. *JAMA,* 76(23):1551-1556. **14.** Day, A. (1867). *Methomania: A Treatise on Alcoholic Poisoning.* Boston: James Campbell (Reprinted in Grob, G. Ed. *Nineteenth-Century Medical Attitudes Toward Alcoholic Addiction.* NY: Arno Press, 1981), p. 213. **15.** Crothers, T.D. (1902). *Morphinism and Narcomainias from other Drugs.* Philadelphia: W.B. Saunders & Company, p. 101. **16.** Mattison, J. (1893). The Modern and Humane Treatment of the Morphine Disease. *Medical Record,* 44:804-806 (December 23). **17.** Day, 1868, p. 230. **18.** Codeine was first introduced as a treatment for morphinism in 1885 by a California Physician named Lindenberger. Mattison, 1893, p. 805. **19.** The "free use of black coffee" as an opium treatment is attributed to Dr. J.M. DaCosta. Collins, S.B. (Circa 1890). The Original and Only Genuine Painless Opium Antidote. (Advertising Material-4 pages). **20.** Morgan, 1981, p. 71; Morgan, H. (1974). *Yesterday's Addicts: American Society and Drug Abuse, 1865-1920.* Norman, Oklahoma: University of Oklahoma Press. **21.** Sceleth, C. (1916). A Rational Treatment of the Morphine Habit. *JAMA,* March. **22.** Nellans, C. and Masse, J. (1929). Management of Drug Addicts in the United States Penitentiary at Atlanta. *JAMA* 29:1153-1155 (April 6). **23.** Lambert, A. And Tilney, F. (1926). The Treatment of Narcotic Addiction by Narcosan. *Medical Journal and Record*, 124:764-768. **24.** Livingston, R. Ed. (1959). *Narcotic Drug Addiction Problems: Proceedings of the Symposium on the History of Narcotic Drug Problems March 27 and 28, Bethesda, Maryland.* Bethesda, Maryland: National Institute of Mental Health. **25.** MacMartin, D. (1921). *Thirty Years in Hell.* Topeka, Kansas: Capper Printing Company. **26.** General references for this section include: Musto, 1973; Latimer, D. and Goldberg, J. (1981). *Flowers in the Blood: The Story of Opium* NY: Franklin Watts; Lindesmith, A. (1965, 1973). *The Addict and the Law.* Bloomington, IN: Indiana University Press; Courtwright, D. (1982); *Dark Paradise: Opiate Addiction in America before 1940.* Cambridge, Massachusetts: Harvard University Press; Courtwright, D. (1987). Willis Butler and the Shreveport Narcotic Clinic. *Social Pharmacology,* 1:13-24; Courtwright, D. (1991). Drug Legalization, The Drug War, and Drug Treatment in Historical Perspective. *Journal of Policy History,* 3:393-414. **27.** Kinder, D. (1991). Shutting Out the Evil: Nativism and Narcotics Control in the United States. *Journal of Policy History,* 3:468-93. **28.** Rippey, J. (1994). *Drug Abuse in America: An Historical Perspective.* Alexandria, Virginia: Behavioral Health Resource Press. **29.** Lindesmith, 1965, 1973; King, R. (1953). The Narcotics Bureau and the Harrison Act: Jailing the Healers and the Sick. *Yale Law Review,* 62: (April), pp. 736-49. **31.** McNamara, J. (1973). The History of United States' Anti-opium Policy. *Federal Probation* 37(2):15-21. **32.** Williams, H. (1938). *Drug Addicts are Human Beings.* Washington, D.C.: Shaw Publishing Company. **33.** Drug Treatment (1919). *Survey,* 42:147; Drug Addicts in the South (1919). *Survey*, 42:147-148. **34.** Payne, E. (1931). *The Menace of Narcotic Drugs: A Discussion of Narcotics and Education.* NY: Prentice-Hall, Inc. **35.** Graham-Mulhall, S. (1920). After-Care for the Narcotic Drug Addict. *Mental Hygiene*, 4:608-610 (July); Terry, C. and Pellens, M. (1928). *The Opium Problem*, Montclair, New Jersey: Patterson Smith. **36.** Jaffe, A. (1976). *Addiction Reform in the Progressive Age: Scientific and Social Responses to Drug Dependence in the United States, 1870-1930.* Ph.D. Dissertation,

University of Kentucky. **37.** Kolb, Lawrence (1962). *Drug Addiction: A Medical Problem.* Springfield, IL: Charles Thomas. **38.** Musto, D. and Ramos, M. (1981). Notes on American Medical History. A Follow-up Study of the New Haven Morphine Maintenance Clinic of 1920. *NEJM*, 304:1071. **39.** Musto, D. (1987)The History of Legislative Control Over Opium, Cocaine, and their Derivatives. In: Homowy, Ed. *Dealing With Drugs: Consequences of Government Control.* San Francisco: Pacific Research Institute for Public Policy. **40.** Federal Bureau of Narcotics (1955). *Narcotic Clinics in the United States.* Washington DC: U.S. GPO, p. 2. **41.** Musto, 1981, p. 1072; Council on Mental Health, American Medical Association (1966). Review of the Operation of the Narcotic "Clinics" Between 1919-1923. In: O'Donnell, J. And Ball, J. Eds. *Narcotic Addiction.* NY: Harper & Row, pp. 180-187. **42.** Musto, 1981, p. 1071. **43.** Payne, E. ,1931, p. 167. **44.** Regulations issued by the Department of Treasury in 1921 stated: "It is well established that the ordinary care of addiction yields to proper treatment, and that addicts will remain permanently cured when addiction is stopped." Austin, G. (1978). *Perspectives on the History of Psychoactive Substance Use.* Rockville, MD: NIDA/U.S. GPO, p. 219. **45.** Council on Mental Health-AMA, 1957, p. 183. **46.** Graham-Mulhall, S. (1926). *Opium: The Demon Flower.* NY: Harold Vinal, p. 125. **47.** Nyswander, M. (1956). *The Addict as a Patient.* NY: Gruene & Stratton, p. 9. **48.** Courtwright, D. (1986). Charles Terry. The Opium Problem and American Narcotic Policy. *JDI,* 16:422-425. **49.** Courtwright, 1986, pp. 421-434. **50.** Graham-Mulhall, S. (1921). Experiences in Narcotic Drug Control in the State of New York. *New York Medical Journal*, 113:106-111; Flowers, M. and Bonner, H. (1923). *The Menace of Morphine, Heroin and Cocaine* Pasadena, CA: Narcotic Education Association, p. 27; Federal Bureau of Narcotics, 1955, p. 5. **51.** Copeland, S. (1920). The Narcotic Drug Evil and the New York City Health Department. *American Medicine,* 15:17-23; Hubbard, S. (1920). Some Fallacies Regarding Narcotic Drug Addiction. *JAMA*, 74: 1439; Graham-Mulhall, 1921, p. 110; Anslinger, H. and Tompkins, W. (1953). *The Traffic in Narcotics.* NY: Funk & Wagnalls Company, p. 195. **52.** Graham-Mulhall, 1921, p. 26. **53.** Jaffe, 1976, p. 222. **54.** Nyswander, 1956, p. 7. **55.** Graham-Mulhall, 1921, p. 109. **56.** Graham-Mulhall, 1926, p. 22. **57.** Graham-Mulhall, 1921, pp. 111, 117. **58.** Hubbard, 1920, p. 1441. **59.** Graham-Mulhall, 1920, p. 606. **60.** Butler, W. (1922). How One American City is Meeting the Public Health Problems of Narcotic Addiction. *American Medicine,* 28:154-162. **61.** See Courtwright, 1987, for Butler's own fascinating account of the methods used to coerce him into closing the clinic. **62.** Waldorf, D., Orlick, M. and Reinarman, C. (1974). *Morphine Maintenance: The Shreveport Clinic 1919-1923.* Washington, DC: The Drug Abuse Council, Inc, p. 48. **63.** Baumohl, J. (1997). "Now We Won't Call it Lobbying": The Federal Bureau of Narcotics and the Depression-Era Maintenance Controversy in California and Washington. Presented at Historical Perspectives on Drug and Alcohol Use in American Society, 1800-1997. College of Physicians of Philadelphia, May 9-11, 1997. **64.** Anslinger and Tompkins (1953), p. 186-189; Rippey, 1994, p. 18. **65.** Anslinger and Tompkins, 1953, p. 196.

Chapter Fourteen: The Treatment of Addiction to Narcotics and Other Drugs: 1925-1950

66. Bishop, E. (1920). *The Narcotic Drug Problem.* NY: MacMillan Company, pp. 122-123. **67.** Terrry, C. (1921). Some Recent Experiments in Narcotic Control. *American Journal of Public Health,* 11:35. **68.** Terry, 1921, p. 38. **69.** Terry, 1921, p. 38. **70.** Williams, 1938, p. 19. **71.** Williams, 1938, p. 227. **72.** Williams, 1938, pp. 266-268. **73.** Williams, H. (1935). *Drugs Against Men.* NY: Robert M. McBride & Company . **74.** Mosely, A. (1959). The Addicts Bag of Tricks. *Journal of the Oklahoma State Medical Association,* 52:309-310. (May). **75.** Blair, T. (1919). Narcotic Addiction as Regulated by a State Department of Health. *JAMA,* 72:1443-1444. **76.** Helbrant, M. (1941). *Narcotic Agent.* NY: Vanguard Press; Musto, D. (1985). Iatrogenic Addiction: The Problem, Its Definition and History. *Bulletin of the New York Academy of Medicine,* 61:694-705 (October). **77.** O'Donnel, John A. (1969). *Narcotic Addicts in Kentucky.* U.S. Public Health Service Publication No. 1881. Chevy Chase, MD: National Institute of Mental Health; Brill, 1977, p. 312. **78.** The Ratigan account is detailed in: King, R. (1972). *The Drug Hang-up: America's Fifty Year Folly.* NY: W.W. Norton & Company; Reference to the McCarthy episode can be found in: Courtwright, D, Herman, J. and Des Jarlais, D. (1989). *Addicts Who Survived: An Oral History of Narcotic Use in America.* Knoxville: The University of Tennessee Press, p. 312. **79.** Lewin, L. (1931). *Phantastica: Narcotic and Stimulating Drugs, Their Use and Abuse.* London: Routledge and Kegan Paul, pp. 75-85. **80.** Sceleth, 1916. **81.** General references for this section include: Latimer, 1981; Livingston, 1959. **82.** Dai, B. (1937). *Opium Addiction in Chicago.* Montclair, NJ: Patterson Smith (1970 Reprint), p. 38. **83.** Bennett, C. (1929). Hospitalization of Narcotic Addicts, U.S. Penitentiary, Leavenworth, KS. *Journal of the Kansas Medical Society,* 30:341-345 (October). **84.** McKelvey, B. (1977). *American Prisons: A History of Good Intentions.* Montclair, NJ: Patterson Smith, pp. 303-304. **85.** Hawkins, J. (1937). *Opium: Addicts and Addictions.* Danville, VA: J.T. Townes , p. 142. **86.** Lowry, J. (1956). The Hospital Treatment of the Narcotic Addict. *Federal Probation,* 15(20) (December). **87.** Berliner, A. (1962). The Helping Process in a Hospital for Narcotic Addicts. *Federal Probation,* 26(3):57 (September). **88.** The reader who would like a more detailed description of the Lexington facility during the 1940s and 1950s can find autobiographical accounts of treatment at Lexington in Barney Ross's *No Man Stands Alone* (1957) and Alexander King's *Mine Enemy Grows Older* (1958). **89.** Kolb, 1962, pp. 38-39. **90.** Lowry, 1956, p. 44. **91.** Weppner, R. (1983). *The Untherapeutic Community: Organizational Behavior in a Failed Addiction Treatment Program.* Lincoln: University of Nebraska, p. 31; Kolb, L. and Ossenfort, W. (1938). The Treatment of Drug Addicts at the Lexington

Hospital. *Southern Medical Journal*, 31:914 (August). **92.** Duncan, T. (1965). *Understanding and Helping the Narcotic Addict.* Philadelphia: Fortress Press, p. 104. **93.** Vogel, V. (1948). Treatment of the Narcotic Addict by the United States Public Health Service. *Federal Probation,* June, pp. 45-50. **94.** No heterosexual bias is intended in this statement. Patients with histories of overt homosexuality were excluded from Lexington, and homosexual activity of any kind resulted in immediate discharge. Weppner, 1983, p. 30. **95.** Rasor, R. (1972). The United States Public Health Service and Institutional Treatment Program for Narcotic Addicts at Lexington, Ky. In: Lieberman, L. and Brill, L. Eds., *Major Modalities in the Treatment of Drug Abuse.* NY: Behavioral Publications, p.4. **96.** Maddux, J. (1978). History of the Hospital Treatment Program: 1935-1974. In: Martin, W. and Isbell, H. *Drug Addiction and the US Public Health Service* DHEW Pub. No. ADM-77-434, pp. 217-250. **97.** Lowry, J. (1956). The Hospital Treatment of the Narcotic Addict. *Federal Probation,* 15(20):51 (December). **98.** Knight, R. And Prout, C. (1951). A Study of Results in Hospital Treatment of Drug Addictions. *AJP,* 108:303-308. **99.** Rasor, 1972. **100.** Serum Injections Used in Prison to Cure Drug Addicts, *Davenport, Iowa Times,* February 17, 1938—AMA Archives, Box 0031-03.

Section 5
Chapter Fifteen: The Birth of Alcoholics Anonymous: A Brief History

1. The history of A.A. has been meticulously recorded within three A.A.-approved texts—*Alcoholics Anonymous Comes of Age*; *"Pass It On": Bill Wilson and the A.A. Message; and Dr. Bob and the Good Oldtimers*—and a more scholarly and definitive history—*Not God: A History of Alcoholics Anonymous*—prepared by historian Ernest Kurtz. These four texts provide the foundation for this chapter. I encourage those interested in A.A.'s early history to read these works. Kurtz' book provides a meticulously researched synthesis of A.A. history as well as an illuminating analysis of the A.A. program. Other highly readable background texts include Bill Pittman's *A.A. The Way It Began*, Robert Thomsen's *Bill W.* and Nell Wing's *Grateful to Have Been There*. **2.** Source abbreviations used in this and the following three chapters include: *AA* (*Alcoholics Anonymous: The Story of How Many Thousands of Men and Women Have Recovered from Alcoholism*, 1955, New York: Alcoholics Anonymous World Services, Inc.); *12&12* (*Twelve Steps and Twelve Traditions*, 1952, New York: Alcoholics Anonymous World Services, Inc.); *AACA* (*Alcoholics Anonymous Comes of Age*, 1957, New York: Alcoholics Anonymous World Services, Inc.); *DBGO* (*Dr. Bob and the Good Oldtimers, 1980*, New York: Alcoholics Anonymous World Services, Inc.); *PIO* (*Pass It On—The Story of Bill Wilson and How the A.A. Message Reached the World*, 1984, New York: Alcoholics Anonymous World Services, Inc.); *LR* (*Lois Remembers*, 1994, Al-Anon Family Group Headquarters, Inc.; and *LOTH* (*Language of the Heart—Bill Wilson's Grapevine Writings*, 1988, New York: The AA Grapevine, Inc.). **3.** Traditions Eleven and Twelve of Alcoholics Anonymous call for "personal anonymity" in the media and define anonymity as the "spiritual foundation" of the fellowship. In keeping with the practices of this tradition, all A.A. members in this book are identified by first name and last initial. Exceptions to this will be the founders of A.A., whose full names were released publicly following their deaths, with the permission of their families and A.A.'s governing authority. **4.** Kurtz, E. (1979). *Not God: A History of Alcoholics Anonymous.* Center City, Minnesota: Hazelden, p. 9. **5.** *DBGO,* 1980. **6.** B., Mel (1991). *New Wine: The Spiritual Roots of the Twelve Step Miracle.* Center City, MN: Hazelden Pittman Archives Press. **7.** In spite of his influential role in the birth of A.A., Ebby T. never achieved stable sobriety. However, Bill Wilson sustained his involvement with Ebby and continued to call Ebby his sponsor. Wing, N. (1992). *Grateful to Have Been There.* Chicago: Parkside Publishing Corporation. **8.** *AACA,* 1957; Kurtz, 1979, pp.9-10. **9.** Given the above-mentioned details, the reader might find it interesting that some historical revisionists have questioned that Bill W. was really alcoholic. John Rumbarger, in a recent critique, argues that Bill suffered more from "a crisis of faith" as a result of business failures than from a specific problem in his relationship with alcohol. Rumbarger, J. (1994). The "Story" of Bill W.: Ideology, Culture and the Discovery of the Modern American Alcoholic. *CDP,* 20:759-782. **10.** Towns was expensive relative to other hospitals, which meant that alcoholics like Bill Wilson had to have affluent friends pay for their episodic drying out. Wilson's seven-day stay in December of 1934 cost $125. *PIO,* 1984, p. 104. **11.** AACA, 1957, p.63. **12.** *Pioneers We Have Known in the Field of Alcoholism.* (1979). Mill Neck, NY: The Christopher D. Smithers Foundation, p. 101. **13.** Wilson, B. (1945). The Fellowship of Alcoholics Anonymous. In: *Alcohol, Science, and Society.* New Haven. *QJSA.,* p. 465. **14.** AACA, 1957, p. 13. **15.** Wilson, B. (1949). The Society of Alcoholics Anonymous. *AJP,* Sesquicentennial Supplement 151(6):259-262 (1994). **16.** LR, 1994, p. 89 **17.** Wilson, 1945, p. 464. **18.** Thomsen, R. (1975). *Bill W.* NY: Harper & Row, Publishers. **19.** *DBGO,* 1980, p. 68. **20.** Mertin M.'s investigations of A.A.'s beginnings raise the possibility that the date of Dr. Bob's last drink may have been June 17, 1935—a date calculated through the dates of the 1935 AMA Convention in Atlanta; Pittman, B. (1988). *AA: The Way It Began.* Seattle, Washington: Glen Abbey Books. **21.** Pittman, 1988; *DBGO,* 1980; AA, 1955. **22.** LR, 1994, p. 103. **23.** Anonymity served two purposes at this time: It protected members from the public stigma associated with alcoholism, and it prevented damage to the group's reputation resulting from the relapse of people who were publicly linked with it. It was only later that anonymity would come to be seen as a spiritual exercise. Some early A.A. groups were so concerned about public knowledge of members' affiliation with A.A. that they rented rooms under the name, "The Wilson Club." Wing, 1992, p.45; Kurtz, personal communication, April, 1996. **24.** Kurtz, 1979, p. 266. **25.** Kurtz, 1979, p. 50. **26.** *DBGO,* 1980, p. 71. **27.** Kurtz, 1979, p. 74. **28.** Pittman, 1988, p. 160. **29.** 12&12, 1952, p. 136. **30.** AACA, 1957, p. 101. **31.** Lois

Wilson later reported that all of the $30 payments Bill received were paid back in full. LR, 1994, p. 129. **32.** AACA, 1957, p. 159; LOTH, 1988. **33.** LOTH, 1988, p. 59. **34.** LOTH, 1988, p. 200. **35.** LOTH, 1988, p. 196; A Fragment of History by Bill, (1953). *AA Grapevine,* 10(2): 2-9, (July). **36.** AACA, 1957, p. 167. **37.** LR, 1994, p.114. **38.** *PIO*, 1984, p. 205. **39.** *A History of Alcoholics Anonymous in Oregon*: 1943-1983. (1995) Portland, OR: The Oregon Area General Service Committee of Alcoholics Anonymous. **40.** Book Notices: Alcoholics Anonymous (1939). *JAMA*, 113(16):1513; Book Reviews. Alcoholics Anonymous (1940). *Journal of Nervous and Mental Disease,* 92(3):399. **41.** P., Wally (1995). *But, For the Grace of God...: How Intergroups & Central Offices Carried the Message of Alcoholics Anonymous in the 1940s.* Wheeling, WV: The Bishop of Books. **42.** According to Wally P., this custom did not take hold until the late 1950s. **43.** Wally P., 1995. **44.** AA Lingo. (1974). *AA Grapevine,* 31(7):16-17. **45.** Alcoholics Anonymous' Own Story, Presentation of Ernest Kurtz, Haymarket House Summer Institute on Addictions, June 26, 1996. **46.** Wilson, 1945, p. 466. **47.** Markey, M. (1939). Alcoholics and God. *Liberty Magazine,* September 30, pp. 6-8. **48.** Davis, E. (1939). Alcoholics Anonymous Makes its Stand Here. *The Cleveland Plain Dealer* (October 21, 23, 24, 25, 26; November 4). **49.** AACA, 1957, p. viii. **50.** Wing, 1992, pp. 12-13. **51.** Thomsen, 1975, p. 319. **52.** Richeson, F. (1978). *Courage to Change.* U.S.A.: M & M Printing. **53.** Blumberg, L. with Pittman, W. (1991). *Beware the First Drink!* Seattle: WA: Glen Abbey Books. **54.** Cited in Wally P., 1995, p. 175. **55.** Thirty Years of Grapevine History, (1974). *AA Grapevine,* 31(1):2-7 (June). **56.** An example of such breaches can be found in a 1946 article that Marty M. wrote using her full name for *The Modern Hospital,* in which she proffered with no subtlety: "I myself am a member of Alcoholics Anonymous, and I owe my recovery from severe and protracted alcoholism to my entry into the New York group of A.A., where I was sent by my psychiatrist in 1939." Mann, M. (1946). Alcoholics Anonymous: A New Partner for Hospitals. *The Modern Hospital,* January, (Reprint). **57.** *A History of Alcoholics Anonymous in Oregon*: 1943-1983. Portland, OR: The Oregon Area General Service Committee of Alcoholics Anonymous. **58.** Wally P., 1995, p. 190. **59.** Wing, 1993, Audio, September 3. **60.** Wilson, B. (1949). The Society of Alcoholics Anonymous. *AJP*, Sesquicentennial Supplement 151(6):262. **61.** Wally P., 1995, pp. 185-186. **62.** Kurtz, 1979, p. 107. **63.** AACA, 1957, p. 119. **64.** Wing, 1992, pp. 21-23. **65.** The A.A. Movement Gains Public Recognition, (1948). *AA Grapevine.* 5(6):15-17. (November). **66.** Kurtz, 1979, p. 161. **67.** Thomsen, 1975, p. 141. **68.** LR, 1994, p. 69. **69.** *PIO*, 1984, p. 81. **70.** Delbanco, 1985, p. 51 **71.** Pittman, 1988, pp. 136-150. **72.** *PIO*, 1984, p. 221. **73.** *PIO*, 1984, p. 299; Fitzgerald, R. (1995). *The Soul of Sponsorship: The Friendship of Fr. Ed Dowling, S.J. and Bill Wilson in Letters.* Center City, Minnesota: Hazelden, p. 37. **74.** Nell Wing suggests that Bill' failure to attend meetings was due to the fact that he couldn't use meetings the way others did, because he would always be asked to speak or would be subjected to non-stop advice about the proper operation of A.A.. Wing, 1992, p. 63. **75.** Kurtz, 1979, p. 142. **76.** *PIO*, 1984, p. 369. **77.** Bill took niacin for the rest of his life and continued to recommend it enthusiastically to others who suffered from depression. **78.** Fitzgerald, 1995, p. 98; *PIO*, 1984, p. 376. **79.** Wing, 1992, p. 54. **80.** LSD—A Controlled Study, (1967). *AA Grapevine,* 23(12):41. (May). **81.** Fitzgerald, 1995, p. 61. **82.** Wing, 1992, p. 28. **83.** Was Dr. Bob the First Two-hatter? (1975). *AA Grapevine,*31(8):14-15. (February). **84.** Dr. Bob. 1975). *AA Grapevine,* 32(6):4. (November). **85.** Blumberg, L. (1977). The Ideology of a Therapeutic Social Movement: Alcoholics Anonymous. *JSA,* 38:2122-2143. **86.** Silkworth, W. (1937). Alcoholism as a Manifestation of Allergy. *MR,* 145:249-251; Silkworth, W. (1937). Reclamation of the Alcoholic. *MR,* 145:321-324 (April 21); Silkworth W. (1939). Psychological Rehabilitation of Alcoholics. *MR,* 150:65-66. **87.** Silkworth, W. (1939). A New Approach to Psychotherapy in Chronic Alcoholism. *Lancet,* (July) pp. 184-187; Silkworth, W. (1941). Highly Successful Approach to Alcoholic Problem Confirmed by Medical and Sociological Results. *MR,* 154(3):105-107. **88.** The Little Doctor Who Loved Drunks, (1951). *AA Grapevine,*7(12):3-8. (May); AACA, 1957. **89.** This brief sketch of Sister Ignatia is drawn primarily from Mary Darrah's well-researched and delightful book *Sister Ignatia: Angel of Alcoholics Anonymous*. **90.** Pittman, 1988, p. 173. **91.** In Memory of Harry, (1966). *AA Grapevine,* 23(2):2-4. (July). **92.** Tiebout, H. (1963a). What Does "Surrender" Mean? *AA Grapevine,* 19(11):30 **93.** Two of the most noted of Tiebout's articles, "The Ego Factors in the Surrender of Alcoholism" and "The Therapeutic Mechanism of Alcoholics Anonymous," are highly recommend. **94.** Tiebout, H. (1951a). The Role of Psychiatry in the Field of Alcoholism; With Comment on the Current Concept of Alcoholism as Symptom and as Disease. *QJAS,* 12:52-57 (March). **95.** Tiebout, H. (1942). The Private Hospital and the Care of Alcoholic Patients. *Diseases of the Nervous System,* 3:202-205. **96.** Tiebout, 1942, pp. 202-203. **97.** Tiebout, H. (1961). Alcoholics Anonymous-An Experiment of Nature. *QJSA,* 22:52-68. **98.** Tiebout, H. (1944). Therapeutic Mechanisms of Alcoholics Anonymous. *AJP*, 100:468-473; Tiebout, H. (1949). The Act of Surrender in the Therapeutic Process, with Special Reference to Alcoholism. *QJSA,*10:48-58. **99.** Robertson, N. (1988). *Getting Better: Inside Alcoholics Anonymous.* NY: William Morrow and Company. **100.** Tiebout, H. (1972). Why Psychiatrists Fail with Alcoholics, *AA Grapevine,* 29(6):14-19. (November) Reprinted September, 1956.

Chapter Sixteen: The Program of Alcoholics Anonymous

101. The understanding of Alcoholics Anonymous by professionals working in the field of addiction treatment has been greatly enhanced by the doctoral work of two individuals: Ernest Kurtz and Milton Maxwell. Kurtz, through his landmark work *Not God: A History of Alcoholics Anonymous* and numerous articles on A.A., has provided definitive accounts of A.A.'s history as well as insightful interpretations of A.A.'s program of recovery. Maxwell did his doctoral research on Alcoholics Anonymous at the University of Texas in the late 1940s. His writings on A.A. and the Washingtonian Movement remain classics in the field. **102.** *AA Grapevine* (1951). 8(6), 24; *AA Grapevine* (1987). 23(12):24-25; "If you are a professional, A.A. wants to work with you," (1972) NY: AA World Services, Inc. **103.** Miller, W. and Kurtz, E. (1994). Models of Alcoholism Used in Treatment: Contrasting AA and Other Perspectives with Which it is Often Confused. *JSA*, pp.159-166 (March). **104.** Wilson, B. (1944). Basic Concepts of Alcoholics Anonymous. *New York State Journal of Medicine,* 44(16)1805-1808. **105.** Maxwell, M. (1962). Alcoholics Anonymous: An Interpretation. In: Pittman, D. and Snyder, C. *Society, Culture and Drinking Patterns.* NY: John Wiley & Sons, Inc. pp. 577-585. **106.** Wing, 1992, p. 82. **107.** Room, R. (1993). Alcoholics Anonymous as a Social Movement. In: McCrady, B. and Miller, W. *Research on Alcoholics Anonymous: Opportunities and Alternatives.* New Brunswick, New Jersey: Rutgers Center of Alcohol Studies. **108.** Kurtz, 1982, p.53. **109.** Some early members described the A.A. program as a "cure" and referred to themselves as "cured." Other early designations such as "ex-alcoholic" or "reformed alcoholic" eventually gave way to debate about the relative merits of two other self-designations: "recovered alcoholic" versus "recovering alcoholic." *DBGO*, 1980, p. 136. **110.** 12&12, 1952, p. 55. **111.** *AA, 1955,* p. 60. **112.** Maxwell, 1962, p. 581. **113.** White, W. (1990). *The Culture of Addiction, the Culture of Recovery.* Bloomington, IL: Lighthouse Institute. **114.** 12 & 12, 1952, p. 89. **115.** Nell Wing, Monterey Bay Conference. Monterey, CA: 9-3-93, Audiotape. **116.** White, 1990, p. 474. **117.** B., Mel (1990). *The Slogans.* Portage, In: Portage Printing.; Our Slogans—Old Sayings Made New. (1971). *AA Grapevine,* 27(10):6-8. (April). **118.** A Disease of Opposites, (1979). *AA Grapevine,* 35(10):20-21. (March). **119.** See Kurtz, AA and Treatment (Rutgers Distance Learning Tape) and Wing, 1992, p. 116, for observations on this role of laughter from two long-term observers of A.A. **120.** *12&12,* 1952, p. 106 **121.** Why I'm Glad I'm an Alcoholic. (1964). *AA Grapevine,* 21(2):21-22 (July). **122.** It cannot be said that A.A. incorporated these elements from their predecessors since the first references to the Washingtonians in A.A. literature didn't appear until 1945 (in the *AA Grapevine*) and even today one finds no references in A.A. literature to the existence of the fraternal temperance societies or the reform clubs. **123.** While this rule generally held, there were exceptions. Robert Fitzgerald notes that there were a number of non-alcoholic "fellow-travelers" in early A.A. who through some kind of implicit agreement were allowed to attend closed meetings. This practice continues today in some groups without open acknowledgment. Fitzgerald, 1995, p. 28. For a flavor of differing opinions within A.A. about open versus closed meetings, see the September, 1948 *AA Grapevine,* pp.20-22. **124.** Kurtz, E. (1996). Spirituality and the Secular Quest: Twelve Step Programs. In: *World Spirituality Encyclopedic History of the Religious Quest,* Vol 22, Ed. Peter Can Ness, NY: Crossroad. **125.** This practice has not been without its controversy within A.A., particularly among fundamentalists who continue to argue that "The person here with the longest sobriety is the one who got up earliest this morning and hasn't taken a drink." **126.** Letter from Doc N. (1944). *AA Grapevine,* 1(3):2. (August). **127.** In the Oxford groups, members received "guidance"—messages of spiritual direction communicated from others. In practice, this meant that members often received from other members strong admonitions of what they should and should not do, couched in the language of "spiritual direction" that had been received. This advice or admonishment did not set well with most alcoholics and was eliminated in A.A. through the general discouragement of cross-talk. For a brief review of informal rules of communication that govern A.A. meetings, see Makela, et.al. (1996). *Alcoholics Anonymous as a Mutual-Help Movement: A Study in Eight Societies.* Madison: University of Wisconsin Press. **128.** Makela, K., et. al. (1996). p.248. **129.** Mercadante, L. (1996). *Victims and Sinners: Spiritual Roots of Addiction and Recovery.* Louisville, KY: Westminster John Knox Press. p. 79 ; Kurtz, E. and Ketchum, K. (1992). *The Spirituality of Imperfection: Modern Wisdom from Classic Stories.* New York: Bantam Books, p. 5 **130.** *AA,* 1955, pp. xvii, 92, 219, 187, 227. **131.** A.A., 1955, pp. 64, 103, 62; *12 & 12,* 1952, p.44. **132.** *12 & 12,* 1952, p., 43, 123; *AA,* 1955, p.21. **133.** *AA, 1955,* p. 172. **134.** Folk sayings within the culture of recovery such as "Act as if" and "Fake it 'till you make it" reflect this view. **135.** Blumberg and Pittman, 1991, pp. 195, 207. **136.** Clark, W. (1951). *The Oxford Group: Its History and Significance.* NY: Bookman Associates, pp.25, 31, 35. **137.** *12 & 12,* 1952, p. 140. **138.** *12 & 12,* 1952, p. 145. **139.** *AA,* 1955, p. 565. **140.** *AA Grapevine.* (1944). 1(3): 2; Letter from Doc M. (1944). *AA Grapevine* 1(4):2. (September). **141.** Women in AA Face Special Problems. (1946). *AA Grapevine,* 3(5):1,6. (October). **142.** This exclusivity would influence most of the later Twelve-Step adaptations. What most Twelve-Step program participants have in common, in addition to the Steps, is mutual identification—a shared pain produced by a single problem, condition or event. Exclusivity ensures that those sitting across the table from one another will communicate out of an equality of shared experience. **143.** See Chapter 24 for additional discussion on the inclusion of people in A.A. who are addicted to drugs other than alcohol. **144.** It is my own view that the best-kept secret about and within A.A. is the existence of large numbers of formerly active members who sustain their sobriety and their emotional well-being long after they have ceased active participation in A.A. meetings. Bill Wilson, A.A.'s co-founder, seemed to elude to these hidden, non-active members in his 1969 testimony during congressional hearings on alcoholism. Statement of Bill W., Co-founder, Alcoholics Anonymous, July 24, 1969, Special Subcommittee on Alcoholism and Narcotics, Washington, D.C., U.S. GPO. **145.** *12&12,* 1952, p. 130. **146.** For samples of the latter, see: On Attending Meetings, (1948). *AA Grapevine,* p. 12 (June); Everyone Quit Coming, (1964). *AA Grapevine,* 20(11):35-36. (April); I want to Share, (1978). *AA Grapevine,* 34(8):35. (January). **147.** *12&12,* 1952, p. 129. **148.** If this analysis is accurate, it has potentially ominous implications for some of the newer mutual-aid societies that offer themselves as alternatives to A.A. Organizations such as Women for Sobriety, Rational Recovery and others posit that individuals should participate only as long as they feel a need for such support. While this position may make sense in the short run for individuals participating during a time of high organizational energy and stable organizational leadership, it might very well doom these organizations to an early demise by depriving new members of stable and mature role models. The lack of a cadre of strong indigenous leaders decreases the organization's ability to sustain itself and the integrity of its message. **149.** Another interesting footnote to this discussion is the reminder from the last Chapter that Bill Wilson was himself criticized for not attending meetings regularly. **150.** Mercadante, 1996, p. 58. **151.** Room, 1993, p. 174. **152.** Levine, H. (1984). The Alcohol Problem in America: From Temperance to Alcoholism, *BJA*, 79:109-119.

Chapter Seventeen: A.A. Critics and A.A. Legacy

153. Tournier, R. (1979). Alcoholics Anonymous as Treatment and as Ideology. *JSA,* 40:230-239. **154.** Tiebout, H. (1958). Direct Treatment of a Symptom. In: Hoch, P. and Zubin, J. *Problems of Addiction and Habituation.* NY: Grune & Stratton, pp. 17-26; Tiebout, H. (1963b). Treating the Causes of Alcoholism. *AA Grapevine,* 20(6):9 **155.** Miller, W. and Hester, R. (1986). The Effectiveness of Alcoholism Treatment. In: Miller, W. And Hester, R. (Eds.) *Treating Addictive Behaviors: Process of Change.* NY: Plenum Press, pp. 121-174.; Emrick, C. (1989). Overview: Alcoholics Anonymous. In: Galanter, M. Ed. *Recent Developments in Alcoholism Treatment Research,* Volume 7, NY: Plenum., p. 4. **156.** Fingarette, H. (1988). Alcoholism: The Mythical Disease. *Utne Reader*, Nov./Dec., pp. 64-69; Peele, S. (1989). *The Diseasing of America.* Lexington, Massachusetts: Lexington, Books, pp. 56-57. **157.** *AA*, p.xx; Wilson, 1944, p. 1805. **158.** Trimpey, J. (1989). *The Small Book.* New York: Delacorte Press, p. 10. **159.** Bean, M. (1975b). Alcoholics Anonymous, Part II. *Psychiatric Annals* 5:7-57. **160.** Ogborne, A. (1989). Some Limitations of Alcoholics Anonymous. In: Galanter, M. Ed. *Recent Developments in Alcoholism,* Volume 7, pp. 55-65. **161.** Cain, A. (1963). Alcoholics Anonymous-Cult or Cure. *Harper's Magazine,* 226:48-52 (February); Alexander, F. And Rollins, M. (1984). Alcoholics Anonymous: The Unseen Cult. *California Sociologist,* 7(1), 33-48; Herman, E. (1988). The Twelve Step Program: Cure or Cover. *Utne Reader,* November/December, pp. 52-63; Bufe, C. (1991). *Alcoholics Anonymous: Cult or Cure?* San Francisco: Sharp Press. **162.** Emrick, 1989, p. 45. **163.** Montgomery, H. Miller, W., and Tonigan, S. (1993). Differences among AA Groups: Implications for Research. *JSA,* 54:502-504. **164.** Bufe, 1991, p. 80. **165.** For a well-written response to this criticism, see Kurtz, L. (1997). Recovery, the 12-Step Movement, and Politics. *Social Work,* 42(4):403-405. **166.** Tournier, 1979. **167.** Tournier, 1979; Emerick, 1989; Cahalan, D. (1979). Why Does the Alcoholism Field Act Like a Ship of Fools? *BJA*, 74:235-238. **168.** The careful reader of this chapter will note that the very activities A.A. is accused of involving itself in are strictly prohibited by A.A. traditions. The failure to delineate the actions of A.A. as an institution from the actions of alcoholism professionals—who may also happen to be A.A. members but who in no way speak for A.A.—and the confusion between A.A. and the broader alcoholism movement are obvious here. **169.** Ellison, J. (1964). Alcoholics Anonymous: Dangers of Success. *Nation,* 198:212-214 (March 2). **170.** *AA Grapevine*, (1944). 1(4):1, 3. **171.** Our Critics Can be Our Benefactors. (1963). *AA Grapevine,* 20(11):2-4. (April). **172.** *DBGO*, 1980, p.235; *PIO, 1984*, p. 202. **173.** The first edition did use the subtitle "The Story of How More Than One Hundred Men Have Recovered From Alcoholism." The second edition replaced the term "Men" with the phrase "Thousands of Men and Women" *PIO*, 1984, p. 202. **174.** Marty M. 4th International Convention, Toronto, Canada (July, 1965). (Audiotape) **175.** Vourakis, C. (1989). *The Process of Recovery for Women in Alcoholics Anonymous: Seeking Groups "Like Me."* Ph.D. Dissertation, San Francisco: University of California. **176.** Later studies would show that recovery rates for women in A.A. were comparable to those for men. Leach, B. and Norris, J. (1977). Factors in the Development of Alcoholics Anonymous (AA). In: Kissen, B. and Begleiter, H. (eds). *The Biology of Alcoholism, Volume 5, Treatment and Rehabilitation of the Chronic Alcoholic.* NY: Plenum Press. **177.** *DBGO*, 1980, p. 240. **178.** *DBGO*, 1980, pp. 97-98. **179.** Maxwell reported that only three of A.A.'s first 100 members were women. Maxwell, M. (1982). Alcoholics Anonymous. In: Gomberg, E., White, H. and Carpenter, J., Eds,. *Alcohol, Science and Society Revisited.* Ann Arbor: The University of Michigan Press, pp. 295-305. **180.** Women Alcoholics Have a Tougher Fight. (1945). *AA Grapevine,* 1(12):3. (May). **181.** Professional observers of A.A. during its first 15 years also noted that women had more difficulty affiliating with A.A. than did men. Bacon, S. (1949). The Administration of Alcoholism Rehabilitation Programs. *QJSA*, 10(1) 1-47. **182.** *AA Grapevine* (1946). 3(5):1,6 (October). **183.** Richeson, 1978, p. 63. **184.** McElrath, D. (1981). *Roses of Dia Linn: A Celebration of 25 Years.* Center City, Minnesota: Hazelden Foundation. **185.** W., Searcy (1993). *A Study Book on My "Alcoholism Recovery" Since May 10, 1946 and A History of How Early A.A. Groups Started.* Dallas Texas: Texas Clinic-Hospital for Alcoholism, Inc. **186.** Alexander, J. (1950). The Drunkard's Best Friend. *Saturday Evening Post,* pp. 17-18, 74-76, 78-79. (April 1). **187.** Vourakis, 1989, p. 30. **188.** For a typical article, see: Lady A.A. Members Get Their Heads Together. (1949). *AA Grapevine,* 5(12):11. (May). **189.** AA in the News: 1940-1942 (1982). *AA Grapevine*, 39(6):25. (November). **190.** McElrath, D. (1987). *Hazelden: A Spiritual Odyssey.* Center City, Minnesota: Hazelden Foundation. **191.** Mel B., Personal Communication, September 29, 1996. **192.** *DBGO*, 1980, p. 247. **193.** AACA, 1957, p. 38. **194.** Kurtz, 1979, p.305; Hudson, H. (1985). How and Why Alcoholics Anonymous Works for Blacks. In: Brisbane, F. and Womble, M. Eds. *Treatment of Black Alcoholics.* NY: Haworth Press. **195.** Mel B., Taped Interview with Jimmy F., 1978. **196.** Dr. Bob and Sister Ignatia also seem

362 Endnotes - Pages 160 - 168

to have been instrumental in opening up some of the early hospital units. At first, Black alcoholics were denied access to St. Thomas' alcoholism ward in the 1940s, because of the widespread practice of designating only certain hospitals or certain sections of a hospital for Blacks. During that time, Sister Ignatia and Dr. Bob were able to get the hospital administration to approve the inclusion of 1-2 "colored beds" in the alcoholism ward. Mel B. Taped Interview with Edward B., 1978. **197.** Hudson, 1985. **198.** The Negro in AA, (1951). *AA Grapevine,* 8(4):47 (September). **199.** The first survey of A.A. members was conducted in the State of New York by the National Council on Alcoholism. It revealed that most New York A.A. members were middle and upper class. Forty-eight percent had completed college and eleven percent had completed professional or graduate education. New York A.A., however, was by no means representative of A.A. around the country. Measuring AA—A Study, (1967). *AA Grapevine,* 23(9):45. (February). **200.** Harper, F. (1976). *Alcohol and Blacks: An Overview.* Alexandria, VA: Douglas Publishers, p. 4. **201.** Hudson, 1974. **202.** Caetano defined this shared view in terms of agreement with three propositions: 1) "Alcoholism is an illness." 2) "Without help problems get worse and worse." and 3) "To recover, alcoholics have to quit forever." **203.** Caetano, R. (1993). Ethnic Minority Groups and Alcoholics Anonymous: A Review. Berkeley, California: Alcohol Research Group; also, In: McCrady, B. and Miller, W. (1993). *Research on Alcoholics Anonymous: Opportunities and Alternatives.* New Brunswick, NJ: Rutgers Center of Alcohol Studies. **204.** Humphreys, K. and Woods, M. (1993). Researching Mutual Help Group Participation in a Segregated Society. *Journal of Applied Behavioral Science,* 29(2):181-201 (June). **205.** Bean, 1975B, p.28. **206.** *DBGO,* 1980, p. 249. **207.** *AA,* 1955, p. xx.; Comments on A.A.'s Triennial Survey; Report on Survey of AA Membership. (1968). *AA Grapevine,* 25(7):p.43 (December); 1996 Membership Survey of Alcoholics Anonymous New York: A.A. World Services. **208.** Makela, 1996, p. 102. **209.** Laundergan, J. (1982). *Easy Does It: Alcoholism Treatment Outcomes, Hazelden and the Minnesota Model.* Center City, Minnesota: Hazelden Foundation., p. 120. **210.** Beckman, L. (1993). Alcoholics Anonymous and Gender Issues. In: McCrady, B. and Miller, W. *Research on Alcoholics Anonymous: Opportunities and Alternatives.* New Brunswick. New Jersey: Rutgers Center of Alcohol Studies. **211.** Maxwell, 1982, p. 297. **212.** Cited in Caetano, 1993. **213.** Heath, D. (1981). Determining the Sociocultural Context of Alcohol Use. In: Heath, D., Waddell, J. and Topper, M. Eds. *Cultural Factors in Alcohol Research and Treatment of Drinking Patterns. JSA,* Supplement 9. New Brunswick, NJ; Caetano, 1983; Jllek-Aall, L. (1981). Acculturation, Alcoholism, and Indian-style Alcoholics Anonymous. *JSA.* (Supplement. 9):143-158. **214.** Makela, 1996, p.244. **215.** Montgomery, H., Miller, W., and Tonigan, S. (1995). Does Alcoholics Anonymous Involvement Predict Treatment Outcome? *JSAT,* 12(4):241-246. **216.** Kurtz. E. (1982). A.A. Works: The Intellectual Significance of Alcoholics Anonymous. *JSA,* 43:38-80. **217.** Trice, H. and Staudenmeier, W. (1989). A Sociocultural History of Alcoholics Anonymous. In: Galanter, M. Ed. *Recent Developments in Alcoholism,* Volume 7, NY: Plenum Press, pp. 11-35. **218.** Room, 1993, p. 186. **219.** Wuthnow, R. (1994). *Sharing the Journey: Support Groups and America's New Quest for Community.* NY: Free Press. **220.** Kurtz, 1982, p. 42. **221.** Leach, B. And Norris, J. (1977). Factors in the Development of Alcoholics Anonymous (A.A.). In: Kissen, B. and Begleiter, H. (eds) *The Biology of Alcoholism, Volume 5, Treatment and Rehabilitation of the Chronic Alcoholic.* NY: Plenum Press. p. 451. **222.** Mercadante, 1996, p. 4.

Chapter Eighteen: A.A. and the Professional Care of Alcoholics: 1935-1960
223. AACA, 1957, p.145. **224.** Heersema, P. (1942). Present Role of 'Alcoholics Anonymous' in the Treatment of Chronic Alcoholism. *Minnesota Medicine,* 25:204-205 (March); Corwin, E. and Cunningham, E. (1944). Institutional Facilities for the Treatment of Alcoholism. *QJSA ,* 5(1):9-85. **225.** *12&12,* 1952, pp. 156,161; See also AACA, 1957, p. 145. **226.** Louisville Plans Clinic. (1966). *AA Grapevine,* 2(9):7. (February). **227.** Appendix, Central Committee Hospital Committee Meeting, September 14, 1941: Proposed Plan for A.A. Hospital. Clarence S. Papers. **228.** Central Committee Meeting Minutes, December 2, 1941, Clarence S. Papers **229.** *DBGO,* 1980, p. 130. **230.** A.A. Central Committee Minutes, February 3, 1942, p. 6. Clarence S. Papers **231.** Trustee Vote Fixes Policy on Gift Funds. (1946). *A.A. Grapevine,* 3(1):2,8. (June). **232.** *AA Grapevine* (1947). 3(1):3-5. (March). **233.** *AA Grapevine,* (1946). P, 2. (June). p. 2. **234.** New York's Long Hard Road to Hospital Facilities. (1952). *AA Grapevine,* 8(9):19-23. (February). **235.** The majority of material for this profile has been drawn from *DBGO,* Mary Darrah's text, *Sister Ignatia: Angel of Alcoholics Anonymous,* and Sister Ignatia's own articles and speeches. **236.** Dr. Bob. (1951). *AA Grapevine,* Special Edition. (January). **237.** *AA Grapevine.* (1969). 26(1):4-8. (June). **238.** For Sister Ignatia: Our Everlasting Gratitude, (1966). *AA Grapevine* 23(3)2-9. (August). **239.** Darrah, M. (1992). *Sister Ignatia: Angel of Alcoholics Anonymous.* Chicago: Loyola University Press. **240.** Sister Ignatia, (1951). The Care of Alcoholics. *Hospital Progress,* 32:294. **241.** Sister Ignatia, (1960). 25th A.A. International Convention, Long Beach, CA. (Audiotape) **242.** Sister Ignatia, 1951; Darrah, 1992. **243.** *AA Grapevine,* 26(1), 54-8, June, 1969; Sister Ignatia, 1951, pp. 294-295. **244.** Hospitalization in Akron Model for A.A. (1945). *AA Grapevine,* 1(9):4. (February). **245.** Silkworth, 1939, p. 314. **246.** MacCormick quite poignantly describes the risk that alcoholics might die in detoxification in his 1941 account of alcoholics in the criminal justice system: *I have known of men who were dying on their feet while they were being lectured by a judge and who died within an hour after being received at the institution to which they had been sentenced.* Quoted in Corwin and Cunningham, 1944, p. 23. **247.** *DBGO,* 1980, p. 102. **248.** *AA Grapevine,* (1969). 26(1): 4-8. (June). **249.** *DBGO,* 1980, p. 202; Wing, 1992, pp. 87-88. **250.** *DBGO,* 1980, p. 177. **251.** AACA, 1957, p. 88. **252.** AACA, 1957, p. 20; Hospital Committee Report, February 3, 1942,

Clarence S. Papers **253.** *DBGO*, 1980, p. 202. **254.** Hospital Facilities. (1951). *AA Grapevine,* 7(9):19-23. (February). **255.** From an Early Secretary's Handbook (Report on Knickerbocker Hospital). *Markings: Your Archives Interchange,* 15(1). **256.** From an Early Secretary's Handbook (Report on Knickerbocker Hospital). Markings: *Your Archives Interchange,* 15(1). **257.** Mann, M. (1948). The Alcoholic in the General Hospital. *Southern Hospitals* (November).pp. 27-31. **258.** AA Ward at Knickerbocker Proves Success. (1946). *AA Grapevine,* 2(9):3. (February). **259.** Philadelphia Story on Hospitalization. (1945). *AA Grapevine,* 1(10):4. (March). **260.** Teddy R.'s story appeared in an October 3, 1952 issue of *Saturday Evening Post* in an article entitled, "I'm a Nurse in an Alcoholic Ward." **261.** AA and Hospitalization. (1950). *AA Grapevine,* 17(2):6-9. (July). **262.** AACA, 1957, p. 6. **263.** *PIO,* 1984, p. 161. **264.** Letter from Allan B., President, New York Intergroup Association of A.A., to Colonel Towns, dated December 18, 1956, Quoted in Wally P., 1995, p. 143. **265.** AACA, 1957, p. 12. **266.** AACA, 1957, p. 12; Anderson, 1941, pp. 11,89; The First Hospital Group. (1977). *AA Grapevine,* 34(1):26-29. (June). **267.** Wing, 1992. **268.** The Brooklyn Group Works Closely with Hospital Patients. (1944). *AA Grapevine,* 1(2):3. (July); Washington D.C. has New Clinic for Alcoholics. (1945). *AA Grapevine,* 2(5):7. (October); *AA Grapevine,* (1946). 2(12):12. (May); Corwin and Cunningham, 1944, p. 68; Hope is Born for Hopeless Behind Doors of State Hospital. (1947). *AA Grapevine,* 4(1):15. (June); Dr. Sam Parker Of Kings County Suggests 'Criteria for A.A. Work in Hospitals' (1945). *AA Grapevine,*1(10):1,8. (March). **269.** McMahan, H. (1942). The Psychotherapeutic Approach of Chronic Alcoholism in Conjunction with the Alcoholics Anonymous Program. *Illinois Psychiatric Journal,* 2:15-20. **270.** Moore, R. and Buchanan, T. (1966). State Hospitals and Alcoholism: A National Survey of Treatment Techniques and Results. *QJSA,* 27:459-468;Moore, R. (1971). Alcoholism Treatment in Private Psychiatric Hospitals. *QJSA,* 32:1083-85. **271.** Searcy W., 1993, p. 112. **272.** Twelfth Step Workshops, (1951). *AA Grapevine,* 7(9):39-44. (January). **273.** Chicago Committee on Alcoholism Sparks Civic Interest. (1947). *AA Grapevine,* 4(4):3. (September). **274.** Shepherd, E. (1950). Reports on Government Sponsored Programs. *QJSA,* 11:351-371. **275.** Corwin and Cunningham, 1944, p. 68; Wally P., 1995, p. 48. **276.** A.A. (Los Angeles) (1952). *AA Grapevine,* 8(10):21-22. (February). **277.** Searcy W. Interview, May 16, 1996. **278.** Searcy W. Interview, May 16, 1996. **279.** Searcy W. Interview, May 16, 1996. **280.** LR, 1994, p. 122. **281.** Harbaugh, L. (1995). *Sister Francie and the Ministry of High Watch: From New Thought to Alcoholics Anonymous.* Bachelor's Thesis, Smith College. **282.** High Watch Board Meeting Minutes, October, 1940. **283.** AACA, 1957, p. 182. **284.** High Watch Board Meeting Minutes, August 21, 1941. **285.** High Watch Board Meeting Minutes, July 5, 1941 and August 21, 1941. **285.** High Watch Board Meeting Minutes, July 5, 1941. **286.** Harbaugh, 1995, p. 37. **287.** High Watch Board Meeting Minutes, July 5, 1941 to October 7, 1943. **288.** Marty M.'s Resignation Letter from the High Watch Board, July 5, 1941; Marty Mann did not always maintain this clear distinction between treatment and A.A. In her 1950 *Primer on Alcoholism*, she described A.A. as "a fellowship and a method of treatment." Mann, M. (1950). *Primer on Alcoholism.* NY: Rinehart and Company. **289.** See Mann. 1948, p. 28. **290.** July 22, 1941 letter from Bill W. to Ray C., High Watch Archives **291.** High Watch Board Minutes, August-November, 1941. **292.** Harbaugh, L. (1994). A Case Study of the Ministry of the High Watch: Political and Economic Pressures on a Non-medical Solution for Alcoholism. Unpublished paper. **293.** Kurtz, L. (1997). *Self-Help and Support Groups.* Thousand Oaks, CA: Sage Publications. **294.** AACA, 1957, p.59. **295.** Richeson, 1978. **296.** Richeson, 1978. **297.** Miller and Kurtz, 1994, p. 161. **298.** *A History of A.A. in Oregon,* 1995, p. 215. **299.** For early sentiments on this issue, see Bacon, 1949, pp. 20, 40. Bacon's position was clear: "A hospital should not play at being A.A., nor should A.A. play at being a hospital." He further thought that the use of A.A. members should be restricted to non-therapist roles, because the therapeutic functions of A.A. and those of professional therapists were different. He called for "cooperation without co-mingling of personnel."

Chapter Nineteen: The "Modern Alcoholism Movement": The Core

300. Chapters Nineteen and Twenty have been enriched by two dissertations: Bruce Holley Johnson's 1973 *The Alcoholism Movement in America* and Ron Roizen's 1991 *The American Discovery of Alcoholism, 1933-1939.* I would like to acknowledge the particular contributions Ron Roizen made to the development of these chapters. His research and writings on this period and our ongoing correspondence about the context, institutions, and people of this period provided invaluable details and perspective. **301.** Levine, H. (1987). The Discovery of Addiction: Changing Conceptions of Habitual Drunkenness in America. *JSA,* 39(2):162. **302.** Roizen, 1991a. *The American Discovery of Alcoholism, 1933-1939.* Ph.D. Dissertation, Berkeley: University of California, p. 18 **303.** Haggard, H. (1945). Editorial: The "Wets" and Drys" Join Against Science. *QJSA,* 6(2):131. **304.** Pattison, E., Bishop, L. And Linsky, A. (1968). Changes in Public Attitudes on Narcotic Addiction. *AJP,* 125:160-167. **305.** Quoted in Roizen, 1991a, p. 31. **306.** Roizen, 1991a, pp. 47-93. **307.** Roizen, 1991a, pp. 180-207. **308.** Roizen, 1991a, p. 130. **309.** Johnson, B. (1973). *The Alcoholism Movement in America: A Study in Cultural Innovation.* Urbana, Illinois: University of Illinois Ph.D. Dissertation, p. 233. **310.** Keller, M (1982). On Defining Alcoholism: With Comment on Some Other Relevant Words. In: Gomberg, L., White, H. and Carpenter, J. *Alcohol, Science and Society Revisited.* Ann Arbor: The University of Michigan Press. **311.** Keller, M. (1979 B). Mark Keller's History of the Alcohol Problems Field. *Drinking and Drug Practices Surveyor,* 14(1):22-28; Roizen, R. (1991c). Research Council on Problems of Alcohol. *Social History of Alcohol Review,* 24:9-16 (Fall). **312.** Roizen, 1991a, p. 107. **313.** Roizen, 1991a, pp. iii-iv. **314.** Moore, H. (1940). Activities of the

Research Council on Problems of Alcohol. QJSA, 1:104-107. **315.** Roizen, R. (1995). Four Unsung Moments in the Genesis of the Modern Alcoholism Movement. Unpublished Manuscript. **316.** Anderson, D. (1942). Alcohol and Public Opinion. *QJSA*, 3(3):376-392. **317.** Research Council on Problems of Alcohol (1943). QJSA, 4:148-150 **318.** *State Programs on Alcoholism Research, Treatment and Rehabilitation.* (1955). NY: Licensed Beverage Industries, Inc., pp. 1-2. **319.** Anderson, D. (1950). *The Other Side of the Bottle.* NY: A.A. Wyn, Inc. **320.** Keller, 1979B, p. 24. **321.** Yale Plan. (1947). *AA Grapevine,*4(5):4-5, 14-15. (October). **322.** Roizen, R. (1994b). Paradigm Sidetracked: Explaining Early Resistance to the Alcoholism Paradigm at Yale's Laboratory of Applied Physiology, 1940-1944 (Revised). Presented at the Alcohol & Temperance History Group's International Congress on the Social History of Alcohol, Huron College, London, Ontario, Canada, May 13-15, 1993. p. 2 **323.** Roizen, 1994b, p. 5n. **324.** This residential summer program was later extended to six weeks, then reduced to three weeks; most recently, the program has operated as a two-week program with two supplemental week-long sessions, one designated as an advanced session for students who have completed the basic school. **325.** Milgram, G. (1986). The Summer School of Alcohol Studies: An Historical and Interpretive Review. In: Strug, D. Priyadarsini and Hyman, M. Eds. *Alcohol Interventions: Historical and Sociocultural Approaches.* NY: The Haworth Press. **326.** Jellinek, E.M. (1944). Notes on the First Half Year's Experience at the Yale Plan Clinics. *QJSA, 5(2):279-302;* Haggard, H. And Jellinek, E. (1944). Two Yale Savants Stress Alcoholism as True Disease. *A.A. Grapevine,* 1(1):1. **327.** Jellinek, 1944, 5(2), p. 282. **328.** McCarthy, R. (1946). A Public Clinic Approach to Certain Aspects Related to Alcoholism. *QJSA,* 6:500-514. **329.** McCarthy, 1946, p. 502. **330.** McCarthy, R. and Douglas, E. (1949). *Alcohol and Social Responsibility.* NY: Thomas Y. Crowell Company and Yale Plan Clinic, p. 98-109. **331.** Jellinek, 1944, 5(2):284; McCarthy, 1946, p. 503. **332.** Keller, 1979B; Pioneers, 1979, p. 115. **333.** Bacon, 1949, p. 20; Myerson, D. (1957). The Study and Treatment of Alcoholism: A Historical Perspective. *NEJM,* 257: 820-25. **334.** McCarthy, 1946, p. 513; Bacon, 1949, p. 21. **335.** McCarthy, 1946, p. 514. **336.** There was not wide concurrence even in Yale on how best to use recovered alcoholics. In 1949, Seldon Bacon advocated a more limited use of recovered alcoholics, not in the role of therapist, but as liaisons with courts or as hospital attendants. Bacon, 1949, p. 30. **337.** Roizen, 1991a. **338.** Keller, 1979B. **339.** Keller, 1979B. **340.** Room, R. (1978). *Governing Images of Alcohol and Drug Problems: The Structure, Sources and Sequels of Conceptualizations of Intractable Problems.* Ph.D. Dissertation, Berkeley, CA: University of California, p. 133. **341.** Johnson, 1973, p. 265. **342.** Johnson, 1973, p. 265. **343.** In a touch of historical irony, an organization called the National Committee on Alcohol Hygiene, which was founded by Dr. Robert Seliger, a psychiatrist with impeccable credentials in alcoholism education and treatment, died out from lack of support. Johnson, 1973, p. 267, 295. **344.** Johnson, 1973, pp. 267-270. **345.** Anderson, 1950, 214-217; Pioneer, 1979, p. 13. **346.** Mann, M. (1944). Formation of a National Committee for Education on Alcoholism. *QJSA,* 5(2):354. **347.** Mann, 1944, p. 354. **348.** Anderson, D. (1944). Committee for Education on Alcoholism Historic Event. *AA Grapevine,* 1(5):1. **349.** Johnson, 1973, p. 286. **350.** *AA Grapevine.* (1947). 4(5):14. (October); Mann, M. (1947). What Shall We Do About Alcoholism? *Vital Speeches,* 13:253-256. **351.** Johnson, 1973, p. 298. **352.** Keller, M. (1985). Alcohol Problems and Policies in Historical Perspective. In: Kyvig, D. Ed. *Law, Alcohol and Order: Perspectives on National Prohibition.* Westport, CT: Greenwood Press, 159-175. **353.** "Special Bulletin," 1949, Marty Mann Collection, Box Number 3, Folder 'NCAA-Yale Severance.' Marty Mann, in a letter to an NCEA colleague, described this announcement as a "pallid and throughly cleaned-up version of what was actually a knock-down-and-drag-out fight." The strain did emerge from growing differences in philosophy, but it was further complicated by money problems—money owed to Yale by NCEA and competition between Yale and NCEA in raising funds. **354.** Letter: Mann to Houston, Marty Mann Collection, Box Number 2, Folder 'Personal Letters,' December 8, 1949.

Chapter Twenty: The "Modern Alcoholism Movement": The Periphery

355. Johnson, 1973, p. 103. **356.** Wilkerson, A. (1966). *A History of the Concept of Alcoholism as a Disease.* DSW dissertation, University of Pennsylvania, pp. 255-256. **357.** Johnson, 1973, pp. 94-99, 321. **358.** General references for this section include: *Pioneers We Have Known in the Field of Alcoholism.* (1979). Mill Neck, NY: The Christopher D. Smithers Foundation;Trice, H. and Schonbrunn (1981). A History of Job-Based Alcoholism Programs: 1900-1955. *JDI,* 11:171-198;McClellan, K. (1984). Work-based Drug Programs. *JPD,* 16(4) October-December, pp. 285-303;and Bickerton, R. (1990). Employee Assistance: A History in Progress. *EAP Digest,* 11(1) 34-42, 82-84, 91. **359.** Bluestone, E. (1944). Foreword: Institutional Facilities of the Treatment for Alcoholism. *QJSA,* 5:5-8. **360.** *AA Grapevine,* (1944). 1(3):1. **361.** Johnson, 1973, p. 298. **362.** Jellinek, E. (1947). What Shall We Do About Alcoholism? *Vital Speeches,* 13:252-253. **363.** Henderson, R. And Bacon, S. (1953). Problem Drinking: The Yale Plan for Business and Industry. *QJSA,* 14:247-262. **364.** Henderson and Bacon, 1953, pp. 257-261. **365.** Surles, C. (1978). *Historical Development of Alcoholism Control Programs in Industry from 1940-1978* D.Ed. Dissertation: University of Michigan. **366.** John, H. (1977). The Church and Alcoholism: A Growing Movement. *AHRW,* 1(4):2-10. **367.** Conley, P. and Sorensen, A. (1971). *The Staggering Steeple: The Story of Alcoholism and the Churches.* Philadelphia: The Pilgrim Press. **368.** General references for this section include: Hirsh, J. (1949). *The Problem Drinker.* NY: Duell, Sloan and Pearce. p.145; Lewis, J. (1955). Summary of Federal and State Alcoholism Programs in the U.S. *American Journal of Public Health,* 45:1417-1419; Chafetz, M. and Demone, H. (1964). Alcoholism: Causes and Treatment. In:

McCarthy, R. Ed. *Alcohol Education for Classroom and Community.* NY: McGraw-Hill Book Company; Johnson, 1973, pp. 100-101; Bacon, S. (1952). Alcoholism, 1941-1951. A Survey of Activities in Research, Education and Therapy. (1952). *QJSA,* 3(3):474. **369.** *AA Grapevine,* (1948), 5(7):332 (December). **370.** Hirsch, 1949, p.177. **371.** State Programs, 1955, p. 8. **372.** *State Programs on Alcoholism Research, Treatment and Rehabilitation in the United States and Canada.* (1956). NY: Licensed Beverage Industries, Inc., p. 3. **373.** State Programs, 1956, pp. 8-11; Shepherd, 1950, p. 362. **374.** Shepherd, 1950, pp. 366-367. **375.** Johnson, 1973, p. 281. **376.** Hirsch, 1949, p. 149 **377.** Johnson, 1973, p. 103. **378.** Morgan, P. (1980). The State as Mediator: Alcohol Problem Management in the Post-War Period. *CDP,* (Spring) pp. 107-140. **379.** Chafetz, M. and Demone, H., 1964, p. 119. **380.** State Programs, 1956, p.5. **381.** Bacon, 1952, p. 433. **382.** State Programs, 1955, pp. 12-13. **383.** Hart, L. (1977). A Review of Treatment and Rehabilitation Legislation Regarding Alcohol Abusers and Alcoholics in the United States: 1920-1971. *IJA,* 12:(5): 667-678. **384.** General sources for this section include Smithers, R.B. (1977). *25th Anniversary Report.* Mill Neck, NY: The Christopher D. Smithers Foundation, Inc.; Smithers, R.B. (1992). *40th Anniversary Report* Mill Neck, NY: The Christopher D. Smithers Foundation, Inc. **385.** Johnson, 1973, p. 274. **386.** Johnson, 1973, p. 323. **387.** Research Council on Problems of Alcohol. (1943). *QJSA,* 4: 141. **388.** Burnham, J. (1993). *Bad Habits: Drinking, Smoking, Taking Drugs, Gambling, Sexual Misbehavior, and Swearing in American History.* NY: New York University Press. **389.** Roizen, Personal communication, September, 14, 1996. **390.** Room, 1978, p.138. **391.** Roizen, 1994, p. 16. **392.** Anderson, D. (1989). *Celebrating Forty Years of Progress: A Look at the History of Alcohol/Drug Treatment.* Presented at the 40th Annual Conference of the Alcohol and Drug Problems Association, August 27-30, Washington, DC. **393.** Silkworth, 1937. **394.** Miller and Kurtz, 1994. **395.** Jellinek, E.M., Ed. (1942). *Alcohol Addiction and Chronic Alcoholism.* New Haven: Yale University Press. p. 62. **396.** Roizen, 1991a, p. 177. **397.** Haggard, H. (1944). Critique of the Concept of the Allergic Nature of Alcohol Addiction. *QJSA,* 5:233-241. **398.** Jellinek, E., Ed. (1945). *Alcohol, Science, and Society.* New Haven. *QJSA.,* p.27. **399.** Room, 1978. **400.** Bowman and Jellinek, 1942; Jellinek, E.M. (1952). The Phases of Alcohol Addiction. *QJSA,*13:672-684. **401.** Jellinek, E.M. (1960). *The Disease Concept of Alcoholism.* Highland Park, New Jersey: Hillhouse. **402.** Tiebout, H. (1955b). Perspectives in Alcoholism. *Selected Papers Delivered at the Sixth Annual Meeting National States' Conference on Alcoholism,* Miami Beach, Florida, October 30-November 2, Portland, Oregon: The National States' Conference on Alcoholism, pp. 1-7. **403.** Bowman and Jellinek, 1942; Jellinek, 1960; Seeley, J. (1962). Alcoholism as a Disease: Implications for Social Policy. In: Pittman, D. and Snyder, C. (Eds). *Society, Culture and Drinking Patterns.* NY: John Wiley & Sons, p. 593.

Section 6
Chapter Twenty-one: The Birth and Spread of the "Minnesota Model"

1. This chapter was constructed using three excellent works: Forrest Richeson's 1978 history of A.A. in Minnesota, Damian McElrath's 1987 history of Hazelden, and Jerry Spicer's 1993 text on the Minnesota Model. This written material was supplemented by interviews with Dan Anderson, Gordon Grimm, Damian McElrath, Jean Rossi, and Jerry Spicer; Anderson, D. (1981). *Perspectives on Treatment--The Minnesota Experience.* Center City, MN: Hazelden Educational Materials. **2.** Richeson, F. (1978). *Courage to Change.* U.S.A.: M & M Printing, p. 2. **3.** This biographical profile of Pat C. is drawn primarily from Richeson, 1978, pp. 3-33. **4.** Richeson, 1978, pp. 3-33. **5.** Shepherd, E. (1950). Reports on Government Sponsored Programs. *QJSA,* 11:353-354. **6.** Shephard, 1950, p. 358. **7.** Spicer, J. (1993). *The Minnesota Model: The Evolution of the Interdisciplinary Approach to Addiction Recovery.* Center City, Minnesota: Hazelden Educational Materials, p. 30. **8.** Bradley, N. (1975). Where We Are at This Point in Time. Presentation at the 40th Anniversary International Convention of Alcoholics Anonymous, July 5-6. Denver, CO, p. 10. **9.** Richeson, 1978, pp. 21-29. **10.** Pioneer House continued its service work into the modern era. Between 1948 and 1973, Pioneer House treated more than 8,500 alcoholics in its 21-day treatment program. New Pioneer House facilities were constructed in 1977 (two 32-bed treatment units). The "Old Pioneer House" programs became known as Pioneer Programs and moved to the Detox Center in Minneapolis. In 1981, Hazelden took over the ownership and management of Pioneer House, which today is now known as the Hazelden Center for Youth and Families. **11.** The primary resource used to construct this sketch of Hazelden was McElrath, D. (1987). *Hazelden: A Spiritual Odyssey.* Center City, Minnesota: Hazelden Foundation. **12.** Anderson, Personal Communication, August 27, 1997. **13.** Crewe, C. (1978). A Short History of Hazelden. (Appendix). Anderson, D. and Burns, J. Hazelden Foundation, Part of the Caring Community, In: Groupe, V., Ed., *Alcoholism Rehabilitation Methods and Experiences of Private Rehabilitation Centers.* NIAAA-RUCAS Alcoholism Treatment Series, No. 3. New Brunswick, New Jersey: Rutgers Center of Alcohol Studies, p. 51 **14.** Laundergan, J. (1982). *Easy Does It: Alcoholism Treatment Outcomes, Hazelden and the Minnesota Model.* Center City, Minnesota: Hazelden Foundation, p. 6. **15.** Dan Anderson, Personal Interview, May 8, 1996. **16.** Richeson, 1978, p. 188. **17.** Richeson, 1978, p. 189. **18.** McElrath, 1987, p. 39. **19.** Richeson, 1978, p. 49. **20.** Richeson, 1978, p. 50. **21.** Bradley, 1974, p. 1. **22.** Bradley, 1974, p. 1. **23.** Bradley, 1974, p. 2. **24.** Evidence of this slow evolution can be found in a 1954 booklet distributed to Willmar patients, which expressed a preference for the term "problem drinker" rather than "alcoholic" and stated that "alcoholism is fundamentally the result of a personality disorder." Anderson, D. (1954). Alcoholism and the Willmar Treatment Program. Millar, MN: Willmar State Hospital., p. i,11. **25.** Dan Anderson, Personal Interview, May 8, 1996. **26.** Anderson, D. (1981),

p. 17. **27.** Bradley, 1960, Audiotape. **28.** There are differing reports on the length-of-sobriety requirement, placing it at between two and five years. Required sobriety time may have increased with the growth of the pool of recovered alcoholics from which staff could be recruited. Richeson, 1978, p. 50. **29.** Gordon Grimm, Personal Interview, May 8, 1996. **30.** Dan Anderson, Personal Interview, May 8, 1996. **31.** Corwin, E. and Cunningham, E. (1944). Institutional Facilities for the Treatment of Alcoholism. *QJSA,* 5(1), pp. 9-85. **32.** Rossi, J., Stach, A. And Bradley, N. (1963). Effects of Treatment of Male Alcoholics in a Mental Hospital: A Follow-up Study. *QJSA,* 24:91-108. **33.** Dan Anderson, Personal Interview, May 8, 1996. **34.** Richeson, 1978, p. 52. **35.** Keller, J. (ND). The History of the Evangelical Lutheran Church in America Mission in Alcoholism/Drug Abuse. Unpublished manuscripts (received from the author June, 1995), p. 4. **36.** Keller, 1995. **37.** Spicer, 1993, p. 133. **38.** Dan Anderson, Personal Interview, May 8, 1996. **39.** Rossi, J. and Bradley, N. (1960). Dynamic Hospital Treatment of Alcoholism. *QJSA,* 21:432-446. **40.** Rossi, Stach, and Bradley, 1963, pp. 91-108. **41.** McElrath, D. (1981). *Roses of Dia Linn: A Celebration of 25 Years.* Center City, Minnesota: Hazelden Foundation. **42.** Crewe, C. (ND). Hazelden History (Unpublished Manuscript). Center City, Minnesota: Hazelden Library, pp. 22-23. **43.** Laundergan, 1982. **44.** Anderson, 1981, p. 28. **45.** Richeson, 1978, pp. 56, 201. **46.** Anderson, 1981; McElrath, 1987; Spicer, 1993, Laundergan, 1982. **47.** Goffman, I. (1961). *Asylums.* Garden City, NY: Anchor Books. **48.** Dan Anderson, Personal Interview, May 8, 1996. **49.** Jerry Spicer, Personal Interview, May 22, 1996. **50.** Spicer, 1993, p. 115. **51.** Dan Anderson, Personal Interview, May 8, 1996. **52.** Gordon Grimm, Personal Interview, May 8, 1996. **53.** This section draws primarily from interviews conducted with Dan Anderson, Gordon Grimm, Jerry Spicer, and Damian McElrath. **54.** Richeson, 1978, p. 165. **55.** Rossi and Bradley, 1960. **56.** White, W., Personal Reflection. **57.** Dan Anderson, Personal Interview, May 8, 1996. **58.** Flexner, A. (1915). Is Social Work a Profession? *National Conference on Charities and Corrections Proceedings,* 42:576-90. **59.** Dan Anderson, Personal Interview, May 8, 1996.

Chapter Twenty-two: Mid-Century Alcoholism Treatment: An Overview

60. Hart, L. (1977). A Review of Treatment and Rehabilitation Legislation Regarding Alcohol Abusers and Alcoholics in the United States: 1920-1971. *IJA,* 12(5):667-678. **61.** Bacon, S. (1952). Alcoholism, 1941-1951. A Survey of Activities in Research, Education and Therapy. *QJSA,* 3(3): 433. **62.** Giesbrecht, N. and Pernanen, K. (1987). Sociological Perspectives on the Alcoholism Treatment Literature Since 1940. In: Galanter, M., Ed., *Recent Developments in Alcoholism.* NY: Plenum Press. pp. 175-202. **63.** Bowman, K. and Jellinek, E.(1941). Alcoholic Mental Disorders. QJSA, 2:312-390.(September). **64.** Rosenwasser, C. (1909). A Plea for the Establishment of Hospitals for the Rational Treatment of Inebriates. In: *The Alcohol Problem and Its Practical Relations to Life* (U.S. Senate Document No. 48). Washington, D.C.: U.S. GPO, pp. 102-108. **65.** Fleming, R. (1937). The Treatment of Chronic Alcoholism. *NEJM,* 217:779-783. (November). **66.** Wellman, W., Maxwell, M., and O'Hallaren, P. (1957). Private Hospital Alcoholic Patients and the Changing Conception of the "Typical Alcoholic." *QJSA,* 18:388-404. (September). **67.** Wellman, Maxwell, O'Hallaren, 1957, p. 402. **68.** Moore, M. and Gray, M. (1937). The Problem of Alcoholism at the Boston City Hospital. *NEJM,* 217:381-388. **69.** Futterman, S. (1953). Personality Trends in Wives of Alcoholics. *Journal of Psychiatric Social Work,* 23:37-41. **70.** Whalen, T. (1953). Wives of Alcoholics: Four Types Observed in a Family Service Agency. *QJSA,* 12:632-641. **71.** Day, B. (1961). Alcoholism and the Family. *Marriage and Family Living,* 23:253-258. **72.** Reddy, B. (1971). The Family Disease--Alcoholism. Unpublished Manuscript, p. 1. **73.** Jackson, J. (1954). The Adjustment of the Family to the Crisis of Alcoholism. *QJSA,* 15:562-86. **74.** See the following for reviews: Jackson, J. (1962). Alcoholism and the Family. In: Pittman, D. and Snyder, C., Eds., *Society, Culture and Drinking Patterns.* NY: John Wiley & Sons, Inc. pp. 472-492; Jackson, J. (1964). Drinking, Drunkenness, and the Family. In: McCarthy, R. Ed. *Alcohol Education for Classroom and Community.* NY: McGraw-Hill Book Company. **75.** Jellinek, E.M., Ed. (1942). *Alcohol Addiction and Chronic Alcoholism.* New Haven: Yale University Press, p. 65. **76.** Hirsh, J. (1949). *The Problem Drinker.* NY: Duell, Sloan and Pearce. **77.** Deutsch, A. (1937, 1949). *The Mentally Ill in America: A History of their Care and Treatment from Colonial Times.* NY: Columbia University Press, p. 455. **78.** Richeson, 1978, p. 56. **79.** Cahn, S. (1969). Alcoholism Halfway Houses: Relationships to Other Programs and Facilities. *Social Work,* 14(2) 50-60. **80.** McMahan, H. (1942). The Psychotherapeutic Approach of Chronic Alcoholism in Conjunction with the Alcoholics Anonymous Program. *Illinois Psychiatric Journal* 2:15-20. **81.** *AA Grapevine.* (1947). 3:12. (May). **82.** Moore, R. and Buchanan, T. (1966). State Hospitals and Alcoholism: A National Survey of Treatment Techniques and Results. *QJSA,* 27:459-468. **83.** Brunner-Orne, Iddings, F. and Rodrigues, J. (1951). Court Clinics for Alcoholics: A Description and Evaluation of the Stoughton Clinic. *QJSA,* 12(4):592-600. **84.** For an interesting profile of one of the Yale-inspired clinics, see: Daley, E. (1952). A Report on the Pilot Plan Alcoholism Rehabilitation Clinic at San Francisco. *QJA,* 13:2 (June), pp. 345-355. **85.** Spicer, 1993, p. 61. **86.** *AA Grapevine.* (1951). 8(4):15-17. (September). **87.** Bacon, S. (1949). The Administration of Alcoholism Rehabilitation Programs. *QJSA,* 10(1):1-47; Myerson, D. (1957). The Study and Treatment of Alcoholism: A Historical Perspective. *NEJM,* 257:820-25. **88.** Searcy, W., Personal Interview, May 16, 1996; W., Searcy (1993). *A Study Book on My "Alcoholism Recovery" Since May 10, 1946 and A History of How Early A.A. Groups Started* Dallas Texas: Texas Clinic-Hospital for Alcoholism, Inc. **89.** McGoldrick, E. (1960). The Bridge House Way of Treating Alcoholics. *Report on Man's Use of Alcohol,* 43 (2):13-16 (March-

April); McGoldrick, E. (1964). Who is Qualified to Treat the Alcoholic? Comment on the Krystal-Moore Discussion. *QJSA* 25:351; McGoldrick, E. (1966). *The Conquest of Alcohol.* NY: Delacorte Press, pp. 8, 31. **90.** McGoldrick, 1966, pp. 73-75. **91.** McGoldrick, 1966, pp. x-xi. **92.** Delaney, G. (1978). Little Hill-Alina Lodge: Nonpermissive Treatment of Alcoholics and Polyaddicts. In: Groupe, V., Ed., *Alcoholism Rehabilitation: Methods and Experiences of Private Rehabilitation Centers.* New Brunswick, New Jersey: Rutgers Center of Alcohol Studies, pp. 64-66; Mell, J. (1995). How a Place of Hope Became Fact (The History of Little Hill - Alina Lodge). Unpublished paper. **93.** *AA Grapevine. (1947).* 4(4):3 (September). **94.** Portal House of Chicago Annual Reports (1952, 1953, 1955). Chicago: Chicago Committee on Alcoholism. **95.** Agrin, A. (1960). The Georgian Clinic: A Therapeutic Community for Alcoholism. *QJSA,* 21(1): 113-124; Krystal, H. and Moore, R. (1963). Who is Qualified to Treat the Alcoholic? *QJSA,* 27:449-59. **96.** Today the Caron Foundation operates a 20-bed medical detoxification facility, two adult residential treatment facilities with a combined capacity of more than 100 beds, a 36-bed adolescent facility, two halfway houses, and two outpatient counseling centers. Dick and Catherine Caron died in 1975 and 1987 respectively, having seen their dream of an "East-Coast Hazelden" fulfilled. Their son, Rick, continues to serve on the board of the Foundation. **97.** Kurtz, E. (1979). *Not God: A History of Alcoholics Anonymous.* Center City, Minnesota: Hazelden, p. 161. **98.** *Lois Remembers.* (1994). NY: Al-Anon Family Group Headquarters, Inc., World Service Office for Al-Anon and Alateen, p. 172. **99.** Family Groups Make Headway in California (1947). *AA Grapevine.* 3(12):1. (May); Non-AA Group Formed in Austin. (1947). *AA Grapevine.* 4(2):3. (July); Non-Alcoholic Wives form AA Auxiliary. (1948). *AA Grapevine.* 4(12):7. (May); NAA Organized. (1948). *AA Grapevine.* 5(2):5 (July); San Diego Non-AAs Celebrate Fifth Anniversary. (1951). *AA Grapevine.* 8(3):38-39. (August); The Al-Anon Story. (1963). *AA Grapevine,* 19(9):2-9. **100.** *Living with an Alcoholic with the Help of Al-Anon.* (1980). NY: Al-Anon Family Group Headquarters, p. 2. **101.** Al-Anon: Then and Now (1986). NY: Al-Anon Family Group Headquarters, Inc. **102.** Corder, B., Hendricks, A. And Corder, R. (1964). An MMPI Study of a Group of Wives of Alcoholics. *QJSA,* 25:551. **103.** Lois, 1994, p. i. **104.** Dunn, J. (1986). *God is for the Alcoholic.* Chicago, IL: The Moody Bible Institute of Chicago, pp. 142-143. **105.** Richeson, 1978, p. 260. **106.** Dunn, 1986, p. 14. **107.** John, H. (1977). The Church and Alcoholism: A Growing Movement. *AHRW,* 1(4):2-10; Fox, B. (1992). Prayer, Sacraments, and Sobriety (The Calix Society). *New Covenant,* December, pp. 30-31.

Chapter Twenty-three: Mid-century Alcoholism Treatment Methods

108. Wallerstein, R. (1957). *Hospital Treatment of Alcoholism.* NY: Basic Books. **109.** Wilson, B. (1993). *Bill Wilson & The Vitamin B-3 Therapy: 1965-1971.* Wheeling, West Virginia: The Bishop of Books, p. 2. **110.** William, R. (1959). Biochemical Individuality and Cellular Nutrition: Prime Factors in Alcoholism. *QJSA,* 20: 452-63. **111.** Ross, B. (1990). *Niacin Can Curb Craving for Alcohol.* Tampa, FL: Mancorp Publishing. **112.** Corwin and Cunningham, 1944. **113.** Feldman, D. (1957). Drug Therapy in Chronic Alcoholism. *Medical Clinics of North America,* 41:381-392. **114.** Sugarman, A. (1982). Alcoholism: An Overview of Treatment Models. In: Gomberg, L., White, H. and Carpenter, J. *Alcohol, Science and Society Revisited.* Ann Arbor: The University of Michigan Press, p. 268. **115.** Kissin, B. and Gross, M. (1968). Drug Therapy in Alcoholism. *AJP,* 125:31-41. **116.** White, J. (1955). *Ward N-1.* NY: A.A. Wyn, Inc. **117.** Feldman, 1957, p. 390. **118.** Miller, W. (1993). Alcoholism: Toward a Better Disease Model. *Psychology of Addictive Behaviors* 7(2):129-136. **119.** Bloomburg, W. (1939). Treatment of Chronic Alcoholism With Amphetamine (Benzedrine) Sulfate. *NEJM,* 220(4):135. **120.** Reifenstein, E. and Davidoff, E. (1938). The Treatment of Alcoholic Psychoses with Benzedrine Sulfate. *JAMA,* 110:1811-1813; Reifenstein, E. and Davidoff, E. (1939). The Psychological Effects of Benzedrine Sulfate. *American Journal of Psychology,* 52:56-64. **121.** Anderson, D. (1950). *The Other Side of the Bottle.* NY: A.A. Wyn, Inc., pp. 106-119; Voegtlin, W. and Lemere, F. (1942). The Treatment of Alcohol Addiction: A Review of the Literature. *QJSA,* 2:717-803. **122.** Hewitt, D. (1957). *Alcoholism: A Treatment Guide for General Practioners.* Philadelphia: Lea & Febiger, pp. 88-89. **123.** Blum, E. (1966). Psychoanalytic Views on Alcoholism. *QJSA,* 27(2):259-299. **124.** Williams, E. (1937). Effects of Alcohol on Workers with Carbon Disulfide. *JAMA,* 109:1472. **125.** Hald, J. and Jacobsen, E. (1948). A Drug Sensitizing the Organism to Ethyl Alcohol. *Lancet,* II, p. 10001. **126.** Hewitt, 1957, pp. 72-73. **127.** Keller, M., McCormick, M., and Efron, V. (1982). *A Dictionary of Words about Alcohol.* New Brunswick, NJ: Rutgers Center of Alcohol Studies, p. 101. **128.** Glud, E. (1949). The Treatment of Alcoholic Patients in Denmark with Antabuse. *QJSA,* 10: 185-96. **129.** Fox, R. (1958). Antabuse as an Adjunct to Psychotherapy in Alcoholism. *New York State Journal of Medicine,* 58(1):1540-1544. **130.** Fox, 1958, pp. 1540-1544 **131.** Miller, W. and Hester, R. (1986). The Effectiveness of Alcoholism Treatment. In: Miller, W. and Hester, R. (Eds.) *Treating Addictive Behaviors: Process of Change.* NY: Plenum Press, pp. 121-174. **132.** Wilson, A. (1975). Disulfram Implantation in Alcoholism Treatment: A Review. *JSA,* 36:555-565; Doherty, J. (1976). Disulfram (Antabuse): Chemical Commitment to Abstinence. *AHRA,* Spring, pp. 2-9; Halikas, J. (1983). Psychotropic Medication Used in the Treatment of Alcoholism. *Hospital and Community Psychiatry,* 34(11):1035-1039. **133.** General references for this section include: Stevens, J. (1987). *Storming Heaven: LSD and the American Dream.* NY: Harper & Row, Publishers; Groff, S. (1970). The Use of LSD in Psychotherapy. *JPD,* 3(1):52-62; Groff, S. (1980). *LSD Psychotherapy.* Pomona, California: Hunter House; Abramson, H. (1967). *The Use of LSD in Psychotherapy and Alcoholism.* NY: Bobbs-Merrill Co. **134.** Hill, T. (1990). Peyotism and the Control of Heavy

Drinking: The Nebraska Winnebego in the Early 1900s. *Human Organization*, 49:255-265; LaBarre, W. (1947). Primitive Psychotherapy in Native American Cultures: Peyotism and Confession. *Journal of Abnormal and Social Psychology*, 42:294-309. **135.** Caldwell, W. (1969). *LSD Psychotherapy*. NY: Grove Press, p. 8 **136.** Hofmann, A. (1983). *LSD: My Problem Child*. Los Angeles: Tarcher, pp. 48-49. **137.** Grinspoon, L. and Bakalar, J. (1986). Can Drugs Be Used to Enhance the Psychotherapeutic Process? *American Journal of Psychotherapy*, 40:393 (July). **138.** Hoffer, A. (1967). A Program for the Treatment of Alcoholism: LSD, Malaria and Nicotinic Acid. In: Abramson , H., Ed., *The Use of LSD in Psychotherapy and Alcoholism*. NY: Bobbs-Merrill Company, Inc, p. 363. **139.** Hoffer, A. and Osmond, H. (1967). *The Hallucinogens*. NY: Academic Press, p. 132. **140.** Stevens, 1987, pp. 173-175; Groff, 1970, pp. 52-53. **141.** Chwelos, N., Blewett, D., Smith, C. and Hoffer, A. (1959). Use of LSD-25 in the Treatment of Chronic Alcoholism. Q*JAS*, 20: 577-590. **142.** Cohen, I. (1970). The Benzodiazepines. In: Ayd, F. and Blackwell, B., Eds., *Discoveries in Biological Psychiatry*. Philadelphia: Lippincott, pp.115-129. **143.** Fox, 1967, p. 775. **144.** Hoffer and Osmond, 1968, p. 102. **145.** Stevens, 1987, p. 175. **146.** Hoffer and Osmond, 1968, pp. 69-70. **147.** Miller, 1986, p. 130. **148.** Brunner-Orne, M. (1967). A Three-Dimensional Approach to the Treatment of Alcoholism. In: Fox, R. *Alcoholism: Behavioral Research, Therapeutic Approaches*. NY: Springer Publishing Company, Inc, pp. 152-163. **149.** Ashworth, W. (1932). Rambling Thoughts About Whiskey and Drug Addiction. *Virginia Medical Monographs*, 58:678. **150.** LaVerne, A. and Herman, M. (1955). An Evaluation of Carbon Dioxide Therapy, *The AJP*, 112(2):111 (August). **151.** LaVerne, 1972. **152.** LaVern also reported that of 50 heroin addicts treated with carbon dioxide, "48% remained drug-free from one to five years; 22% who had relapses were put on maintenance treatment of once a week and remained drug-free up to five years; 30% were failures." Ashley, R. (1972). *Heroin: The Myths and the Facts*. NY: St. Martin's Press, p. 213. **153.** Keller, O. and Alper, B. (1970). *Halfway Houses: Community-Centered Correction and Treatment*. Lexington, Massachusetts: Heath Lexington Books, pp. 1-15; McKelvey, B. (1977). *American Prisons: A History of Good Intentions*. Montclair, New Jersey: Patterson Smith, p. 84. **154.** This reference by Raush is to a 1953 article by Louis Reik, which appeared in the journal *Mental Hygiene*, 37: 615-618. **155.** Raush, H. with Raush, C. (1968). *The Halfway House Movement*. NY: Appleton Century Crofts, pp. 3-8. **156.** Holmes, T. (1899). Habitual Inebriates. *The Contemporary Review*, 75:740-746. **157.** Lois Looks Back on Early Days with Bill. (1959). *AA Grapevine*, 16(1):8-10. (March). **158.** *Pass I t On—The Story of Bill Wilson and How the A.A. Message Reached the World*. (1984). New York: Alcoholics Anonymous World Services, Inc., p. 165. **159.** Rubington, E. (1970). The Future of the Halfway House. *QJSA*, 31:167-174. **160.** Keller, McCormick, Efron, 1982, p. 122. **161.** Crewe, 1978, p. 53. **162.** Rubington, 1977. **163.** Rubington, 1970; Rubington, E. (1967). The Halfway House for the Alcoholic. *Mental Hygiene*, 51:552-560. (Reprinted in *Addictions* (1973) 20(3):19-31). **164.** Barrows, D. (1979). The Residential Rehabilitation Program for the Alcoholic (Working Paper, pp. 1-38). Berkeley, CA: The Alcohol Research Group. **165.** Barrows, 1979, p. 16. **166.** Blacker, E, and Kantor, D. (1960). Half-way Houses for Problem Drinkers. *Federal Probation*, 24(2):18-23. **167.** Martinson, R. (1964). The California Recovery Home: A Sanctuary for Alcoholics. *Mental Hygiene*, 48:432-438. **168.** Pittman, D. And Gordan, C. (1958). Revolving Door. New Haven, CT: Center of Alcohol Studies. Pittman, pp. 321-327. **169.** Larson, K. (1982). Salute to Minnesota (Willmar State Hospital: Birthplace of "The Minnesota Model"). *Alcoholism/The National Magazine*, 3(2):34-39. **170.** Fox, V. (1977). *Community-Based Corrections*. Englewood Cliffs, New Jersey: Prentice-Hall, Inc. **171.** Rubington, 1970, 1973.

Chapter Twenty-four: Midcentury Addiction Treatment: The Rise of New Approaches

172. Weston, P. Ed. (1952). *Narcotics, U.S.A.* NY: Greenburg Publisher. **173.** Modern, F.S. (1932). Insulin in the Treatment of Chronic Morphinism. *Medical Journal and Record*, 136:163. **174.** Deutsch, A. (1937, 1949). *The Mentally Ill in America: A History of Their Care and Treatment from Colonial Times*. NY: Columbia University Press, p. 409. **175.** Thigpen, F. Thigpen, C. and Cleckley, H. (1955). Use of Electric-Convulsive Therapy in Morphine, Meperidine, and Related Alkaloid Addictions. In: Podolsky, E. Ed. *Management of Addictions*. NY: Philosophical Library, pp. 383-393. **176.** Mason, T. and Hambry, W. (1948). Relief of Morphine Addiction by Prefrontal Lobotomy. *JAMA*, 136:1039 (April 17); Wikler, A., Pescor, M., Kalbaugh, E., and Angelucci, R. (1952). Effects of Frontal Lobotomy on the Morphine-abstinence Syndrome in Man. A.M.A. *Archives of Neurological Psychiatry*, 71: pp. 510-521; Maurer, D. and Vogel, V. (1973). *Narcotics and Narcotic Addiction* . Springfield, Illinois: Charles C. Thomas; Milby, J. (1981). *Addictive Behavior and its Treatment*. NY: Springer Publishing Company. **177.** Serum Injections Used in Prison to Cure Drug Addicts, AMA Archives, Box 0031-02. **178.** Brill, L, (1977). Historical Evolution of the Current Drug Treatment Perspective. In: Schecter, A. *Rehabilitation Aspects of Drug Dependence* Cleveland, OH: CRC Press, pp. 11-21. **179.** Knight, R. And Prout, C. (1951). A Study of Results in Hospital Treatment of Drug Addictions. *AJP*, 108:303-308. **180.** Freedman, A. (1963). Treatment of Drug Addiction in a Community Hospital. *Comparative Psychiatry*, 4:199; Wilner, D. and Kassebaum, G. (1965). *Narcotics*. NY: McGraw-Hill Book Company, pp. 177-192. **181.** Chafetz, M. and Demone, H. (1964). Alcoholism: Causes and Treatment. In: McCarthy, R. Ed. *Alcohol Education for Classroom and Community*. NY: McGraw-Hill Book Company, p. 201. **182.** Gamso, R. and Mason, P. (1958). A Hospital for Adolescent Drug Addicts. *Psychiatric Quarterly, Supplement*, 32:99-109. **183.** Wakefield, D. (1992). *New York in the 1950's*. Boston: Houghton Mifflin, pp. 98-99. **184.** Maddux, J. (1978). History of the Hospital Treatment Program:

1935-1974. Martin, W. and Isbell, H. *Drug Addiction and the US Public Health Service.* DHEW Pub. No. ADM-77-434, pp. 217-250. **185.** Brill, L. (1972). *The De-Addiction Process.* Springfield, IL: Charles C. Thomas, p. 142. **186.** Wilner and Kasenbaum, 1965, pp. 249-262. **187.** Leon Brill. In: Wilner and Kassebaum, 1965, p. 219. **188.** Boshes, B., Sewell, L. and Koga. M. (1956). Management of the Narcotic Addict in an Outpatient Clinic. *AJP,* 113:158-162. (August). **189.** Harney, M. (1962). Current Provision and Practices in the United States of America Relating to the Commitment of Opiate Addicts. *Bulletin on Narcotics,* 14(July-September), pp. 19-21 **190.** Smith, D. and Luce, J. (1971). *Love Needs Care: A History of San Francisco's Haight-Ashbury Free Medical Clinic and Its Pioneer Role in Treating Drug-Abuse Problems.* Boston: Little, Brown and Company, p. 15; Brecher, E. (1972). *Licit and Illicit Drugs.* Boston: Little, Brown and Company, p. 282. **191.** Langrod, Josephy, and Valdes (1972). The Role of Religion in the Treatment of Opiate Addiction. In: Brill, L. and Lieberman, L. *Major Modalities in the Treatment of Drug Abuse.* NY: Behavioral Publications, 167-189. **192.** Duncan, T. (1965). *Understanding and Helping the Narcotic Addict.* Philadelphia: Fortress Press, p. 104. **193.** Duncan, 1965. **194.** Pitcaithly, W. And Fisher, C. (1973). *From Dope to Hope: The Story of Father Pit and the Samaritan Halfway Society.* Garden City, NY: Doubleday & Company, Inc. **195.** Another program that could be placed in this category is The Damascus Program (The Christian Youth Crusade), which was founded in 1963 by the Reverend Leonicia Rosado and Bishop Francisco Rosado of the Damascus Christian Church in the South Bronx. Brill, 1972, p. 144; Langrod, Josephy, and Valdes,1972. **196.** Wilkerson, D. (1963). *The Cross and the Switchblade.* NY: Bernard Geiss Associates, p. 108. **197.** Glasscotte, R.; Sussex, J.; Jaffe, J.; Ball, J.; and Brill, L. (1972). *The Treatment of Drug Abuse: Programs, Problems, Prospects.* Washington, DC: American Psychiatric Association; Wilkerson, 1963. **198.** Wilkerson, 1963, p. 167. **199.** Wilkerson, 1963, p. 76. **200.** Glasscotte, 1972, p. 166. **201.** Hesse, R. (1977). Primary Prevention: A Brief Review of Policy Development. Washington, DC: National Association of State Drug Abuse Program Coordinators. **202.** General references for this section include Barboza, S. (1993). *American JIhad: Islam After Malcolm X.* NY: Doubleday; Banks, W. (1997). *The Black Muslims.* Philadelphia: Chelsea Publishers. **203.** Banks, 1997. **204.** Barboza, 1993, p. 133. **205.** Brill, 1972, p. 121. **206.** Langrod, J., Alksne, L. and Gomez, E. (1981). A Religious Approach to the Rehabilitation of Addicts. In: Lowinson, J. and Ruiz, P. (Eds.) *Substance Abuse, Clinical Problems and Perspectives.* Baltimore, MD: Williams & Wilkins, p. 419; Miller, J. (1973). The Seed: Reforming Drug Abusers with Love. *Science,* 182:40-42. **207.** AA *Grapevine.* (1965). 21(8). (January). **208.** *AA Grapevine.* (1949). 6(2):21. (July); Stone, B. (1997). *My Years with Narcotics Anonymous.* Joplin, Missouri: Hulon Pendleton Publishing Co. pp. 3-4. **209.** Vogel, V. (1948). Treatment of the Narcotic Addict by the United States Public Health Service. *Federal Proba*tion, June, pp. 45-50; Gerstel, D. (1982). *Paradise Incorporated: Synanon.* Novato, California: Presidio Press. **210.** Ellison, J. (1954). These Drug Addicts Cure One Another. *Saturday Evening Post,* 227(6):22-23,48-52. (August 7). **211.** Patrick, S. (1965). Our Way of Life: A Short History of Narcotics Anonymous, Inc. In: Harmes, E. Ed. *Drug Addiction and Youth.* Oxford: Pergammon Press. **212.** Stone, 1997, pp. 21-22. **213.** Nurco, D., et. al., (1983). *Ex-Addicts' Self-Help Groups.* NY: Praeger Scientific, p. 114. **214.** Stone, 1997, pp. 47, 125, 532. **215.** *N.A.: A Resource in Your Community* (Pamphlet). **216.** Duncan, 1965, pp. 106-107. **217.** Winick, C. (1957). Narcotics Addiction and Its Treatment. *Law and Contemporary Problems,* 22:9. **218.** Glaser, F. (1974). Some Historical Aspects of the Drug-Free Therapeutic Community. *American Journal of Drug and Alcohol Abuse,* 1:37-52. **219.** This story has been constructed from the six major texts on Synanon: Casriel, D. (1963). *So Fair a House: The Story of Synanon.* Englewood Cliffs, NJ: Prentice-Hall, Inc.;Yablonsky, L. (1965). *Synanon: The Tunnel Back.* Baltimore, Maryland: Penguin Books; Endore, G. (1968). *Synanon.* Garden City, NY: Doubleday & Company, Inc.; Olin, W. (1980). *Escape from Paradise: My Ten Years in Synanon.* Santa Cruz: Unity Press; Mitchell, D, Mitchell, C. and Ofshe, R. (1980). *The Light on Synanon.* Wideview Books; Gerstel, D. (1982). *Paradise Incorporated: Synanon.* Novato, California: Presidio Press. References to the effectiveness of therapeutic community approaches to drug addiction are based primarily upon: DeLeon, G. Ed. (1984). *The Therapeutic Community: Study of Effectiveness.* Treatment Research Monograph. Washington, D.C.: U.S. GPO. **220.** Gerstel, 1982, p. 35. **221.** Casriel, 1963, p. 25. **222.** Endore, 1968, p. 166. **223.** Yablonsky, L. (1962). The Anti-Criminal Society: Synanon. *Federal Probation,* 16(3):50-56. **224.** Gerstel, 1982, p. 37. **225.** Mitchell, Mitchell and Ofshe, 1980, p. 146. **226.** Endore, 1968, p. 56. **227.** Deitch, D. And Zweben, J. (1981). Synanon: A Pioneering Response in Drug Abuse Treatment and A Signal for Caution. In: Lowinson, J. and Ruiz, P. Eds. *Substance Abuse, Clinical Problems and Perspectives.* Baltimore, MD: Williams & Wilkins, pp. 289-302. **228.** Mitchell, Mitchell and Ofshe, 1980, pp. 73, 126. **229.** Deitch and Zweben, 1981, p. 296. **230.** Sells, S. Ed. (1966). *Rehabilitating the Narcotic Addict.* Washington, DC: GPO. **231.** Endore, 1968. **232.** White, W. (1997). *The Incestuous Workplace.* Center City, MN: Hazelden. **233.** Bourne, P. and Ramsey, A. (1975). The Therapeutic Community. *JPD,* 7(2):203-207. **234.** Yablonsky, L. (1989). *The Therapeutic Community.* NY: Gardner Press. **235.** Glazer, F. (1971). Gaudenzia, Incorporated: Historical and Theoretical Background of a Self Help Addiction Treatment Program. *IJA,* 6(4):617-618. **236.** General references for this section include Casriel, D. and Amen, G. (1971). *Daytop: Three Addicts and Their Cure.* NY: Hill and Wang. **237.** Shelly, J. and Bassin, A. (1965). Daytop Lodge–A New Treatment Approach for Drug Addicts. *Corrective Psychiatry,* 2(4).186-195. **238.** Casriel and Amen, 1971, p. xv. **239.** Sugarman, B. (1974). *Daytop Village: A Therapeutic Community.* NY: Holt, Rinehart and Winston, Inc, pp. 121-123. **240.** Sugarman, 1974, pp. 121-127; Casriel and Amen, 1971. **241.** Glaser, 1974, p. 48. **242.** Malikin, D. (1973). *Social Disability: Alcoholism, Drug Addiction, Crime and Social*

Disadvantage. NY: New York University Press, p. 116. **243.** Casriel and Amen, 1971, p. x. **244.** Yablonsky, 1962, p. 55. **245.** Casriel, D. And Deitch, D. (1966). Permanent Cure of Narcotic Addicts. *The Physician's Panorama,* (October), pp. 5-12. **246.** Olin, W. (1980). *Escape from Paradise: My Ten Years in Synanon.* Santa Cruz: Unity Press, p. 162. **247.** Gerstel, 1982, p. 17. **248.** Sugarman, 1964, p. 89. **249.** While the addiction treatment field has been quite enamored with confrontation as a therapeutic tactic, research on confrontation suggests the need for great care in the use of this technique. William Miller's review of studies on confrontation concluded that such approaches "must be undertaken with great care because of the potential for precipitating dropout, negative emotional states, lowered self-esteem, and proximal relapse." Miller, W. and Hester, R. (1986). The Effectiveness of Alcoholism Treatment. In: Miller, W. And Hester, R. (Eds.). *Treating Addictive Behaviors: Process of Change.* NY: Plenum Press, p.135. **250.** Johnson, G. (1976). Conversion as a Cure: The Therapeutic Community and the Professional Ex-addict. *CDP,* 5:187-206. **251.** Milby, 1981, pp. 209-210. **252.** Bourne and Ramsey, 1975, p. 204. **253.** Glasscote, R.; Sussex, J.; Jaffe, J.; Ball, J.; and Brill, L. (1972). *The Treatment of Drug Abuse: Programs, Problems, Prospects.* Washington, DC: American Psychiatric Association. **254.** Johnson, 1976, p. 210. **255.** Hart, L. (1972). Milieu Management for Drug Addicts: Extended Drug Subculture or Rehabilitation? *BJA,* 67:297-301. **256.** Bourne and Ramsey, 1974, p. 204. **257.** Deitch, D. (1973). Treatment of Drug Abuse in a Therapeutic Community. In: *Technical Papers of the Second Report of the National Commission on Marijuana and Drug Abuse* Appendix, Vol. IV, p. 173. **258.** Yablonsky, 1989, pp. 41-48.

Chapter Twenty-five: Midcentury Addiction Treatment: Part Two

259. General references for this section include Kramer, J. (1970). The Place of Civil Commitment in the Management of Drug Abuse. In: Harris, R., McIsaac, W. and Schuster, C. Eds. *Drug Dependence.* Austin, Texas: University of Texas Press. **260.** Speer, W. (1958). Documentation of the Narcotic Addiction Problem in the United States. In: Hoch, P. and Zubin, J. *Problems of Addiction and Habituation.* NY: Grune & Stratton, p. 151. **261.** Voegtlin and Lemere, 1942, p. 718. **262.** Harvey, 1962, p. 17. **263.** Wood, R. (1973). 18,000 Addicts Later: A Look at California's Civil Addict Program. *Federal Probation,* pp. 26-31. **264.** Sells, 1966, p. 149. **265.** Wood, 1973, p. 26. **266.** Glasscote, 1972, p. 124. **267.** Similarly poor outcome data is reported for New York's civil commitment program. Inciardi (1988) cites reports of only a small number of addicts completing the program, and of those, only 25% were reported abstinent at follow-up. **268.** Inciardi, J. (1988). Compulsory Treatment in New York: A Brief Narrative History of Misjudgment, Mismanagement, and Misrepresentation. *JDI,* 18:547-560. **269.** Harney, M. (1962). Current Provision and Practices in the United States of America Relating to the Commitment of Opiate Addicts. *Bulletin on Narcotics,* 14:11-23. (July-September). **270.** Folklore would later claim that Dolophine was named after Adolf Hitler, but Inciardi's research into the early history of methadone reveals no such connection. Dolophine is an Eli Lilly and Company trade name for methadone selected after the war. Its name comes from the Latin *dolor,* which means pain. Inciardi, J. (1986). *The War on Drugs: Heroin, Cocaine, Crime and Public Policy.* Palo Alto, CA: Mayfield Publishing Company, p. 146. **271.** Williams, H. (1935). *Drugs Against Men.* NY: Robert M. McBride & Company, p. 147. **272.** Senay, E. & Renault, P. (1971). Treatment Methods for Heroin Addicts: A Review. *JPD,* 3(2):47-54. **273.** Brown, J., Mazze, R., Glaser, D. (1974). *Narcotics Knowledge and Nonsense.* Cambridge, MA: Balinger Publishing Company, p. 56. **274.** Dole, V. (1988). Implications of Methadone Maintenance for Theories of Narcotic Addiction. *JAMA,* 260(20):3025-3029). **275.** Courtwright, D. (1997). The Prepared Mind: Marie Nyswander, Methadone Maintenance, and the Metabolic Theory of Addiction. *Addiction,* 92(3)257-265. **276.** Senay and Renault, 1971, p. 49. **277.** National Commission on Marihuana and Drug Abuse (1973). *Drug Use in America.* Washington, D.C.: U.S. Government Printing, p. 312. **278.** Senay and Renault, 1971, p. 47. **279.** Dennis, M. (1995). *Individual Substance Abuse Counseling (ISAC) Manual.* Bloomington, Illinois: Chestnut Health Systems / Lighthouse Institute. **280.** Senay, E. (1981). Multi-modality Programming in Illinois: Evolution of a Public Health Concept. In: Lowinson, J. and Ruiz, P. (Eds.). *Substance Abuse: Clinical Problems and Perspectives.* Baltimore, Maryland: Williams & Wilkins, pp. 396-402. **281.** Dole, V. (1980). Addictive Behavior. *Scientific American,* 243:138-140, 142, 144, 146, 148, 150, 154. (December). **282.** General references for this section include Epstein, E. (1977). *Agency of Fear: Opiates and Political Power in America.* NY: G.P. Putnam's Sons; Inciardi, 1986. **283.** Epstein, 1977, p. 128. **284.** The methadone strategy was one of the more reasonable strategies that emerged from the Office of Drug Abuse Law Enforcement inside the Nixon White House. This was, after all, an era in which narcotic control policy was being heavily influenced by people like G. Gordon Liddy and E. Howard Hunt who would be best known for their later role in Watergate. The era included such exotic strategies as recruiting Elvis Presley to lead a national anti-drug campaign, proposals to assassinate Latin-American drug kingpins, proposals to distribute poisoned cocaine, and a proposal to develop an insect that would eat Southeast Asia's opium fields. Epstein, 1977. **285.** Kandall, S. (1996). *Substance and Shadow: Women and Addiction in the United States.* Cambridge, MA: Harvard University Press. **286.** Conrad, P. And Schneider, J. (1980). *Deviance and Medicalization: From Badness to Sickness.* St. Louis: C.V. Mosby, p. 139. **287.** Platt, J. (1986). *Heroin Addiction: Theory, Research and Treatment.* (Second Edition). Malabar, FL: Robert F. Krieger Publishing Company, p. 58. **288.** Maisto, S. Galizio, M., and Connors, G. (1991). *Drug Use and Misuse.* Forth Worth: Harcourt Brace Jovanovich College Publishers, p. 282. **289.** Shelly and Bassin, 1965, p. 46. **290.** Casriel, 1963, p. 205. **291.** Smith and Luce, 1971, p. 267. **292.** Senay and Renault, 1971, pp. 51-52. **293.** Washton, A., Gold, M., and Pottash, A. (1984). Successful Use of Naltrexone in Addicted Physicians and Business Executives. In: Stimmel, B., Ed., (1984). *Alcohol and Drug Abuse in the Affluent.* NY: Haworth Press. **294.** Dole, 1988, p. 3028. **295.** *Federal Drug Abuse Programs.* (1972). Washington, DC: The Drug Abuse Council. **296.** Savage, C. and McCabe, O. (1971). Psychedelic (LSD) Therapy of Drug Addiction. In: *The Drug Abuse Controversy.* Brown, C. and Savage, C. Eds. Baltimore, MD: National Educational Consultants, Inc., pp. 145-163. **297.** General references for this section include: Senay, E.; Jaffe, J.; Chappel, J.; Renault, P.; Wright, M.; Lawson, C.; Charnett, C.; and DiMenza, S. (1973). IDAP–Five Year Results. *Proceedings of the 5th National Conference on Methadone Treatment,* pp. 1-28; Senay, E. (1981). Multi-modality Programming in Illinois: Evolution of a Public Health Concept. In: Lowinson, J. and Ruiz, P. (Eds.). *Substance Abuse: Clinical Problems and Perspectives.* Baltimore, Maryland: Williams & Wilkins, pp. 396-402; Senay, E. (1989). Drug Abuse Treatment in Illinois: 1966-1984. In: Arif, A. and Westermeyer, J. *Methadone in the Management of Opiate Dependence* NY: Praeger, Glasscote, 1972. **298.** Hageman, L. (1973). Drug Abuse--Past and Present. In: Malikin, D. *Social Disability: Alcoholism, Drug Addiction, Crime and Social Disadvantage.* NY: New York University Press, pp. 66-77. **299.** Glasscote, 1972, p. 207. **300.** General references upon which this discussion are based include Senay, 1981, Senay et. al., 1973; Senay, 1989. **301.** Glasscote, 1972, pp. 150-151. **302.** Glasscote, 1972. **303.** Senay, 1981, p. 399. **304.** Senay, 1989, p. 219. **305.** Senay, et. al., 1973, pp. 2-6; Senay, 1981, p. 9. **306.** Dr. Ed Senay, Personal Interview, March 5, 1996. **307.** Dr. Ed Senay, Personal Interview, March 5, 1996. **308.** Senay, 1981, p. 398. **309.** Glasscote, 1972. **310.** Dr. Ed Senay, Personal Interview, March 5, 1996. **311.** Dr. Ed Senay, Personal Interview, March 5, 1996. **312.** Senay, 1989, p. 224. **313.** Conrad, H. (1972). NIMH Clinical Research Center Lexington, Kentucky: Current Status. In: Lieberman, L. and Brill, L. Eds., *Major Modalities in the Treatment of Drug Abuse.* NY: Behavioral Publications. **314.** Weppner, R. (1973). Some Characteristics of an Ex-Addict Self-Help Therapeutic Community and Its Members. *BJA,* 68:243-250. **315.** Weppner, R. (1983). *The Untherapeutic Community: Organizational Behavior in a Failed Addiction Treatment Program.* Lincoln: University of Nebraska, p. 31; Kolb, L. and Ossenfort, W. (1938). The Treatment of Drug Addicts at the Lexington Hospital. *Southern Medical Journal,* 31:914 (August).; Maddux, J. (1978). History of the Hospital Treatment Program: 1935-1974. Martin, W. and Isbell, H. *Drug Addiction and the US Public Health Service* DHEW Pub. No. ADM-77-434, pp. 217-250. **316.** Walsh, J. (1973). Lexington Hospital Narcotics Hospital: A Special Sort of Alma Mater. *Science,* 128:1004-1008. **317.** Maddux, 1978, p. 217. **318.** Simmel, E. (1970). History of Legal and Medical Roles in Narcotic Abuse in the U.S. In: Ball, J. and Chambers, C. *The Epidemiology of Opium Addiction.* Springfield, IL. **319.** Wilner and Kassebaum, 1965, p. 47.

Section 7
Chapter Twenty-Six: The Modern Evolution of Addiction Treatment

1. My references to "community-based" treatment programs in this chapter refer to programs that, through support from public funds, are accessible to a broad spectrum of alcoholics and addicts—including the indigent. "Private" programs are treatment institutions that are supported primarily through client self-pay or non-governmental third-party payors. **2.** Institute of Medicine (1990). *Broadening the Base of Treatment for Alcohol Problems.* Washington, DC: Academy of Science Press, p. 99. **3.** Plaut, T. (1967). *Alcohol Problems: A Report to the Nation by the Cooperative Commission on the Study of Alcoholism.* New York: Oxford University Press, p. 53. **4.** Plaut, 1967. **5.** Blume, S. (1977). Role of the Recovered Alcoholic in the Treatment of Alcoholism. In: Kissin, B. And Beglieter, H. Eds. *The Biology of Alcoholism, Vol 5, Treatment and Rehabilitation of the Chronic Alcoholic.* New York: Plenum Press, p. 552. **6.** *Pioneers We Have Known in the Field of Alcoholism.* (1979). Mill Neck, New York: The Christopher D. Smithers Foundation., pp. 31, 79-80. **7.** Johnson, B. (1973). *The Alcoholism Movement in America: A Study in Cultural Innovation.* Ph.D. Dissertation. University of Illinois, p. 107. **8.** Glasscotte, R. Sussex, J., Jaffe, J., Ball, J. and Brill, L. (1972). *The Treatment of Drug Abuse: Programs, Problems, Prospects.* Washington, DC: American Psychiatric Association; Wilkerson, A. (1966). *A History of the Concept of Alcoholism as a Disease.* DSW Dissertation, University of Pennsylvania, p. 25. **9.** National Commission on Marihuana and Drug Abuse (1973). *Drug Use in America.* Washington, D.C.: U.S. Government Printing , p. 313. **10.** Glasscotte, 1972. **11.** National Commission on Marihuana and Drug Abuse,1973, p. 303.**12.** Johnson, 1973, pp. 103-113. **13.** Smithers, R.B. (1977). *25th Anniversary Report* Mill Neck, New York: The Christopher D. Smithers Foundation, Inc., p. 24. **14.** Nancy Olson, Professional Staff of the Alcoholism and Drug Abuse Subcommittee, Personal Interview, November 3, 1997. **15.** Anderson, D. (1989). *Celebrating Forty Years of Progress: A Look at the History of Alcohol/Drug Treatment.* Presented at the 40th Annual Conference of the Alcohol and Drug Problems Association, August 27-30, Washington, DC, p. 11. **16.** Gordis, E. (1988). Milestones. *AHRW,* 12(4):236-269. **17.** Lewis, J. (1982). The Federal Role in Alcoholism Research, Treatment and Prevention. In: Gomberg, L., White, H. and Carpenter, J. *Alcohol, Science and Society Revisited.* Ann Arbor: The University of Michigan Press, p. 393. **18.** NIDA (1978). *Report on Manpower and Training Issues.* Rockville, MD, p. 19. **19.** Brown, B. (1993). Observations on the Recent History of Drug User Counseling. *IJA,* 28(12) 1243-1255. **20.** Cook, F. (1992). *TASC: Case Management Models Linking Criminal Justice and Treatment. NIDA Research Monograph # 127.* Rockville, MD, p. 368. **21.** Crisis Seen in Alcoholism Field. (1980). *AA Grapevine,* 37(4):43. **22.** Barrows, D. (1979). The Residential Rehabilitation Program for the Alcoholic (Working Paper, pp.

1-38). Berkeley, CA: The Alcohol Research Group. **23.** Later clinical studies actually demonstrated that more than half of the narcotic addicts treated at the federal narcotics "farm" in Lexington eventually developed problems with alcohol. Croughan, J., et.al., (1981). Alcoholism and Drug Dependence in Narcotic Addicts: A Prospective Study with a Five Year Follow-up. *American Journal of Drug and Alcohol Abuse*, 8:85-94. **24.** Schmidt, L. and Weisner, C. (1993). Developments in Alcoholism Treatment. In: Galanter, M., Ed., *Recent Developments in Alcoholism, Volume II: Ten Years of Progress.* New York: Plenum Press, pp. 365-396. **25.** Fisk, E. (1916). Alcohol and Life Insurance. *The Atlantic Monthly,* 118:624-635 (November). **26.** Fisk, 1916, p. 629. **27.** Allen, W. (1909). *Civics and Health.* Boston: Ginn and Company, p. 359. **28.** Keeley Institute Records, Illinois State Historical Library, Box 76, "Insurance Survey". **29.** NIAAA, (1977). Health Insurance Coverage for Alcoholism. *Alcohol Topics in Brief.* Rockville, MD: National Clearinghouse for Alcoholic Information, p. 1. **30.** Pioneers, 1979, pp. 107-108. **31.** James Kemper, Jr., Personal Interview, June, 1995. **32.** Boynton, S. (1975). Capital Blue Cross Alcoholic Rehabilitation Benefit Program: Description and Initial Experience. Unpublished paper. **33.** Hallan, J. and Montague, B. (1975). Health Insurance Coverage for Alcoholism. Presented at the National Alcoholism Forum. Milwaukee, Wisconsin, April, 1975; Graham, G., Occupational Programs and their Relation to Health Insurance Coverage for Alcoholism. Presented at the National Conference on Health Insurance Coverage for Alcoholism Treatment, National Institutes of Health. Bethesda, Maryland, October 28-29, 1980; McClellan, K. (1984). Work-based Drug Programs. *JPD,* 16(4):285-303 (October-December). **34.** Hallan and Montague, 1975. **35.** Hallan and Montague, 1975. **36.** Shepherd, E. (1958). Current Resources for Therapy, Education and Research. In: Bacon, S., Ed., *Understanding Alcoholism* Philadelphia: The Annals of the American Academy of Political and Social Science, pp. 133-143. **37.** Korcok, M. (1983). Alcoholism Treatment Moving Swiftly into Mainstream of Health Care in U.S. *The U.S. Journal of Drug and Alcohol Dependence,* January, pp. 8-9. **38.** Holcomb, J. (1981-82). Alcohol and the Armed Forces. *AHRW,* 6(2):2-17. **39.** Institute of Medicine, 1990, p. 118. **40.** ASAM Introduction. (1997). *Journal of Maintenance in the Addictions,* 1(1):121-123. **41.** *National Drug and Alcoholism Treatment Unit Survey (NDATUS): 1991 Main Findings Report* (1993). Rockville, MD: SAMSA., p. 50. **42.** Rosenberg, C. (1892). The Paraprofessionals in Alcoholism Treatment. In: Pattison, E. And Kaufman, E. Eds. *Encyclopedic Handbook of Alcoholism* New York: Gardner Press, pp. 802-809. **43.** Staub, G. and Petree, C. (1970). Rehabilitation Aides at Sacramento's Alcoholism Center. *Rehab. Rec.* 11(1):8-12. **44.** McGovern, T. (1992). Alcoholism and Drug Abuse Counseling: A Personal Reflection. *TC,* 10(3):38-46. **45.** Staub and Petree, 1970, pp. 8-12. **46.** Kalb, M. and Propper, M. (1983). The Future of Alcohology: Craft or Science? *AJP,* 133(6):644. **47.** Krystal, H. and Moore, R. (1963). Who is Qualified to Treat the Alcoholic? *QJSA,* 27:705-719. **48.** Brown, B. (1993). Observations on the Recent History of Drug User Counseling. *IJA,* 28(12):1243-1255. **49.** McInerney, J. (1973). Alcoholics Anonymous Members as Alcoholism Counselors. In: Staub, G. and Kent, L. *The Para-Professional in the Treatment of Alcoholism.* Springfield: Illinois: Charles C. Thomas Publisher. **50.** White, W. (1978). *Relapse as a Phenomenon of Relapse in Recovering Counselors.* HCS, Inc.: Rockville, Md. **51.** Kinney, J. (1983). Relapse among Alcoholics who are Alcoholism Counselors. *JSA,* 44:744-748. **52.** McGovern, T. And Armstrong, D. (1987). Comparison of Recovering and Non-Alcoholic Counselors: A Survey. *ATQ,* 4(1):43-60. **53.** Not all recovered people working professionally in the field lacked academic credentials. LeClair Bissell reported in 1982 that there were more than 200 members of International Doctors in A.A. who were working full time in the alcoholism treatment field. Bissell, L. (1982). Recovered Alcoholic Counselors. In: Pattison, E. and Kaufman, E. Eds., *Encyclopedic Handbook of Alcoholism,* pp. 810-817. New York: Gardner Press. **54.** Kaldry, J. (1997). NAADAC Celebrates 25 Years of Vision and Leadership. *TC,* 15(4):9-20. **55.** Blume, 1977, p. 556. **56.** NIDA, 1978, *Report on Manpower and Training Issues,* p.5. **57.** Roy Littlejohn Associates, Inc; 1974. **58.** Banken, J. And McGovern, T. (1992). Alcoholism and Drug Abuse Counseling: State of the Art Consideration. *ATQ,* 9(2).29-53. **59.** NDATUS, 1991, pp. 49-50. **60.** Weisner, C. (1981). *The Politics of Alcoholism: Building an Arena Around a Social Problem.* New Brunswick, NJ: Transaction Books, p. 218. **61.** Institute of Medicine, 1990, p. 103. **62.** This explosive growth in hospital units was in part sparked by changes in the federal Medicare program in 1983. According to the new regulations, reimbursement was based on fixed prices for particular diagnostic categories. This change created a drop in lengths of stay and occupancy rates. The empty beds created by this policy shift created a vacuum that was often filled by addiction treatment units—an area exempted from the Medicaid reimbursement system for the first three years. Schmidt and Weisner, 1993, p. 376. **63.** Institute of Medicine, 1990, p. 121. **64.** *Overview of the FY94 National Drug and Alcoholism Treatment Unit Survey (NDATUS): Data From 1993 and 1980-1993.* (1995). Rockville, MD: SAMSA, p. 6. **65.** Schmidt and Weisner, 1993, p. 20. **66.** Anderson, D. (1989). *Celebrating Forty Years of Progress: A Look at the History of Alcohol/Drug Treatment.* Presented at the 40th Annual Conference of the Alcohol and Drug Problems Association, August 27-30, Washington, DC., p. 12; Spicer, J. (1993). *The Minnesota Model: The Evolution of the Interdisciplinary Approach to Addiction Recovery.* Center City, Minnesota: Hazelden Educational Materials, p. 67; NDATUS, 1991, p. 13 ; In 1995, the NDATUS Survey identified 11,800 specialty addiction service providers. Rouse, B. Ed., (1995). *Substance Abuse and Mental Health Statistics Sourcebook.* Washington D.C.: U.S. GPO. **67.** Schmidt and Weisner, 1993, p. 20; NDATUS, 1991, p.25. **68.** llinois' Investment History (1995). *FOCUS (Newsletter of the Illinois Alcoholism and Drug Dependence Association.* p. 4. **69.** NAADAC Survey Profiles Counselors. (1990). *TC,* July/August, p. 31; NAADAC 1997 Member Needs Assessment, p. 1. **70.** NAADAC (1995). *NAADAC Income and Compensation Study of Alcohol and Drug*

Counseling Professionals, Arlington, VA., p. 8. **71.** Schmidt, L. (1993). Private Practice: Wave of the Future? *TC,* Sep/Oct, pp. 25-29; Rosenberg, C. (1982). The Paraprofessionals in Alcoholism Treatment. In: Pattison, E. And Kaufman, E., Eds., *Encyclopedic Handbook of Alcoholism.* NY: Gardner Press, p. 805. **72.** Betty Ford Center (1997). *TC,* 15(4) p.39. **73.** Makela, K., et. al. (1996). *Alcoholics Anonymous as a Mutual-Help Movement: A Study in Eight Societies.* Madison: University of Wisconsin Press, p. 10. **74.** For a discussion of this commodification of A.A. spirituality, see: Kurtz, E. (1996). Spirituality and the Secular Quest: Twelve Step Programs. In: Can Ness, P., Ed., *Spiritual and The Secular Quest World Spirituality Encyclopedic History of the Religious Quest*, Volume 22. New York: Crossroad, p. 12. **75.** Armstrong, D. and Armstrong, E. (1991). *The Great American Medicine Show.* New York: Prentice Hall, p. 50; Anderson, 1989, p. 13; Makela 1996, p. 99. **76.** Kurtz, E., AA and Treatment, Rutgers Distance Learning Tape, p. 9 transcribed. **77.** Delbanco, A. and Delbanco, T. (1988). A.A. at the Crossroads. *New Yorker,* 61(4):50-63. **78.** Such groups include Vie Libre and Croix d'Or in France, Danshukai groups in Japan, the Abstainers Clubs in Poland, the Clubs of Treated Alcoholics in Yugoslavia, and the Swedish Links. Makela, 1996, pp. 207-209. **79.** Kaskutas, L. (1994). What do Women Want out of Self-Help? Their Reasons for Attending Women for Sobriety and Alcoholics Anonymous. *JSAT,* 11(3):186. **80.** Kirkpatrick, J. (1978). *Turnabout: Help for a New Life.* Garden City, NY: Doubleday and Company; Kirkpatrick, J. (1981). *A Fresh Start.* Dubuque: Kendall/Hunt Publishing; Kirkpatrick, J. (1986). *Goodbye Hangovers, Hello Life.* New York: Ballantine Books. **81.** Kaskutkas, L. (ND). Pathways to Self-Help among Women for Sobriety. Working Paper, Alcohol Research Group, p. 7, 21. **82.** Kaskutkas, 1994, p. 186. **83.** Christopher, J. (1988). *How to Stay Sober: Recovery without Religion.* Buffalo, NY: Prometheus Books; Christopher, J. (1989). *Unhooked: Staying Sober and Drug Free.* Buffalo, NY: Prometheus Books; Christopher, J. (1992). *SOS Sobriety: The Proven Alternative to 12-Step Programs.* Buffalo, NY: Prometheus Books. **84.** Christopher, 1992, p. 62. **85.** McCrady, B. And Delaney, S. (1995). Self-Help Groups In: Hester, R. And Miller, W. *Handbook of Alcoholism Treatment Approaches: Effective Alternatives.* Boston: Allyn and Bacon. (Second Edition), p. 161. **86.** Trimpey, J. (1989). *The Small Book.* New York: Delacorte Press. **87.** McCrady, 1995, p. 161. **88.** McCrady and Delaney, 1995, pp. 167-168. **89.** For a sample of such approaches, see: Kishline, A. (1994). *Moderate Drinking.* Tucson, Arizona: See Sharp Press. **90.** Dan Anderson, Personal Interview, May 8, 1996. **91.** Zimmerman, R. (1986). "Get Your Act Together"--Kemper. *U.S. Journal of Alcohol and Drug Dependence,* March 4. **92.** OSAP-NAADAC 1990 Survey of AODA Counselor Certification and Training: Management Summary. **93.** Conrad, P. And Schneider, J. (1980). *Deviance and Medicalization: From Badness to Sickness.* St. Louis: C.V. Mosby, p. 103. **94.** Fingarette, H. (1989). *Heavy Drinking: The Myth of Alcoholism as a Disease.* Berkeley: University of California Press, p. 1; Peele, S. (1989). *The Diseasing of America.* Lexington, Massachusetts: Lexington, Books. **95.** Fingarette, 1989, p. 51. **96.** Peele, 1989, p. 65; Peele, S. and Brodsky, A., with Arnold, M. (1992). *The Truth About Addiction and Recovery.* New York: Simon and Schuster, p. 28. **97.** Fingarette, 1989, pp. 34-38, 41-44. **98.** Fingarette, 1989, pp. 72, 87; Peele and Brodsky, 1991, p. 28. **99.** Peele, 1989, p. 57. **100.** Peele, 1989, p. 73. **101.** Fingarette, H. (1988). Alcoholism: The Mythical Disease. *Utne Reader*, Nov./Dec., pp. 64-69; Peele and Brodsky, 1992, pp. 30-31. **102.** Lewis, J. (1982). Adverse Publicity on Raleigh Hills Hospitals Has Spawned Federal Inquiries... *Alcoholism Report,* 10(10):1-2, (March). **103.** Miller, W. and Hester, R. (1986). Inpatient Alcoholism Treatment: Who Benefits? *American Psychologist,* 41:794-805. **104.** Hazelden's occupancy ran at 80% in 1993. Spicer, 1993, p. 69. Faced with deepening financial crises, many free-standing programs and hospital-based addiction treatment units downsized or closed. Managed care led to the estimated closing of between 40% and 60% of the private programs that had operated in the mid-1980s. As many as 200 private programs closed in 1990 alone, and others were "downsized." Schmidt and Weisner, 1993, p. 377. **105.** Rehab Centers Run Dry. (1996). *Time* February 5, pp. 44-45.

Chapter Twenty-Seven: Modern Addiction Treatment: Seminal Ideas and Evolving Treatment Technology
106. For a prototype of the single-pathway model, see: Milam, J. and Ketchum, K. (1983). *Under the Influence: A Guide to the Myths and Realities of Alcoholism.* New York: Bantam Books. **107.** Valliant, G. (1983). *The Natural History of Alcoholism: Causes, Patterns, and Paths to Recovery.* Cambridge, Massachusetts: Harvard University Press. **108.** For reviews of these early studies, see: Watts, T. (1981). The Uneasy Triumph of a Concept: The 'Disease' Conception of Alcoholism. *JDI,* 11(Fall):451-60; Caddy, G.R. (1983). Alcohol Use and Abuse: Historical Perspective and Present Trends. In: Tabakoff, B., Sutker, P. and Randall, C. Eds. *Medical and Social Aspects of Alcohol Abuse.* NY: Plenum, pp. 1-33. What all of these studies began to challenge was the proposition that America's alcohol problems resulted from a singular clinical entity labeled alcoholism. Room, R. (1980). Treatment-Seeking Populations and Larger Realities. In: Edwards, G. and Grant, M., Eds., *Alcoholism Treatment in Transition.* London: Croom Helm, pp. 211-214. **109.** Pattison, E. Sobell, M. And Sobell, L. (1977). *Emerging Concept of Alcohol Dependence.* New York: Springer, pp. 4-5; Caddy, G.R. (1983). Alcohol Use and Abuse: Historical Perspective and Present Trends. In: Tabakoff, B., Sutker, P. and Randall, C., Eds., *Medical and Social Aspects of Alcohol Abuse.* NY: Plenum, p. 17; White, W. (1990). *The Culture of Addiction, the Culture of Recovery.* Bloomington, Illinois: Lighthouse Institute. **110.** Miller, W. (1991). Emergent Treatment Concepts and Techniques. *Annual Review of Addictions Research and Treatment,* pp. 283-296. **111.** Bowman, K. and Jellinek, E. (1941). Alcohol Addiction and Its Treatment. *QJSA,* 2:98-176. (September); Jellinek, E.M. (1960). *The Disease Concept of Alcoholism.* Highland Park, New Jersey: Hillhouse. **112.** Blum, E. (1966).

Psychoanalytic Views on Alcoholism *QJSA,* 27(2) 259-299. **113.** Glendorf, P. (1982). Endorphins: Ifs, Buts, Maybes. *The U.S. Journal of Alcohol and Drug Dependence,* 11(1):16; Restak, R. (1994). *Receptors.* New York: Bantam Books, p. 186. **114.** Cloninger, C.; Bohman, M.; and Sigvardsson, S. (1981). Inheritance of Alcohol Abuse: Cross-fostering analysis of Adopted Men *.Archives of General Psychiatry,* 38:861-868; Goodwin, D. (1978). The Genetics of Alcoholism: A State of the Art Review. *AHRW* ,2(3):2-12; Schuckit, M. (1988). Reactions to Alcohol in Sons of Alcoholics and Controls. *Alcoholism Clinical and Experimental Research* 15:537-542. **115.** *Alcoholism: An Inherited Disease.* (1985). Rockville, MD: NIAAA, p. 35. **116.** Blum, K; Noble, E.; Sheridan, P.; Montgomery, A.; Ritchie, T.; Jagadeeswaran, P.; Nogami, H.; Griggs, A.; and Cohn, J. (1991). Allelic Association of Human D2 Receptor Gene in Alcoholism. *JAMA,* 263(15):2055-2060; Gelernter, J.; Goldman, D.; and Risch, N. The A1 Allele at the D2 Dopamine Receptor Gene and Alcoholism. *JAMA,* 269(13):1673-1677. **117.** Lester, D. (1989). The Heritability of Alcoholism: Science and Social Policy. In: Gomberg, E. (Ed). *Current Issues in Alcohol/Drug Studies* New York: Haworth Press, pp. 31, 62-62. **118.** Goldman, D. (1993). Genetic Transmission In: Galanter, M. *Recent Developments in Alcoholism* Volume 11, p. 232. **119.** The Genetics of Alcoholism (1992). *Alcohol Alert No. 18* (October), p. 3. **120.** Levin, J. (1990). *Alcoholism: A Bio-Psycho-Social Approach.* New York: Hemisphere Publishing Corporation, pp.75-81. **121.** Luks, A. (1983). *Will America Sober Up?* Boston: Beacon Press, p. 111. **122.** Wallace, J. (1974). *Tactical and Strategic Use of the Preferred Defense Structure of the Recovering Alcoholic.* New York: National Council on Alcoholism, Inc. **123.** McClellan, T.; Luborsky, L.; O'Brien, C.; Woody, G.; and Druley, K. (1982). Is Treatment for Substance Abuse Effective? *JAMA,*247(10):1423-1428. **124.** Michael Dennis, Personal Interview, October 7, 1997. **125.** Johnson, V. (1980). *I'll Quit Tomorrow.* San Francisco: Harper & Row, Publishers; Johnson, V. (1986). *Intervention: How to Help Someone Who Doesn't Want Help.* Minneapolis, Minnesota: The Johnson Institute. **126.** White, W. (1990). *PROJECT SAFE Program Manual.* Chicago, IL: Illinois Department of Children & Family Services. **127.** Prochaska, J.; Norcross, J.; and DiClemente, C. (1994). *Changing for the Good.* New York: Avon Books. **128.** Stryker, J. and Smith, M. (1993). *Needle Exchange: Dimensions of HIV Prevention.* Menlo Park, California: Henry J. Kaiser Family Foundation, p. 82. **129.** Hooker, T. (1992). Getting the Point: HIV, Drug Abuse and Syringe Exchange in the United States. *State Legislative Report,* July, 17(14):1-16; Stryker and Smith, 1993. **130.** Beard, G. (1871). *Stimulants and Narcotics.* New York: G.P. Putnam and Sons, p. 136. **131.** Prochaska, Norcross, and DiClemente, 1994. **132.** Parish, J. (1883). *Alcoholic Inebriety: From a Medical Standpoint.* Philadelphia: P. Blakiston, Son & Company, p. 126. **133.** Durfee, C. (1937). *To Drink or Not to Drink.* Boston: Longmans, Green, p. 58. **134.** Lemere, F. (1953). What Happens to Alcoholics? *AJP,* 109:674-682. **135.** Lemere, 1953, p. 675. **136.** Cahalan, D. and Room, R. (1974). *Problem Drinking among American Men.* New Brunswick: Rutgers Center of Alcohol Studies. **137.** Tuchfield, B. (1981). Spontaneous Remission in Alcoholics: Empirical Observations and Theoretical Implications. *JSA,* 42(7):626-641; Smart, R. (1976). Spontaneous Recovery in Alcoholics: A Review and Analysis of the Available Research. *Drug and Alcohol Dependence,* 1:277-285. **138.** Biernacki, P. (1986). *Pathways from Heroin Addiction: Recovery Without Treatment.* Philadelphia: Temple University Press, pp. 57, 179. **139.** Heather, N. (1986). Changes Without Therapists: The Use of Self-help Manuals by Problem Drinkers. In: Miller, W. and Heather, N., Eds., *Treating Addictive Behaviors: Process of Change.* New York: Plenum, pp. 331-359; Heather, N. (1989). Brief Intervention Strategies. In: Hester, R. and Miller, W., Eds., *Handbook of Alcoholism Treatment Approaches.* Boston: Allyn and Bacon, pp. 93-116. **140.** For samples of such manuals, see Dorsman, J. (1994). *How To Quit Drinking Without A.A.: A Complete Self-Help Guide.* Rocklin, CA: Prima; Tate, P. (1997). *Alcohol: How to Give It Up and Be Glad You Did.* Tucson, AZ: Sharp Press. **141.** Shea, J. (1954). Psychoanalytic Therapy and Alcoholism. *QJSA,* 15:595-605. **142.** Selzer, M. And Holloway, W. (1957). A Follow-up Study of Alcoholics Committed to a State Hospital. *QJSA,* 18:98-120. **143.** Davies, D. (1962). Normal Drinking in Recovered Alcohol Addicts. *QJSA,* 23:94-104. **144.** Davies, 1962; Miller, W. (1983). Controlled Drinking: A History and a Critical Review. *JSA* 44(1):68-83. **145.** Cain, A. (1964). *The Cured Alcoholic.* New York: John Day. **146.** Sobell, M. and Sobell, L. (1973). Alcoholics Treated by Individualized Behavior Therapy: One-Year Treatment Outcome. *Behavior Research and Therapy,* 11:599-618; Pendery, M., Maltzman, I., West, L. (1982). Controlled Drinking by Alcoholics? New Findings and a Reevaluation of a Major Affirmative Study. *Science,* 217:169-175; Sobell, M. and Sobell, L. (1984). The Aftermath of Heresy: A Response to Pendery et. al's (1982) Critique of "Individualized Behavior Therapy for Alcoholics." *Behavior Research and Therapy,* 22:413-440; Roizen, R. (1987). The Great Controlled-Drinking Controversy. In: Glanter, M. *Recent Developments in Alcoholism,* Vol 5, New York: Plenum, pp. 245-279; Hester, R.; Nirenberg, T.; and Begin, A. (1990). Behavioral Treatment of Alcohol and Drug Abuse: What Do We Know and Where Shall We Go? In: Glanater, M. (1990). *Recent Developments in Alcoholism.* Volume 8, p. 311. **147.** Hare, F. (1912). *On Alcoholism: Its Clinical Aspects and Treatment.* London: J. & A. Churchill, p. 242. **148.** Chein, I. (1959). The Status of Sociological and Social Psychological Knowledge Concerning Narcotics. In: Livingston, R.,Ed.,*Narcotic Drug Addiction Problems: Proceedings of the Symposium on the History of Narcotic Drug Problems March 27 and 28, Bethesda, Maryland.* Bethesda, Maryland: National Institute of Mental Health, p. 148. **149.** Kane, H. (1882). *Opium-Smoking in America and China.* New York: G.P. Putnam & Sons, p. 73. **150.** Jacobson, R. and Zinberg, N. (1975). *The Social Basis of Drug Abuse Prevention.* Washington, DC: The Drug Abuse Council, Inc. **151.** See "What A.A. Won't Tell You," *U.S. News and World Report,* September 8, 1997, pp. 55-65. **152.** Cork, M. (1969). *The Forgotten Children.* Toronto: Addiction Research Foundation. **153.** Greenleaf, J. (1981). Co-

Alcoholic Para-Alcoholic: Who's Who and What's the Difference. Presented at the National Council on Alcoholism Forum New Orleans, Louisiana April 12. **154.** Melody, P.; Miller, A.; and Miller, J. (1989). *Facing Codependence*. San Francisco: Harper San Francisco, p. 214. **155.** Black, C. (1982). *It Will Never Happen to Me!* Denver, Colorado: M.A.C. Printing and Publishing; Wegscheider-Cruse, S. (1985). *Choice-Making for Co-dependents, Adult Children and Spirituality Seekers*. Pompano Beach, FL: Health Communications. **156.** Robertson, N. (1988). *Getting Better: Inside Alcoholics Anonymous*. New York: William Morrow and Company, p. 177. **157.** For an excellent review of the ACOA movement, see: Brown, S. (1995). Adult Children of Alcoholics: The History of a Social Movement and Its Impact on Clinical Theory and Practice. In: Galanter, M. *Recent Developments in Alcoholism*, Vol. 9, New York: Plenum Press, pp. 267-285. **158.** Cermak, T. (1986). Diagnostic Criteria for Codependency. *JPD,* 18(1)15-20; Cermak, T. (1986). *Diagnosing and Treating Codependency* Minneapolis. Minnesota: Johnson Institute Books. **159.** Makela, K., et. al. (1996). *Alcoholics Anonymous as a Mutual-Help Movement: A Study in Eight Societies*. Madison: University of Wisconsin Press, p. 228. **160.** For sample critiques of the Co-dependency Movement, see: Katz, S. and Liu, A. (1991). *The Codependency Conspiracy*. New York: Warner Books; Kaminer, W. (1992). *I'm Dysfunctional, You're Dysfunctional*. Reading, MA: Addison-Wesley Publishing Company, Inc. **161.** SAMSA (1995). *Substance Abuse and Mental Health Statistics Sourcebook*. Rockville, MD: Substance Abuse and Mental Health Service Division, p. 94; *National Admissions to Substance Abuse Treatment Services: The Treatment Episode Data Set (TEDS) 1992-1995*, p. 28. **162.** Johnson, 1959, p. 365; Conrad, P. And Schneider, J. (1980). *Deviance and Medicalization: From Badness to Sickness*. St. Louis: C.V. Mosby, p. 100. **163.** Conrad and Schneider, 1980, p. 100. **164.** Hart, L. (1977). A Review of Treatment and Rehabilitation Legislation Regarding Alcohol Abusers and Alcoholics in the United States: 1920-1971. *IJA,* 12:(5): 667-678. **165.** Wallace, S. (1965). *Skid Row as a Way of Life*. Totowa: The Bedminister Press, Inc. **166.** Anderson, D. (1989). *Celebrating Forty Years of Progress: A Look at the History of Alcohol/Drug Treatment*. Presented at the 40th Annual Conference of the Alcohol and Drug Problems Association, August 27-30, Washington, DC. **167.** Rubington, E. (1982). The Chronic Public Offender on Skid Row. In: Gomberg, L.; White, H.; and Carpenter, J. *Alcohol, Science and Society Revisited*. Ann Arbor: The University of Michigan Press, p. 327. **168.** Rubington, 1982, pp. 328-331. **169.** Room, R. (1976). Comment on the Uniform Alcoholism and Intoxication Treatment Act. *JSA,* 37:113-44. **170.** Lender, M and Martin, J. (1982). *Drinking in America*. New York: The Free Press, p. 108. **171.** Transeau, E. (1934). The Problem of the Drunken Driver. *STJ,* 42(4),85-89; Cameron, T. (1979). The Impact of Drinking-Driving Countermeasures: A Review of the Literature. *CDP,* 8(4):495-565. **172.** Pioneers, 1979, p. 175. **173.** Marshall, M. And Oleson, A. (1996). "Madder Than Hell," *Qualitative Health Research,* 6:6-22. **174.** SADD changed its name in 1997 to Students Against Destructive Decisions in order to reflect its broadened agenda against drug use, suicide, violence, and HIV/AIDS. **175.** Crancer, A. (1986). The Myth of the Social Drinker-DUI Driver. Presented at the Joint Meeting of the American Medical Society on Alcoholism and other Drug Dependencies and the Research Society on Alcoholism, April 18-22; Kramer. A. (1986). Sentencing the Drunk Driver: A Call for Change. *ATQ,* 3(2):25-35). **176.** Jones, K.; Smith, D.; Ulleland, C.; and Streissguth, A. (1973). Pattern of Malformation in Offspring of Chronic Alcoholic Mothers. *Lancet,* 1:1267-1271. **177.** Kandall, S. (1996). *Substance and Shadow: Women and Addiction in the United States*. Cambridge, MA: Harvard University Press, pp. 252, 265. **178.** Examples include: Mayes, L.; Granger, R.; Bornstein, M.; and Zuckerman, B. (1992). The Problem of Prenatal Cocaine Exposure: A Rush To Judgment. *JAMA,* 267(3):406-408; Neuspiel, D. (1993). On Pejorative Labeling of Cocaine Exposed Children. *JSAT,*10:407. **179.** Mathias, R. (1992). Developmental Effects of Prenatal Drug Exposure May be Overcome by Postnatal Environment. *NIDA Notes,* January/February, p. 14. **180.** Major Trial Finds Only Subtle Fetal Injury from Cocaine (1997). *The Journal of NIH Research,* 9:29-32. **181.** For a representative literature review, see: Johnson, S. (1991). Recent Research: Alcohol and Women's Bodies. In: Roth, P. *Alcohol and Drugs Are Women's Issues*. London: Scarecrow Press; Kandall, 1996. **182.** Schmidt, L. and Weisner, C. (1995). The Emergence of Problem-Drinking Women as a Special Population in Need of Treatment. (1995). *Recent Developments in Alcoholism, Vol 12*, Galanter, M., Ed., New York : Plenum Press, p. 323. **183.** See, for example: Center for Substance Abuse Treatment. (1994). *Practical Approaches in the Treatment of Women Who Abuse Alcohol and Other Drugs*. Rockville, MD: Department of Health and Human Services, Public Health Service. **184.** NDATUS, 1991, p. 63. **185.** Kaminer, Y. (1994). *Adolescent Substance Abuse: A Comprehensive Guide to Theory and Practice*. New York: Plenum Medical Book Company, pp 198, 20. **186.** Bukstein, O. (1995). *Adolescent Substance Abuse: Assessment, Prevention and Treatment*. NY: John Wiley & Sons, Inc.; Liddle, H. and Dakof, G. (1995). Family-based Treatment for Adolescent Drug Use: State of the Science. In: Rahdert, E. and Czechowicz, D. *Adolescent Drug Abuse: Clinical Assessments and Therapeutic Interventions*. Rockville, MD: NIDA, pp. 218-254; Kaminer, Y. (1995). Pharmacotherapy for Adolescents with Psychoactive Substance Abuse Disorders. In: Rahdert and Czechowicz, pp. 291-324. **187.** Kaminer, Y. (1991). Adolescent Substance Abuse. In: Frances, R. and Miller, S., Eds., *Clinical Textbook of Addictive Disorders*. New York: Guilford Press, pp. 320-346. **188.** Surles, C. (1978). *Historical Development of Alcoholism Control Programs in Industry from 1940-1978*. D.Ed. Dissertation: University of Michigan, p. 23; Steele, P. (1989). A History of Job Based Alcoholism Programs: 1955-1972. *JDI,* 19:511-532; McCarthy, R. (1964). The Fellowship of Alcoholics Anonymous: Alcoholism in Industry. In: McCarthy, R. Ed. *Alcohol Education for Classroom and Community*. New York: McGraw-Hill Book Company, p. 237. **189.** ALMACA-EAPA, 1971-1991, "Birth of a Nation", p. 20. **190.** Steele, 1989, p. 525. **191.**

Roman, P. (1981). From Employee Alcoholism to Employee Assistance. *JSA*, 42(3):244-272; Milgram, G. and McCrady, B. (1986). *Employee Assistance Programs* (Center of Alcohol Studies Pamphlet Series). New Brunswick, NJ: Alcohol Research Documentation, Inc, p. 3. **192.** Roman, 1981, p. 251. **193.** Blum, T., Roman, P., and Tootle, D. (1988). The Emergence of an Occupation. *Work and Occupations,* 15:96-114. **194.** Blum, Roman, Tootle, 1988, p. 99. **195.** Roman, 1981, p. 267. **196.** Jim Wrich, Personal Interview, May 11, 1995. **197.** The designation "pedestal professional" usually includes clergy, health-care professionals, lawyers, and pilots. **198.** Rush, B. (1814). *An Inquiry into the Effect of Ardent Spirits upon the Human Body and Mind, with an Account of the Means of Preventing and of the Remedies for Curing Them.* 8th rev. ed. Brookfield: E. Merriam & Co., p. 23. **199.** Clum, F. (1888). *Inebriety: Its Causes, Its Results, Its Remedy.* Philadelphia: Lippincott, p. 106; Cobbe, W. (1895). *Doctor Judas: A Portrayal of the Opium Habit.* Chicago: Griggs and Company, p. 188; Crothers, T.D. (1902). *The Drug Habits and Their Treatment.* Chicago: G.P. Englehard & Company, p. 152; Pettey, G. (1913). *Narcotic Drug Diseases and Allied Ailments.* Philadelphia: F.A. Davis Co., p. 27; Snowden, J. (1917). Home Treatment and Cure of Opium and Morphine Addicts. *Kentucky Medical Journal*, 15:125-131 (March 1). **200.** Reddy, B. (1984). The History of LAP (Lawyer Assistance Program). *Illinois Bar Association,* 73:(1): 22. **201.** Lonhart, P., Reddy, B. and Clarno, J. (1991). *Suggested Principles for the Treatment of Chemical Dependency in Health Care Professionals.* Park Ridge, Illinois: Parkside Publishing Company, pp. 5-7. **202.** Bissell. L. and Haberman, P. (1984). *Alcoholism in the Professions.* New York: Oxford University Press; Coombs, R. (1997). *Drug-Impaired Professionals.* Cambridge, MA: Harvard University Press. **203.** Fiman, B., Conner, D. And Segal, C. (1973). A Comprehensive Alcoholism Program in the Army. *The AJP*, 130(5):532-535. **204.** Maurer, D. and Vogel, V. (1973). *Narcotics and Narcotic Addiction.* Springfiled, Illinois: Charles C. Thomas, p. 29. **205.** Ruben, H. (1974). Rehabilitation of Drug and Alcohol Abusers in the U.S. Army. *IJA,* 9(1):41-55. **206.** West, L. and Swegan, W. (1956). An Approach to Alcoholism in the Military Service. *AJP,* 112:1004-1009. **207.** Pursch, J. (1976). From Quonset Hut to Naval Hospital: The Story of an Alcoholism Rehabilitation Service. *JSA*, 37(11):1655-1665. **208.** Pursch, 1976, pp. 1655-1665. **209.** Zuska, J. (1978). Beginnings of the Navy Program. *Alcoholism: Clinical and Experimental Research,* 2:352-357. **210.** Krivanek, J. (1988). *Heroin: Myths and Realities.* Sydney: Allen & Unwin, pp. 64-65. **211.** Robins, L. (1974). *The Vietnam Drug User Returns.* Special Action Office Monograph Series, A, Number 2, Washington, D.C: U.S. GPO. **212.** Newcomb, M. (1988). *Drug Use in the Workplace.* Dover, Massachusetts: Auburn House Publishing Company, p. 8. **213.** Peterson, K.; Swindler, R.; Phibbs, C.; Recine, B.; and Moos, R. (1994). Determinants of Readmission Following Inpatient Substance Abuse Treatment: A National Study of VA Programs. *Medical Care* 32(6):542. **214.** Harper, F. (1976). *Alcohol and Blacks: An Overview.* Alexandria, VA: Douglas Publishers, p. 7. **215.** Institute of Medicine (1990). *Broadening the Base of Treatment for Alcohol Problems.* Washington, DC: Academy of Science Press, p. 119; Weibel-Orlando, J. (1989). Treatment and Prevention of Native American Alcoholism. In: Watts, T. and Wright, R. Eds. (1989). *Alcoholism in Minority Populations.* Springfield, Illinois: Charles C. Thomas, pp. 125-126. **216.** Williams, C. with Laird, R. (1992). *No Hiding Place: Empowerment and Recovery for Troubled Communities.* NY: Harper San Francisco, p. 8. **217.** Williams, 1992. **218.** Meyer, R. (1972). *Guide to Drug Rehabilitation.* Boston: Beacon Press. **219.** White and Chaney, (1993). *Metaphors of Transformation: Feminine and Masculine.* Bloomington, IL: A Lighthouse Institute Monograph. **220.** Vigdal, G. (1995). *Planning for Alcohol and Other Drug Abuse Treatment for Adults in the Criminal Justice System* (Treatment Improvement Protocol Series 17) Rockville, MD: SAMSA, p. 13; Timrots, A. *Drugs and Crime Facts.* (1994). Rockville, MD: National Drug Control Policy Drugs and Crime Clearinghouse. **221.** Inciardi, J. And McBride, D. (1991). *Treatment Alternatives to Street Crime: History, Experiences, and Issues.* DHHS Publication No. (ADM). 91-1749, Rockville, Maryland: NIDA; Cook, F. (1992). TASC: Case Management Models Linking Criminal Justice and Treatment NIDA Research Monograph # 127. Rockville, MD: NIDA. **222.** Falkin, G.; Wayson, B.; Wexler, H.; and Lipton, D. (1991). *Treating Prisoners for Drug Abuse: An Implementation Study of Six Prison Programs.* New York: Narcotic and Drug Research, Inc. **223.** Inciardi, J., McBride, D. and Rivers, J. (1996). *Drug Control and the Courts.* Newbury Park, CA: Sage Publications. **224.** Vigdal, 1995, p. 6. **225.** Sells, S. and Simpson, D. Eds. (1976). *The Effectiveness of Drug Abuse Treatment.* (Volume 3). Cambridge, MA: Ballinger; DeLeon, G. (1988). Legal Pressure in Therapeutic Communities. In: Leukefeld, C. and Tims, F., Eds., *Compulsory Treatment of Drug Abuse: Research and Clinical Practice.* NIDA Research Monograph No. 86. Rockville, MD: NIDA, pp. 160-177. **226.** Faltz, B. and Madover, S. (1988). Treatment of Substance Abuse Patients with HIV Infection. In: Siegel, L. *AIDS and Substance Abuse.* New York: Harrington Park Press, p. 146 **227.** Siegel,1988. **228.** Tilleraas, P. (1990). *Circle of Hope: Our Stories of AIDS, Addiction, & Recovery.* New York: Harper & Row Publishers. **229.** White, W. (1994). *Voices of Survival, Voices of Service: AIDS Case Management in Chicago.* Chicago, Illinois: AIDS Foundation of Chicago, p. 109. **230.** NDATUS, 1991, p. 47. **231.** Early texts included: Meyer, R. Ed. (1986). *Psychopathology and Addictive Disorders.* New York: Guilford Press; Evans, K. and Sullivan, J. (1990). *Dual Disorders: Counseling the Mentally Ill Substance Abuser.* New York: Guilford Press. **232.** For sample descriptions of such techniques, see Godley, S. (1995). *A Case Manager's Manual for Working with Adolescent Substance Abusers.* Bloomington, IL: Lighthouse Institute; Siegel, H. and Rapp, R., Eds., (1996). *Case Management and Substance Abuse Treatment: Practice and Experience.* New York: Springer Publishing Co.; White, W., Woll, P. and Godley, S. (1997)*The Delivery and Supervision of Outreach Services to Women.* Chicago, IL: Illinois Department of Alcoholism and Substance Abuse. **233.** Miller, W. (1987). Techniques to Modify Hazardous Drinking Patterns. In: Galanter, M. *Recent Developments in Alcoholism: Volume 5.* New York: Plenum Press, pp. 425-438; Miller, W. (1992). Building Bridges over Troubled Waters: A Response to "Alcoholism, Politics, and Bureaucracy: The Consensus against Controlled-Drinking Therapy in America." *Addictive Behavior*, 17:79-81. **234.** Miller, W. and Page, A. (1991). Warm Turkey: Other Routes to Abstinence. *JSAT*, 8:227-232. **235.** Azrin, N; Sisson, R.; Meyers, R.; Godley, M. (1982). Alcoholism Treatment by Disulfiram and Community Reinforcement Therapy. *Journal of Behavioral Therapy and Experimental Psychiatry*, 13:105-112. **236.** Meyers, R. and Smith, J. (1995). *Clinical Guide to Alcohol Treatment: The Community Reinforcement Approach.* New York: The Guilford Press; Miller, W. and Hester, R. (1986). The Effectiveness of Alcoholism Treatment. In: Miller, W. And Hester, R. (Eds.) *Treating Addictive Behaviors: Process of Change.* NY: Plenum Press, p. 152. **237.** Brown, S. (1994). What is the Family Recovery Process? *The Addiction Letter*, 10(10):1,4 (October). **238.** Edwards, M. and Steinglass, P. (1995). Family Therapy Treatment Outcomes for Alcoholism. *Journal of Marital and Family Therapy*, 21(4):475-509; Liddle, H. and Dakof, G. (1995). Family-based Treatment for Adolescent Drug Use: State of the Science. In: Rahdert, E. and Czechowicz, D. *Adolescent Drug Abuse: Clinical Assessments and Therapeutic Interventions.* Rockville, MD: NIDA, pp. 218-254. **239.** Landry, M. (1997). *Overview of Addiction Treatment Effectiveness.* SAMSA (DHHS Publication No. (SMA) 97-3133), p. 42. **240.** Halikas, J. (1983). Psychotropic Medication Used in the Treatment of Alcoholism. *Hospital and Community Psychiatry*, 34(11):1035-1039; Dorus, W., et.,al., (1989). Lithium Treatment of Depressed and Nondepressed Alcoholics. *JAMA*, 262:1646-1652. **241.** Gottheil, E. (1993). Overview. In: Galanter, M. *Recent Developments in Alcoholism: Ten Years of Progress,* Volume 11. New York: Plenum Press, pp. 366-367. **242.** Volpicelli, J.; Alterman, A.; Hayashida, M.; O'Brien, C. (1992). Naltrexone in the Treatment of Alcohol Dependence. *Archives of General Psychiatry,* 49:876-880; Korsten, T. (1996). Naltrexone and Alcoholism. *Newsletter Insert--American Academy of Addiction Psychiatry*, 11(2):1-4. **243.** NDATUS, 1991, p. 48. **244.** Restak, R. (1994). *Receptors.* New York: Bantam Books, p. 152; Kaminer, 1994, p. 237. **245.** Rawson, R. (1993). *Psychosocial and Pharmaco-Therapies for Cocaine and Dependency*, American Society of Addiction Medicine, 24th Medical/Scientific Meeting, April 29-May 2, 1993, Los Angeles. **246.** Crothers, T.D. (1902). *Morphinism and Narcomanias from other Drugs.* Philadelphia: W.B. Saunders & Company, p. 164; Lambert, A. (1912). Care and Control of the Alcoholic. *BMSJ,* 166:615-621; Towns, C. (1932). *Drug and Alcohol Sickness.* New York: M.M. Barbour Co. In: Grob, G. (1981). *The Medical Profession and Drug Addiction.* New York: Arno Press, p. 38. **247.** Bien, T. And Barge, R. (1990). Smoking and Drinking: A Review of the Literature. *IJA,* 25(12).1429-1454. **248.** White, W. (1990). *The Culture of Addiction, the Culture of Recovery.* Bloomington, IL: Lighthouse Institute, p. 353. **249.** Hoffman and Slade, 1993, pp. 153-160. **250.** Parrish, J. (1883). *Alcoholic Inebriety: From a Medical Standpoint.* Philadelphia: P. Blakiston, Son & Company, p. 181. **251.** Marlatt, G. and Gordon, J. (1985). *Relapse Prevention.* London: Guilford Press. pp. xii-xiii. **252.** McElrath, D. (1987). *Hazelden: A Spiritual Odyssey.* Center City, Minnesota: Hazelden Foundation, p. 132. **253.** Molloy, J. (1992). *Self-Run, Self-Supported Houses for More Effective Recovery from Alcohol and Drug Addiction.* Rockville, MD: Center for Substance Abuse Treatment; Oxford House (1991). Oxford House National Vacancy Report: December 30, 1991. **254.** Hoffman, N. and Miller, N. (1993). Perspectives of Effective Treatment for Alcohol and Drug Disorders. *Psychiatric Clinics of North America,* 16(1):128. **255.** Michael Dennis, Personal Communication, 1997. **256.** Michael Dennis, Personal Communication, October, 1995; Hubbard, R.; Marsden, M.; Rachal,, J.; Harwood, H.; Cavanaugh, E.; and Ginzberg, H. (1989). *Drug Abuse Treatment: A National Study of Effectiveness.* Chapel Hill, NC: University of North Carolina Press; Simpson and Sells, 1982. **257.** Allison, M. And Hubbard, R. (1985). Drug Abuse Treatment Process: A Review of the Literature. *IJA,* 20: 1321-1345. **258.** Miller, W. and Hester, R. (1986). The Effectiveness of Alcoholism Treatment. In: Miller, W. and Hester, R., Eds., *Treating Addictive Behaviors: Process of Change.* NY: Plenum Press, pp. 156, 162-163; ; Miller, W. (1991). Emergent Treatment Concepts and Techniques. *Annual Review of Addictions Research and Treatment,* p. 287. **259.** Hoffman and Miller, 1993, pp. 130-131; Landry, 1997, pp. iii-vi. **260.** Patient-Treatment Matching. (1997). *Alcohol Alert,* No. 36, Rockville, MD: NIAAA. **261.** For an excellent review of cost-benefit studies of treatment, see: Holder, H.; Lennox, R.; and Blose, J. (1992). The Economic Benefits of Alcoholism Treatment: A Summary of Twenty Years of Research. *Journal of Employee Assistance Research,* 1(1):63-82. **262.** Lennox, R. (1993). Costs Offsets of Drug Abuse Treatment Provided in the Private Sector. Presented at the Annual Meeting of the Association for Health Services Research. **263.** California Department of Alcohol and Drug Programs. (1994). *Evaluating Recovery Services: The California Drug and Alcohol Assessment (CALDATA).* Sacramento: California Department of Alcohol and Drug Programs. **264.** Rajkumar, A. and French, M. (1997). Drug Abuse, Crime Costs, and the Economic Benefits of Treatment. *Journal of Quantitative Criminology,* 13(3):293-323. **265.** NTIES (1996). *National Treatment Improvement Evaluation Study (Preliminary Report: The Persistent Effects of Substance Abuse Treatment–One Year Later.* Center for Substance Abuse Treatment, p.1. **266.** Michael Dennis, Personal Communication, October, 1995.

Chapter Twenty-Eight: Parkside: A Rich Legacy and a Cautionary Tale

267. Jean Rossi, Personal Interview, July 8, 1995. **268.** Bradley, N., Keller, J. and McElfresh, O. (ND). Lutheran General Hospital Alcoholics Rehabilitation Center for Treatment, Training and Research. Unpublished Manuscript, p. 1. **269.** Keller, J. (1978). Alcoholism Center for Treatment, Training and Research: Lutheran General Hospital. In: Goby, M. and Keller, J.

Perspectives on the Treatment of Alcoholism. Park Ridge, Illinois: Lutheran General Hospital, pp. 2-3. **270.** Bradley, Keller, McElfresh, 1978, p. 94. **271.** Rossi, J. and Filstead, W. (1973). The Application of Social Psychological Forces in the Treatment of Illness in a General Hospital. In: Rossi, J. and Filstead, W. (1973). *The Therapeutic Community.* NY: Behavioral Publications, p. 318. **272.** Jim M., Personal Interview, July 12, 1995. **273.** McInerney, J. (1971). Bridge Group: A Bridge Between Treatment and Community. Presented at the 22nd meeting of the North American Association of Alcohol Programs, Hartford, Connecticut, p. 1. **274.** McInerney, J. (1973). Alcoholics Anonymous Members as Alcoholism Counselors. In: Staub, G. and Kent, L. *The Para-Professional in the Treatment of Alcoholism.* Springfield: Illinois: Charles C. Thomas Publisher, p. 101. **275.** Jim M., Personal Interview, July 12, 1995. **276.** Jim M., Personal Interview, July 12, 1995. **277.** It was not uncommon during the early years of emerging programs for "paraprofessional" recovering counselors to be paid several thousand dollars less than their "professional" counterparts, in spite of sometimes almost simultaneous duties. **278.** Jim M., Personal Interview, July 12, 1995. **279.** Jim M., Personal Interview, July 12, 1995. **280.** Keller, 1978, p. 3. **281.** From "Dedication of the Nelson J. Bradley Center for Research, Education, and Training," 1985. **282.** Filstead, W. (1991). *Two Year Treatment Outcome: An Evaluation of Substance Abuse Services for Adults and Youth.* Park Ridge, Illinois: Parkside Medical Services Corporation. **283.** Parkside Medical Services Corporation later returned to a not-for-profit status. **284.** Parkside Plans to Shut up to 11 Treatment Units (1990). *Chicago Tribune* (November 8).

Chapter Twenty-Nine: Some Closing Reflections on the Lessons of History

285. Green, W. (1995). *Dysfunctional by Design: The Rebirth of Cultural Survivors.* Evanston, IL: Chicago Spectrum Press. **286.** Gordon, A. (1981). The Cultural Context of Drinking and Indigenous Therapy for Alcohol Problems in Three Migrant Hispanic Cultures: An Ethnographic Report. *JSA,* Supplement 9:217-240. **287.** Wilson, W. (1944). *AA Grapevine,* 1(4):4. **288.** Davies, D. (1962). Normal Drinking in Recovered Alcohol Addicts. *QJSA,* 23:94-104; Burglass, M/ and Shaffer, H. (1981). The Natural History of Ideas in the Treatment of the Addictions. In: Shaffer, H. and Burglass, M. (Eds.). *Classic Contributions in the Addictions.* New York: Brunner/Mazel, pp. 33-35; Kalb, M. and Propper, M. (1983). The Future of Alcohology: Craft or Science? *AJP,* 133(6):641-645; Chiauzzi and Liljegren, 1993, pp. 303-304. **289.** Agar, M. (1995). Concept Abuse in the Drug Field. *IJA,* 30(9):1165-1168. **290.** Nancy Olson, Personal Communication, October, 1997. **291.** Rogalski, C. (1993). The Political Process and Its Relationship to the Psychotherapy of Substance Misusers: An Historical Perspective. *IJA,* 28(1):1-46. **292.** Blocker, J. (1989). *American Temperance Movements: Cycles of Reform.* Boston: Twayne Publishers, p. 29. **293.** Weisner, C. (1983). The Alcohol Treatment System and Social Control: A Study of Institutional Change. *JDI,* (Winter):119-120 **294.** Howard, C. and Hurdum, H. (1940). Therapeutic Problems in the Alcoholic Psychoses. *Psychiatric Quarterly,* 14:347-359. **295.** Kurtz, E. (1996). Spirituality and Recovery: The Historical Journey. *The Blue Book,* 47:5-29. **296.** Bishop, E. (1920). *The Narcotic Drug Problem.* New York: MacMillan Company, p. 58. **297.** Weisner, 1983, p. 117. **298.** Erlenmeyer, 1889, p. xiii. **299.** Moore, R. And Murphy, T. (1961). Denial of Alcoholism as an Obstacle to Recovery. *QJSA,* 22:597-609; Allison and Hubbard, 1985, p. 1335; Landry, M. (1997). *Overview of Addiction Treatment Effectiveness.* SAMSA (DHHS Publication No. (SMA) 97-3133), p. 84. **300.** Chiauzzi, E., and Liljegren, S. (1993). Taboo Topics in Addiction Treatment: An Empirical Review of Clinical Folklore. *JSA,* 10:310. **301.** Deitch, D. (1973). Treatment of Drug Abuse in a Therapeutic Community. In: *Technical Papers of the Second Report of the National Commission on Marijuana and Drug Abuse* Appendix, Vol.IV, pp.158-175; Dole, V. (1997). What is "Methadone Maintenance Treatment"? *Journal of Maintenance in the Addictions,* 1(1):8. **302.** Campbell, J. with Bill Moyers. (1988). *The Power of Myth.* New York: Anchor Books, p. 73. **303.** Allison and Hubbard, 1985, p. 1330. **304.** Watts, T. (1981). The Uneasy Triumph of a Concept: The 'Disease' Conception of Alcoholism. *JDI,* 11:451-60 (Fall). **305.** Baumohl, J. (1990). Inebriate Institutions in North America, 1840-1920. *BJA,* 85:1187-1204. **306.** Wodak, A. (1995). The Language of Industry: Toward a Definition of Liquorspeak. *Addiction,* 90:133-139. **307.** Room, R. (1983). Sociological Aspects of the Disease Concept of Alcoholism. In: *Research Advances in Alcohol and Drug Problems, Volume 7,* New York: Plenum Press, pp. 47-91. **308.** Gusfield, J. (1963). *Symbolic Crusade: Status Politics and the American Temperance Movement.* Urbana: University of Illinois Press. **309.** Room, R. (1978). *Governing Images of Alcohol and Drug Problems: The Structure, Sources and Sequels of Conceptualizations of Intractable Problems.* Ph.D. Dissertation, Berkeley, CA: University of California, p. 18. **310.** Room, 1978, p. 40. **311.** For an expanded discussion of implosion and inversion, see White, W. (1997). *The Incestuous Workplace.* Center City, MN: Hazelden.

Name Index

Name Index

Subject / Institution / Product Index

About the Author

William White has a Master's Degree in Addiction Studies and more than thirty years of experience working in the addiction treatment field as a clinician, clinical director, administrator, researcher, and well-traveled trainer and consultant. He is currently a Senior Research Consultant at Chestnut Health Systems' Lighthouse Institute where he pursues his interests in clinical research, writing and training. His previous books include *Critical Incidents: Ethical Issues in Substance Abuse Prevention and Treatment; The Incestuous Workplace: Stress and Distress in the Organizational Family; Pathways from the Culture of Addiction to the Culture of Recovery*; and *Voices of Survival, Voices of Service: AIDS Case Management in Chicago*. He is also the co-author of *The Call to Write* and *The Training Life: Living and Learning in the Substance Abuse Field*. For information regarding any of these publications, visit the Chestnut Health Systems web site at http://www.chestnut.org or call toll free 1-888-547-8271.

About The Lighthouse Institute

Chestnut Health Systems (CHS) has provided addiction treatment and related human services since the opening of its first treatment facility in 1973. The Lighthouse Institute, a division of CHS, conducts clinical and health services research under grants from several state and federal agencies. The Institute also provides advanced technical education and training for health and human service professionals across the country and publishes books, curricula, monographs and manuals related to the prevention and treatment of addiction.

Bibliographic Information

For information on how to obtain a complete bibliography of all the resources used in *Slaying the Dragon*, call our toll free number 1-888-547-8271.